History of the Canadian Peoples

VOLUME 2 | 1867 to the Present

D1441789

History of the Canadian Peoples

VOLUME 2 | 1867 to the Present

Fifth Edition

Margaret Conrad • **Alvin Finkel**

University of New Brunswick *Athabasca University*

PEARSON
Longman

Toronto

Library and Archives Canada Cataloguing in Publication

Conrad, Margaret
    History of the Canadian peoples / Margaret Conrad, Alvin Finkel. — 5th ed.

CD-ROM containing primary documents in the pocket of the inside back cover.
Copyright date: 2009.

Includes bibliographical references and index.
Contents: v. 1. Beginnings to 1867 — v. 2. 1867 to the present.
ISBN 978-0-321-52430-0 (v. 1) — ISBN 978-0-321-53908-3 (v. 2).

    1. Canada—History—Textbooks. 1. Canada—Histoire—Manuels scolaires.
I. Finkel, Alvin, 1949– II. Title.

FC164 H57 2009   971   C2008-901920-2   FC164

ISBN-13: 978-0-321-53908-3
ISBN-10: 0-321-53908-7

Vice President, Editorial Director: Gary Bennett
Editor-in-Chief: Ky Pruesse
Senior Acquisitions Editor: Laura Paterson Forbes
Executive Marketing Manager: Judith Allen
Senior Developmental Editor: Joel Gladstone
Production Editor: Richard di Santo
Copy Editor: Sally Glover
Proofreader: Lu Cormier
Production Coordinator: Avinash Chandra
Composition: ICC Macmillan Inc.
Photo and Permissions Research: Lisa Brant
Art Director: Julia Hall
Interior and Cover Design: Anthony Leung
Cover Image: Christopher Kontoes / Getty Images

1 2 3 4 5   12 11 10 09 08

Printed and bound in the United States of America.

PEARSON
Longman

Contents

List of Maps

List of Figures and Tables

List of Boxes

Voices from the Past

Preface

The fifth edition of *History of the Canadian Peoples* tries to preserve our primary objective of an inclusive history of Canada. In addition to the achievements of the rich and powerful, we include developments in the lives of Aboriginal peoples, women, racial and ethnic minorities, and the poor, who also helped create the Canada we know today.

Part I, "Inventing Canada, 1867–1914," begins with a chapter surveying the conditions in Canada at the time of confederation and continues with three chapters tracing the political processes by which Canada was transformed from a string of isolated British colonies in the 1860s into a nation that was ready to make its mark on the world stage during the First World War (1914–1918). Although we focus here on the policies championed by national leaders such as John A. Macdonald, Wilfrid Laurier, and Robert Borden, we also highlight the alternative visions of Canada that inspired people such as Joseph Howe, Louis Riel, and Henri Bourassa to lead political protests. The conflict of visions and values reminds us that Canada's national policy is always a subject for negotiation rather than a predetermined path followed by leaders.

Part II, "Economy and Society in the Industrial Age, 1867–1918," covers much of the same time frame as Part I but focuses on the important economic, social, and cultural developments that characterized Canada's rise to industrial maturity. Following confederation, Canadians were swept up in a tide of change that included rapid industrialization, immigration, urbanization, and the emergence of new secular values. In Chapters 5 through 8, we explore these transforming processes and the ways Canadians responded to them. The First World War consolidated pre-war trends and further exposed the divisions based on class, culture, gender, race, and region that had marked the period since 1867. In Chapter 9, we focus on developments at home and abroad during the First World War, highlighting its multifaceted impact on individuals, groups, and the nation as a whole.

Part III, "Transitional Years: Canada 1919–1945," traces Canada's evolution through three turbulent decades characterized by the rise of mass consumer culture, the Great Depression, and the Second World War. Left reeling under the impact of these developments, Canadians began to question long-held beliefs about economic goals, political structures, and social institutions. Chapters 10 and 11 describe political and economic developments in the 1920s and 1930s, respectively, while Chapters 12 and 13 focus on social and cultural themes of that time period. In Chapter 14, we turn to the events and impact of the Second World War, which, like the first, consolidated earlier trends and created a new international context in which Canada would play an important role.

In Part IV, "Reinventing Canada, 1945–1975," we begin by looking at the new liberal consensus based on the goals of balancing profit-oriented capitalism with state intervention to guarantee high levels of employment and social programs that would help to improve disparities among individuals and regions. The overweaning influence of the United States in defining the parameters of the post-war consensus, which emerged in the context of an ideological and geopolitical contest with the Soviet Union and its allies, is discussed in Chapter 16. Although disagreement around issues relating to economic development, the role of the state, and social welfare emerged in the mid 1970s following the OPEC oil crisis, the three decades of relative economic prosperity following the Second World War inspired Canadians to support policies that sought to achieve a better standard of living for disadvantaged groups, encourage homegrown cultural industries, and champion peace-keeping around the world. Developments in this period also led groups such as Aboriginal peoples, Quebecers, and women to demand a greater voice in shaping the nation's destiny.

Part V, "Post-Modern Canada," addresses Canadian responses to the new era of economic globalization and the neo-liberal agenda that followed in its wake. Public protests increased as Canadians found themselves tied into international agreements, most notably a free-trade treaty with the United States, that weakened the role of the federal government in making decisions to benefit Canadians. In the final chapter, we chronicle developments in the twenty-first century, in particular the changing global scene precipitated by the attacks on the World Trade Center in New York and the Pentagon in Washington by Muslim extremists on 11 September 2001, and by new policy directions spearheaded by a minority Conservative federal government under the leadership of Stephen Harper. With many people in Quebec demanding independence from Canada, the gap between rich and poor provinces widening, disadvantaged groups and individuals mounting increasingly aggressive protests, and the environment under siege from industrial pollutants, Canada entered the twenty-first century with its future still in question. The United Nations has designated Canada as one of the best nations in the world to live in—a ranking that seems to underscore the fact that Canadians have achieved much together and, whether divided or united, have much to look forward to in the future.

In revising and updating this edition, we have maintained the pedagogical features of the fourth edition—"A Historiographical Debate," "More to the Story," "Voices from the Past," and "Biography"—but modified some of the topics covered. Beyond these existing features, there is an end-of-chapter section called "Related Readings in This Series," which directs readers both to complementary articles in *Nation and Society: Readings in Post-Confederation Canadian History* and to primary source selections on the accompanying Primary Documents CD-ROM. The CD-ROM contains 129 original newspaper articles, essays, acts of parliament, and pictures organized by chapter. We have also updated the two appendices: "Appendix A: Population of Canada" and "Appendix B: Prime Ministers of Canada." As in the previous edition, timelines appear at the beginning of each chapter to place events in chronological perspective and we have continued to incorporate the Selected Reading feature at the end of each chapter.

The maps in this edition have been updated to be both more useful and more accessible. These maps appear not only in the text but also for the first time on our open-access website with additional interactive features. The website can be found at www.pearsoned.ca/conrad-finkel.

As you will see, the interior of the fifth edition now has enhanced colour. We have increased the number of photos in the text to maximize this new design and to provide further visual support to the narrative.

Weaving together the rich tapestry of Canada's social, political, and economic story is a daunting task, and, as we note below, we have many people to thank for helping us across the four editions of this text.

Our debts to others continue to grow as we pass from edition to edition of this text, and we apologize to those who have contributed but whom we have passed over here. We thank Veronica Strong-Boag, Michael Behiels, Brian Henderson, and Cornelius Jaenen for their roles in the initial conceptualization of this project. We owe a particular debt to our editors of the four editions. Barbara Tessman and Dawn du Quesnay contributed immeasurably to the organization, content, and writing of Volume II. We would also like to express our thanks and appreciation to the team at Pearson Education Canada: to Laura Forbes, Joel Gladstone, Suzanne Schaan, and Richard di Santo; to our copyeditor Sally Glover and our proofreader Lu Cormier; and to our photo, art, and literary researcher Lisa Brant. Your efforts and hard work have been most appreciated in the creation of this new edition.

Many people read and suggested improvements for some or all of these chapters. For the first edition, we thank Veronica Strong-Boag, Michael Behiels, Jim Pritchard, Adrian Shubert, Brian Young, John Dickinson, Douglas Baldwin, and Barry Moody. For the second edition, we thank John Dickinson, Cornelius Jaenen, Gerald Friesen, Mark McGowan, Ruth Brouwer, Graham Decarie, Kathryn McPherson, Norman Hillmer, Marilyn Barber, Jim Miller, Lorne Hammond, Suzanne Zeller, Patricia Dirks, Suzanne Morton, Carmen Miller, Ken Munro, Peter Nunoda, Wendy Mitchinson, Cecilia Danysk, Sharon Myers, Robert Sweeny, and Del Muise. We received helpful input on the third edition from James Hiller (Memorial University), John Belshaw (University College of the Cariboo), Roger Hall (University of Western Ontario), Sean Cadigan (Dalhousie University), Catherine Desbarats (McGill University), Linda Kerr (Concordia University College), Rusty Bitterman (Saint Thomas University), Jan Noel (University of Toronto at Mississauga), David Murray (University of Guelph), Ron Stagg (Ryerson Polytechnic University), Jeff Keshen (University of Ottawa), Raymond Huel

(University of Lethbridge), Shawn Cafferky (University of Victoria), Norman Hillmer (Carleton University), Jeff Webb (Memorial University), and Cynthia Comacchio (Wilfrid Laurier University). For the fourth edition, we thank our reviewers, including Peter A. Russell (Okanagan University College), David Bright (University of Guelph), Paula Young (Camosun College), Todd McCallum (Dalhousie University), and Ernest LeVos (Grant MacEwan College).

For the fifth edition, we would like to thank the following reviewers for their contributions and suggestions: Clarence Bolt (Camosun College), Tim Cook (Canadian War Museum), Thor Frohn-Nielsen (Kwantlen University College), George Davison (College of New Caledonia), Alan Gordon (University of Guelph), David Mills (University of Alberta), Gillian Poulter (Acadia University), and Robert Rutherdale (Algoma University College).

SUPPLEMENTS FOR STUDENTS

Primary Documents CD-ROM: Included in the back of each text, this CD-ROM includes PDF versions of 129 original newspaper articles, essays, acts of parliament, and pictures organized by chapter. A list of each chapter's readings can be found at the end of each chapter under "Related Readings in This Series."

Companion Website (www.pearsoned.ca/conrad-finkel): This website is an online study guide that includes self-tests and links to other online resources for further research. The maps that appear in your text are also posted in interactive form on the site.

SUPPLEMENTS FOR INSTRUCTORS

Instructor's Resource CD-ROM (0-321-54626-1): This CD-ROM includes the following instructor supplements:

- **Instructor's Resource Manual:** This manual includes chapter-by-chapter lecture outlines, discussion points, assignments, and other resources for instructors.
- **Test Item File:** Chapter-by-chapter test questions, including multiple-choice, fill-in-the-blank, short answer, and essay questions. The test item file is available in Word on the IRCD and online with MyTest.

    MyTest for *History of the Canadian People*, Volume II, fifth edition, is a powerful assessment generation program to help instructors easily create and print quizzes, tests, exams, and homework or practice handouts. Questions and tests can be authored online, allowing instructors ultimate flexibility and the ability to efficiently manage assessments at any time from any location. Go to http://www.pearsonmytest.com to get started.
- **PowerPoints:** PowerPoint presentations highlight the key points in each chapter.
- **Image Archive:** The archive provides selected maps and images from the text in PowerPoint format.

Most of these instructor supplements are also available for download from a password-protected section of Pearson Education Canada's online catalogue, http://vig.pearsoned.ca. Navigate to your book's catalogue page to view a list of available supplements. See your local sales representative for details and access.

Interpreting Canada's Past

In 1829, Shanawdithit, the last surviving Beothuk on the island of Newfoundland, died of tuberculosis. Thirty-eight years later, three British North American colonies united to form the Dominion of Canada. The second of these two events has always had a central place in Canadian history textbooks. The first, until recently, has been ignored. For students of history, it is important to understand why the focus of historical analysis changes and what factors influence historians in their approaches to their craft.

WHAT IS HISTORY?

Simply stated, history is the study of the past, but the past is a slippery concept. It is impossible to recover everything that happened in the past. The best we can do is preserve and pass on what we think is important for the next generation to remember. In non-literate societies, people passed oral traditions from one generation to the next, with each generation fashioning the story to meet the needs of the time. When writing was invented, history became fixed in texts. The story of the past was often revised, but earlier texts could be used to show how interpretations changed over time. Although ordinary people continued to tell their stories, they were considered less important than "official" written histories that reflected the interests of the most powerful members of society. Some of the official texts, such as the Bible and the Koran, were deemed to be divinely inspired and therefore less subject to revision than the accounts of mere mortals.

In the nineteenth century, history became an academic discipline in Europe and North America. Scholars in universities began to collect primary historical documents, compare texts, develop standards of accuracy, and train students to become professional historians. At first, professional historians focused on political and military events that chronicled the evolution of empires and nation-states. Gradually, they broadened their scope to include economic, social, and cultural developments.

THE CONTEXT OF THIS TEXT

The authors of this book are university-trained historians, schooled in the theories and methods of what was once called "the new social history." Since the new social history is now nearly four decades old, it can no longer be considered new, but its findings have informed our decisions about what to include in this introductory textbook.

Social historians have made a concerted effort to broaden the scope of historical inquiry beyond well-documented political and military developments. To fill the gaps in written sources, they have taken an interdisciplinary approach, drawing upon other disciplines (including archeology, anthropology, demography, and geography) to answer their questions. Such sources as oral traditions and the findings of archeological excavations have enabled historians to explore the lives of the silent majority in past times. When personal computers became widely available in the 1970s, historians were able to process more efficiently large amounts of information found in such sources as censuses, immigration lists, and church registers. The science of demography, which analyzes population trends and draws upon vast quantities of data, has proven particularly useful in helping historians trace changes in family size, migration patterns, and life-cycle choices.

At the same time that new methodologies extended the scope of history, historians were being influenced by new theoretical approaches. Scholars who studied minorities, women, and the working class brought insights from multicultural studies, feminism, and Marxism to their analyses. Canadian history was also enriched by regional studies that integrated the perspectives of West, North, and Atlantic Canada into the larger national story hitherto dominated by Quebec and Ontario. By focusing on social structures such as class, culture, gender, race, and region, social historians raised new questions about old topics and revolutionized the way Canada's past is perceived.

Social history also has its critics. They argue that it focuses the energy of historians into narrow topics, that it yields interesting but ultimately insignificant findings, and that it destroys the unifying national focus offered by earlier political studies.[1] In response to such charges, we argue that social history offers a more comprehensive view of what happened in the past. We also maintain that there cannot be and never was an official version of Canada's history. The claim that there is only one way to view the past is, we believe, as damaging to the historical enterprise as are theories that dismiss history—and the belief that the present can be informed by an understanding of the past—as a figment of the modernist imagination.

WHY STUDY HISTORY?

Given that the story of the past is so contested, students may wonder if there is any value in studying history at all. We maintain that a study of history and engagement in debates about the meaning of the past is a critical component of an informed intelligence. Because history can be invoked to support a wide range of causes, both for good and ill, it is essential for citizens to have a working knowledge of what happened in the past and to be able to identify arguments that rely on a distortion or trivialization of historical evidence.

While most Canadians encounter the past in their everyday lives, students of history are encouraged to reflect on the standards for producing reliable representations of the past. In history classrooms, students develop skills in historical thinking that enable them to work comfortably with such concepts as evidence, significance, interpretation, continuity and change, progress and decline, empathy and perspective, moral judgment, and agency. They learn to deal responsibly with the dimension of time, to situate past events in their contexts, and, perhaps most importantly, to include reflections on their own assumptions before they come to a final judgment about some aspect of the past.

Like other fields in the humanities and social sciences, history has value as a way of understanding the place of human beings in the world. Along with literature, history has long been central to identifying, interpreting, and sharing the values upon which civil society depends. It is an essential discipline for building community, for encouraging empowerment, for expanding our horizons, and for developing skills in discerning how knowledge and power intersect across time and place.

History, well presented, is also an intoxicating stimulus to the imagination, enabling us to walk in other people's shoes in other times and places. Through the study of history we gain a perspective on the range of human behaviour, the potential and limits of human agency, and the continuum of past, present, and future in which we live our short lives. This kind of knowledge, much discounted in a society driven by stock market swings, the clash of civilizations, and doomsday scenarios, is important, perhaps even crucial, to our well-being as a species.

The academic discipline of history is, of course, only one way of knowing the past. In Canada, people engage the past in a variety of other ways, including watching history television, reading historical novels, visiting museums and historic sites, constructing family trees, learning ancestral stories, collecting artifacts, or playing history computer games. The study of history as a discipline increasingly involves an effort to dissect both academic histories and public approaches to the past to reveal what they tell us about the assumptions and priorities of the societies that produced them. So, for example, historians today will study the ways in which key historical figures such as Samuel de Champlain or Jeanne Mance have been commemorated in different eras less as a way of learning more about these individuals than as a means of decoding the social values of the era in which the commemoration took place. In the future, no doubt, historians will learn about our society's shifting social values by examining current interpretations of past events from sources such as various editions of this textbook.[2]

CONSTRUCTING A TEXT

From the foregoing discussion, it is clear that history is a dynamic and evolving discipline. Debates rage, methods come and go, new sources are discovered, and different conclusions are drawn from the same body of evidence. We want students who use this text not only to learn about developments in Canada's past but also to gain some understanding of how history is written. At the beginning of and at various points throughout each chapter we cite from primary sources that historians use. We also discuss historiography—that is, reflections on historical interpretation—in sections entitled "A Historiographical Debate." We conclude each chapter with a list of Selected Reading to acknowledge the sources that have informed our thinking and to offer direction for students who wish to explore topics in more depth.

Ultimately, our goal is to integrate social and cultural history into the text so that readers can develop a clearer understanding of how economic and political developments influenced people's lives and vice versa. There is, we maintain, nothing inevitable about historical processes. At times in this text the limitations on an individual's behaviour set by age, class, culture, gender, race, or region may appear to suggest that many—perhaps most—of our ancestors were hopeless victims of forces beyond their control. A closer reading should reveal that people sought in various ways to transcend the limits placed on their lives. Social struggles of every sort changed or at least sought to change the course of history.

WHAT'S IN A NAME?

Contemporary political movements that are changing the face of Canada are also forcing historians to think about the words they use. A half-century ago, most textbooks referred to people with black skin as "Negroes." In the 1960s, the term was replaced by "black," and more recently by "African Canadian," despite the fact that not all Africans are black. Similarly, the words used to describe Aboriginal peoples have changed in recent years. "Savages" was quickly dropped from textbooks in the 1960s. Although the

misnomer "Indian" has particular applications that seem as yet unavoidable, the preferred terms are now "First Nations" or "Native peoples."

Women, too, have insisted on being described in more respectful terms. Feminists have objected strongly to the use of the word "girl" when adult women are being discussed, and dismiss "lady" as condescending or elitist. Because "man" was adequate for the male of the species, "woman," they argued, was the most appropriate term, although some radical feminists prefer a different spelling, such as "wymyn." Only the most hidebound of scholars still insist that the word "man" can be used to describe the entire human species.

Many scholars complained loudly about being asked to abandon words long established in their vocabularies. A few even argued that "political correctness" restricted freedom of speech. We do not hold such views. Since English is a living language and changes over time, we see no reason why it should not continue to reflect the new consciousness of groups in Canadian society. In our view, the term "politically conscious" more accurately describes attempts by groups to name their own experiences.

Language, of course, is not only about naming things; it is also about power. Attempts by oppressed groups to find new words to fit their experiences should be seen in the context of their struggles for empowerment. In this text, we attempt to keep up with the changing times while bearing in mind that people in the past used a different terminology. We are also aware that in the future we may revise the words we use as groups continue to reinvent their identities. Even the word "Canada" has changed in meaning over the past 500 years, and it is our job as historians to shed light on the way this term came to be applied, for a time at least, to all the people living on the northern half of the North American continent.

NOTES

1 The now classic critique of social history in general and the first edition of our text in particular can be found in J.L. Granatstein, *Who Killed Canadian History?* (1998; 2nd ed. Toronto: Phyllis Bruce Books, 2007). For a more nuanced critique see Michael Bliss, "Privatizing the Mind: The Sundering of Canadian History, the Sundering of Canada," *Journal of Canadian Studies* 26, 4 (Winter 1991–92): 5–17. A.B. McKillop offers a thoughtful response in "Who Killed Canadian History? A View from the Trenches," *Canadian Historical Review* 80, 2 (June

1999): 269–99. See also Jocelyn Létourneau, *A History for the Future: Rewriting Memory and Identity in Quebec Today* (Montreal: McGill-Queen's University Press, 2004 and Linda Kealey et al., "Teaching Canadian History in the 1990s: Whose 'National' History Are We Lamenting?" *Journal of Canadian Studies* 27, 2 (Summer 1992): 129–31.

2   For a thoughtful reflection on the value of history education see Ken Osborne, "'To the Past': Why We Need to Teach and Study History," in *To the Past: History Education, Public Memory, and Citizenship in Canada*, ed. Ruth Sandwell (Toronto: University of Toronto Press, 2006), 103–131. Peter Seixas and his colleagues at the Centre for the Study of Historical Consciousness at the University of British Columbia have spearheaded a Benchmarks of Historical Thinking project in collaboration with Historica to encourage teachers to make explicit efforts to introduce historical thinking into their classrooms. See Peter Seixas, "What is Historical Consciousness?" in Sandwell, ed., *To the Past*, 3-10. Information on the Benchmarks of Historical Thinking project can be found on the Historica website: http://www.histori.ca/benchmarks.

Selected Reading

Students interested in the writing of Canadian history should start with the following: Carl Berger, *The Writing of Canadian History: Aspects of English-Canadian Historical Writing Since 1900, 2nd* ed. (Toronto: University of Toronto Press, 1986); Beverly Boutilier and Alison Prentice, eds., *Creating Historical Memory: English-Canadian Women and the Work of History* (Vancouver: UBC Press, 1997); Serge Gagnon, *Quebec and Its Historians: 1840–1920* (Montreal: Harvest House, 1982) and *Quebec and Its Historians: The Twentieth Century* (Montreal: Harvest House, 1985); Ronald Rudin, *Making History in Twentieth Century Quebec* (Toronto: University of Toronto Press, 1997); and M. Brook Taylor, *Promoters, Patriots, and Partisans: Historiography in Nineteenth-Century English Canada* (Toronto: University of Toronto Press, 1989). Essays on history education, public history, and the relation of history to citizenship can be found in Ruth Sandwell, ed., *To the Past:*

History Education, Public Memory, and Citizenship in Canada (Toronto: University of Toronto Press, 2006. See also Ged Martin, *Past Futures: The Impossible Necessity of History* (Toronto: University of Toronto Press, 2004).

More sources on various topics in pre-confederation Canadian history can be found in Doug Owram, ed., *Canadian History: A Reader's Guide, Vol. 2: Confederation to the Present* (Toronto: University of Toronto Press, 1994). Students of Canadian history should also become familiar with four important reference works: *The Dictionary of Canadian Biography* (15 volumes to date) and *Historical Atlas of Canada*, 3 vols., both published by the University of Toronto Press, Gerald Hallowell, ed., *The Oxford Companion to Canadian History* (Toronto: Oxford University Press, 2004), and *The Canadian Encyclopedia*, 4 vols. (Edmonton: Hurtig, 1988).

Weblinks

The Atlas of Canada
http://atlas.gc.ca/site/index.html
  Developed by Natural Resources Canada, this bilingual online atlas offers a collection of maps and related information about all regions of Canada.

Canada's Digital Collections
http://collections.ic.gc.ca
  Canada's Digital Collections is one of the largest sources of Canadian content on the internet, featuring over 600 collections celebrating Canada's history, geography, science, technology, and culture.

Canada's National History Society
www.historysociety.ca
  Canada's National History Society, publisher of *The Beaver, Canada's History Magazine and Kayak, Canada's History Magazine for Kids*, hosts a website that includes, among other things, past issues of *The Beaver*.

The Canadian Encyclopedia
www.thecanadianencyclopedia.com
  This electronic version of the Canadian Encyclopedia offers a variety of interactive activities and links.

Canadian Heritage Information Network
www.chin.gc.ca
  The Canadian Heritage Information Network works with Canadian museums to create, present, and manage Canadian digital content.

Early Canadiana Online
www.canadiana.org
  This site posts early printed Canadian materials, including books, annuals, and periodicals.

CENTRE FOR THE STUDY OF HISTORICAL CONSCIOUSNESS
www.cshc.ubc.ca

This site includes academic articles on matters relating to historical understanding and the teaching of history in addition to a comprehensive bibliography on these topics.

DICTIONARY OF CANADIAN BIOGRAPHY
www.biographi.ca

Hosted by the Library and Archives of Canada, this electronic version of the Dictionary of Canadian Biography facilitates searching across the 15 volumes of the dictionary currently in print.

DOMINION INSTITUTE
www.dominion.ca

Using public opinion research and innovative TV, new media, and in-school programs, the Dominion Institute helps Canadians connect in meaningful ways with the country's history, shared citizenship, and democratic institutions and values.

HISTORICA
www.histori.ca

This is the home page of Historica, a foundation whose mandate is to provide Canadians with a deeper understanding of their history and its importance in shaping their future.

LIBRARY AND ARCHIVES CANADA
www.collectionscanada.ca

Library and Archives Canada hosts the largest collection of materials related to the nation's history. The site includes electronic resources and research tools. View exhibits and conduct some research at this site.

OUR ROOTS
www.ourroots.ca

The Our Roots project is designed to present an online coast-to-coast record of Canadian local histories.

PARKS CANADA
www.pc.gc.ca

The online home of Parks Canada includes information on Canada's national historic sites.

STATISTICS CANADA
www.statcan.ca

The Statistics Canada website contains a remarkable amount of historical and contemporary data.

VIRTUAL MUSEUM OF CANADA
www.virtualmuseum.ca

This site showcases the distinct culture entrusted in Canadian museums and includes a series of attractive virtual exhibits and an image gallery.

Inventing Canada, 1867–1914

Between 1867 and 1914, Canada was transformed from a string of isolated British colonies into a nation that was ready to make its mark on the world stage during the First World War (1914–1918). In this period, immigration, western settlement, the growth of cities, and new social values signalled the onset of what historians call "the modern age." Two trends are particularly noteworthy: first, the emergence of the state—federal, provincial, and municipal—as a major force in nation-building; and second, the role of industrial capitalism in defining Canada's economic and social realities. Together, the interventionist state and vigorous industrial growth changed the lives of all Canadians and "invented" a nation that was vastly different from the one that had come together so inauspiciously in 1867. Part I provides a bird's eye view of Canada in 1867 and describes the political processes that brought the scattered British colonies together to form an industrial nation. In Part II, we explore the economic and social impact of the new industrial order on Canadians.

Photo: Library and Archives Canada, C-001466

A People in Search of a Nation, 1867

TIMELINE

1846	Great Britain adopts free trade policy
1848–55	Responsible government granted to United Canadas and Atlantic colonies
1854–56	Crimean War
1854–66	Reciprocity Treaty provides for limited free trade with United States
1858	Gold Rush on Fraser and Thompson rivers; British Columbia becomes Crown colony
1859	Grand Trunk Railway completed; Darwin's *The Origin of Species* published
1861–65	American Civil War
1863	London bankers buy Hudson's Bay Company
1867	British North America Act, creating the Dominion of Canada, passed in British parliament

B orn: On Monday last, at 12:05 a.m. (premature) the Dominion of Canada—illegitimate. This prodigy is known as the infant monster Confederation.[1]

On 1 July 1867, the British North America Act came into effect, joining the British colonies of New Brunswick, Nova Scotia, and the United Canadas—now divided into the provinces of Ontario and Quebec—into the Dominion of Canada (see Map 1.1). The reaction among Canada's citizens was mixed. In Nova Scotia, the New Glasgow *Eastern Chronicle* captured the colony's strong opposition to the union with a satirical birth announcement. Toronto, in contrast, celebrated the occasion with band concerts, troop reviews, garden parties, and a balloon ascension from Queen's Park, clear testimony to the city's enthusiasm for the new political arrangement.

Although regional and cultural tensions were defining features of the Dominion of Canada, the fledgling nation survived and even thrived in the half-century following its birth. By the 1880s, Canada's territorial jurisdiction had been extended to the Pacific and Arctic oceans, making it physically the second largest nation on Earth. In the twentieth century, Canada emerged as one of the world's industrial giants. Even the most optimistic supporters of confederation would have been surprised by the success of their venture. In this chapter, we will outline the defining features of what on the surface looked like a most improbable nation.

THE STATE OF THE UNION, 1867

Canada had a population of fewer than 3.5 million at the time of confederation (see Table 1.1). Clustered along the Great Lakes–St. Lawrence waterway and the northeast coast of North America, the individual provinces were in closer communication with Great Britain and the United States, the two empires that dominated their existence, than they were with each other. They had had scarcely any links with the other British colonies in North America—British Columbia, Prince Edward Island, and Newfoundland and Labrador—or with the vast Northwest Territories, known as Rupert's Land and administered by the British-chartered Hudson's Bay Company since 1670. The Arctic Archipelago, also claimed by Great Britain, was out of bounds for most "southerners," who tended to succumb to the rigours of its cold weather and difficult terrain.

In the settled areas, railroads were beginning to supplement the stagecoach services that had linked major communities, but there was no direct rail communication, and only a poor excuse for a road, between Quebec and New Brunswick. Portland, Maine, was the eastern terminus and winter port of the Grand Trunk Railway, the longest rail line in Canada in 1867. When Canadians travelled to the Northwest, they usually did so through the United States, which boasted a transcontinental railroad by 1869. Even telegraph lines, the fastest form of communication, were often routed through the United States rather than directly from one colony to another.

Their isolation from each other notwithstanding, the citizens of the new nation were all subjects of Great Britain, the world's most powerful empire in the nineteenth century. Like the Dominion of Canada—which remained a dependency of Great Britain under the BNA Act—all of the British North American colonies possessed, to a greater or lesser degree, the political, legal, and social institutions of their mother country.

Queen Victoria, who ascended the British throne in 1837, was popular in Canada. When she died in 1901, many Canadians looked back fondly on the Victorian Age, which they associated with progress and social propriety. It was this shared heritage, and Great Britain's eagerness to relinquish direct involvement in the internal administration of its North American colonies, that enabled the Canadian government to move quickly in expanding its borders following confederation.

Canada's closest neighbour, and the object of grudging admiration, was the United States. When 13

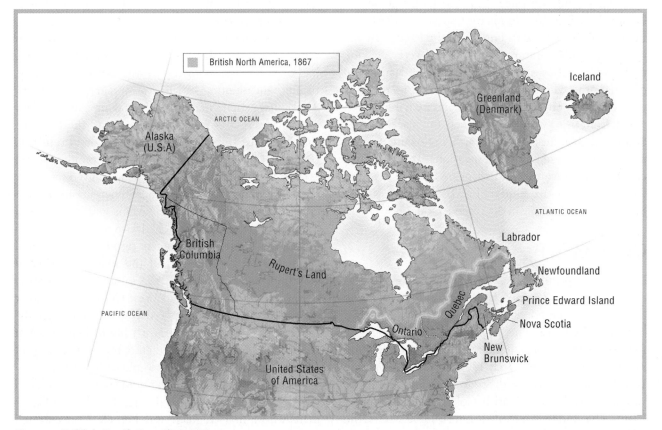

MAP 1.1 **British North America, 1867.**

Measuring the Canadian Population

In the nineteenth century, reformers argued that statistical tables revealed patterns that could help governments develop public policy. Section 91(6) of the BNA Act made census enumeration and vital statistics—that is, the record of births, marriages, and deaths—a responsibility of the federal government. Beginning in 1871, the federal government conducted census enumerations every 10 years (and, since 1956, every five years).

Covering the four original provinces of confederation, the 1871 census provided a record of population distribution (see Table 1.1) and indicators of economic growth. The quality of the data depended to a large extent on the diligence and ability of the enumerators. Notwithstanding its flaws, the manuscript

TABLE 1.1   Population of Canada, 1871

Ontario	1 620 851
Quebec	1 191 516
New Brunswick	285 594
Nova Scotia	387 800
Total	3 485 761

Source: Census of Canada, 1871.

census remains one of the best sources available for historians and genealogists to gain information on the lives of ordinary Canadians at the time of confederation.

of Great Britain's colonies declared independence in 1776, they were not much larger in population and territory than Canada in 1867. The United States made good its claim to independence from Great Britain in the bloody American Revolutionary War (1775–1783) and then quickly expanded its borders to the Pacific. By the mid-nineteenth century, Americans were making threatening noises about their "manifest destiny" to dominate the whole North American continent. This goal was temporarily deflected by a bitter Civil War that raged from 1861 to 1865 between the slave-owning South and the industrializing North. Following the war, the Americans resumed their expansionary policies, purchasing Alaska from the Russians in 1867 and casting covetous eyes toward Rupert's Land. Fear of the United States played a key role in the confederation movement.

CANADA'S PEOPLES

In 1867, the peoples of Great Britain's North American colonies were a mixed lot, scarcely the building blocks of a nation bound together by ties of a common history and culture. The land's First Nations could be found in every region, but their numbers were declining rapidly. Of the approximately 130 000 Native peoples in British North America at the time of confederation, the vast majority lived in British Columbia and Rupert's Land. That number included some 10 000 Métis, the

progeny of European traders and Native women. Inuit peoples, close to 10 000 in total, confined themselves to the northern regions of the continent, where, perhaps to their benefit, they had only sporadic contact with European culture.

The vulnerable condition of most Native peoples at mid-century was a far cry from the independence they had once known. With the invasion of their farming, fishing, and hunting territories by European settlers, Aboriginal peoples had difficulty making a living. They now lacked the resources to live well off the fur trade that had once sustained many of them or to return to traditional lifestyles. In the eastern colonies, about 20 000 Algonkian and Iroquois peoples lived primarily on reserves that were often encroached upon by rapacious settlers. Meanwhile, the Métis and Blackfoot of the southwestern plains watched with dismay as western settlement in the United States resulted in the virtual extinction of the buffalo and the marginalization of Aboriginal peoples. Would the same process destroy them? First Nations on the West Coast already knew the answer. They had prospered from the fur trade in the first half of the nineteenth century but had lost much of their land as settlers poured into the new colony of British Columbia following the gold rush of 1858.

The legacy of the French regime in North America (1604–1760) was present in the nearly a third of Canadians whose first language was French. Concentrated in Quebec, the heartland of the old French empire, the population of French-speaking Canadians also included the Acadians in the Maritimes and a growing number of Francophone settlers in the eastern sections of Ontario. The French-speaking Métis of Red River and other areas of the Northwest testified to the earlier influence of France in the fur trade.

Although it had been well over a century since the Acadian deportation (1755–1763) and the conquest of Quebec (1763), the historical memory of the bitter conflict between the British and French for ascendancy in North America was still very much alive. The creation of the Dominion of Canada in no way erased the Francophone nationalism that was fast emerging, in differing forms, in Quebec and the Maritimes, and was a central feature of Métis identity in Rupert's Land.

British immigrants began settling the eastern seaboard a century before Great Britain officially gained control of the French colonies in North America by the Treaty of Utrecht (1713) and the Treaty of Paris (1763). Between 1713 and 1867 as many as 1 500 000 British subjects migrated to British North America. While an unknown number of these immigrants eventually drifted to the United States, enough stayed in the colonies to ensure a British majority in every province except Quebec by 1867. British heritage did not guarantee a common culture or even a strong allegiance to the British Empire. The English, Welsh, Scots, and Irish differed from one another in significant ways and were divided by internal conflicts. People who traced their origins to Great Britain's former Thirteen Colonies—arriving as Loyalists following the American Revolutionary War or as the pioneers along the leading edge of the North American settlement frontier—added yet another ingredient to the "English" culture.

People who traced their origins to the German-speaking states—German unification was achieved only in 1871—comprised the largest ethnic group in Canada other than British and French in 1867. Although most Germans were not recent immigrants, they retained their cultural identity in areas where their settlements were concentrated, such as Lunenburg County, Nova Scotia and Waterloo County, Ontario. In Waterloo County, the town of Berlin had Lutheran, Mennonite, Evangelical, and Roman Catholic churches and German-language newspapers and schools to serve

At the time of confederation, the bead and quill work of Aboriginal artists was highly prized, selling well in domestic and foreign markets. This nineteenth-century cradle, fashioned by Christianne Morris, is covered with panels of Mi'kmaq porcupine quill work. Panels by Christianne Morris/Des Brisay Museum, Bridgewater, Nova Scotia. Photo by Ron Merrick/Courtesy of the History Collection of the Nova Scotia Museum, Halifax

its overwhelmingly German citizens. The close relationship of the British monarchy to Germany assured the place of Germans in the Canadian mosaic, at least until 1914 when antagonism between Germany and Great Britain erupted in war.

In 1867, as many as 30 000 people of African descent lived in Canada. The first Africans in the colonies in both the French and British regimes were usually slaves. After the American Revolution, 3500 free blacks arrived in the Loyalist migration. Wealthy Loyalists also brought their black slaves to British-controlled colonies. Slavery was abolished in Upper Canada in 1793, ceased elsewhere in British North America early in the nineteenth century, and was formally abolished throughout the British Empire in 1833. As a result, African Americans seeking escape from the United States, where slavery was legally sanctioned until 1863, often turned their sights northward.

In the wake of the 1858 gold rush, the West Coast became home to some 7000 Chinese, the majority of whom came from the gold fields of California. Most Chinese immigrants were men who worked as merchants, prospectors, and servants, but a few women worked with their merchant husbands or made a living as prostitutes. When the gold fields were depleted, fewer than 2000 Chinese remained to form the basis of Canada's oldest Chinese community. The hostility of

Harriet Tubman. In the 1850s, a secret process known as the "underground railroad" was developed to bring escaped slaves into British North America, most of them to Canada West. One of the best-known "conductors" on the underground railway was Harriet Tubman, who made an estimated 19 trips into slave states to rescue more than 300 people. Between 1851 and 1857, Tubman was based in St. Catharines, Canada West, where she made a living cleaning and cooking for people in the town.
Library of Congress

the white majority, a lack of work, and difficulty finding marriage partners encouraged many Chinese to return either to California or to their homeland.

While over 90 percent of Canadians at the time of confederation traced their origins to France or Great Britain, most had never set foot in Europe. Fully 93 percent of the inhabitants of Quebec and Nova Scotia had been born in Canada. The percentages were lower in New Brunswick and Ontario—87 percent and 73 percent, respectively—but it was clear that Canada was no longer a preferred destination for immigrants. By the mid-nineteenth century, even the Canadian-born were beginning to move to the United States in large numbers, where frontier lands and industrial employment offered attractive opportunities.

LIFE AND DEATH

With over half of its citizens under the age of 21, Canada was a young nation in 1867. Fertility—the number of births per thousand women between ages 15 and 49—was high, especially in Francophone families and rural areas of the country. In urban centres, there was evidence of a dramatic decline in family size that demographers call the "fertility transition." People began limiting the size of their families for reasons that seem to be linked to a lower death rate and the adoption of new values associated with industrialism. On average, women born in 1825 gave birth to 7.8 children. The figure dropped to 6.3 for women born in 1845. By the end of the century the average was under 4.

Ninety-five percent of Canadians in 1867 were married or would enter into a marriage relationship at some point in their lives. Community proscriptions against premarital sex were part of a rigid sexual code that also included harsh legal penalties against intimate relations between people of the same sex. There may have been networks of gays and lesbians—terms that did not exist to describe same-sex relationships in 1867—but, because the legal system forced homosexuals to keep their intimate lives secret, their history remained largely unrecorded.

Average life expectancy in early Victorian Canada was 40 years. One in five children died before their first birthday, primarily as a result of diseases spread by impure water and contaminated milk. Those who survived childhood and adolescence had an average life expectancy of close to 60 years. At any age, death was likely, and no Canadian could be assured of a long life or robust health. Illness was an ever-present threat, and cures were often worse than the disease. Epidemics of cholera, the most recent in 1854, killed thousands in cities, and diseases such as tuberculosis, smallpox, and diphtheria were common. Although some municipal jurisdictions had taken steps to improve sanitation, urban water and sewer systems were rudimentary.

THE INDUSTRIAL AGE

The leading cities in the new dominion owed their growth to the Industrial Revolution that was fast transforming the lives of all Canadians. The term "Industrial

Revolution" refers to changes in technology, transportation, and the organization of production that swept the North Atlantic world in the nineteenth century. Strongly influenced by Great Britain, the world's leader in industrial development, British North Americans were quick to adopt new transportation and production processes. Steam-propelled machines, trains, and ocean-going vessels changed the ways that people performed their most basic activities and created the context that made confederation possible.

With its pivotal location on the St. Lawrence trading system, Montreal was Canada's leading industrial city in 1867. Factories built along the Lachine Canal benefited from nearby hydraulic power and an abundant labour supply, enabling them to establish a dominant position in a variety of consumer and heavy industries.

Toronto Rolling Mills. At the time of confederation, illustrated newspapers often included lithographic scenes of industrial sites such as this one of the Toronto Rolling Mills. The size and complexity of operations associated with railway development elicited much comment and symbolized Canada's entry into the industrial age.
J. Ross Robertson Collection/T10914, Toronto Public Library

Between 1851 and 1871, Toronto was transformed from a city of independent artisans to one where over 70 percent of the labour force worked in shops employing more than 30 people. Saint John, thriving on its shipbuilding, foundry, footwear, and clothing industries, was the industrial leader in the Maritimes.

Railroad companies were Canada's largest corporations in 1867. With their personnel departments, complex accounting systems, quality control procedures, and specialized division of labour, they were at the forefront of practices associated with the Industrial Revolution. Every community in the new dominion longed for a railroad to bring capital investment, quicken the pace of travel, and put them on the map. Significantly, Maritimers made an intercolonial railroad link one of their few conditions for joining confederation, and the promise of a railway, or of assuming the debt of one already in existence, clinched the confederation negotiations with British Columbia and Prince Edward Island.

Industrialism not only revolutionized production processes, it also changed the way that people related to each other and to their work. In pre-industrial society, artisans had controlled their workplace, making a product from start to finish and determining their own standards and prices. Machines, in contrast, encouraged the division of labour into repetitive tasks and the centralization of production in factories owned by a few wealthy capitalists who could finance such expensive ventures. Under the factory system, labourers lost control of their work and often found it difficult to make a living wage.

At the time of confederation, only a tiny minority of workers belonged to unions, but, whether unionized or not, wage earners were determined not to become slaves to their capitalist masters. On 10 June 1867, just three weeks before the first Dominion Day, more than 10 000 workers in Montreal took to the streets in a show of worker solidarity.

In addition to changing the ways that people made a living, the Industrial Revolution also prompted changes in the political structures governing the colonies. The British Empire had been built on a policy of mercantilism that required the colonies to trade exclusively with the mother country. As the world's industrial leader, Great Britain could now dominate global markets without imposing formal trade regulations. In 1846, Great Britain adopted a policy of global free trade and began dismantling the old mercantile system. The introduction of free trade created consternation among colonial producers who believed that their fortunes depended on privileged access to the British market. A few merchants, especially those tied to the timber and wheat trades, even advocated annexation to the United States as the only solution to economic chaos.

Although the crisis passed, it produced three new strategies that would have a profound impact on the British North American colonies. First, Great Britain negotiated a free trade treaty with the United States as a means of relieving some of the economic distress experienced by the colonies. In effect from 1854 to 1866, the Reciprocity Treaty applied only to primary products such as fish, timber, minerals, and agricultural products, but it proved particularly valuable when these commodities were in high demand during the American Civil War. Second, changing economic policy was accompanied by political reform. Between 1848 and 1855, the British North American colonies with elected assemblies were granted a limited form of colonial self-rule known as "responsible government." Armed with their new powers, the colonies embarked on a third strategy to meet the challenges of the age: free trade among themselves and tariff protection against imports from the rest of the world. Following confederation, protectionism would become the cornerstone of Canada's national policy.

RURAL LIFE AND PRIMARY PURSUITS

We know now that the Industrial Revolution transformed Canadian society, but it is important not to overestimate the degree of social change it caused before 1867. At the time of confederation, 80 percent of Canadians lived in communities of fewer than 1000 inhabitants and over half of the working adult population made a living by farming, fishing, lumbering, and trapping animals (compared to fewer than 5 percent by the beginning of the twenty-first century). While some areas of the nation had been farmed for more than 200 years, huge sections, especially in more remote regions, were not far from the frontier stage.

The goal of owning a farm had been within reach of many British North Americans in the century before confederation. In 1871, fully 85 percent of farmers in Ontario over the age of 50 owned land. Those who remained tenants on the estates of others, as was the case of the Irish immigrants who lived on Amherst Island in Lake Ontario, often did so because it was profitable. In Ontario's bustling towns and cities "working on one's own account" as an artisan or small

Women's Work on a Canadian Farm, 1867

When 27-year-old Juliana Horatia Ewing, an accomplished writer of children's literature and the wife of a British officer stationed in Fredericton, was asked to provide advice on a woman's domestic responsibilities to friends in England who were planning to emigrate to Canada in 1868, she wrote the following:

> She must learn to make her own soap & candles if not to spin her own yarn. She must get her neighbours to tell her if she ought to have her house banked for the winter with sawdust to keep the frost from the cellar. She must keep a strong (metal if she can get it) saucer or pot of water on her stove if she feels giddy from the stove heat. She must keep her wood ashes to make soft soap . . . & be very, very careful as to where she stores them till the heat has gone out because of fire. Wood ashes & water make ley [sic] to scrub the floors with. Hard soap is made with lime & grease—so she must save her bits of fat. In the winter the children had better wear 2 pairs of socks & moccasins instead of boots. She can learn to make them herself I think. What I should especially advise them to take are good seeds for next year. At least in Fredericton vegetable seeds were got out from England and dear. In the short & hot summer vegetation is wonderful. Squash & cucumbers & vegetable marrows will rampage over the ground. Everything is luxuriant. I advise plenty of carrots & beetroots, things that will store in a frost proof cellar for winter consumption as one gets a little tired of the monotony of winter fare. She will have to pack butter & eggs in autumn for winter consumption. . . . I used to grease my eggs all over with butter & pack them in coarse salt the narrow end downwards. Meat is frozen and keeps any length of time, & is "thawed out" for cooking. It is best to thaw it gradually. Tell her not to frighten herself with thoughts of a barbarian outlandish life. I have gone through all of that & it is a great mistake.[2]

shopkeeper was a widespread phenomenon, not yet eclipsed by factory production and corporate practices.

As Canada's frontier province, Ontario was exceptional in the degree of opportunity it offered its citizens. People in other parts of Canada, where settlement had proceeded earlier and often under less liberal regimes, were facing difficult choices. In Quebec, seigneurialism, a system of landholding that predated the conquest, had been abolished in 1854 but had left a legacy of small and overcrowded farms. Prince Edward Island was still struggling to rid itself of the system of proprietary land ownership that had been imposed on the colony in 1767. Despite a generation of efforts to solve the "land question," some 60 percent of the island's farmers in 1861 were either tenants or squatters. Because of the importance of the timber trade to the New Brunswick economy, much of the land there remained locked up in Crown leases. Nova Scotia's land frontier was entirely gone, and the physical extent of settlement, much of it on marginal agricultural land, was greater in the 1860s than it is today.

The speed with which Canadians were gobbling up resources was evident to even the casual observer. In most settled regions, wild animals no longer existed in sufficient quantities to make the fur trade profitable, while several species of birds, such as the great auk, had become extinct from over-exploitation. The stands of white pine, much in demand for the shipbuilding industry, were also fast disappearing. In 1867, Canadians relied almost entirely on wood for their fuel, with the result that there was little forested land remaining near major cities. Coal comprised less than 10 percent, and oil scarcely any, of energy production.

By 1867, farmers living on the best agricultural lands had moved well beyond the subsistence stage, producing significant surpluses for markets at home and abroad. Stimulated by mechanization, new seeds

Carleton House on the North Saskatchewan River was a favourite stopping point for fur traders making the long trek between the Red River Colony and Edmonton.
Glenbow Archives/NA-1408-8

and breeds, better methods of transportation, and expanding markets, commercial agriculture grew dramatically in the mid-nineteenth century. Ontario was Canada's breadbasket, producing 84 percent of the nation's wheat, much of it destined for export. Ontario farmers also produced livestock, butter, milk, and wool in exportable quantities. Quebec specialized in livestock, potatoes, and coarse grains, most of which was consumed locally. Surplus grains, potatoes, apples, and other foodstuffs from Maritime farms found markets in Newfoundland and the Caribbean. Such sales increased a family's disposable income without threatening its primary goal of producing for subsistence.

In areas where farming alone could not sustain a family, members combined a number of activities to ensure survival. Fathers and older sons often worked in the fisheries or the woods for part of the year, while adolescent children moved to the cities to find work and wages to supplement the family income. When these strategies failed, entire families moved to industrial towns to take work in expanding factories. The family-based labour practices of rural farm life often worked effectively in the unregulated urban landscapes of Victorian Canada. If the income of the head of household was insufficient for a family's needs, one or

This photograph, taken in 1867 by Frederick Dally (1838–1914), shows a mule team and a freight wagon at the Great Bluff along the Thompson River in British Columbia.
British Columbia Archives and Records Service/A-00350

more children were sent out to work and, if space was available, boarders were taken in.

By 1867, the fur trade was experiencing a period of transition. The Hudson's Bay Company dominated the industry, but its days as a privileged monopoly were numbered. Although the depletion of fur-bearing animals posed some difficulties for the company, its major problems were economic and political. Competition from free traders and the eagerness of visionaries to convert the great Northwest to an agricultural frontier meant that the company would have to expand its range of activities and transform itself from a monopoly into a competitive corporation.

The challenges facing ocean fisheries, the resource that first drew Europeans to northern North America, were more complex. While cod was still the mainstay of most families and the chief export of communities in Newfoundland, a mixed fishery had developed along the coasts of the Maritimes. Increased competition from Americans, who were granted access to inshore fisheries by the Reciprocity Treaty, added to the problem of more people chasing fewer fish. With its base on Saint-Pierre and Miquelon and rights to fish along the west coast of Newfoundland (commonly

called the French Shore), France brought still more pressure on the beleaguered Atlantic fisheries. On the West Coast, commercial fishery was still in its infancy.

The riches beneath the vast Canadian terrain offered exciting prospects for a nation on the verge of an industrial boom. While the gold rush on the West Coast was running down, a smaller rush in Nova Scotia peaked in 1867. The expansion of coal mining in Nova Scotia was one of the success stories of the decade. Between 1858, when the General Mining Association's monopoly over Nova Scotia coal was abolished, and 1865, 14 new coal mines were opened in Cape Breton and more on the mainland. Nova Scotia was the mineral capital of Canada in 1867, with more than 3000 men and boys employed in coal mines and another 700 in the gold industry.

FAMILY AND COMMUNITY

In 1867, the family was the basic unit of Canadian society. Most families worked together to ensure the survival of each individual member, but families were more than economic entities. They were the context in which children learned gender roles, heard stories of their ancestors, received their earliest lessons on the meaning of life, and were taught their "place" in society. That place was largely determined by socially constructed categories such as class, ethnicity, and religion. While an individual might move from one class to another, change religious affiliation, or lie about ethnic origins, it was rarely done. Even more difficult to escape were colour, gender, and age, which also played major roles in determining individual destiny.

No distinction in Canadian society was more fundamental than that between the sexes. Men and women contributed different skills to the family economy and were treated separately under the law. Upon marriage, all personal property belonging to a wife and any wages she earned were under the absolute control of her husband. Husband and wife were declared to be one under

British common law, which prevailed outside Quebec. In common law jurisdictions, it was impossible for a wife to sign a contract, sue or be sued in her own name, or take her husband to court if he mistreated her. Nor could a married woman engage in business separate from her husband without his consent. The husband also had complete control over the children of the marriage and had easier access to divorce than did his wife.

The subordination of women was based on the pre-industrial ideal of a male-headed household in which women, children, apprentices, and servants were provided for and protected. Although it is unlikely that this patriarchal ideal was ever entirely reflected in practice, the gulf between the ideal and reality widened in the nineteenth century. Women were excluded from the boards of banks and railways, professional and skilled occupations, university education, and formal politics. Despite the changes taking place around them, women were told that they must continue to take the status of their husbands and inhabit the private sphere of the home. Women who avoided their roles as wives and mothers to stay in the paid labour force or who espoused the doctrines of "woman's rights" were the objects of criticism and ridicule. So, too, were men who failed to maintain their wives in a domestic setting.

Racial prejudices were also a source of individual and institutional discrimination. Notwithstanding the great range in ability and wealth among Aboriginal, African, and Asian peoples, they were all, virtually without exception, treated shabbily by the white majority of Canadians. Rather than disappearing following the abolition of slavery, racism was becoming more deeply entrenched. New scientific theories about the origins of species were quickly adapted to make claims about the superiority of the white "race." Such ideas in turn fed prejudices against racial intermarriage that fuelled segregationist tendencies. As a result, people of African and Asian descent were often segregated into separate schools and churches, excluded from skilled trades and professions, and confined to the outskirts of communities dominated by whites.

In 1867, Aboriginal peoples could still be seen in the towns and cities of Canada, but they were being pressured to live on reserves, out of the sight of white communities. Native peoples living on reserves were denied the vote, allegedly on the grounds that they were wards of the state. They were also often forced to endure religious schooling and, on many occasions, were subjected to physical and sexual abuse from the very people who professed to be helping them. Because of such treatment, many Natives living in Canada questioned the wisdom of adapting to the world taking shape around them.

Hereditary privileges that existed in Europe failed to take root in North America, but people in Canada still managed to sort themselves on the basis of class. Tight cliques of businessmen, professionals, and politicians dominated all aspects of public life. With the exception of Quebec, where the elite was predominantly Francophone and Roman Catholic, most members of Canada's ruling class were white, English-speaking, Protestant men. These men, along with their wives, imposed their values on Canadian society to a degree out of proportion to their numbers and in direct proportion to their wealth—and they were destined to increase in power as the century advanced.

The middle class of farmers and artisans constituted the backbone of the nation, but there were wide variations in wealth and status in this occupational group. While many families lived close to subsistence on the margins of society, others were poised to expand their operations and join the ranks of the economic elite. Most of the "middling sort" were facing pressures that would result in the erosion of their status. In retrospect, they would view the mid-nineteenth century as a golden age, before the factory system, corporate management practices, and commercial agriculture completely undermined their independence.

In both town and country, a class of propertyless labourers survived by doing manual work, often on a seasonal basis. This class was expanding rapidly and was anything but uniform in its composition. For some Canadians, wage labour was only a stage in their life cycle—a chance to earn a little money before returning to the family farm or setting up in a business or profession. Others who joined the working class were destined to stay there for the rest of their lives, their status defined by the skills they could acquire and the occupational choices that came their way.

Wealth, like power, was unevenly distributed in the new nation. For example, 20 percent of the farmers in Ontario owned 60 percent of the land, while in cities such as Toronto the wealthiest 10 percent of householders held well over half of the assessed estate and personal wealth. Among the middle class it was becoming increasingly fashionable to display one's wealth in fine homes. The Victorian parlour—crammed with furniture, knick-knacks, photographs, and paintings—became a popular site for conspicuous consumption and a source of much grumbling by the growing army of domestic servants whose job it was to dust the objects that cluttered the room.

COMMUNITY AND CULTURE

In 1867, Canadians were moving quickly toward new ways of defining their sense of community. Older ways, based on local identities, face-to-face relationships, oral communication, and a holistic sense of community, were gradually being replaced by literate societies where written documents bound people through commercial, religious, and political institutions across greater expanses of time and space. As railways, newspapers, and state institutions diminished distance and accelerated the pace of change, people were wrenched from their local contexts of kin and community. Many Canadians were illiterate, but everyone was aware of written texts, such as the Bible, calendars, constitutions, laws, and contracts, and understood their importance.

Formal education, with its emphasis on teaching the skills of reading and writing, offered the key for improving one's prospects in life. By the mid-nineteenth

century, 60 percent of children claimed at least a few years of schooling. Once seen as the responsibility of parents and left to the voluntary sector, schooling had become a state responsibility in most provinces by the time of confederation. Under new education acts, taxes were assessed on all property holders to finance state-operated schools. This policy was considered such an invasion of privacy that in some communities there were violent protests against it.

Despite the goals of school reformers, the common schools—or "free" schools as they were sometimes called—were not equally accessible to all children and were certainly not uniform in their curriculum and administration. In Quebec, Roman Catholics ran their own schools and shared government grants equally with Protestant schools. The Newfoundland government also provided assistance to a school system that was developed entirely along denominational lines. While school attendance under the new system increased impressively, many children attended erratically and for only a few years. Most parents viewed their children as contributors to the family economy and took them out of school to work in the fields or to perform household chores. In the 1860s, the policy of compulsory school attendance was still too controversial to force upon reluctant citizens.

Religion played a central role in defining identity in Canada. In the mid-nineteenth century, the growth in membership and power of Christian churches was a trend of major significance. Nearly every individual claimed to be a Christian, and those who did not were under intense pressure to become one. Not only were religious leaders reaching out to the unconverted both at home and abroad, they were also mounting campaigns to build new churches, establish universities, and support social services. Churches had a higher profile than the state in most communities and were pivotal to the spiritual, economic, social, and political life of the nation.

The energy displayed by the institutional church was in part fuelled by competition among the various denominations. At the time of confederation, over 40 percent of Canadians were Roman Catholic (see Table 1.2). They were a majority in Quebec

Cull's schoolhouse in West Garafraxa, Ontario, in 1867. Many communities in Victorian Canada boasted new one-room schoolhouses, built to the latest specifications of heat, light, and ventilation and staffed by teachers hired by the government.
From the collection of the Wellington County Museum and Archives/PH6130

TABLE 1.2 Religious Affiliation in Canada, 1871

Denomination	Percentage
Church of England	14.00
Baptist	6.80
Jewish	0.03
Lutheran	1.00
Roman Catholic	43.00
Congregationalist	0.60
Methodist	16.30
Presbyterian	16.20
Other	2.07

Source: Census of Canada, 1871 (Statistics Canada).

and Rupert's Land and formed a significant minority nearly everywhere else. Roman Catholics had participated in the political life of most of the colonies before it was possible to do so in Great Britain, where "Catholic Emancipation" was achieved only in 1829. The deep roots of Roman Catholicism in British North America, combined with a reinvigorated papacy in Rome and the arrival of a large number of Irish Roman Catholics in the colonies, virtually guaranteed a growing rivalry with Protestants.

By the mid-nineteenth century, the Roman Catholic Church was asserting its authority everywhere, but especially in Quebec. Papal enthusiasts resisted the separation of church and state, maintained a tight control over social services and education, and intervened directly in political matters when secular authorities threatened their power. In social terms, the Roman Catholic Church touched the lives of its adherents at every level. The number of priests and nuns grew dramatically at mid-century, and church-sponsored institutions ran the gamut from day nurseries and orphanages to universities such as Laval, based in Quebec City.

At the time of confederation, Ontario was the most Protestant province, with over 80 percent of its population belonging to one of the Protestant denominations. There was little uniformity among Protestants except in their determined opposition to Roman Catholicism. By the mid-nineteenth century, the Church of England was rapidly losing ground to the Baptist, Methodist, and Presbyterian churches, whose evangelical message often had a greater appeal to ordinary folk. The diversity of religious beliefs in colonial society made separation of church and state and voluntary support for church organization the preferred option for the majority of Protestants.

Although Protestants subscribed to the voluntary principle in religious matters, it did not mean that they recoiled from political action. Protestant alliances came together during elections to ensure the defeat of Roman Catholic candidates, while organizations such as the Orange Order were devoted to the exclusion of Roman Catholics from all areas of public life. Initially comprising of Irish Protestants, the Orange Order broadened its membership by offering assistance and camaraderie to anyone eager to fight papal influences. Violent clashes between Orange and Green (Irish Catholic) groups often accompanied parades marking important events in the history of Ireland, while a "mixed" marriage between a Protestant and a Roman Catholic might result in a noisy and even violent charivari by disapproving neighbours.

Brute strength often outweighed notions of Christian charity in motivating individual behaviour in Victorian Canada, where political conflict, drunken brawls, and family violence were common. Many parents and teachers encouraged discipline in children by beating them, and the law permitted husbands to use physical force to control their wives. Popular pastimes such as cockfighting, bear-baiting, wrestling, and fisticuffs carried violence into recreation. Along the waterfront in Quebec City's Lower Town and on Water Street in Halifax, violent crimes and brawls along with prostitution and drunkenness were commonplace. While there were laws against fighting duels, upper-class men continued to challenge each other to physical contests to defend their honour against even the most trivial verbal slights.

There was a growing concern within the middle class about the ignorance and violence that characterized Canadian society. Dedicated to individual discipline and self-help, middle-class reformers urged others to follow their lead in establishing "companionate" marriages, displaying good manners, and practising moderation in their public behaviour. Only a minority of people were committed to such a degree of self-discipline in 1867. But as the middle class grew and gained power in the later decades of the nineteenth century, concern for moderation and control became features of a set of "modern" values that would increasingly govern behaviour in Canada.

INTELLECTUAL REVOLUTIONS

The transformation sweeping Canada at the time of confederation had an enormous impact on belief systems. As material wealth and technological innovation became the order of the day, people began to advance the view that human beings were essentially good and that worldly progress was a desirable end of human endeavours. This was in sharp contrast to the older Christian belief that humans were born in sin and that release from the pain of human existence came only in a heavenly afterlife. For those adopting the modern perspective, education and moral training were seen as key to creating a reformed society.

Middle-class reformers in the mid-nineteenth century turned their zeal on the poor, criminal, and insane. Once considered the world's unfortunate souls, less advantaged groups were now believed to be "curable." Reformers urged the establishment of Houses of Industry (where the poor could be taught useful work habits), model prisons (where criminals could be reformed), and asylums (where the mentally ill could get remedial treatment). Like many other developments in this period, the reform impulse was documented by imposing buildings that testified to the public nature of the perceived solution to society's problems.

Concerned about the widespread consumption of alcoholic beverages, many reformers saw temperance as the single most effective solution to the complex problems facing a rapidly changing society. The Sons of Temperance was the largest temperance organization in 1867, with branches in every province. Not content to encourage individuals to discipline themselves in such matters as alcohol consumption, many temperance advocates were urging the passage of laws prohibiting the manufacture and sale of liquor.

Nothing symbolized the progressive impulse of the confederation period better than the promise and practice of science in Canada. Science stimulated industry, advanced civilization, filled hours of leisure time, and even, some believed, brought people closer to an understanding of God's purpose for the universe. By the 1860s, most Canadian universities had scientists on their faculties, and travelling lecturers could almost always guarantee a good audience if they spoke on a scientific subject. Practical inventions were the stock-in-trade of Canadians who, like their southern neighbours, were obsessed with finding better ways of doing things.

Cricket Club in Vancouver. At the time of confederation, there was little that could be called a Canadian literary or artistic culture, but Canadians had developed their own unique contribution to leisure and sports activities. Lacrosse and snowshoeing clubs, first organized in Montreal, reflected the popularity of sports introduced by Canada's Aboriginal peoples. By the 1860s, these activities were giving way to European leisure pursuits—cricket, racing, yachting, rowing, skating, and curling. Although a form of ice hockey was played in a few places before 1867, it was not the popular sport it would later become.
Vancouver Public Library/2417

Most Canadians accepted new science as part of a larger movement toward a better society. In 1859, their complacency was shaken when British scientist Charles Darwin published *On the Origin of Species*. Darwin's view that all living things evolved from a single primitive form of life and had developed by a process of natural selection and survival of the fittest flew in the face of Christianity's human-centred view of creation and the notion of a God who, if not benevolent, was at least not deliberately cruel. Darwinism was hotly debated in intellectual circles, but did little to dampen religious enthusiasm or deflect the rage for reform.

In their quest for improvement, Canadians had laid the foundations for 17 universities by the time of confederation. Most institutions of higher learning were sponsored by churches, and those claiming to be non-denominational, including Dalhousie, the University of New Brunswick, McGill, and the University of Toronto, often had close ties to one of the major churches. Open only to men, universities catered primarily to a small elite. Only about 1500 students attended Canadian universities in 1867. While law and medicine were taught in a few of the larger universities, the liberal arts, dominated by courses in Greek, Latin, and philosophy, was the most popular program of study.

Other than by word of mouth, people in 1867 received their information largely from newspapers. There were 380 newspapers published in British North America, one for every 10 000 people. Most newspapers appeared once or twice weekly and consisted of four pages crammed with editorials, shipping information, local items, serialized novels, advertisements, and news of the wider world. With the successful laying of the Atlantic cable in 1866, news from Europe was suddenly available in a few minutes rather than a week or two. Newspapers were sustained by political parties or religious denominations and by their subscribers, not by advertisements. As the purveyors of "knowledge," Canada's newspaper editors—men such as George Brown, Thomas D'Arcy McGee, and Joseph Howe—wielded considerable political power, and their high profiles often led them to careers in politics.

POLITICAL CHANGE

Political values in Victorian Canada reflected developments in the wider North Atlantic world. In Europe, the old order, in which power was concentrated in the hands of a small hereditary elite bolstered by a state-supported church and a standing army, was crumbling. The growing middle class demanded that power be shared by all men with a stake in society through elective representatives rather than monopolized by an appointed elite. These contrasting ways of organizing power, labelled "conservative" and "liberal," were challenged by a few people who argued that every man—and even every woman—should be given an equal political voice, and that equality of condition, not just equality of opportunity, should be the goal of public policy. Although such doctrines, labelled "radical" or "socialist," were quickly dismissed by the colonial elite, they developed a larger following as the Industrial Revolution gained ground.

The struggle between conservatives and liberals dominated colonial legislatures in British North America for the first half of the nineteenth century. Although there were rebellions in Upper and Lower Canada in 1837 and 1838, the transition to "responsible government"—the term used to describe the limited form of liberalism prevailing in the colonies—was a relatively peaceful affair. Political parties became the vehicle for choosing candidates to stand for election, and in most colonies they assumed the names of the theoretical positions they espoused: Conservative (Tory) and Liberal (Reform). In Quebec these parties were known by their colours: Bleu (Conservative) and Rouge (Liberal). By the time of confederation, the Conservative Party, inspired less by liberal doctrines than by its ambition to undermine the opposition, sported the name Liberal-Conservative Party, one which it continued to use on official documents until the 1920s.

The Roman Catholic Church in Quebec remained adamantly opposed to liberalism under firm instructions from Rome. It subscribed to the belief that the pope was infallible, proscribed controversial books listed on the papal Index, and excommunicated Roman Catholics who became members of the liberal-inspired Institut Canadien. At election time, leaders of the Roman Catholic Church threw their considerable weight behind Conservative candidates, who, in their view, represented the least of the evils on the political spectrum.

Even outside the Roman Catholic hierarchy, there was only qualified support for liberalism in Canada. It might be acceptable to support public schools, provide government funding to railway companies, and dismantle proprietary property relations, but few were

Thomas D'Arcy McGee

One of the most eloquent advocates of Canadian nationalism was Thomas D'Arcy McGee. A native of Ireland and a participant in the Irish rebellion of 1848, McGee immigrated to North America and finally settled in Montreal in 1857. As editor of *New Era,* a newspaper that catered to the growing Irish community in Montreal, McGee quickly gained a high profile and was elected to the assembly of the United Canadas. Rejecting the militant practices of his youth, he supported a new "northern nationality" for the British North American colonies within the larger imperial context. For McGee, a moderate nationalism based on economic progress offered an alternative to the ethnic and sectional conflicts that he felt impeded the progress of British North America, just as they had poisoned the potential of his beloved Ireland. In a speech delivered to the assembly of the United Canadas on 2 May 1860, McGee captured the enthusiasm that westward expansion and economic development inspired in many British North Americans:

> I look to the future of my adopted country with hope, though not without anxiety; I see in the not remote distance one nationality bound, like the shield of Achilles, by the blue rim of Ocean. I see it quartered into many communities, each disposing of its internal affairs, but all bound together by free institutions, free intercourse, and free commerce; I see within the round of that shield the peaks of the Western mountains and the crests of the eastern waves—the winding Assiniboine, the five-fold lakes, the St. Lawrence, the Ottawa, the Saguenay, the St. John, and the Basin of Minas—by all these flowing waters, in all the valleys they fertilize, in all the cities they visit on their courses, I see a generation of industrious, contented moral men, free in name and in fact—men capable of maintaining, in peace and in war, a Constitution worthy of such a Country.

McGee's views were highly unpopular among militant Irish nationalists, who in the 1850s banded together to form the Irish Republican Brotherhood and Clan-na-Gael, popularly known as the Fenians. With supporters on both sides of the Atlantic, their goal was to lift the yoke of British oppression and secure independence for Ireland by any means possible—including violence. They were opposed to any plan whereby the British North American colonies willingly chose to remain part of the British Empire and are believed to have been responsible for McGee's assassination in 1868.

Funeral procession of Thomas D'Arcy McGee, 1868.
Library and Archives Canada, C-084323

willing to take the notion of equality before the law too far. Colonial politicians toyed with the idea of adopting universal manhood suffrage but fell back on property and rental qualifications as the basis for political citizenship. No public figure suggested that women should be granted suffrage. When elections were called for the Canadian parliament in 1867, only about 20 percent of the population was eligible to vote.

The blending of a liberal economic regime with a conservative social order was particularly evident in the way colonial politicians approached legal reform. In an effort to embrace the opportunities of the industrial age, new laws relating to contract, debt, and bankruptcy were adopted in most colonies prior to confederation. The acceptance of liberal principles in family law took much longer to achieve. Legal reform was particularly complicated in Quebec, where a new civil code (1866) and the Code of Civil Procedure (1867) introduced liberal thinking with respect to commercial relations but maintained a more conservative approach to laws relating to family, marriage, inheritance, and the legal position of women.

The confederation movement itself was inspired by a new idea—nationalism—that was modified to accommodate particular Canadian circumstances. In Europe, national independence became the goal of peoples who could point to a common cultural identity, often linguistic or religious. Nationalism was unleashed during the American and French revolutions and quickly took hold in Latin America and Europe. In the mid-nineteenth century, British North Americans watched with growing interest the movements to unify the German and Italian states and efforts by Irish patriots to liberate Ireland from its hated union with Great Britain.

Many British North Americans saw nationalism as something that could spur the colonies to greater achievements, but nationalist sentiment posed problems in a society where culture divided rather than united its people. French Canadians, whose common language, religion, and history provided the basis for a separate national identity, were particularly leery of romantic talk about a larger British North American cultural identity. Safer ground for the new nationalism was the economic potential of the northern half of the continent, which stirred the hearts and imaginations of both the romantic idealist and the practical businessman. In the late 1850s, with the discovery of gold in British Columbia and scientific studies proclaiming the agricultural potential of the Prairies, the possibility of a transcontinental nation rivalling the United States suddenly seemed more than a pipe dream.

CONCLUSION

Divided by culture and geography, the British North American colonies in the 1860s seemed unlikely candidates for national greatness. While external pressures—changes in British colonial policy, fear of the United States, and the social chaos accompanying the Industrial Revolution—were powerful inducements to political experimentation, it was unclear whether First Nations and Europeans, English and French, Roman Catholic and Protestant, East and West, rich and poor could come together to produce anything more than unending conflict. Finding unity in diversity was the major challenge facing Canada's political leaders as they set about to create a transcontinental nation out of Great Britain's scattered North American colonies.

NOTES

1 *Eastern Chronicle* (New Glasgow), 3 July 1867.

2 Donna McDonald, *Illustrated News: Juliana Horatia Ewing's Canadian Pictures, 1867–1869* (Toronto: Dundurn Press, 1985), 44–45.

RELATED READINGS IN THIS SERIES

From Primary Documents CD-ROM, Volume II
Canadian Railways by 1860
Learners
Infants' Home, Toronto

SELECTED READING

This chapter summarizes material in the later chapters of *History of the Canadian Peoples*, Volume I, which should be consulted for published sources relating to Canada in the confederation era.

CHAPTER 2

Nation-Building, 1867–1880

TIMELINE

1864	Charlottetown and Quebec conferences discuss union of British North American colonies
1866	End of Reciprocity Treaty; Fenian raids; London conference
1867	Confederation; federal and provincial elections; Nova Scotia secession movement
1867–73	John A. Macdonald serves as Canada's first prime minister
1869	Nova Scotia and Ottawa come to terms; Newfoundland rejects confederation
1869–70	Red River Resistance
1870	Province of Manitoba created
1870–77	First Nations in the Northwest sign treaties with Ottawa
1871	British Columbia joins confederation
1872	Dominion Lands Act passed
1873	Prince Edward Island joins confederation; North-West Mounted Police established
1876	Native policy consolidated in Indian Act
1880	Great Britain transfers Arctic Archipelago to Canada

In his Speech from the Throne opening Canada's first parliamentary session on 7 November 1867, Governor General Lord Monck expressed his gratification at being able to assist "at every step taken in the creation of this great Confederation." He congratulated his listeners "on the Legislative sanction which has been given by the Imperial Parliament to the Act of Union," and which, in his view, "laid the foundations for a new Nationality that I trust and believe will, ere long, extend its bounds from the Atlantic to the Pacific."[1]

As witness to the events leading to confederation, Lord Monck was well aware of the hard bargaining that made it possible and the obstacles that still had to be overcome in extending its boundaries and creating a "new Nationality" that would inspire the allegiance of all Canadians. Even the selection of members for the first cabinet under Sir John A. Macdonald's leadership

proved to be a delicate balancing act of regional and religious representation. Would the new federation hold or would it dissolve into warring factions? Only time would tell.

This chapter explores the background to the confederation of the original four provinces of Canada in 1867 and the territorial expansion of the nation to the Pacific and Arctic oceans and to Prince Edward Island, which, like Newfoundland, had initially rejected the idea of British North American union.

THE ROAD TO CONFEDERATION, 1864–1867

Confederation was achieved relatively easily and without the violence and bloodshed typical of many national movements elsewhere. As with most successful undertakings, the context was critical to the final outcome. The revolution in imperial policy signalled by the adoption of free trade and the granting of responsible government was an important prerequisite. So, too, were the rapid advances in communication and transportation made possible by telegraph and the railroad. The Civil War in the United States (1861–1865) and its troubled aftermath added an air of urgency to constitutional discussions. Despite fierce provincial loyalties and long-held cultural identities, the fact that most people in 1867 had been born in British North America helped to make them more receptive to notions of homegrown nationalism.

Leadership, it could be argued, was also essential to the outcome of the confederation movement. Both at centre stage and behind the scenes during the negotiations was a purposeful group of businessmen and politicians, mostly based in the United Canadas, who were determined to make their vision a reality. With a generation of experience behind them in colonial administration and capitalist development, they drew up the confederation agreement, manoeuvred it through colonial and imperial legislatures, and played a central role in defining the policies that governed the new nation through its early years of development.

The event that set the ball rolling early in 1864 was the collapse of yet another administration in the United Province of Canada. Engineered by Great Britain before the colonies had been granted responsible government, the union of Upper and Lower Canada in 1840 had been designed to solve the problems of ethnic antagonism, economic stagnation, and political conflict in the two colonies. It failed to produce the desired results. Instead, sectional politics became entrenched, with a predominantly Roman Catholic Francophone population in Canada East aligned against a largely Protestant Anglophone population in Canada West.

Under the conditions laid down by the Act of Union, Canada East (formerly Lower Canada) and Canada West (formerly Upper Canada) had equal representation in the assembly. This situation became increasingly unacceptable to the rapidly growing population of Canada West. Policies favoured by one side were invariably imposed on the other, creating hard feelings on both sides. While Canada West tended to support public schools, ambitious economic programs, expansion of the militia, and a more democratic distribution of seats in the assembly, Canada East resisted such policies. By the late 1850s, the opposing parties in the assembly were so equally balanced that it became difficult to form a government. The resignation of another coalition government in March 1864 was the last in a long string of administrative failures that frustrated politicians and made capitalists uneasy about the investment potential of the colony.

By this time, too, the government of the United Canadas was deeply in debt, much of it generated by the loan guarantees and massive subsidies given to the Grand Trunk Railway. Although the Grand Trunk linked the colony from Sarnia to Quebec City, it carried less traffic than was predicted, was badly administered, and threatened to take the government with it if it filed for bankruptcy. Investors in the Grand Trunk saw confederation as the best way to recoup their failing fortunes. If the colonies united and expanded westward, the Grand Trunk could become a transcontinental railway carrying foodstuffs from a new agricultural frontier and products from Asia to markets in Great Britain. With this vision before them, some of the Grand Trunk's British investors bought controlling interest in the Hudson's Bay Company in 1863, planning to link the Northwest to the eastern colonies once, and if, confederation was achieved.

George Brown, leader of the Reform Party in Canada West, took the initiative in calling for a legislative committee with representatives from all parties to find a solution to the constitutional impasse. The committee met in May and early June of 1864. Although Brown preferred a smaller federation encompassing only Canada East and Canada West, he was prepared to accept the majority view that a larger federation should be attempted. When the government collapsed on 14 June—the very day the committee brought down its report—Brown became part of the so-called Great Coalition, which included his long-time rivals John A. Macdonald and George-Étienne Cartier. Its sole purpose was to settle the constitutional difficulties in the United Canadas. The first step in achieving this goal was to approach the Maritime colonies with a proposal for the union of British North America.

The Fathers of Confederation, by Robert Harris.
Library and Archives Canada/C-001466

FORGING AN AGREEMENT

The political crisis in the United Canadas coincided with discussions in the Maritimes on the topic of Maritime union. Primarily of interest to Nova Scotians and New Brunswickers who were riding high on their success in shipbuilding and international trade, Maritime union had become a fall-back position when the Canadians abruptly withdrew from discussions relating to an intercolonial railway in 1862. Maritime union offered the prospects of creating a larger stage for local politicians and, with any luck, the weight necessary to get British investors to look favourably on their railway proposals. The ice-free ports of Halifax and Saint John stood to benefit from any railway project the union could mount, and the region's rich reserves of coal would fuel the engines that ran the trains and factories.

When the Canadians sent letters asking to be invited to a proposed Maritime union conference, they initiated a chain of events that led to three conferences: one in Charlottetown in September 1864, a second a month later in Quebec City, and a final one in London in the fall and winter of 1866–1867. Prince Edward Island and Newfoundland opted out of negotiations after the Quebec Conference, but the advocates of confederation in the other self-governing colonies persevered, and, at the end of March 1867, the British North America Act (BNA Act) passed in the British parliament.

The Canadians who had signed the act all had different expectations about what the new federation would accomplish, and therein lay seeds of discord. While Ontario businessmen and farmers saw it as a chance to expand their markets and take a lead in developing the western plains, leaders of church and state in Quebec saw it as an opportunity to create a province with a Francophone and Roman Catholic majority. Even the skeptical Maritimers sometimes allowed themselves to imagine a future in which their ports bulged with the imports and exports of a great transcontinental nation. The BNA Act reflected these diverse interests and the power relationships that prevailed in the colonies in the 1860s.

The confederation agreement was largely the handiwork of politicians from the United Canadas.

Construction on Parliament Hill, 1863.
Library and Archives Canada, C-000773

For them, the most important goal was to preserve the liberal principle of majority rule while satisfying the demands of the Francophone minority. This was achieved through the creation of a federal system by which the powers of the state were divided between national and provincial administrations. Canada West and Canada East would each have provincial status, thus ending once and for all the indignities imposed by the Act of Union. To protect the Protestant minority in Canada East, the separate school system in place there was specifically guaranteed. Representation by population, with seats being weighted slightly in favour of rural ridings, would prevail in the House of Commons. Sectional equality was the proposed basis for appointments to the Senate: Ontario and Quebec were each allotted 24 seats, the same number that the Canadians were prepared to let the Maritimers divide among themselves.

The Canadians presented this blueprint for union at the Charlottetown Conference and hammered out the details in resolutions adopted at the October meetings in Quebec City. So determined were they to adhere as closely as possible to their principles that they even refused Prince Edward Island's request for an extra seat in the House of Commons. According to the formula developed for representation by population, the island received only five seats, an awkward number to divide among its three constituencies. The delegates were also unwilling to find a solution to the island's land problem. With little inducement, the islanders withdrew from the negotiations to enter confederation. Newfoundlanders were equally unimpressed by the proposals presented by the Canadians, whose interests in railways and westward expansion were far removed from the issues that dominated the Newfoundland economy.

There were also dissenting voices in Nova Scotia and New Brunswick. Anti-confederates in the Maritimes noted, with some justification, that confederation was a scheme of Canadian politicians and business interests who regarded the proposed new nation as an extension of the boundaries of the United Canadas. By virtue of the concentration of over three quarters of the colonial population within its territory, it would dominate the new federation. Moreover, anti-confederates argued, the financial proposals in the Quebec Resolutions gave the provinces inadequate income to pay for the responsibilities assigned to them, such as schools, roads, and social services. All customs duties, the main source of government funds in the 1860s, would be absorbed into the federal coffers, while the provinces would be forced to manage on a per capita grant. The small population base in the Maritimes meant that their provincial administrations would have little money to work with. Although Maritimers desperately wanted to be connected to the other colonies by an intercolonial railway, they saw little benefit coming their way from a line to the Pacific or indeed from an agricultural frontier on the distant Prairies. Many Acadians and Irish Roman Catholics in the region were suspicious, on principle, of any union that reflected British models in Ireland, Scotland, and Wales.

In Quebec, too, there were strong anti-confederate arguments, most of them voiced by Rouge leader Antoine-Aimé Dorion. He maintained that the federal government, with control over trade, foreign affairs, interprovincial railways, justice, and defence and armed with the right to take on extraordinary powers in times of emergency, would dictate to the provinces. Under such an arrangement Quebec would have little control over its destiny. Eventually its culture would be eroded and its people assimilated into an Anglophone Protestant state. The Rouges pressed for an election or a referendum on confederation, but to no avail. Despite tensions among its leaders, the Great Coalition held together. The Bleu majority from Canada East joined Reformers and Conservatives from Canada West to give the confederation proposals a comfortable majority in the legislature of the United Canadas in the winter of 1865.

The opposition to confederation in the Maritimes was not so easily brushed aside. Early in 1865, in a hotly contested election in New Brunswick, Samuel Leonard Tilley's pro-confederation forces were defeated by an anti-confederation coalition headed by A.J. Smith. Resistance to confederation in Nova Scotia developed so quickly under Joseph Howe's leadership that Conservative premier Dr. Charles Tupper decided against introducing the Quebec Resolutions in the assembly for fear that they would be rejected. Since Prince Edward Island and Newfoundland also showed little interest in confederation, it looked as if the Maritimes were out of the picture entirely.

CONFEDERATION ACHIEVED

Pro-confederation forces soon showed their hand. By 1865, the colonial office was fully behind confederation as a vehicle for reducing imperial commitments in North America, and it instructed its representatives in the colonies to use their influence to see that the scheme succeeded. Lieutenant-Governor Arthur Gordon in New Brunswick, demonstrating how imperial pressure could be exercised even in a colony that had responsible government, forced the resignation of his recently elected government and called another election. At the polls, Tilley's pro-confederation party, which promised to negotiate substantial alterations to the Quebec Resolutions to make them more acceptable to the voters, won a resounding victory.

Gordon's influence was not the only factor determining the outcome of the 1866 election. With the Reciprocity Treaty due to come to an end in 1866, timber interests in New Brunswick sought alternative economic strategies. The Roman Catholic hierarchy, originally opposed to confederation, was also coming around to a more positive view. For those who were still wavering, money supplied by the Canadians and their Grand Trunk allies helped legitimize the confederation forces. Further drama was added to the contest when, in the days leading up to the election, an American wing of the Fenian Brotherhood launched raids on New Brunswick and Canada West from their bases in the United States. Although easily deflected, the attacks gave emphasis to the pro-confederate position that defence could be better handled by a strong federal government for all of the colonies.

The end of reciprocity, which threatened markets for coal, timber, potatoes, and fish, also put Nova Scotia in a vulnerable position. In 1866, the prospects were so bleak that a few Nova Scotians even argued that annexation to the United States was the only sensible course of action. Tupper saw his main chance and took it. Unable to convince his own party to support the hated Quebec Resolutions, he managed to get the Nova Scotia assembly to authorize further negotiations on union. Since neither the Nova Scotian voters nor their elected representatives gave their approval to the proposals that ultimately became the basis of the BNA Act, there was certain to be trouble ahead.

John A. Macdonald

Born in Glasgow, Scotland, in 1815, John A. Macdonald immigrated to Upper Canada with his parents five years later. He attended school and studied law in Kingston, where he established his practice and became involved in various business ventures. In 1844, at age 29, he was elected to the legislature of the United Canadas and quickly became a leading figure in the Conservative Party. He helped engineer an alliance with the French-Canadian bloc and in 1856 emerged as co-premier of the United Canadas.

As Canada's first prime minister, Macdonald proved himself a quick-witted and practical politician. He kept close control over his party and used patronage to legitimize confederation among those who resisted its charms. An innovator and a builder rather than an ideologue, he believed that it was essential that Canada maintain British institutions in the face of American influences and was tenacious in pursuing this goal. His accommodation of Quebec was based on political necessity rather than any liberal notion of minority rights.

Macdonald's fondness for alcohol frequently caused embarrassment for his colleagues. Indeed, it may have contributed to the mismanagement of the railway negotiations that resulted in the Pacific Scandal and the defeat of his government in 1873. Nevertheless, Macdonald remained leader of the Conservative Party and led it to victory in 1878. Championing a national policy of industrialization, railway building, and western settlement, he remained in office until his death in May 1891.

John A. Macdonald.
Library and Archives Canada/PA12848

At the meetings in London, the Canadians were adamant that the Quebec Resolutions remain the basis of negotiations. Assurances were provided that the Intercolonial Railway would be built and that subsidies to provincial governments would be improved, but no substantial changes were made to the federal structure to meet the concerns of the Maritimers. The pressure from the Roman Catholic hierarchy for protection of separate schools outside Quebec was handled by including guarantees to separate schools legally in existence at the time the act went into effect and by the possibility of appeal to the federal government for remedial legislation should the laws be violated.

Federal and provincial powers were defined in the BNA Act of 1867. Section 91 enumerated a wide range of federal powers—running the gamut from trade and commerce to patents and copyright—that were, in the words of the act, deemed to be in the interest of the "Peace, Order and Good Government" of Canada as a whole. The list of responsibilities delegated to the provinces in section 92 of the act seemed modest when it was drawn up in 1867. In later years, with the expansion of matters of a "local or private Nature," such as municipal institutions, social services, and education, the provinces faced the challenge of finding money to pay for the responsibilities that fell to them under the BNA Act.

The finishing touches to the agreement included giving the new union a title, name, and rank. It was decided to refer to the union as a "confederation" rather than a "federation" on the grounds that the latter term implied a loose political arrangement that many of the architects of confederation sought to avoid. Agreement was quickly reached that it should be called Canada. Although suggestions were made that Canada should be ranked as a kingdom or viceroyalty, it was finally decided that it should be a "dominion," a term drawn, at Tilley's suggestion, from a biblical reference in Psalm 72: "He shall have dominion also from sea to sea, and from the river unto the ends of the earth."

CONSOLIDATING THE UNION

It had taken nearly three years to bring Nova Scotia, New Brunswick, and the United Province of Canada into confederation, but the work of creating a nation had only just begun. In addition to convincing the original signatories to the BNA Act to stay in the federation,

political leaders were also determined to round out boundaries and develop a national policy that would appeal to the hearts and minds of the diverse peoples in an immense territory. They had their work cut out for them.

The task of choosing the nation's first prime minister was assigned to the governor general, Lord Monck. He selected John A. Macdonald, an opponent of confederation before 1864, but thereafter its most energetic promoter. If anyone could bring the scattered elements of the new nation together, it would be John A., whose ability to charm his opponents and sustain the faithful with well-placed patronage was legendary.

Macdonald had hoped to maintain the coalition that had championed confederation, but there were defections. In 1865, George Brown resigned over disagreements regarding the handling of negotiations to renew the reciprocity treaty with the United States. Macdonald persuaded the remaining Reform ministers in the coalition to support his leadership and also maintained his partnership with the Bleus, led by

MORE TO THE STORY

Voting in the New Dominion

In 1867, elections were carried out very differently from the way they are today. Except in New Brunswick, where vote by secret ballot came into effect in 1857, voters openly announced the candidate of their choice, often to jeers from the crowd around the polls and under the watchful eyes of relatives, employers, and party workers. Violence between supporters of opposing sides was not uncommon. For example, no member was elected for the riding of Kamouraska in 1867 because a family feud between the Chapais and the Letelliers led to riots that made polling impossible.

The lack of a national franchise policy also caused difficulties. From 1867 to 1884, provincial election lists were used to determine who could vote. The 1867 contest was particularly confusing because all the provinces were electing new assemblies, and in Ontario and Quebec, candidates were allowed to sit in both the federal and provincial legislatures. Except in Nova Scotia, where voting occurred simultaneously in all constituencies on 18 September, elections were conducted at different times across the dominion. Thus, voting took place from late

July to September in the 180 constituencies electing members to the first Canadian House of Commons. As government leader, Macdonald could ensure that elections were held in the easy ridings first so that momentum could be used to sway votes in the constituencies where government support was uncertain.

The number of people eligible to cast a ballot was relatively small. All provinces at the time of confederation limited the vote to men over 21 years of age who owned or rented property of a certain value. Status Indians, regarded as wards of the state, had no vote, and property qualifications kept most unskilled workers and farm labourers off electoral lists. As a result of gender, property, and age restrictions, only 15 percent of the Quebec population, for example, could vote in provincial or federal elections in the early years of confederation, and only about 20 percent had this right by the end of the century. Today, by contrast, under universal suffrage for people over 18 years of age, almost 70 percent of the population has the right to vote, with most of the disenfranchised being either children or immigrants who have not yet fulfilled the requirements for citizenship.

George-Étienne Cartier. Samuel Leonard Tilley, the Liberal premier of New Brunswick, and Charles Tupper, Conservative premier of Nova Scotia, also agreed to bring their pro-confederation forces into Macdonald's Liberal-Conservative party.

The regional, religious, and cultural issues that had plagued the colonies before confederation lingered. When Macdonald created his first cabinet, he was obliged to accommodate various interests—Protestant and Catholic, French and English, province and nation. Although the Liberal-Conservative coalition carried 108 of the 180 seats in the first election, almost half of the popular vote went to candidates supporting George Brown's Reformers, A.A. Dorion's Rouges, and the Maritime anti-confederates. In time, they would form a coalition that would become the basis of the Liberal Party.

NOVA SCOTIA'S SECESSIONIST MOVEMENT

The election results also highlighted another serious problem. Although the Liberal-Conservatives won huge majorities in Ontario and Quebec, pro-confederation candidates won barely half the seats in New Brunswick, while Tupper was the only government candidate in Nova Scotia to scrape through. Tupper's Conservative government was also defeated in the elections to the provincial assembly, where all but two seats went to anti-confederation candidates. With such a clear indication of discontent in his native province, Joseph Howe felt that he had a mandate to transform his anti-confederation campaign into a demand for repeal of the union. A Repeal League quickly took shape, and Howe was dispatched to London to get permission to take Nova Scotia out of confederation.

Many Maritimers believed that they had every reason to feel aggrieved. The Liberal-Conservative Party proved little more than the old Conservative-Bleu alliance of the United Canadas writ large; the federal cabinet was dominated by politicians from Ontario and Quebec who held nine of the 13 ministerial positions; and the nation's capital, Ottawa, was run by public servants who had formerly served the United Canadas. When the Canadian parliament opened on 8 November 1867, it endorsed policies that fuelled

Nova Scotia's discontent, including a rise in the tariff rate from 10 to 15 percent, which angered Maritime shippers dependent on international trade.

In London, Howe's request for repeal of the union fell on deaf ears. Accepting defeat, Howe began negotiating with the Canadians for better terms for Nova Scotia in confederation. Howe's willingness to compromise was due in part to growing militancy among his anti-confederate supporters. Neither a populist nor a republican, Howe was repulsed by talk of popular revolt or annexation to the United States, which many Repealers saw as their only alternatives to the hated union. Howe reasoned that it was better to make the best of a bad bargain than risk the possibility of severing ties with the mother country, and even of bloody conflict.

At meetings held in Portland, Maine, over the winter of 1868–1869, Howe and Finance Minister John Rose hammered out "better terms" for Nova Scotia. The federal government agreed to pay an additional $1 million of pre-confederation Nova Scotia debt and to increase the province's annual grant by $82 698 per year for 10 years to help it meet the ongoing costs of government. In a rare gesture of conciliation, Howe and Hugh MacDonald, another anti-confederate from Nova Scotia, were given seats in the cabinet. The strategy was only partly successful. Despite his high profile, Howe had difficulty winning his own seat in Hants County and proved unable to deliver all of the anti-confederates from Nova Scotia into Macdonald's hands.

In conjunction with Tupper, who was awarded a seat in the cabinet in 1870, Howe urged his colleagues to move quickly on the construction of the Intercolonial Railway and to press for a new reciprocity treaty with the United States. All regions of Canada lamented the end of free trade with the United States in 1866, but Maritimers were particularly eager to restore American markets. As a result of negotiations in 1866 in which Great Britain gave Americans access to the inshore fisheries without offering anything in return, Maritimers were convinced that their interests were being sacrificed on the altar of larger Canadian and imperial goals.

Macdonald hoped that negotiations between the United States and Great Britain to resolve difficulties resulting from the American Civil War would provide an opportunity to pressure the Americans to accept free trade. In 1871, he represented Canada in a British delegation that met with its American counterparts in Washington. Macdonald's strategy was to exchange American access to Canadian inshore fisheries for a new reciprocity treaty, but he was unable to do so because of opposition from the protectionist Republican Congress. While there would be no general access to American markets, the Treaty of Washington offered some relief to Canadians involved in the fisheries. Their fish was granted free entry into the United States, and financial compensation, to be decided by arbitration, would be forthcoming in return for American access to Canada's inshore waters.

There were cries of "sell-out" in Nova Scotia, but only two Nova Scotian members of parliament voted against the treaty. By the time of the 1872 election, two-thirds of Nova Scotia MPs supported Macdonald. Anti-confederates remained strong in the provincial assembly, but much of the energy had gone out of their fight. The threat of secession, it seemed, had passed—at least for the time being.

ANNEXING THE NORTHWEST: THE RED RIVER RESISTANCE

The first parliamentary session of the Dominion of Canada moved swiftly to negotiate the transfer of the Northwest to the new country. By 1869, an agreement had been reached with the Hudson's Bay Company, which held legal title over the region, to sell its claim to the land for £300 000 (about $1.5 million) and a grant to the company of one-twentieth of the land most suitable for farming. This agreement proved lucrative to the financiers who had bought control of the company in 1863. They received a cash return on their initial investment of about £1.5 million, retained their fur-trading operations, and stood to gain immensely from the sale of land once the area was settled. Eventually, the land sales netted the company $120 million.

The Métis and Aboriginal peoples living in the Northwest were not included in these negotiations. Nor were they consulted when the federal government began to implement policies to open the region to

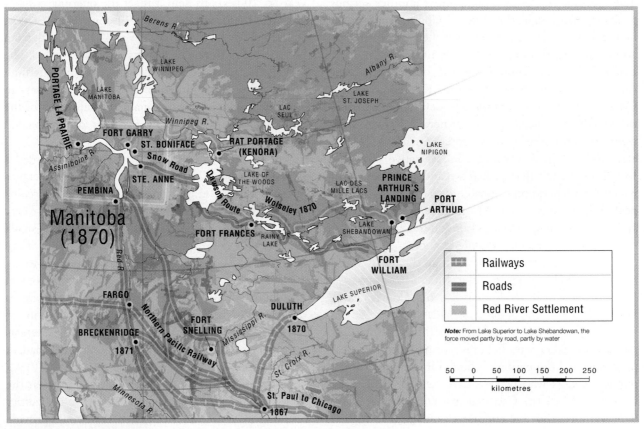

MAP 2.1 **Red River colony.**

immigrants. In August 1869, Ottawa sent land surveyors to the Red River colony to prepare for the influx of settlers expected when the official transfer of title occurred in December. Métis fears that they would lose possession of the land they farmed seemed confirmed when the surveyors began measuring the land in square lots, ignoring the narrow river-lot system used by the Métis to mark off their property.

The behaviour of Canadians already living in the Red River area reinforced the Métis's well-founded anxieties. Unlike the fur traders, who were often paternalistic but rarely contemptuous toward Aboriginal and Métis peoples, the so-called Canadian Party regarded Natives as uncivilized people whose presence in the region was a deterrent to European settlement. Canadians were a minority in the community, which, according to the 1871 census, included 5757 French-speaking Métis, 4083 English-speaking Métis—the offspring of English traders and Aboriginal women—1500 whites, and 558 Natives, but they had the ear of Ottawa. Many of them

were land speculators who hoped to make their fortunes when Canada acquired the Northwest.

On 11 October 1869, a group of unarmed Métis stopped a road-building party from its work, angry that the contract had been given to John Snow, an openly racist Canadian land speculator. Five days later, the Métis National Committee was formed. The committee's goal was to block the Canadian takeover of Red River until firm guarantees for Métis land rights had been granted. The Métis chose Louis Riel as secretary of this committee. Twenty-five-year-old Riel had spent nearly 10 years in Catholic educational institutions in Quebec. Literate and articulate, he was seen as someone who could negotiate with the Canadians on their own terms but who, as a Métis, could be counted on not to sell out his people.

Meanwhile, William McDougall, the minister of Public Works in Macdonald's cabinet, was appointed the first lieutenant-governor of what became known as the Northwest Territories, and immediately set out

Louis Riel (second row, centre) with his provisional government.
Library and Archives Canada/C6692

to take possession of Canada's new colony. When McDougall attempted to enter Hudson's Bay territory on 2 November, he was prevented from doing so by a group of armed Métis. Early in December, the Métis established a provisional government under John Bruce and Louis Riel to coordinate resistance to Canadian imperialism.

The heart of the resistance lay with French-speaking Métis. Although many residents of the Red River area opposed the provisional government's actions, they were reluctant to take sides. The English-speaking Métis were particularly torn and shifted allegiance depending upon the circumstances. Macdonald tried to undermine the resistance by encouraging divisions between the French-speaking Métis and their English-speaking counterparts and by using the influence of the Roman Catholic Church over the leaders of the provisional government, but his efforts failed.

The Canadians in Red River attempted to overthrow the provisional government soon after it was established, but they were no match for the well-organized Métis. Sixty-five conspirators were captured and imprisoned in Fort Garry. Yet another attempt to seize control of the colony was foiled in February 1870. One of the prisoners captured in the second incident was Thomas Scott, an Orangeman from Ontario who had been employed as a road builder before the rebellion began. Showing contempt for his Métis guards, he called on his fellow prisoners to escape so they could continue their resistance to the provisional government. Riel, pressured by angry Métis guards bent on vengeance and by the challenge to his government's legitimacy, agreed to have Scott executed in March 1870.

The situation was further complicated by the presence of American agents in Red River. Afraid that the United States would take advantage of the political crisis to seize control of the region, Macdonald reluctantly agreed to negotiate with representatives of the provisional government. They were led by Abbé N.J. Ritchot, who had the confidence not only of Riel but also of the Bishop of St. Boniface, A.A. Taché. Church officials opposed the rebellion but supported Métis land claims and demands for protection of the French language and Roman Catholic religion.

By May 1870, negotiations between the Canadian and provisional Red River governments had concluded with an agreement that, on the surface, met Métis demands. The Red River colony and its environs would become the province of Manitoba, a tiny jurisdiction that initially encompassed only the area around Red River. Like the other provinces, it would have an elected legislative assembly and an appointed upper chamber. Both English and French were officially recognized in legislative and court proceedings; denominational schools, Protestant and Roman Catholic, would be maintained. Unlike other provinces, Manitoba would, until the federal government decided otherwise, have its land and other resources controlled by Ottawa. For the Métis, the major victory was the guarantee in the Manitoba Act that they would receive title for lands they currently farmed in addition to 1.4 million acres of farmland for the use of their children.

The victory soon proved hollow. With a settlement in hand, Macdonald convinced British authorities that a military expedition should be sent to Red River to assert Canadian control against American designs and any further difficulties from the Métis. Led by Colonel Garnet Wolseley, the army included in its ranks Ontario Orangemen who saw Riel and his followers as the agents of Roman Catholic domination in the West. They imposed a virtual reign of terror on the Métis. Riel fled to the United States, and other members of the provisional government went into hiding. In the wake of the army, white settlers poured into the province and received title for land while the Métis were kept waiting for their promised land grants. With the buffalo in Manitoba disappearing, no land settlement in sight, and continued hostility from their white neighbours, many Métis moved west to territory that is now part of Saskatchewan, where they could still hunt buffalo and where they could establish communities under their own control.

THE INDIAN TREATIES

The Macdonald government was determined not to repeat the Métis experience with the Natives in newly acquired territories. Between 1871 and 1877, seven treaties were concluded with Aboriginal peoples living east of the Rockies, whose estimated population was 34 000. Adams Archibald, the first lieutenant-governor of Manitoba, was the negotiator of Treaty 1, which covered the area around Lower Fort Garry. In his speech to those assembled for the occasion, he made clear the intentions of the federal government: "Your Great Mother [Queen Victoria] wishes the good of all races under her sway. She wishes her red children to be happy and contented. She wishes them to live in comfort. She would like them to adopt the habits of the whites, to till land and raise food, and store it up against a time of want."[2]

The Natives agreed to the treaties because they were facing starvation and feared the changes that were taking place around them. They wanted guarantees for their future well-being, which was being threatened by the disappearance of the buffalo and the influx of settlers. Like the six subsequent treaties, Treaty 1 established reserves where Aboriginal peoples would have farms and promised implements, seed, and training to launch them in agricultural careers. It also promised that traditional hunting and fishing rights would be recognized.

Aboriginal peoples were soon frustrated by the failure of the Canadian government to live up to its promises. Indian Commissioner Wemyss Simpson interpreted the Lower Fort Garry treaty to imply that

implements and seed would be provided only when Native peoples had settled on reserves and built homes to demonstrate their readiness for agricultural life. The distraught Lower Fort Garry Natives replied eloquently but with little impact: "We cannot tear down trees and build huts with our teeth, we cannot break the prairie with our hands, nor reap the harvest when we have grown it with our knives."[3]

THE INDIAN ACT

The political status of Native peoples on the Prairies was determined before the treaties were negotiated. Under the BNA Act, Aboriginal peoples throughout Canada were placed under the jurisdiction of the federal government. Those living on reserves in the eastern colonies were registered by the federal government, as were the "Treaty Indians" in the new areas acquired by Canada. In 1876, Ottawa consolidated its policies with respect to "Status Indians" in the comprehensive

During the American Civil War, the British North American colonies feared an invasion from the United States. African Americans living in Victoria formed the Victoria Pioneer Rifle Corps to help defend the colony.
British Columbia Archives and Records Service/C-6124

Indian Act. The act was revised periodically over the following century, but its basic premise—that Natives were still incapable of integrating into "civilized" society and therefore needed supervision in their economic, political, and social activities—remained unchanged.

The act made provision for replacing traditional political practices with band chiefs and councils and subjected all reserve activities to the supervision of regional and national structures dominated by white bureaucrats. In defining Indian status, the act made gender distinctions: the wives, widows, and children of registered men were declared Status Indians even if they had no Indian heritage. Meanwhile, an Aboriginal woman who married a white man lost her status as an Indian, as did her children. In later revisions to the act, Status Indians were denied the right to perform traditional religious practices or drink alcohol. In theory, reserves were designed to isolate Aboriginal peoples so that they could learn European ways at their own pace and be introduced to white society when they were ready; in practice, it brought them together in closed political and social arrangements that made future integration highly unlikely.

As the provisions of the Indian treaties and Indian Act suggest, the government's priority in the Northwest was European settlement, not Aboriginal. In 1872, the Dominion Lands Act granted free homesteads of 160 acres to farmers who cleared 10 acres and built homes within three years of registering their intention to settle. In 1873, the North-West Mounted Police was established to maintain law and order in the Northwest. Although planning for the force was already in the works, its speedy approval by parliament was assured after the massacre of 22 Assiniboine in the Cypress Hills by American wolf hunters bent on avenging the alleged theft of horses. This atrocity emphasized the threat from Americans who eyed the lands claimed by Canada. Threats from the United States also stiffened Macdonald's resolve to negotiate the entry of British Columbia and Prince Edward Island into confederation.

BRITISH COLUMBIA

The gold rush in British Columbia was over by the mid-1860s, resulting in a large outflow of prospectors, miners, and merchants. Before the economic downturn, the two West Coast colonies—Vancouver Island and British Columbia—had spent liberally to build courts, roads, and other public works and were now facing bankruptcy. The colonial office engineered their union in 1866, but, with a combined debt of $1.3 million, the new colony of British Columbia was not in a position to embrace new programs for development. Jealousy between mainlanders and islanders further complicated the colony's politics. For two years, New Westminster and Victoria fought over which one would be the capital before the latter prevailed. The lack of full responsible government also drew fire from the growing number of immigrants.

By the early 1870s, new economic activities had taken root on the West Coast. Coal mines were operating in Nanaimo, sawmills had been established along Alberni Canal and Burrard Inlet, a British naval base was located in Esquimalt, and small agricultural settlements were scattered throughout the colony. Victoria continued its role as the centre of banking, commerce, and shipbuilding. Although British capital dominated these economic initiatives, close economic ties developed with the American territories south of the border during and after the gold rush.

While a few business people in Victoria called for admission of British Columbia into the United States, the idea was denounced by the dominant British interests in the colony. The latter tended to support the status quo. As in Red River, immigrants from the eastern colonies were inclined to support annexation to Canada. They did so not only because Canada was their original homeland but also because they found the political system in British Columbia, which was dominated by appointed officials, antiquated and oppressive. They reasoned, quite correctly, that confederation would bring with it representative and responsible government. In constructing their political visions, immigrants in British Columbia invariably excluded Native peoples who, if allowed to vote in British Columbia, could have dominated the electoral processes.

The confederation option was slow to take hold in part because the British elite concentrated on Vancouver Island tended to view Canadians, most of whom had settled on the mainland, as a "poor mean slow people."[4] Nevertheless, one Canadian, who certainly defied the stereotype, kept the confederation option at the forefront. Amor de Cosmos was a colourful Victoria-based newspaper editor whose adopted name—he was plain William Smith from Nova Scotia—reflected his flamboyant style. In March 1867, de Cosmos countered annexationist proposals with a resolution in the legislative council that British Columbia be included as a province of Canada. Great Britain rejected the proposal at the time on the grounds that it was premature to incorporate the Pacific coast into the new federation before the Northwest had been acquired by Canada. Undaunted, de Cosmos and his allies established the Confederation League in 1868 to mobilize support for their cause.

Once the fate of the Northwest had been sealed, the colonial office was quick to let the colonists know that Great Britain favoured British Columbia's entry into confederation. Lieutenant-Governor Andrew Musgrave was sent to the colony in 1869 to actively promote the union. After an inconclusive debate in the legislative council on the merits of union with Canada, it was agreed that a delegation would meet with representatives of the dominion government. The council's terms for British Columbia's entry into confederation included the immediate building of a wagon road connecting New Westminster to Fort Garry, with a railroad along that route to follow in due course; the assumption by Canada of British Columbia's existing debt; and a grant to the province of $100 000 per annum to enable it to undertake necessary public works.

In June 1870, three delegates from British Columbia—Dr. Robert Carrall, Joseph Trutch, and John Sebastian Helmcken—met in Ottawa with the Canadian delegation led by George-Étienne Cartier. He proved more than willing to accept the conditions demanded by the British Columbians and even agreed to start building the railway within two years and complete it within 10 years of British Columbia's joining confederation. These generous terms raised more than one eyebrow in Ottawa. How could a railway be built across such difficult terrain in such a short time? What would the other provinces say about the $100 000 per annum grant that was much more on a per capita basis than they had been offered? British Columbia would have needed a non-Aboriginal population of 120 000 to justify its grant request. Instead, it had only about 10 500: 8576 Europeans, 1548 Chinese, and 462 African-origin residents. Despite these concerns, the Macdonald government stood by the agreement.

Amor de Cosmos. In 1852 William Smith left his job in a Halifax grocery business for the gold fields of California, where he changed his name to Amor de Cosmos, claiming that the name "tells what I love most . . . order, beauty, the world, the universe." In 1858 he moved to Victoria, where he established a newspaper—the *British Colonist*—and became involved in politics. A promoter of both responsible government and confederation for British Columbia, he served as premier of the province from 1872 to 1874. He proved to be a poor politician and was defeated by the voters of Victoria in 1882 for advocating Canadian independence from Great Britain.
Library and Archives Canada/PA-025397

British Columbia would give Canada a Pacific boundary and fulfill the confederation promise of a dominion from sea to sea. It could not be lost to the Americans.

Under the terms of the confederation agreement, the federal government assumed responsibility for "the Indians, and the trusteeship and management of the lands received for their use and benefit." As for future land negotiations, Ottawa agreed to continue "a policy as liberal as that pursued by the British Columbia Government." The province was required to release for reserves only "tracts of land of such extent that has hitherto been the practice of the British Columbia Government to appropriate for that purpose." As historical geographer Cole Harris has noted, this "dubious bargain" imposed a new constitutional rigidity on the province and inflicted years of federal-provincial conflict on the Native land question.[5] With the province in control of the land and its resources and Ottawa responsible for Aboriginal policy, the Native land issue quickly became a political football.

Elections in November 1870 gave every seat in the British Columbia legislature to supporters of confederation on the terms worked out in the June negotiations. On 18 January 1871, the legislative council unanimously agreed to bring the colony into confederation, and in June British Columbia became the sixth province of Canada. Few people in British Columbia—and certainly not the First Nations, who made up 80 percent of the population—felt any real attachment to Canada. The economic stimulus of the proposed railway and Canadian government grants made confederation appear to be a lucrative economic arrangement that should not be rejected.

PRINCE EDWARD ISLAND

Similar economic reasons led Prince Edward Island into confederation in 1873. In the 1860s, the promise of an intercolonial railway connecting the Maritimes to

potential markets in central Canada seemed irrelevant to residents of the island colony. The 1867 election was fought not over confederation but over the persistent land question, the role of the Conservative government in repressing the Tenant League—organized to intimidate landlords—and denominational schools, an issue of intense interest to Roman Catholics, who made up 45 percent of the island's population.

Supported by a majority of Roman Catholic voters, the Liberals defeated the Conservatives in the 1867 election. Once in office, the Liberals proved as unwilling as their Conservative predecessors to establish a system of publicly funded denominational schools. Consequently, they lost much of their support and, in turn, suffered defeat in the 1870 election. The Conservatives under James Pope, a leading island businessman and one-time supporter of confederation, formed a new government in alliance with Roman Catholic independents who had broken away from the Liberals.

When the Conservatives took office, the economy of the island colony was stable, if not thriving. Its 94 021 inhabitants found export markets for the

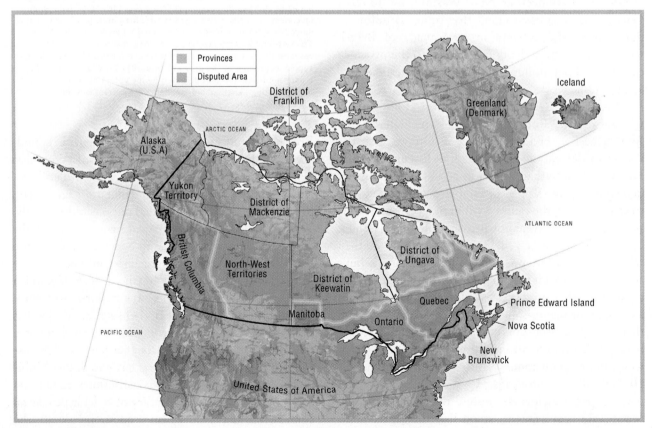

MAP 2.2 **Canada, 1882.**

products of their farms and fisheries and, like other Maritimers, boasted a healthy shipbuilding industry. In the wake of several decades of steady growth, the island's elite had established three banks and several newspapers. Only one thing was missing: railroads. An apostle of progress, Pope set out to fill the gap with a line that wound a serpentine route through many of the island's communities. Islanders soon found, as had others before them, that railway building was hard on the public purse. Faced with huge public debt, Pope argued that only by joining Canada and letting Ottawa assume the island's debt could they avoid the paralysis that repayment would entail.

Macdonald agreed not only to assume the railway debt and establish year-round communications between the island and the mainland, but also to use federal money to buy out the remaining absentee landlords so that tenants could become freeholders. With its interests thus addressed, Prince Edward Island agreed to become the seventh province of Canada in 1873.

NEWFOUNDLAND'S PERSPECTIVE

There was little prospect that Newfoundland, the remaining Atlantic colony, would follow in Prince Edward Island's footsteps. Dependent largely on fisheries, the island's 150 000 people looked out to sea and international trade for their livelihood. The economy was experiencing difficulties in the 1860s, but confederation promised more problems than it solved. British North America bought only 5 percent of Newfoundland's exports and provided 16 percent of its imports. With markets in southern Europe, the West Indies, and Brazil, and 70 percent of its imports supplied by Great Britain and the United States, confederation threatened Newfoundland's long-standing trading patterns with tariffs against foreign trade and policies designed to create an integrated national economy.

Other issues influencing the mainland colonies also had little resonance in Newfoundland. In any attack, the island would be defended by the British navy and not an enlarged Canadian militia, mention of which only conjured up fears that the colony's young men would be conscripted to fight Canadian wars. Nor did the colonial office use pressure to force compliance. The merchants of St. John's and Conception Bay, who dominated the local economy, were firmly set against union with Canada, and most of the island's

Roman Catholic population—and particularly the church leaders in the colony, many of whom were Irish immigrants—wanted no part of a union backed by Great Britain. With so little support for it, confederation was not even an issue in the 1865 election.

Nevertheless, Conservative premier Frederick Carter, a principled man who had done much to mute sectarian politics in his province, supported the idea of union. In the months preceding the 1869 election, he persuaded the assembly to pass draft terms for union, and a generous agreement was negotiated with the Canadian government. This initiative proved to be Carter's undoing. Led by the merchant Charles Fox Bennett, anti-confederation forces won over two-thirds of the seats in the Newfoundland legislature. Even Protestant areas of the colony, which usually voted Conservative, deserted the party that had flirted with "the Canadian wolf." Several generations would pass before Newfoundlanders debated the issue of confederation again.

THE NORTH

In 1880, by an imperial order-in-council, the Arctic Archipelago was added to Canadian jurisdiction as the District of Franklin. This move was precipitated by a request from the United States in 1874 for mineral rights on Baffin Island. There was no thought of developing or settling the region on the part of British or Canadian authorities. As one member of the colonial office remarked at the time, the main reason for turning the islands over to Canada was "to prevent the United States from claiming them, not from their likelihood of their being any value to Canada."[6]

CONCLUSION

Despite the refusal of Newfoundland to join confederation, by 1880 the Dominion of Canada stretched from sea to sea to sea. There was, of course, nothing inevitable about the union of the British North American colonies. Nor was there any guarantee that the wobbly structure put in place primarily to promote railways and accommodate certain cultural sensibilities would survive any length of time. Federations are notoriously unstable political arrangements and often last only a few years. In the case of Canada, however, the naysayers were proven wrong.

NOTES

1 Canada, House of Commons Debates, 7 November 1967, 5.

2 Alexander Morris, *The Treaties of Canada with the Indians of Manitoba and the North-West Territories* (1880; Toronto: Coles, 1971), 28.

3 Quoted in Manitoba Indian Brotherhood, *Treaty Days: Centennial Commemorations Historical Pageant* (Winnipeg: Manitoba Indian Brotherhood, 1971), 24.

4 Quoted in Jean Barman, *The West Beyond the West: A History of British Columbia*, rev. ed. (Toronto: University of Toronto Press, 1996), 92.

5 Cole Harris, *Making Native Space: Colonialism, Resistance, and Reserves in British Columbia* (Vancouver: UBC Press, 2002), 73.

6 Cited in Shelagh D. Grant, *Sovereignty or Security: Government Policy in the Canadian North, 1936–1950* (Vancouver: UBC Press, 1988), 5.

RELATED READINGS IN THIS SERIES

From *Nation and Society: Readings in Post-Confederation Canadian History*

D.N. Sprague, "Dispossessed vs. Accommodation in Plaintiff vs. Defendant Accounts of Métis Dispersal from Manitoba, 1870–1881," 4–20.

From Primary Documents CD-ROM, Volume II

Declaration of the People of Rupert's Land and the North-West

The Execution of Thomas Scott: Ontario's Reaction

The Dominion Lands Act

The Stone Fort and Manitoba Post Treaties, Numbers One and Two

Settlers Moving West Through Winnipeg in Response to the Dominions Land Act of 1872

Western Canada: The New Eldorado

SELECTED READING

There is an extensive literature on confederation. The standard surveys include W.L. Morton, *The Critical Years: The Union of British North America, 1857–1873* (Toronto: McClelland & Stewart, 1964); P.B. Waite, *The Life and Times of Confederation, 1864–1867* (Toronto: University of Toronto Press, 1962); and Donald Creighton, *The Road to Confederation: The Emergence of Canada, 1863–1867* (Toronto: Macmillan, 1964). A useful analysis of party politics in the confederation era can be found in Gordon T. Stewart, *The Origins of Canadian Politics: A Comparative Approach* (Vancouver: UBC Press, 1986). Stanley Ryerson's *Unequal Union: Roots of Crisis in the Canadas* (Toronto: Progress Books, 1968) provides a Marxist perspective on the period. Several important essays on confederation appear in Ramsay Cook, ed., *Confederation* (Toronto: University of Toronto Press, 1967); and Ged Martin, ed., *The Causes of Canadian Confederation* (Fredericton: Acadiensis Press, 1990). The Maritime perspective is insightfully analyzed by Phillip A. Buckner, P.B. Waite, and William M. Baker, "The Maritimes and Confederation: A Reassessment," *Canadian Historical Review* 71, no. 1 (March 1990), 1–45. Individual provinces are the focus of A.I. Silver, *The French-Canadian Idea of Confederation, 1864–1900* (Toronto: University of Toronto

Press, 1982); Kenneth G. Pryke, *Nova Scotia and Confederation, 1864–74* (Toronto: University of Toronto Press, 1979); Donald F. Warner, "The Post-Confederation Annexation Movement in Nova Scotia," *Canadian Historical Review* 28, no. 3 (September 1947), 156–65; William M. Baker, "Squelching the Disloyal, Fenian-Sympathizing Brood: T.W. Anglin and Confederation in New Brunswick, 1865–1866," *Canadian Historical Review* 55, no. 22 (June 1974), 141–58; Alfred G. Bailey, "The Basis and Persistence of Opposition to Confederation in New Brunswick," *Canadian Historical Review* 23, no. 4 (December 1942), 374–97; Carl M. Wallace, "Albert Smith, Confederation and Reaction in New Brunswick, 1852–1882," *Canadian Historical Review* 64, no. 4 (December 1963), 285–312; Ian Ross Robertson, "Prince Edward Island Politics in the 1860s," *Acadiensis* 15, no. 1 (Autumn 1985), 35–58; David Weale and Harry Baglole, *The Island and Confederation: The End of an Era* (Summerside, PEI: Williams and Crue, 1973); F.W.P. Bolger, *Prince Edward Island and Confederation* (Charlottetown: St Dunstan's University Press, 1964); and James Hiller, "Confederation Defeated: The Newfoundland Election of 1869," *Newfoundland in the Nineteenth and Twentieth Centuries: Essays in Interpretation*, ed. James Hiller and Peter

Neary (Toronto: University of Toronto Press, 1980), 67–94. On railways and railway promoters in the confederation era, see A.A. den Otter, *The Philosophy of Railways: The Transcontinental Railway Idea in British North America* (Toronto: University of Toronto Press, 1997). See also Bruce Curtis, *The Politics of Population: State Formation, Statistics, and the Census of Canada, 1840–1985* (Toronto: University of Toronto Press, 2003).

American designs and other designs on the Northwest are discussed in Sarah Carter, *Aboriginal People and Colonizers of Western Canada to 1900* (Toronto: University of Toronto Press, 1999); and Alvin C. Gluek, *Minnesota and the Manifest Destiny of the Canadian Northwest* (Toronto: University of Toronto Press, 1965). The Red River Resistance is discussed in George F.G. Stanley, *The Birth of Western Canada: A History of the Riel Rebellions* (Toronto: University of Toronto Press, 1970); W.L. Morton, ed., *Alexander Begg's Red River Journal* (Toronto: Champlain Society, 1956); Gerhard J. Ens, *Homeland to Hinterland: The Changing Worlds of the Red River Métis in the Nineteenth Century* (Toronto: University of Toronto Press, 1996); D.N. Sprague, *Canada and the Métis, 1869–1885* (Waterloo, ON: Wilfrid Laurier University Press, 1988); Thomas Flanagan, *Métis Lands and Manitoba* (Calgary: University of Calgary Press, 1991); Frits Pannekoek, *The Social Origins of the Riel Resistance, 1869–70* (Winnipeg: Watson and Dwyer, 1991); and J.M. Bumsted, *Reporting the Resistance: Alexander Begg and Joseph Hargrave on the Red River Resistance* (Winnipeg: University of Manitoba Press, 2004).

On British Columbia and confederation, see Margaret Ormsby, "Canada and the New British Columbia," *Canadian Historical Association Report* (1948), 74–85, and the relevant chapters of Robin Fisher, *Contact and Conflict: Indian-European Relations in British Columbia, 1774–1890* (Vancouver: UBC Press, 1977); Jean Barman, *The West Beyond the West: A History of British Columbia*, rev. ed. (Toronto: University of Toronto Press, 2007); Adele Perry, *On the Edge of Empire: Gender, Race, and the Making of British Columbia, 1849–1871* (Toronto: University of Toronto Press, 2001); and Cole Harris, *Making Native Space: Colonialism, Resistance, and Reserves in British Columbia* (Vancouver: UBC Press, 2002).

Biographies of major political leaders of the period include Brian Young, *George-Étienne Cartier: Montreal Bourgeois* (Montreal: McGill-Queen's University Press, 1981); A.A. den Otter, *Civilizing the West: The Galts and the Development of Western Canada* (Edmonton: University of Alberta Press, 1982); D.G. Creighton, *John A. Macdonald*, 2 vols. (Toronto: Macmillan, 1965); Richard Gwyn, *John A. The Man Who Made Us: The Life and Times of John A. Macdonald* (Toronto: Random House, 2007); J.M.S. Careless, *Brown of the Globe*, 2 vols. (Toronto: Macmillan, 1959); J. Murray Beck, *Joseph Howe*, 2 vols. (Montreal: McGill-Queen's University Press, 1985/88); William M. Baker, *Timothy Warren Anglin, 1822–1896: Irish Catholic Canadian* (Toronto: University of Toronto Press, 1977); George F.G. Stanley, *Louis Riel* (Toronto: McGraw-Hill Ryerson, 1963); George Woodcock, *Amor de Cosmos: Journalist and Reformer* (Toronto: Oxford University Press, 1975); and entries on these and other politicians in the printed and online versions of the *Dictionary of Canadian Biography*.

Forging a National Policy, 1873–1896

TIMELINE

1868	Canada First founded
1871	New Brunswick Common Schools Act passed
1873	Catholic Program launched; Pacific Scandal
1873–78	Liberals under Alexander Mackenzie hold power in Ottawa
1875	Caraquet Riot
1878–96	Conservatives hold power in Ottawa
1879	Increase in tariffs marks implementation of the National Policy
1880	Canadian Pacific Railway contract awarded
1881	Société nationale des Acadiens founded
1884	Imperial Federation League founded
1885	Northwest Resistance, CPR completed
1886	Parti national wins Quebec provincial election; Repealers win Nova Scotia election
1887	Provincial premiers' conference; British-American joint high commission on inshore fisheries
1888	Jesuits' Estates Act passed
1889	Federal government concedes to Ontario area from Kenora to Thunder Bay
1890	Manitoba Public Schools Act passed
1891	Federal election focuses on issue of US relations and the National Policy; John A. Macdonald dies
1891–92	John Abbott heads Conservative government in Ottawa
1892	Northwest Territories legislative assembly restricts French-language education
1892–94	John Thompson serves as prime minister
1894–96	Mackenzie Bowell serves as prime minister of Canada
1896	Charles Tupper serves briefly as prime minister; Wilfrid Laurier leads Liberals to victory

Next summer, or at the latest next fall, the railway will be close to us, and the whites will fill the country and they will dictate to us as they please. It is useless to dream that we can frighten them; that time has passed; our only resource is our work, our industry, our farms. The necessity of earning our bread by the sweat of our brows does not discourage me. There is only one thing that discourages me— what is it?—if we do not agree amongst ourselves; let us be like one man, and work will show quick, and there will be nothing too hard. Oh! Allow me to ask you all to love each other; that is not diffi- cult. We have faced the bullets of our enemies more than once, and now we cannot hear a word from each other.[1]

In this address to his people on 1 January 1882, Poundmaker outlined the difficult situation facing the First Nations of the Plains. The acquisition of the Northwest Territories by the Dominion of Canada led to dramatic changes in the lives of Native peoples. Although they seemed to have little choice other than to relinquish their land in return for assistance from the government, Natives understood that the ex- change was an unequal one. Canada's National Policy, which included building a railway to the Pacific and encouraging immigrants to farm the Prairies, would displace the land's original inhabitants and threaten their very survival.

Canada's Aboriginal peoples experienced the most brutal consequences of the changes transforming Canadian society, but they were not alone in feeling uneasy about the impact of federal policies. Divided by ethnicity and geography, some Canadians thought that the fledgling nation would be better off joining the United States. Annexation sentiment was never far from the surface in the early years of confederation, but other forces in the closing decades of the nine- teenth century, including close ties to the British

Empire and a national policy that appealed to powerful economic interests, helped to point the new nation in a direction that, for better or worse, would define it for nearly a century.

THE PACIFIC SCANDAL

John A. Macdonald's success in creating a transcontinental nation was not enough to win him widespread support at the polls in the 1872 election. When the final tally was in, the Conservatives could claim a small majority in the House of Commons, but their position was precarious. Without the nine seats contributed by the new provinces of Manitoba and British Columbia, Macdonald would have had difficulty continuing to govern. Even Cartier lost his seat in Montreal East and only re-entered parliament through a by-election in Manitoba.

Macdonald's biggest threat came from Ontario, where Alexander Mackenzie's Reformers—or Liberals, as they were increasingly called—revived criticisms of the Liberal-Conservatives as corrupt spendthrifts and papist sympathizers. In the wake of the Red River uprising, sectarian issues intensified, and Ontario Liberals were not above reminding Protestants that Macdonald had failed to bring the Métis murderers of Thomas Scott to justice. Such views clashed dramatically with those of opposition members from Quebec, who denounced Cartier for having done nothing to settle Métis land claims or win amnesty for Louis Riel.

Other issues also surfaced during the campaign. Macdonald had failed to convince the United States to sign a new reciprocity agreement, a major item on the wish list of most primary producers. Nor, apparently, had his government been able to resolve the question of who was to build the Pacific railway. Moreover, as a means of appealing to skilled workers, many of whom had sufficient property holdings to allow them to vote, Macdonald had legally recognized unions. George Brown, the éminence grise of the Ontario Liberals, was particularly outraged by this move, which scuttled the union-breaking tactics practised in his *Globe* newspaper offices.

In May 1871, the government introduced legislation to provide for the construction of a railway to the Pacific coast. The bill offered $30 million in cash and 20 million acres of land as an incentive to any company

CONFEDERATION!
THE MUCH-FATHERED YOUNGSTER.

This spoof on confederation is one of many drawn by Canada's first great cartoonist, J.W. Bengough, who between 1873 and 1892 produced the satirical weekly newspaper *Grip*, named for the raven in Charles Dickens's *Barnaby Rudge*. Born in Toronto in 1851, Bengough worked for the *Globe* before launching his own publication. The Pacific Scandal of 1873 gave him ample material for satire and launched him on a successful career as a newspaper editor, cartoonist, and public lecturer.
Library and Archives Canada/C78676

that would sign a contract to build the line. Opposition members, led by Alexander Mackenzie's Ontario contingent, balked at such extravagance and confidently predicted that the awarding of a railway charter would be marked by political corruption. They were right.

Two companies sought the lucrative railway-building contract. One was headed by Ontario senator David MacPherson and included the leading lights of the Toronto business community. The other, headed by Hugh Allan, president of Allan Steamship Lines, represented Montreal business interests and had backing from the Northern Pacific Railway in the United States. Attempts by the Macdonald administration to effect a merger of these two Canadian groups—and to keep the Americans out—proved futile.

Cartier was eager to see his city prevail in the contest with Toronto. Politically vulnerable, he also wanted to ensure a Liberal-Conservative Party victory in the

Alexander Mackenzie.
Library and Archives Canada/C-020052

1872 federal election. As election day approached, a beleaguered Cartier, suffering from Bright's disease that would take his life a year later, promised to do his utmost to deliver the contract to Allan in return for a contribution of at least $162 000, and perhaps as much as $360 000, to the party's election coffers.

In February 1873, the Macdonald government named Hugh Allan as president of the Canadian Pacific Railway Company (CPR). Two months later, Lucius Huntington, a Liberal MP, charged that Allan had bought his presidency with $360 000 in donations to the Conservative Party. Macdonald reluctantly appointed a select committee to examine the charges. It soon became apparent that the Liberals had a mole in the Conservative organization: incriminating letters and telegrams proved Cartier's corruption and left little doubt of Macdonald's.

Even more damaging was the fact that Allan was being financed by American investors, who were poised to assume control of Canada's major railway company. They might even have been planning to undermine the project so that Canadian traffic would be forced to use the Northern Pacific, which was dominated by Allan's American backers. Sensing that the government was doomed, many independents joined the Liberal opposition. On 5 November 1873, Macdonald informed Governor General Lord Dufferin that he no longer enjoyed a parliamentary majority and therefore, following the principle of responsible government, was resigning as prime minister.

THE LIBERALS AT THE HELM

Dufferin invited Alexander Mackenzie, member for Lanark, Ontario, to form a government. A Highland Scot, stonemason, and a Baptist, Mackenzie had quit school at the age of 13 to contribute to the family economy. He was a teetotaller and had a tremendous capacity for hard work, but like many self-made men Mackenzie had little sympathy for anyone who was unable to succeed. He had taken the position of prime minister more out of duty than ambition after Edward Blake and A.-A. Dorion had turned it down. Mackenzie cobbled together a Liberal coalition consisting of Ontario Reformers, Quebec Rouges, moderate Liberals, and Maritimers of all political stripes disillusioned by Macdonald's government.

Hoping to use the Pacific Scandal to win a majority in support of his government, Mackenzie called an election for the winter of 1874. Macdonald, who remained Conservative leader, campaigned on a nationalist platform that emphasized the need for the Pacific railway to hold the Northwest and fulfill pledges to British Columbia. In keeping with the more cautious program favoured by his followers, Mackenzie promised a new Pacific railway contract that did not involve large public expenditures for the benefit of private entrepreneurs. Emphasizing provincial rights and the need for economy, he presented a less ambitious vision for the new dominion than that promoted by the Conservatives. Mackenzie won a majority of seats in every province except British Columbia, whose voters returned Conservatives in all six ridings.

Despite their strong mandate, the Liberals survived only one term in office. Canada was gripped in a worldwide recession in the 1870s, which meant less money for state initiatives. When the United States rejected the new government's efforts to negotiate a reciprocity treaty, the Liberals had no economic strategy other than retrenchment. It did not inspire enthusiasm. British

Columbia threatened secession if the federal government failed to build a railway within the time frame promised by their confederation agreement, and Canadians continued to move to the United States to find work.

The Liberal interlude nevertheless left its mark on the new nation. In addition to introducing electoral reforms that included simultaneous voting, the secret ballot, and trial of disputed elections by the courts, the Liberals tried to enlarge the powers of Canada within the British Empire. This was the special goal of Edward Blake, who agreed to serve in a number of portfolios under Mackenzie's leadership. A brilliant but thin-skinned individual, Blake had briefly associated himself with the Canada First movement, which was dominated by a group of young Canadian nationalists based in Ontario. The Canada Firsters envisioned a vigorous Anglo-Saxon and Protestant nation allied with Great Britain. In a speech delivered in Aurora, Ontario, in October 1874, Blake captured the essence of the Canada First position:

> The future of Canada, I believe, depends very largely upon the cultivation of a national spirit. We are engaged in a very difficult task—the task of welding together seven Provinces which have been accustomed to regard themselves as isolated from each other, which are full of petty jealousies, their Provincial questions, their local interests. How are we to accomplish our work? How are we to effect a real union between these Provinces? Can we do it by giving a sop now to one, now to another, after the manner of the late Government? . . . Do you hope to create or preserve harmony and good feeling upon such a false and sordid and mercenary basis as that? Not so! That day I hope is gone for ever, and we must find some other and truer ground for Union than that by which the late Government sought to buy love and purchase peace.[2]

Blake resisted the attempts of Canada Firsters to recruit him as leader of their short-lived party, the Canadian National Association, founded in the wake of the Pacific Scandal. But he remained sympathetic to their demand that Canada be given greater autonomy within the British Empire. As Mackenzie's minister of justice, Blake extended the nation's powers to create admiralty courts, exercise authority over shipping on the Great Lakes, and pardon criminals. He also established the Supreme Court of Canada in 1875 but failed in his attempts to make it the final court of appeal, which remained the Judicial Committee of the Privy Council of Great Britain until 1949.

CANADA FIRST

Blake's decision to resist the blandishments of the Canada First movement was only one of the reasons that it failed to take root. More important was the narrow definition of nationalism that motivated its supporters. The group formed in 1868 following the assassination of Thomas D'Arcy McGee, one of the most articulate proponents of national idealism. The leading Canada Firsters included Ottawa civil servant and author Henry J. Morgan, Nova Scotia Coal Owners' Association lobbyist Robert Grant Haliburton, poet Charles Mair, militia officer and lawyer George Taylor Denison III, and lawyer W.A. Foster. They claimed as their mission the promotion of "national sentiment" worthy of a great transcontinental nation.

Canada Firsters presented Canada as a country peopled by robust Nordic races disciplined by their efforts to survive in a harsh environment. In *Canadian Monthly and National Review* and *Nation*, two journals spawned by the expanding circle of Canada Firsters in the early 1870s, they expounded the notion of a new nationality based on a combination of race and geography. They took their cue from R.G. Haliburton, who in 1869 argued that the identifying feature of Canada "must ever be that it is a Northern country inhabited by the descendants of the Northern races." For Haliburton, the superiority of the "Northern races" was self-evident. "If climate has not had the effect of moulding races," he queried, "how is it that southern nations have almost invariably been inferior to and subjugated by the men of the north?"[3]

The place of French Canadians in the new nation was problematic. Although Haliburton and other Canada Firsters were willing in theory to include the "Norman French" among the Nordic elite, they failed in practice to demonstrate even this limited tolerance. Their bigoted attitudes toward French Canadians—and complete contempt for Aboriginal peoples—were fully exposed in their efforts to suppress the Red River Resistance. In Toronto, Denison threatened civil insurrection if Macdonald pardoned Riel and abandoned the West to the Métis. Mair, who had moved to the Red River Colony in 1869, was particularly outspoken, concluding that French Canadians were the principal "bar to progress, and to the extension of a great Anglo-Saxon Dominion across the continent."[4]

Racist and ethnocentric, Canada Firsters wanted white English Canadian values to prevail in the new dominion. Their movement was too narrowly based to be successful and following the 1874 election both the movement and the party it sponsored quickly collapsed. The views they expressed nevertheless continued to thrive.

MACDONALD'S NATIONAL POLICY

It was widely conceded that the voters preferred Sir John A. drunk to Mackenzie sober, and the federal election of 1878 confirmed that verdict. Despite the Pacific Scandal and a weak performance in the House while the Liberals were in office, Macdonald's Conservatives won 142 of the 206 seats in the House and carried majorities in every province except New Brunswick. During the campaign, Macdonald advocated a development program that is often described as the National Policy. The centrepiece of the program was a policy of

high tariffs to stimulate a strong manufacturing sector in the Canadian economy. In addition, Macdonald underlined the importance of a rapid completion of the Pacific railway and the encouragement of population growth through immigration. Inspired by the slow economic climate of the 1870s, these policies would form the framework of national development under both Conservative and Liberal administrations until the First World War.

Following the election, the Macdonald government acted quickly to implement the National Policy. In 1879, Finance Minister Tilley raised the tariff from 15 percent to levels ranging from 17.5 to 35 percent. Manufacturers were delighted with a policy that they had long been promoting to support their industries against foreign competition. Counting the members of the Canadian Manufacturers' Association among his principal supporters, Macdonald increased tariffs throughout the 1880s, reportedly relying on casual billiard-room discussions with entrepreneurs to determine the appropriate level of protection.

Meanwhile, the government moved on a second aspect of the National Policy in 1880 when it entered into negotiations for a new CPR. Headed by George Stephen, president of the Bank of Montreal, and his cousin Donald Smith, a major stakeholder in the Hudson's Bay Company, the company included Norman Kittson and James J. Hill, two men who in the 1870s had developed a successful partnership with Stephen and Smith in the St. Paul, Minnesota, and Manitoba Railway Company. The CPR was from the outset a multinational enterprise. In the early years of the company's existence, only about a sixth of CPR stock was held in Canada; the rest was purchased by investors in New York, Paris, and London.

The Macdonald government offered the CPR syndicate generous support for its efforts: a cash grant of $25 million in aid of construction; a land grant of 25 million acres (half of the land within 32 kilometres of the CPR's main line would be set aside until the company decided which parcels it wished to claim); an additional land grant for railway stations and road beds; the 1100 kilometres

In both Canada and the United States, railway companies employed Chinese labourers to do some of the most dangerous and backbreaking work. They were responsible for the jobs of tunnelling and handling explosives, which helped account for the deaths of 600 Chinese workers during the CPR construction process. In the words of the 1884 Royal Commission on Chinese Immigration, they were "living machines" working for the benefit of the capitalists who employed them and the fragile nation that was bound together by iron rails.
Notman Photographic Archives, McCord Museum of Canadian History, Montreal

of completed track built in the Mackenzie years, valued at more than $37 million; a guarantee of a 20-year monopoly on western rail traffic; exemption of the company from the tariff on all materials required in railway construction; and a 20-year exemption for all CPR properties from federal and provincial taxation and from taxation by municipalities not yet incorporated. More grants were required before the line was completed in 1885, and in 1888 the government guaranteed a $15-million bond issue in compensation for dropping the monopoly clause in the original contract.

In the third area of the National Policy—immigration—the Macdonald government had less obvious success. More than 900 000 immigrants arrived in Canada in the 1880s, but this was balanced against the million plus people who had left in the same time period. The exodus of people from the Maritimes and Quebec to the United States was a cause of some alarm in both regions. In Ontario, people were more likely to take up the challenge of western settlement, but the numbers were not large. The population of the Prairies was only about 400 000 by 1901, not the millions that optimists had predicted a few decades earlier.

THE NORTHWEST

In the two decades following confederation, no region of the nation experienced greater changes than the old Northwest. Outside Manitoba, whose boundaries were extended in 1881, the Northwest Territories remained under the jurisdiction of the federal government. The North-West Territories Act of 1875 determined that the area would be governed by an appointed council until such time as the population warranted the inclusion of elected officials. Since no provision was made for responsible government, power was concentrated in the hands of the lieutenant-governor and his Ottawa advisers. The act guaranteed denominational schools, and, by an amendment in 1877, French and English were made the official languages of the courts and council. The capital of the vast region was Battleford until 1882, when, with the arrival of the railway, it was moved to Regina.

The heavy hand of Ottawa was soon called into question. In 1879, the council, by then called the legislative assembly, resigned en masse, charging that

Lieutenant-Governor Edgar Dewdney often ignored its advice. The federal government responded two years later by granting the assembly most powers held by provinces except the right to borrow money. Despite this concession, discontent continued to percolate. Natives, who had no voice in the territorial government, were particularly discouraged.

As historian Gerald Friesen has pointed out, Native peoples of the western interior experienced a revolution in the last half of the nineteenth century.[5] The disappearance of the buffalo, the building of the railway, the influx of white settlers, and the arrival of the federal government in the form of police, law courts, and legislatures were each occurrences of profound significance. The fact that they all happened in the short period between 1875 and 1885 meant that special care was needed to prevent disaster for both Native and newcomer. Unfortunately, administrators in the Northwest Territories and their political masters in Ottawa proved ill-equipped to handle the volatile situation developing in their rapidly changing western colony.

With the disappearance of the buffalo and other game, Native peoples on the Plains reluctantly accepted treaties that they believed guaranteed them government help to become farmers. The transition proved difficult. Before the promised government assistance arrived, Dewdney reduced rations as a cost-cutting measure. This policy was implemented in the early 1880s, just as the buffalo were disappearing from the Canadian Prairies—the last Canadian hunt occurred in 1879. The crisis facing the Aboriginal peoples was real. Between 1880 and 1885, an estimated 3000 Natives in the Northwest died from starvation.

The government's response in the House of Commons to reports of starvation was provided by Sir Hector Langevin in 1886:

> We do not propose to expend large sums of money to give them food from the first day of the year to the last. We must give them enough to keep them alive; but the Indians must, under the regulations that have been sanctioned by Parliament, go to their reservations and cultivate their land. They must provide partially for their wants. And therefore, if, by accident, an Indian should starve, it is not the fault of the Government nor the wish of the Government.[6]

In desperation, some Natives stole cattle from settlers in the region. This inevitably got the culprits into

North-West Mounted Police at the Regina training camp.
Canadian Pacific Archives NS5649

trouble with the North-West Mounted Police (NWMP), which was charged with the responsibility of upholding laws against theft. As the situation worsened, Cree militants began to organize against the whites in the region, who symbolized the threat to the old way of life on the Plains. Cree chiefs such as Big Bear and Poundmaker played key roles in Aboriginal resistance. From the outset of negotiations with

VOICES FROM THE PAST

The "Bill of Rights," 1885

Métis demands suggest that Riel's program was neither separatist nor racist, as Canadian opponents of Riel charged at the time. While the concerns of the Métis were uppermost in Riel's mind, the Bill of Rights included calls for better treatment of all peoples in the Northwest Territories. Following is a condensed version of the demands:

1. That the half-breeds of the Northwest Territories be given grants similar to those accorded to the half-breeds of Manitoba by the Act of 1870.

2. That patents be issued to all half-breeds and white settlers who have fairly earned the right of possession to their farms; that the timber regulations be made more liberal; and that the settler be treated as having rights in the country.

3. That the provinces of Alberta and Saskatchewan be forthwith organized with legislatures of their own, so that the people may be no longer subject to the despotism of Lieutenant-Governor Dewdney; and, in the proposed new provincial legislatures, that the Métis shall have a fair and reasonable share of representation.

4. That the offices of trust throughout these provinces be given to residents of the country, as far as practicable, and that we denounce the appointment of disreputable outsiders and repudiate their authority.

5. That this region be administered for the benefit of the actual settler, and not for the advantage of the alien speculator; and that all lawful customs and usages which obtain among the Métis be respected.

6. That better provision be made for the Indians, the parliamentary grant to be increased, and lands set apart as an endowment for the establishment of hospitals and schools for the use of whites, half-breeds, and Indians, at such places as the provincial legislatures may determine.

7. That the Land Department of the Dominion Government be administered as far as practicable from Winnipeg, so that settlers may not be compelled, as heretofore, to go to Ottawa for the settlement of questions in dispute between them and land commissioners.[7]

Ottawa, Big Bear regarded the treaty provisions as insulting. He refused to sign Treaty 6 until starvation among his band forced his hand in 1882. Like his white counterparts in Ottawa, Big Bear dreamed of creating a larger political organization, but his confederation was one in which the Plains tribes would unite to force the Canadian government to renegotiate the treaties and provide Native peoples with ironclad assurances of the right to hunt and live in their traditional territories.

In 1884, about 2000 Cree from several reserves gathered outside Battleford in an attempt to coordinate their resistance. Several councils held that year demonstrated a growing cohesion among the Cree in protesting their treatment. When the government response was slow in coming, young militants in the band began calling for armed struggle. Unrest among the First Nations coincided with growing discontent among the Métis, many of whom were migrants from Manitoba, living along the South Saskatchewan River. While the Métis had come to terms with the fact that hunting would have to give way to a largely agricultural existence, they wanted the same assistance as was offered other settlers in the West. Encouraged by the clergy, the Métis began to petition Ottawa for land, agricultural aid, schools, and a locally run police force. Their biggest concern was that they be able to maintain community control over new institutions and thereby preserve their distinct way of life.

BIOGRAPHY

Poundmaker

Born around 1842, Poundmaker was the son of a Stony father and Métis mother of French and Cree descent. He was adopted by Crowfoot, chief of the Blackfoot, in 1873, and quickly rose to prominence. During the negotiations leading to Treaty 6 with the Canadian government, Poundmaker held out for better terms but ultimately signed the treaty on 23 August 1876. With the dwindling of the buffalo, he settled on a reserve near Battleford, Saskatchewan, and in 1881 was chosen to accompany the Marquis of Lorne, governor general of Canada, on a tour of the region.

During the Northwest Resistance, Poundmaker counselled restraint as his followers ransacked the abandoned village of Battleford and placed the fort under siege. He also was instrumental in preventing the warriors from pursuing Colonel Otter's forces, who retreated under heavy fire after the bruising battle at Cut Knife Hill. Arrested and tried for treason in Regina, he told the court: "Everything I could do was done to stop the bloodshed. Had I wanted war, I would not be here now. I should be on the prairie. You did not catch me. I gave myself up. You have got me because I wanted justice." He was found guilty and sentenced to three years in prison. After serving less than a year in Stony Mountain Penitentiary near Winnipeg, he was released, broken in health and spirit. He died four months later in July 1886.[8]

Surrender of Poundmaker.
Library and Archives Canada/C-002769

The Northwest Resistance

When Ottawa ignored their petitions, the Métis decided in 1884 to invite Riel to return to Canada from his home in the United States to lead his people. During his years in exile, Riel had suffered from mental problems and had increasingly become obsessed with what he viewed as his mission to establish a new North American Catholicism with Bishop Bourget of Montreal as the pope of the "New World." He eventually became an American citizen, joined the Republican Party, and was teaching school in Montana when he received the call from his people in the Northwest. Despite his emotional instability, Riel still had the skills required to make Ottawa listen.

Initially, Riel attempted to pursue the peaceful route of pressuring the Macdonald government for concessions. With this approach, he had the support of many white settlers in the region, who were growing impatient with their own treatment by Ottawa and Lieutenant-Governor Dewdney. Ottawa ignored Riel's petitions with predictable results. On 18 March 1885, Riel proclaimed a provisional government and demanded that Ottawa grant the moderate demands outlined in the Bill of Rights. Riel still hoped for a peaceful settlement to the standoff, but many Métis, including Riel's military adviser, Gabriel Dumont, felt that militant action was called for.

Dumont advocated seizing government buildings, attacking NWMP detachments, and blowing up the railway tracks used by the federal government to send troops westward. Skirmishes between Métis and NWMP at Batoche and Duck Lake resulted in more than 40 deaths and prompted the federal government's decision to send a militia force under Major-General Frederick Middleton to the scene. Within two weeks of the Duck Lake incident, the first detachment of militia arrived on CPR trains.

When word of the Métis rebellion reached Cree ears, the young militants attacked the base at Frog Lake, killing a hated Indian agent and eight others. In another incident, two farming instructors regarded as hostile to Natives were murdered in the Battleford district. These developments alarmed white settlers, who feared nothing so much as an "Indian War." Forced to choose sides, they volunteered to help the army sent by Ottawa to put down the uprising.

Riel withdrew his supporters to Batoche, where they held out against the army for six weeks before surrendering. In the end, at least 35 Natives and 53 non-Natives lost their lives in the Northwest Resistance.

Tried for treason, Riel was found guilty by an all-white jury in a Regina courtroom and was hanged in November 1885. Riel's defence of his actions during his trial was a mixture of a madman's confused ramblings and a clear-sighted analysis of the plight of the First Nations and Métis. Since his death, Riel has become a symbol of his people, and assessments of his behaviour have often varied greatly. It is more generally conceded now than it was a century ago that, whatever the merits of this complicated man, the cause for which he fought in 1885 was a noble one.

The Aboriginal peoples paid dearly for their acts of frustration. Of the 81 arrested during the turmoil, 44 were convicted. Of these, eight were hanged, three were sentenced to life imprisonment, and many others were incarcerated for shorter periods. Even Big Bear and Poundmaker, who had tried to prevent violence, were sentenced to three-year prison terms on charges of felony-treason. While the hanging of Riel was an issue of public debate for many years, a similar fate for eight Aboriginal leaders and long jail sentences for many of their followers created little interest outside Native communities.

Military might and the legal system had broken organized resistance to white colonialism, but Aboriginal peoples continued to perform individual acts of defiance. They secretly practised religious ceremonies that were banned under the Indian Act and protected each other against attempts by the NWMP to arrest them when accused, often falsely, of failing to meet the standards of the white man's laws.

RELIGION, LANGUAGE, AND POLITICS

Natives were not the only people questioning Macdonald's interpretation of confederation. For Francophones, Ottawa's handling of guarantees for French-language rights and denominational schools was a major cause of concern. Both policies were resisted by provincial legislatures outside Quebec. Dominated by representatives of the English Protestant majority, the federal government also remained unmoved by pleas for legislation that would have protected Francophone and Roman Catholic minorities throughout the country.

At the time of confederation, Cartier led a Conservative bloc in Quebec, known as ultramontanists, that included both moderates and ultra-conservatives The latter were determined to organize society according to the principles of the Roman Catholic Church, which would have had control over the most important institutions in society. In the 1871 provincial election in Quebec, the ultramontane wing of the Conservative Party launched the Catholic Program, which required that all candidates make Catholic doctrine the basis of their political action and comply with directives issued by Roman Catholic bishops. The *programmistes*, as they were called, won only one seat, but they were a force to be reckoned with in the Conservative Party both in Quebec City and in Ottawa.

The Caraquet Riot of 1875 resulted in two deaths and encouraged leaders in church and government to compromise on the issue of school policy in New Brunswick.
Courtesy Charles P. de Volpi Collection, Special Collections/Dalhousie University Libraries

New Brunswick Schools

The first contest over denominational schools occurred in New Brunswick. The New Brunswick Common Schools Act of 1871 authorized municipalities in the province to tax all ratepayers to support the public school system, whose institutions henceforth would be the only ones to benefit from government funding. The omission from the act of Roman Catholic schools—which had hitherto received public funding, though by convention rather than by law—was intentional. When Premier George King went to the polls in 1872 to defend the new legislation, he campaigned under the slogan, "Vote for the Queen against the Pope." He won a resounding victory.

In response to what they perceived as an unfair law, Roman Catholics in New Brunswick, who constituted a third of the population, appealed to the courts. The legislation was declared valid, so they turned to the federal government. Education was normally a provincial matter, but the British North America Act (BNA Act) authorized the federal government to intervene when education laws in place at the time of confederation were violated. Since grants to Roman Catholic schools in the province had been the practice but not the law, the government let the New Brunswick legislation stand. Roman Catholics responded by refusing to pay their tax assessments and were prosecuted for non-payment. When the assessment legislation was ruled unconstitutional on a technicality, the government moved to close the loopholes in the act.

Again, Roman Catholics in New Brunswick appealed to Ottawa. To Macdonald's embarrassment, the motion to disallow the New Brunswick assessment act was carried with votes from Francophone Quebec members in his party. Macdonald passed the responsibility to the imperial government, which advised the governor general to sign the act to confirm the principle of provincial responsibility in education.

While most Roman Catholics in New Brunswick vigorously opposed the school legislation, resistance was especially fierce among the province's Acadian population. They made up about half of provincial adherents to Roman Catholicism. Since only one Acadian child in six received any schooling, most Acadians balked at taxes to support any school, much less a school that excluded Catholic education.

Tensions came to a head in the village of Caraquet in January 1875, when violence erupted between Acadians and Protestant police and volunteers. During the fracas, one volunteer and one Acadian were shot. The trial of nine Acadians for murder became a cause célèbre and forced the government to compromise. It dismissed charges against the accused Acadians and permitted religious orders to teach Roman Catholics in areas where numbers warranted.

The Acadian Renaissance

Confrontations over separate schools and language rights reflected a growing sense of political awareness among Acadians. By the time of confederation, an Acadian sense of identity was taking shape, strongly influenced by the publication of Longfellow's poem "Evangeline" (1847) and François-Edme Rameau de Saint-Père's historical treatment of the Acadian experience in *La France aux colonies* (1859). In 1867, Israel-D. Landry, a native of Quebec, established the first French-language Acadian newspaper, *Le Moniteur Acadien*, based in Moncton. At the same time, the Collège Saint-Joseph, founded in nearby Memramcook in 1864, began educating an Acadian professional elite that would take the lead in defining Acadian goals and values.

In 1880, the Société Saint-Jean-Baptiste of Quebec invited all French-speaking communities in North America to a congress in Quebec. Acadians followed up this event with their own congress at Collège

Built in 1896 in memory of Father Camille Lefebvre, who founded the Collège Saint-Joseph, the Monument Lefebvre in Memramcook, New Brunswick, became a symbol of the Acadian renaissance.
La Société du Monument Lefebvre

Saint-Joseph in July 1881, at which the Société nationale des Acadiens was founded. More than 5000 people attended. In this and a subsequent congress in 1884 at Miscouche, Prince Edward Island, the Acadians chose a national holiday (the Feast of the Assumption), a national flag (the French tricolour with the gold star), and a national hymn ("Ave Maris Stella"). Acadians were proud of their French heritage but were determined to develop cultural symbols distinct from those already established in Quebec.

Ontario versus French Canada

By the 1880s, religious and cultural concerns had become as important as economic issues in determining party loyalties and shaping national policies. This was amply revealed in the aftermath of Riel's hanging in 1885. Because the Métis involved in the rebellion were primarily French-speaking Roman Catholics, neither Orangemen nor Quebec nationalists took account of the regional and Aboriginal concerns behind the uprising. Instead, Orangemen regarded Riel as a French-speaking Roman Catholic determined to deprive the British Empire of the Northwest, while Quebec nationalists saw him as a hero whose undoing proved that French-Canadian rights would not be respected outside Quebec.

Macdonald's decision to let Riel hang was undoubtedly calculated to reassure Anglophones that he was not a pawn of Roman Catholics, but it was also a decision made with the tacit support of the Roman Catholic hierarchy, who found Riel's religious beliefs increasingly unacceptable. Such evidence was conveniently forgotten by the extremists on both sides. After Riel's execution, an outpouring of grief and rage, including a demonstration in Montreal attended by more than 50 000 people, testified to the extent of Quebecers' alienation.

Building on Francophone discontent, Honoré Mercier led the Parti national, which included Quebec's Liberals along with Conservative dissidents, to a provincial election victory in 1886. Mercier's success demonstrated the erosion of the political alliance between the Conservatives and the

Roman Catholic Church that had exercised power both federally and in Quebec in the post-confederation era. By using the word "national" in the party name, Liberals also reminded the Francophone majority in Quebec that they were a nation even if it was submerged in the larger nation-state of Canada.

French Canadians in Ontario, who numbered more than 100 000 by the 1880s, became hostages to the cultural bigotry spreading across the country. Unlike New Brunswick, Ontario's denominational schools were protected by the BNA Act, but French linguistic rights had no similar guarantees. Before 1885, provincial officials tolerated education in both French and German. In the wake of Quebec campaigns against Riel's execution, the Ontario government limited the hours of instruction in languages other than English and required teachers to be tested to ensure proficiency in the English language. Since local school boards were left to enforce this regulation, most initially chose to ignore it.

The Jesuits' Estates Act of 1888 galvanized the anti–Roman Catholic forces of Ontario into more concerted action. When the Jesuits returned to Quebec in the 1840s, they demanded compensation for the properties confiscated by Great Britain following the conquest in 1763. The Quebec government, at a loss as to how to arbitrate among the contending Roman Catholic claimants, invited Pope Leo XIII to help to determine monetary compensation. Although the final settlement included funds for Protestant universities in Quebec, Protestant extremists in Ontario decried Vatican involvement in Canadian affairs. An Ontario-based group calling itself the Equal Rights Association launched a campaign to rid the province and the nation of papal influences of any kind. Riding the wave of anti–Roman Catholic sentiment, D'Alton McCarthy, one of the Conservative Party's most able lieutenants, urged the abolition of public funding for separate schools and called for the assimilation of French Canadians.

In an effort to curry favour with its overwhelmingly English and Protestant electorate, the Liberal government of Ontario removed all French textbooks from its authorized list of books in 1889. Meanwhile, local school boards threw roadblocks in the way of instruction in the French language. In Caledonia Township, for example, where Francophones made up a third

of the population, Anglophone Roman Catholics refused to establish any French-language schools to supplement the nine English-language schools in operation by 1871.

The Manitoba Schools Question

While Anglophone and Francophone Roman Catholics fought for control within the Ontario separate schools system, their counterparts in Manitoba were forced to cooperate to defend the right to have publicly supported separate schools at all. The Manitoba Act of 1870 and the North-West Territories Act of 1875 provided for official bilingualism on the Prairies, but demography worked against such a policy. Although Francophones were half the population of Manitoba in 1870, they represented only 11 000 of the 152 000 residents in 1891. Across the West, including British Columbia, only 4.6 percent of the population reported French as their mother tongue in 1901. The anti–French, anti–Roman Catholic rhetoric of English Protestant settlers in the West and the ingrained image of the western lands as bleak and infertile discouraged extensive migration of Quebecers to Canada's frontier.

In 1890, Thomas Greenway's Liberal government, influenced by developments in Ontario, passed legislation to eliminate official bilingualism and the separate schools system guaranteed by the Manitoba Act. Following Manitoba's lead, in 1892 the Northwest Territories legislated an end to education in French after the third grade and removed French as an official language in legislative proceedings. The Roman Catholics of Manitoba (and the Anglicans, who also ran their own schools) decided to challenge the validity of the schools legislation in the courts.

The Manitoba schools legislation became a national issue for those fighting the battle over separate schools. When the Judicial Committee of the Privy Council in Great Britain ruled that Manitoba had acted legally but that the federal government had the constitutional right to pass remedial legislation to restore public funding for denominational schools, the Conservatives were caught in a quandary. Should they offer assistance to the aggrieved minorities of Manitoba or insist that education remain a matter for provincial jurisdiction?

Macdonald enjoyed exercising federal authority over the provinces, but he died in 1891, leaving the decision to his successors. In 1896, the federal Conservatives included remedial legislation as part of their election platform. Since they lost the election, it was left to the new prime minister, Wilfrid Laurier, to negotiate a compromise acceptable to Liberals, who supported the principle of provincial rights. The Manitoba schools legislation was allowed to stand, but religious instruction and instruction in a language other than English (the French language was not specifically mentioned) were permitted in areas where the number of pupils warranted such practices.

EMPIRE ONTARIO

As the foregoing discussion suggests, the defence of provincial interests emerged as a major feature of the Canadian federal system. Macdonald had hoped to create a strong federal state with the provinces as subordinate political entities. Instead, he was faced with ambitious principalities that claimed powers equal and even superior to those of the federal government in areas under their jurisdiction. Macdonald made extensive use of the power of disallowance, which enabled the federal government to set aside provincial legislation, but the provinces challenged his actions in the courts. Much to Macdonald's dismay, the Judicial Committee of the Privy Council in Great Britain, which was the final court of appeal in cases relating to the interpretation of the BNA Act, often sustained the less centralized view of confederation favoured by the provinces.

The tension between Ottawa and the provinces was in part a natural result of the give-and-take of party politics. When Liberal parties were in office provincially it was easy for them to take the Conservative government in Ottawa to task. This was certainly true in the case of Ontario, where the Liberal Party held office from 1871 to 1905. But Ontario's battles with Ottawa involved more than partisan politics. At stake was the issue of who would dominate the new federation: the national government or the government of the province with nearly half the nation's population.

Oliver Mowat, premier of Ontario from 1872 to 1896, emerged as the undisputed champion of provincial

rights in the generation following confederation. A lawyer and former articling student in Macdonald's law firm, Mowat was an implacable foe of Macdonald's centralizing vision of confederation. Mowat insisted that it was an agreement among provinces and that the provinces retained the jurisdiction they had held prior to confederation except for the specific responsibilities they had granted to the federal government. From this "provincial compact" point of view, there was no new "political nationality" formed in 1867. Such a reading of the constitution meant that the federal power to legislate for the "peace, order, and good government" of the nation should never intrude upon provincial jurisdiction in matters of a "local or private" nature.

Mowat believed that the federal government's frequent disallowances of provincial legislation amounted to unconstitutional interference in Ontario's sovereign areas of authority. He also resented Macdonald's favouritism toward provinces that supported Conservative administrations. When Macdonald attempted to have Ontario's boundaries restricted by placing territories north and west of Lake Superior within the province of Manitoba, Mowat challenged the decision in the courts and argued the case before the Privy Council in London. Only after several judicial decisions upholding Ontario's claim did Macdonald agree in 1889 to concede the boundary demanded by Ontario.

Macdonald's attempt to restrict Ontario's boundaries was motivated by more than his opposition to a Liberal premier. The discovery of rich mineral deposits in the disputed region, discovered while building the CPR, was a prize worth fighting for. Since Manitoba's public lands and natural resources were controlled by Ottawa—unlike those of Ontario—the federal government would benefit from a decision favouring Manitoba. Macdonald was no doubt also becoming uncomfortable with the growing wealth and population of Ontario, whose concerns increasingly dominated the fledgling dominion.

THE PROVINCES IN REVOLT

The Ontario boundary dispute was in full swing when Quebec premier Honoré Mercier suggested to the other premiers that they meet to discuss matters of common interest. Not surprisingly, Mowat was enthusiastic about the idea. In the Maritimes, provincial governments were also open to constitutional change. They were having difficulty managing on their federal subsidies and were alarmed by the impact of federal economic policies on their regional economies.

In May 1886, Liberal premier W.S. Fielding introduced a resolution in the Nova Scotia legislature calling for repeal of the BNA Act and establishment of a Maritime union. The Liberal premier of New Brunswick, A.G. Blair, was not prepared to go that far, but he, like Fielding, was interested in cooperating with other premiers in a revision of the terms of confederation. In Manitoba, economic growth encouraged plans for railways to the United States, but these were banned by the CPR's monopoly clause. John Norquay, Canada's first premier of Métis descent, was sued by the CPR and harassed by the federal government for his defiant approach to such matters. Although a Conservative, he, too, agreed to attend a conference of premiers.

In October 1887, five of Canada's seven premiers—the Conservative premiers of Prince Edward Island and British Columbia stayed home—met in Quebec City to demand changes in federal-provincial relations. The 22 resolutions passed by the premiers included calls for a million-dollar increase in subsidies to the provinces (which then stood at $3.2 million); the handing of the power of disallowance from the federal to the British government; provincial selection of half of all senators; provincial consent before local works could be placed under dominion control; and recognition of Ontario's boundary. Macdonald ignored the conference, accusing the four Liberal premiers of partisan mischief, but federal-provincial tensions would not disappear.

THE NORTH ATLANTIC TRIANGLE

Canada had no department of external affairs until 1909. The self-governing dominions and crown colonies within the British Empire accepted British primacy in the international arena and had little desire

The first provincial premiers' conference.
Library and Archives Canada/C-011583

to establish foreign policy at odds with British interests. Nonetheless, Canada's leaders expected to be consulted by the British government on diplomatic initiatives that affected the new nation's interests. In the discussions leading to the Treaty of Washington in 1871 and on several occasions thereafter, Great Britain included Canadian representatives on its negotiating teams, but Canadians could never be certain that they would not be sacrificed to good international relations by British negotiators.

Many of the problems between Canada and the United States revolved around fish. Fishing disputes grew out of the Anglo-American convention of 1818 that had excluded Americans from British North American inshore fisheries—defined as a three-mile limit from shore—and from access to the harbours, bays, and creeks of British North America except for shelter, repairs, and supplies of wood and water. During the periods in which the Reciprocity Treaty (1854–1866) and Treaty of Washington (1871–1883) prevailed, Americans had free access to the inshore fisheries, but thereafter American access again became a point of contention.

When the terms of the Treaty of Washington came to an end, Americans showed little interest in coming to the bargaining table, with the result that Canada began enforcing measures to protect its fisheries. In 1886, nearly 700 vessels were boarded and some were seized for violations; the number doubled the following year. The Americans threatened to retaliate by cutting off all commercial relations with Canada if satisfactory redress for the seizures was not forthcoming.

In 1887, a British-American joint high commission was established to deal with the problem. Canada was invited by Great Britain to name a representative to the British delegation. Although Canada's delegate, Charles Tupper, was eager to secure Canadian access to the American market for fish and, if possible, a larger reciprocity agreement, he ran into a brick wall of American resistance. Again there would be no reciprocity treaty. Even the limited arrangement negotiated by the British delegation, which gave Canadians free access to the American market for fresh fish, was rejected by the American senate. Americans paid a licence fee for access to Canadian ports, and Canadian fishermen were left high and dry.

Canada fared better with regard to its sealing industry in the North Pacific. After buying Alaska from the Russians in 1867, the Americans claimed exclusive rights to the Bering Sea. The United States leased sealing rights off the Pribilof Islands in the Bering Sea to the North American Commercial Company, which was enraged when British Columbia interests also began sealing in the region. The Americans charged that indiscriminate sealing was destroying the seal herd and seized Canadian vessels. Great Britain countered that the North American Commercial Company was the major perpetrator of the slaughter. In the face of a standoff, the two sides agreed to an arbitration panel, which met in Paris in 1893 and decided largely in Great Britain's favour. The slaughter of the seals could continue, with all sides participating, until a moratorium on sealing in the Bering Sea was imposed in 1911.

CANADA IN QUESTION

Notwithstanding the protectionist sentiment in the United States, the Liberals, under their new leader Edward Blake, still clung to their free trade agenda. It did little to enhance their popularity with voters in the 1882 election, which Macdonald, trumpeting the virtues of the National Policy, won handily in every province except Ontario. In Quebec, Blake's principled Protestantism was rewarded with only seven of the province's 75 seats.

Blake and Macdonald battled it out on the same issues in 1887 and again Macdonald won a majority, but this time the Quebec votes were split almost evenly between Liberals and Conservatives. With Francophones now willing to vote for Liberals like Honoré Mercier, it was only a matter of time before the Liberal Party turned to Quebec to find a leader. Their choice was Wilfrid Laurier, who assumed leadership of the federal Liberal Party in June 1887. Within a decade, he had reshaped it into an election-winning machine, but he had to deal with the free trade issue first.

The idea of closer trade relations with the United States was popular with many Liberal Party supporters. Among party radicals, there was even support for commercial union, a policy that would harmonize the tariff structures of the two North American nations and open the border to trade in natural and manufactured products. Those who championed the National Policy pointed out that such a union would compromise Canada's ability to determine its own economic policy, but primary producers considered such concerns irrelevant. In 1887, the Conservatives tried to spike the Liberal guns by securing a limited trade agreement with the United States, but the Americans were moving in a more protectionist direction for reasons that had little to do with Canadian interests. When the United States introduced the McKinley Tariff Act in 1890, the latest in a series of tariff increases, Macdonald's hopes for a reciprocity treaty were completely dashed.

Opposition to reciprocity usually rested on economic arguments, but emotional issues also entered the debate. Among many Canadians, there was a lingering fear that overly close commercial ties with the United States would weaken economic and cultural relations with Great Britain. Even Canadians who were not of British origin recognized that the British connection and the institutions it represented were one of the main pillars of the Canadian identity. They argued that any policy threatening Canada's ties to the world's greatest empire should be avoided since British power and prestige gave Canada a higher international profile than its population and wealth warranted.

Imperial sentiment was on the rise in the late nineteenth century. During the 1880s, many Canadian communities were celebrating the centenary of their Loyalist origins, while in Great Britain there was

The Métis Migrations

In the decade and a half following the 1869–1870 Red River Resistance, about 40 percent of the Red River Métis moved farther west, either joining existing communities in the Northwest or founding new ones. The migrants, many of whom had figured among the rebels of 1869, also played key roles in the 1885 rebellion. Why did they move and why did they join in a second rebellion against Canadian authority?

For most historians before the 1970s, there was a simple answer. The Métis were "half-savages" with little interest in becoming part of the new agriculture-based European society that was emerging in Red River. They wanted to hunt, not farm, and moved to areas free of agricultural settlement. Disillusioned when their nomadic lifestyles again became threatened by settler society, they engaged in the futile Northwest Resistance in 1885. From this perspective, the "pull" of a promised "primitive" life farther west explained the Métis migration.

In the 1980s, several historians suggested that "push" factors were more important than the lure of a pre-agricultural existence. Using archival evidence of government policy in this period, Douglas Sprague outlined the mistreatment of the Métis and the stalling tactics used by the federal government to deprive them of lands promised to them in 1870, to which both the federal and Manitoba governments turned a blind eye, causing the Métis to give up in frustration and move farther west. As settlement and the railway again began to stretch into their new territories at the same time that the buffalo disappeared, the Métis demanded guarantees from Ottawa that they would not again be dispossessed. The government made a pretence of dealing with these demands, but its previous duplicity in Manitoba and continuing inaction in the Northwest Territories provoked a violent Métis reaction.[9]

The dispossession thesis has been disputed by political scientist Thomas Flanagan and historian Gerhard Ens. Flanagan provides evidence to bolster the older view that the Métis did not want to farm. This, he argues, rather than government delays, official hostility, or mistreatment by European settlers, persuaded them to abandon or sell their land claims and move farther west. He also argues that delays in the Manitoba and Northwest land settlements resulted from disagreements and misunderstandings between the Métis and the federal government and not from deliberate stalling by the latter.[10]

Ens, meanwhile, suggests that a desire to participate in the flourishing trade of buffalo robes with American merchants informed the Métis decision to migrate. Ens uses censuses of the population of older, established communities in Red River at different periods to demonstrate that the move west had begun before the rebellion, as buffalo hunters came to terms with declining numbers of buffalo in the Red River region. He infers that many Métis, though once "peasants" content to eke out a living from hunting and small-scale farming, had become consumers on the European model, trading robes for consumer goods.[11]

Diane Payment takes issue with Ens's suggestion that migrants to the territories were in search of buffalo robes and in retreat from a subsistence agriculture/hunting economy. In her study of the evolution of the Métis community of Batoche, she demonstrates that the Métis sought a settled, not a nomadic, life. They built stores, schools, and churches and started farms. Although they also hunted buffalo, the robe trade was only one of multiple strategies for making a living. Payment concludes that the "push" factors—the racism of the Manitoba settlers and the broken promises of governments regarding land—caused the Métis to migrate, since they established new communities much like those they had left behind.[12]

Payment also raises questions about the tendency of most historians of the Métis to leave gender out of the equation. Observing the important role of women in establishing institutions in Batoche, Payment argues that women's networks played an important role in migration and community life. "The general resettlement pattern," she notes, "was by extended families; grandparents, parents, brothers, sisters, cousins, and cross-cousins but closer analysis reveals a particularly strong female kinship tie."[13]

Far from a purely academic matter, the debate about Métis migration patterns has become entangled in Métis land claims. The Manitoba Métis Federation hired Sprague, who questioned some of Ens's findings,[14] to make its case that the federal government has failed to fulfill its 1870 promises, while the federal Department of Justice contracted with both Flanagan and Ens to help prepare its case against the Métis claims.

support for strengthening the bonds of empire. Imperial enthusiasts established the Imperial Federation League in 1884 and called for a conference to take place in 1887 on the occasion of Queen Victoria's Golden Jubilee. Thereafter, imperial conferences were held periodically in London. Canadians, representing the senior dominion in the empire, usually played a leading role in their deliberations. Although imperialists disagreed among themselves about what form closer imperial ties should take, most discussion centred on a common imperial tariff, colonial representation in an imperial parliament, and cooperation in imperial defence.

During the 1891 election, a scandal erupted that seemed to confirm a conspiracy between members of the Liberal Party and American business interests to sever Canada's ties with Great Britain. The Conservative Party secured a copy of a private pamphlet written by Edward Farrer, editor of the *Globe*, which suggested ways of pressuring Canada into union with its southern neighbour. The Conservatives used this seemingly clear evidence of treason to help them win the election, but they could not stop people from voting with their feet and moving to the United States.

In this, his last election, Macdonald offered no new remedies for his divided country. The Conservative slogan in the campaign—"The Old Man, The Old Flag and The Old Policy"—said it all. With Macdonald at the helm, the British flag as their inspiration, and the tariff as their crowning achievement, the Conservatives squeaked through. The Liberals boldly declared their support for "unrestricted reciprocity." Such a position, which retreated from the idea of commercial union, appealed to the radical wing of the party, but made many Liberals—and many Canadians—extremely nervous. It failed, however, to deter Francophones in Quebec, who, for the first time since the Pacific Scandal, elected Liberals in a majority of their constituencies.

As Macdonald lay on his deathbed in June 1891, he must have wondered what manner of political entity he had helped to shape. Canadians were still at odds with each other, and there were few signposts offering a clear direction for the future. Even the party he had worked so hard to build was in disarray. Following his death, it broke into squabbling factions and had four leaders—John Abbott, John Thompson, Mackenzie Bowell, and Charles Tupper—in five years.

John Sparrow Thompson (1845–1894) was born in Halifax, trained as a lawyer, and served briefly as premier of Nova Scotia. In 1885 he joined Macdonald's cabinet as minister of Justice. Raised a Methodist, Thompson had converted to Roman Catholicism as an adult, which gave him a unique perspective on the religious and cultural wars that raged in the final decades of the nineteenth century. He was the logical successor to Macdonald but because of his religious affiliation was passed over in 1891 in favour of John Abbott, who was a Protestant. Following Abbott's retirement in 1892, Thompson became prime minister, but his tenure in the office was short-lived. He died in Windsor Castle, England, in December 1894, shortly after being sworn by Queen Victoria as a member of the Imperial Privy Council.
Library and Archives Canada/C-012206

CONCLUSION

Rounding out the borders of the new Dominion of Canada proved to be the easy part of nation-building. Holding it together was more difficult, as both Macdonald and Mackenzie soon discovered. For many Canadians, the adjustment to new national policies as defined in the first three decades of confederation brought only hardship and heartache. Aboriginal peoples experienced defeat and marginalization, while the outlying regions of West and East still wondered about their place in a Canadian firmament dominated by Ontario and Quebec. Throughout Canada, religious and cultural differences focusing on school and language policy made some people feel that imperial federation, annexation, or provincial independence were happier alternatives to being yoked in a federation where every national policy was ringed with compromise and bitterness. Perhaps most disappointing of all, the rapid economic growth sought by Canada's leaders proved elusive. Would the Liberals under Wilfrid Laurier be able to do any better?

NOTES

1 Cited in Don Gillmor, Achille Michaud, and Pierre Turgeon, *Canada: A People's History*, vol. 2 (Toronto: McClelland & Stewart, 2001), 19.

2 Cited in P.B. Waite, *Canada, 1874–1896: Arduous Destiny* (Toronto: McClelland & Stewart, 1971), 35.

3 Cited in Carl Berger, "The True North Strong and Free," in *Nationalism in Canada*, ed. Peter Russell (Toronto: McGraw-Hill, 1965), 6.

4 Cited in David P. Gagan, "The Relevance of Canada First," *Journal of Canadian Studies* 5 (1970), 38.

5 Gerald Friesen, *The Canadian Prairies: A History* (Toronto: University of Toronto Press, 1984), 129.

6 Hugh Shewell, *"Enough to Keep Them Alive": Indian Welfare in Canada, 1873–1965* (Toronto: University of Toronto Press, 2004), 41.

7 *Bill of Rights*, 13 April 1885, Provincial Archives of Alberta.

8 Hugh A. Dempsey, "Pīitikwahanapiwīyin (Poundmaker)," *Dictionary of Canadian Biography*, vol. XI (1881–1890), 697.

9 D.N. Sprague, *Canada and the Métis, 1869–1885* (Waterloo: Wilfrid Laurier University Press, 1988).

10 Thomas Flanagan, *Riel and the Rebellion: 1885 Reconsidered* (Saskatoon: Western Producer Prairie Books, 1983).

11 Gerhard J. Ens, *Homeland to Hinterland: The Changing Worlds of the Red River Métis in the Nineteenth Century* (Toronto: University of Toronto Press, 1996).

12 Diane Payment, *"The Free People—Otipemisiwak," Batoche, Saskatchewan, 1870–1930* (Ottawa: National Historic Parks and Sites, 1990).

13 Diane Payment, "'La Vie en Rose?' Métis Women at Batoche, 1870–1920," in *Women of the First Nations: Power, Wisdom and Strength*, eds. Christine Miller, Patricia Chuchryk et al. (Winnipeg: University of Manitoba Press, 1996), 20.

14 D.N. Sprague, "Dispossession vs. Accommodation in Plaintiff vs. Defendant Accounts of Métis Dispersal from Manitoba, 1870–1881," *Prairie Forum* 16, no. 2 (Fall 1991), 137–56.

RELATED READINGS IN THIS SERIES

From *Nation and Society: Readings in Post-Confederation Canadian History*
Christopher Armstrong, "Remoulding the Constitution," 21–43.
Veronica Strong-Boag, "The Citizenship Debates: The 1885 Franchise Act," 44–62.
Sarah Carter, "Categories and Terrains of Exclusion: Constructing the 'Indian Woman' in the Early Settlement Era in Western Canada," 63–78.

From Primary Documents CD-ROM, Volume II
Big Bear
Poundmaker and Wife
Gabriel Dumont
Riel Addressing the Jury at His Regina Trial, July 1885
Macdonald Introduces the National Policy
Riel's Last Interview
French Aggression
Sir Charles Tupper on Remedial Legislation
A Great Northwest Victory
The Northwest Question

SELECTED READING

Regional studies that cover this period include Jean Barman, *The West Beyond the West: A History of British Columbia* (Toronto: University of Toronto Press, 1996); Margaret Ormsby, *British Columbia: A History* (Toronto: Macmillan, 1971); Cole Harris, *The Resettlement of British Columbia: Essays on Colonialism and Geographical Change* (Vancouver: UBC

Press, 1997); and *Making Native Space: Colonialism, Resistance, and Reserves in British Columbia* (Vancouver: UBC Press, 2002); Morris Zaslow, *The Opening of the Canadian North, 1870–1914* (Toronto: McClelland & Stewart, 1971); William R. Morrison, *True North: The Yukon and Northwest Territories* (Toronto: Oxford University Press, 1998); W.L. Morton, *Manitoba: A History* (Toronto: University of Toronto Press, 1957); Lewis H. Thomas, *The Struggle for Responsible Government in the North-West Territories, 1870–97* (Toronto: University of Toronto Press, 1978); Gerald Friesen, *The Canadian Prairies: A History* (Toronto: University of Toronto Press, 1987); John Herd Thompson, *Forging the Prairie West* (Toronto: Oxford University Press, 1998); J.M.S. Careless, *The Union of the Canadas: The Growth of Canadian Institutions, 1841–1857* (Toronto: McClelland & Stewart, 1967); John A. Dickinson and Brian Young, *A Short History of Quebec*, 2nd ed. (Toronto: Copp Clark Pitman, 1993); Paul-André Linteau, René Durocher, and Jean-Claude Robert, *Quebec: A History, 1867–1929* (Toronto: Lorimer, 1983); Fernand Ouellet, *Economic and Social History of Quebec, 1760–1850* (Toronto: Macmillan, 1981); Susan Mann Trofimenkoff, *The Dream of Nation: A Social and Intellectual History of Quebec* (Toronto: Gage, 1983); E.R. Forbes and D.A. Muise, eds., *The Atlantic Provinces in Confederation* (Toronto and Fredericton: University of Toronto Press and Acadiensis Press, 1993); W.S. MacNutt, *The Atlantic Provinces: The Emergence of Colonial Society, 1712–1857* (Toronto: McClelland & Stewart, 1965); Margaret R. Conrad and James K. Hiller, *Atlantic Canada: A Region in the Making* (Toronto: Oxford University Press, 2001). See also Sarah Carter et al., *Unsettled Pasts: Reconceiving the West Through Women's History* (Vancouver: University of British Columbia Press, 2006).

The causes and events of the 1885 North-West Rebellion are detailed in the two Stanley works cited in Chapter 2 and in Bob Beal and Rod Macleod, *Prairie Fire: The Northwest Rebellion of 1885* (Edmonton: Hurtig, 1984). A qualified defence of Canadian government actions is found in Thomas Flanagan, *Riel and the Rebellion: 1885 Reconsidered* (Saskatoon: Western Producer Prairie Books, 1983). The military aspects of the rebellion are outlined in Desmond Morton, *The Last War Drum* (Toronto: Hakkert, 1972). Biographies of the major Métis protagonists of the 1885 rebellion include George F.G. Stanley's *Louis Riel* (Toronto: McGraw-Hill Ryerson, 1973); and George Woodcock's *Gabriel Dumont: The Métis Chief and His Lost World* (Edmonton: Hurtig, 1975). An examination of representations of Riel from the time of the rebellion to the present can be found in Albert Braz, *The False Traitor: Louis Riel in Canadian Culture* (Toronto: University of Toronto Press, 2003). Life for Native peoples in the West following the defeat of the rebellions is the subject of several essays in F.L. Barron and

James B. Waldrom, eds., *1885 and After: Native Society in Transition* (Regina: Canadian Plains Research Center, 1986). An important community study focusing on the Métis is Diane Payment, *Batoche, 1870–1910* (St. Boniface: Les Éditions du Blé, 1983). The gender discourse of the rebellion's opponents is discussed in Sarah A. Carter, *Capturing Women: The Manipulation of Cultural Imagery in Canada's Prairie West* (Montreal McGill-Queen's University Press, 1997).

Two books establish a valuable framework for analyzing the fate of the First Nations in western Canada: Sarah Carter, *Aboriginal People and Colonizers of Western Canada to 1900* (Toronto: University of Toronto Press, 1999); and Treaty 7 Elders and Tribal Council with Walter Hildebrandt, Sarah Carter, and Dorothy First Rider, *The True Spirit and Original Intent of Treaty 7* (Montreal: McGill-Queen's University Press, 1996). On Native women, see Sarah Carter, *The Importance of Being Monogamous: Marriage and Nation-Building in Western Canada to 1915* (Edmonton and Athabasca: University of Alberta Press and AU Press, 2008). Other important works on Aboriginal issues include surveys by Arthur J. Ray, *I Have Lived Here Since the World Began: An Illustrated History of Canada's Native People*, Revised edition (Toronto: Lester/Key Porter, 2005); Olive P. Dickason, *Canada's First Nations: A History of Founding Peoples from Earliest Times*, 3rd ed. (Toronto: Oxford University Press, 2001); and J.R. Miller, *Skyscrapers Hide the Heavens: A History of Indian White Relations in Canada* (Toronto: University of Toronto Press, 2000). See also Hugh Shewell, *"Enough to Keep Them Alive": Indian Welfare in Canada, 1873–1965* (Toronto: University of Toronto Press, 2004); Frank Tough, *"As Their Resources Fail": Native People and the Economic History of Northern Manitoba, 1870–1930* (Vancouver: UBC Press, 1996); Katherine Pettipas, *Severing the Ties That Bind: Government Repression of Indigenous Religious Ceremonies on the Prairies* (Winnipeg: University of Manitoba Press, 1994); Sheila McManus, *The Line Which Separates: Race, Gender, and the Making of the Alberta-Montana Borderlands* (Edmonton: University of Alberta Press, 2005); Brian Titley, *A Narrow Vision: Duncan Campbell Scott and the Administration of Indian Affairs in Canada* (Vancouver: UBC Press, 1986); Sarah Carter, *Lost Harvests: Prairie Indian Reserve Farmers and Government Policy* (Montreal: McGill-Queen's University Press, 1990); R.E. Cail, *Land, Man and Law: The Disposal of Crown Lands in British Columbia, 1871–1913* (Vancouver: UBC Press, 1974); Adele Perry, *On the Edge of Empire: Gender, Race, and the Making of British Columbia, 1849–1871* (Toronto: University of Toronto Press, 2001); and Tina Loo, *Making Law, Order, and Authority in British Columbia, 1812–1871* (Toronto: University of Toronto Press, 1994).

On the formation of political parties in Canada, see Gordon T. Stewart, *The Origins of Canadian Politics: A Comparative Approach* (Vancouver: UBC Press, 1986); and R. Kenneth Carty and W. Peter Ward, eds., *National Politics and Community in Canada* (Vancouver: UBC Press, 1986). Ideological debates are traced in Denis Monière, *Ideologies in Quebec: The Historical Development* (Toronto: University of Toronto Press, 1981); and Douglas V. Verney, *Three Civilizations, Two Cultures, One State: Canada's Political Traditions* (Durham, NC: Duke University Press, 1986). On Canada's external relations, see R.C. Brown, *Canada's National Policy, 1883–1900: A Study of American-Canadian Relations* (Princeton: Princeton University Press, 1964); J.L. Granatstein and Norman Hilmer, *For Better or for Worse: Canada and the United States to the 1990s* (Toronto: Ryerson, 1991); Edelgard E. Mahant and Graeme S. Mount, *An Introduction to Canadian-American Relations* (Toronto: Methuen, 1984) and relevant articles in Phillip Buckner and R. Douglas Francis, eds., *Canada and the British World* (Toronto: University of British Columbia Press, 2006). The Canada First movement and aspects of early Canadian nationalism are discussed in Carl Berger, *The Sense of Power: Studies in the Ideas of Canadian Imperialism, 1867–1914* (Toronto: University of Toronto Press, 1970). See also David P. Gagan, "The Relevance of Canada First," *Journal of Canadian Studies* 5 (November 1970), 36–44 and a new biography on the early years of one of Canada First's heroes, David A. Wilson, *Thomas D'Arcy McGee: Vol. 1, Passion, Reason, and Politics, 1825–1857* (Montreal: McGill-Queen's University Press, 2008). Legal matters are discussed in Jonathan Swainger, *The Canadian Department of Justice and the Completion of Confederation, 1867–78* (Toronto: University of Toronto Press, 2001); and the early chapters of James G. Snell and Frederick Vaughan, *The Supreme Court of Canada* (Toronto: The Osgoode Society, 1985).

General background on French-English and Protestant-Roman Catholic conflict is provided in Ramsay Cook, *Provincial Autonomy, Minority Rights and the Compact Theory, 1867–1921* (Ottawa: Queen's Printer, 1969); Ramsay Cook, R. Craig Brown, and Carl Berger, eds., *Minorities, Schools and Politics* (Toronto: University of Toronto Press, 1969); Robert Choquette, *Language and Religion: A History of English-French Conflict in Ontario* (Ottawa: University of Ottawa Press,

1975); Richard Wilbur, *The Rise of French New Brunswick* (Halifax: Formac, 1989); Jean Daigle, ed., *Acadia of the Maritimes: Thematic Studies* (Moncton: Chaire d'études acadiennes, Université de Moncton, 1995); Sheila A. Andrew, *The Development of Elites in Acadian New Brunswick, 1861–1881* (Montreal: McGill-Queen's University Press, 1996); Jacques Paul Couturier et Phyllis E. LeBlanc, dir., *Économie et société en Acadie, 1850–1950* (Moncton: Éditions d'Acadie, 1996); Robert Painchaud, "French-Canadian Historiography and Franco-Catholic Settlement in Western Canada, 1870–1915," *Canadian Historical Review* 59, no. 4 (December 1978), 447–66; Paul Crunican, *Priests and Politicians: Manitoba Schools and the Election of 1896* (Toronto: University of Toronto Press, 1974); Kenneth Munro, "Official Bilingualism in Alberta," *Prairie Forum* 12, no. 1 (Spring 1987), 37–48; and Chad Gaffield, *Language, Schooling and Cultural Conflict: The Origins of the French-Language Controversy in Ontario* (Montreal: McGill-Queen's University Press, 1987). The Acadian renaissance is discussed in Cecile Gallant, *Women and the Acadian Renaissance* (Moncton: Les Éditions d'Acadie, 1992); and the Daigle collection mentioned earlier; Phyllis LeBlanc, "The Vatican and the Roman Catholic Church in Atlantic Canada: Policies Regarding Ethnicity and Language, 1878–1922," in *Papal Diplomacy in the Modern Age*, ed. Peter C. Kent and John F. Pollard (Westport: Praeger Press, 1994), 65–74; and George F.G. Stanley, "The Flowering of the Acadian Renaissance," in *Eastern and Western Perspectives*, ed. David Jay Bercuson and Phillip A. Buckner (Toronto: University of Toronto Press, 1981), 19–46.

Norman Knowles explores the Loyalist tradition as it developed in Ontario after confederation in *Inventing the Loyalists: The Loyalist Tradition and the Invention of Usable Pasts* (Toronto: University of Toronto Press, 1997). For the New Brunswick experience, see Murray Barkley, "The Loyalist Tradition in New Brunswick," *Acadiensis* 4, no. 2 (Spring 1975), 3–8211;45.

Biographies of major national political figures include Donald Creighton, *Sir John A. Macdonald: The Old Chieftain* (Toronto: Macmillan, 1955); Dale C. Thompson, *Alexander Mackenzie: Clear Grit* (Toronto: Macmillan, 1960); Joseph Schull, *Edward Blake*, 2 vols. (Toronto: Macmillan, 1975/76); and P.B. Waite, *The Man from Halifax: Sir John Thompson, Prime Minister* (Toronto: University of Toronto Press, 1985).

CHAPTER 4

Entering the Twentieth Century

1896–1911	1897	1898	1899–1902	1903	1904	1905	1906	1908	1909	1910	1911	1911–20	1913	1913–14	1914–18

Liberals under Wilfrid Laurier hold power in Ottawa

Klondike gold rush begins

Treaties signed with the Dene

South African War

Laurier's government supports building two new transcontinental railways; Alaska Boundary decision; La Ligue nationaliste canadienne founded

L'Association catholique de la jeunesse canadienne-française founded

Saskatchewan and Alberta become provinces

British troops withdrawn from Halifax and Esquimalt

Indian Act amendments give the federal government power to expropriate reserve lands

Department of External Affairs established

Le Devoir begins publication; Naval Service Bill passed

Reciprocity Treaty negotiated with the United States, rejected in federal election

Conservatives under Robert Borden hold power in Ottawa

Vilhjalmur Stefansson leads expedition to the North under Canadian auspices

Economic recession

First World War

As the twentieth century dawned, the Canadian economy was booming. Even Prime Minister Wilfrid Laurier got caught up in the optimism of the period, claiming: "The nineteenth century was the century of the United States. I think we can claim that it is Canada that shall fill the twentieth century."[1]

In retrospect, Laurier's comment, made during a speech to the Ottawa Canadian Club in 1904, proved over-optimistic. The United States dominated the twentieth century even more than the nineteenth and continued to have a major impact on Canada. Nevertheless, the opening years of the twentieth century brought the economic growth that Canadian leaders had sought for their nation. Industries flourished, immigrants flocked to the West, and two more transcontinental railways were built.

Although federal policy seemed to change little as the reins of government passed from the Conservatives to the Liberals, Canada changed dramatically during Laurier's term in office. When the United States finally agreed to the long-sought-after Reciprocity Treaty in 1911, the Liberals were convinced that it would buy them another victory at the polls. They were wrong. The Conservatives under Robert Borden won the election and North American free trade was rejected by a nation that was increasingly confident of its future.

LAURIER LIBERALISM

Laurier became prime minister of Canada in 1896 at the age of 55. Trained as a lawyer, he joined the Parti Rouge as a young man and edited a newspaper, *Le Défricheur*, in the Eastern Townships of Quebec. He was among those who opposed confederation, but, after serving a term in the Quebec legislature (1871–1874), he decided to run federally in 1874. For a short time, he was minister of inland revenue in the Mackenzie cabinet. A stout defender of political liberalism and Canadian unity, Laurier was Edward Blake's choice as party leader and

Railroading Canada

Encouraged by what seemed to be unending growth, Laurier decided to assist the eastern-based Grand Trunk Railway and the western-based Canadian Northern Railway companies to complete transcontinental lines. The vast sums of taxpayers' money invested in the projects meant that they, like the CPR, encouraged extravagance and political corruption. Unlike the CPR, the two new railways failed to make a profit and continued to be a drain on the federal budget long after Laurier had departed the scene.

The Canadian Northern Railway was the brainchild of Donald Mackenzie and Donald Mann, both originally subcontractors for Canadian Pacific Railway Company (CPR). In 1895 the pair formed a partnership to build a railway to Hudson Bay. This project failed to materialize, but Mackenzie and Mann began buying short rail lines in Manitoba and soon had the basis for a second transcontinental railway. With bond guarantees and land grants from the Manitoba government, they marketed $14 million of securities in London and New York for their Canadian Northern Railway. Neither promoter put up any of his own money: a third of the capital was guaranteed by governments at various levels, while Mackenzie's Toronto associate, George Cox, added the financial muscle of the Canadian Bank of Commerce.

The Grand Trunk Railway, whose conservative London-based directors saw their future survival as dependent on tapping the booming West, tried to buy the Canadian Northern, but negotiations for a merger of the two companies failed. Under their new American general manager, Charles M.

Hayes, the Grand Trunk embarked on a project to build its own new railway, incorporated as the National Transcontinental. Both companies would demand and get land grants, subsidies, and loan guarantees from the Laurier government. When Quebec and the Maritimes complained that they were left out of the investment in railways, the federal government agreed to build the Grand Trunk's Eastern Division from Moncton to Winnipeg and lease it to the company. Not to be outdone, Mackenzie and Mann knit together eastern lines to establish their claim to an Atlantic terminus.

Extravagance, greed, and patronage dogged the two ventures. When a royal commission was struck in 1911 to look into the skyrocketing costs of the Eastern Division, it was discovered that the project cost $70 million (out of $160 million) more than it should have. Nevertheless, the two companies pressed forward with construction, floating new security issues in London and demanding more subsidies and loan guarantees from Ottawa. Hayes was planning even grander schemes when he died in the sinking of the *Titanic* in 1912.

Mackenzie and Mann continued to expand their railroad empire, but their days were numbered. European investors were beginning to have second thoughts about investing in Canadian railways, and the outbreak of the First World War closed European financial markets completely. Faced with bankruptcy, Mackenzie and Mann were forced to let their railway empire be amalgamated with other government-owned railways into the Canadian National Railway system, which was created in a series of mergers between 1917 and 1923.

was chosen over the objections of a number of prominent Liberals.

Laurier's opposition to the *programmistes* earned him few friends among ultramontanists in Quebec. At the same time, it endeared him to the majority of English Protestants, who admired his courage in standing up to conservative forces in his province. Like Macdonald, Laurier had a personality for politics. He was a gifted orator and developed into a skillful politician who sought compromise among the discordant groups battling for ascendancy.

Canadians voted for the Liberals in 1896 for a variety of reasons. Laurier's success in improving the party's

organization was one of them. Another was the party's retreat in 1893 from its rigid free trade philosophy, which was increasingly alienating voters in Ontario, where the tariff was credited with much of the province's recent economic growth. Laurier's talent for political management and his sensitivity to provincial aspirations no doubt also helped. These qualities were evident in the formation of his first cabinet. In it he included powerful local chieftains—W.S. Fielding of Nova Scotia, Oliver Mowat of Ontario, and A.G. Blair of New Brunswick—and rising newcomers like Clifford Sifton of Manitoba, who in 1897 became minister of the interior, responsible for development of the West.

A view of Chilkoot Pass.
Library and Archives Canada, C-014260

tariff preference. This policy pleased those with imperialist leanings and did little to hurt Canadian manufacturers, whose main competition came from the United States.

It was fortunate for the Liberals that they came into office just as international economic conditions were on the upswing and when most of the farmland on the American frontier had been taken up. Under the supervision of Clifford Sifton, immigration was vigorously pursued, and the results were spectacular. More than 2 million people came to Canada between 1896 and 1911, many of them settling in the four western provinces. In 1905, the Laurier government created two new provinces—Alberta and Saskatchewan—out of the Northwest Territories. Laurier invited Liberals to form the government in both new provinces, giving his party a substantial patronage advantage over the rival Conservatives. In deciding, as Macdonald had in the case of Manitoba, to keep public lands and natural resources under federal control, Laurier created a continuing source of federal-provincial relations in the Prairie region.

Laurier's willingness to compromise was reflected in the tariff policy developed early in his adminstration. In 1897, his Finance minister, W.S. Fielding, introduced the so-called British preference, which applied lower tariffs to any country admitting Canadian products on a preferential basis. Since Great Britain had a policy of global free trade, it was automatically granted

Martha Munger Black. The Yukon gold rush drew many people into the Canadian North, including Martha Munger, who married George Black and in 1935 became the second woman to hold a seat in the Canadian House of Commons.
Yukon Archives, Martha Louise Black Collection, #3258

THE KLONDIKE GOLD RUSH

Coinciding with Laurier's success at the polls was the discovery of gold in the Klondike in 1896. The last great find in a series that began with California in 1849 and British Columbia in 1858, the Klondike gold rush began after California-born George Cormack, together with two Tagish brothers, Skookum Jim and Dawson Charlie, discovered gold nuggets at Rabbit Creek, which was renamed Bonanza Creek. The three men and other prospectors in the region staked their claims well before the inrush of gold-seekers in 1897.

Although the Klondike gold rush made a few instant millionaires, most of the 40 000 people who flooded into Canada's new Eldorado returned home empty-handed. The shrewdest man of all was Joe Ladue, a trader and prospector who bought land in what would become the major settlement in the region. Within two years of the gold find at Bonanza Creek, the lure of instant wealth transformed Dawson from a tiny fur-trading post into western Canada's second-largest city. The land that Ladue purchased for $10 an acre fetched as much as $1000 for a small building lot.

For those with plenty of money, the trip to the Yukon could be made by a steamer that ran from Seattle or Victoria to the mouth of the Yukon River, and from there along the river to Dawson City. There were several routes to the Klondike from Edmonton, British Columbia, and Alaska, most of them onerous and time-consuming. For those with little money and great hopes, the best way to reach the Klondike was over the Chilkoot or White passes from the two Alaskan communities that sprang up to serve them, Dyea and Skagway on the Lynn Canal. The trek through the passes was strenuous, but it was not a formidable obstacle to reaching Dawson City. The problem was getting supplies to the region: the North-West Mounted Police (NWMP) decreed that no one could enter the Yukon without enough money or supplies to last six months.

At the height of the gold rush, Dawson City was a rough-and-ready place, with saloons and dance halls open 24 hours a day—though they closed on Sunday. Its reputation for lawlessness was nevertheless greatly exaggerated. Unlike Skagway, a roaring American frontier town ruled for a time by a gangster named Soapy Smith, Dawson was under the firm control of the NWMP, who were dispatched to the Yukon as soon as the news of the gold discovery reached Ottawa. By 1898 there were 300 NWMP in Dawson in addition to 200 members of the Yukon Field Force, a military unit created to protect the newly established Yukon Territory. Under Superintendent Sam Steele, the NWMP rigidly enforced the regulation banning firearms from being carried in town and handed out stiff penalties to those who broke the law. The police kept the three main routes carefully guarded, not only to catch criminals, but also to make sure that the royalty on gold was paid. Between 1897 and 1911, gold worth over $22 million (about $3.5 billion in today's dollars) was extracted from the Yukon, and the royalties added substantial sums to Ottawa's coffers. A railway connected the Yukon with Skagway on the Pacific coast in 1900, but by that time the discovery of gold in Nome, Alaska, had shifted the attention of gold-seekers elsewhere.

Meanwhile, Canada's northern frontier settled into a more mundane existence. Individual prospectors gave way to international corporations and the territorial government gradually became less authoritarian. Like

Fond du Lac, on the east end of Lake Athabasca, became the site of a Hudson's Bay post in 1853. Soon thereafter, the Oblate mission was established, named Our Lady of Seven Sorrows. Despite the ravages of European diseases and suspicions that priests were the sources of their difficulties, the Dene gradually began to incorporate aspects of Roman Catholicism into their world view.
Courtesy of the Thomas Fisher Rare Book Library, University of Toronto

other territorial governments, the Yukon was originally governed by a commissioner and appointed officials, backed by the NWMP. Elected officials were gradually added to the council.

NORTHERN EXPOSURE

The Klondike gold rush had little impact on the North's Aboriginal residents, who still dominated the region north of the 60th parallel, the line that in this period increasingly defined what Canadians believed to be "the true North." The area south of this boundary was gobbled up by the provinces of Quebec, Ontario, Manitoba, Saskatchewan, and Alberta, which only took on their present configuration in the early decades of the twentieth century.

As the southern areas of the old Northwest were opened to settlement, Aboriginal peoples in the North were increasingly drawn into the fur trade. This was particularly the case among the Dene who inhabited the Mackenzie River Valley. In the second half of the nineteenth century, free traders (many of them Métis), missionaries, and scientists (most of them associated with the Geological Survey and the Dominion Lands Branch of the Department of the Interior) increasingly encroached on the North. The Dene also became the target for salvation by two missionary organizations, the Oblate Missionaries of Mary Immaculate and the Anglican Church Missionary Society. Like other Aboriginal peoples who became Christians, the Dene responded to the spiritual message of Christianity while shaping their religious practices to their own traditions and needs.

The potential wealth of the North, especially the oil-laden Athabasca tar sands and the iron-bearing rocks of Ungava, was gradually recognized by the federal government. In 1895 and 1897, orders-in-council affirmed the British cession of the Arctic to Canada, laid claim to all territory between 141 degrees west longitude and a vague line running west of Greenland, and created three new northern administrative districts—Mackenzie, Yukon, and Franklin. As early as 1891, the federal government declared its determination to negotiate treaties with the Dene but was slow to do so until the discovery of gold in the Klondike galvanized them into action. Treaties 8, 10, and 11 were signed with various Dene bands beginning in 1898.

Because Canada's claim to its Arctic sector was called into question by other nations, the federal government sponsored forays into the North by Captain Joseph Bernier between 1906 and 1911. Canada's pretensions notwithstanding, American explorer Robert Peary claimed the North Pole for the United States in 1909, but the Americans failed to follow up the claim. In 1913, Vilhjalmur Stefansson led an expedition under Canadian auspices to study the marine biology, oceanography, and Inuit people of the North. Soon after setting out, the primary government vessel, the *Karluk*, was crushed in the ice, and most of its crew, who had set out on foot, were never heard from again. A few managed to reach Wrangel Island, 110 miles off the coast of Siberia. Rumours that they had claimed the island for Canada set in motion a protracted sovereignty debate with the Soviet Union in the 1920s.

Although the Inuit of the eastern Arctic remained largely outside European influences until the 1930s, the peoples of the central and western Arctic were not so fortunate. The uncontrolled slaughter of whales and walrus from the 1860s to the 1880s left starvation in its wake among a people already weakened by European diseases. As a result, the original Inuvialuit people disappeared from the region and were replaced by Alaskan Inuit.

PROVINCIAL RIGHTS AND THE MANAGEMENT OF PROGRESS

While the prosperity that characterized the early years of the twentieth century helped cover up the cracks in confederation, it did not stop the growing regional disparity that increasingly defined the country. Nor did it stop the provinces from demanding that Ottawa pursue their interests, whether or not they conflicted with national policies. For better or for worse, federal-provincial tensions had become an enduring feature of the new nation.

Throughout the West, a political storm was brewing over the high tariffs that favoured eastern manufacturers and forced farmers to pay higher prices for their agricultural machinery and supplies. After 1905, Manitoba became insistent that its northern boundary be pushed to the 60th parallel to give it a territorial base equal to Saskatchewan and Alberta. Westerners also wanted a railway to a Hudson Bay port to provide an alternative route to export markets. In British Columbia, the white majority were alarmed by the growing number of Asians arriving on their shores and insisted that Ottawa restrict Asian immigration.

In the Maritimes, regional resentment flourished as all three provinces fell behind the rest of the nation in economic growth. The expansion of industries related to coal and steel in the first decade of the twentieth century masked some of the deep structural problems facing the region's economy, but no one could deny that the Maritimes were generally losing power within confederation. In 1867, the region held over 20 percent of the seats in the House of Commons; by 1914, its representation had dropped to 13 percent. Declining representation made it difficult for the Maritime region to shape national policies to meet its needs.

Like Macdonald, Laurier built his success on support in Canada's two largest provinces. Yet Laurier could not count on Ontario to keep him in office. The province's seats were split evenly between Conservatives and Liberals in 1896, but thereafter the Conservatives won a majority of Ontario's seats in federal elections. In 1905, James Whitney's Conservatives put an end to the 34-year reign of the Liberals in Ontario's provincial government. Holding more than a third of the seats in the House of Commons, Ontario wielded considerable influence in the corridors of power and caused Laurier as many problems as the other provinces put together. The strength of the province's industrial interests threatened the delicate balance between regional and national interests, while growing imperial sentiment within Ontario's overwhelmingly Anglophone population continued to clash with nationalist sentiment in Quebec.

Laurier won large majorities in Quebec throughout his political career, but the nationalist movement remained an ongoing threat to his Francophone support. Henri Bourassa, the grandson of Louis-Joseph Papineau—the Patriote leader in the rebellion of 1837–1838—emerged as the new leader of the nationalist cause. Although he was widely respected in his native province, Bourassa's vision of a bilingual and bicultural Canada put him at odds with some nationalists, who felt that Quebec should pursue a destiny independent from the rest of Canada. Bourassa concentrated on influencing public opinion and existing parties rather than forming a new organization to promote his policies. Founded in 1910, his newspaper, *Le Devoir*, emerged as a major force in developing public opinion in Quebec.

THE SOUTH AFRICAN WAR AND THE IMPERIAL QUESTION

The growing rivalry between Germany and Great Britain for imperial and industrial ascendancy inevitably created problems in Canada. So, too, did the jingoistic attitude of the United States, whose leaders continued to resist Canada's efforts to secure a free trade treaty or a generous settlement of the Alaska boundary. Laurier's genius for compromise was sorely tested in his efforts to steer a middle course in the conflicting demands generated by the two English-speaking empires that played a major role in Canada's political and economic life.

When Great Britain declared war against Dutch settlers—called Boers—in South Africa in 1899, many Anglophone Canadians felt it was their war too. Laurier faced enormous pressure to send a Canadian contingent to South Africa, not only from imperialist-minded English Canadians but also from Governor General Lord Minto, from the British-appointed general officer commanding the Canadian militia, Edward Hutton, and from British Colonial Secretary Joseph Chamberlain.

In sharp contrast, Bourassa and other French-Canadian nationalists in Laurier's party were determined that Canada not be involved in the conflict. It had nothing to do with Canada's interests, they argued. Rather than seeing imperialism as another form of Canadian nationalism, French Canadians identified with the Boers, who were fleeing the clutches of an aggressive world empire.

True to form, Laurier offered a compromise: Ottawa would equip and raise volunteers, but once in South Africa they would be paid by the British. On the grounds that the effort would cost Canada little financially, he refused to debate the issue in the commons. Laurier's compromise pleased neither side: it lost him the support of Bourassa, who resigned from the House of Commons in 1899 to protest the Liberal Party's policy on the war; at the same time, it did little to improve his image among the jingoistic imperialists.

More than 7000 Canadians eventually saw service in the so-called Boer War. Laurier's refusal to give more assistance to the British war effort encouraged a number of private initiatives. Donald Smith, raised to the British peerage as Lord Strathcona, funded an entire contingent. In Montreal, Margaret Polson Murray launched a

A one-time protégé of Wilfrid Laurier (left), Henri Bourassa (right) resigned from his seat in the House of Commons over Liberal policy on the South African War in 1899. He returned to parliament as an independent in 1900 and soon emerged as the intellectual and moral leader of French-Canadian nationalism.
Library and Archives Canada/A-119 (right) and C27360 (left)

patriotic organization of women, the Imperial Order Daughters of the Empire (IODE), to support empire unity and assist in the war effort. Its motto, "One flag, one throne, one country," appealed to many women who identified Canada's interests with those of Great Britain, and branches of the IODE sprang up across the country. The enormous interest that the war sparked on the home front also inspired the establishment of a patriotic fund, a Canadian branch of the Soldiers' Wives League, and the Canadian Memorial Association. This latter organization was dedicated to marking the graves of the 244 Canadian fatalities and erecting monuments to the men who fought in South Africa.

The South African War increased tensions between English and French Canadians, especially in Montreal, where Anglophone imperialists and Francophone nationalists lived in close proximity. On 5 March 1900, a group of McGill University students attacked the offices of two French-language newspapers and then paraded to the Montreal campus of Laval University (now the Université de Montréal), where they tried to provoke the French students into retaliatory action. The following day, the Laval students held a peaceful demonstration to protest the behaviour of the McGill students, which, in turn, provoked a crowd of English-speaking students and townspeople, armed with sticks, clubs, and frozen potatoes, to march on Laval University. The mob was dispersed by police with water hoses, but the militia had to be called out to preserve public order in the ethnically divided city.

For those fighting in South Africa, the glamour of warfare quickly wore off. The Boers inflicted humiliating defeats on British forces in the first few weeks of the war, and when the empire finally threw enough troops into the field to win formal engagements, the Boers refused to surrender. Instead, they resorted to guerrilla warfare, which prolonged the war for two years. Most of the Canadian casualties were a result of the diseases that ravaged the military camps rather than of the shooting skills of the Boers.

Following the war, Laurier was determined to find a middle ground between subordination to imperial authorities and total independence, but the task proved difficult. Canada still needed British support in negotiating with the Americans, who, like the British, seemed to be entering another expansionary phase. In 1898, the Americans trounced the Spanish in a nasty little war over Cuba and then took Puerto Rico, Guam, and the Philippines from the humiliated Spaniards. Would they use the same tactics with Canada?

The disputed boundary between Alaska and the Yukon became the testing ground. With the discovery of gold in the Klondike, the width of the Alaska Panhandle suddenly became important for determining who owned the ports through which people and goods entered the fabled gold fields. Canada's dependence on Great Britain in foreign affairs was reflected in the

The Manitoba Transvaal Contingent.
Library and Archives Canada/C-024604

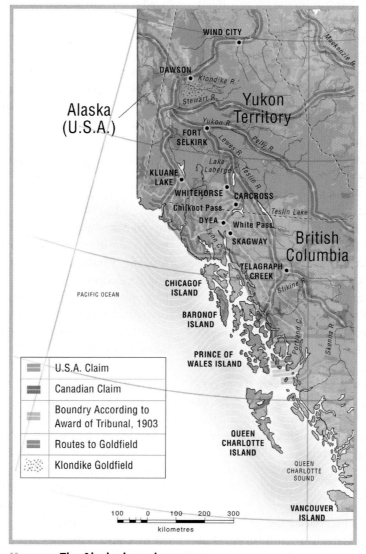

MAP 4.1 **The Alaska boundary, 1903.**

makeup of an international judicial tribunal to decide the issue in 1903. The two Canadian delegates on the three-man British negotiating team (A.B. Aylesworth and Sir Louis Jetté) found an uncertain ally in the British appointee, Lord Alverstone. In their negotiations with three American commissioners, all loyal appointees of President Theodore Roosevelt, Alverstone sided with the United States, demonstrating, at least in the minds of many Canadians, that Anglo-American friendship was more important to Great Britain than were good relations with its senior dominion.

As a result of the meddling of British officers in Canada's affairs during the South African War and the bad feelings lingering from the Alaska boundary decision, the Laurier government insisted in 1904 that the officer commanding the Canadian militia be appointed by Canada rather than by Britain. Canada also theoretically assumed greater responsibility for its own defence in 1906, when Britain withdrew its troops from Halifax and Esquimalt, the last two British bases in Canada.

In 1909, John A. Macdonald's former secretary, Joseph Pope, was charged with the task of establishing a department of external affairs for Canada. Although Great Britain was still technically in control of Canada's external relations, the growing volume of paperwork surrounding trade, boundary disputes, and other matters pointed in the direction of better organization of—and more autonomy over—the nation's foreign affairs.

The major question facing Laurier as he entered his fourth mandate in 1908 was naval defence. Given the escalating Anglo-German naval rivalry, Canadians were pressed either to make a direct financial contribution to the British Admiralty or establish their own navy. Laurier once again took a compromise position. His Naval Service Bill, introduced in 1910, proposed a Canadian navy that, in times of war, could be placed under imperial control. United in their disdain for Laurier's "tinpot navy," the Conservatives were nevertheless deeply divided between an English-Canadian majority demanding a direct contribution to the British Admiralty and a small band of French Canadians who opposed any money being spent on naval defence.

COMPETING NATIONALISMS

Like his predecessors, Laurier faced the problem of competing definitions of Canadian nationalism. The passage of time did little to mute cultural differences and in some respects divisions actually deepened and intensified. In Quebec, nationalist sentiment reached a fever pitch while notions of Anglo-Saxon superiority continued unabated among Anglophones. Laurier, as was his wont, tried to steer a middle course but increasingly found himself unable to satisfy anyone.

The rising tide of European imperialism at the end of the nineteenth century exacerbated tensions between English and French Canadians. When industrialized nations led by Great Britain began seizing control of the resources of Africa and Asia, definitions of the new nationality became even more ethnocentric. Many supporters of closer links between Canada and Great Britain ignored the exploitative character of imperialism, claiming that it was, at least potentially, a means of spreading the message of Christianity throughout the world. While many of the leading imperialists were social reformers, their social critique tended to emphasize the lack of Christian values rather than the excesses of capitalism. The imperial goal, it was hoped, would rekindle spiritual purpose and bind Canadians together in a mission to help Great Britain to elevate the world.

Reverend G.M. Grant, a native of Nova Scotia, typified this brand of imperialism. Appointed principal of Queen's University, a Presbyterian institution, in 1877, he remained in that post for more than two decades. Grant pressed for unity among Protestant churches and played a key role in the union of four previously independent Presbyterian denominations into the Presbyterian Church in Canada in 1875. The concepts of "Christian," "imperial," and "Canadian unity" were all part of the same organic whole for people like Grant, who believed that by helping to bring the spiritual and cultural benefits of Western civilization to "heathen" peoples around the world, Canadians were contributing to global progress.

Another Canadian imperialist was New Brunswick–born George Parkin. As the self-styled "wandering evangelist of empire," he became a leader in the Imperial Federation Movement. His book *Imperial Federation: The Problem of National Unity*, published in 1892, called for a single British imperial nation that would assume the burden of governing the world's "weak and alien races." In 1902, Parkin left his position as principal of Upper Canada College to become secretary of the scholarship trust established by Cecil Rhodes, an

Empire Day in Canada

One expression of the growth of imperialist sentiment was the establishment of Empire Day as a national holiday. The idea was suggested by Clementine Fessenden, a prominent club woman in Hamilton, and promoted in the wake of Queen Victoria's Golden Jubilee by Ontario's minister of education, George Ross. First celebrated in Ontario, Nova Scotia, and the Protestant schools of Quebec on 23 May 1898–the day before Queen Victoria's birthday–it was designed to provide an opportunity to use public schools for the promotion of patriotic sentiments. In his directive to all school inspectors, George Ross nicely blended national and imperial sentiments:

> Part of the forenoon might be occupied with a familiar talk by the teacher on the British Empire, its extent and resources; the relations of Canada to the Empire; the unity of the Empire and its advantages; the privileges which, as British subjects, we enjoy; the extent of Canada and its resources; readings by Canadian and

British authors by the teacher; interesting historical incidents in connection with our own country. The aim of the teacher in all of his references to Canada and the empire should be to make Canadian patriotism intelligent, comprehensive and strong.

> The afternoon, commencing at 2:30 p.m., might be occupied with patriotic recitations, songs and readings by the pupils, and speeches by the trustees, clergymen and others as may be available. The trustees and public generally should be invited to be present at the exercises. During the day the British Flag or the Canadian Ensign should be hoisted over the school building.[2]

Although Victoria Day is still celebrated in Canada, it has lost its imperial overtones. Busy school teachers may use the occasion to encourage civic engagement among their students, but, for most people, it marks the unofficial beginning of the summer–something all Canadians can celebrate.

ardent imperialist and successful entrepreneur who had made provision in his will for young men throughout the empire to study at Oxford with the help of Rhodes scholarships.

Support for imperialism among English Canadians was by no means unanimous. As the high degree of interest in closer economic links with the United States suggests, many English Canadians were comfortable with the view that Canada was a North American nation, free from the weight of tradition that plagued Europe. Goldwin Smith, a British-born academic who had settled in Toronto in 1871, argued that annexation to the United States was the best option for Canada. In his book *Canada and the Canadian Question* (1891), Smith maintained that annexation would consolidate the peoples of North America into one progressive nation, enhance the global power of English-speaking peoples, and resolve, in one bold stroke, the nationalist issue in Quebec.

Goldwin Smith was not alone in seeing Canada's destiny firmly bound with that of the United States. Especially in the Maritimes and the West, there was strong support for commercial union with the United States among primary producers, though few went so far as calling for political annexation. Canadians who had moved to the United States to find work were also more receptive to closer relations between the two North American nations. In the Canadian Clubs that sprang up at the turn of the century in cities such as Boston, New York, and San Francisco, businessmen argued for closer Canada–United States relations, especially in matters of trade. Annexationism was always a latent force, ready to be called into service when economic circumstances looked bleak.

Before 1914, few voices in English Canada called for Canada to cut its ties with Great Britain and forge an independent national identity. John S. Ewart, who served as legal counsel for the French-speaking minority of Manitoba, wrote a series of essays arguing for Canada to become constitutionally independent, but there was little popular support for achieving such a goal until the First World War spurred Canadians into re-evaluating their lingering colonial relationship with Great Britain.

FRENCH-CANADIAN NATIONALISM

Few Francophones in Canada found much in the national identity debate that appealed to them, though their leading spokesman, Henri Bourassa, shared Goldwin Smith's anti-imperialism. When Laurier gave way to pressure from imperialists in Canada and Great Britain to participate in the South African War in 1899, Bourassa embarked down an intellectual road that made him one of Canada's most original and controversial critics of Canadian public policy. In 1901, he introduced a bill into the House of Commons that would make the Canadian parliament the only authority that could declare war on behalf of Canada. Although the resolution was voted down, it put the nation's colonial relationship to Great Britain on the agenda of public debate.

Bourassa also took the position that Canada should be an Anglo-French nation, with two cultures having equal rights throughout the country. During the debate surrounding the creation of the provinces of Alberta and Saskatchewan in 1905, he argued that Roman Catholics should have control of their own schools in the new provinces, warning that the equality of cultures was an absolute condition of French Canadians continuing to accept confederation. Bourassa gradually retreated from his notion of a bilingual, bicultural Canada because English Canada was so unreceptive to the idea. Instead, he began to emphasize the Roman Catholic nature of French-Canadian society and the need to protect Quebec's special identity, which, he felt, was being threatened by secularism and materialism. Much troubled by the emergence of big corporations, Bourassa championed the rights of small business and farming families against the greed of corporate capitalism.

Bourassa increasingly became a spokesman for the nationalist forces that had been gaining momentum in Quebec since the Northwest Resistance. Following the defeat of Honoré Mercier's Parti national government in 1891, nationalist sentiment continued to thrive in a variety of voluntary organizations. The most important of these was La Ligue nationaliste canadienne, established in 1903. Bourassa was a leading figure in the Ligue, which stood for Canadian autonomy within the British Empire, provincial rights, linguistic dualism, separate Roman Catholic schools, and the economic development of Canada by and for Canadians. Although the Ligue had only a few active members, its doctrines were widely disseminated through its newspaper, *Le Nationaliste*, and the speeches and writings of Bourassa and his coterie of young followers.

The enthusiasm of young people for nationalist ideas was captured in L'Association catholique de la jeunesse canadienne-française (ACJC), founded in 1904. Growing out of the determination of male college students to protect French-Canadian and Roman Catholic interests, it was encouraged by church officials and journalists who believed that French Canada was in the midst of a religious and national crisis. The ACJC's motto was "notre maître le passé" (our master the past), and its constitution embodied its idealistic goals:

1. The members of the Catholic Association of French-Canadian Youth believe that the French-Canadian race has a special mission to fulfil on this continent and that it must, for this end, guard its distinct character from that of other races.
2. They believe that the progress of the French-Canadian race is in a special fashion attached to the Catholic faith, which is one of the essential and specific elements.[3]

This approach was further developed by one of the organization's most prominent members, Lionel Groulx, a priest who taught at the Valleyfield Seminary. In his numerous publications, beginning with *Croisade d'adolescents*, Groulx proclaimed a mission for French Canadians, who, he argued, had been especially chosen by God to advance the cause of Roman Catholicism in North America. When he was appointed to teach history at Laval's Montreal campus in 1915, he had a platform from which to promote his providential view of French-Canadian history, an understanding of which he and other nationalistes felt was essential to the struggle for cultural survival.

Few people in Quebec dared to voice the idea of complete independence. Not surprisingly, perhaps, the idea was taken up by a Franco-American. Born in Kentucky, Jules-Paul Tardivel moved to Quebec in 1868 and quickly became a spokesperson for French-Canadian nationalism and ultramontanism. He advanced his idea of an independent French Roman Catholic nation on the banks of the St. Lawrence in his newspaper, *La*

Vérité, and in a futuristic novel, *Pour la Patrie*, published in 1895. Although few people championed his cause, it would not be long before cultural nationalism would prompt others to dream of a separate nation-state to support it.

NATIVE PEOPLES AND THE DOMINANT CULTURE

Despite their presence in all provinces and territories, Aboriginal peoples throughout industrializing Canada found themselves largely outside of the national debate. Victims of blinding racism, their voices went unheard and their living conditions deteriorated. The combination of immigration and high death rates quickly reduced both the absolute and relative numbers of Aboriginal people, especially in western Canada. In Alberta, for example, Native peoples constituted a mere 3 percent of the population in 1911. Fifty years earlier, they had been the overwhelming majority in the territory. With numbers dipping below 200 000 at the beginning of the twentieth century, the very survival of Canada's First Nations seemed seriously in doubt.

Because white settlers tended to view Native peoples as a nuisance in the path of "progress," the major goal of federal policy became the removal of Aboriginal peoples from their lands without provoking a violent reaction. In 1908, Frank Oliver introduced a measure that would allow Status Indians to be removed from reserves near towns with more than 8000 residents. Oliver won a further amendment to the Indian Act in 1911 that allowed portions of reserves to be expropriated by municipalities or companies for roads, railways, or other public purposes. Under this legislation, almost half of the Blackfoot reserve was sold for slightly over $1 million. The McKenna-McBride Commission, created in 1912 to resolve federal-provincial differences regarding Native land claims in British Columbia, ignored Native claims and exchanged over 14 000 hectares of reserve land for larger but significantly less valuable holdings.

Education policies were similarly ill conceived. The federal government delegated responsibility for Native education to the major churches, which had sent missionaries to reserves to convert their charges to Christianity. While the churches professed support for the assimilation of Aboriginal peoples into white society, their school curricula suggested that Natives were only welcome in the lower ranks of the social hierarchy. Little time was devoted to academic subjects; instead, much of the day was divided between religious instruction and training in manual labour for boys and in household work for girls.

Native parents complained that boarding schools separated children from their families and forbade pupils the use of their birth languages. They also argued that youngsters were overworked, poorly fed, and subject to corporal punishment and sexual abuse. Although about two-thirds of the Native children enrolled in schools at the end of the century attended day schools on their reserves, the government's policy favoured schools well away from reserves. A cabinet minister expressed the government's philosophy in 1883: "If these schools are to succeed, we must not have them too near the bands; in order to educate the children properly we must separate them from their families. Some people may say that this is hard, but if we want to civilize them, we must do that."[4]

Remedies for injustice did not come easily. As litigants in a European-based judicial system, Natives faced major social, cultural, and economic obstacles. They gradually responded by using the tactics of their adversaries: cooperation among themselves, organized protests, and demands that laws relating to property rights and personal freedom be applied equally to Native peoples. The Grand Indian Council of Ontario and Quebec, founded in 1870 by Iroquois and Ojibwa, protested Ottawa's legislation designed to expropriate their land near towns and cities. Land claims in British Columbia were the subject of a Squamish delegation to King Edward VII in London in 1906 and of a petition from the Nisga to the Judicial Committee of the Privy Council in 1913. Pan-Indian revival movements such as the Council of Tribes were even more outspoken, stating bluntly that whites had demoralized and defrauded Native peoples, who should now fight back. Pressure from the Department of Indian Affairs, the indifference and outright hostility of most Canadians, and the military might of the majority doomed such protests.

As a last resort, Natives practised widespread defiance of measures taken to restrict their freedom.

Native industrial school students and their father, Saskatchewan, ca. 1900.
Library and Archives Canada/C37113

When a pass system was introduced on reserves in the Northwest Territories after the rebellion of 1885, this regulation proved largely unenforceable. Attempts to ban the sun dances of the Prairie Natives in the 1890s simply drove them underground: the dances were an essential component of communion with the spirit world and, like all dances among Native peoples, were an expression of group solidarity. In British Columbia, Natives similarly defied the 1885 government ban on potlatches, elaborate gift-giving ceremonies widely practised in West Coast cultures.

THE LOST MÉTIS NATION

The Métis, whose sense of purpose was badly fractured in the years following the Northwest Resistance of 1885, fared little better than other Aboriginal peoples. Although they continued to demand lands as their Aboriginal right, the Métis met a brick wall of government indifference. Meanwhile, the pressures of white settlement forced them to inhabit areas with little agricultural potential. They hunted, fished, and trapped in

VOICES FROM THE PAST

The Land Question

Native peoples often expressed disbelief at the heavy-handedness by which they were dispossessed of their lands and resources. This letter to the *Victoria Daily Colonist,* published on 15 May 1880, expressed views common among Native leaders.

> I am an Indian chief and a Christian. "Do unto others as you wish others should do unto you" is Christian doctrine. Is the white man a Christian? This is a part of his creed—"take all you want if it belongs to an Indian"? He has taken all our land and all the salmon and we have nothing. He believes an Indian has a right to live if he can on nothing at all. . . .
>
> The Indians are now reduced to this condition—THEY MUST ROB OR STARVE. Which will they do? I need not answer. An Indian is a man; and he has eyes. If you stab him he will bleed; if you poison him he will die. If you wrong him shall he not seek revenge? If an Indian wrongs a white man what is his humility? Revenge. If want compels us to execute the villainy they teach they may discover when it is

> TOO LATE that an Indian can imitate the lightning and strike in a thousand places at the same time. We are not beggars. In the middle of the magnificent country that was once our own we only ask for land enough to enable us to live like white men by working in the fields. If the Indians get no land this spring you MAY BE SURE the white man will have a very bad harvest this year, and the Indians will eat beef next winter. Fine talk won't feed an Indian. "Her Majesty's Indian subjects," whose rights are limited to living on nothing at all if they can, are prepared to face the worst—anything but death by starvation. In a court of justice we could prove that we are the only persons who have any right or title to this land. If the Queen has no power to aid us; if all the power belongs to the parliament, then I say again may the Lord have mercy on the Indians—AND ON THE WHITE-MEN.
>
> WILLIAM,
> Chief of the Williams Lake Indians[5]

unsettled territories and moved on when white settlers arrived.

Instead of the unified nation that the rebels of 1885 had hoped to create, the Métis were dispersed across the Prairies in communities such as Green Lake, Saskatchewan, and Lac Ste. Anne and Lac La Biche, Alberta. The Métis in Batoche finally won a land settlement in 1899–1900, receiving individual land grants rather than a reserve. Since farming required capital that the Métis lacked, many sold their lands. For decades, the Métis remained a forgotten people, invisible even in the census until 1981, when, for the first time, "Métis" was recognized as an ethnic group.

The 1911 Election

The plight of Canada's Native peoples was not high on the list of Laurier's concerns on the eve of the 1911 election. With nationalist forces in Quebec, western alienation, and charges of corruption dominating newspaper headlines, it was clear that the Liberals were in danger of defeat at the polls. A timely economic initiative by the Americans seemed to provide an issue that would unite the country and defeat the prime minister's opponents. Under President William Howard Taft, the Americans proposed a comprehensive trade agreement that allowed the free entry of a wide range of natural products and set lower rates on a number of manufactured goods, including agricultural implements dear to the hearts of Canadian farmers. Here, it seemed, was the solution to agrarian grievances and a means of satisfying those who had long worked for closer trade relations between Canada and the United States.

At first glance, the phlegmatic Robert Laird Borden, federal Conservative leader since 1901, was not the man to challenge the charismatic Laurier. Yet this respectable Halifax lawyer had managed to rebuild a party shattered by the divisions of the 1890s. Like his predecessors, Borden was determined to pursue policies that would foster economic growth, but unlike Macdonald and Laurier, he was a progressive in his approach to policy. Borden emphasized morality, duty, and efficiency in government and struggled, in a way typical of progressives, to eliminate some of the worst abuses of the old patronage-ridden system.

At a meeting in Halifax in 1907, the Conservatives unveiled a new platform designed to emphasize their

During the 1911 election campaign, companies opposed to free trade bought advertising space in their local newspapers to promote their anti-free-trade position. This cartoon was drawn by Donald McRitchie, who had previously published much of his work in the *Eye Opener*, a Calgary-based journal.
The *Gazette* (Montreal), 22 and 23 September 1911

progressive program. It included endorsement of progressive policies such as free rural mail delivery, civil service reform, and federal aid to technical education. The Halifax platform failed to win many votes in 1908, but it remained the foundation for many of the policies promoted by the Conservatives in the 1911 campaign. By 1911, the Conservatives were also backed by effective local organizations.

Conservative spirits were raised further still by the defection of two key interest groups from the Liberal fold. Enraged by the prospect of reciprocity, 18 prominent Toronto businessmen and financiers, along with long-time National Policy advocates such as the Canadian Manufacturers' Association, deserted the party they had formerly supported so generously. Together with dissident Liberal MPs such as Clifford Sifton, they denounced reciprocity as a threat to Canadian survival, a step toward absorption by the United

States, and a threat to the dominion's manufacturing interests. Laurier's Quebec stronghold also crumbled as Bourassa's nationalists, damning the naval policy as a sell-out to English Canada, found common cause with Quebec Francophone Conservatives.

The federal election of 1911 was preceded by months of heated debate and pamphleteering. Borden crisscrossed the country, promising to introduce the merit system into the civil service, establish a permanent tariff commission to set a "scientific tariff," create a board of grain commissioners to regulate the grain trade, implement free rural mail delivery, and provide subsidies to the provinces to improve roads and agricultural education. Prepared to accept increased state intervention in a number of areas, Borden was even quietly considering taking full control over the Liberal-sponsored Grand Trunk Pacific and Canadian Northern railways if they continued to sap the federal treasury. He also planned to scrap Laurier's "tinpot navy." In its place, he proposed to make an "emergency" $35-million contribution to Great Britain's efforts to keep the imperial navy—upon which Canada depended—strong and efficient. This would buy time, Borden argued, for Canadians to reflect more deeply on their defence policy.

Reciprocity and the naval policy, the two issues that more than any other posed the question of Canada's future, combined with the usual appeal of patronage, local issues, and individual candidates to defeat the Liberals. Although the popular vote was close, the distribution of seats was decisive. The Liberals won only 13 of Ontario's 86 constituencies and altogether won only 87 ridings; the Conservatives took 134 seats, including 27 in Quebec, where the alliance with nationalists boosted Conservative fortunes. Neither Laurier's liberalism nor his efforts to steer a middle course between differing visions of Canada proved sufficient to address the problems of the day.

THE BORDEN ADMINISTRATION, 1911–1914

Having come to power in 1911 with the support of Quebec nationalists and the anti–free trade business community, Borden faced the challenge of keeping the Conservative coalition together. To make matters worse, the economy began to sink into a recession in 1913. People across the country were thrown out of work, and the unemployed began drifting to cities, where they stretched municipal and charitable resources to the limit. Most frustrating for Borden was his inability to get some of his most innovative policies passed by parliament. Although the Conservatives had a majority in the House of Commons, the Liberal-dominated Senate rejected or severely amended much of the government's legislation.

Borden's cabinet included people who had not caught up with the style of progressive politics, but Borden had a strong ally in his minister of finance, Thomas White. The vice-president of National Trust, White represented the Toronto Liberals who had defected from Laurier in 1911 and was a powerful figure in the Canadian financial community. Bourassa also supported Borden in 1911 and might have added a progressive voice to the cabinet, but he refused to consider such a role. As the leader of the Quebec contingent of the cabinet, F.D. Monk was uncomfortable in the predominantly Anglophone milieu of Ottawa and, like Bourassa, held views on imperial policy that were diametrically opposed to those promoted by Borden and many of his imperialist-minded colleagues. Quebec nationalists had formed an alliance with the Conservatives in 1911 because they opposed Laurier, but a common enemy was not enough to keep them together once the party came to power. A little over a year after taking office as minister of public works, Monk resigned over the naval question. Like other Quebec nationalists, he was opposed to any policy that smacked of excessive subservience to the British.

Monk's defection from the cabinet did not make it easier to resolve the naval issue. When the Conservative Party's Naval Aid Bill was introduced into the House of Commons, it encountered such fierce opposition from the Liberals that the government invoked closure, a manoeuvre designed to limit debate. This was the first time that such a procedure had been used in Canada, and Laurier pointed to it as justification for instructing the Liberals in the Senate to defeat the bill. In making this decision, Laurier undoubtedly took into consideration the views of the nationalists in his native province, but he was probably also taking revenge for Borden's scrapping of his naval program.

Bills creating the tariff commission and providing subsidies to provincial highways also fell victim to the Senate's powers to veto and amend bills. In justifying

Robert Laird Borden

Born in Grand Pré, Nova Scotia, in 1854, Robert Borden grew up in modest circumstances. After a brief education in nearby Acacia Villa Academy, he began a teaching career at the age of 14. He taught school for five years in Nova Scotia and New Jersey before articling in law with Weatherbe and Graham in Halifax. Called to the bar in 1878, he became a junior partner in the law firm of Graham, Tupper, and Borden in 1882. Close ties to Charles Tupper gave Borden opportunities to take cases to the Supreme Court of Canada in Ottawa and the Judicial Committee of the Privy Council in London. It also brought pressure on the loyal and hard-working Borden to run in the 1896 election. The Conservative Party under Tupper's leadership went down to defeat, but Borden won his Halifax seat handily.

When Tupper stepped down as leader after the party's defeat in 1900, there were few men willing to take his place. The dutiful Borden, after much pressure, agreed to do so. The leader and his party were defeated by the triumphant Liberals in 1904, but Borden refused to give up. He won a by-election in Carleton, Ontario, early in 1905 and moved with his wife Laura to Ottawa. Forsaking his legal practice, Borden devoted his energies to reorganizing the party and developing a winning platform. Laurier whipped the Conservatives again in the 1908 election, but, after a decade in opposition, Borden finally tasted victory in 1911.

Robert Borden in London with a young Winston Churchill, 1913.
Library and Archives Canada/C-002082

their obstructionism, Liberal senators argued that the Borden administration was usurping powers that were not authorized by the British North America Act. Even the Grain Act of 1912, which created the Board of Grain Commissioners and gave the federal government the power to own and operate terminal grain elevators, had to be carefully administered in order not to invoke the wrath of the Liberal senators.

Not all programs foundered on the rock of Senate intransigence. In the West, Borden's popularity soared when he agreed to support the construction of a railroad to Hudson Bay to provide another outlet for growing grain exports. Farmers were doubtless also pleasantly surprised when many of the provisions of the aborted free trade agreement of 1911 were made available in the Underwood Tariff Act adopted by the United States in 1913. In 1912, Borden made good on his promise to

Canada's most powerful provinces—Quebec, Ontario, and Manitoba—that he would grant them huge sections of federally administered territories on their northern borders. (No effort was made to consult the largely Aboriginal populations who lived there.) Maritime and western provinces and bankers and brokers were relieved when the federal government saved the nation's two faltering railway companies from impending bankruptcy in 1914.

On the matter of civil service reform, the government was forced to move more slowly than it had planned. A commission, headed by Sir George Murray, a British public servant with impeccable credentials, had been established in September 1912 to investigate the federal civil service. In his report, Murray recommended a complete overhaul of a system that had become top heavy, patronage-ridden, and inefficient.

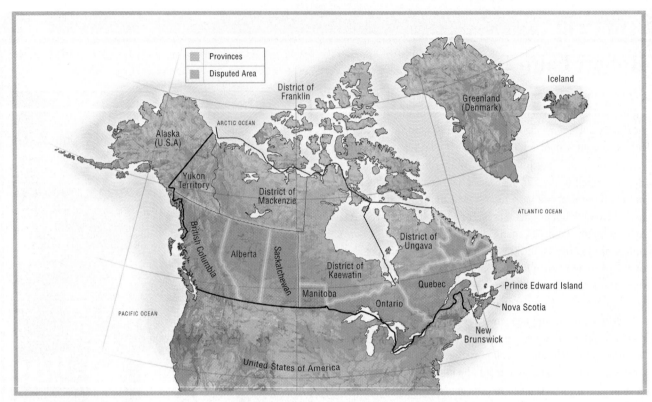

MAP 4.2 **Canada, 1905.**

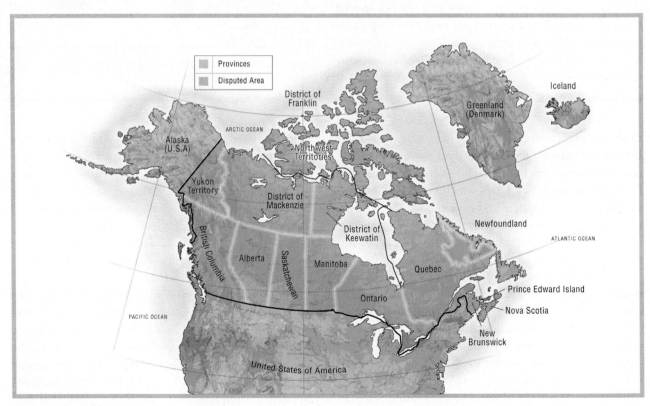

MAP 4.3 **Canada, 1912.**

Borden's government took steps to introduce reforms, but the existing system was so inadequate that it was unable—and probably not all that eager—to preside over its own transformation.

Perhaps nothing was as disturbing in the long run as the economic recession that descended in 1913. While business and government leaders understood that a credit crunch and over-expansion had created the crisis, most people experienced it as bankruptcy, unemployment, and having inadequate income to purchase the necessities of life.

The federal government responded by appointing a commission on the cost of living and by urging the railways to maintain high levels of employment. In the larger cities, municipal governments established employment bureaus. These efforts proved inadequate. Many people were facing real misery and, with immigrants still pouring into the country, there was every possibility that social unrest would be more than local police forces could manage. In May 1914, 2000 immigrants marched through the streets of downtown Winnipeg waving shovels and shouting, "Work or bread." This incident was a harbinger of what could come if economic conditions failed to improve.

CONCLUSION

Borden's concerns over the economy and the Senate's obstructionism were quickly superseded with the outbreak of the First World War in the summer of 1914. Other concerns, some older than confederation itself, would remain to complicate wartime planning. Despite impressive economic growth and successful political compromises, Canada was still a fragile nation-state. Alternative destinies, including provincial independence, union with the United States, and imperial federation, continued to attract those who were disappointed with what Canada had to offer. When wartime stresses were added to the curious brew called Canada, the very survival of the nation would be called into question.

NOTES

1 "First Annual Banquet," January 18, 1904, Addresses Delivered before the Canadian Club of Ottawa, 1903–1909 (1910), cited in *Colombo's Canadian Quotations*, ed. John Robert Colombo (Edmonton: Hurtig, 1974), 332.

2 Cited in Robert Craig Brown and Ramsay Cook, *Canada, 1896–1921: A Nation Transformed* (Toronto: McClelland & Stewart, 1974), 316.

3 Ibid., 140.

4 J.R. Miller, *Skyscrapers Hide the Heavens: A History of Indian-White Relations in Canada* (Toronto: University of Toronto Press, 1989), 298.

5 Quoted in Penny Petrone, ed., *First People, First Voices* (Toronto: University of Toronto Press, 1983), 68–69.

RELATED READINGS IN THIS SERIES

From *Nation and Society: Readings in Post-Confederation Canadian History*
William R. Morrison, "Eldorado," 65–75.

From Primary Documents CD-ROM, Volume II
The Story of a National Crime

The French Canadian in the British Empire
Pioneer Migrants Travelling to Dawson City During the Klondike Gold Rush
The Sarcee Sundance

SELECTED READING

A good survey of the Laurier and Borden administrations can be found in Robert Craig Brown and Ramsay Cook, *Canada, 1896–1921: A Nation Transformed* (Toronto: McClelland & Stewart, 1974). Biographies of Laurier include Joseph Schull, *Laurier* (Toronto: Macmillan, 1965); Richard Clippendale, *Laurier: His Life and World* (Toronto: McGraw-Hill Ryerson, 1979); and Réal Bélanger, *Wilfrid Laurier: quand la politique devient passion* (Quebec: Presses de l'Université Laval, 1986). Borden's administration is discussed in Robert Craig Brown, *Robert Laird Borden*, 2 vols. (Ottawa: Carleton University

Press, 1969); and John English, *The Decline of Politics: The Conservatives and the Party System, 1901–1920* (Toronto: University of Toronto Press, 1977).

The Alaska boundary dispute is the focus of Norman Penlington, *The Alaska Boundary Dispute: A Critical Appraisal* (Toronto: McGraw-Hill Ryerson, 1972) and John Munro, *The Alaska Boundary Dispute* (Toronto: Copp Clark, 1970). It is also touched on by William R. Morrison, *The Mounted Police and Canadian Sovereignty in the North, 1894–1925* (Vancouver: UBC Press, 1985). On the Yukon in this period, see William R. Morrison, *True North: The Yukon and Northwest Territories* (Toronto: Oxford University Press, 1998); William R. Morrison and Ken Coates, *Land of the Midnight Sun: A History of the Yukon* (Edmonton: Hurtig, 1988); and Charlene Porsild, *Gamblers and Dreamers: Women, Men and Community in the Klondike* (Vancouver: UBC Press, 1998). Missionary work among Native peoples in the North is discussed in John Webster Grant, *Moon of Wintertime: Missionaries and the Indians of Canada in Encounter since 1534* (Toronto: University of Toronto Press, 1984); Martha McCarthy, *From the Great River: Oblate Missions to the Dene, 1847–1921* (Edmonton: University of Alberta Press, 1995); and Robert Choquette, *The Oblate Assault on Canada's Northwest* (Ottawa: University of Ottawa Press, 1995).

The general context of Canadian-American relations in this period is covered in the books by Granatstein/Hilmer and Mahant/Mount cited in the previous chapter in addition to C.C. Tansill, *Canadian-American Relations, 1875–1911* (Toronto: Ryerson, 1943). The 1911 election is explored in Paul Stevens, ed., *The 1911 General Election: A Study in Canadian Politics* (Toronto: Copp Clark, 1970). On the Department of External Affairs, see John Hilliker, *Canada's Department of External Affairs*, vol. 1, *The Early Years, 1909–1946* (Montreal/Kingston: McGill-Queen's University Press, 1990). On imperial relations, see Carl Berger, *The Sense of Power: Studies in the Ideas of Canadian Imperialism, 1867–1914* (Toronto: University of Toronto Press, 1970) and *Imperial Relations in the Age of Laurier*, ed. Carl Berger (Toronto: University of Toronto Press, 1969). The South African War is extensively covered in Carman Miller, *Painting the Map Red: Canada and the South African War, 1899–1902* (Montreal: McGill-Queen's University Press, 1993); and Robert Page, *Imperialism and Canada, 1895–1903* (Toronto: Holt, Rinehart and Winston, 1972). George Parkin's career is discussed in David E. Torrance, "Instructor to Empire: Canada and the Rhodes Scholarship, 1902–39," in Phillip Buckner and R. Douglas Francis, eds., *Canada and the British World* (Toronto: University of British Columbia Press, 2006), 250–269.

Clerical nationalism is explored in Susan Mann Trofimenkoff, *L'Action Française: French-Canadian Nationalism in the Twenties* (Toronto: University of Toronto Press, 1975); Joseph Levitt, *Henri Bourassa and the Golden Calf: The Social Program of the Nationalists of Quebec, 1900–1914* (Ottawa: University of Ottawa Press, 1969); Jean Hamelin and Nicole Gagnon, *Histoire du Catholicisme québécois*, Part 3, *Le XXe siècle* (Montreal: Boréal Express, 1984); and Arthur Silver, *The French Canadian Idea of Confederation, 1864–1900* (Toronto: University of Toronto Press, 1982).

In addition to works cited earlier on Native peoples in this period, see J.R. Miller, *Shingwauk's Vision: A History of Native Residential Schools* (Toronto: University of Toronto Press, 1996); Maureen K. Lux, *Medicine That Walks: Medicine, Disease, and Canadian Plains Aboriginal People, 1880–1945* (Toronto: University of Toronto Press, 2001); John Sutton Lutz, *Makúk: A New History of Aboriginal-White Relations* (Vancouver: UBC Press, 2008); Susan Neylan, *The Heavens Are Changing: 19th-Century Protestant Missions and Tsimshian Christianity* (Montreal: McGill-Queen's University Press, 2002); Douglas Cole and Ira Chaikin, *An Iron Hand upon the People: The Law Against the Potlatch on the Northwest Coast* (Vancouver: Douglas and McIntyre, 1990); Rolf Knight, *Indians at Work: An Informal History of Native Indian Labour in British Columbia, 1858–1930* (Vancouver: New Star Books, 1978); Paul Tennant, *Aboriginal Peoples and Politics: The Indian Land Question in British Columbia, 1849–1989* (Vancouver: UBC Press, 1990); David C. Mandelbaum, *The Plains Cree: An Ethnographic, Historical and Comparative Study* (Regina: Canadian Plains Research Center, 1978); Peter Schmalz, *The Ojibwa of Southern Ontario* (Toronto: University of Toronto Press, 1990); Ellice B. Gonzalez, *Changing Economic Roles for Micmac Men and Women: An Ethnohistorical Analysis* (Ottawa: National Museum, 1981); Ruth Holmes Whitehead, *The Old Man Told Us: Excerpts from Micmac History, 1500–1950* (Halifax: Nimbus, 1991); Keith J. Crowe, *A History of the Original Peoples of Northern Canada* (Montreal: McGill-Queen's University Press, 1991); two books by Ken S. Coates, *Best Left as Indians: Native-White Relations in the Yukon Territory, 1840–1973* (Montreal: McGill-Queen's University Press, 1991) and *The Marshall Decision and Native Rights* (Montreal: McGill-Queen's University Press, 2000). See also Lyle Dick's impressive study *Muskox Land: Ellesmere Island in the Age of Conflict* (Calgary: University of Calgary Press, 2001).

Economy and Society in the Industrial Age, 1867–1921

Canadians who lived during the half-century between confederation and the end of the First World War witnessed a transformation of their economy and society. While national policies designed to produce economic growth and industrial development at first seemed slow to bear fruit, by the turn of the century the economy was growing by leaps and bounds. So, too, was the population, swelled at last by massive numbers of immigrants, most of them from Europe and the United States. Rapid growth created new problems in Canadian society and social movements to resolve them. Armed with a sense of their own ability to reform the industrial order, which heightened inequality while at the same time increasing material wealth, Canadians organized pressure groups, commissioned studies, collected signatures for petitions, buttonholed mayors and councillors, marched in the streets, and even clashed with militias in an effort to make their demands known. There was also a new energy and complexity in cultural life. Everything from schools and universities to sports and fine arts adjusted to the challenges of the modern age and, in the process, laid the foundations for many of the institutions and values that still define Canadian society.

The New Industrial Order, 1867–1921

TIMELINE

1872	Trade Union Act passed
1873–79	Economic recession
1876	Intercolonial Railway completed; Alexander Graham Bell invents the telephone
1879	National Policy tariff implemented
1884	Ontario passes first provincial Factory Act; Standard time adopted
1885	Canadian Pacific Railway completed
1886–89	Royal Commission on the Relations of Labor and Capital
1893–96	Economic recession
1896	Canadian economy begins long period of growth
1897	Alien Labour Act passed; wheat boom begins
1901	First transatlantic wireless signal received by Guglielmo Marconi in St. John's
1909	J.A.D. McCurdy becomes the first person in the British Empire to fly an airplane
1910	Steel Company of Canada created by mergers of smaller companies
1913	Economic recession begins
1914–18	First World War
1916	Advisory Council for Science and Industrial Research established

Dairy farming became a major business enterprise at the end of the nineteenth century as farmers increasingly sold their milk to mechanized dairies. In 1905, F.E.A. Gagnon revealed his enthusiasm for modernization in his description of the dairy facilities at Sainte-Marie de la Beauce in Quebec.

> The centrifugal machine is truly marvelous: it separates the cream from the milk at a rate of 1000 pounds per hour. Thanks to its use, the one hundred and six farmers who supply the creamery, of which MM. Duchesnay, Lindsay, Chaperon, and others are the owners, need only transport their milk once a day. The evening milk is mixed with the morning milk. The light cream formed during the night is remixed with the milk during transport, but the centrifugal separator undoes all that.
>
> . . . The apparatus is put in motion by a six horse-power steam engine, a jewel! You must see the separator work, the mixer, the vacuum suction devices, etc. Above all, be sure to have every thing

explained to you by the intelligent director of the school-factory, Mr. Stanislas Barré.

> Go and see. I tell you just this, because one must always be careful not to promise more butter than bread.[1]

Gagnon's enthusiasm for the technological marvels of the industrial age was shared by many Canadians, who embraced the efficiency of new machinery and the promise of easily accomplishing tasks that had once involved back-breaking work. As mechanization increased across all sectors of the economy, it soon became clear that some benefited while others did not. People who once produced the necessities of life by hand lost their livelihoods, while the factory jobs created by mechanization were often organized to force workers to perform at inhuman speeds with endless repetition of the same tasks. Even the farm women, who rejoiced when the new creameries relieved them of the drudgery of separating cream and churning butter, soon realized that tasks that they once controlled

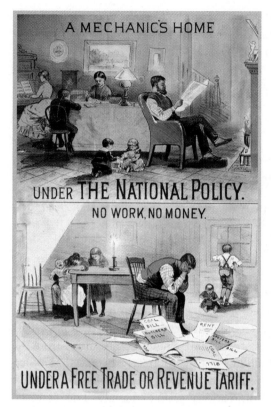

A MECHANIC'S HOME

UNDER THE NATIONAL POLICY.

NO WORK, NO MONEY.

UNDER A FREE TRADE OR REVENUE TARIFF.

An electoral campaign poster against free trade from 1891.
Library and Archives Canada, C-095466

in the home were now managed by their husbands and sons in the public sphere. This chapter explores the contours of the new industrial order and its dramatic impact on the way many Canadians made a living.

ASSESSING THE NATIONAL POLICY

While not everyone had an easy ride on the rocky road to industrialization in Canada, the overall economic trends were in the direction of impressive growth. The total output of goods and services, known as the gross national product (GNP), multiplied several times between 1867 and 1921 as the population rose from 3.5 million to 8.5 million. By 1915, three rail lines stretched across the continent, linking cities, towns, and villages, many of which had not even existed in 1867. Wherever it went, the railway spurred economic growth and laid the foundations for a national economy dominated by the banks and businesses in Montreal and Toronto.

Three policies—a protective tariff, transcontinental railways, and sponsored immigration—emerged as the cornerstones of the federal government's national development strategy. By linking the provinces, the railways enabled tariff-protected goods to find national markets. Immigration ensured passengers for railways and markets for Canadian products. Together, these policies were designed to bring Canada into an age of sustained industrial growth. In retrospect, the National Policy looks impressively integrated, but it actually developed in a piecemeal fashion and was challenged by regional, occupational, and individual agendas.

The importance of the National Policy in promoting industrial growth and economic expansion has long been debated. Detractors of the policy then and now charge that the tariff benefited producers at the expense of consumers and encouraged investors to establish firms destined for failure. By protecting domestic manufacturers from foreign competition, they argue, the National Policy encouraged the development of industries that could never compete in international markets. Regional critics maintain that the policy encouraged economic development in central Canada to the detriment of the Maritimes and the West.

In contrast, supporters of the National Policy have argued that protection is necessary to allow infant industries to succeed against competition from established companies in other countries. Canada's model, after all, was the United States, where the importance of tariffs in promoting industrial development is generally conceded. Moreover, supporters point to statistics showing that, in the decade following the implementation of the National Policy tariff, capital investment increased 114 percent, total wages paid by manufacturers rose by 68 percent, and the number of manufacturing establishments grew by 52 percent over the previous decade. They also argue that, because of the National Policy, Canada was in a better position to take advantage of improved economic conditions in the late 1890s.

While the role of tariffs in Canadian economic development remains controversial, there are several points of agreement. It is clear, for example, that under the protective cloak of the National Policy tariff, Canadian entrepreneurs moved to fill needs hitherto met by American imports. Southern Ontario, in particular, became the centre of specialized industries that served a national market. The agricultural implements industry is a good case in point. Using American patents in addition to developing their own lines, the firms of Massey Manufacturing of Toronto and A. Harris and Son of Brantford had emerged as leaders in the industry before confederation. The implementation of a 35 percent tariff on imported agricultural machinery in 1883 gave them a tremendous boost in the Canadian market. In 1891, when the two companies merged as Massey-Harris, capitalized at $5 million, they formed Canada's largest corporation, controlling over half the Canadian sales of agricultural machinery and accounting for 15 percent of the manufactures exported from Canada between 1890 and 1911.

There is also clear evidence that the National Policy laid the foundations for a branch-plant economy in Canada. Despite the success of such companies as Massey-Harris, many new companies, including Singer Sewing Machine, Gillette, Swift's, Coca-Cola, and Westinghouse, were American-owned. Their managers built factories in Canada to sell in a market that was protected from direct imports by high tariffs. In this period, the government welcomed foreign companies that sought to scale the tariff wall, and remained unconcerned about the nationality of company owners or the address to which profits were delivered.

The National Policy did little to shield Canada from dependence on foreign countries—primarily Great Britain and the United States—for capital and technology. Nor did it protect Canadians from international economic trends. Rising tariffs in the United States, fluctuating capital markets in Great Britain, and recessions in either country were immediately felt in Canada, and there was little Canadians could do economically or politically to alter that reality. International trends meant that economic growth remained sluggish from 1867 to 1896, then soared upward until 1912; the First World War sent it soaring again. Shorter business cycles resulting in slowdowns from 1873–79, 1893–96, 1903–07, and 1913–14 were also felt in Canada.

It is impossible to determine whether another approach to economic development would have been more successful. No matter what they did, Canadians lived in a world dominated by the British Empire and situated on the border of the United States, an emerging industrial giant. When the Canadian economy was experiencing healthy growth, the American economy was often performing even better, encouraging people to move across the border to find work. In global terms, Canada's economic performance in this period was spectacular, but compared to the United States, the results seemed less impressive.

TRANSPORTATION AND COMMUNICATION

Railways played a major role in Canada's Industrial Revolution. By 1915, Canadians boasted over 55 000 kilometres of track capable of shuffling goods and people from the Atlantic to the Pacific and even into the Yukon. By reducing transportation costs, railways expanded the geographic range in which products could be marketed. With the introduction of lower freight rates on eastbound grain under the Crow's Nest Pass Agreement of 1897 and competition resulting from the railway-building orgy of the early twentieth century, Prairie wheat farmers emerged as highly competitive players in international grain exchanges. The increased efficiency of rail communication was reflected in the inauguration of daily postal service across the nation in 1886 and rural postal delivery in 1908.

Ocean travel was also improving in safety and capacity. Reliable steamship service carried Prairie wheat, Ontario bacon, and Nova Scotia apples to British markets on time and usually in good condition. Under the auspices of the federal government, which held responsibility for navigational aids, Canada's coasts and inland waterways sprouted lighthouses, channel markers, and wharves. When the *Titanic* was sunk by an iceberg in 1912, it shocked Canadians, who had become less accustomed to marine disasters than their grandparents had been. Increased capacity and lower rates also encouraged the traffic in immigrants.

The major threat to the supremacy of steam-powered transportation was the internal combustion engine, used in automobiles and aircraft. After the first manufacturing plant—a Ford branch plant—opened in Windsor, Ontario, in 1904, the auto industry thrived in Canada. By contrast, aircraft transportation was, literally, slow to get off the ground. Aeronautical experiments by J.A.D. McCurdy and F.W. Baldwin, under the auspices of Alexander Graham Bell's Aerial

Experiment Association in Cape Breton, managed the first manned flight in the British Empire in 1909, with McCurdy at the controls, but it had few practical results.

Developments in transportation were matched by equally revolutionary advances in communication. Before he experimented in aviation, Alexander Graham Bell had become a household name with his highly publicized telephone call between Brantford and Paris, Ontario, in 1876. Initially perceived as a novelty, the telephone quickly became a popular necessity for business and personal use. Another communication first occurred in 1901 when Guglielmo Marconi received a wireless signal from the other side of the Atlantic by hoisting an antenna on a kite on Signal Hill in St. John's. Meanwhile, Canadian-born Reginald Fessenden was experimenting with wireless telegraph and voice transmissions, conducting the first broadcast of the human voice by radio from his laboratory in Massachusetts in 1906.

This conquest of time and space through developments in transportation and communication made

The Silver Dart was the plane that flew the first manned flight in 1909.
Library and Archives Canada, PA-122520

traditional ways of telling time awkward. In 1867, clocks were set by astronomical calculations in each major locality. This meant, for example, that 12:00 noon was 15 minutes earlier in Halifax than in Moncton. The railway and telegraph demanded a more standardized approach, especially in a country as big as Canada. Appropriately, it was a Canadian, Sandford Fleming, who

MORE TO THE STORY

Measuring the Canadian Economy

Economists divide the economy into three sectors: primary or staple industries such as hunting, fishing, forestry, farming, and mining; secondary or manufacturing industries that add value through the processing of primary resources; and tertiary or service industries that facilitate the use and development of primary and secondary resources. The tertiary sector includes financial services, trade, transportation, utilities, and public administration and services ranging from street cleaning to teaching. Together, the output of goods and services is called the gross national product (GNP). In 1986, Statistics Canada adopted the gross domestic product (GDP) to measure the nation's economic performance. The GDP is calculated in the same way as the GNP except that it excludes payments on foreign investment. Since goods and services produced outside of the market economy, such as housework and voluntary labour, are not included in calculations of GNP, the national

output is considerably greater than the official figures indicate. In 1996, Census Canada began collecting data on unpaid labour in and outside of the household, which accounts for much of the work performed by Canadians.

TABLE 5.1 Percentage Sectoral Distribution of the GNP, 1880–1920

Year	Primary	Secondary	Tertiary	Other
1880	43.5	22.7	22.4	11.4
1890	36.6	28.1	26.7	8.6
1900	36.5	25.0	29.4	9.1
1910	30.2	27.8	33.6	8.4
1920	26.6	29.7	35.3	8.4

Source: William L. Marr and Donald Paterson, *Canada: An Economic History* (Toronto: Gage, 1980) 22.

convinced those attending the International Prime Meridian Conference in 1884 in Washington to adopt a global system of telling time based on hourly variations from a standard mean, which is still in use today.

SECONDARY INDUSTRY

In the 50 years following confederation, secondary industry went from strength to strength. The first phase of Canada's Industrial Revolution, which occurred roughly between 1850 and 1900, was characterized by a rapid expansion of consumer goods industries, such as textiles, clothing, footwear, and cigars. The second phase, beginning around 1900, was fuelled by a surge in capital goods industries, such as machinery and equipment, and new technologies that spurred development in mining, pulp and paper, and electrical and chemical industries. By 1921, nearly 30 percent of Canada's GNP was derived from manufacturing and construction (see Table 17.1), a proportion that remained virtually constant to the end of the twentieth century.

The emergence of a vigorous iron and steel industry at the turn of the century signalled Canada's arrival as an industrial nation. Located in convenient proximity to coal mines on Cape Breton Island and an abundant supply of iron ore shipped from Bell Island, Newfoundland, Sydney became home to two industrial giants: Nova Scotia Coal and Steel and Dominion Iron and Steel. After several false starts, the Hamilton Steel and Iron Company began pouring open-hearth steel in 1900 and established its dominance in the field following its reorganization as Stelco in 1910. By that time, American visionary Francis Hector Clergue had capped his industrial empire at Sault Ste. Marie with a massive steel and iron works. Between 1877 and 1900, Canadian iron production increased more than sixfold and multiplied tenfold again by 1913.

Canada's heavy industry expanded impressively during the first two decades of the twentieth century. In addition to the rails and rolling stock required for the railways, Canadian factories turned out binders and seed drills, bicycles and carriages, furniture, and appliances to supply the Canadian market. Stimulated by economic growth, construction materials such as lumber, bricks, glass, stone, and cement figured prominently in the secondary sector. The demand for factories, public buildings, homes, and tenements sustained a construction industry that accounted for over 5 percent of the GNP by 1921.

As manufacturing became more complex, intermediate goods required in the production process became a larger segment of secondary industry. Among the most successful intermediate goods industries were those producing bolts, nails, nuts, screws, and similar products. Acids, alkalis, and heavy chemicals, essential ingredients in pulp and paper, iron and steel, oil refining, the electrical industry, and agriculture, also experienced increased demand.

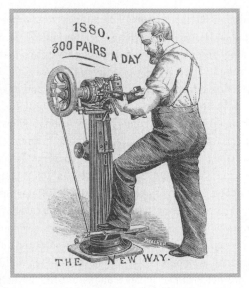

What a difference a century makes in the shoe industry.
McCord Museum of Canadian History, Montreal, M930.50.262 and M930.50.5.142

There was a clear geographical structure to the Canadian economy as it emerged under the National Policy. Neither the Maritimes nor the western provinces managed to emulate the manufacturing success of the central Canadian provinces, whose head start in the Industrial Revolution was evident even before confederation. By 1901, Ontario accounted for fully half of the gross value of Canadian manufacturing and Quebec for nearly a third. Once set, this pattern remained remarkably constant.

THE NEW FACE OF AGRICULTURE

Primary industries were also transformed in the industrial age. As agriculture evolved from a way of life to an industry, successful farms became larger and more highly mechanized, while subsistence farms on marginal lands were quickly abandoned. The decline in the relative importance of farming in this period reflects the fact that fewer farms were required to meet the Canadian and international demand for food.

Stimulated by local demand and the almost insatiable British market for staple foods, commercialized farming flourished in Ontario. With rail and steamship service offering more reliable transportation, cold storage facilities, and lower freight rates, huge quantities of Ontario's bacon, cheese, butter, and eggs found their way to British larders by the end of the nineteenth century. Ontario farmers also branched into industrial crops such as sugar beets, grapes, and tobacco and grew most of the fruit and vegetables that were canned in Canada prior to 1920. By the end of the century, the William Davies Company in Toronto slaughtered nearly 450 000 Canadian-grown hogs, employed 300 workers, and boasted export sales of more than $3.5 million. The export sales of Canadian cheese, much of it produced in Ontario, skyrocketed from 8.3 million pounds in 1871 to 189.8 million in 1899. Although Canadian producers made their reputation with cheddar, they also invented processed cheese, upon which A.F. McLaren of Ingersoll built a thriving business. Following the First World War, he was bought out by another Canadian-born cheesemaker, J.L. Kraft, who, in 1905, had moved to Chicago, where he became the world's most successful cheesemaker.

Ontario's farms remained more productive than those of Quebec, where families were larger, mechanization slower, and farm surpluses less abundant. Nevertheless, cattle raising in Quebec's Eastern Townships proved a highly profitable venture, and Quebec farmers exported butter and cheese to Great Britain. The Maritimes, like Quebec, had a large number of marginal farms, but, in fertile areas such as the St. John River Valley, the Annapolis Valley, and Prince Edward Island, farmers took up commercial farming to take advantage of expanding urban markets at home and abroad. Potatoes were a successful crop throughout the region, and in the Annapolis Valley of Nova Scotia, the production of apples, destined primarily for the British market, increased nearly tenfold between 1881 and 1911.

The Prairie wheat boom was the most spectacular agricultural success story of this period. Between 1901 and 1913, wheat production expanded from 56 million to 224 million bushels, grain exports increased by 600 percent, and wheat soared from 14 to 42 percent of total Canadian exports. A variety of factors came together to make the wheat boom possible: faster maturing strains of wheat, the chill steel plough (which could

Milk wagon at St. Roch, Quebec. As Canada urbanized, farm families earned money by supplying creameries and city markets with milk, butter, eggs, and other foodstuffs. Before the age of the automobile, milk wagons pulled by horses or oxen were a common sight in city streets.
Library and Archives Canada/PA11677

handle the prairie sod), gas-driven tractors, rising world prices, lower transportation costs, a steady supply of immigrant labour, and encouragement from public and private agencies. Together, these factors transformed the Prairies from a fur-trade frontier into the breadbasket of the world, its wheat production second in volume only to that of the United States.

Although significant, wheat was by no means the only product of western agriculture. Dairy farming was important in Manitoba, as was mixed farming in the Park Belt of the Prairies and in British Columbia. Between 1885 and 1905, cattle ranching flourished in the Alberta foothills. Canada's "wild West" was developed by "gentlemen farmers" such as Senator Matthew Cochrane, a pioneer cattle breeder and successful shoe manufacturer from the Eastern Townships. With an embargo on American imports, generous terms for leasing land, and the completion of the CPR—all provided by the obliging Macdonald government in the 1880s—ranching fever gripped Alberta. Cattle ranching also flourished in the Okanagan Valley in the wake of the gold rush. Despite their initial success, ranchers in Alberta and British Columbia

were soon fighting a rearguard action against farmers who, armed with dryland farming techniques, insisted on breaking up the cattle range.

Scientific and technological innovation had an enormous impact on agricultural production. It has been estimated that the development of the fast-maturing Marquis wheat by dominion cerealist Charles E. Saunders added over $100 million to farm income between 1911 and 1918. While horse and human power continued to be the chief sources of energy on Canadian farms, engine power was introduced as early as 1877 when the first steam threshing machine was used in Woodbridge, Ontario. Steam threshers could process more in a day than the average farmer produced in a year and soon transformed the harvesting process. Gasoline engines and tractors became practical in the second decade of the twentieth century.

FISH, FOREST, AND FURS

East Coast fisheries, like agriculture, adjusted unevenly to the new economic order. In the second half of the nineteenth century, the inshore fisheries came under increasing competition from deep-sea fleets, while canning and cold storage emerged as new ways of preserving fish, supplementing salting, drying, and pickling. Investment poured into canning factories designed to process lobster, herring, and sardines, and into cold storage facilities to handle fresh fish. While technology and transportation dictated that the fresh fish industry would become centralized in a few communities, the canned and salt fishery remained dispersed and uncoordinated. Because virtually every fishing port had a canning factory, the product varied widely in quality, and workers were relegated to seasonal employment. Quality control also plagued the salt-fish industry, which was beginning to face stiff competition in its traditional Latin American and southern European markets.

On the West Coast, the salmon fishery developed quickly in the

The influx of immigrants and the rapid spread of salmon canneries in British Columbia at the turn of the twentieth century resulted in a series of laws that restricted salmon-fishing licences in the interests of canning and recreational fisheries. Invariably, the laws had a negative impact on Native peoples, who were less likely than immigrants to own canning companies. This picture shows a federal fisheries officer removing an "illegal" Kwakwaka'wakw salmon trap on the Marble River, Quatsino Sound, Vancouver Island, in 1912.
Vancouver Public Library/13904

final decades of the nineteenth century, and by 1900 salmon had become the most profitable fishery in Canada, surpassing cod in the value of sales. Steveston, where a large number of canneries were built, became known as the sockeye capital of the world, exporting its canned salmon largely to a British market. In 1902, much of the industry was centralized under the British Columbia Packers Association. A company backed by eastern Canadian and American capital, it was based in New Jersey, a state whose liberal incorporation laws made it a popular base for companies avoiding anti-trust legislation. The new company consolidated and mechanized the packing process, increasing its profits by reducing the costs of labour and fish supply. The Smith butchering machine, whose popular name, the "Iron Chink," reflected racist attitudes toward Asian cannery workers, processed 60 to 75 fish a minute and encouraged the mechanizing of filleting, salting, and weighing. When the sanitary can and double seamer were introduced in 1912, the automated assembly line became a reality.

Aboriginal peoples suffered most from the commercialization of the salmon fishery. For centuries, the economies and cultures of Natives on the Pacific coast had been based on salmon fisheries. Indeed, the commercial fishery in the early years depended on Natives' skills as fishers, processors, boat builders, and net makers. By the end of the nineteenth century, federal and provincial governments began passing legislation to control the fishery. Historian Dianne Newell traced the process by which fishery regulations were used to deny Natives access to their traditional fishing sites and methods. She concludes: "As the industry spread and mechanized in the twentieth century, changes in labour supply, in markets for fish, in technology, and in government regulation rendered Indians less central to fishing, and eventually to fish processing."[2] By adapting to new technologies, new regulations, and white hostility, Native families and villages managed to maintain a toehold in the industry until the second half of the twentieth century, but they were no longer central to the industry they once had dominated.

The introduction of manufactured goods eroded the advantage of Aboriginal peoples in most of their labour-intensive crafts. Snowshoes, however, remained a vital trade commodity for Native peoples in the North, who found a ready buyer in the Hudson's Bay Company.
Library and Archives Canada/C38174

British Columbia was also Canada's new timber frontier. By the 1880s, most of the white pine forests of eastern Canada had been laid to waste. The demand for lumber for construction in rapidly growing North American cities was met by the majestic Douglas fir and cedar trees of the West Coast. Between 1871 and 1880, some 350 million board feet of timber were cut in British Columbia; in the second decade of the twentieth century, the figure had risen to a staggering 13.5 billion, and lumbering had emerged as one of British Columbia's most lucrative industries. The forests of eastern Canada continued to produce lumber, fine woods for furniture, pit props for mines, railway ties, shakes, shingles, and laths, and contributed to the production of pulp and paper, an industry that expanded rapidly at the end of the nineteenth century.

New technology and modern business practices also transformed the fur industry. By the first decade of the twentieth century, fur farming had begun to emerge as an alternative to hunting and trapping. Based primarily on Prince Edward Island, the raising of fox, mink, and other fur-bearing animals in captivity was made more practical by the introduction of woven wire enclosures in the late 1890s. Thereafter, the industry developed quickly, stimulated by improved breeding methods, the growing demand of the fashion industry, and the declining population of the world's wild fur-bearing animals. By 1910, Prince Edward Island breeders fetched as much as $15 000 a pair for their silver fox on the London market. Faced with this form of competition, the Hudson's Bay Company introduced bureaucratic management structures, used railways and steamships where possible, and pushed into new fur trade frontiers.

THE MINING INDUSTRY

Canada's mining industry grew dramatically in the years following confederation. The new era of mining activity got off to a dramatic start when gold was discovered in the Klondike in 1896, but it had relatively less impact on the Canadian economy and business community than other mining ventures. Since the Industrial Revolution was built on resources of coal, iron, and other base metals, the discovery and exploitation of these resources drew most of the investment, if not the popular attention.

Coal mining in the Maritimes, Alberta, and British Columbia expanded in the late nineteenth century to supply Canadian trains, factories, and homes. By the beginning of the twentieth century, huge quantities of coal and iron were processed in Canada's steel plants. Surveys conducted for the CPR and the Canadian Geological Survey revealed the potential wealth locked in the Canadian Shield and the western mountain ranges. When chemical and mechanical processes for separating complex ores were developed at the turn of the century, the nickel-copper deposits around Sudbury and zinc-lead-silver deposits in British Columbia became profitable fields for exploitation. Capital poured into Canada from all over the world to bring the vast storehouse of mineral wealth into production.

The discovery of copper-gold deposits at the base of Red Mountain in 1887 created an instant boom town at Rossland, British Columbia. By that time, an American promoter, F.A. Heinze, had built a smelter at Trail, which was connected to Rossland by a narrow-gauge railway. Following its decision to build a line through the Crow's Nest Pass, the CPR bought Heinze's interests and incorporated them in the Consolidated Mining and Smelting Company of Canada (Cominco) in 1906. As a CPR subsidiary, Cominco had access to extensive capital resources, which were used to develop hydro-electrical power in the region and to solve the metallurgical problem of separating ores. By 1910, British Columbia's mineral output was second in value only to Ontario's, much of it extracted from the Kootenay region.

Rich mineral resources were concentrated in "New Ontario," the area between Sudbury and Hudson Bay, which was granted in huge sections to Ontario by the federal government and the courts between 1874 and 1912. Following the discovery of copper sulphides in the Sudbury Basin in 1883, American promoter Samuel J. Ritchie established the Canadian Copper Company to develop Sudbury's deposits for refining by the Orford Copper Company in New Jersey. In 1888, a smelter was constructed at Copper Cliff to concentrate the nickel-copper matte prior to shipping.

In 1902, Canadian Copper and Orford merged to form the International Nickel Company, or Inco, of New Jersey. Increasing demand for nickel-steel armour plate in a rapidly militarizing Europe led Mond Nickel

Franklin Carmichael, *A Northern Silver Mine*, 1930.
McMichael Canadian Art Collection, 1971.9

of Wales to establish a base in Sudbury, which emerged as the world's major supplier of nickel. At the same time, discoveries of gold, silver, and cobalt along the route of the Timiskaming and Northern Ontario Railway put the names of Cobalt, Timmins, Kirkland Lake, and Porcupine on the map. The value of minerals produced in Ontario increased fourfold between 1900 and 1910 and nearly doubled again in the next decade, making Ontario Canada's leading province in the mining industry.

Quebec's rich mining frontier was slow to develop, but its extraordinary range of mineral resources inspired a variety of initiatives. At the end of the nineteenth century, foreign companies began working asbestos deposits in the Eastern Townships. Although Quebec quickly became the world's leading producer of this rare mineral, most of the processing was done outside Canada, and the fierce competition between mining companies resulted in overproduction, gluts, and slowdowns that made the industry highly unstable. The copper and gold deposits of the Abitibi region of Quebec, though identified, were not seriously exploited until the 1920s.

With nearly 80 percent of Canada's electrical generating capacity, Ontario and Quebec dominated the second industrial revolution based on mining, chemicals, and pulp and paper, which relied on abundant energy resources. Ontario's initiative in developing Niagara Falls gave the province a massive source of hydro-electric power. In Quebec, American capital developed the mighty Shawinigan Falls on the St. Maurice River. Shawinigan soon attracted an aluminum smelter, pulp mill, and chemical factories. Unlike Ontario, which made hydro a government-run service in 1906, Quebec left the hydro industry to private enterprise. Whether publicly or privately owned, the abundant supply of hydro-electric power served as a magnet to industry.

SERVING THE INDUSTRIAL ECONOMY

The Industrial Revolution in Canada and elsewhere was carried forward by a growing army of clerks, cleaners, cab drivers, cooks, and secretaries in addition to managers, bankers, lawyers, engineers, and civil servants. In 1921, as many people worked in service industries as in the primary sector, performing jobs that could scarcely have been imagined in 1867, such as electrical repair, automobile sales, and switchboard operation.

Clerical work was one of the fastest-growing occupations in an industrializing Canada. While the general labour force grew by 10.4 percent between 1891 and 1901, the clerical sector rose 73.3 percent. This growth continued in the first decade of the twentieth century and reached an astounding 109.3 percent between 1911 and 1921. By the latter date, clerical workers represented nearly 7 percent of the labour force. Another change had also taken place in this 30-year period. In 1891, women comprised only 14.3 percent of those working in clerical positions; by 1921, 41.8 percent of clerical workers were women, and the trend toward the feminization of clerical work continued throughout the twentieth century.

As transportation improved and nationwide markets emerged, retail operations grew and changed. The changes in retailing activity can be seen in the meteoric rise of the T. Eaton Company. In 1869, Timothy Eaton opened a dry-goods and clothing store on Yonge Street in Toronto. His method of selling, which included fixed prices, cash only, and money-back guarantees, proved so popular that he moved to larger premises, equipped with an elevator, in 1883. A year later, Eaton reached across the country to grab business from local retailers when he issued his first mail-order catalogue. The expansion in sales allowed Eaton's to manufacture its own merchandise, thus bypassing wholesalers and suppliers. In 1893, Eaton's established the first of a number of overseas operations in London. Eaton's also opened a branch in Winnipeg in 1905, the first in a chain-store business that would expand dramatically in the 1920s. Robert Simpson, also of Toronto, paralleled the Eaton experience. No corner of Canada reached by the postal service was left unchanged by the rise of the great department stores and their dream-selling catalogues.

MASS PRODUCTION AND MODERN MANAGEMENT

Market expansion led to a reorganization of the structure of industry, encouraging small-scale, owner-operated businesses to evolve into bureaucratic, multipurpose, and multinational corporations. The limited liability corporation separated individual wealth from corporate wealth and made corporations independent legal entities. No longer tied to the fate of a single person or a few individuals, the corporation took on a life of its own. At the same time, ownership was divorced from management functions, which were increasingly carried out by salaried employees. No individual, no matter how energetic or gifted, could keep on top of the details of such rapidly expanding businesses. Nor was such control desirable. Chief executive officers needed their time to mobilize capital and plot long-range corporate strategy.

Control over day-to-day operations of large corporations was achieved through structural reorganization. At the turn of the century, management techniques became the focus of attention for business people trying to maximize the profits of their enterprises. Scientific management, a term coined by the American Frederick W. Taylor, advocated that managers take responsibility for coordinating work processes and employees be deprived of any initiative or authority in deciding how to do their work. On the shop floor, this meant that the labour process was broken down into simple repetitive tasks and that employee output was closely monitored by supervisors.

At the management level, rigid hierarchies with clear lines of authority were developed and new accounting procedures implemented to control production and labour costs. When American entrepreneur Henry Ford perfected the assembly line for his Model T in 1914, artisans who had once performed the most skilled of manufacturing operations—the assembly of complex machinery—were forced to submit to the dictates of management and the machine.

SURVIVAL OF THE FITTEST

Driven by the Darwinian logic that held that only the fittest survived, corporate managers were forced to keep ahead of the competition or go to the wall. Not surprisingly, entrepreneurs were decidedly unenthusiastic about unrestrained competition. While giving lip-service to free enterprise, they secretly agreed to fix prices and agitated publicly for policies that would guarantee them a "living profit." Nationwide associations, such as the Dominion Wholesale Grocers Guild, Retail Merchants Association, Canadian Manufacturers Association, and Canadian Bankers Association, tried to regulate the activities of their members, but restrictions on "unfair" trading practices often failed to bring order to the marketplace because it took only one entrepreneur to break an agreement.

For most businesses, growing bigger meant becoming more efficient, reaping the benefits of economies of scale, and gaining an edge over competitors. If a company could become big enough, it might be possible to sweep all competition aside and establish a monopoly over the marketplace. Although "monopoly" was a bad word in industrializing Canada, anti-combine laws, first introduced in 1889, had little impact on corporate practices. A spate of mergers in the 1880s was followed by an even bigger merger movement in the early twentieth century. Between 1909 and 1912, some 275 Canadian firms were consolidated into 52 enterprises, capitalized at nearly half a billion dollars.

The merger movement brought to the fore some of Canada's major corporate giants. Vertically integrated companies were capable of handling all the functions of the industry, including supplying their own raw materials and shipping their products in company-owned boxcars. Their vast assets enabled them to mobilize capital on a scale hitherto unimaginable. Although such companies were not technically monopolies, their size gave them tremendous power in the reorganized marketplace. They could outbid and outlast their smaller competitors and make it difficult for new competitors to break into the industry. Many of the companies established at the turn of the twentieth century became household names in Canada—Imperial Oil, Bell Canada, General Electric, Stelco, and Canada Cement Company—visible testimony to their triumph over the "invisible forces" of the marketplace.

Consolidation was also the order of the day in banking. In 1871, Ottawa passed an act requiring banks to have assets of at least $500 000, resulting in the eventual dissolution of small banks. Between 1880 and 1920, while the number of branches rose from under 300 to 4676, the number of banks operating under dominion charter declined from 44 to 18. No longer simply vehicles for facilitating exchange, banks encouraged savings accounts by paying interest on deposited money, transferred funds from their many branches to profitable investment frontiers, and

Max Aitken

Canada's most flamboyant financier was Max Aitken. The son of a Presbyterian minister, Aitken grew up in northern New Brunswick and turned to selling bonds and insurance after failing the entrance examination to Dalhousie Law School. As the protégé of Halifax businessman John Stairs, Aitken became president of Stairs's new holding company, Royal Securities, in 1903. After speculating in utilities in the Caribbean and Latin America, Aitken moved to Montreal, used Montreal Trust to take over Royal Securities, and was a key figure in the merger movement of 1909–12.

His crowning achievement was putting together the Steel Company of Canada in 1910, a conglomerate that included Montreal Rolling Mills, Hamilton Steel and Iron, Canada Screw, and Canada Bolt and Nut. Having made his fortune, Aitken moved to London, where he had marketed much of his speculative stock, became a member of parliament, bought himself a title—Lord Beaverbrook—and continued to keep an eye on his Canadian interests. Among Beaverbrook's merger-making associates was a future Canadian prime minister, R.B. Bennett, whose millions were earned in part by collaborating with Aitken to merge grain elevators and hydro-electric stations on the Prairies.

Max Aitken.
National Archives of Canada/PA-006478

developed modern management structures. By 1920, four of the five Canadian banks that still tower over the business centres of most Canadian towns and cities—Scotia, Commerce, Montreal, and Royal—had established their positions in the financial firmament.

PRIVATE INITIATIVE AND PUBLIC POLICY

In Canada, as in the United States and Great Britain, private capitalists were the preferred agents for undertaking risky economic ventures. Governments at all levels encouraged and assisted private enterprise but became directly involved only as a last resort. Largely unfettered by government regulation before the First World War, capitalists also reaped most of the profit of their risk-taking activities. Successful entrepreneurs paid no income tax whatsoever before 1917, were subject to few estate or corporation taxes, and were often the beneficiaries of huge government grants.

In the first decade of the twentieth century, entrepreneurs came under increasing criticism, and governments were encouraged to take action to protect the public against private greed. Regulatory commissions became a popular means of establishing some control over the activities of private corporations. In 1903, the Board of Railway Commissioners was set up to serve as a buffer between the disgruntled public and the railways. Federally chartered telephone companies came under the commission's jurisdiction in 1906.

Public money continued to provide much of the infrastructure, or basic services, upon which private fortunes were built. Apart from involvement in railways, Ottawa sponsored the Geological Survey of

Canada, established a system of experimental farms, and subsidized cold storage facilities to enhance economic development. In 1916, at the height of the First World War, the federal government created the Honorary Advisory Council for Science and Industrial Research (later renamed the National Research Council of Canada) to take the initiative in scientific research, increasingly the key to economic development.

Provincial governments enjoyed important economic powers, especially if Ottawa did not control their natural resources. Most provinces passed legislation to encourage settlement and disposed of timber and mineral rights by sale or lease. From 1897 to 1900, Ontario imposed an excise tax on the export of unprocessed logs to encourage manufacturing in the province. As a result of this legislation, sawmills and pulp and paper plants were established in Ontario, leading other timber-producing provinces such as Quebec and New Brunswick to adopt similar legislative measures.

The Ontario government also took the dramatic step of establishing the provincially controlled Hydro-Electric Power Commission in 1906 to regulate private power companies, distribute power, and ultimately generate its own power. Promoted as a policy to bring "power to the people," Ontario Hydro was supported by entrepreneurs throughout southwestern sections of the province who wanted access to a cheap and reliable source of power for industrial purposes. Like Ontario, the Prairie provinces experimented with government-owned utilities, but most provincial administrations preferred to avoid the political pitfalls of direct government ownership.

Municipal governments could not afford the luxury of remaining aloof. As cities grew and services became more complex, direct involvement seemed increasingly necessary. Private companies providing water, sewage, street lighting, communication, and transportation services in urban settings were often granted monopoly powers, and, in the opinion of consumers, many abused their privileged position. After the 1890s, many municipal governments either assumed direct control over utilities or created regulatory commissions to keep an eye on private corporations. The result of the spate of utility development in a burgeoning industrial economy was a typically Canadian system of mixed public and private services reflecting the circumstances of individual localities.

HUMAN CAPITAL

Life in the industrial workplace was hard. In many occupations, 12-hour days were common. Conditions were sometimes better in small businesses where people worked with kin or in community settings, but in such cases there was even less recourse from a cruel or capricious boss. Children in the workforce were particularly vulnerable. Punishments were imposed to exact conformity, break a child's independence, and ensure regular work habits. In families where the child's income was critical to survival, it was not uncommon for parents to support employers in their efforts to "train" young workers.

Given their value to the family economy, many children no doubt preferred workplaces to schools. In Cumberland County, Nova Scotia, where children made up 16 percent of the coal-mining workforce in the 1880s, young boys were proud to be doing "a man's job." Coal miners, working with relatively uncomplicated technology, produced an indispensable product, and their ability to shut down a mine gave them power within the workplace and the community. Boys shared with men the dangers of the job. In 1891, the first of many mining disasters in Springhill, Nova Scotia, resulted in the deaths of 125 men and boys.

In keeping with the gendered notions of work that prevailed in industrializing Canada, skill, while arguably an objective concept, was also socially constructed. Certain jobs were treated as requiring special abilities or training while others were not. For example, though it required little talent or training, printing was a well-paid "skilled" occupation that excluded women. Meanwhile, dressmaking, which required considerable skill, was a poorly paid "unskilled" line of work in which women were employed. Although women were the food manufacturers at home, in a candy-making factory such as Ganong Brothers in St. Stephen, New Brunswick, only men were confectioners. Women were hired at low wages to decorate and box prepared candies. As the structures of industrialization were gradually put in place, it became the ideal that married men earned incomes in the marketplace while their wives stayed home to do housework and rear the children or, in middle-class families, supervise the servants who did this work.

Professionals and unionized craftsmen could often earn a wage sufficient to maintain a family, but the vast majority of wage earners could not. Nevertheless, the belief that the male head of household should—and could—earn enough to feed, clothe, and shelter a family was used to justify underpaying women workers. Writing in 1897 on the sweatshops of the clothing-manufacturing sector in Toronto, future prime minister William Lyon Mackenzie King quoted an owner who noted: "I don't treat the men bad, but I even up by taking advantage of the women. I have a girl who can do as much work, and as good work as a man; she gets $5 a week. The man who is standing next to her gets $11. The girls, however, average $3.50 a week, and some are as low as two dollars."[3]

A clothing factory in London, Ontario.
Library and Archives Canada/PA-074737

On the railroads and in the highly mechanized manufacturing sectors, late-nineteenth-century employers capitulated to male workers' demands that women and children not be hired as cheap labour. Such demands were often ignored in unskilled labour-intensive industries where competition to provide goods at the lowest possible cost occurred mainly on the backs of workers. For example, the cigar makers of London, Ontario, learned in the 1880s how easily a well-paid skilled occupation could be turned into a poorly paid "unskilled" job. While unionized cigar makers tried to maintain quality, restrict new entrants to the trade, and hold the line on wages, their employers were eager to reduce labour costs. When unionized workers refused to accept a cut in wages, their employers replaced most of them with women and children. By the mid-1880s, only 13 of the 150 cigar makers in town were adult men.

Company owners also kept Canadian labour in line by supporting an open-door policy for immigrant labourers who agreed to work as strikebreakers or under conditions that Canadians found unacceptable. In response to demands from workers, the Laurier government passed an Alien Labour Act (1897) designed to make it unlawful to bring in foreign labourers. Despite its sweeping scope, the Alien Labour Act failed to prevent companies from importing contract labour and strikebreakers when they were determined to do so. The act was rarely enforced and applied only to the importation of labour from the United States.

Modern management techniques and hiring practices reduced the autonomy of many workers; so did the company-town phenomenon. Mining and textile-mill towns were frequently owned by companies, with homes, stores, schools, doctors, and even churches firmly under corporate control. Cape Breton, Alberta, and British Columbia coal, Quebec asbestos, and Ontario gold, silver, and nickel were mined primarily by workers who lived in company towns. While some factory owners took a paternal attitude toward their workers, most resorted to authoritarian control if workers threatened to strike or otherwise were perceived as stepping out of line.

Disease and injury were often the fate of industrial workers. Although the 1889 Royal Commission on the Relations of Labor and Capital had reported dangerous working conditions and recommended reform, little action was taken. Workers stricken by injury or disease were in the difficult position of having to prove employer negligence in order to sue for compensation. In the second decade of the twentieth century, Ontario, Nova Scotia, British Columbia, Alberta, and New Brunswick passed Workmen's Compensation acts, which conceded a limited right to industrial compensation. Still, many employees found no protection from the high levels of zinc, mercury, asbestos, dry-cleaning fluids, dyes, and other chemicals that went unregulated. Coal miners and textile workers "retired"

The Impact of Immigrant Labour

Both skilled and unskilled Canadian workers were opposed to a liberal immigration policy, which they saw as a means of keeping their wages depressed. For cities such as Montreal, where wages were relatively low to begin with, the arrival in the spring of 1905 of a large number of Italian men, many of them sojourners who planned to return home with their earnings, brought howls of complaint. The federal government felt obliged to respond to the uproar by appointing the Royal Commission on Immigration of Italian Labourers to Montreal and the Alleged Fraudulent Practices of Employment Agencies. Its report left little doubt about the impact of immigrant labourers.

Charles Hodgson Osler, a superintendent employed by the Montreal Light, Heat and Power company, testified that 100 of the roughly 250 men employed by the company were Italians and that wages had been reduced as a result of their arrival in the city.

Q. You remember the influx of Italian labour last April and May? – A. Yes.

Q. Would that affect the scale of labour for labourers? – A. Yes, I think it would.

Q. These Italians only received from $1.25 to $1.35 a day? – A. Yes.

Q. Are there others besides Italians only receiving that amount? – A. Yes, quite a number.

Q. Who are they? – A. Well, some English and some French speaking men.

Q. You get as many men as you require on your work without difficulty? – A. We have done it so far, we have had no trouble at all; we had a little trouble last year, but we increased the wages to $1.45. We got lots of men this year at $1.25, whereas we had to pay $1.45 last year.

Q. I suppose there are the same number employed this year as last? – A. No, I have nearly double the quantity this year.

Q. The wages then dropped 20 cents? – A. Yes, there was a large influx of men, and we took advantage of labour as it came in.[4]

exhausted and prematurely aged, their lungs so damaged by coal dust and fabric fibres that they coughed themselves to death. Anonymous graves along rail tracks or near remote mines bear testimony to the existence of immigrant labourers who worked under draconian conditions in industrializing Canada.

FAMILY AND WORK

The shift to an industrial economy had an enormous impact on the Canadian family. While self-sufficiency was rare even in pre-industrial British North America, a majority of family units produced a substantial proportion of the goods they consumed, relying only peripherally on the sale of their products and labour in the marketplace. By the twentieth century, the market played a major role in the lives of virtually every Canadian. Urban dwellers, in particular, lacked the resources to produce most of their own food, clothing, or shelter, but even in the countryside, the fully subsistent farm family was becoming rare and was, in most cases, desperately poor.

Families responded to the new market economy in a gendered way. In many mid-nineteenth-century farming families, women began to increase their production for off-farm sales, becoming major producers in dairying, poultry raising, market gardening, and fruit growing. As these areas of farming expanded and wheat farming declined east of Ontario, men took over what had previously been considered women's work. Dairying was entirely transformed in the second half of the nineteenth century. Pasturing, feeding, calving, and milking, once regarded as women's work, were increasingly appropriated by men. For many women, this shift in farm responsibilities was welcomed as a reduction of the heavy physical labour that characterized their daily lives, but it also reduced their power in the family and community context.

Most families depended on the labour of all their members, including their children. Although a romantic view of childhood innocence was maintained by middle-class families who had the money to keep servants to perform household chores, the working classes could rarely afford to be sentimental about their children. Children in farm and factory households fetched water from wells, ran errands, and helped with the cooking, cleaning, gardening, babysitting, and care of the aged and infirm. In rural areas, children were frequently kept home from school during planting and harvesting seasons. When the household economy was faced with a crisis such as the death or illness of a parent, older children were called upon to take on adult roles.

Children, rather than wives, were the secondary wage earners in early industrializing Canada. Working-class children often entered the paid labour force at age 11 or 12—and even younger—and lived with their parents for perhaps another 15 years before marrying. The 1871 census reported that 25 percent of boys and 10 percent of girls between the ages of 11 and 15 had occupations outside the home. Factory acts passed in Ontario and Quebec in the mid-1880s and later replicated in other provinces prohibited employment of boys under 12 and girls under 14 in factories, but these laws were poorly enforced and frequently circumvented by families facing destitution.

Most working-class families were poor at some stage in their evolution. Generally, at the time of marriage, savings and two incomes allowed a couple to enjoy an acceptable, if modest, standard of living, but poverty was especially pronounced for large families with children too young to work or be left unsupervised while their mothers entered the labour force. In such cases, the wife's marginal earnings from piecework, laundry, or boarders often meant the difference between a family's subsistence and destitution.

Families headed by women—those who had never married, were widowed, or whose husbands had deserted them—and families where the husband was too ill to work were in a particularly precarious position. Legislation passed in 1869 made it a criminal offence for a man to refuse to provide his wife with food, clothes, and lodging, but few women were successful in pursuing their claims. Nor could a woman expect the state or private charity to offer anything more than temporary assistance, if that. Families and individuals in early industrializing Canada were largely left to sink or swim. In this respect there was little change from the pre-industrial era, when luck and good health played a greater role than planning in determining income levels.

NATIVES AND THE NEW ECONOMY

As we have seen in earlier chapters, Canada's Aboriginal peoples had difficulty embracing the opportunities that the new industrial order had to offer. They possessed neither the capital nor the networks to make capitalism work for their benefit. Nevertheless, they adapted as best they could to the changes taking place around them. Those lucky enough to hold on to good lands in the face of predatory settlers often prospered. In the Cowichan and Fraser River valleys and in many areas of the Prairie provinces, Natives raised livestock, cereals, and market produce. On many reserves, Natives made a reasonable living as carpenters, blacksmiths, and craftspeople; others owned trading schooners, hotels, inns, cafés, and small logging and sawmill operations.

Like many other Canadians facing the challenges of industrialization, Native peoples sought jobs in the industrial economy developing around them. The Iroquois of Kahnawaké, near Montreal, were widely known as skilled construction workers. Cree women and girls did laundry and cleaning for wages while men worked on railway construction. In the Maritimes, a few Mi'kmaq worked in the coal mines, on the railroads, and in the steel mills. On the West Coast, women and men from Native communities found work in lumber mills, mines, canneries, and the commercial fishery. With the rise of tourism, many Natives worked as guides for recreational hunters and fishers. Unfortunately, the position of Aboriginal peoples in the industrial economy was often marginal, and grew even more so as economic growth became defined in terms of the immigrant population.

The National Policy and Regional Development

It is a common belief in western and Maritime Canada that the National Policy of the late nineteenth century was biased in favour of central Canada. Some historians confirm popular perceptions and suggest that central Canadian industrialization occurred at the expense of the outlying regions as a result of deliberate public policy. There are also scholars, past and present, who argue that the National Policy had negligible impact on the economic fate of these two regions. Who is right?

S.A. Saunders argued in the 1930s that the economic problems of the Maritimes stemmed from a decline in demand or price for key staple exports. When British demand for timber and ships fell off in the 1880s, the region's economy began a decline from which it could not recover. The region's carrying trade, meanwhile, suffered a fatal blow from the competition of steam and steel ships.[5] This explanation, of course, does not address the issue of why the region's entrepreneurs did not adjust to changing economic times. According to T.W. Acheson, the failure of the Maritimes to generate a major metropolitan centre in the age of the National Policy contributed to the region's drift to outside control and industrial stagnation. "With its powerful mercantile interests," Acheson argues, "Halifax could have most easily adapted to this role, but its merchants preferred, like their Boston counterparts, to invest their large fortunes in banks and American railroad stocks than to venture them on building a new order."[6] Historian E.R. Forbes points a finger at high freight rates for the problems facing Maritime producers in supplying Canadian markets, but it seems unlikely that lower freight rates alone would have changed the region's economic fate.[7]

Economist Ken Norrie and historian Doug Owram, authors of an economic history of Canada, are skeptical about the possibility of extensive industrialization of the Maritime region in the late nineteenth century. They are even more skeptical of attempts to pin the blame on the National Policy: "To find the argument credible, one would need to believe that fairly small changes in transportation rates or in Dominion subsidies could have had enormous effects on industrial prospects. Simply putting the issue in that manner suggests the probable answer."[8]

Norrie and Owram are equally skeptical of claims that the National Policy discriminated against western Canada. T.D.

Regehr, for example, states, "[t]here has been deliberate and admitted freight-rate discrimination against the West."[9] Only constant battles by westerners resulted, over time, in partial amelioration of these rates, argues Regehr. In contrast, Norrie and Owram claim flatly that "rail freight rates in the development phase of the wheat economy were at least as low as they would have been under the next most likely alternative to the national policy."[10] Norrie rejects the view that federal tariff and freight-rate policies hindered western industrialization:

> In some instances, Prairie industrialization being perhaps the best example, the problem lies in being small and isolated rather than with discriminatory treatment. The present economic structure of the region is adequately explained by standard location theory concepts. It is incorrect to suggest that the federal government or other institutions have industrialized the East at the expense of the West. It must be recognized rather that any significant decentralization of industry in Canada can only be achieved by committing real resources to that end and that this means a subsidy for persons residing in the recipient regions at the expense of other Canadians.[11]

Norrie's argument perhaps makes too little allowance for the role the state has played in the marketplace, demonstrating a strong central Canadian bias in its purchasing policies, for example. But he correctly points out a fallacy in the claims of many who focus on alleged discrimination against the regions: the assumption that the free market, left to its own workings, would have produced a more equitable distribution of industry in Canada. The tendency of capital left on its own to concentrate in a few areas with transportation and population advantages is a universal phenomenon of the capitalist system. In some countries, the state has intervened to force industries to locate in less favoured areas, but there is little evidence that in late-nineteenth-century Canada there were significant sections of popular opinion in any region that favoured more draconian intervention in the marketplace than that envisaged by John A. Macdonald and his business community supporters.

CONCLUSION

By the turn of the century, few people could ignore the inequality that characterized the age of industry. American investigative journalist Gustavus Myers claimed in 1914 that fewer than 50 men controlled $4 billion, or a third, of Canada's wealth. Certainly no one could have made such a claim in 1867. The total estate of Nova Scotia's Enos Collins, who was reputed to have been one of the wealthiest men in Canada when he died in 1871, was little more than $6 million. The conflict between labour and capital was a troubling feature of the industrial age, but it was by no means the only problem facing the new nation. As we shall see in the next chapter, immigration and urbanization were changing Canada's social fabric in ways totally unanticipated by the Fathers of Confederation.

NOTES

1 F.E.A. Gagnon, *Choses d'Autrefois, feuilles éparses* (Montreal, 1905), 51–53. Cited in B. Sinclair, N.R. Ball, and J.O. Petersen, eds., *Let Us Be Honest and Modest: Technology and Society in Canadian History* (Toronto: Oxford University Press, 1974), 133–34.

2 Dianne Newell, *The Tangled Webs of History: Indians and the Law in Canada's Pacific Coast Fisheries* (Toronto: University of Toronto Press, 1993), 206.

3 Quoted in Ruth Frager, "Class and Ethnic Barriers to Feminist Perspectives in Toronto's Jewish Labour Movement, 1919–1939," *Studies in Political Economy* 30 (Autumn 1989), 148.

4 Report of the Royal Commission on Immigration of Italian Labourers to Montreal and the Alleged Fraudulent Practices of Employment Agencies, Canada, Sessional Papers 1905 (36b), cited in Jeffrey Keshen and Suzanne Morton, *Material Memory: Documents in Post-Confederation History* (Toronto: Addison-Wesley, 1998), 69.

5 S.A. Saunders, *Economic History of the Maritime Provinces* (Ottawa: Royal Commission on Dominion-Provincial Relations, 1940).

6 T.W. Acheson, "The National Policy and the Industrialization of the Maritimes, 1880–1910," *Acadiensis* 1, no. 2 (Spring 1972), 27–28.

7 For a summary of the freight rate debate and the publications that fuelled it, see E.R. Forbes, "The Intercolonial Railway and the Decline of the Maritime Provinces Revisited," and Ken Cruikshank, "With Apologies to James: A Response to E.R. Forbes," in *Acadiensis*, XXIV, 1 (Autumn 1994), 3–34.

8 Kenneth Norrie and Douglas Owram, *A History of the Canadian Economy* (Toronto: Harcourt Brace Jovanovich, 1991), 402.

9 T.D. Regehr, "Western Canada and the Burden of National Transportation Policies," in *Canada and the Burden of Unity*, ed. D.J. Bercuson (Toronto: Macmillan, 1977), 115.

10 Norrie and Owram, *A History of the Canadian Economy*, 327.

11 Kenneth H. Norrie, "Some Comments on Prairie Economic Alienation," *Canadian Public Policy* 2, no. 2 (Spring 1976), 222.

RELATED READINGS IN THIS SERIES

From *Nation and Society: Readings in Post-Confederation Canadian History*

Bill Parenteau, "'Care, Control and Supervision': Native People in the Canadian Atlantic Salmon Fishery, 1867–1900," 94–113.

Sandra Rollings-Magnusson, "Necessary for Survival: Women and Children's Labour on Prairie Homesteads, 1871–1911," 114–130

From *Primary Documents CD-ROM, Volume II*

Women in Clerical and Commercial Positions
Alien Labour Act, 1897
Signor Marconi and Wireless Telegraphy
Japanese Women Working at Richmond Canneries with Babies

SELECTED READING

Major economic histories include Kenneth Norrie and Douglas Owram, *A History of the Canadian Economy* (Toronto: Harcourt Brace Jovanovich, 1991); W.T. Easterbrook and Hugh G.J. Aitken, *Canadian Economic History* (1956; repr., Toronto: University of Toronto Press, 1988); and William L. Marr and Donald G. Paterson, *Canada: An Economic History* (Toronto: Gage, 1980). Business developments are discussed in Graham D. Taylor and Peter A. Baskerville, *A Concise History of Business in Canada* (Toronto: Oxford University Press, 1994); Michael Bliss, *Northern Enterprise: Five Centuries of Canadian Business* (Toronto: McClelland & Stewart, 1987) and *A Living Profit: Studies in the Social History of Canadian Business, 1883–1911* (Toronto: McClelland & Stewart, 1974); Tom Naylor, *The History of Canadian Business, 1867–1914*, 2 vols. (Toronto: Lorimer, 1975); Christopher Armstrong, *Blue Skies and Boiler Rooms: Buying and Selling Securities in Canada* (Toronto: University of Toronto Press, 1997); and David Monod, *Store Wars: Shopkeepers and the Culture of Mass Marketing, 1890–1939* (Toronto: University of Toronto Press, 1996). State-business relations are illuminated in H.V. Nelles and Christopher Armstrong, *Monopoly's Moment: The Organization and Regulation of Canadian Utilities, 1830–1930* (Toronto: University of Toronto Press, 1988). Biographies of early Canadian tycoons include Michael Bliss, *A Canadian Millionaire: The Life and Business Times of Sir Joseph Flavelle, Bart., 1858–1939* (Toronto: Macmillan, 1978); Gregory P. Marchildon, *Profits and Politics: Beaverbrook and the Gilded Age of Canadian Finance* (Toronto: University of Toronto Press, 1996); and Joy L. Stantik, *Timothy Eaton and the Rise of the Department Store* (Toronto: University of Toronto Press, 1990). A good history of one of the "big five" banks is found in Duncan McDowall, *Quick to the Frontier: Canada's Royal Bank* (Toronto: McClelland & Stewart, 1993). See also Russell Johnston, *Selling Themselves: The Emergence of Canadian Advertising* (Toronto: University of Toronto Press, 2001).

Geographically focused studies include Richard Rajala, *Up-Coast: Forests and Industry on British Columbia's North Coast, 1870–1905* (Victoria: Royal B.C. Museum, 2006); Ruth W. Sandwell, *Contesting Rural Space: Land Policy and Practices of Resettlement on Saltspring Island, 1859–1891* (Montreal: McGill-Queen's University Press, 2005); Cole Harris, *Making Native Space: Colonialism, Resistance, and Reserves in British Columbia* (Vancouver: UBC Press, 2002); James Murton, *Creating a Modern Countryside: Liberalism and Land Resettlement in British Columbia* (Vancouver: UBC Press, 2007); Morris Zaslow, *The Opening of the Canadian North, 1870–1914* (Toronto: McClelland & Stewart, 1971);

Chester Martin, *Dominion Lands Policy* (Toronto: Carleton Library, 1973); V.C. Fowke, *The National Policy and the Wheat Economy* (Toronto: University of Toronto Press, 1957); John Herd Thompson, *The Harvests of War: The Prairie West, 1914–1918* (Toronto: McClelland & Stewart, 1978); David W. Leonard, *The Last Great West: The Agricultural Settlement of the Peace River Country to 1914* (Calgary: Detselig, 2006); Warren M. Elofson, *Cowboys, Gentlemen, and Cattle Thieves: Ranching on the Western Frontier* (Montreal: McGill-Queen's University Press, 2007); Kenneth M. Sylvester, *The Limits of Rural Capitalism: Family, Culture, and Markets in Montcalm, Manitoba, 1870–1940* (Toronto: University of Toronto Press, 2001); Ian M. Drummond, *Progress Without Planning: The Economic History of Ontario from Confederation to the Second World War* (Toronto: University of Toronto Press, 1987); H.V. Nelles, *The Politics of Development: Forests, Mines and Hydro-electric Power in Ontario, 1849–1941* (Toronto: Macmillan, 1974); Jean Hamelin and Yves Roby, *Histoire Économique du Québec, 1851–1896* (Montreal: Fides, 1971); J.I. Little, *Crofters and Habitants: Settler Society, Economy and Culture in a Quebec Township, 1848–1881* (Montreal: McGill-Queen's University Press, 1991); Normand Séguin, *La Conquête du sol au 19e siècle* (Montreal: Boréal, 1977); J.H. Dales, *Hydroelectricity and Economic Development: Quebec, 1898–1940* (Cambridge: Harvard University Press, 1957); William F. Ryan, *The Clergy and Economic Growth in Quebec, 1896–1914* (Quebec: Les Presses de l'Université Laval, 1966); Robert Armstrong, *Structure and Change: An Economic History of Quebec* (Toronto: Gage, 1984); Ronald Rudin, *Banking en français: The French Banks of Quebec, 1835–1935* (Toronto: University of Toronto Press, 1985); René Hardy, *La Sidérurgie dans le monde rural* (Quebec: Les Presses de l'Université Laval, 1995); Gérard Bouchard, *Quelque arpents de l'Amérique: Population, économie, famille au Saguenay, 1838–1971* (Montreal: Boréal, 1996); S.A. Saunders, *Economic History of the Maritime Provinces* (Ottawa: Royal Commission on Dominion-Provincial Relations, 1940); David G. Alexander, *Atlantic Canada and Confederation: Essays in Canadian Political Economy* (Toronto: University of Toronto Press, 1983); and Eric W. Sager with Gerald E. Panting, *Maritime Capital: The Shipping Industry in Atlantic Canada, 1820–1914* (Montreal: McGill-Queen's University Press, 1990).

Ontario's relative success over other regions is explored in John Isbister, "Agriculture, Balanced Growth and Social Change in Central Canada since 1850: An Interpretation," in *Perspectives on Canadian Economic History*, ed. Douglas McCalla (Toronto: Copp Clark Pitman, 1987), 58–80; Douglas McCalla, *Planting the Province: The Economic History of Upper Canada, 1784–1870* (Toronto: University of Toronto

Press, 1993); and N.R.M. Seifried, *The Regional Structure of the Canadian Economy* (Toronto: Nelson, 1984).

On the post-confederation fur trade, see Arthur J. Ray, *The Canadian Fur Trade in the Industrial Age* (Toronto: University of Toronto Press, 1990). On changes in the fishery, see Dianne Newell and Rosemary E. Ommer, eds., *Fishing Places, Fishing People: Traditions and Issues in Canadian Small-Scale Fisheries* (Toronto: University of Toronto Press, 1999); Rosemary E. Ommer, *From Outpost to Outport: A Structural Analysis of the Jersey-Gaspé Fishery* (Montreal: McGill-Queen's University Press, 1991); and Peter S. Sinclair, *From Traps to Draggers: Domestic Commodity Production in Northwest Newfoundland* (St. John's: ISER, Memorial University, 1985). The structure of the fishing industry is discussed in Rosemary E. Ommer, ed., *Merchant Credit and Labour Struggles in Historical Perspective* (Fredericton: Acadiensis Press, 1990).

On the Aboriginal economy in the industrial age, see Bruce W. Hodgins and Jamie Benidickson, *The Temagami Experience* (Toronto: University of Toronto Press, 1989); Sarah Carter, *Lost Harvests: Prairie Indian Reserve Farmers and Government Policy* (Montreal: McGill-Queen's University Press, 1990); Kerry Abel, *Drum Song: Glimpses of Dene History* (Montreal: McGill-Queen's University Press, 1993); Dianne Newell, *The Tangled Webs of History: Indians and the Law in Canada's Pacific Coast Fisheries* (Toronto: University of Toronto Press, 1994); Douglas Harris, *Landing Native Fisheries: Indian Reserves and Fishing Rights in British Columbia, 1849-1925* (Vancouver: UBC Press, 2008), and William J. Turkel, *The Archive of Place: Unearthing the Pasts of the Chilcotin Plateau* (Vancouver: University of British Columbia Press, 2007).

Railway development is assessed in W. Kaye Lamb, *History of the Canadian Pacific Railway* (New York: Macmillan, 1977); G.R. Stevens, *History of the Canadian National Railways* (New York: Macmillan, 1973); T.D. Regehr, *The Canadian Northern Railway: Pioneer Road of the Northern Prairies, 1895–1918* (Toronto: Macmillan, 1976); John Eagle, *The Canadian Pacific Railway and the Development of Western Canada* (Montreal: McGill-Queen's University Press, 1989); and Ken Cruikshank, *Close Ties: Railways, Government, and the Board of Railway Commissioners, 1851–1933* (Montreal: McGill-Queen's University Press, 1991). The impact of telecommunications is discussed in Jean-Guy Rens, *The Invisible Empire: A History of the Telecommunications Industry in Canada, 1846-1956* (Montreal: McGill-Queen's University Press, 2001).

Vernon Fowke's *National Policy and the Wheat Economy* (Toronto: University of Toronto Press, 1957) makes the Prairie case against the National Policy. An opposing view is presented in Kenneth H. Norrie, *The National Policy and the*

Prairie Region (New Haven, CT: Yale University Press, 1971). Maritime assessments of national economic policies should begin with the much-reprinted essay by T.W. Acheson, "The National Policy and the Industrialization of the Maritimes, 1880–1910," *Acadiensis* 1 (Spring 1972), 3–28. On the foreign ownership debate, see Glenn Williams, *Not for Export: Toward a Political Economy of Canada's Arrested Industrialization* (Toronto: McClelland & Stewart, 1983); and Gordon Laxer, *Open for Business: The Roots of Foreign Ownership in Canada* (Toronto: Oxford University Press, 1989). On the evolution of the tariff, see Ben Forster, *A Conjunction of Interests: Business, Politics, and Tariffs, 1825–1879* (Toronto: University of Toronto Press, 1986); and J.H. Dales, *The Protective Tariff in Canada's Development* (Toronto: University of Toronto Press, 1966).

Working-class life, described more fully in Chapter 6, is analyzed in Terry Copp, *The Anatomy of Poverty: The Condition of the Working Class in Montreal, 1897–1929* (Toronto: McClelland & Stewart, 1974); Michael Piva, *The Conditions of the Working Class in Toronto, 1900–1921* (Ottawa: University of Ottawa Press, 1979); Judith Fingard, *The Dark Side of Life in Victorian Halifax* (Halifax: Pottersfield Press, 1989); Paul Craven, ed., *Labouring Lives: Work and Workers in Nineteenth-Century Ontario* (Toronto: University of Toronto Press, 1995); and Bryan D. Palmer, *Working Class Experience: Rethinking the History of Canadian Labour, 1800–1991* (Toronto: McClelland & Stewart, 1992).

The impact of industrial capitalism on women and children's work is explored in Marjorie Cohen, *Women's Work, Markets and Economic Development in Nineteenth Century Ontario* (Toronto: University of Toronto Press, 1988); Mary Kinnear, *A Female Economy: Women's Work in a Prairie Province, 1870-1970* (Montreal: McGill-Queen's University Press, 1999); Joy Parr, *Labouring Children: British Immigrant Apprentices to Canada, 1869–1924* (Montreal: McGill-Queen's University Press, 1980) and *The Gender of Breadwinners: Women, Men and Change in Two Industrial Towns, 1880–1950* (Toronto: University of Toronto Press, 1990); Bettina Bradbury, *Working Families: Age, Gender, and Daily Survival in Industrializing Montreal* (Toronto: McClelland & Stewart, 1993); Robert McIntosh, *Boys in the Pits: Child Labour in Coal Mines* (Montreal: McGill-Queen's University Press, 2000); John Bullen, "Hidden Workers: Child Labour and the Family Economy in Late Nineteenth-Century Urban Ontario," *Labour/Le Travail* (Fall 1986), 163–88; Janice Acton, Penny Goldsmith, and Bonnie Shepard, eds., *Women at Work: Ontario, 1850–1930* (Toronto: Women's Press, 1974); Ruth A. Frager and Carmela K. Patrias, *Discounted Labour: Women Workers in Canada, 1870–1939* (Toronto: University of Toronto Press, 2005); Lindsay McMaster, *Working Girls in the West: Representations of Wage-Earning Women* (Vancouver: UBC Press, 2008); Franca Iacovetta and Mariana Valverde, eds., *Gender Conflicts: New Essays in Women's History* (Toronto: University of Toronto Press, 1992); Paula Bourne, ed., *Women's Paid and Unpaid Work: Historical and Contemporary Perspectives* (Toronto: New Hogtown, 1986); Graham Lowe, *Women in the Administrative Revolution: The Feminization of Clerical Work* (Toronto: University of Toronto Press, 1987); Elaine Bernard, *The Long Distance Feeling: A History of the Telecommunications Union* (Vancouver: New Star, 1982); Kathryn McPherson, *Bedside Matters: The Transformation of Canadian Nursing, 1900–1990* (Toronto: Oxford University Press, 1996); Mary Kinnear, *In Subordination: Professional Women in Manitoba, 1870–1970* (Montreal: McGill-Queen's University Press, 1995), and Elizabeth Smyth et al., *Challenging Professions: Historical and Contemporary Perspectives on Women's Professional Work* (Toronto: University of Toronto Press, 1999).

CHAPTER 6

A Nation on the Move, 1867–1921

TIMELINE

- 1869 First Canadian Immigration Act passed
- 1877 Disastrous fire in Saint John leaves 15 000 homeless
- 1885 Head tax imposed on Chinese immigrants
- 1892 St. John's fire leaves 10 000 homeless
- 1901–21 3 million immigrants arrive in Canada
- 1906 Major revisions made to the Immigration Act
- 1907 Anti-Asian riots in Vancouver; Doukhobors in Saskatchewan have half their land confiscated
- 1914 Komagata Maru incident

In 1901, census-taker Charles P. McRosite arrived at the one-room home of a Chinese immigrant in Nelson, British Columbia. He recorded the name of its occupant as Juin Yen, noting that he was a 40-year-old man living with his son Sing. Juin had arrived in 1898 and Sing in 1899. Sing's mother was nowhere in evidence, perhaps because immigration laws made it expensive for Yen to bring his wife to Canada. The lone-parent status of the Yen family was not unusual in industrializing Canada. In her research on the 1901 census, historian Bettina Bradbury found that 12 percent of the families in Canada in which there were children living in the home and where the parent was under 55 were headed by lone parents.[1]

Nearly 5 million immigrants arrived in Canada between 1871 and 1921 (see Table 6.1). Some prospered; others clearly did not. The same could be said for most Canadians, more than 4 million of whom left Canada in the same period. Whatever their hopes and fears,

| | **Natural** | | | **Net** | |
Year	increase	Immigration	Emigration	migration	Population
1861					3230
1861–71	650	186	376	−191	3689
1871–81	720	353	438	−85	4325
1881–91	714	903	1108	−205	4833
1891–01	719	326	507	−181	5371
1901–11	1120	1782	1066	716	7207
1911–21	1349	1592	1360	233	8788

TABLE 6.1   Canada's Population (in thousands), 1861–1921

Source: David C. Corbett, *Canada's Immigration Policy: A Critique* (Toronto: University of Toronto Press, 1957), 121.

Canadians old and new were on the move in the half-century following confederation. They struggled—sometimes individually, increasingly together—to come to terms with a country whose families, communities, and institutions were changing, often dramatically.

THE PROBLEM OF OUTMIGRATION

In the early years of confederation, the slow rate of population growth was as great a concern for Canadian leaders as railways and tariffs. Despite the passage of the Dominion Lands Act in 1872, most immigrants to North America in the late nineteenth century preferred to settle in the United States. So, too, it seemed, did many Canadians. Frontier lands, industrial jobs, and a better climate attracted Canadians like a magnet, and there seemed to be nothing that the nation's leaders could do to stop the exodus.

In Maritime Canada, close family ties and geographic proximity had long made New England a place to find work. Once the trend was set, other family members followed, producing what demographers describe as a chain migration. Nearly half a million people left the Maritimes between 1880 and 1921, a number representing over a third of the total population remaining in the region. Maritime carpenters thrown out of work by the collapse of the shipbuilding

Lumber mills such as this one on the Rimouski River enabled some families in the colonization regions of Quebec to survive the difficulties of farming in marginal agricultural regions.
Library and Archives Canada/PA22075

industry helped build the suburbs of American cities, former farm boys delivered milk in horse-drawn vans, and fishing families found the protected American markets easier to supply from Gloucester and Salem in Massachusetts than they did from Maritime fishing communities. Women, who outnumbered men in the exodus, worked as domestics, factory hands, clerks, secretaries, teachers, and nurses.

Newfoundland experienced a similar trend. While most Newfoundlanders moved to Massachusetts or New York, a significant number also found work in the industrializing areas of the Maritimes, particularly Halifax and Cape Breton. The development of the iron reserves on Bell Island to supply Nova Scotia's steel industry led naturally to the migration of labour across the Cabot Strait to Cape Breton. From there, Newfoundlanders often joined Nova Scotians moving to better opportunities in the United States.

In the same period, large families and limited agricultural opportunities encouraged more than 700 000 Quebecers to leave Canada, many of them destined for mill towns in New England. With factories employing men, women, and children, whole families joined the exodus and thereby became the founders of a Franco-American community that still retains its distinctiveness. Quebec's Roman Catholic Church tried to keep its flock at home by developing colonization societies to settle frontier areas of the province, but such efforts had little success.

The Canadian West had little attraction for Quebec's rural migrants. Efforts by Bishop Taché and his successors in St. Boniface to repatriate Francophones from New England bore some fruit in the 1870s, but the numbers trickled off despite attempts to maintain interest through a federally sponsored newspaper, *Le Colonisateur*, distributed throughout Quebec and New England in the 1880s. In 1901, there were only 23 000 French-speaking settlers on the Prairies, many of them from France, Belgium, and Switzerland rather than Quebec. Francophones were scattered throughout the West in communities such as St. Albert,

Grande Clairière, Montmartre, St. Brieux, and Gravelbourg. Together they had an important influence on the culture and politics of the region, but they found their culture increasingly submerged in a flood of immigrants who spoke any language but French.

At the same time, the number of Francophones living in Ontario and the Maritimes increased significantly in the half-century following confederation. Quebecers crossed the border into eastern and northern Ontario to take advantage of employment opportunities in farming, resource development, and the federal bureaucracy. The number of Franco-Ontarians jumped from 102 743 in 1881 to 202 442 in 1911, an increase that brought their numbers to nearly 10 percent of the provincial population. Although some Acadians were attracted to jobs in New England, they were less likely than their Anglophone neighbours to leave the Maritimes. They were also more likely than Anglophones to have large families. As a result, those claiming a French heritage in New Brunswick rose from less than 16 percent of the population in 1871 to over 31 percent in 1921. By the latter date, Francophones had increased to 10.8 percent of the population in Nova Scotia and 13.5 percent in Prince Edward Island.

Rural Ontario lost population to the developing western territories and the agricultural, forest, and urban frontiers of the United States in the last three decades of the nineteenth century. However, unlike the Maritimes and Quebec, where outmigration exceeded immigration until the 1930s, Ontario was able to stem the outward flow in the first decade of the twentieth century. Ontario's rapidly developing industrial economy and resource frontier employed not only the surplus population from the rural areas of the nation but also a rising tide of immigrants who flooded into Canada in the early years of the twentieth century.

IMMIGRATION POLICY

Under the British North America Act, immigration was a responsibility shared by federal and provincial jurisdictions. Ottawa took an early lead with the passage of an act defining immigration and citizenship procedures in 1869. The Immigration Act established immigration offices in Great Britain and continental

A poster from 1911 to encourage American immigration.
Library and Archives Canada, C-056088

Europe, quarantine stations in Halifax, Saint John, and Quebec, and immigration branches in various Canadian cities. On paper, Canada's immigration policy was an open one; only criminals were denied admission. In practice, people who were deemed destitute, physically unfit, or mentally disabled were required to post a bond and were often turned away.

In the first three decades following confederation, Canada's ethnic balance changed very little. The 1901 census reported that 88 percent of Canadians were of British or French descent, just 4 percent fewer than in 1871. Although many Canadians were skeptical, Clifford Sifton, minister of the interior from 1896 to 1905, was prepared to welcome eastern Europeans, assessing them as good prospects to survive the rigours of pioneering on the Canadian Prairies. "I think a stalwart peasant in a sheep-skin coat, born on the soil, whose forefathers have been farmers for ten generations, with a stout wife and a half-dozen children is good quality," Sifton declared.[2] Business people were similarly enthusiastic about such recruits, seeing them as ideal candidates for the hard, low-wage labour needed in factories, resource industries, and homes.

Under Sifton's direction, the Department of the Interior, in cooperation with transportation companies and other private recruitment agencies, advertised extensively in Europe and the United States for immigrants to settle the Prairies and work in Canada's expanding industries. These efforts coincided with a number of global trends that combined to make immigration an attractive option for many people. In Europe, ethnic and religious tensions, outright persecution, industrial upheaval, and the collapse of peasant farming systems "pushed" many potential emigrants to seek a new life in Canada. An upswing in the international economy, vigorous recruitment campaigns, improved transportation by steam and rail, technological breakthroughs in farming, and the relatively high wages in Canada "pulled" people to what was increasingly perceived as a land of opportunity.

Sifton's successor, Frank Oliver, who served as minister of the interior from 1905 to 1911, pursued a much more restrictive immigration policy: "It is not merely a question of filling the country with people," he opined. "It is a question of the ultimate efforts put forward for the building up of a Canadian nationality. This can never be accomplished if the preponderance of the people should be of such a class and character as will deteriorate rather than elevate the condition of our people and our country at large."[3] In 1906, the Immigration Act was revised to exclude the "feeble minded;" those "afflicted with a loathsome disease;" professional beggars, prostitutes, and those living off their avails; persons convicted of crimes of "moral turpitude;" and anyone "likely to become a public charge" or who "may become dangerous to the public health." Later amendments barred women or girls from coming to Canada for "any immoral purpose" and anyone suffering from alcoholism, mental or physical defects, or a condition of "constitutional psychopathic inferiority." Because these terms were vague, immigration officials had considerable latitude to make arbitrary judgments about the suitability of applicants.

These laws failed to stem the flow of people into the country before the First World War. From a low of 16 835 arrivals in 1896 to a high of 400 000 in 1913, immigrants came from Great Britain, Europe, the United States, and Asia, many of them settling in the four western provinces. In total between 1901 and 1921, more than 3 million immigrants arrived in Canada. The majority of them—perhaps as many as two-thirds—came from the United States and Great Britain, but enough came from other nations of the world to alter the ethnic composition of Canada. By 1920, over 20 percent of Canadians traced their origins to countries other than Great Britain and France.

Between 1896 and 1914, nearly a million immigrant farmers were found for Canada's agricultural economy. Other immigrants found work as farm labourers, usually on a temporary basis. In 1891, 6300 seasonal workers were employed in the wheat harvest; by 1921 the number had increased tenfold. Many of the people employed on western farms came from the eastern provinces on "harvest trains," placed in service specifically to cater to the labour needs of the wheat economy. Immigrants were also attracted to the jobs opening up in Canada's industrial cities.

Immigrant workers were most likely to be found in the mining, lumbering, and railway camps scattered throughout industrializing Canada. With the assistance of the federal government and private agencies, company officials recruited Slavs, Scandinavians, and Italians for these jobs, but when their numbers proved insufficient, companies pressed the government to admit Chinese, Japanese, and East Indian labourers. Historian Donald Avery estimates that between 1907 and 1914, when all three of Canada's transcontinental railway systems were engaged in construction projects, 50 000 to 70 000 workers were required annually by the railway companies alone.[4]

The three Prairie provinces, with 54 percent of the foreign-born, were entirely transformed by the newcomers. There, Canadian, British, and American settlers lived side by side with eastern and western Europeans, each of whom contributed about 20 percent to the population. On the Pacific coast, the cultural mix varied again. Sixty percent of the 40 000 Chinese and virtually all of the 16 000 Japanese enumerated by the 1921 census were located in British Columbia, which otherwise was 60 percent British. Only the Maritime region, with its agricultural frontier taken up and its industrial base languishing, failed to attract a significant number of immigrants outside its coal-mining and steel-making communities.

Because of the high birth rate among Francophones, their percentage of the population of Canada dropped only marginally, from 31.1 percent in 1871 to 28.2 percent in 1921. The percentage of non-Francophones and non-Anglophones (generally referred to as Allophones today) in Quebec rose from 1.6 percent in 1871 to 4.9 percent in 1921. While this increase did not represent a major demographic shift, its effect was particularly noticeable in Montreal, where 80 percent of the Allophones—and 60 percent of the Anglophones—chose to live.

By the second decade of the twentieth century, the population patterns of "new" Canada were beginning to take shape. Over half of the dominion's population continued to live in Quebec and Ontario, but the proportion of Canadians living in these two provinces dropped from nearly 75 percent in 1891 to 60 percent in 1921. Maritimers accounted for only 11.4 percent, down from 18.2 percent three decades earlier. By contrast, the West registered explosive growth. Prairie populations rose from 7.8 percent to 22.3 percent of the Canadian total in the first two decades of the twentieth century, while British Columbia accounted for 6 percent of the nation's people in 1921.

Canadians harboured deep fears about immigration. For many English-speaking Canadians, the tide of foreigners threatened the dominance of British culture. Francophones were even more cautious. Since most immigrants came from English-speaking countries—and those who did not quickly assimilated to the Anglo-Canadian culture—French Canadians saw themselves disappearing in a sea of English-speaking North Americans. Between 1900 and 1940, virtually all nationalist organizations in Quebec went on record as opposing Canada's "open door" immigration policy. As a result of such views, there was little likelihood of Canada becoming a "mosaic" of different but equal peoples, or the "melting pot" favoured in the United States. Rather, the nation became a battleground for many cultures trying to establish their place in a rigid social pecking order.

SETTLERS AND SOJOURNERS

The federal government's early difficulties in attracting large numbers of farmers to the West created an interest in sponsoring block settlements for ethnic minorities. In the 1870s, about 7400 German-speaking Mennonites left their homes in western Russia to settle in Manitoba; two decades later, their descendants spread into the area that would become the province of Saskatchewan. The Mennonites proved excellent farmers, introducing crop rotation and planting trees as wind breaks. Because they were pacifists, farmed communally, and kept to themselves, they were initially viewed with suspicion by their neighbours. Despite their exclusiveness, the Mennonites created prosperous farming communities and soon established good relations with the people living around them.

Also in the 1870s, 2000 Icelanders settled in Gimli ("Paradise"), Manitoba, driven from their homeland by economic depression and volcanic eruptions. Just after the colony was founded, a devastating outbreak of smallpox resulted in an armed quarantine of the settlement and the deaths of 100 people, mainly young children. This tragedy was followed by floods in 1879 and 1880. Religious tensions between adherents of the Church of Iceland and more conservative Lutherans also racked the community and pushed a number of the settlers to move to the United States. Such difficulties notwithstanding, the colony thrived. Within a generation, its members had begun to adapt to English-Canadian norms while retaining pride in their distinct culture, which was reflected in their own schools, churches, and Icelandic-language newspaper.

In the 1880s, the first wave of Jewish immigrants, fleeing persecution in the Russian Empire, established farming settlements in what would become Saskatchewan. It was a new experience for a people who had been barred by law from farming in their homeland. By the end of the century, Jews subjected to discriminatory policies in Poland, Austria-Hungary, and Germany also turned to Canada as a place of refuge, but found that Canada was not without its own discriminatory practices. General hostility toward non-Christians forced Jewish immigrants to stick together, despite their diverse cultural backgrounds. At the same time, discrimination in employment and quotas restricting Jewish entrance into legal and medical schools focused them into a narrow range of occupations. In Winnipeg, Jews took up jobs as unskilled labourers, pedlars, and small shopkeepers and congregated in the city's north end. Wherever they settled, socialist political beliefs distinguished many Jewish settlers from their usually more conservative neighbours.

The Cardston Temple of the Church of Jesus Christ of Latter-Day Saints.
Glenbow Archives/ND27-12

The Prairies were home to about 25 000 Jews by 1921. Even more could be found in Quebec and Ontario, which each counted almost 50 000 Jews in their populations in 1921. Because Montreal and Toronto had Jewish communities and offered urban employment, many Jews chose to make these cities their home, and Montreal's Jewish community quadrupled between 1901 and 1911. The Jewish presence in Quebec put tremendous pressure on Protestant English-language schools, which the Jews attended because they could not get provincial grants to create their own schools. By a 1903 ruling, Jews were considered Protestants for the purposes of school taxes, but they received few benefits from this ruling. By the 1920s, nearly 40 percent of the Protestant school board's students were Jewish, but there were no Jewish high school teachers. Protestant prayers and religious instruction were imposed upon Jewish children, and they were also denied the right to stay at home on Jewish holidays.

Not all group settlers came from Europe. Mormons, adherents of the Church of Jesus Christ of Latter-Day Saints, began moving to Canada from their base in Utah in the 1880s. The first eight families, under the leadership of Charles Ora Card, arrived in the Northwest Territories in 1887. Using dryland farming techniques developed in Utah, the Mormons brought into agricultural production areas of the Prairies that had hitherto supported only open-range ranching. The aim of permanent settlement was reflected in one of Card's

With their strongly held beliefs about appropriate spheres for men and women, middle-class Canadians objected to the hard physical labour performed by women in Doukhobor families and the extreme patriarchal control that Doukhobor men held over women and children.
Library and Archives Canada/C8891

advertisements: "Come along with your capital and build our flouring mills, sugar refineries, electric railways and electric lights, and aid to establish other industries and grow up with an enterprising and healthy country. Don't forget to secure a good farm adjacent to one of the grandest irrigation systems of modern times."[5]

The Mormon population in Alberta rose to 7000 by 1912. In the following year, building began on a temple located in Cardston, Alberta. Completed 10 years later, it was distinctive not only for its size and style of architecture but also because it was the first Mormon temple to be built outside the United States. Like other religiously defined cultural groups, the Mormons often felt the prejudice of neighbours who condemned their religious beliefs, most notably their advocacy of polygamy. Most Mormons gave up this practice soon after their arrival in Canada, but Canadians were slow to forget that this had once been a distinguishing feature of Mormon culture.

One of the first groups to respond to Sifton's stepped-up recruitment program in the 1890s was a block of Doukhobors in Russia who were being persecuted by the tsar for their ethnic traits and religious practices. Under an agreement negotiated in 1898 with the help of Russian intellectual Leo Tolstoy and University of Toronto professor James Mavor, some 7400 Doukhobors settled on 400 000 acres of land near Yorkton, Saskatchewan. Mainly followers of visionary leader Peter Veregin, who required his flock to live communally, they soon became divided over the degree of loyalty to their leader's beliefs the group should maintain.

The most fervent followers, called the Sons of Freedom, began to destroy their property in 1902 and conduct nude demonstrations as visible evidence of their faith. For shocked Canadians, such behaviour was visible evidence that the whole group should be brought into conformity with Anglo-Canadian practices. In 1906, the government began forcing Doukhobors to follow the strict letter of the homestead law with respect to their communal landholdings. About a third of the

Galicians at an immigration shed in Quebec City.
Library and Archives Canada/C4745

group agreed to abandon their communalism and remained in Saskatchewan under their leader Peter Makaroff. In 1912, the rest joined Veregin in the creation of a new utopia in the interior of British Columbia.

During the First World War, the Hutterites, a German-speaking pacifist group with communal practices, negotiated entry into Canada. Most of them had spent one or two generations in South Dakota before moving northward. Settling in Manitoba and Alberta, they established communities that resisted all efforts at assimilation. Their distinctive communal arrangements included a children's nursery, women's spinning hall, and common dining room. When a community reached a population of between 100 and 200 people, another one was established, which remained as self-sufficient, remote, and autonomous as its predecessor.

Canada also became the homeland for thousands of people from the Hapsburg provinces of Galicia and Bukovina. Known today as Ukrainians, they were the largest and the most visible of all European peasant cultures to come to Canada. As many as 150 000 Ukrainians had arrived by 1914 and another 70 000 came in the interwar years. The exact numbers are difficult to determine since the newcomers were designated in a variety of ways in immigration records and came from countries whose boundaries were notoriously fluid. Often poor, illiterate, and oppressed in

Chinatowns such as this one in Victoria are among the legacies of racial segregation in Canada.
Library and Archives Canada/C23415

their homeland, they were the prototype of Sifton's peasant in a sheepskin coat.

Prior to 1910, the vast majority of Ukrainian migrants were men, the most destitute of whom began their Canadian experience clustered in tenements in the north end of Winnipeg and worked as railway navvies and farm labourers. As soon as they could, they moved to their own farms, many of them in the vicinity of Dauphin, Manitoba; Yorkton, Saskatchewan; or the Edna-Star district northeast of Edmonton. The Ukrainians quickly earned a reputation for hard work and determination, though their cultural practices brought widespread criticism from their Canadian-born neighbours.

The onion-shaped dome of their church architecture was the most visible symbol of Ukrainian presence in the dominion. Thatched-roof homes built by first-generation Ukrainians were also unlike any others found in the West, and they elicited much comment. Because of their numbers and varied political experiences, the Ukrainians were never a uniform cultural group. They held political views ranging from socialist to conservative and subscribed to a wide range of religious beliefs, although a majority of those who came before the First World War were Roman Catholics of the Byzantine Rite. As a group, Ukrainians left an indelible mark on Canada. In their insistence on maintaining their cultural distinctiveness, historian Gerald Friesen argues, Ukrainians, as much

as any other single ethnic group, "were responsible for the official adoption of today's bilingual-multicultural definition of Canadian society."[6]

The majority of newcomers came to stay, but another category of immigrant, called sojourners, planned to return to their homelands with money in their pockets. Most Chinese and Japanese immigrants fell into this category. So, too, did a number of eastern Europeans, such as people from the mountain villages where the borders of Greece, Bulgaria, Serbia, and Albania meet. Now known as Macedonians, they began migrating to Canada to find work in the first decade of the twentieth century. Overwhelmingly, they were single or young married men, and many found jobs in Toronto's factories, abattoirs, and construction sites. While in Toronto, they lived in boarding houses located in ethnic enclaves such as Cabbagetown. During the recession of 1907, some 300 Macedonian sojourners were deported to prevent their becoming objects of Canadian charity, but their numbers continued to grow. Mutual support soon found expression in the creation in 1910 of a "national" Eastern Orthodox parish centred in SS Cyril and Methody Church in Toronto. When the Balkan Wars in 1912–1913 divided their homeland, many Macedonian sojourners decided to become permanent settlers, a decision confirmed by the difficulties of returning to Europe during the First World War.

Italians came both as settlers and sojourners, their numbers swelling in the first two decades of the twentieth century when more than 120 000 Italians arrived in Canada. Like the Macedonians, most of the early Italian immigrants were young single men. They were often recruited by Italian labour agents (*padroni*) based in Montreal and Toronto who sponsored contract labour for railway and mining companies. The majority of the Italians who chose to stay in Canada lived in Montreal and Toronto; others settled in communities across the nation. The low proportion of women among them—10 834 out of a population of 45 411 in 1911—suggests one of the reasons why 10 years later only 66 769 people of Italian origin were reported living in Canada. Some men returned to their homeland once their work contracts expired; others moved to the United States, where the vast majority of Italian immigrants to North America chose to settle.

"White Canada Forever"

While eastern and southern Europeans were subjected to discrimination, non-white immigrants bore the brunt of Canadian hostility. The Chinese, who performed the most dangerous jobs in the construction of the Canadian Pacific Railway (CPR), were almost universally despised. In defending his policy of importing Chinese workers, John A. Macdonald revealed his contempt when he told a Toronto political meeting: "Well, they do come and so do rats. I am pledged to build the great Pacific Railroad in five years, and if I cannot obtain white labour, I must employ other."[7] Following the completion of the railway, many labourers stayed in Canada because their families in China depended on the money they sent home. Angry whites complained that they were unfair competition for jobs and began to lobby for their deportation.

Responding to pressure from the province of British Columbia, where most of the Chinese had settled, the federal government imposed a $50 head tax on Chinese immigrants in 1885. The tax was raised to $100 in 1901 and $500 in 1904, equivalent to a year's wages. The result was a gender imbalance in the Chinese-Canadian population. In the period before the First World War, most of the small number of Chinese women in the country were the wives of merchants who could afford to pay the tax or prostitutes who were already in Canada when the tax was instituted. Shunned by broader society, the Chinese lived in segregated Chinatowns, where support was available for the homeless, ill, and aged.

Like the Chinese, most Japanese immigrants to Canada (known as *Issei*) viewed themselves as sojourners who would return home after making some money. Many did so, but by 1910 a number of Japanese men in Canada had established themselves in farming, fishing, and trade in the Vancouver and Steveston areas of British Columbia. Soon they began to bring in Japanese women and establish families. Known as "picture brides" because prospective husbands had only their

William Peyton Hubbard (third from right, foreground) laying the last stone for Toronto's new city hall, 1898. Canada's treatment of blacks was not always characterized by prejudice and exclusion. Once the chauffeur for George Brown, Hubbard became a successful businessman and in 1894 was elected alderman in Toronto. He was re-elected 13 times and often served as acting mayor.
City of Toronto Archives/Fonds 1268, Item 216

pictures when they "proposed," the women were married by proxy in Japan after negotiations between the couple's families. The economic success of the Japanese drew the ire of their racist neighbours, who made no secret of the fact that they wanted to keep British Columbia "white forever."

Whether immigrant or Canadian-born, Chinese and Japanese were denied the franchise in the western provinces, barred from access to the professions, subjected to discriminatory housing covenants, and segregated in public places. They were also threatened with physical violence. In 1907, whites marched through Japanese and Chinese sections of Vancouver, breaking windows and shouting racist slogans. While an isolated example, the incident indicated the depth of the hostility faced by Asian immigrants. The federal government responded to these racist sentiments by negotiating an agreement with Japan that restricted the number of Japanese allowed to enter the country to 400 annually.

While it was difficult for Canadians to impose restrictions on immigrants from India, which, like Canada, was a colony of the British Empire, it did not stop them from trying. The federal government passed an order-in-council in 1908 requiring East Indians to come to Canada by continuous passage from India. Since there was no direct steamship line between the two countries, the regulation virtually precluded immigration. In 1913, a group of 38 Sikhs contested the restriction and were admitted. This experience encouraged others to charter the *Komagata Maru*, a Japanese-owned freighter, to bring 376 Punjabis, mostly Sikhs, to Canada in 1914. Detained on board for two months in Vancouver harbour while their case was heard before the courts, the would-be immigrants were eventually ordered to leave. To give point to the court order, the Royal Canadian Navy cruiser *Rainbow* was sent to the scene. Due to such policies, only 1016 East Indians were enumerated in Canada in 1921, down from 2342 (2315 men and 27 women) 10 years earlier.

By the late nineteenth century, most whites had become adherents of racist beliefs that held blacks to be mentally and morally inferior. Even Wilfrid Laurier was heard to proclaim in 1910 that "[W]e see in the United States what grave problems may arise from the presence of a race unable to become full members of the same social family as ourselves."[8] Thus the arrival between 1910 and 1912 of some 1300 African-American homesteaders from Oklahoma, where statehood brought deteriorating conditions for blacks, caused a major uproar. Because they were healthy American citizens and held property, immigration regulations could not be used to keep them out.

Public petitions from all three Prairie provinces urged Ottawa to ban further admission of black immigrants and the federal government prepared an order-in-council to do so for a year, but it was never proclaimed.

Fears that relations with the United States would be damaged and that black voters in Ontario and the Maritimes would be alienated apparently caused politicians to exercise restraint. Instead, agents were sent into the United States to discourage black immigrants and border officials were rewarded for the rigorous application of immigration regulations against blacks trying to enter the country—policies that, sadly, had the effect that was intended.

REINFORCING THE DOMINANT CULTURE

The majority of immigrants in this period were Caucasian and came from Great Britain and the United States. Because most of them spoke English and came as individuals, they attracted less attention from nativistic Canadians. This was especially the case with the English-speaking Canadians living in the United States who took advantage of the incentives offered in the Canadian West to return to the land of their birth. Not only were they better able to adapt to institutions that were familiar to them, they were also likely to have extended family members in Canada upon whom they could draw for assistance.

Between 1904 and 1914, some 90 000 British women came to Canada to work in domestic service: 60 percent came from England, 29 percent from Scotland, and 10 percent from Ireland. This breakdown

Home Children

Between the 1860s and the 1920s, nearly 100 000 poor and orphaned children from Great Britain were sent to Canada. They were known as "home children" because they came from British orphanages, commonly called "homes," which sponsored their placement overseas. While their experiences in Canada varied widely, most home children were indentured to farm families as cheap labour and seldom received the love and care reserved for "blood" children.

Maggie Hall, a child immigrant, described a typical work day to her friend in 1890:

I have to get my morning's work done by 12 o'clock every day to take the children for a walk then I have to get the

table laid for lunch when I come in then after dinner I help to wash up then I have to give the little boy his lessons then for the rest of the afternoon I sew till it is time to get afternoon tea and shut up and light the gas then by that time it is time for our tea after which I clear away get the table ready for Miss Smith's dinner then put the little boy to bed & after Miss Smith's dinner I help wash up which does not take very long then I do what I like for the rest of the evening till halfpast nine when we have Prayers then I take Miss Smith's hot water & hot bottle, the basket of silver & glass of milk to her bedroom shut up & go to bed which by the time I have done all it is just about ten.[9]

meant that the Irish servant typical of the 1870s had almost vanished by the early twentieth century. British sources made up about three quarters of the immigrants who came to work as domestic servants in this period. Others came from Scandinavia and central and eastern Europe. Domestic servants were believed to be especially desirable immigrants because they made the most likely marriage partners for the male farmers and labourers who were the majority of newcomers in the migration process. Not surprisingly, the open door for domestics and wives did not include African, West Indian, or Asian women.

Despite their talk about keeping the country British, Anglo-Canadians were not always welcoming of immigrants from their imperial homeland. Many Canadians found the superior attitude adopted by some British immigrants particularly hard to swallow. An even greater cause for concern, especially for employers, was the socialist perspective held by those who had been associated with labour politics in Great Britain. Because many British immigrants came from urban backgrounds, they often made disgruntled homesteaders. Dubbed "green Englishmen" by their neighbours, they drifted to Prairie towns to find work, where they were sometimes met with signs indicating that "No Englishmen need apply."

While many British immigrants came as single men looking for work in Canadian towns and cities, in at least one instance it was British women who were actively sought as factory operatives. John Penman, the owner of Penman's woollen factories in Paris, Ontario, recruited 700 skilled hosiery workers from the East Midlands of England between 1907 and 1928. Many were single women who were accustomed to life-long wage earning. In her investigation of these women, Joy Parr found that they maintained this tradition in Paris, relying on female networks, public services, and family practices to sustain their continued labour-force participation. The commercial provision of laundry services, the hours for Saturday shopping, and early school-leaving laws all reflected that Paris was a "woman's town."[10]

SETTLING IN

Immigrants faced special challenges in establishing a sense of community. Whether they settled in rural or urban areas and came as individuals, families, or in groups, they were caught between their old world and the new. Their lot might have been marginally easier than that of pre-confederation immigrants, but both faced hostility from native-born Canadians and the difficult task of making a living in a rapidly changing economy. The *Missionary Outlook* in 1910 embodied an attitude that was all too general across Canada: "Every large city on this continent has its fourfold problem of the slum, the saloons, the foreign colony and the districts of vice. The foreign colony may not properly be called a slum, but it represents a community that is about to become an important factor in our social life and will become a menace in our civilization unless it learns to assimilate the moral and religious ideals and the standards of citizenship."[11]

Despite such views, immigrants at the turn of the twentieth century almost always had an easier experience settling in than did earlier immigrants. Atlantic crossings, while not always pleasant, usually lasted less than two weeks and rarely resulted in marine disaster. Train travel, even in roughly fitted colonist cars, was palatial compared with the discomfort of crossing the country before the advent of the railway. All the same, survival in Canada proved a good deal harder than settlers and sojourners had been led to expect by the optimistic pamphlets, films, and lectures supplied by recruitment agencies. Once at their destination, immigrants were left to fend for themselves, without public assistance. On the Prairies, new arrivals faced the back-breaking work, poor living conditions, and homesickness that pioneers in other regions had experienced. Historians estimate that as many as 40 percent of those who filed for homesteads eventually sold or abandoned their claims.

The Canadian homestead policy of 160 acres for a $10 fee and minor settlement duties seemed a bonanza to many people, but families settling on the land needed more than hope and industry to succeed. The minimum investment required in ploughs, oxen, cattle, poultry, wagons, and basic household utensils, in addition to seed and sufficient supplies to tide families over until the first harvest, was reckoned to cost even thrifty families close to $1000. Few came with such a sum: it had to be earned in Canada. Many immigrants worked as labourers and domestics on more prosperous farms or took jobs with the railways or in mines before taking up farming. While husbands and older sons and daughters worked elsewhere to earn the cash stake to guarantee the family's future, married women regularly

The Pioneering Experience

The Prairie pioneering experience offered singular hardship. One of the sons of Maria Aho, a founding settler of a Finnish community established in southwest Saskatchewan in 1888, recalled how difficult the early years were for his family:

> My mother was so homesick, she never allowed us to dismantle her trunk insisting that she would not stay in this bush with no roads, nothing, just a small two-room hut with branches as a roof. The roof leaked. But every second year she had a new baby until there were twelve of us. She worked all the time, I never saw her sleep and still she kept insisting we act civilized. I was not allowed out to the nearest town till I could read and write. She taught us all that and she told us about Finland, her hometown Lapua. We dug a well by hand, but it kept drying up. Still we had a sauna every week and we were all scrubbed. Then we read the Bible and sang from the hymn book. . . . Mother never saw Finland again, she died at seventy-six, and I have never seen that country, but still if people ask me I tell them that I am a Finn.[12]

Belonging to the dominant Anglo-Canadian culture did not always make matters better. For example, Roy and Verna Benson, who settled in Munson, Alberta, were less than enthusiastic about their experience. Roy wrote in January 1911:

> I suppose you are wondering what kind of country we have struck well there are a lot of people right here that are doing the same thing wondering. This past year has made a lot of them sit up and notice. Some have left the country, some couldn't. . . . I had a 10 a[cres] broke a year ago (cost me $50) last July. Last spring I let a fellow put in on shares and put $20 into a fence—this fall I told him he could have it all but the fence.

In May of the same year, Verna offered her perspective:

> I surely don't care anything about putting in another winter like last winter. I went to one of the neighbours New Years day and I wasn't away from home again until the last of April. There was two months last winter I never saw a woman and in fact the only persons I did see during that time was Roy and our bachelor neighbor. Then the men all wonder why the women don't like it here and the women all wonder what there is about the country that the men like so well.[13]

Verna's bachelor neighbour probably also suffered from loneliness. In her study of male labour in Prairie agriculture, Cecilia Danysk cites the case of Ebe Koeppen from Germany, who recorded in his diary that he had reached a "very sad point." For Koeppen, life without a wife was "slow spiritual death." He admitted that he did not write home about such things because "the staggering drearyness of such existence is too difficult to make understandable." A popular Prairie song, "The Alberta Homesteader," made light of this familiar lament of single men:

> My clothes are all ragged, my language is rough,
> My bread is case-hardened and solid and tough
> My dishes are scattered all over the room
> My floor gets afraid of the sight of a broom.[14]

Hot meals served at all hours: the reality for harvest workers in Saskatchewan.
Saskatchewan Archives Board/R-A8634–1

maintained homesteads, living for long, lonely winter months in what were often little more than shacks—or in the somewhat less uncomfortable "soddies" constructed out of the prairie land itself—caring for young children and tending livestock.

Despite the hard times, uncertain reception, and lack of women, newcomers found encouragement and support in both rural and urban settings. Mutual aid societies, church organizations, cooperatives, and just plain neighbourliness rescued many families and individuals from destitution. Ethnic solidarities proved invaluable. Minority communities such as Vancouver's "Little Tokyo" and Saskatchewan's Jewish agricultural colonies near Wapella, Hirsch, Cupar, Lipton, and Sonnenfeld gave inhabitants opportunities to share cherished customs and to work out collective ways of dealing with life's many hardships. In the Ukrainian settlements of east-central Alberta, more than 90 community halls had been built by 1913 to host meetings, lectures, plays, concerts, dances, and choir practices. For navvies and sojourners, the fellowship found in the boarding houses, stores, cafés, and restaurants run by their compatriots sometimes helped to compensate for Canadian inhospitality.

This is not to say that ethnic solidarity was an entirely positive experience. Among immigrant Italians, for example, the middlemen who arranged contract labour for Canadian companies often extorted substantial commissions from their desperate clients. On the West Coast, Chinese prostitutes were sometimes virtual slaves of the merchants who sold their sexual services to Chinese and white customers. Police records of Canadian cities show a high incidence of crime, especially assault and theft, within immigrant communities. While this evidence perhaps reflects the fact that immigrants were more likely to be singled out by the forces of law and order, it also testifies to the tensions that, not surprisingly, surfaced among unhappy immigrants thrown together in less than ideal circumstances.

URBANIZATION

Emigration, immigration, and the growth of population in the western and northern frontiers were paralleled by an unprecedented movement of people from rural to urban areas of the country. In the boom years

TABLE 6.2 Population of Selected Canadian Cities, 1871–1921 (ranked in order of size for 1921)

City	1871	1891	1901	1921
Montreal	115 000	219 616	328 172	618 506
Toronto	59 000	181 215	209 892	521 893
Winnipeg	241	25 639	42 340	179 087
Vancouver	0	13 709	29 432	163 220
Hamilton	26 880	48 959	52 634	114 151
Ottawa	24 141	44 154	59 928	107 843
Quebec	59 699	63 090	68 840	95 193
Calgary	0	3 867	4 392	63 305
London	18 000	31 977	37 976	60 959
Edmonton	0	700	4 176	58 846
Halifax	29 582	38 437	40 832	58 375
Saint John	28 805	39 179	40 711	47 166

Source: Adapted from Alan Artibise, *Winnipeg: A Social History of Urban Growth* (Montreal: McGill-Queen's University Press, 1975), 132; George A. Noder, *Cities of Canada*, vol. 2, *Profiles of Fifteen Metropolitan Centres* (Toronto: Macmillan, 1976).

from 1901 to 1921, the population of Montreal nearly doubled and that of Toronto increased about 150 percent. Even this growth paled in comparison with that of Winnipeg, Calgary, Edmonton, and Vancouver (see Table 6.2). Urbanization changed the way people thought about community and left rural areas scrambling to respond to the loss of population. Despite the problems surfacing in congested cities, they were exciting places to live, offering amenities and opportunities that rural folk were hard-pressed to emulate.

Cities in western Canada grew out of nowhere to dominate their rural hinterlands. A sleepy village in 1871, Winnipeg would have remained a backwater except for the determination of local merchants to have the CPR put its main line through the town and construct its western yards and shops there. The CPR Syndicate had planned to build through Selkirk, northeast of Winnipeg, but the railway directors could always be persuaded to change their minds. By building a bridge across the Red River and securing two rail loops that could link a Pacific railway with the United States, Winnipeg had something other locations lacked. It offered the CPR free passage on the bridge, a $200 000 bonus, free land for its station, and a permanent exemption from municipal taxes on railway property.

Jasper Avenue in Edmonton, 1890 (top) and 1910.
Provincial Archives of Alberta, E. Brown Collection/B4755 and Library and Archives Canada/C7911

With the railway in place and Prairie agriculture under way, Winnipeg grew quickly and emerged as the third-largest city in Canada by 1911. Other Prairie cities, including Edmonton, Calgary, Saskatoon, and Regina, had begun to expand by the end of the century, but the railyards and Winnipeg's position as the main distribution point for the region gave it an advantage in attracting new industry. It became the home of the grain exchange, whose speculators bid on the wheat crop, and developed a substantial manufacturing sector, including clothing, furniture, and food processing firms and metal shops dependent on the railway.

Like Winnipeg, Vancouver owed its growth to the CPR. To become the terminus of that company's transcontinental line, Vancouver provided subsidies and tax holidays to the company. Competing with Victoria, whose commission merchants continued to control trade with Great Britain and California for another 20 years, Vancouver's merchants sought to

dominate the British Columbia economy. They convinced city council to provide a $300 000 subsidy to local promoters of a railway to the Upper Fraser Valley, spent $150 000 on a bridge across False Creek to connect the city with roads to the Fraser Valley, and gave subsidies to the initiators of a sugar refinery and graving dock.

CANADIAN CITIES IN TRANSITION

Wherever they were located, cities harboured the worst features of uncontrolled growth in this period. Noise, overcrowding, poor sewage systems, pollution from smokestacks, and inadequate roads combined to make life unpleasant for most city dwellers. Despite the problems experienced in Canada's congested cities, some people lived in much better circumstances than others. The gap between rich and poor was evident in the stark contrast between the spectacular homes and office buildings of the wealthy and the substandard housing and dust-ridden factories of workers.

Montreal, Canada's largest city, was a textbook case of the problems caused by industrialization. By the end of the nineteenth century, most of its working-class citizens lived in rundown tenements, its infant mortality rate was among the highest in the Western world, and the hierarchy of ethnic privilege was rigidly maintained.

In 1896 Herbert Ames, a businessman and social reformer, conducted a survey of living conditions in Montreal. Ames focused on two areas of the city, areas he labelled "the city below the hill" and "the city above the hill." The former consisted of the part of west-end Montreal bounded by Westmount, the city limits, and the St. Lawrence River; the latter encompassed the high terraces along the base of Mount Royal. The city below the hill was home to about 38 000 people—divided into an almost equal number of French, English, and Irish Canadians; the city above the hill was peopled largely by those of English and Scottish background.

Above the hill, Ames noted, there were "tall and handsome houses, stately churches and well-built schools," while below the hill "the tenement house replaces the single residence, and the factory with its smoking chimney is in evidence on every side." Beautiful parks and abundant greenery added to the charms of the homes in the upper city; below, "one paltry plot of ground, scarce an acre in extent, dignified by the title of Richmond Square, is the only spot where green grass can be seen free of charge." Above the hill, all the homes had modern plumbing and looked out on wide, well-paved, clean streets; below the hill, half the houses lacked running water and made use of pit-in-the-ground privies. Below the hill, population density was more than double the city average, and residents suffered disproportionately from disease, crime, drunkenness, poverty, and early death. Summing up the conditions below the hill, Ames noted that for every 10 families in the area, "One family might secure an entire house to itself, but nine families must needs share theirs with another."[15]

Later studies confirmed the view that there were two cities in Montreal, with the rich and poor living completely different lives. As late as the 1920s, children of Montreal's wealthier families had a much higher life expectancy than those who were born into poor families. The continuing high infant-mortality rate in poor districts of Montreal can be traced in large part to contaminated milk and water. While affluent families could afford to purchase milk that was certified pure, 90 percent of the milk shipped to Montreal in freight cars was unfit for human consumption. The elite were also more likely to be able to afford better food and live in areas served by adequate water, sewage mains, and municipal parks. Moreover, when bad weather or epidemics rendered urban life especially unsafe or uncomfortable, they could escape to hideaways outside the city, like those in Ontario's Kawarthas or along Quebec's North Shore.

Because the rich could avoid most of the problems created by poverty, urban improvements were often a long time coming. It was not until 1926 that the province of Quebec made the pasteurization of milk mandatory, and only the threat posed to wealthy residents by disease helped to encourage some early public health efforts such as compulsory vaccination for smallpox in 1903 and a water filtration plant in 1914.

Toronto, Canada's second-largest city, was only marginally better off than Montreal. Although falling land prices made home ownership possible for an increasing number of Toronto's working families, slum conditions prevailed in the back-lane cottages of St. John's Ward and in areas close to railyards, factories, and packing houses. As in Montreal, Toronto's

In the 1890s, Halifax, like most Canadian cities, switched from horse-drawn to electric streetcars.
Public Archives of Nova Scotia/N-0405

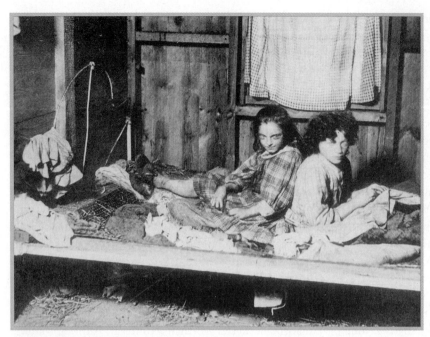

Slum conditions in Montreal at the turn of the twentieth century.
Library and Archives Canada, C-030936

leading citizens spent as much energy bemoaning the morality of those living in poverty as the economic and political conditions that produced their sad condition.

The requirement that a person had to own property to acquire the municipal franchise ensured that local governments attended mainly to the needs of ratepayers in all Canadian cities. Even in small cities such as Charlottetown, where waterworks, sewerage, and improved sanitation appeared in the last two decades of the century, the *Patriot*, a local newspaper, complained in 1874:

> The rich citizen can have his residence in the suburbs where the air and water are both pure, or if he chooses to live in the city he can afford to buy spring water, and he has always a doctor at hand to attend to any of his family who shows any symptoms of being unwell. [The poor man] must bring up his family in the neighbourhood of reeking cesspools and filthy pig-sties. He can not well afford to buy pure water at a very expensive rate; and he has to think twice before he calls in a doctor.[16]

Despite the general recognition by the 1870s of the role of polluted water in carrying disease, many city governments were slow to install better water systems outside wealthy neighbourhoods. Vancouver was an ugly, smelly city without sewers or any hint of planned development in the 1880s. By the late 1890s, the city had acquired a waterworks and extended water mains to most areas. With the mountains supplying pure water, Vancouver's water-related disease problems were minor compared with most cities.

In Winnipeg, just 10 percent of the population had sewers and waterworks in 1890. Only in central Winnipeg, where the commercial elite lived and conducted their business, was the water supply adequate. In the working-class north end, water was delivered to homes but the sewage system emptied into the river, with the result that deadly Red River fever (typhoid) was a continuing problem in the area. The combination of wooden buildings and a poor water supply could translate into uncontrolled fires that destroyed many homes. Winnipeg was not unique in this regard. A major fire left 15 000 people homeless in Saint John in 1877, and 15 years later the homes of 10 000 people were destroyed by fire in St. John's.

The nation's capital was not immune to problems facing urban dwellers. While the city named a health officer in 1874 to demand that householders dispose of garbage, Ottawa had no dump. Smallpox spread through the tenements of Lower Town in 1875. It has been estimated that a quarter of the population of Ottawa were working poor—people able to find work during part of the year, but unemployed and often destitute during the winter. There were also people who could not find work at all: men maimed in mill, construction, and bush accidents; pregnant serving girls; the handicapped and those ill with diseases such as tuberculosis. Both the working poor and the unemployables required aid from private charities to survive when relatives or friends were unable or unavailable to help.

Halifax, with its military base, was unique among Canadian cities. When the British withdrew their troops from Canada in 1871, they retained their garrison in Halifax, which served as Great Britain's naval and military base for the North Atlantic. The bishop of the Church of England declared in 1889 that "the military were a curse to this city and were the cause of a great deal of demoralization among the poor."[17] Since cities without military bases also had demoralized poor in their midst, it is doubtful that the good bishop was correct in laying the entire blame on the military. It was nevertheless the case that grog shops, brothels, and disreputable boarding houses thrived on Barrack Street just below the Citadel and helped sustain the lifestyle of the repeat offenders committed to Rockhead Prison, a substantial octagonal building located in the north end of the city. After Barrack Street was closed to the military and its name changed to South Brunswick in the early 1870s, "soldiertown" drifted to adjacent areas and continued to be a major cause for concern among urban reformers.

CONCLUSION

By the turn of the twentieth century, immigration and urbanization were changing the face of Canada. The influx of settlers, who made their homes primarily in cities and in the western provinces, helped fuel the economic boom that characterized the early 1900s and performed much of the back-breaking labour that made economic growth possible. Immigrants also made Canada a more culturally diverse nation, forcing English, French, and Aboriginal Canadians to reassess their own identities and adjust to the values and practices of newcomers who brought their own ways of doing things. In the end, native-born and immigrant Canadians faced a similar challenge: how to make a living and create a sense of community in a nation in a state of rapid transition.

NOTES

1 Bettina Bradbury, "Children Who Lived with One Parent in 1901," in *Household Counts: Canadian Households and Families in 1901*, eds. Eric W. Sager and Peter Baskerville, (Toronto: University of Toronto Press, 2007), 247–248.

2 Cited in J.W. Dafoe, *Clifford Sifton in Relation to His Times* (Toronto: Macmillan, 1931), 142.

3 Quoted in Reg Whittaker, *Canadian Immigration Policy Since Confederation* (Ottawa: Canadian Historical Association, 1991), 8.

4 Donald H. Avery, *Reluctant Host: Canada's Response to Immigrant Workers, 1896–1994* (Toronto: McClelland & Stewart, 1995), 30.

5 Cited in Jacqueline Hucker, "Temple of the Church of Jesus Christ of the Latter-Day Saints" (Agenda Paper No. 32, Historic Sites and Monuments Board, November 6–7, 1992), 163.

6 Gerald Friesen, *The Canadian Prairies: A History* (Toronto: University of Toronto Press, 1984), 265.

7 *Daily Globe*, 7 June 1882.

8 Cited in James W. St. G. Walker, *Racial Discrimination in Canada: The Black Experience* (Ottawa: Canadian Historical Association, 1985), 4.

9 John Bullen, "Hidden Workers: Child Labour and the Family Economy in Late Nineteenth-Century Urban Ontario," *Labour/Le Travail* 18 (Fall 1986), 181.

10 Joy Parr, *The Gender of Breadwinners: Women, Men, and Change in Two Industrial Towns, 1880–1950* (Toronto: University of Toronto Press, 1990), 94–95.

11 Cited in Robert Harney, "Ethnicity and Neighbourhoods," in *Cities and Urbanization: Canadian Historical Perspectives*, ed. Gilbert A. Stelter (Toronto: Copp Clark Pitman, 1990), 228.

12 Varpu Lindström-Best, *Defiant Sisters: A Social History of Finnish Immigrant Women in Canada* (Toronto: Multicultural History Society of Ontario, 1988), 27.

13 Cited in John W. Bennett and Seena B. Kohl, *Settling the Canadian-American West, 1890–1915: Pioneer Adaptation and Community Building* (Lincoln: University of Nebraska Press, 1995), 68.

14 Cecilia Danysk, *Hired Hands: Labour and the Development of Prairie Agriculture, 1880–1930* (Toronto: McClelland & Stewart, 1995), 71–72.

15 Herbert Brown Ames, *The City Below the Hill* (Toronto: University of Toronto Press, 1972), 103, 105, 48.

16 Quoted in Douglas Baldwin, "'But Not a Drop to Drink': The Struggle for Pure Water," in *Gaslights, Epidemics and Vagabond Cows: Charlottetown in the Victorian Era*, eds. Douglas Baldwin and Thomas Spira (Charlottetown: Ragweed Press, 1988), 110.

17 Cited in Judith Fingard, *The Dark Side of Life in Victorian Halifax* (Porters Lake, NS: Pottersfield Press, 1989), 16.

RELATED READINGS IN THIS SERIES

From Primary Documents CD-ROM, Volume II

Clifford Sifton's Immigration Policy

The Curse of Chinese Immigration: What It Has Done for Other Countries and What It Is Doing for Canada

A Circle of Good Company

Clifford Sifton

Hand-Picked Only

Shut Out

To Deport Undesirable Immigrants

SELECTED READING

On immigration and immigrants, the major surveys are Ninette Kelley and Michael Trebilcock, *The Making of the Canadian Mosaic: A History of Canadian Immigration Policy* (Toronto: University of Toronto Press, 1998); Jean Burnet with Howard Palmer, *"Coming Canadians": An Introduction to the History of Canada's Peoples* (Toronto: McClelland & Stewart, 1988); Dirk Hoerder, *Creating Societies: Immigrant Lives in Canada* (Montreal: McGill-Queen's University Press, 1999); Gerald Tulchinsky, ed., *Immigration in Canada: Historical Perspectives* (Toronto: Copp Clark Longman, 1994); and Franca Iacovetta et al., *A Nation of Immigrants: Women, Workers, and Communities in Canadian History, 1840s–1860s* (Toronto: University of Toronto Press, 1998). Among other key works are Lisa Chilton, *Agents of Empire: British Female Migration to Canada and Australia, 1860s–1930* (Toronto: University of Toronto Press, 2007); David Goutor, *Guarding the Gates: The Canadian Labour Movement and Immigration* (Vancouver: UBC Press, 2007); Donald Avery, *Reluctant Host: Canada's Response to Immigrant Workers, 1896–1994* (Toronto: McClelland & Stewart, 1995); Howard Palmer, *Patterns of Prejudice* (Toronto: McClelland & Stewart, 1982); and Barbara Roberts, *Whence They Came: Deportation from Canada, 1900–1935* (Ottawa: University of Ottawa Press, 1988). Much valuable information on immigration and settlement in this period is condensed in the pamphlets of the Canadian Historical Association's *Canada's Ethnic Groups* series, several of which are cited in this chapter. See also D.J. Hall, *Clifford Sifton*, 2 vols. (Vancouver: UBC Press, 1985). For a thoughtful discussion of the impact of immigration on the land and its people, see Cole Harris, *The Resettlement of British Columbia: Essays on Colonialism and Geographical Change* (Vancouver: UBC Press, 1997). Also see Catherine Cavanaugh and Jeremy Mouat, eds., *Making Western Canada: Essays on European Colonization and Settlement* (Toronto: Garamond Press, 1996); Veronica Strong-Boag et al., eds., *Painting the Maple: Essays on Race, Gender, and the Construction of Canada* (Vancouver: UBC Press, 1998); and Marlene Epp, Franca Iacovetta, and Frances Swyripa, *Sisters or Sojourners? Immigrant, Ethnic, and Racialized Women in Canadian History* (Toronto: University of Toronto Press, 2004).

Publications dealing with specific groups and regions include Orest Martynowych, *The Ukrainian Bloc Settlement in East Central Alberta, 1890–1930: A History* (Edmonton: Alberta Culture, 1985); Lubomir Luciuk and Stella Hryniuk, eds., *Canada's Ukrainians: Negotiating an Identity* (Toronto: University of Toronto Press, 1991); Vadim Kukushkin, *From Peasants to Labourers: Ukrainian and Belarussian Immigration from the Russian Empire to Canada* (Montreal: McGill-Queen's University Press, 2007); Frederick Engelmann, *History of the Austrian Migration to Canada* (Ottawa: Carleton University Press, 1996); George Woodcock and Ivan Avakumovic, *The Doukhobors* (Ottawa: Carleton Library, 1977); Lillian Petroff, *Sojourners and Settlers: The Macedonian Community in Toronto to 1940* (Toronto: University of Toronto Press, 1995); Bruno Ramirez, *The Italians of Montreal: From Sojourning to Settlement, 1900–1921* (Montreal: Éditions du Courant, 1980); John Zucchi, *Toronto Italians* (Montreal: McGill-Queen's University Press, 1988); Irving Abella, *A Coat of Many Colours: Two Centuries of Jewish Life in Canada* (Toronto: Lester and Orpen Dennys, 1990); Gerald Tulchinsky, *Taking Root: The Origins of the Canadian Jewish Community* (Toronto: Lester Publishing, 1992); Hans Lehmann, *The German Canadians, 1750–1937: Immigration, Settlement and Culture* (St. John's: Bassler Gerhard, 1986); Frank H. Epp, *Mennonites in Canada, 1786–1920: The History of a Separate People* (Toronto: Macmillan, 1974); Royden K. Loewen, *Family, Church, and Market: A Mennonite Community in the Old and the New Worlds, 1850–1930* (Toronto: University of Toronto Press, 1993) and *Hidden Worlds: Revisiting the Mennonite Migrants of the 1870s* (Winnipeg: University of Manitoba Press, 2001); Bruno Ramirez, *On the Move: French-Canadian and Italian Migrants in the North Atlantic Economy, 1860–1914* (Toronto: McClelland & Stewart, 1990); Hugh Johnson, *The Voyage of the* Komagata Maru: *The Sikh Challenge to Canada's Colour Bar* (Delhi: Oxford University Press, 1979); Patricia E. Roy, *A White Man's Province: British Columbia Politicians and Chinese and Japanese Immigrants, 1858–1914* (Vancouver: UBC Press, 1989); W. Peter Ward, *White Canada Forever: Popular Attitudes and Public Policy Toward Orientals in British*

Columbia, 2nd ed. (Montreal: McGill-Queen's University Press, 1990); and J. Brian Dawson with Patricia Dawson, *Moon Cakes in Gold Mountain: From China to the Canadian Plains* (Calgary: Detselig, 1991). On child immigrants, see Roy Parker, *Uprooted: The Shipment of Poor Children to Canada, 1867–1917* (Bristol, UK: Policy Press, 2008); Joy Parr, *Labouring Children: British Immigrant Apprentices to Canada, 1896–1924* (Montreal: McGill-Queen's University Press, 1980); and John Bullen, "Hidden Workers: Child Labour and the Family Economy in Late Nineteenth-Century Urban Ontario," *Labour/Le Travail* 18 (Fall 1986), 163–87.

On outmigration, see Bruno Ramirez with Yves Otis, *Crossing the 49th Parallel: Migration from Canada to the United States, 1900–1930* (Ithaca, NY: Cornell University Press, 2001); Yolande Lavoie, *L'émigration des Canadiens aux États-Unis avant 1930* (Montreal: Les Presses de l'Université de Montréal, 1972); Serge Courville, *Immigration, colonisation, et propagande: du rêve Américain au rêve colonial* (Sainte-Foy: Éditions Multimondes, 2002); Betsy Beattie, *Obligation and Opportunity: Single Maritime Women in Boston, 1870–1930* (Montreal: McGill-Queen's University Press, 2000); and Patricia A. Thornton, "The Problem of Outmigration from Atlantic Canada, 1871–1921: A New Look," *Acadiensis* 15, no. 1 (Autumn 1985), 3–34. Jean Barman analyzes the impact of two migrants from eastern Canada on British Columbia in *Sojourning Sisters: The Lives and Letters of Jessie and Annie McQueen* (Toronto: University of Toronto Press, 2003).

For a detailed demographic analysis of Canadian family life based on the 1901 Canadian census, see the essays in Eric W. Sager and Peter Baskerville, eds., *Household Counts: Canadian Households and Families in 1901* (Toronto: University of Toronto Press, 2007). A good case study of social mobility in an Ontario town is David G. Burley, *A Particular Condition in Life: Self-Employment and Social Mobility in Mid-Victorian Brantford, Ontario* (Montreal: McGill-Queen's University Press, 1994). On western settlement, see James Murton, *Creating a Modern Countryside: Liberalism and Land Resettlement in British Columbia* (Vancouver: University of British Columbia Press, 2007); John W. Bennett and Seena B. Kohl, *Settling the Canadian-American West, 1890–1915: Pioneer Adaptation and Community Building* (Lincoln: University of Nebraska Press, 1995); David Jones and Ian Macpherson, eds., *Building Beyond the Homestead* (Calgary: University of Calgary Press, 1988); David Jones, *Empire of Dust: Settling and Abandoning the Prairie Dry Belt* (Edmonton: University of Alberta Press, 1987); Paul Voisey, *Vulcan: The Making of a Prairie Community* (Toronto: University of Toronto Press, 1988); Elizabeth B. Mitchell, *In Western Canada Before the War:*

Impressions of Early Twentieth Century Prairie Communities (Saskatoon: Western Producer Prairie Books, 1981); David Breen, *The Canadian Prairie West and the Ranching Frontier* (Toronto: University of Toronto Press, 1983); Sarah Carter et al., *Unsettled Pasts: Reconceiving the West Through Women's History* (Vancouver: University of British Columbia Press, 2006); Susan Jackel, ed., *A Flannel Shirt and Liberty: British Gentlewomen in the Canadian West* (Vancouver: UBC Press, 1982); Frances Swyripa, *Wedded to the Cause: Ukrainian-Canadian Women and Ethnic Identity, 1891–1991* (Toronto: University of Toronto Press, 1993); Eliane Silverman, *The Last Best West: Women on the Alberta Frontier, 1880–1930* (Montreal: Eden Press, 1984); and Catherine A. Cavanaugh and Randi R. Warne, eds., *Telling Tales: Essays in Western Women's History* (Vancouver: UBC Press, 2000). See also two memoirs: Nellie McClung, *Clearing in the West* (New York: Revell, 1936) and Georgina Binnie-Clark, *Wheat and Women* (Toronto: University of Toronto Press, 1979).

On city life, see the works by Bettina Bradbury, Terry Copp, Paul Craven, Judith Fingard, and Bryan D. Palmer cited in Chapter 5. See also G. Stelter and A.F.J. Artibise, eds., *The Canadian City: Essays in Urban History* (Toronto: Copp Clark Pitman, 1984); A.F.J. Artibise, ed., *Town and City: Aspects of Western Canadian Urban Development* (Regina: University of Regina, 1981); and J.M.S. Careless, *The Rise of Cities: Canada Before 1914* (Ottawa: Canadian Historical Association, 1978). A series of illustrated urban histories published by James Lorimer is useful for studying the growth of the late-nineteenth-century city. Included are *Winnipeg* by Alan Artibise (1977); *Calgary* by Max Foran (1978); *Vancouver* by Patricia Roy (1980); *Toronto to 1918* by J.M.S. Careless (1984); *Hamilton* by John C. Weaver (1984); and *Ottawa* by John H. Taylor (1986). Also see Bettina Bradbury and Tamara Myers, eds., *Negotiating Identities in 19th- and 20th-Century Montreal* (Vancouver: University of British Columbia Press, 2005); Richard Harris, *Unplanned Suburbs: Toronto's American Tragedy, 1900 to 1950* (Baltimore: Johns Hopkins University Press, 1996) and *Creeping Conformity: How Canada Became Suburban, 1900–1960* (Toronto: University of Toronto Press, 2004); Robert Lewis, *Manufacturing Montreal: The Making of an Industrial Landscape* (Montreal: McGill-Queen's University Press, 2001); Jill Wade, *Houses for All: The Struggle for Social Housing in Vancouver, 1919–1950* (Vancouver: UBC Press, 1994); Doug Baldwin and Thomas Spira, eds., *Gaslights, Epidemics and Vagabond Cows: Charlottetown in the Victorian Era* (Charlottetown: Ragweed, 1988); John English and Kenneth McLaughlin, *Kitchener: An Illustrated History* (Waterloo, ON: Wilfrid Laurier University Press, 1983); Paul André Linteau, *Maisonneuve: Comment des promoteurs fabriquent une ville*

(Montreal: Boréal, 1981); Robert A.J. McDonald, *Making Vancouver: Class, Status and Social Boundaries, 1863–1913* (Vancouver: UBC Press, 1996); Judith Fingard, *The Dark Side of Life in Victorian Halifax* (Porters Lake, NS: Pottersfield Press, 1989); and Judith Fingard, Janet Guildford, and David Sutherland, *Halifax: The First 250 Years* (Halifax: Formac, 1999). An examination of legal and police systems can be found in John C. Weaver, *Crimes, Constables and the Courts: Order and Transgression in a Canadian City, 1816–1970* (Montreal: McGill-Queen's University Press, 1995). A critical study of law-making can be found in Carolyn Strange and Tina Loo, *Making Good: Law and Moral Regulation in Canada, 1867–1939* (Toronto: University of Toronto Press, 1997), while policing generally

is treated in Greg Marquis, *Policing Canada's Century* (Toronto: University of Toronto Press, 1993).

Several studies of regions of Quebec address issues of mobility in this period, including Gérard Bouchard, *Quelques arpents d'Amérique: population, économie, famille au Saguenay, 1838–1971* (Montreal: Boréal, 1996); J.I. Little, *Nationalism, Capitalism, and Colonization in Nineteenth-Century Quebec: The Upper St. Francis District* (Montreal: McGill-Queen's University Press, 1989); and Peter Gossage, *Families in Transition: Industry and Population in Saint-Hyacinthe* (Montreal: McGill-Queen's University Press, 1999). Racism in law and culture is discussed in Constance Backhouse, *Colour Coded: A Legal History of Racism in Canada, 1900–1950* (Toronto: University of Toronto Press and The Osgoode Society, 1999).

CHAPTER 7

Community Responses to the Age of Industry, 1867–1921

TIMELINE

1870	First branch of the Young Women's Christian Association established in Saint John
1872	Trade Union Act removes prohibition against unions
1874	Woman's Christian Temperance Union of Canada and Dominion Grange founded
1876	Toronto Women's Literary Club established
1878	Canada Temperance Act (Scott Act) passed
1879	Provincial Workmen's Association founded
1883	Trades and Labour Congress founded
1885	Banff National Park and Rocky Mountain Park established
1886	Royal Commission on the Relations of Labor and Capital appointed; morality department established in Toronto
1892	Criminal Code outlaws contraceptives and abortifacients
1893	National Council of Women of Canada founded; Wilfred Grenfell opens first mission at Battle Harbour, Labrador
1897	Victorian Order of Nurses established
1898	National referendum on prohibition
1901	Territorial Grain Growers' Association founded
1902	Trades and Labour Congress formally affiliated with American Federation of Labor
1907	Industrial Disputes Investigation Act (Lemieux Act); Lord's Day Act passed; Moral and Social Reform Council founded
1908	Fishermen's Protective Union founded in Newfoundland
1909	Canadian Commission on Conservation founded; Cooperative Union of Canada founded
1909–11	Twenty-two-month strike by coal miners in Springhill, Nova Scotia
1914	United Farmers of Ontario established

The farmers of the prairie lands are massing in their might
Exulting in a Principle, a cause for which they fight;
The sacred cause of Justice, the establishment of Right
And Equal Rights to all.

Refrain:
Oh! 'Tis time to get together;
Join and help us get together;
We have vowed to stand together,
For the day of Peace and Right.

The farmers of the prairie lands have right upon their side,
The platform is the people's—democratic, nation-wide;
Their cause, the ancient cause for which brave-hearted men have died—
Of Equal Rights to all.[1]

This rallying cry, sung to the tune of "The Battle Hymn of the Republic," was popular among farmers in the Canadian West, many of whom advocated cooperatives as a means of reforming an economic system that seemed to be stacked against them. The cooperative movement was only one of many organizational activities that drew the support of Canadians in the early decades of the twentieth century. Hallmarks of an engaged citizenry, voluntary organizations laid the foundations for a strong civil society in industrializing Canada. Not only did they respond in a timely fashion to the needs of their supporters and provide forums in which new ideas could be debated, they also exerted strong pressure on governments and corporations to address the dislocation caused by industrial development, urban growth, and rural depopulation. In this chapter, we explore the progressive impulse

Beer parlour, Boisetown, New Brunswick, 1912.
National Archives of New Brunswick/P145-61

that inspired this organizational activity and its dramatic impact on the new nation.

THE PROGRESSIVE IMPULSE

In the early years of confederation, reformers commonly blamed the poor for their own plight, observing that people needing assistance to get by often drank too much or failed to attend church. Ignoring the economic causes of human misery, reformers emphasized the need for self-discipline and better work habits. Able-bodied men were often required to work for charity, usually at breaking stones or sawing wood. If the poor would just "shape up," the conservatives argued, they

Toronto Department of Health well-baby clinics instructed new mothers on how to care for their infants.
City of Toronto Archives/Series 372/DPW 32-234

would soon be on the road to living healthier and happier lives.

By the turn of the century, many "progressive" thinking people had come to the conclusion that reforming the individual would not produce a reformed society. Larger forces, it was clear, were a cause of destitution, and the power of the state would be necessary to achieve deep and lasting changes. Progressivism drew together an impressive coalition of forces, including professionals, journalists, church leaders, union organizers, and women's rights activists. Through their voluntary agencies and carefully documented studies, they shed a bright light on the darkest corners of Canadian society and promoted the view that, through judicious laws, scientific management, and reformed political structures, everyone could enjoy the benefits of the industrial system.

Churches played a major role in promoting progressive reform efforts. By the turn of the century, Methodists, Presbyterians, and Baptists, in particular, had adopted what is termed the "social gospel" approach to their work. While still concerned with spiritual salvation and social purity, they expanded their charitable activities to address the appalling conditions created by the industrial system. Protestant churches cooperated with union leaders, through the Lord's Day Alliance, to pressure the federal government to legislate Sunday observance. Passed in 1907, the Lord's Day Act banned paid employment, shopping, and commercial leisure activities on Sunday, a policy the churches argued not only conformed to Canada's Christian beliefs but also gave working people a day of rest.

Canadian churches established missions, labour churches, and settlement houses in the inner cities to minister to the spiritual and physical needs of the working class. In Halifax, the Methodist Church's Jost Mission reached out to working-class mothers, while the Fred Victor Mission in Toronto ministered to the needs of destitute people. Between 1907 and 1913, Methodist minister J.S. Woodsworth served as superintendent of Winnipeg's All People's Mission, which catered to the city's culturally diverse immigrant population. His surveys of social conditions in Winnipeg, *Strangers Within Our Gates* (1909) and *My Neighbor* (1911), offered sensitive analyses of the situation facing his clients, but they also revealed the condescending attitude toward immigrants and the poor that typified many of those who championed the progressive movement.

Methodist and Presbyterian churches established social reform agencies that came together in 1907 as the Moral and Social Reform Council of Canada. In 1913, the council changed its name to the Social Service Council of Canada and hosted a congress in Ottawa the following year. The program, with sessions on such topics as child welfare, commercialized vice, urban and rural problems, and prison reform, testified to the broad range of interests that motivated the social gospellers. Wartime tensions would drive a wedge between the reformers and the radicals in the social gospel movement, but in 1914 great plans were afoot for a mass effort to establish "God's kingdom on earth."

At the forefront of many reform initiatives was an army of health professionals led by medical doctors and nurses. They argued that public health should be a priority of reform and provided municipal officials and school boards with scientific evidence of the need for vaccinations, medical inspection, and better nutrition. Throughout the country, energies were marshalled to build new hospitals, establish clinics for young mothers and their babies, and teach school children that "Cleanliness is next to Godliness." Campaigns against smoking and spitting—both connected for those who pursued the popular pastime of chewing tobacco—encouraged habits that would lead to healthier Canadians.

The Temperance Movement

Alcohol had long been a favoured target of conservative reformers, who saw it as the cause of many of Canada's social problems. Over the course of the nineteenth century, the movement to encourage temperance in the consumption of alcohol had given way to a demand that the state impose laws to prohibit its manufacture, sale, and consumption. This transition from the personal to the political prompted a mass movement for legislative action. By the end of the nineteenth century, Protestant churches, led by the Baptists, Methodists, and Presbyterians, forged a formidable alliance with

voluntary associations such as the Sons of Temperance and the Woman's Christian Temperance Union (WCTU). In their zeal to achieve prohibition, they conducted a vigorous education campaign, solicited signatures for enormous petitions, and lobbied politicians at all levels of government.

Pressed by the mounting support for action, the federal government passed the Canada Temperance Act in 1878. Known as the Scott Act, it allowed municipalities to hold a plebiscite to determine whether liquor could be sold within their boundaries. Many areas of Canada voted "dry," and the consumption of alcohol actually declined, but it never totally stopped. A royal commission investigation reported in 1895 that, with bootleggers and a dramatic increase in medical prescriptions, liquor flowed almost as freely in supposedly dry municipalities as in "wet" ones.

There is no doubt that drinking was a real problem in early industrializing Canada, where liquor was consumed in great quantities. As a result, temperance in the consumption of alcohol was supported by Roman Catholics and Protestants and by people in all classes and regions of the country. What separated the "wets" from the "drys" was not the problem itself but the means of addressing it. For many people, the demand for state intervention went too far. This was the position taken in Quebec, where the Roman Catholic Church scorned state intervention on the issue and where people were less likely than other Canadians in other provinces to exercise the local option to ban alcohol.

Prime Minister Laurier tried to avoid immediate action by agreeing to a national referendum on the issue. Held in 1898, it yielded a predictable result: a majority for the drys in every province outside Quebec. The relatively small overall majority and a low voter turnout allowed Laurier to sidestep the issue that bitterly divided the country. Undaunted, prohibitionists turned to their provincial governments for action on the liquor trade. They also demanded a wholesale reform of the political system, including giving women, who were believed to be more supportive of the temperance cause, the right to vote.

Legislating Morality

Most conservative reformers focused on the moral issues associated with the problems they were trying to address. Nowhere was this approach more diligently pursued than in Toronto, which earned the appellation "Toronto the Good" for its earnest efforts to legislate morality. In 1886, Toronto's reforming mayor, William Howland, established a morality department in the city police force. Anyone involved in prostitution, the illicit sale of liquor, gambling, or the mistreatment of children and animals was hauled into court by the new morality squad. Under the charge of vagrancy, young women innocently walking on the streets at night could be interrogated by the morality police.

Women and children were the special concern of moral reformers, who had difficulty accepting the freedom from parental and patriarchal control that city life encouraged. As Carolyn Strange points out in her study of the "girl problem" in Toronto, that city took the lead in the social purity movement, creating a flurry of institutions designed specifically to focus on the plight of women and female children. A children's aid society, two industrial schools for girls, a children's court, and a women's court were all established in the period between 1880 and 1910. Women in Toronto also had access to the expanded services of the Young Women's Christian Association (YWCA), Big Sisters, the WCTU, and a variety of "safe" settlement houses.[2] Despite this energetic response, young women in Toronto continued to ply their trade as prostitutes, practise infanticide, and sink into destitution. Journalist C.S. Clark, in an 1898 exposé entitled *Toronto the Good*, shocked the citizens of Toronto with his lurid account of the vice that flourished under the noses of morality department officers.

Sexual Purity

Class and racial biases were reflected in the pseudo-scientific theories of eugenics, which gained wide currency among progressives. Drawing on scientific findings relating to reproduction in the plant and animal world, eugenicists argued that society could be improved by preventing people with undesirable mental and physical traits from reproducing. Those who embraced eugenics believed that inherited traits rather than social conditions predisposed people to poverty and crime. Because of such views, reform leaders such as Reverend S.D. Chown, moderator of the Methodist

Church, could make statements such as the following without fear of being challenged:

> The immigration question is the most vital one in Canada today, as it has to do with the purity of our national life-blood. It is foolish to dribble away the vitality of our own country in a vain endeavour to assimilate the world's non-adjustable, profligate, and indolent social parasites. . . . It is most vital to our nation's life that we should ever remember that quality is of greater value than quantity and that character lies at the basis of national stability and progress.[3]

Concern for racial purity and social control led the progressives to focus on the reform of sexual practices. Although 1892 Criminal Code legislation prohibiting birth control and abortifacients made it difficult for progressives to champion eugenics, they were determined to educate people in sexual hygiene and self-control. The Methodist Church, for example, distributed sex manuals targeted at various age levels for women and men. While criticized today as moralistic and wrong-headed, they incorporated the thinking of the time in the field of "sexology" and moved some distance from the puritanical approach to sex characteristic of the Victorian age.

Support for controlling sexuality sprang from a number of motives. With the rise of prostitution and the increasing incidence of venereal disease, many Canadians felt that some form of social control over sexuality was necessary. Women in particular were eager to eliminate the double standard of sexual behaviour by extending to men the strict codes that governed female sexuality. For most reformers, a lifelong monogamous marriage—what the WCTU described as "the pure white life for two"—was the bedrock of the nation. With correct family formation, reformers argued, a wide range of social evils would be eliminated, including divorce, wife and child abuse, sexually transmitted disease, and prostitution.

The desire for social control and scientific analysis led to same-sex relationships being labelled "homosexual" and deemed unnatural. Social purity advocates insisted that homosexuals be put in jail and were instrumental in having homosexuality punished more vigorously under the Criminal Code. Meanwhile, the medical profession, taking what was believed to be a more progressive approach, began describing same-sex

Wilfred Grenfell

In Newfoundland, the social gospel movement was dramatically represented by the mission of Wilfred Grenfell. Born in England in 1865, Grenfell was a student at London Medical School when he was converted to active Christianity by American evangelist Dwight L. Moody. He subsequently joined the Royal National Mission to Deep-Sea Fishermen. In 1892, he visited the coasts of Newfoundland and Labrador, where he saw a great opportunity to combine medical and missionary work among people who rarely saw a doctor or minister. The following year, he opened his first mission at Battle Harbour, and by the end of the century had established his mission headquarters at St. Anthony's on the northern tip of Newfoundland. Backed by supporters in the United States, Canada, and Great Britain, Grenfell expanded his activities to include nursing stations, schools, cooperatives, and an orphanage. His well-publicized efforts to bring services to isolated areas—including a close brush with death on an ice floe in 1908—made him a popular hero and enabled him to earn more money for his mission through the lecture circuit. Following his marriage to a Chicago heiress in 1909, Grenfell spent less time in missionary work, which was carried on by dedicated men and women inspired by Grenfell's pioneering efforts.

Wilfred Grenfell.
Courtesy of Grenfell Historic Properties

attraction as a form of insanity requiring confinement in a lunatic asylum rather than a prison. Practising homosexuals could face either fate in a society that still subscribed to the view that sex should be confined only to married couples. In Victoria, two men convicted of sodomy in 1891 were each sentenced to 15 years in prison, a sentence later commuted to seven years. Sentences of a year or two were more common. Sometimes the offenders were simply asked to leave town.

Environmental Reform

Progressives also took up the cause of environmental reform, arguing that Canada lagged behind other industrialized nations in attending to the problems of pollution and resource depletion. The example of the United States inspired the federal government to set aside Banff Hot Springs Reserve and Rocky Mountain Park for public use in 1885. Following the North American Conservation Conference called by President Theodore Roosevelt in 1909, the federal government established a Canadian Commission of Conservation (CCC). Under the energetic direction of Clifford Sifton, the CCC investigated everything from fur farming and migratory birds to urban planning and power development.

Frustration with jurisdictional disputes and federal inaction caused Sifton to resign in 1918, and the commission was abolished three years later. Nevertheless, a number of the issues it raised continued to preoccupy environmental reformers, and its achievements were considerable. It produced more than 200 studies of environmental conditions, encouraged the creation of parks and game reserves, inspired the passage of laws to protect migratory birds and wild animals, and forged a link between conservation and urban planning that left a legacy in a number of Canadian cities.

Urban Reform

The "city beautiful" movement, with its notions of rational planning, handsome buildings, and public spaces, appealed to many progressives. Originating in Europe and the United States, the movement soon had Canadian converts, including Herbert Ames, who, as we have seen, catalogued Montreal's problems in his book *The City Below the Hill*. Urban reformers established their own voluntary associations, such as Montreal's City Improvement League, and enlisted the support of the Union of Canadian Municipalities. Urban planning experts argued that changing cities would also change the people who lived in them.

Determined to eliminate urban slums, progressives advanced programs for subsidized housing that would replace overcrowded tenements. Ames recommended that the City of Montreal enter into arrangements with developers to build working-class homes at cost, with a 5-percent profit factored into the calculations. Although the scheme failed to catch on with developers or the city, progressives continued to press their case for improved urban housing. The "garden city" movement in Great Britain, with its most celebrated example in Letchworth Garden City north of London, offered a model for action. While the city beautiful movement emphasized urban aesthetics, garden city planners stressed health and housing. Parks, playgrounds, sewers, public baths, water filtration systems, and planned housing developments, it was argued, would offer urban dwellers better health and, by extension, make them better citizens.

Progressive reformers were suspicious of private utilities in water, power, telephones, and transport, arguing for government control of such essential services. Municipal and provincial governments in the first decade of the twentieth century often responded to pressure from urban reformers to take over utilities from private developers. Montreal's private utilities weathered the tide of consumer grievance, while Edmonton's streetcars, electricity, and telephones became publicly owned. In Toronto, Bell survived as a private monopoly, but the Toronto Transit Commission assumed control of the street railways.

As progressives encountered resistance from municipal governments, they became critical of political processes. The ratepayers, critics argued, had become passive pawns in the hands of corrupt developers who could influence voting in the poorer wards. To counter the power of "special interests," cities were urged to establish boards of control elected on a city-wide franchise. Because middle-class voters were more likely to vote than the working class, they could influence the results in a city-wide election, thereby putting an end to corrupt ward politics. Boards of control were adopted in Winnipeg (1906), Ottawa (1907), Montreal (1909), Hamilton (1910), and London (1914) prior to the First World War. A more extreme attempt to wrest power from the masses was the trend of delegating authority to "expert" city managers and appointed

MORE TO THE STORY

Urban Parks

Even before the "city beautiful" and "garden city" movements began to have a major impact on urban design, Canadian cities had begun to sprout parks and open spaces within their boundaries. In 1874, Montreal invited Frederick Law Olmstead, who designed New York City's Central Park in the 1860s, to develop Mount Royal according to his design principles. One of Olmstead's pupils, Frederick Todd, established a practice in Montreal and designed projects from Newfoundland to British Columbia. Like his mentor, Todd believed that nature had to be carefully integrated into the park environment and blended into a unified urban plan. Such views inspired the City of Halifax to take over the Public Gardens from the local horticultural society in 1875 and the City of Vancouver to create Stanley Park in 1889, named for the governor-general. Manitoba created a public parks board in 1893. By the turn of the century, most cities were creating parks, large and small, as "breathing spaces" for people wearied by the hustle and bustle of urban life.

commissioners, policies adopted in Edmonton in 1904, Saint John in 1908, and a few years later in Regina, Saskatoon, and Prince Albert.

The progressive agenda gained limited support from the poorer districts of many cities. In Montreal, for example, the Francophone working class, resentful of the self-serving policies of the Anglophone elite who took little interest in their well-being, gave a resounding victory to populist mayoral candidate Médéric Martin in 1914.

The Union Movement

At the time of confederation, unionized labour was still too weak to exert much political pressure. The Trade Union Act of 1872 removed common-law prohibitions against unions as combinations in restraint of trade, but no laws forced employers to bargain collectively with their employees or prevented employers from dismissing employees who supported unionization.

Despite the obstacles, workers organized resistance. In 1871, Toronto printers struck all of the city's newspapers in an attempt to force the nine-hour day on the entire publishing industry. The publishers, led by Liberal Party notable George Brown, successfully prosecuted the strikers for seditious conspiracy, while 10 000 people paraded in support of the accused and their strike demands. Throughout 1872, the movement for the nine-hour day reverberated throughout industrial Canada, only to be quelled by the crushing recession of 1873. While the movement failed to achieve its objective, it produced a degree of solidarity among workers that re-emerged once the recession lifted.

In the 1880s and 1890s, the strike became firmly established as labour's chief method of attempting to win improvements for workers. A key player in the strike wave was the Noble and Holy Order of the Knights of Labor. The Knights originated in 1869 among Philadelphia garment cutters concerned about the loss of worker control in their industry and spread quickly across the United States. By the early 1880s, it had a foothold in Canada. Unlike craft unions, which organized workers according to their trade, the Knights were open to all workers regardless of skill and encouraged workers to support each other's struggles.

It was not only employers who recoiled at the class consciousness promoted by the Knights. Craft union leaders claimed that the exclusive right of workers to practise certain trades would be whittled away if the Knights succeeded in developing all-inclusive "industrial" unions. During the recession of the late 1880s, craft unions began to force workers to choose between the Knights and separate craft unions. The Knights retained many locals, especially in Quebec, but their isolation increased as the Trades and Labour Congress (TLC), created in 1883, emerged as the major political voice of Canadian labour.

Dominated by craft-based unions, the TLC fought against industrial unions almost as hard as it did against employer intransigence. It also adopted the policy of its counterpart in the United States—the American Federation of Labor—of calling for higher wages and improved working conditions rather than for radical changes to the capitalist system. In 1902, at a meeting in Berlin, Ontario, the TLC formally affiliated with the American Federation of Labor. It then proceeded to expel industrial unions such as the Knights of Labor from its ranks and to consolidate its position as the dominant labour organization in the country. TLC exiles established a rival organization, the National Trades and Labour Congress, in 1907. Although its numbers were small, it offered a nationalist alternative for Canada's working men and women.

Labour, Culture, and Region

During Canada's rise to industrial maturity, labour organizations were fragmented along regional and cultural lines. In Nova Scotia, the Provincial Workmen's Association (PWA), established in 1879, emerged as the most powerful voice of the province's working class. Militant in its early years, the PWA shut down all the province's mines on two occasions, and its fiercely independent locals waged over 70 strikes before 1900. When strike activity increased during the first decade of the twentieth century, Maritime coal miners turned to the even more radical American-based United Mine Workers (UMW) of America to help them in their struggles.

Miner militancy on the East Coast was matched in British Columbia, where the Mutual Protective Society was established in 1877 among workers at Dunsmuir, Diggle and Company. The society protested wage cuts and the short-weighing of coal on company scales (the workers were paid by the ton) and closed down the Wellington mine on Vancouver Island. Robert Dunsmuir, the province's leading capitalist,

Bunkhouse men experienced some of the worst working and living conditions in industrializing Canada.
Library and Archives of Canada/PA-115432

convinced the government to use the militia to force miners back to work, but a long history of miner organization and militancy in British Columbia had begun. By 1905–06, the UMW had gained a foothold in the coal fields of southwestern British Columbia and Alberta.

In Quebec, Francophone workers were encouraged to look for assistance from the Roman Catholic Church rather than from secular unions, which the church condemned as foreign-dominated and materialistic. Church-sponsored unions were initially conservative in their approach to labour rights, but priests assigned to the unions soon became sensitive to the plight of working people. In 1921, Catholic unions came together as the Confédération des travailleurs catholiques du Canada with an outlook similar to that of the TLC.

While many unionized workers held their own in the workplace, the position of common labourers remained precarious. The most vulnerable among male wage labourers were the navvies—men who worked in construction gangs that built the railways and other public works. Living in grim bunkhouses and eating stale bread, a navvy had experiences of the work world far removed from those of the proud craftsman. Such workers were ripe for the message of Industrial Workers of the World (IWW), an American-based organization founded in 1905 that rejected both the parliamentary process and traditional unionism. The Wobblies, as

they were called, focused on the strike as the most effective political weapon and urged their members to walk off the job collectively when a fellow worker was unjustly treated by an employer.

Women were largely excluded from labour organizations, but the exclusion did not stop them from protesting labour practices in the trades they dominated. In 1900, female spoolers in Valleyfield's cotton industry walked off the job when apprentices were hired to perform their work. The women had limited bargaining power because textile workers could easily be replaced, but women in more skilled occupations also fared poorly in their confrontations with management. In 1907, over 400 Bell telephone operators in Toronto went on strike to protest a reduction in hourly rates for their highly skilled and physically taxing work. The strikers agreed to submit their grievances to a federal arbitration commission, whose members were more concerned about the impact of dangerous working conditions on the maternal potential of the women—most of whom were between the ages of 17 and 22—than the ability of the women to make a living wage.

Since most Asians and blacks were excluded from unions, they worked in manual jobs, many of them seasonal and part-time, which made it difficult for them to form their own unions. One exception was the occupation of railway porters. Although their hours were long and the pay low, working on the trains was almost a rite of passage for many African-Canadian men. In 1918, porters of the Canadian Northern Railway, then in the process of becoming part of the CNR system, organized Canada's first black union, the Order of Sleeping Car Porters. The Canadian Brotherhood of Railway Employees initially refused to accept the union but relented in 1919, thus becoming the first craft union to abolish racial restrictions on membership.

Unions made their presence felt during Canada's rise to industrial maturity, but they had little success in restructuring capitalist development in the interests of labour or in expanding their membership. Only 5.6 percent of the labour force in Ontario and 8.4 in Quebec was organized by 1911. While some of the difficulties can be attributed to the conservative agenda promoted by the international unionism of the TLC, this was only partly the cause. Union leaders were often overtly racist and sexist, thereby alienating a significant proportion of their potential membership. Many employers, harking back to the paternalism that they felt characterized pre-industrial relations, tried to earn the loyalty of their skilled and experienced employees by sponsoring company picnics, excursions to nearby tourist sites, and even company bands. When such inducements failed to work, employers used force, calling upon governments to send in police, militia, and troops to put down strikes and coerce labour into compliance.

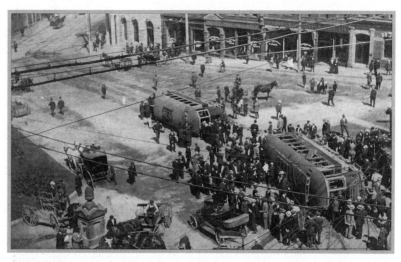

As this photo of the 1914 Street Railway Strike in Saint John suggests, peaceful demonstrations sometimes led to violence when police tried to disperse demonstrators.
Provincial Archives of New Brunswick Harold Wright Collection/P338-200

Labour and the State

Alarmed by the growing class conflict, governments at all levels tried to find a "middle way" that would reduce the worst excesses of the capitalist system while leaving its structure largely intact. The Report of the Royal Commission on the Relations of Labor and Capital, submitted in 1889, provided a wealth of information on the shocking conditions in Canadian factories, but the commissioners' recommendations yielded few immediate reforms other than the declaration in 1894 of a holiday—Labour Day—for Canada's working people.

One Hundred and Two Muffled Voices

The royal commissioners studying the relations between labour and capital in Canada between 1886 and 1889 heard the testimony of nearly 1800 witnesses. Only 102 of those who testified were women. Although women made up over 20 percent of the paid labour force in 1891, nobody on the commission was very interested in hearing from them. As historian Susan Mann Trofimenkoff revealed, it took a great deal of courage for working people generally and women in particular to speak before a formal body such as a royal commission.[4] Saying something that offended employers might threaten a worker's job. Nearly half of the women testified anonymously; only 30 out of nearly 1700 male witnesses did so.

The most dramatic testimony relating to women's work came from a woman identified as Georgina Loiselle. Beaten by her employer for her "impertinent" refusal to make a hundred extra cigars, she was still employed at the factory five years later when she gave her testimony. Her employer justified his behaviour to the commissioners on the grounds that "her mother had prayed me . . . to correct her in the best way I could." With three of Georgina's brothers also employed by the company, the factory's owner had assumed the role of disciplinarian to the fatherless Loiselle children. Georgina was 18 at the time of the beating, and no one, including Georgina herself, seemed particularly surprised by her employer's brutality.

When the commissioners submitted their report, they indicated much greater concern over the moral consequences of women working in unchaperoned settings and using common washrooms with men than they did about the poor salaries and working conditions that were uniformly the lot of wage-earning women in Victorian Canada.

In 1900, the federal Liberals established the Department of Labour and hired a university-trained labour relations expert, William Lyon Mackenzie King, to be its first deputy minister. In 1907, King helped to engineer the Industrial Disputes Investigation Act (Lemieux Act), which prohibited strikes and lockouts in public utilities and mines until the dispute had been investigated by a tripartite board of arbitration representing labour, capital, and government. By establishing a compulsory cooling-off period, the act deprived organized labour of its strongest weapon, the surprise strike, without any compensatory protection against retaliation by the employer, such as hiring strikebreakers. The TLC asked the Conservatives to repeal the act when they were elected to power in 1911, but Robert Borden let the legislation stand.

THE RADICAL RESPONSE

By 1914, a growing number of Canadians were pursuing more radical visions than those championed by progressives and labourites, whose main goal was to impose rational order on capitalism. Those advocating socialism were in the forefront of an international movement to abolish a system that they believed put property ahead of people and pitted labour against capital in an uneven struggle refereed by a state clearly biased in favour of the rich. Socialists disagreed on the best means of achieving a society where each would receive according to his or her needs, but the goal nevertheless had wide appeal in early industrializing Canada.

The socialist movement that took root in Canada was a strange amalgam of Marxism, Christian socialism, and reformism. At one end of the spectrum, radicals such as the IWW preached syndicalism, the view that labourers should join forces to overthrow the yoke of capitalism. These hardliners argued that a cataclysmic conflict between labour and capital was the only way the new order could be born. In contrast, the Christian Socialist League, whose leading spokesman was G. Weston Wrigley, maintained that Christ was the first socialist and advocated a more gradual approach to a socialist utopia.

One of the earliest spokesmen for the gradual approach was T. Phillips Thompson. Born into a Quaker family in Newcastle-on-Tyne in 1843, Thompson arrived in Canada at the age of 14. After studying law, he became a journalist and intellectual based in Toronto. Unlike most Anglo-Canadians, he sympathized with the Francophone and Métis minorities and advocated the abolition of the monarchy. A free thinker, he was influenced by the work of American critic Henry George, whose book *Progress and Poverty*, published in 1879, caused a stir throughout Canada. George's message—that industrialism had unleashed an insupportable burden of poverty and distress—was not new, but his solution was: a tax on the property of the rich. Dubbed the "single tax," it had the virtue of simplicity.

Thompson met George on several occasions and incorporated his ideas into a book entitled *The Politics of Labour*, published in 1887. "In the place of the monopolistic rule, which in the true sense now governs the people by prescribing whether they shall work or not, and how they shall receive," Thompson reasoned, "let us have a representative, popular recognized government, conducted on business principles, doing the same thing not for the profit of a few but in the interests of all."[5] While taxing profits and expanding the role of the state may not sound very radical to people today, such ideas were roundly condemned in the nineteenth century.

With the arrival of thousands of immigrants with a tradition of socialist politics, efforts to achieve unity in the cause of socialism were further complicated. No sooner had local socialist groups on the West Coast come together to produce the Socialist Party of Canada in 1904 than they were weakened by the defection of members who founded the more moderate Social Democratic Party (SDP) in 1907. With its language locals, the SDP appealed to Finnish, Ukrainian, and Russian communities on the Prairies, who felt excluded from the established political parties. The SDP also proved more open to women's issues, including the problems of unpaid domestic labour and prohibition, than the Socialist Party of Canada, whose leaders considered such issues as detracting from "scientific" socialist goals.

THE RURAL RESPONSE

While cities served as a focus for reform, people living in rural communities were far from passively resigned to the changes taking place around them. The prohibition movement, for example, was widely supported in rural areas of eastern Canada. When the Prairies filled up with settlers, the region added weight to the rural voice that had been losing ground in the decades following confederation. Western farmers began to question the power of eastern-based institutions such as railways, banks, and government. In the eastern provinces, rural people were also disturbed by the growing power of urban-based institutions, and their concerns focused on the depopulation of rural areas, which had few of the amenities available to their city-bound neighbours.

The transformation of rural life and the flight of large numbers of people to the city also troubled many urban dwellers. In Montreal, Henri Bourassa wrote frequently and eloquently about the danger to society of abandoning the values associated with rural life. So, too, did Andrew Macphail, a Montreal-based medical doctor who edited *University Magazine* between 1907 and 1920. Macphail looked back nostalgically upon his childhood in rural Prince Edward Island and lamented the rapid disappearance of what he saw as a superior way of life. In 1912, the Board of Moral and Social Reform and Evangelism of the Presbyterian Church established a summer school on the "country church problem" and asked John MacDougall, a pastor from Spencerville, Ontario, to lecture on the topic. His lectures were incorporated in *Rural Life in Canada: Its Trend and Tasks*, a publication that documented the crisis apparently facing rural Canada. For all of these men, rural living was as crucial to the moral and spiritual well-being of the nation as it was to physical survival and food production.

The flight of women from the farm was a particular concern of reformers. When markets became the focus of production, the balance of power in the family enterprise shifted in favour of men. Profits from farming, if there were any, were more likely to be invested in farm machinery than in appliances to relieve domestic drudgery. The situation in the West—Canada's much-vaunted land of opportunity—was particularly telling.

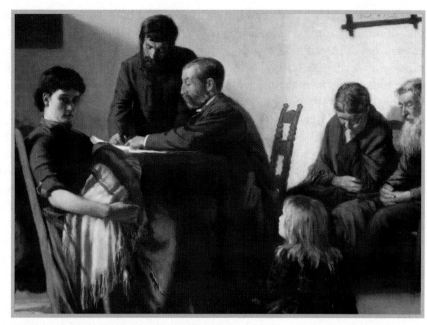

Mortgaging the Homestead, by George Reid, 1890.
National Gallery of Canada

Discouraged by discriminatory homestead laws, unequal inheritance patterns, and the unending domestic toil that confronted them, women resisted taking up the farming life. Desperate bachelor farmers advertised for women to join them on the farm and many accepted their proposals, but few women counselled their daughters to marry farmers. Throughout the nation, young women between the ages of 15 and 30 left farms in droves to find jobs in the cities. Industrial wages were lower for women than men, but at least in the cities women had access to an income that was often denied them on the farm.

Rural discontent blossomed into a full-blown movement that demanded major changes in Canada's political structures. In central Canada and the Maritimes, the Grange movement of the 1870s paralleled efforts by labour and capital to use collective action to achieve their goals. Granges spread from the United States into Canada, and by 1874 a Dominion Grange was formed. Although the Grange movement focused on educational activities and avoided direct political action, it was soon paralleled by another American import, the Patrons of Industry, whose brief political success in the early 1890s led to the election of candidates to the Ontario and Manitoba legislatures and the House of Commons. The Patrons of Industry dissolved as quickly as it began but was succeeded by the Ontario Farmers' Association, which in 1902 emerged as a critic of high transportation costs and the protective tariff. By 1914, farm organizations had come together to form the United Farmers of Ontario. Led by E.C. Drury and J.J. Morrison, it was determined to make Ottawa listen to the concerns of the farming community.

Meanwhile, on the Prairies, agrarian discontent led to the creation of the Territorial Grain Growers' Association in 1901, which became the basis for provincial associations following the creation of the provinces of Saskatchewan and Alberta in 1905. The Manitoba Grain Growers' Association was founded in 1902. In 1908, the *Grain Growers' Guide*, a newspaper based in Winnipeg, was established as a mouthpiece for agrarian discontent. Francis Marion Beynon's column in the *Guide* gave women plenty to think about. Recognition of women's contribution to farm life led to the creation of women's auxiliaries of the prairie farm organizations and to support for female suffrage.

Rural areas of Newfoundland were also ripe for the message of social reform. Under the dynamic leadership of William Coaker, the Fishermen's Protective Union (FPU), founded in 1908, swept through the outports gaining support from the workers in the fishing and forest industries. It soon earned the hostility of merchants in St. John's and the Roman Catholic Church, which forbade its adherents from becoming members of the "godless" organization. The FPU motto was "To each his own." Does the fisherman receive "his own," Coaker asked, "when he boards a coastal steamer . . . and has to sleep like a dog, eat like a pig and be treated like a serf? . . . At the seal fishery where he has to live like a brute, work like a dog and be paid like a nigger? Do they receive their own when they pay taxes to keep up five splendid colleges at St. John's . . . while thousands of fishermen's children are growing up illiterate? Do they receive their own when forced to supply the funds to maintain a hospital at St. John's while fishermen, their wives and daughters, are dying daily in the outports for want of hospitals?"[6]

The FPU demanded state intervention to ensure fair return to the people who caught and processed fish, improvements in education and health care in the outports, and the implementation of an old-age pension program. In alliance with the Liberal Party, the FPU won eight seats in the Newfoundland legislature in 1913 and applied pressure on the government of the day, led by Sir Edward Morris, to legislate reforms.

One of the most significant challenges to capitalist industrial development came from the cooperative movement, which was particularly strong in rural Canada. Originating in Great Britain in the 1840s, cooperatives were organized on the principle of cooperation rather than competition and were owned by their members rather than by anonymous investors. Between 1860 and 1900, farmers in the Maritimes, Quebec, and Ontario established more than 1200 cooperative creameries and cheese factories. Alphonse Desjardins in Quebec used cooperative principles to establish a chain of credit unions, the caisses populaires. In the West, grain farmers, led by E.A. Partridge, organized the Grain Growers' Grain Company in 1906 to market directly to buyers in Europe.

The creation of the Cooperative Union of Canada in 1909 brought like-minded cooperators together for education and lobbying activities. In the same year, Ontario farmers and western grain growers established the Canadian Council of Agriculture. Tariff policy emerged as the organization's major grievance. Condemned as a charge on society's producers for the benefit of manufacturers, tariffs were seen by farmers as an instrument of oppression by a class of businessmen who were sucking the nation dry through their greed and corruption.

In June 1910, Prime Minister Laurier set out on a three-month tour of the West, where he was besieged by petitions from well-organized farmers. Later in the year, nearly 1000 farmers from across the country descended on Parliament Hill demanding lower tariffs, better rail and grain elevator service, and legislation supporting cooperative enterprises. When the Laurier government negotiated a free trade treaty with the United States in the winter of 1911, it did so not as a throwback to the earlier goals of the Liberal Party but because a clear majority of rural Canadians demanded an end to high tariffs. The fact that the Liberals lost the election late that year only confirmed the belief held by farmers that industrial interests controlled the levers of power in the nation.

THE WOMEN'S MOVEMENT

The involvement of women in a variety of reform causes was fuelled by enormous changes in their lives and by new ideas about the role of women in society. With the introduction of manufactured clothes, food-stuffs, and household products, and the tendency toward smaller families and educating children in public schools, much of what was considered women's work moved outside the home. At the same time, middle-class women were told that their place was in the home. To reinforce that injunction, women were denied access to higher education, the professions, boardrooms, and political office. The careful delineation of separate spheres was thus established: men dominated the public sphere, with all its opportunities, while women were relegated to the private sphere of motherhood, domesticity, morality, and good works.

The contradictions embodied in the doctrine of separate spheres were particularly obvious in working-class families. When the family economy failed, as it so often did, women could not simply remain "angels in the house." Yet when they ventured into the public sphere, women were faced with discrimination and exploitation. For working-class women, the notion of living a life of middle-class domesticity no doubt looked attractive, but it was no solution to the problems that arose because women of all classes took their status from their husbands and fathers and were confined to a narrow range of options.

The doctrine of separate spheres led middle-class women to organize separately from men in a variety of voluntary organizations. In the 1870s, Women's Missionary Aid societies sprouted in various Protestant churches. Designed to spread the gospel at home and abroad, missionary aid societies sponsored single women for overseas service in countries such as India, China, and Korea and taught women valuable organizational skills. While consistent with women's long-standing role in charitable activities, missionary work provided a source of employment for women in the public sphere, often in areas such as medicine and administration, which were largely denied to them at home.

Two of the earliest women's organizations, the Young Women's Christian Association (YWCA) and the Woman's Christian Temperance Union (WCTU),

took middle-class women another step along the road to public service. Founded in Great Britain as a counterpart to the YMCA, the Canadian YWCA was first established in Saint John in 1870. The "Y" provided lodging and job training, largely in domestic service, for girls arriving in the "dangerous" urban environment. The WCTU was an American organization that took root in Canada in 1874, when Letitia Youmans founded a branch in Picton, Ontario. Although it initially focused women's energies in the cause of prohibition, the WCTU soon took on other reform causes. Spreading quickly throughout the nation, the WCTU formed a dominion union in 1883, and by the 1890s claimed over 10 000 members.

Many of the voluntary organizations that appealed to women originated in Great Britain and the United States, but Canada made its own contribution to the voluntary cause in the form of the Women's Institutes. The first Women's Institute was established in Stoney Creek, Ontario, in 1897 by Adelaide Hoodless. As a mother who had watched her youngest child die as a result of drinking impure milk, Hoodless wanted to improve women's domestic skills through education on matters relating to nutrition and sanitation. Her major causes included domestic science courses in schools, pure milk legislation, and public health reforms. These goals were taken up with zeal by the Women's Institutes after the Ontario government began subsidizing their efforts in 1900. By the 1920s, the Women's Institutes had spread throughout Canada and had taken root in rural areas of Great Britain and around the world.

In Quebec, Francophone women found an outlet for their energies in religious orders, which had responsibility for education, health care, and social services. Between 1837 and 1899, 34 new female religious communities were established in Quebec. By 1901, 6.1 percent of the province's single women over 20 years of age were nuns. Nuns took up many reform causes. For example, the Grey Nuns in Montreal organized day-care centres for working-class families in the early 1870s. By the turn of the century, lay women in Quebec began to resist the conservative injunctions of their clerical leaders. In 1907, Marie Lacoste-Gérin-Lajoie played a leading role in founding the Fédération nationale Saint-Jean-Baptiste, an organization that pushed for access to higher education for

The Hospital of the Sisters of Charity in Rimouski, 1890.
R.E. Mercier, Archives nationales du Québec à Québec/P600-6/438-1

women, improvements in their legal status, and reform of working conditions.

The growth in Canadian women's activism was capped by the formation of a national federation of women's clubs in 1893. Known as the National Council of Women of Canada (NCWC), it was the brainchild of Lady Aberdeen, the wife of the governor-general. An enthusiastic supporter of reform causes, Lady Aberdeen was a founder of the Aberdeen Association (1890), which distributed reading material to isolated settlers, and the Victorian Order of Nurses (1897), an organization that provided nursing services in areas where trained medical help was not available. The NCWC began cautiously but soon encompassed a wide range of organizations and causes, including temperance, child welfare, and professional advancement for women. Through local councils, they mobilized the volunteer energies of women across the country. While the NCWC tried not to alienate male legislators, whose votes were needed, they refused to back away from controversial issues once their membership had reached a consensus. In 1910, the NCWC endorsed women's suffrage, the final step in recognizing women as having public power in their own right.

Women's efforts to gain access to university education began to bear fruit in the 1870s with the opening of Mount Allison to women. When she graduated from the Mount in 1875, Grace Annie Lockhart became the first woman in the British Empire to receive a university degree. By the 1880s, most other universities had followed Mount Allison's lead, although the numbers of women who registered for classes remained low until the twentieth century. Even when their numbers increased, women tended to be channelled into arts programs, steered away from science courses, and excluded completely from professional schools offering degrees in law, medicine, engineering, and theology.

Men jealously guarded their monopoly on the professions. In 1895, Toronto's Clara Brett Martin became Canada's first woman law graduate, but she faced great resistance from the Law Society of Upper Canada not only in her efforts to seek education in the legal field but also in attempts to practise. In medicine,

A group of women in front of a YWCA boarding house at 689 Ontario Street, Toronto.
Library and Archives Canada/PA126710

Women in Action

To be an active member of the WCTU, a woman needed strong will. The *Ottawa Daily Citizen* published this account of a WCTU action on 5 February 1890:

> A Band of evangelistic workers announced a few days ago by handbills distributed throughout Hull, that meetings would be held every Tuesday evening in that city in a hall on the corner of Duke and Queen Streets. . . . It seems that preparations were made by a gang of roughs, headed by an unlicensed saloon keeper, to give the new-comers a warm reception; in fact, the intention was more or less openly expressed to "clean them out." The band of evangelists was composed of Miss Bertha Wright, accompanied by a considerable number of young ladies. . . . On opening the doors of the Hall a crowd of about TWO HUNDRED MEN well primed with liquor rushed in and filled the place. For a time, their interruptions were confined to noises, etc., but on being remonstrated with they made an attack on the speaker and singers. For a time everything was in confusion, and there was reason to fear the worst, missiles being thrown and blows freely given, but not returned. The young women then joined hands and formed a circle around the speakers, and the roughs refrained from striking them but confined their efforts to separating the little band. . . . Finally the police managed to clear the hall and took the Ottawa people to the station, fighting off the crowd with their batons all the way. At this time some of the young women were badly hurt by the missiles that were thrown.[7]

Despite the "warm reception," Bertha Wright and her "little band" from the Ottawa Young Woman's Christian Temperance Union were back in Hull the following week, this time to take on an angry mob of 400 "roughs."

Emily Howard Stowe and Jennie Trout were forced to train as physicians in the United States because no Canadian medical school would admit women. Upon their return to Canada, they successfully pressured Queen's University and the University of Toronto to open facilities to train women doctors in 1883. The administrators of these universities responded by creating separate female medical colleges. Women's College Hospital in Toronto, incorporated in 1913, became the base for many women doctors in the city who found other hospital surgeries closed to them.

While few women became doctors, the number of female nurses was growing rapidly by the end of the nineteenth century. Nurses were expected to be selfless servants of patients and to remain subordinate to doctors, much like the idealized mother in the home. Similarly, many women took up teaching as a profession in this period, but they remained subordinate to male principals and trustees and, like nurses, were paid low salaries compared with those of the men in their profession. Secretarial work for women began to expand rapidly with the invention of the typewriter, and by the turn of the century, men were beginning to avoid an occupation that was increasingly being viewed as "women's work." Although women remained subordinates in hierarchies of gender and income, their movement in such large numbers into the professions open to them represented their quest for economic independence and social respectability.

The Campaign for Female Suffrage

By the 1890s, an increasing number of reformers supported what was known at the time as "woman suffrage." People came to the cause in a variety of ways: from lengthy struggles to open universities, professions, and businesses on an equal basis to women; from groups condemning married women's subordination under the law; and from reform movements that felt their goals might be advanced by the support of women. Two feminist perspectives were evident in the suffragists' arguments: equal rights and maternal, or social, feminism. Equal rights advocates hoped to sweep away the unfair laws and attitudes that encouraged discrimination against women. Maternal feminists wanted special laws to support women in their roles as wives and mothers. In both lines of thinking, women's suffrage became a key element in the struggle for reform.

The equal rights perspective tended to dominate in the years immediately following confederation, but by the turn of the century the rhetoric of maternal feminism prevailed. Expanding on the view that a woman's place was in the home, maternal feminists argued that women's special qualities hitherto practised in the private sphere were increasingly needed in the public sphere to reform the abuses of the industrial system. Maternal feminists exploited the widespread nineteenth-century belief that women were instinctively better than men—or at least more sensitive and nurturing—to justify their demands for greater power in the private and public spheres.

Like other middle-class reformers, suffragists were likely to express unflattering views of the working class and immigrants, and frequently pointed to the injustice of allowing illiterate peasant men to vote while Canadian-born women were denied the franchise. Whatever the justification offered by suffrage advocates, the demand

Nellie McClung (left), with Alice Jamieson (centre) and Emily Murphy (right).
British Columbia Archives/B-06791

The Suffragists

Middle-class reformers, imbued with the progressive spirit of the age, were convinced that political action and social reform could eliminate many of the "social evils" that they saw around them. For many historians, these reformers have become the heroes of Canadian history, and people such as feminist Nellie McClung have been praised for their clarity of vision. Other historians have taken a more critical approach to reformers, viewing them less as people of vision than as a privileged group who tried to impose their narrow middle-class values on all Canadians. The clash of opinion is clearly drawn around the women's movement, which culminated in the granting of suffrage to women in Canada during and immediately following the First World War.

In her pioneering study of the Canadian women's suffrage movement, published in 1950, Catherine Cleverdon argued: "Political equality is a prize not to be lightly held. Though it came to Canadian women without the harshness and bitterness of the struggle in Great Britain, it was won by the hard work and heartaches of small groups of women throughout the dominion who had the courage and vision to seek it."[8] Cleverdon's perspective was shaped by her strong commitment to the democratic process and her identification with the suffrage leaders, many of whom she interviewed while conducting her research.

When interest in women's history resurfaced in the 1970s and 1980s, Carol Lee Bacchi, following the direction taken by feminist scholars internationally, was less inclined to see suffragists only as women with courage and vision. She concluded from her study of some 200 suffrage leaders that most of them were elite women who had hoped to impose Protestant morality, sobriety, and family order on Canadian society. In many suffrage circles, it was revealed, racist and class-bound solutions—including eugenics, exclusive immigration laws, and restrictive voting practices—were openly advocated. Even more damning, especially from the point of view of left-wing scholars, was the fact many middle-class suffrage leaders had the time to devote to "good causes" because they exploited an underclass of household servants. Since a narrow maternal feminist vision—many suffrage leaders saw women's primary role and rationale for public action as rooted in their status as mothers—seemed to motivate most Canadian suffragists, they were ultimately seen as unworthy predecessors to the more purposeful feminists of the modern women's movement. To quote Bacchi, "[t]he female suffragist did not fail to effect a social revolution for women; the majority never had a revolution in mind."[9]

The rejection of the early suffrage leaders as "foremothers" to modern feminism has elicited a vigorous response. In a critique of Bacchi's book, historian Ernest R. Forbes used the experience of women in Halifax, who were described by both Cleverdon and Bacchi as being invariably "conservative" in their approach to female suffrage, to expose the parochialism and present-mindedness of such a position. Halifax suffrage leaders took on a whole range of feminist reforms, Forbes argued, and used any available argument to promote their clearly radical goals. "Reading only the leaders' statements in the newspapers one might conclude that the scheme was motivated chiefly by class interests and social control. Having read the minutes [of the Local Council of Women] I do not believe it. Neither, apparently, did the men who rejected their proposals."[10] In her study of women involved in left-wing organizations such as the Social Democratic Party of Canada before 1914, Janice Newton found that many socialist women also espoused maternal feminist goals, often in defiance of their male colleagues. Newton maintains that there was nothing inherently conservative about maternal feminism in this period because many women on the left wanted "nothing less than the socialist transformation of women's maternal and domestic roles."[11]

Contemporary political concern about what constitutes modern feminism motivates such a debate and may obscure more important questions that should be asked about the suffrage movement. Australian scholar Judith Allen, for instance, has called upon scholars to adopt a comparative and international approach to suffrage. By looking at such issues as temperance and sexual consent laws in the context of suffrage, Allen shows that feminist causes were rooted in time and place. For example, developments following the granting of the vote to women in New Zealand and parts of Australia in the 1890s were different from those that followed the success of suffrage in Great Britain, Canada, and the United States, where suffrage was granted a generation later.[12]

By analyzing suffrage and other reform activities in the context of the larger changes taking place in society and in comparison with developments elsewhere, historians can understand individual reform leaders on their own terms. The question then becomes not whether suffrage leaders were heroes or villains, or whether their policies were right or wrong, but why they responded to their world in the way they did.

for female suffrage remained fundamentally radical, seeking a direct connection between women and the state rather than allowing male family members to act as mediators.

The hardships of the suffrage campaign wore out several generations of women and deterred the less courageous from publicly expressing their opinions. Misogyny and anti-feminism were widely expressed both orally and in print by people determined to keep women in their place. In Quebec, Henri Bourassa lashed out against feminism as a dangerous import from a godless Anglo-Saxon culture that would destroy Roman Catholic Quebec. English-Canadian intellectuals such as Stephen Leacock were equally appalled by the notion of equality for women and resorted to the comfortable view that because women were superior to men they should be shielded from the realities of the public sphere. Canada's union leaders were no better than their middle-class employers, who argued that women should be segregated in the workforce and receive lower wages. When immigrants brought with them traditional views about the subordination of women, further weight was added to the patriarchal perspective. Even Protestant church leaders, whose congregations were increasingly dominated by women, preached against defying the divinely sanctioned subordination of women.

Not surprisingly, given their education and sense of purpose, many of the first generation of professional women became active in the suffrage movement. Dr. Emily Howard Stowe, for example, took the lead in establishing Canada's first women's suffrage organization in 1876, whose purpose was concealed under the name the Toronto Women's Literary Club. By 1883, the group felt confident enough to change its name to the Toronto Women's Suffrage Association and at the same time launch the Canadian Women's Suffrage Association. Pressure from women's organizations led to gradual municipal enfranchisement of unmarried and widowed women who met the property qualification. Ontario granted this right in 1884, New Brunswick in 1886, Nova Scotia in 1887, and Prince Edward Island in 1888, but many municipalities still refused women the right to hold public office.

The right of women to vote in provincial and national elections was steadfastly resisted. In Nova Scotia, the lobbying of women's groups produced a narrow majority in favour of women's suffrage in the legislative assembly in 1893, but manoeuvring by the anti-suffragist attorney-general, J.W. Longley, forestalled passage of the relevant bill. Women's franchise bills in other provincial jurisdictions were invariably voted down. By the end of the century, the tide seemed to have turned firmly against women's suffrage, in part because so many reforms, including prohibition, were predicted to succeed if women ever got a chance to clean up the political system.

In this discouraging context, Nellie McClung emerged as Canada's most prominent leader of the suffrage cause. Born in Grey County, Ontario, she migrated to Manitoba as a young girl, married a druggist, raised five children, and had a successful career as a fiction writer. Her sense of humour and clever repartee enabled her to survive the many taunts that came her way. In 1914, she packed Winnipeg's Walker Theatre for a performance of "How the Vote Was Won." To thundering applause, she played the role of premier of a woman's parliament and punctured the pretensions of Conservative premier Sir Rodmond Roblin with her speech to an imaginary group of franchise-seeking males: "We wish to compliment this delegation on their splendid gentlemanly appearance. If, without exercising the vote, such splendid specimens of manhood can be produced, such a system of affairs should not be interfered with. . . . If men start to vote, they will vote too much. Politics unsettles men, and unsettled men means unsettled bills, broken furniture, broken vows, divorce."[13] Such events put the anti-suffrage forces on the defensive and paved the way for opposition parties to embrace a cause whose time had come.

CONCLUSION

By the turn of the twentieth century, Canadians were becoming involved in a wide range of voluntary organizations designed to address the worst abuses of the industrial order. Some visionaries even imagined a world in which everyone would benefit from the material wealth made possible by new technological processes. Although reformers had scored some spectacular victories by 1914, most felt that they still had a long way to go to bring about the brave new world that they envisioned. Their struggles contributed to an emerging national culture that, like other aspects of Canadian life, was dramatically changing. It is to aspects of this cultural development that we now turn our attention.

NOTES

1 Quoted in Paul F. Sharp, *The Agrarian Revolt in Western Canada* (New York: Octagon Books, 1971), 63.

2 Carolyn Strange, *Toronto's Girl Problem: The Perils and Pleasures of the City, 1880–1930* (Toronto: University of Toronto Press, 1995), 91.

3 Cited in Mariana Valverde, *The Age of Light, Soap, and Water: Moral Reform in English Canada, 1885–1925* (Toronto: McClelland & Stewart, 1991), 106.

4 Susan Mann Trofimenkoff, "One Hundred and Two Muffled Voices: Canada's Industrial Women in the 1880s," *Atlantis* 3, no. 1 (Fall 1977), 66–82.

5 T. Phillips Thompson, *The Politics of Labour* (Toronto: University of Toronto Press, 1975), 221–22.

6 Cited in James K. Hiller, "Newfoundland Confronts Canada, 1867 to 1949," in *The Atlantic Provinces in Confederation*, eds. E.R. Forbes and D.A. Muise (Toronto: University of Toronto Press, 1993), 363.

7 Cited in Sharon Anne Cook, *"Through Sunshine and Shadow": The Woman's Christian Temperance Union,*

Evangelicalism and Reform in Ontario, 1874–1930 (Montreal: McGill-Queen's University Press, 1995), 3.

8 Catherine L. Cleverdon, *The Woman Suffrage Movement in Canada*, 2nd ed. (1950; repr., Toronto: University of Toronto Press, 1974), 67.

9 Carol Lee Bacchi, *Liberation Deferred? The Ideas of the English Canadian Suffragists, 1877–1918* (Toronto: University of Toronto Press, 1983), 148.

10 Ernest R. Forbes, "The Ideas of Carol Bacchi and the Suffragists of Halifax," *Atlantis* 10, no. 2 (Spring 1985), 122.

11 Janice Newton, *The Feminist Challenge to the Canadian Left, 1900–1918* (Montreal: McGill-Queen's University Press, 1995), 13.

12 Judith Allen, "Contextualizing Late Nineteenth-Century Feminism: Problems and Comparisons," *Journal of the Canadian Historical Association*, n.s., no. 1 (1990), 17–39.

13 Cleverdon, *The Woman Suffrage Movement in Canada*, 59.

RELATED READINGS IN THIS SERIES

From *Nation and Society: Readings in Post-Confederation Canadian History*

Gillian Crease, "Exclusion or Solidarity? Vancouver Workers Confront the 'Oriental Problem,'" 100–20.
Sarah-Jane (Saje) Mathieu, "North of the Colour Line: Sleeping Car Porters and the Battle Against Jim Crow on Canadian Rails, 1880–1920," 121–37.

From Primary Documents CD-ROM, Volume II

Knights of Labor Procession in Hamilton, Ontario, 1885
Victoria Chief of Police Is Examined by the Royal Commission on Liquor Traffic
National Council of Women of Canada: What It Means and What It Does
Labour Day
The New Chivalry
Nellie McClung

SELECTED READING

Social reform in this period is discussed in Paul Rutherford, ed., *Saving the Canadian City: The First Phase, 1880–1920* (Toronto: University of Toronto Press, 1974); Mariana Valverde, *The Age of Light, Soap, and Water: Moral Reform in English Canada, 1885–1925* (Toronto: McClelland & Stewart, 1991); Ramsay Cook, *The Regenerators: Social Criticism in Late Victorian English Canada* (Toronto: University of Toronto Press, 1985); Joseph Levitt, *Henri Bourassa and the Golden Calf: The Social Program of the Nationalists in Quebec, 1900–1914* (Ottawa: University of Ottawa Press, 1969); Paul Rompkey, *Grenfell of Labrador: A Biography* (Toronto:

University of Toronto Press, 1991); Richard Allen, *The Social Passion: Religion and Social Reform in Canada, 1914–1928* (Toronto: University of Toronto Press, 1990); Nancy Christie and Michael Gauvreau, *"A Full-Orbed Christianity": The Protestant Churches and Social Welfare in Canada, 1900–1940* (Montreal: McGill-Queen's University Press, 1996); George Emery, *The Methodist Church on the Prairies, 1896–1914* (Montreal: McGill-Queen's University Press, 2002); and Peter Bush, *Western Challenge: The Presbyterian Church in Canada's Mission on the Prairies and the North, 1885–1925* (Winnipeg: J. Gordon Schillingford, 2000).

Issues relating to the prohibition movement are well summarized in Craig Heron, *Booze: A Distilled History* (Toronto: Between the Lines, 2003). See also Mariana Valverde, *Diseases of the Will: Alcohol and the Dilemmas of Freedom* (Cambridge: Cambridge University Press, 1999).

Prison reform is discussed in Peter Oliver, *"Terror to Evil Doers": Prisons and Punishment in Nineteenth-Century Ontario* (Toronto: University of Toronto Press, 1998).

On changing approaches to mental and physical health, see James E. Moran, *Committed to the Asylum: Insanity and Society in Nineteenth-Century Quebec and Ontario* (Montreal: McGill-Queen's University Press, 2002); Benoît Gaumer, Georges Desrosiers, et Othmar Keel, *Histoire du Service de santé de la ville de Montréal, 1865–1975* (Sainte Foy: Presses de l' Université Laval, 2002); David Gagan and Rosemary Gagan, *For Patients of Moderate Means: A Social History of the Voluntary Public General Hospital: Canada, 1890–1950* (Montreal: McGill-Queen's University Press, 2002); Cheryl Krasnick Warsh, *Moments of Unreason: The Practice of Canadian Psychiatry and the Homewood Retreat, 1883–1923* (Montreal: McGill-Queen's University Press, 1989).

Books on the emerging social welfare state include Edgar-André Montigny, *Foisted Upon the Government? State Responsibilities, Family Obligations, and the Care of the Dependent Aged in Late Nineteenth-Century Ontario* (Montreal: McGill-Queen's University Press, 1997); and Yolande Cohen, *Profession Infirmière: Une histoire des soins dans les hôpitaux du Québec* (Montreal: Les Presses de l'Université de Montréal, 2000).

Surveys of the working-class experience and the labour movement include Craig Heron, *The Canadian Labour Movement: A Brief History* (Toronto: James Lorimer, 1996); Bryan D. Palmer, *Working Class Experience: Rethinking the History of Canadian Labour, 1800–1991* (Toronto: McClelland & Stewart, 1992); Desmond Morton, *Working People: An Illustrated History of the Canadian Labour Movement* (Toronto: Summerhill, 1990); Jean Hamelin, ed., *Les Travailleurs Québécois, 1851–1896* (Montreal: Presses de l'Université du Québec, 1973); Jacques Rouillard, *Histoire du syndicalisme au Québec* (Montreal: Boréal, 1989); and Susan Mann Trofimenkoff, "One Hundred and Two Muffled Voices: Canada's Industrial Women in the 1880s," *Atlantis* 3, no. 1 (Fall 1977), 67–82. Labour organization and political values are discussed in Ian McKay, *Rebels, Reds, and Radicals: Rethinking Canada's Left History* (Toronto: Between the Lines, 2005); Gregory S. Kealey and Bryan D. Palmer, *"Dreaming of What Might Be": The Knights of Labour in Ontario* (New York: Cambridge University Press, 1982); A. Ross McCormack, *Reformers, Rebels and Revolutionaries* (Toronto: University of Toronto Press, 1977); Martin Robin, *Radical Politics and Canadian Labour* (Kingston: Industrial

Relations Centre, Queen's University, 1971); Donald Avery, *Dangerous Foreigners: European Immigrant Workers and Labour Radicalism in Canada* (Toronto: McClelland & Stewart, 1979); Linda Kealey, *Enlisting Women for the Cause: Women, Labour and the Left in Canada, 1890–1920* (Toronto: University of Toronto Press, 1998); and Ian McKay, "'By Wisdom, Wile or War': The Provincial Workmen's Association and the Struggle for Working-Class Independence in Nova Scotia," *Labour/Le Travail* (Fall 1986), 13–62. See also Judy Fudge and Eric Tucker, *Labour Before the Law: the Regulation of Workers' Collective Action in Canada, 1900–1948* (Toronto: Oxford University Press, 2001). First-hand accounts of working conditions and attitudes are found in Greg Kealey, ed., *Canada Investigates Industrialism: The Royal Commission on the Relations of Labor and Capital, 1889* (Toronto: University of Toronto Press, 1973); Michael Cross, ed., *The Working Man in the Nineteenth Century* (Toronto: Oxford University Press, 1974); T. Phillips Thompson, *The Politics of Labour* (1887; repr., Toronto: University of Toronto Press, 1975); and Edmund Bradwin, *The Bunkhouse Man* (Toronto: University of Toronto Press, 1972). Peter Baskerville and Eric Sager focus on the unemployed in *Unwilling Idlers: The Urban Unemployed and Their Families in Late Victorian Canada* (Toronto: University of Toronto Press, 2000).

Developments in specific industries and regions are the subject of many books and articles, including Bryan D. Palmer, *A Culture in Conflict: Skilled Workers and Industrial Capitalism in Hamilton, Ontario* (Montreal: McGill-Queen's University Press, 1979); Gregory S. Kealey, *Toronto Workers Respond to Industrialism, 1867–1892* (Toronto: University of Toronto Press, 1980); Craig Heron, *Working in Steel: The Early Years in Canada, 1883–1935* (Toronto: McClelland & Stewart, 1980); David Bright, *The Limits of Labour: Class Formation and the Labour Movement in Calgary, 1883–1929* (Vancouver: UBC Press, 1998); Robert A.J. McDonald, "Working-Class Vancouver, 1886–1914: Urbanism and Class in British Columbia," *BC Studies* (Spring/Summer 1986), 33–69; Ian McKay, *The Craft Transformed: An Essay on the Carpenters in Halifax, 1885–1985* (Halifax: Holdfast Press, 1985); Eric Sager, *Seafaring Labour: The Merchant Marine of Atlantic Canada, 1820–1914* (Montreal: McGill-Queen's University Press, 1989); Ian Radforth, *Bushworkers and Bosses: Logging in Northern Ontario, 1900–1980* (Toronto: University of Toronto Press, 1987); Gordon Hak, *Turning Trees into Dollars: The British Columbia Coastal Lumber Industry, 1888–1913* (Toronto: University of Toronto Press, 2000); Jeremy Mouat, *Roaring Days: Rossland's Mines in the History of British Columbia* (Vancouver: UBC Press, 1995); John Douglas Belshaw, *Colonization and Community: The Vancouver Island Coalfield and the Making of the British*

Columbia Working Class (Montreal: McGill-Queen's University Press, 2002); and Ian McKay, "The Realm of Uncertainty: The Experience of Work in the Cumberland Coal Mines, 1873–1927," *Acadiensis* 16, no. 1 (Autumn 1986), 3–57.

Rural responses are discussed in Vernon C. Fowke, *The National Policy and the Wheat Economy* (Toronto: University of Toronto Press, 1957); Paul F. Sharp, *The Agrarian Revolt in Western Canada* (New York: Octagon Books, 1971); David Laycock, *Populism and Democratic Thought in the Canadian Prairies, 1910–1945* (Toronto: University of Toronto Press, 1990); Ian Macpherson, *Each for All: A History of the Cooperative Movement in English Canada, 1900–1945* (Ottawa: Carleton University Press, 1979); Margaret C. Kechnie, *Organizing Rural Women: The Federated Women's Institutes of Ontario, 1897–1919* (Montreal: McGill-Queen's University Press, 2003); Bradford James Rennie, *The Rise of Agrarian Democracy: The United Farmers and Farm Women of Alberta, 1909–1921* (Toronto: University of Toronto Press, 2000); Ronald Rudin, *In Whose Interest? Quebec's Caisses Populaires, 1900–1945* (Montreal: McGill-Queen's University Press, 1990); Jeffery Taylor, *Fashioning Farmers: Ideology, Agricultural Knowledge and the Manitoba Farm Movement, 1890–1925* (Regina: Canadian Plains Research Center, 1994); Ian McDonald, *"To Each His Own": William Coaker and the Fishermen's Protective Union in Newfoundland Politics, 1908–1925* (St. John's: ISER, Memorial University, 1987); and Terry Crowley, "Rural Labour," in *Labouring Lives: Work and Workers in Nineteenth-Century Ontario*, ed. Paul Craven (Toronto: University of Toronto Press, 1995), 13–104. See also John MacDougall, *Rural Life in Canada: Its Trend and Tasks* (1913; repr., Toronto: University of Toronto Press, 1973); and Andrew Macphail, *The Master's Wife* (1939; repr., Toronto: University of Toronto Press, 1977). Recent work in rural history is explored in R.W. Sandwell, ed., *Beyond City Limits: Rural History in British Columbia* (Vancouver: UBC Press, 1999) and Daniel Samson, ed., *Contested Countryside: Rural Workers and Modern Society in Atlantic Canada, 1800–1950* (Fredericton: Acadiensis Press, 1994).

On the general context of women's history in this period, see the relevant chapters of the Clio Collective, *Quebec Women: A History* (Toronto: Women's Press, 1987); Alison Prentice et al., *Canadian Women: A History*, 2nd ed. (Toronto: Harcourt Brace, 1996); and Sharon Anne Cook, Lorna McLean, and Kate O'Rourke, eds., *Framing Our Past: Canadian Women's History in the Twentieth Century* (Montreal: McGill-Queen's University Press, 2001). On women and the church, see Marta Danylewycz, *Taking the Veil: An Alternative to Marriage, Motherhood and Spinsterhood in Quebec, 1840–1920* (Toronto: McClelland & Stewart, 1987); Ruth Compton Brouwer, *New Women for God: Canadian*

Presbyterian Women and India Missions, 1876–1914 (Toronto: University of Toronto Press, 1990); Rosemary R. Gagan, *A Sensitive Independence: Canadian Methodist Women Missionaries in Canada and the Orient* (Montreal: McGill-Queen's University Press, 1992); Myra Rutherdale, *Women and the White Man's God: Gender and Race in the Canadian Mission Fields* (Vancouver: UBC Press, 2003); and Lynne Marks, *Revivals and Roller Rinks: Religion, Leisure, and Identity in Late-Nineteenth-Century Small-Town Ontario* (Toronto: University of Toronto Press, 1996). The careers of early female journalists are the subject of Marjory Lang, *Women Who Made the News: Female Journalists in Canada, 1880–1945* (Montreal: McGill-Queen's University Press, 1999). Regional studies of women include Sharon Anne Cook, *"Through Sunshine and Shadow": The Woman's Christian Temperance Union, Evangelicalism and Reform in Ontario, 1874–1930* (Montreal: McGill-Queen's University Press, 1995); Denise Lemieux and Lucie Mercier, *Les femmes au tournant du siècle, 1880–1940: Ages de la vie, maternité et quotidien* (Quebec: Institut québécois de recherche sur la culture, 1989); Barbara K. Latham and Roberta J. Pazdro, eds., *Not Just Pin Money: Selected Essays in the History of Women's Work in British Columbia* (Victoria: Camosun College, 1984); Franca Iacovetta and Mariana Valverde, eds., *Gender Conflicts: New Essays in Women's History* (Toronto: University of Toronto Press, 1992); Linda Kealey, ed., *Pursuing Equality: Historical Perspectives on Women in Newfoundland and Labrador* (St. John's: ISER, 1993); Carmelita McGrath, Barbara Neis, and Marilyn Porter, eds., *Their Lives and Times: Women in Newfoundland and Labrador, A Collage* (St. John's: Killick Press, 1995); Margaret Conrad, Toni Laidlaw, and Donna Smyth, *No Place Like Home: Diaries and Letters of Nova Scotia Women, 1771–1939* (Halifax: Formac, 1988); Janet Guildford and Suzanne Morton, eds., *Separate Spheres: Women's Worlds in the Nineteenth-Century Maritimes* (Fredericton: Acadiensis Press, 1994); and Karen Dubinsky, *Improper Advances: Rape and Heterosexual Conflict in Ontario, 1880–1929* (Chicago: University of Chicago Press, 1993). Victorian medical notions about women are dissected in Wendy M. Mitchinson, *The Nature of Their Bodies: Women and Their Doctors in Victorian Canada* (Toronto: University of Toronto Press, 1991). Women and the law are the subject of Constance Backhouse, *Petticoats and Prejudice: Women and Law in Nineteenth-Century Canada* (Toronto: Women's Press, 1991). For a demographic analysis of the teaching profession in this period, see Eric Sager, "Women Teachers in Canada, 1881-1901: Revisiting the 'Feminization' of an Occupation," *The Canadian Historical Review* 88, 2 (June 2007), 201–236.

Social histories dealing with changing notions of families and sexuality include Carolyn Strange, *Toronto's Girl Problem: The Perils and Pleasures of the City, 1880–1930*

(Toronto: University of Toronto Press, 1995); Carolyn Strange and Tina Loo, *Making Good: Law and Moral Regulation in Canada, 1867–1939* (Toronto: University of Toronto Press, 1997); Angus McLaren and Arlene Tigar McLaren, *The Bedroom and the State: The Changing Practices and Politics of Contraception and Abortion in Canada, 1880–1980* (Toronto: McClelland & Stewart, 1986); Angus McLaren, *Our Own Master Race: Eugenics in Canada, 1885–1945* (Toronto: McClelland & Stewart, 1990); Gary Kinsman, *The Regulation of Desire: Homo and Hetero Sexualities*, 2nd ed. (Montreal: Black Rose Books, 1996); Sharon Dale Stone, *Lesbians in Canada* (Toronto: Between the Lines, 1990); Neil Sutherland, *Children in English-Canadian Society: Framing the Twentieth-Century Consensus* (Toronto: University of Toronto Press, 1976); Patricia Rooke and Rudy Schnell, *Discarding the Asylum: From Child Rescue to the Welfare State in English Canada, 1800–1950* (Lanham, MO: University Press of America, 1983); Xiaobei Chen, *Tending the Garden of Citizenship. Child Saving in Toronto, 1880s–1920s* (Toronto: University of Toronto Press, 2005); James G. Snell, *In the Shadow of the Law: Divorce in Canada, 1900–1939* (Toronto: University of Toronto Press, 1991) and *The Citizen's Wage: The State and the Elderly in Canada, 1900–1951* (Toronto: University of Toronto Press, 1996); Nancy Christie, ed., *Households of Faith: Family, Gender and Communities in Canada, 1760–1969* (Montreal: McGill-Queen's University Press, 2002); and Paul Axelrod, *The Promise of Schooling: Education in Canada, 1800–1914* (Toronto: University of Toronto Press, 1997). Motherhood is the focus of Katherine Arnup, *Education for Motherhood: Advice for Mothers in Twentieth-Century Canada* (Toronto: University of Toronto Press, 1994); Cynthia R. Comacchio, *"Nations Are Built of Babies": Saving Ontario's Mothers and Children, 1900–1940* (Montreal: McGill-Queen's University Press, 1994) and *The Infinite Bonds of Family: Domesticity in Canada, 1850–1940* (Toronto: University of Toronto Press, 1999). See also Pauline Greenhill and Diane Tye, eds., *Undisciplined Women: Tradition and Culture in Canada* (Montreal: McGill-Queen's University Press, 1997).

On reform and suffrage movements, see Janice Newton, *The Feminist Challenge to the Canadian Left, 1900–1918* (Montreal: McGill-Queen's University Press, 1995); Linda Kealey, ed., *A Not Unreasonable Claim: Women and Reform in Canada* (Toronto: Women's Press, 1979); Veronica Strong-Boag, *The Parliament of Women: The National Council of Women of Canada, 1893–1929* (Ottawa: National Museum of Civilization, 1976); Naomi Griffiths, *The Splendid Vision: Centennial History of the National Council of Women, 1893–1993* (Ottawa: Carleton University Press, 1993); Carol Lee Bacchi, *Liberation Deferred? The Ideas of the English-Canadian Suffragists, 1877–1918* (Toronto: University of Toronto Press, 1983); Catherine L. Cleverdon, *The Woman Suffrage Movement in Canada* (1950; repr., Toronto: University of Toronto Press, 1972); and Margot I. Duley, *Where Once Our Mothers Stood We Stand: Women's Suffrage in Newfoundland, 1890–1925* (Charlottetown: Gynergy Books, 1993). See also Nellie McClung, *In Times Like These* (1913; repr., Toronto: University of Toronto Press, 1972); and E.R. Forbes, "Battles in Another War: Edith Archibald and the Halifax Feminist Movement," in *Challenging the Regional Stereotype*, ed. E.R. Forbes (Fredericton: Acadiensis Press, 1989), 69–89.

CHAPTER 8

Cultural Currents in the Industrial Age, 1867–1918

TIMELINE

1872	Public Archives of Canada founded	
1880	Ned Hanlan wins world rowing championship	
1882	Royal Society of Canada established	
1884	Amateur Athletics Association of Canada founded	
1891	Pope Leo XIII issues encyclical Rerum Novarum	
1893	Stanley Cup donated by Governor-General Lord Stanley	
1904	Canada sends first team to Olympic Games; Jack Miner establishes Canada's first bird sanctuary at Kingsville, Ontario	
1907	Canadian Art Club founded	
1908	Boy Scouts founded; L.M. Montgomery publishes Anne of Green Gables; Eastern Canada Hockey Association turns professional	
1909	Girl Guides founded; Grey Cup donated by Governor-General Earl Grey; National Hockey Association founded	

In March 1888, Jessie McQueen, a 27-year-old school teacher from Pictou County, Nova Scotia, took the train to British Columbia, where she had been hired to teach school. Her younger sister Annie had made the same journey a year earlier and a cousin, Jessie Olding, would soon join them. As this letter from Jessie's brother George, who was working in the United States, suggests, the McQueens carried their Scottish and Presbyterian values with them when they moved in search of work.

> So you and Jessie Olding and I suppose several more would-be cow girl maidens are going to storm the home of the deceitful mustang and lordly wheat. Are you all going to buy revolvers like the small boys in the novels . . .? It was awful for that harum scarum George to go away off to New York 60 hours from home, but its [it's] nothing for the little birdlings to go clean across the Continent.

> One word of advice don't marry a man unless he's three quarters Scotch & one quarter English and has been brought up a Scotch Presbyterian. It's the best mixture in the world and we says it who ought to know.[1]

Jessie and Annie McQueen were drawn to British Columbia by higher salaries than they could earn in the Maritimes. In their roles as teachers and members of voluntary associations, including the Presbyterian churches they helped to establish, they played a major role in Canadianizing the West. By making decisions about their lives—where to live and work, what to believe about the nature of the universe, how long to stay in school, and which leisure activities to pursue—all Canadians helped lay the foundations of a nation that in 1914 was culturally and intellectually much different from the one that had been created in 1867.

RELIGION AND SOCIETY

The changing economic and intellectual climate of the late nineteenth century had a profound impact on Canadian churches. Following the publication of Charles Darwin's works on evolution, the literal truth of church teachings was called sharply into question. If humans were simply the products of millions of years of evolution, where did that leave the Old Testament account of creation? Declining church attendance in cities also challenged church leaders. If city life was not conducive to spiritual concerns, how was the church to make itself relevant in an increasingly urbanized society?

Many church leaders responded to the Darwinian challenge by rejecting the theory of evolution as speculative nonsense. In taking this position, they had support from some members of the scientific community, including geologist Sir William Dawson, principal of McGill University and the most influential scientist of his generation. Dawson used scientific evidence to challenge the claims of evolutionists and attempted to reconcile the Bible's account of a six-day creation by suggesting that the term "day" in Genesis be understood as a longer period than a literal day.

Other scientists and theologians moved further along this intellectual road by arguing that biblical stories were figuratively rather than literally true. Protestant "higher critics" borrowed critical methods from contemporary German and British scholars, treating the Bible like any other literary work and interpreting its truths in mythical rather than literal terms. By the end of the nineteenth century, a widening gulf was developing between church leaders who accepted higher criticism and those who remained faithful to the literal teachings of the Bible.

The social problems accompanying industrialization also sparked tensions in Canadian churches. While many religious leaders continued to ascribe poverty to personal failings, others began to criticize the new economic order. In the 1880s, the *Canadian Baptist*, under the editorship of Ebenezer William Dadson, called for such legislative measures as prohibition, a guaranteed right to unionize, and legal reforms with respect to the treatment of women, children, and Native peoples. Dadson declared the law of supply and demand "unchristian," a position warmly received by many rank-and-file Baptists.

Presbyterian, Methodist, and Anglican leaders were also increasingly disposed to focus on social problems. Young candidates for the ministry in the Methodist Church, such as J.S. Woodsworth and Albert Edward Smith, were influenced by higher criticism in their classes at Wesley College in Winnipeg and became avid social gospellers in the course of working in the slum-ridden north end of the city. Agnes Machar, a popular author and the daughter of a Presbyterian clergyman, argued that the churches needed to embrace reform so that working people were not driven toward atheistic communism. A keen critic of the oppression of women in the workplace, Machar was in little doubt about the source of the problem: "The answer lies in the hard necessities of poverty which compels them to take the work on the terms offered, and makes them so much afraid of dismissal that they will seldom ever complain of oppression."[2]

Most mainstream Protestant churches were eventually drawn into the social gospel movement. By focusing on the physical and material condition of people on Earth, social gospellers moved away from an evangelical preoccupation with individual spiritual development and life after death. This direction troubled many church members, who became concerned about the abandonment of what they believed to be the fundamental issues of Christianity. As the split between conservatives and social gospellers widened, Protestant churches faced losing the support of leaders on one side or other in the debate.

Ordinary church members were not directly involved in disputes over either the Bible or social action. Although working-class attendance at church was worrisomely low to religious leaders, the middle classes in towns and cities and most people living in rural areas joined a church and regularly attended Sunday services. The establishment of missions, settlement houses, and labour churches helped Protestant denominations maintain church membership in working-class areas of cities. There is also little doubt that the church had a major influence within society as a whole—otherwise, it is unlikely that legislators would have acceded to demands for Sunday closings or that so many people would have joined missionary societies and prohibition organizations.

Nevertheless, in mainstream churches, revivalism, which emphasized intense personal experience, was increasingly downplayed. For example, Methodist camp meetings that included several days of open-air preaching to people housed in rudimentary tents gave way to "camps" featuring summer cottages, boat services, and other amenities for the middle class, who did not wish their religious observance to interfere with creature comforts. By seeking middle-class respectability, many churches lost members to religious movements that emphasized old-time religious values. The Salvation Army was the most successful and enduring of the new evangelical churches, especially among the urban working class. A variety of millenarian groups, who believed in the imminent return of Christ, came and went during this period, attracting followers who were disillusioned with the apparent secularization of the established churches. These groups, in turn, often disillusioned their followers when the predicted Second Coming failed to occur.

In the late nineteenth century, skepticism about the teachings of mainstream churches was evident in the spread of spiritualism and theosophy. The range of spiritualist practices varied widely, but all spiritualists shared the belief that the human soul remained alive after the death of the physical body and could be communicated with by the living. Some spiritualists also believed in reincarnation. Theosophists proposed that there was a universal soul to which all individual souls were ultimately identical. Opposed to all forms of discrimination, theosophists proclaimed that individuals of both genders and every race must find their identity in the universal soul. Social reform was integral to theosophical beliefs, which no doubt helped attract adherents such as Emily Stowe and T. Phillips Thompson. Unitarianism, which proclaimed the essential unity of all religious beliefs and, like theosophy, embraced social reform and human equality, also won adherents. Most shocking to the churches were freethought societies that promoted atheism and agnosticism founded by intellectuals who equated Christianity with superstition.

A Combative Catholicism

Although the Roman Catholic Church was not without skeptics and social reformers, the clerical hierarchy was limited in how far it could deviate from the injunctions of papal pronouncements. The church banned books that it considered irreligious and forbade the faithful from joining secular organizations, such as the

The Salvation Army in winter lumber camps, hamming it up for their primarily male audience.
Archives of Ontario, 10014126

Noble and Holy Order of the Knights of Labor, that it felt distracted people from their religious duties. While clerical rules usually failed to stop Roman Catholics from reading banned literature or joining trade unions, they often pitted the rank and file of church members against their clerical leaders.

Nowhere was clerical control more successful than in Quebec, where Roman Catholicism claimed the allegiance of 85 percent of the population. A celebrated case of the church's confrontation with its critics occurred in 1869 when it refused to allow the burial of an activist of the Institut canadien in a Roman Catholic cemetery. Founded in Montreal in 1844 to foster French-Canadian culture, the Institut sponsored public forums on controversial issues, championed freedom of conscience, and established a library that included publications placed on the papal index of forbidden books.

Not surprisingly, the Institut earned the opposition of clerical leaders in Quebec, who had it condemned by Rome and its yearbook placed on the index in 1868. Many members resigned from the Institut because of the church's position, but Joseph Guibord explicitly refused to renounce his membership. When he died in 1869, Bishop Bourget of Montreal denied him burial in consecrated ground. Guibord's widow took the case to court and, in 1874, after a series of appeals, the Judicial Committee of the Privy Council ordered that Bourget's ruling be overturned. Because feelings ran high over the issue, Guibord's body, which had rested in a Protestant cemetery for five years, had to be accompanied by an armed military escort while it

John Joseph Lynch, the archbishop of the Roman Catholic Church in Toronto who tried to stop his parishioners from attending free-thought meetings, is portrayed here as slaying the serpent of free thought with the sword of faith.
By J.W. Bengough. *Grip*, 22 May 1880

was transferred to its final resting place. Even then, Bishop Bourget had the last word: he immediately deconsecrated the ground where Guibord's body lay. Although the Institut waned and eventually closed its doors in 1885, its ideas could not be entirely suppressed.

While significant, the church's political influence in Quebec was never all-embracing. Although many clerics subscribed to the ultramontanist view that all political policy should be based on papal teachings, they were unable to force compliance. Even the Conservative Party, which dominated Quebec politics until 1886, was split between those who accepted ultramontane injunctions and those who believed that politicians must govern without interference from the church. The election of the Parti National as the provincial government in 1886, in defiance of continued church support for the Conservatives, demonstrated that many Roman Catholics refused to recognize the right of bishops to dictate their political decisions. However, the Parti National could not afford to be too anti-clerical, nor did it challenge church control over education or social services.

By the end of the nineteenth century, the Roman Catholic Church became more receptive to reform ideals. Pope Leo XIII lifted an ineffectual ban on the Knights of Labor in 1887, and in his encyclical of 1891, *Rerum Novarum*, he condemned an uncontrolled market economy. While he supported private ownership of industry, the pope urged that capitalism be guided by government regulation. This position contrasted sharply with that of the Roman Catholic hierarchy in Quebec, which continued to distrust the state and positive government action.

The pope's position that a remedy be found quickly for the misery of the working class eventually spurred a Roman Catholic social action movement. In Quebec, this was centred in the Montreal-based École sociale populaire, established in 1911, which trained Roman Catholic activists to work in the community. The growth of Roman Catholic activism was also reflected in the expansion of the Roman Catholic press, including such clerically controlled newspapers as *Le Droit* in Ottawa, *L'Action catholique* in Quebec City, and *Le Bien public* in Trois-Rivières. In addition, the church supported a Roman Catholic trade union movement—a deliberate attempt to eclipse the secular and increasingly socialist organizations taking root among the working class, but also a check on the exploitation of its flock by profit-seeking capitalists.

Although its influence remained the greatest in Quebec, the Roman Catholic Church expanded throughout Canada, building churches, hospitals, orphanages, and schools to serve its increasingly diverse clients. In the case of Polish immigrants, traditional Roman Catholicism was closely allied to Polish nationalism, a connection that in 1901 turned the congregation of the Winnipeg Holy Ghost parish against the German-speaking Oblate Fathers. At the same time that it was suppressing Native languages in its residential schools, the Roman Catholic Church played an essential role in maintaining minority eastern European languages through its networks of parochial schools. By 1916, for instance, there were 11 Polish and Ukrainian Roman Catholic schools in Manitoba.

SCHOOLING AND SOCIETY

During the second half of the nineteenth century, school attendance increased dramatically. It also varied according to region and culture. By 1891, it was estimated that 6 percent of Ontario residents and 13 percent of Maritime Canadians were totally illiterate. In Quebec, where compulsory schooling was enacted only in 1943, 26 percent of the population was deemed unable to either read or write; in Newfoundland, the figure was 32 percent.

In all provinces except Quebec, the education system was under a state-directed Department of Education, which set minimum standards for schools. Quebec, in contrast, had two systems, one Roman Catholic and one Protestant, each eligible for provincial subsidies. Two denominational committees made education policy for the province. The Roman Catholic committee consisted of all Catholic bishops in the province and an equal number of government-appointed lay Catholics, a system guaranteeing that the influence of the church would remain paramount in the Catholic school board. Francophones from working-class and farm backgrounds in Quebec continued to receive far less education than their Anglophone counterparts inside and outside the province. As late as 1926, only one Catholic child in 20 in Montreal stayed in school beyond the primary grades.

While the trade union movement in Quebec battled for free compulsory schooling, the Catholic Church opposed compulsory education, tuition-free schooling, and free textbooks. The church was supported in its conservatism by the textile, tobacco, and shoe industries, which employed many older children, and often by poor working-class and farm families, who relied on the labour and wages of their children for survival. The migration of rural Quebecers to New England's textile factories decreased after 1900 because enforcement of laws against child labour in New England made it difficult for poor families to make a living.

Elsewhere in Canada, education was undergoing a rapid transformation. Faith in the value of education, fear of social breakdown, and conviction that new skills were required in the industrial labour market contributed to the growth of schools and changes in curriculum. Beginning in Ontario in 1871, the introduction of high schools offered parents who could afford it a chance to further educate their children. By 1905, with the exception of Quebec, all provinces had legislated free schooling and compulsory attendance for youngsters under the age of 12. Between 1891 and 1922, elementary and secondary enrolments in Canada more than doubled from 942 500 to 1 939 700. The number of teachers grew still faster, from 21 149 in 1890 to 54 691 in 1920. Teachers' qualifications improved steadily, and women increased their numerical dominance of the profession to over 82 percent in 1921.

Under pressure from parents, teachers, and administrators, schools became more humane and child-centred and more practical and relevant. Kindergartens, with their goal of improving family life for the poor and nurturing creativity and independence in young children, expanded slowly from their urban Ontario base. In all grades, more stress was placed on reasoning with the child and less on corporal punishment. Pressure was also increasing for the establishment of minimum standards of health and safety. Montreal's schools set the pace in 1906 with Canada's first regular and systematic medical inspection of pupils. As an integral part of the health-reform effort, formal instruction in physical education was introduced in many schools. For boys this often meant cadet training, an option that regularly pitted peace advocates against more militaristically inclined nationalists.

Other reformers advocated making the curriculum more applicable to the world of work. Under the leadership of Canada's first dairy commissioner, James W. Robertson, philanthropist Sir William Macdonald, and social activist Adelaide Hoodless, manual training and household science were introduced in many schools. Boys were encouraged to think in terms of practical pursuits, in particular a future in agriculture and industry. Girls' training in up-to-date menus and housekeeping was to compensate for the shortcomings of education within the family and reaffirm female responsibility in the home. The notion of specialized education for girls had particular appeal in Quebec, where écoles ménagères were established to give girls a non-academic education designed to make them good housekeepers and bearers of traditional Roman Catholic family values.

Although a national consensus emerged among English-Canadian education reformers about the ideal school system, the reality of schooling often varied dramatically from the ideal. The scattered settlement characteristic of northern areas, with their isolated families of farmers, small mill operators, railway workers, and Native trappers, hunters, and fishers, was never addressed adequately by public schooling. Equally problematic was the situation encountered by the disabled. By 1914, school medical inspection meant that children with mental or physical handicaps were more likely to be identified. For those with minor tooth, eye, and ear problems, remedies were possible. Children with serious disabilities found relatively few options. They were likely to be kept at home or to enter the labour force earlier than their contemporaries.

Schools served as a vehicle for assimilating new Canadians, especially on the Prairies. As the region filled with people from diverse cultures, education systems based on the cultural conditions of eastern

Canada came entirely unstuck. The 1897 compromise over French and Roman Catholic schools in Manitoba, for example, had permitted a limited number of Catholic teachers, Catholic instruction at the end of the day, and bilingual teaching in English and any other language spoken by at least 10 pupils in a school. What was not anticipated in 1897 was the flood of new Canadians who would take advantage of the right to bilingual schooling. Immigrant parents proved intensely interested in preserving their cultures and securing the best schooling possible for their children. In urban areas, they frequently established their own evening schools and sent their children to learn English and Canadian ways in the public system during the day.

The English majority in the western provinces refused to accommodate linguistic pluralism in their schools. In the face of strong opposition from French-Canadian, Polish, Mennonite, and Ukrainian communities, the Manitoba government withdrew funding from all bilingual schools in 1916. Despite the compromise of 1905, Saskatchewan abolished instruction in languages other than English beyond the first grade in 1918. The Roman Catholic clergy in Alberta had made separate schools, not language, its cause in 1905. The result was that, at least officially, there were no bilingual schools to outlaw. Nor were there any in British Columbia.

In Ontario, Anglo-Canadians resisted efforts of the growing Francophone minority to secure education in its own language. The ultra-Protestant Orange Lodges and English-speaking Roman Catholics worked together to push Ontario's Department of Education to enact Regulation 17 in 1912. Under this law, only schools with English-speaking teachers, where English instruction was begun upon admission, and where French was not used beyond the second year could be eligible for government funding. Public protests were staged and legal challenges were launched, but the courts supported the Ontario government.

By the end of the nineteenth century, multi-room schools such as the Lunenburg Academy, built in 1895, were emerging in towns and cities as monuments to the faith in education as a panacea for society's ills.
Peter Zwicker

In the Maritimes, the school battles of the second half of the nineteenth century gave way to compromise. The New Brunswick government established a French department in its teacher-training program in 1885, and after 1907 made French-language textbooks available to students. In 1902, Nova Scotia appointed a commission to study Acadian education. Its recommendations resulted in the use of French textbooks and the hiring of bilingual teachers in Acadian areas. On Prince Edward Island, an inspector responsible for Acadian schools was appointed in 1892. Acadians in many parts of the Maritimes were often still subjected to English textbooks and teachers, but they nevertheless retained some concessions to language and culture that were increasingly officially denied to Francophones in Ontario and the West.

Universities in the Industrial Age

While universities served a much smaller clientele than schools, they were important barometers of change in post-confederation Canada. Most of Canada's 17 degree-granting institutions in 1867 managed on meagre endowments, tuition fees, and small government grants. Despite pressure from provincial governments in Nova Scotia and Ontario for consolidation, denominational colleges survived and more were founded, including the Anglican-inspired University of Western Ontario in 1878 and McMaster University in 1887, the latter a special project of Baptist businessman William McMaster and his wife Susan Moulton.

In the newly created western provinces, governments asserted control over universities from the beginning. Manitoba combined Saint Boniface (Roman Catholic), St. John's (Anglican), Manitoba College (Presbyterian), and Wesley College (Methodist) under the umbrella of the University of Manitoba in 1877. In each of the other three western provinces, a single provincial university was established: the universities of Alberta (1906), Saskatchewan (1907), and British Columbia (1908). Modelling themselves after state colleges in the United States, they combined teaching and research functions in the service of their provinces.

In Quebec, higher education remained divided between the two major language groups. McGill and Bishop's, both established before confederation, catered to Anglophone elites, while Laval University,

under the control of the Roman Catholic Church, maintained a campus in Quebec City and, after 1876, had a branch campus in Montreal. Following the First World War, the Université de Montréal gained independence from Laval and emerged as a modern multi-university, including under its auspices the École polytechnique, the École des hautes études commerciales, the Oka Agricultural Institute, and a school of veterinary medicine.

Most Canadian Anglophone universities opened their doors to women in the 1880s and 1890s but female students remained a minority in the student body and were often unwelcome in science and professional programs. By 1921, women made up about 15 percent of the professoriate but could be found primarily in the bottom ranks. People of colour and cultural minorities, such as Jews, were often not welcomed as students or professors.

Despite their reputation for conservatism, universities were changing. The number of subjects was expanding to include natural and social sciences; students were less preoccupied with piety than with social issues and participated in a wide range of extracurricular activities; and ornate buildings, housing laboratories, lecture theatres, and lounges proliferated on growing landscaped campuses.

By 1914, students attending universities were participants in a youth culture that scandalized their elders. Unchaperoned interaction between male and female students was a particular cause of gossip and concern. Sometimes worse was suspected, as was the case in 1913 when the *Toronto News* broke the story that the University of Toronto campus had been the site of a "tango party" involving five men and some "Chorus girls."[3]

The growth of technical colleges and professional schools in universities reflected an increasing demand for career-related education. In their efforts to restrict entry into their fields, professionals pressured the state to grant them self-regulation. Increasingly, a specific university degree became a condition for receiving a licence to practise a profession. Physicians, lawyers, and engineers had succeeded in winning self-regulation in most jurisdictions by the end of the century and required university training as a condition of licensing. As well, in most provinces, specialized technical and agricultural colleges were established to bring academic rigour to practical pursuits. Like other professionals, university professors expanded their training and increasingly turned to research as the basis for their academic credentials. The PhD, a German innovation, was emerging as the most coveted degree in arts and sciences, though few Canadian universities offered it.

Critics warned against the creation of narrow professional monopolies that used education as a means of eliminating rivals. In the health field, for example, homeopaths, midwives, and other proponents of natural medicine complained that "professionalization" was a crude effort to bestow legitimacy on a single approach to medicine—the "scientific" approach stressing chemical-based medicines and surgical solutions espoused by medical societies. Despite such views, the trend toward professionalization and the scientific approach to the study of human and natural phenomena carried the day both inside and outside institutions of higher education.

REINVENTING NATURE

Industrialization and urbanization led Canadians to approach the natural environment in a different way. While Aboriginal peoples had long treated nature with reverence, early European settlers were more likely to see the rugged Canadian landscape as a cause for panic, an obstacle in their path to progress, or a storehouse of wealth to be exploited. A few colonials commented ruefully on the rapid disappearance of forests, birds, and wild animals, but there was little effort to stop the trend toward greater exploitation of Canada's clearly abundant resources.

Influenced by romantic notions of the untamed wilderness emanating from Great Britain and the United States, Canadians in the second half of the nineteenth century began to see the natural environment as a benevolent and healing mother who offered respite from the competition and anxiety of "modern times." In 1899, journalist J.W. Dafoe, writing in the first issue of *Rod and Gun*, the official journal of the Canadian Forestry Association, noted that "in these days the country has been discovered anew. No fact of contemporary life is more significant or more hopeful than this return to nature, for breathing space, for those whose daily walk is the tumultuous city streets."[4] Inevitably, such views were most popular among city

dwellers, who encountered "nature" only in small doses, if at all.

The back-to-nature movement had an enormous impact on the way all Canadians experienced their country. Organizations such as the Alpine Club and the Field-Naturalists' Club initiated many adults into nature's mysteries, while social reformers set up foundations to provide slum children with summer vacations in rural areas. Schools were also enlisted in the cause. Through the efforts of naturalist societies, farm organizations, and the Central Experimental Farm in Ottawa, nature study classes were introduced in the public schools of British Columbia (1900), Nova Scotia (1901), Ontario (1904), and Alberta (1908). In many towns and cities, branches of the Society for the Prevention of Cruelty to Animals gave practical focus to the growing sympathy for the "lower orders."

With urban life increasingly redefining what it meant to be a man, boys became the particular focus of reformers who saw nature as the vehicle for inculcating survival skills and manly virtues. Ernest Thompson Seton, who achieved fame as a naturalist and animal-story writer, inspired a club movement dedicated to teaching boys the skills of tracking, camping, canoeing, and woodcraft. Hundreds of Woodcraft Clubs sprang up all over North America in the first decade of the twentieth century before they were superseded in Canada by the Boy Scout movement. Founded in Great Britain in 1908 by South African War veteran Robert Baden-Powell, the Boy Scout movement was based on the view that the frontier experience toughened up boys so that they would make better men—and better soldiers.

Baden-Powell launched the Girl Guides as a counterpart to the Boy Scouts in 1909 and by January 1910 Canada had its first guide group in St. Catharines, Ontario. Even more popular among girls was the Canadian Girls in Training (CGIT), an organization established by the Young Women's Christian Association (YWCA) in cooperation with the major Protestant denominations in 1915. Dedicated to training young women between the ages of 12 and 17 in Christian leadership, the outdoor experience was prominent in CGIT activities.

Even religion could not escape the call of nature. The notion that spiritual and natural phenomena were in conflict had been a feature of Christian thought since the Middle Ages, but Darwinism called this view into question. Humans, in the post-Darwinian world, seemed not so much enemies of nature but its offspring. Among theologians and creative writers, it became fashionable to refer to nature as a medium whereby people could communicate with God. Poets such as Bliss Carman, Archibald Lampman, and Charles G.D. Roberts wrote eloquently about the kinship between people and nature.

Nature enthusiasts took the lead in demanding state-legislated conservation. Under the combined assault of environmentalists, governments in most provinces passed Game Acts and people were encouraged to hunt with cameras rather than guns. In 1904, Jack Miner established Canada's first bird sanctuary in Kingsville, Ontario, thereby launching a lifelong career devoted to the preservation of birds. The federal government followed up its initiative in Banff by creating more federally designated national parks, including Yoho (1886) and Jasper (1907); the Ontario government established the first provincial park reserve, Algonquin, in 1893. Although Canadians continued to gobble up resources at an alarming rate, there was a growing sense that some control over their exploitation was necessary.

Rural people and minorities bore the brunt of the regulatory regimes that were put in place to conserve nature. Parks and game reserves were closed to hunters and hunting for sport was privileged over the killing of wild animals for consumption. Unable to police an area the size of Canada, wardens tended to target Native people, foreigners, and the rural poor as most likely to defy the law. In Victoria, for example, "Lee, a Chinaman" who supplied the Hotel Driard with grouse and pheasant, was prosecuted in 1908, but the hotel proprietors were not. Three years earlier, the chiefs of the Lillooet band stated clearly the impact of new provincial hunting regulations: "This new game

With the rise in the late nineteenth century of what today would be called eco-tourism, guiding became an important economic activity for Native peoples in many parts of Canada. The Fridays, a Cree family who ran a tourist lodge in Temagami, Ontario, were popular guides. (Here, Bill Friday is shown in 1905 with his companions after a successful day's fishing.) While tourists travelling with guides had glimpses into Native life that few Canadians experienced, they tended to romanticize the Native "instinct" for "wilderness" skills, thus reinforcing the belief in racial differences that informed most encounters between whites and Aboriginal peoples.
Archives of Ontario/Acc 9348, S 14651

act as a whole is hurting us altogether. Should it be put in execution it would mean our entire destruction. Hunting and fishing is our living. It is our daily bread for which we have a right and which no law can take away from us. We have a right to live."[5]

The idea of nature as a refuge from urban life led those who could afford it to buy or rent summer cottages in attractive rural areas outside the cities. With railways providing access to hitherto remote areas, people flocked to the Lake of the Woods, Georgian Bay, and the Muskoka regions of Ontario and the Lower Lakes region and Murray Bay in Quebec. In the Maritimes, the options for seaside bliss were endless, but St. Andrew's-by-the-Sea, New Brunswick; Cavendish Beach, Prince Edward Island; and the Bras d'Or Lakes in Cape Breton became favourite haunts of the rich and famous from all over North America. For many well-heeled tourists, hunting and fishing with a Native guide was the ultimate wilderness experience, taking them back to simpler times when survival in the great outdoors, rather than in some stifling office tower, was what life was all about.

THE GROWTH OF ORGANIZED SPORTS

As with tourism, sporting activities were shaped by the opportunities and values of the industrial age. Competitive games, the codification of rules regulating play, and commercialization paralleled trends in the marketplace and sparked debates about the purpose of games. The expansion of railway and road networks enabled teams to develop regular schedules of inter-community, interregional, and even international play. Electrically lit indoor facilities, such as ice rinks, tracks, and gymnasia, made conditions more predictable for sports that could be played indoors. By the 1890s, specialized sports pages had become common in most newspapers, an indication that such activities were becoming commercially viable.

The middle class clung tenaciously to the amateur ideal, with its prohibition of payment to participants and gentlemanly codes of conduct. Amateurism became the defining feature of the Olympic Games when they were reinstated in 1896 and also prevailed in athletic programs established in schools, universities, and most social clubs before 1914. The Montreal Athletic Association (1881) was the first organization to serve as an umbrella for amateur sports enthusiasts and became the driving force behind the Amateur Athletics Association of Canada, founded in 1884. In 1893, the governor-general, Lord Stanley, donated a cup to the Canadian amateur hockey champions, and his successor, Earl Grey, provided a trophy for the football champions on the condition that it be awarded only to amateur teams.

Canada ultimately followed the United States down the slippery slope toward the professionalization of sports. The Montreal Wanderers, after winning the last amateur Stanley Cup in 1908, immediately turned professional. In that same year, the Eastern Canada Hockey Association turned professional, and in 1909 the rival National Hockey Association was formed. Although football and hockey inspired enthusiastic fans, professional baseball emerged as the most popular spectator sport in this period, attracting a huge working-class audience throughout English and French Canada.

For many Canadians, the rise of professionalism not only violated their much-cherished ideal of amateurism, it also opened the door to other undesirable, even "un-Canadian," practices. In 1885, these issues were addressed by Toronto lawyer W.A. Frost in a letter to the editor of the *Varsity*, the University of Toronto's student newspaper. According to Frost, baseball "has been degraded by Yankee professionalism until the name of baseball cannot fail to suggest a tobacco-chewing, loud-voiced, twang-nosed bar-tender, with a large diamond pin and elaborately oiled hair."[6] Despite such views, professional sports continued to attract a wide following.

Given the migration of many Canadians to the United States in this period and the lure of professional salaries, it is not surprising that many Canadians earned their sporting reputations in events sponsored south of the border. Nat Butler, a native of Halifax, began his career in bicycle racing in Boston and broke all records at the Winter Velodrome in Paris in 1905. Although basketball was developed by a Canadian—James Naismith from Almonte, Ontario—it was pioneered at the YMCA International Training School in Springfield, Massachusetts, where Naismith was a student and later a teacher.

Sports were often closed to racial minorities because whites would not allow them to join their teams and clubs. In the

The Royals Baseball Club of Saint John, New Brunswick. Intermediate Champions, 1921.
Public Archives of New Brunswick Harold Wright Collection/P338-2

Maritimes, blacks began forming their own baseball teams in the 1880s and by the 1890s were hosting an annual regional championship. Tom Longboat, a rare exception to the increasing exclusion of Native peoples from competitive athletics, came first in the 1907 Boston Marathon. Like whites, individuals from racial minorities often found sporting opportunities in the United States. Gabriel Dumont, for example, toured in the United States as a crack marksman in Buffalo Bill's Wild West show in the 1880s, and two black boxers from Nova Scotia, George Dixon and Sam Langford, won acclaim at home and in the United States for their successes in the ring.

Sporting activities were also beginning to open up to women. In the 1880s, bicycling joined tennis, curling, and skating as amusements for middle-class women and as a cause for worry among those who identified an increase in women's physical freedom and scandalously scant sporting attire with moral laxity and, worse still, feminist sympathies. The participation of women in school and university sports such as basketball, field hockey, and ice hockey helped to break down proscriptions against female participation in competitive play.

By 1914, the prevalence of school athletics and the multitude of programs run by groups such as the YWCA, YMCA, CGIT, Girl Guides, and Boy Scouts had given sports an unprecedented place in the lives of most Canadians. The discovery by sports promoters that good money could be made presenting professional baseball, football, and hockey on a regular basis meant that Canadian sport was well on its way to becoming a major North American industry. And, for all the dominance of middle-class Anglophones, a shared interest in sporting activity may have helped to begin to knit together diverse groups of Canadians.

ARCHITECTURE IN THE MODERN AGE

By 1918, cities looked nothing like they had a half-century earlier. With their banks and department stores, universities and hospitals, museums and libraries, palatial homes, and apartment buildings, parks, and public baths, urban landscapes catalogued the exuberant optimism of the industrial age. For both newcomers and long-time residents, many buildings

must have seemed almost the equivalent of medieval cathedrals, highly visible symbols of success and power. Railway hotels such as Quebec City's Château Frontenac and Victoria's Empress and private residences such as Toronto's Casa Loma or Edmonton's Beaulieu spoke volumes about the social aspirations of the Canadian business community. Like the fashionable clothes worn by the wealthy, "style" in architecture was essential to the display of conspicuous consumption.

In the 1870s, Victorian versions of medieval or Renaissance buildings were popular. The ornamental mansard roof on Toronto's Opera House was modelled on buildings in Napoleon III's France, while Gothic features reminiscent of the Middle Ages could be found in structures ranging from the Parliament Buildings in Ottawa to modest homes of the working class. Second Empire and neo-Gothic styles in Canadian architecture were succeeded by a monumental Beaux-Arts style with Roman columns, cornices, and vaults, of which Toronto's Union Station (1915–1920), the Saskatchewan Legislature (1908–1912), and Montreal's Sun Life Building (begun 1914) are some of the best examples.

Construction advances, notably fireproofed steel framing and reinforced concrete, and the introduction of elevators changed the type of buildings that could be designed. Under the influence of the Chicago school of architects, early skyscrapers such as the Calgary Grain Exchange (1909) and Edmonton's Tegler Building (1911) began to alter the urban landscape in ways that made Canadian cities increasingly indistinguishable from their British and American counterparts. Since many important buildings were designed by American and British firms, the similarity is not surprising. McGill University established the first Canadian department of architecture only in 1896, and it was not until 1907 that provincial architectural associations created a national organization.

Buildings in small-town and rural Canada reflected, though more modestly, international trends in architecture. From the Maritimes to the Yukon, Greek columns, Gothic elements, and mansard roofs showed the influence of more than 2000 years of European architectural history. William Critchlow Harris, for example, produced designs for more than 90 high Victorian Gothic buildings in the Maritimes, many of

Union Station, Toronto, and Union Mine, Cumberland, British Columbia (inset). While cities were becoming architectural monuments to the Industrial Age, company towns on the resource frontier bore a remarkable similarity to one another in their undistinguished architecture and lack of amenities.
City of Toronto Archives/SC244-594 and British Columbia Archives/A-04531

them elegant churches, from his base in Charlottetown. Using architectural texts from Europe and the United States, Canadians easily adapted international designs to their needs, often creating their own unique architectural traditions in the process.

Between confederation and the First World War, the federal government erected more than 300 public buildings to house national services such as post offices, customs offices, and prisons. All federal buildings were constructed under the direction of the Department of Public Works, whose chief architect from 1881 to 1897 was Thomas Fuller. A native of Bath, England, Fuller was involved as a young man in the design of Canada's Parliament Buildings and was determined to create an imposing government presence across the country.

In rural areas, Canadians displayed architectural distinctiveness in the crafting of barns and storage facilities designed to handle the expanding output of commercialized farming. Across Canada, farmers erected barns to house their expanding herds of cattle, the source of a year-round supply of milk in the rapidly growing cities. The same changes in construction techniques that transformed the urban landscape also

made grain elevators a classic form on the Prairie landscape. Grain storage facilities in Calgary, Port Arthur, Toronto, and Montreal are said to have been inspirations to world-renowned European architects Walter Gropius and Le Corbusier.

THE ARTS

In the half-century following confederation, Canadians lamented their lack of a distinctive artistic and literary culture. The dominion's youth, colonial inheritance, and proximity to the United States were advanced as reasons why Canadian writers, painters, and sculptors rarely achieved international recognition. At the end of the nineteenth century, novelist and essayist Sara Jeannette Duncan commented:

> In our character as colonists we find the root of all our sins of omission in letters. . . . Our enforced political humility is the distinguishing characteristic of every phase of our national life. We are ignored, and we ignore ourselves. A nation's development is like a plant's, unattractive under ground. So long as Canada remains in political obscurity, content to thrive only at the roots, so long will the leaves and blossoms of art and literature be scanty and stunted

products of our national energy. . . . A national literature cannot be looked for as an outcome of anything less than a complete national existence.[7]

The dead weight of religious conservatism also helped keep Canada behind developments in the arts in Europe and the United States. In Quebec, where the Roman Catholic Church remained powerful, most authors presented their province as a devout Catholic nation with a mission to spread Catholicism throughout the world. The peasant novel, a popular European genre that idealized rural life, took firm root in Quebec. The most enduring example of this genre is Louis Hémon's *Maria Chapdelaine* (1913), which dealt with the difficult choice facing many French Canadians of moving either to New England to find work or to communities on Quebec's agricultural frontier. A few writers resisted clerical dictates. Influenced by French modernists like Baudelaire and Rimbaud, bohemian Montreal poets such as Émile Nelligan and members of the École littéraire de Montréal espoused a highly individualistic literature preoccupied with the meaning of life, death, and love. Such writers risked clerical censure and faced minuscule markets for their work.

In the late nineteenth century, English-Canadian literary production was, on the whole, as conservative and prone to romanticizing the past as was its French-Canadian counterpart. Loyalist themes, common in works from the 1820s onward, remained popular and were reinforced by centennial celebrations of Loyalist settlement. Both the initial Loyalist flight from the mad republic to the south and the defence of Canada in War of 1812 were mythologized in Egerton Ryerson's *The Loyalists of America and Their Times* (1880). In 1876, Sarah Curzon, a Toronto suffrage and temperance advocate, produced a play called *Laura Secord, the Heroine of 1812*, which used popular Loyalist themes to promote a positive view of women's abilities. Canada Firster Charles Mair won praise for his poems drawing on the history of the Loyalists. Ironically, Mair, who harboured racist attitudes toward Riel and his Métis followers, presented the Native leader, Tecumseh, who had supported the British in 1812, as the hero of an 1886 drama.

Novelists and poets found that the centres of English-language publishing were located in London and, increasingly, New York and Boston, where there was only a limited market for Canadian themes. Indeed, one of the reasons that Canadians remained in the romantic literary tradition after other countries had abandoned it was that the popular demand for stories about New France, Acadia, Aboriginal peoples, and rural life remained strong in foreign markets. Dramatic

VOICES FROM THE PAST

Stephen Leacock on Industrial Society

Stephen Leacock, in heavily ironic volumes such as *Sunshine Sketches of a Little Town* (1912) and *Arcadian Adventures with the Idle Rich* (1914), questioned the values and virtues of North American liberal capitalism. In his *Literary Lapses* (1910), he used a humorous interview to condemn North American business ethics:

> So one evening I asked one of the millionaires how old Bloggs had made all his money.
>
> "How he made it?" he answered with a sneer. "Why, he made it by taking it out of widows and orphans."
>
> Widows and orphans! I thought, what an excellent idea. But who would have suspected that they had it?
>
> "And how," I asked pretty cautiously, "did he go at it to get it out of them?"
>
> "Why," the man answered, "he just ground them under his heels, and that was how."[8]

Stephen Leacock
© Bettman/CORBIS

readings by Pauline Johnson, Canada's "Mohawk Princess," on stages in and outside Canada drew on her Native heritage to conjure a distinctive northern nationality that was far removed from the experience of most of her listeners.

By the end of the nineteenth century, literary production began to increase in range and output, fuelled in part by the growing tendency of newspapers to run serialized novels. Women, who were increasingly able to make livings as writers or journalists, particularly excelled as novelists. In *Roland Graeme Knight*, Agnes Machar fused reformist, feminist, religious, and patriotic concerns in her highly romantic portrayal of a Knight of Labor and the woman who loved him. Margaret Marshall Saunders, the daughter of a Nova Scotia Baptist minister, published *Beautiful Joe*, the story of an abused dog, in 1894. After winning first prize in an American Humane Society competition, *Beautiful Joe* became a best-seller, reputedly the first work by a Canadian author to sell a million copies.

BIOGRAPHY

E. Pauline Johnson

In the period before the First World War, E. Pauline Johnson was one of only a handful of Canadian authors who achieved an international audience for their work. The youngest child of an English mother and a Mohawk father, Johnson was born in 1861 and grew up in Chiefswood, an elegant home on the Grand River's Six Nation Reserve near Brantford, Ontario. Educated in both Native and Euro-Canadian cultures, she drew upon her mixed heritage to produce poetry and prose that addressed such issues as racism, feminism, and Canadian national identity.

Johnson began writing to support herself following the death of her father in 1884. In 1892, she launched a career as a performance artist, reading her poems to primarily white audiences in Canada, the United States, and Great Britain. Wearing a Native costume for the first half of her program and a drawing-room gown for the second, "the Mohawk Princess" thrilled audiences with dramatic recitations of such poems as "The Song My Paddle Sings," "A Cry from an Indian Wife," and "As Red Men Die." Her first book of poems, *The White Wampum*, appeared in 1895 and her second collection, *Canadian Born*, in 1903.

While touring in England in 1906, she met Joseph Capilano [Su-á-pu-luck] and his delegation, who were protesting recent hunting and fishing restrictions on Natives in British Columbia in a meeting with King Edward VII. Johnson's friendship with "Chief Joe" reinforced her growing attraction to the West Coast and its Native history, which was being ignored by new immigrants to the region. In 1909, ill with breast cancer, Johnson retired to Vancouver, where editor Lionel Waterloo Makovski and journalist Isabel McLean established a committee that included representatives of the Canadian Women's

Pauline Johnson.
Library and Archives Canada/PA-111473

Press Club and the local Women's Canadian Club to raise money for her care and help with the publication of *Legends of Vancouver* in 1911 and *Flint and Feather* in 1912. Johnson died in 1913 and, as she requested, was buried in Stanley Park within sight of Siwash Rock.

The Writing of History

In the nineteenth century, history emerged as a vehicle for "inventing" Canadian identity. Historians drew on the past to provide support for nation-building efforts, while public commemorations encouraged a common, if selective, understanding of past events. In this context, Samuel de Champlain, Dollard des Ormeaux, Madeleine de Verchères, Tecumseh, and Laura Secord, among others, became heroic, larger-than-life figures who stood for virtues that they might not have possessed in large measure. By the early twentieth century, commemorations such as the one held to mark the tercentenary of Quebec City in 1908 were attended by thousands of people and left in their wake statues, monuments, and plaques to remind Canadians of their debt to the past.

Efforts to bring Canadians together around a common understanding of their past encountered major obstacles. English-Canadian historians tended to portray Canada as a collection of peaceful, Crown-loving, moderately liberal colonies. In such texts as John Charles Dent's *The Last Forty Years: Canada Since the Union of 1841* (1881) and *The Story of the Upper Canadian Rebellion* (1885), both oligarchies and radical reformers were given short shrift, while those who supported responsible government, such as Robert Baldwin and Louis-Hippolyte LaFontaine, were portrayed more positively. These historians subscribed to what is known as a Whig view of history—the notion that history is the story of events that reveal the progress of human development.

Nowhere was this view of history more explicitly revealed than in the popular 10-volume *History of Canada,* published by civil engineer William Kingsford between 1887 and 1898. Kingsford was touted as English Canada's counterpart to the famous French-Canadian nationalist historian François-Xavier Garneau, whose multi-volume *Histoire du Canada,* published in the 1840s, extolled the history and culture of his people. Although both historians shared a progressive view of history, they differed in their interpretation of events. Garneau regretted the conquest, while Kingsford and most English-Canadian historical writers regarded it as a blessing in disguise for French Canadians and a necessary step in the march toward civilization.

In French Canada, the liberal, anti-clerical perspective typified by Garneau gave way to histories that emphasized the role of the clergy in developing French-Canadian society. Abbé Jean-Baptiste-Antoine Ferland's histories in the 1860s, for example, painted a portrait of New France as a missionary colony whose history was guided by providence and its earthly representatives in the form of self-sacrificing bishops, nuns, and priests. Even Garneau modified his earlier views in light of the clerical assault. While a few anti-clerical historians such as Benjamin Sulte championed secular forces, they tended to glorify rural life and paid little attention to the economic history of French Canada.

By the end of the nineteenth century, the historian's craft was being taught in universities. Chairs in history were established at Dalhousie in 1880, Toronto in 1894, and McGill in 1895. The naming of George Wrong to the chair of history at the University of Toronto and the introduction at Queen's University of Adam Shortt's lectures on the economic and social history of Canada, both in 1894, marked the beginning of academic approaches to the nation's past. Between 1913 and 1917, Adam Shortt teamed up with Arthur Doughty to produce the multi-volume series *Canada and Its Provinces.* While Shortt and Doughty shared the progressive view of history, they abandoned the romanticism of earlier writers for a detailed analysis of the nation's social and economic development. Abbé Lionel Groulx's lectures in Canadian history at the Montreal campus of Laval University (now the Université de Montréal) in 1915 led to his appointment as the first full-time professor of Canadian history at a Francophone university.

These men were not charting new directions in a vacuum. In 1872, the founding of the Public Archives of Canada (now Library and Archives Canada) under the direction of Douglas Brymner testified to a growing interest in the collection of historical documents. A decade later, the formation of the Royal Society of Canada gave academic historians a forum in which to disseminate their scholarly research.

While university-based historians were preoccupied with national themes, amateurs continued to practise their craft, producing county, community, and regimental histories. Female historians, some of them university-trained but denied university postings, served as custodians of local history, worked as unacknowledged writers and research assistants for their male relatives and employers, and chronicled social and cultural topics neglected by professional historians. Throughout the nation, Canadians whose stories were not reflected in the dominant narratives and public commemorations passed on oral and written traditions about their experiences.

One of Canada's best-known writers was Lucy Maud Montgomery, whose first published novel, *Anne of Green Gables*, became an instant international success when it appeared in 1908.

A new realistic tradition was reflected in the work of Sara Jeannette Duncan, a disciple of the American novelist Henry James and the first woman to be hired as a full-time journalist at the Toronto *Globe*. Her novel *The Imperialist* (1904) dissected small-town Ontario life and explored the need to balance British sentiment with the reality of North American life. Leading periodicals of the day, such as *Saturday Night* (established 1887), *Busy Man's Magazine* (1896–1911)—which became *Maclean's Magazine*—and *Canadian Magazine* (1893–1939) were somewhat more inclined to express liberal sentiments but were often narrowly provincial in their focus.

Throughout this period, people met in each other's homes at regular intervals to make music, read poetry, and perform plays. Some of these groups gradually became more formal in their efforts to promote cultural activities. The Eclectic Reading Club in Saint John, established in 1884, had a long waiting list of people wanting to join. The Cavendish Literary Society, founded in 1886 for "the mutual improvement of its members," gave a young Lucy Maud Montgomery a place to test her ideas, while the Vagabond Club of Vancouver, established in 1914, offered men "an outlet for whatever small talents we possessed in a city in which buying and selling of real-estate was the preoccupation of the majority of inhabitants."[9] In Toronto, the Arts and Letters Club, founded in 1908, brought artists together to feed off each other's creativity. The Women's Art Association, established in 1890, spawned branches throughout the dominion to bring women together for mutual help and improvement.

Painting and Sculpture

Academic art tended to follow international trends, though often at some distance. In 1868, the Society of Canadian Artists was established to promote formal Canadian artwork in a variety of exhibits. The Royal Academy of Arts and the National Gallery of Canada were created in 1880 at the urging of the governor-general, the Marquis of Lorne. Before the end of the century, a number of art schools had been established in urban centres. Overwhelmingly, professional artists were men who, like William Brymner, Robert Harris, and George Reid, trained either in the academic style of the Paris Salon school or later, like Edmund Morris and Curtis Williamson, found inspiration in the atmospheric Hague school. An exception to the habit of European training was Homer Watson, who, like the French-Canadian Ozias Leduc, was self-taught and visited Europe only later in life.

As a major sponsor of painting, sculpture, and architecture in its great cathedrals, the Catholic Church encouraged some of the most impressive religious art produced anywhere in the world. A combination of church and private commissions supported fine contributions in the art nouveau tradition by painters such as Ozias Leduc and

Demonstration by the Association catholique de la jeunesse canadienne-française at the Monument Champlain in 1908, the 300th anniversary of the founding of Quebec.
Archives de la Ville de Quebec #5465

In the late nineteenth century, an important cultural event in most black communities across Canada was Emancipation Day, an annual celebration of the freeing of slaves in the British Empire on 1 August 1834. The parade depicted here took place in 1894 in Amherstburg, Ontario.
Archives of Ontario/Acc 2537, S 12008

sculptors such as Alfred Laliberté. In Montreal, Louis-Philippe Hébert's monuments to Jacques Cartier and Maisonneuve stand out as some of the best sculpture produced in Canada. Outside of the commissions sponsored by the church, Quebec painters of the late Victorian period focused on landscapes and romanticized portraits of people's lives. Before the First World War, Quebecers in search of more liberated artistic expression moved to Paris.

Secular artists regularly took up identifiably Canadian subjects, particularly landscapes of settled areas of the country. In 1907, the creation of the Canadian Art Club (CAC) encouraged showings by early Canadian impressionists. These painters, who focused their attention on light, colour, and mood, were roundly criticized by traditionalists who felt that art, like photographs, should strive to represent objects as they were, not as imagined. By the time of its last exhibition in 1915, the CAC was being overtaken by men such as Lawren Harris and J.E.H. MacDonald, who, along with Tom Thomson, Frank Carmichael, Frank Johnston, Arthur Lismer, Fred Varley, and A.Y. Jackson, began applying new approaches to art in their sketches of Algonquin Park. The war and the death of Thomson in 1917 postponed the public arrival of the painters, who came to be known as the Group of Seven, but they were part of a significant pre-war effort to find artistic expression for what was deemed uniquely Canadian.

On the West Coast, Emily Carr was beginning to develop her own powerful, post-impressionist style to convey the majesty of Native life and the coastal landscape. Lacking the sympathetic community available to her eastern male contemporaries, she was forced to support herself by running a boarding house. Both Carr and the Algonquin Group, like the great majority of earlier Canadian painters, tended to avoid the city and its problems. Their world, like that of many writers, most often symbolized an effort to come to terms with the natural rather than the human world of early twentieth-century Canada.

Art for a New Nation

In the early decades of confederation, photography was fast replacing art as a way of representing landscape and society. Artists therefore sought to render the deeper meaning of their subjects or find new ways to "see" the world around them. Often ridiculed for "poor" artistic style, they nevertheless created a body of work, represented here by Clarence Gagnon, Tom Thomson, and James Wilson Morrice, that is greatly valued today. Aboriginal artists, of course, followed a long tradition of representing spiritual values in their work, as had painters who were influenced by the artistic style of the Roman Catholic Church.

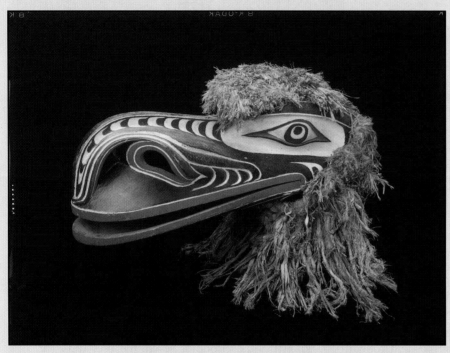

Kwakiutl Mask, ca. 1900.
Crooked Beak of Heaven mask, unknown Kwakwaka'wakw artist. McMichael Canadian Art Collection, Purchase 1977; 1977.2.3

Clarence Gagnon (1881–1942), *La Croix du Chemin, l'automne,* ca. 1915. National Gallery of Canada

Tom Thomson (1877–1917), *Northern River,* **1915.**
National Gallery of Canada

James Wilson Morrice (1865–1924), *Ice Bridge over the St. Charles River,* **1908.**
Montreal Museum of Fine Arts, 1925.333

The Dramatic Arts

Canadians were enthusiastic spectators of a host of foreign and domestic touring theatre companies that crossed the country on the expanding railway networks. In 1897, Corliss Powers Walker, an impresario with a string of small theatres in North Dakota, settled in Winnipeg, which he used as a base for controlling bookings and theatre management throughout the West. His flagship theatre seated 2000 people and hosted productions, some of them direct from Broadway, six nights a week, 52 weeks a year. The seven touring companies of the Marks Brothers entertained in small towns across the dominion.

In the 1890s, the first home-grown professional French-language companies were founded, following on the phenomenal success of Parisian companies that toured Quebec. The British Canadian Theatrical Organization Society (1912) attempted to balance the extensive American influence by organizing tours of British theatrical troupes. Although the Trans-Canada Theatre Society (1915) was Canadian-owned, it stayed in business by organizing tours of foreign companies. Britons and Americans gradually acquired controlling interests in Canadian theatres, effectively monopolizing the booking of entertainment by 1914.

The difficulties faced by Canadian talent did not escape notice. In 1907, Governor-General Earl Grey created the Earl Grey Music and Dramatic Competition for the dramatic arts, but this venture collapsed in 1911 and had only a minimal influence. There was significant progress in amateur little theatre, notably with the creation in 1905 of the Toronto Arts and Letters Players and the Ottawa Drama League in 1913. With the opening of the Hart House Theatre at the University of Toronto in 1919, financed by the Massey family, many distinguished Canadian actors, directors, and playwrights had a forum for their talents.

Canadian audiences were also introduced to the international world of dance, though not without earning the disapproval of church leaders. Acclaimed dancers Lois Fuller and Anna Pavlova and Nijinsky and the Diaghilev Ballet Russe made Canadian appearances. Many dance performances were aimed at well-to-do audiences, but the crowds they drew included Canadians from many walks of life. Spectators also found much to entertain them in dance halls, burlesque theatres, and taverns, where hypnotists, magicians, circuses, and vaudeville drew audiences into a rich world of political satire, popular music, risqué dancing, and bawdy comedy.

These years also saw the appearance of the "movie," a popular entertainment that would soon outdraw all others. In 1896, 1200 citizens of Ottawa paid 10 cents each to watch a production of Thomas Edison's "Vitascope." Because of the obvious potential of the medium to attract viewers, the Department of the Interior experimented with film in its efforts to promote western settlement. By 1914, sporadic screenings were beginning to give way to regular shows offered in movie theatres that charged each enthusiastic customer a nickel: hence the name *nickelodeon*. With more comfortable theatres, better story lines, and higher prices, films appealed to the middle class, who had at first scorned the medium's reputed vulgarity.

CONCLUSION

When Canada went to war in 1914, there was still little consensus on what it meant to be a Canadian. There was no distinctive Canadian flag, and while the beaver and the maple leaf seemed to sum up what was distinctive about Canada, they were not adopted as official symbols of the country. Calixa Lavallée, a composer born in Quebec, penned the words to "O Canada" in 1880, but the song was not heard in English Canada until the turn of the century. Outside of Quebec, "The Maple Leaf Forever," with its triumphant imperialist lyrics, was much more popular. Growing cultural diversity and rapid economic development in the first decade of the twentieth century only compounded the natural tendency to emphasize differences. As participants in the new industrial order, however, Canadians shared more than they realized, including an expanding literacy, a rich popular culture, and a small but growing number of nationwide organizations. Whether these cultural trends were sufficient to hold the nation together under the impact of a world war would remain to be seen.

NOTES

1 George McQueen to Jessie McQueen, 7 January 1888, Greenville. The McQueen Family Papers, Atlantic Canada Virtual Archives, no. 3347_05_02. University of New Brunswick, Fredericton, NB, Canada. On the McQueen family, see Jean Barman, *Sojourning Sisters: The Lives and Letters of Jessie and Annie McQueen* (Toronto: University of Toronto Press, 2003).

2 Cited in Ramsay Cook, *The Regenerators: Social Criticism in Late Victorian English Canada* (Toronto: University of Toronto Press, 1985), 4.

3 A.B. McKillop, *Matters of Mind: The University in Ontario, 1791–1951* (Toronto: University of Toronto Press, 1994), 251–52.

4 Cited in George Altmeyer, "Three Ideas of Nature, 1893–1914," *Journal of Canadian Studies* 11, no. 3 (August 1976), 23.

5 Tina Loo, *States of Nature: Conserving Canada's Wildlife in the Twentieth Century* (Vancouver: University of British Columbia Press, 2006), 43–46.

6 Colin D. Howell, *Northern Sandlots: A Social History of Maritime Baseball* (Toronto: University of Toronto Press, 1995), 55.

7 Cited in Gerald Lynch and David Ramptons, eds., *The Canadian Essay* (Toronto: Copp Clark Pitman, 1991), 12.

8 Stephen Leacock, *Literary Lapses* (1910; repr., Toronto: McClelland & Stewart, 1957), 21.

9 Cited in Maria Tippett, *Making Culture: English-Canadian Institutions and the Arts before the Massey Commission* (Toronto: University of Toronto Press, 1990), 6.

RELATED READINGS IN THIS SERIES

From *Nation and Society: Readings in Post-Confederation Canadian History*

Jarrett Rudy, "Unmaking Manly Smokes: Church, State, Governance and the First Anti-Smoking Campaigns in Montreal, 1892–1914," 169–184.
Ramsay Cook, "The Roots of Modernism: Darwinism and the Higher Critics," 185–199.

From Primary Documents CD-ROM, Volume II

Lucy Maud Montgomery
Revelstoke Women's Hockey Team
The Middleton School, 1906
Baton and Buckskin

SELECTED READING

On the intellectual history of late Victorian Canada, see A.B. McKillop, *A Disciplined Intelligence: Critical Inquiry and Canadian Thought in the Victorian Era* (Montreal: McGill-Queen's University Press, 1979); Ramsay Cook, *The Regenerators: Social Criticism in Late Victorian English Canada* (Toronto: University of Toronto Press, 1985); David B. Marshall, *Secularizing the Faith: Canadian Protestant Clergymen and the Crisis of Belief, 1850–1940* (Toronto: University of Toronto Press, 1992); René Hardy, *Contrôle social et mutation de la culture religieuse au Québec* (Montreal: Boréal, 1999); Yvan Lamonde, *Histoire sociale des idées au Québec, 1760–1896* (Montreal: Fides, 2000); Yvan Lamonde et Claude Corbo, dir., *Les rouges et les bleus : une anthologie de la pensée au Québec de la conquête à la revolution tranquille* (Montreal: Les Presses de l'Université de Montréal, 1999); Denis Monière, *Ideologies in Quebec: The Historical Development* (Toronto: University of Toronto Press, 1981);

Susan Sheets-Pyenson, *John William Dawson: Faith, Hope, and Science* (Montreal: McGill-Queen's University Press, 1996); and Allen Mills, *Fool for Christ: The Political Thought of J.S. Woodsworth* (Toronto: University of Toronto Press, 1991). See also Suzanne Zeller, *Inventing Canada: Early Victorian Science and the Idea of a Transcontinental Nation* (Toronto: University of Toronto Press, 1987); Allan Smith, *Canada—An American Nation? Essays on Continentalism, Identity and the Canadian Frame of Mind* (Montreal: McGill-Queen's University Press, 1994); and Carl Berger, *The Sense of Power: Studies in the Ideas of Canadian Imperialism, 1867–1914* (Toronto: University of Toronto Press, 1970) and *Honour and the Search for Influence: A History of the Royal Society of Canada, 1882–1994* (Toronto: University of Toronto Press, 1996).

For other perspectives on the modern age, see Keith Walden, *Becoming Modern in Toronto: The Industrial Exhibition and the Shaping of Late Victorian Culture* (Toronto: University of Toronto Press, 1997); Gerald Friesen, *Citizens and Nation: An Essay on History, Communication, and Canada* (Toronto: University of Toronto Press, 2000); and articles in James Opp and John Walsh, eds., *Home, Work and Play: Situating Canadian Social History, 1840–1980* (Toronto: Oxford University Press, 2006).

On the writing of Canadian history, see M. Brook Taylor, *Promoters, Patriots and Partisans: Historiography in Nineteenth-Century English Canada* (Toronto: University of Toronto Press, 1990); Carl Berger, *The Writing of Canadian History* (Toronto: University of Toronto Press, 1976); Serge Gagnon, *Quebec and Its Historians, 1840–1920* (Montreal: Harvest House, 1982); Beverley Boutilier and Alison Prentice, *Creating Historical Memory: English-Canadian Women and the Work of History* (Vancouver: UBC Press, 1997); and Micheline Dumont, *Découvrir la mémoire des femmes. Une historienne face à l'histoire des femmes* (Montreal: Éditions du remue-ménage, 2001).

Public commemoration of the past in this period is explored in several recent studies: Ronald Rudin, *Founding Fathers: The Celebration of Champlain and Laval in the Streets of Quebec, 1878–1908* (Toronto: University of Toronto Press, 2003); Alan Gordon, *Making Public Pasts: The Contested Terrain of Montreal's Public Memories, 1891–1930* (Montreal: McGill-Queen's University Press, 2001); Patrice Groulx, *Pièges de mémoire: Dollard des Ormeaux, les Amérindiens et nous* (Hull: Vents d'Ouest, 1998); H.V. Nelles, *The Art of Nation-Building* (Toronto: University of Toronto Press, 1998); and Colin Coates and Cecilia Morgan, *Heroines and History: Representations of Madeleine de Verchères and Laura Secord* (Toronto: University of Toronto Press, 2002).

Religion is explored in William Westfall, *Two Worlds: The Protestant Culture of Nineteenth-Century Ontario* (Montreal: McGill-Queen's University Press, 1989); John Webster Grant, *A Profusion of Spires: Religion in Nineteenth-Century Ontario* (Toronto: University of Toronto Press, 1988); Neil Semple, *The Lord's Dominion: The History of Canadian Methodism* (Montreal: McGill-Queen's University Press, 1996); John S. Moir, *Enduring Witness: A History of the Presbyterian Church in Canada* (Toronto: Presbyterian Church of Canada, 1987); Harry A. Renfree, *Heritage and Horizon: The Baptist Story in Canada* (Mississauga, ON: Canadian Baptist Federation, 1988); Michael Gauvreau, *The Evangelical Century: College and Creed in English Canada from the Great Revival to the Great Depression* (Montreal: McGill-Queen's University Press, 1991); George Rawlyk, ed., *The Canadian Protestant Experience* (Montreal: McGill-Queen's University Press, 1990); Terrence Murphy and Gerald Stortz, eds., *Creed and Culture: The Place of English-Speaking Catholics in Canadian Society, 1750–1930* (Montreal:

McGill-Queen's University Press, 1993); Terrence Murphy, ed., *A Concise History of Christianity in Canada* (Toronto: Oxford University Press, 1996); Terrence J. Fay, *A History of Canadian Catholics: Gallicanism, Romanism, Canadianism* (Montreal: McGill-Queen's University Press, 2002); and Lucia Ferretti, *Brève histoire de l'Église au Québec* (Montreal: Boréal, 1999).

Schools are discussed in Susan Houston and Alison Prentice, *Schooling and Scholars in Nineteenth-Century Ontario* (Toronto: University of Toronto Press, 1988); Donald Wilson, ed., *An Imperfect Past: Education and Society in Canadian History* (Vancouver: UBC Press, 1984); Nancy Sheehan, David C. Jones, and Robert M. Stamp, eds., *Shaping the Schools of the Canadian West* (Calgary: Detselig, 1979); Paul Axelrod, *The Promise of Schooling: Education in Canada, 1800–1914* (Toronto: University of Toronto Press, 1997); and Roger Magnuson, *A Brief History of Quebec Education* (Montreal: Harvest House, 1980). The best treatment of universities is Brian McKillop, *Matters of Mind: The University in Ontario, 1791–1951* (Toronto: University of Toronto Press, 1994). For a close look at one institution, see Sara Z. Burke, *Seeking the Highest Good: Social Service and Gender at the University of Toronto, 1887–1937* (Toronto: University of Toronto Press, 1996).

Nature, tourism, environment, and conservation are the focus of articles in David Freeland Duke, ed., *Canadian Environmental History: Essential Readings* (Toronto: CSPI and Women's Press, 2007) and Chad Gaffield and Pam Gaffield, eds., *Consuming Canada: Readings in Environmental History* (Toronto: Copp Clark, 1995) and of a growing list of monographs, including Tina Loo, *States of Nature: Conserving Canada's Wildlife in the Twentieth Century* (Vancouver: University of British Columbia Press, 2006); Matthew D. Evenden, *Fish versus Power: An Environmental History of the Fraser River* (New York: Cambridge University Press, 2004); George W. Colpitts, *Game in the Garden: A Human History of Wildlife in Western Canada to 1940* (Vancouver: UBC Press, 2003); Karen Dubinsky, *The Second Greatest Disappointment: Honeymooning and Tourism at Niagara Falls* (Toronto: Between the Lines, 1999); Patricia Jasen, *Wild Things: Nature, Culture, and Tourism in Ontario, 1790–1914* (Toronto: University of Toronto Press, 1995); Michel Girard, *L'Écologisme retrouvé: Essor et déclin de la Commission de la Conservation du Canada* (Ottawa: Les Presses de l'Université d'Ottawa, 1994); Carl Berger, *Science, God, and Nature in Victorian Canada* (Toronto: University of Toronto Press, 1983); and Janet Foster, *Working for Wildlife: The Beginning of Preservation in Canada* (Toronto: University of Toronto Press, 1978/1998). On parks, see James C. Taylor, *Negotiating the Past: The Making of Canada's National Historic Parks and Sites* (Montreal: McGill-Queen's

University Press, 1990) and J.G. Nelson, ed., *Canadian Parks in Historical Perspective* (Montreal: Harvest House, 1970). The Boy Scouts are discussed in Robert H. MacDonald, *Sons of the Empire: The Frontier and the Boy Scout Movement, 1890–1918* (Toronto: University of Toronto Press, 1993).

On sports and recreation, see Alan Metcalfe, *Canada Learns to Play: The Emergence of Organized Sport, 1807–1914* (Toronto: McClelland & Stewart, 1987); Colin Howell, *Blood, Sweat, and Cheers: Sport in the Making of Modern Canada* (Toronto: University of Toronto Press, 2001) and *Northern Sandlots: A Social History of Maritime Baseball* (Toronto: University of Toronto Press, 1995); Nancy B. Bouchier, *For the Love of the Game: Amateur Sport in Small-Town Ontario, 1838–1895* (Montreal: McGill-Queen's University Press, 2003); Bruce Kidd, *Contested Identities: The Struggle for Canadian Sport* (Toronto: University of Toronto Press, 1996); and M. Ann Hall, *The Girl and the Game: A History of Women's Sport in Canada* (Peterborough: Broadview Press, 2002).

Architecture in this period is comprehensively surveyed in the second volume of Harold Kalman's *A History of Canadian Architecture* (Toronto: Oxford University Press, 1994); Janet Wright, *Crown Assets: The Architecture of the Department of Public Works, 1867–1967* (Toronto: University of Toronto Press, 1997); Peter Ward, *A History of Domestic Space: Privacy and the Canadian Home* (Vancouver: UBC Press, 1999); and Peter Ennals and Deryck W. Holdsworth, *The Making of the Canadian Dwelling over Three Centuries* (Toronto: University of Toronto Press, 1998).

Literary history is discussed in Yvan Lamonde, Patricia Lockhart Flemming, and Fiona Black, eds., *History of the Book in Canada, 1840-1918* (Toronto: University of Toronto Press, 2005) and Carl F. Klinck, ed., *Literary History of Canada* (Toronto: University of Toronto Press, 1976). E. Pauline Johnson is the subject of two biographies: Veronica Strong-Boag and Carole Gerson, *Pulling Her Own Canoe: The Times and Texts of E. Pauline Johnson* (Toronto: University of Toronto Press, 2000) and Charlotte Gray, *Flint and Feather: The Life and Times of E. Pauline Johnson, Tekahionwake* (Toronto: HarperFlamingoCanada, 2002). The

explosion in newspaper publication and newspaper readership is analyzed in Minko Sotiron, *From Politics to Profit: The Commercialization of Canadian Daily Newspapers, 1890-1920* (Montreal: McGill-Queen's University Press, 2005) and Robert Rutherford, *A Victorian Authority: The Daily Press in Late Nineteenth-Century Canada* (Toronto: University of Toronto Press, 1982). On literary societies, see Heather Murray, *Come, Bright Improvement! The Literary Societies of Nineteenth Century Ontario* (Toronto: University of Toronto Press, 2002).

On artistic developments, see Carman Cumming, *Sketches from a Young Country: The Images of Grip Magazine* (Toronto: University of Toronto Press, 1997); Maria Tippett, *Making Culture: English-Canadian Institutions and the Arts Before the Massey Commission* (Toronto: University of Toronto Press, 1990); J. Russell Harper, *Painting in Canada: A History*, 2nd ed. (Toronto: University of Toronto Press, 1977); Dennis Reid, *"Our Own Country Canada": Being the Account of the National Aspirations of the Principal Landscape Artists in Montreal and Toronto, 1860–1890* (Ottawa: National Gallery, 1980); Guy Robert, *La peinture au Québec depuis ses origines* (Ste-Adèle, PQ: Iconia, 1978); and Laurent Mailhot and Pierre Nepveu, *La poésie québécoise des origines à nos jours* (Montreal: L'Hexagone, 1986). For an introduction to Canadian theatre history, see Don Rubin, ed., *Canadian Theatre History: Selected Readings* (Toronto: Copp Clark, 1996). Helmut Kallmann et al., eds., *The Encyclopedia of Music in Canada*, 2nd ed. (Toronto: University of Toronto Press, 1992) is an excellent resource for matters musical. Folklore is explored in Edith Fowke and Richard Johnston, *Folk Songs of Canada* (Waterloo, ON: Waterloo Music, 1954) and in several volumes by Edith Fowke: *Sally Go Round the Sun* (Toronto: McClelland & Stewart, 1969), *Folklore of Canada* (Toronto: McClelland & Stewart, 1976), and *Ring Around the Moon* (Toronto: McClelland & Stewart, 1977). For a study of one of Canada's foremost photographers, see Roger Hall, Gordon Dobbs, and Stanley Triggs, *The World of William Notman: The Nineteenth Century Through a Master Lens* (Toronto: McClelland & Stewart, 1993).

CHAPTER 9

The Great War and Reconstruction, 1914–1921

1911–20	Robert Laird Borden serves as prime minister
1914–18	First World War
1915	Battle of Ypres
1916	First Battle of the Somme; Female suffrage granted in Manitoba, Saskatchewan, and Alberta; Canadian Council of Agriculture develops Farmers' Platform
1917	Battle of Vimy Ridge; Military Service Act (conscription) passed; Wartime Elections Act; Halifax Explosion; Union government wins election; Military Voters Act passed
1917–23	Canadian National Railways created
1918	Battle of Amiens; women win the right to vote federally and in Nova Scotia
1918–19	Robert Borden sends Canadian troops to help quell the Russian Revolution
1919	Farmer-Labour government elected in Ontario; Winnipeg General Strike and other general strikes across the country; New Brunswick women win the right to vote; Progressive Party formed; Canada signs Treaty of Versailles
1920–21	Arthur Meighen serves as prime minister

A head of me I see men running. Suddenly their legs double up and they sink to the ground. Here's a body with the head shot off. I jump over it. Here's a poor devil with both legs gone, but still alive.[1]

As he described it, Private George Bell's experience in the battle of Ypres in April 1915 was shockingly gruesome. It certainly was not the triumphant march to victory that many people expected when Great Britain entered the First World War on 4 August 1914. The conflict turned out to be a tragedy of unprecedented proportions with battles raging in Europe until an armistice was finally signed on 11 November 1918.

Until the outbreak of the Second World War in 1939, the earlier conflict was known as the Great War, and its impact on Canada was deep and long lasting.

Out of a population of only 8 million, more than 600 000 Canadians were involved in military service, 430 000 of them serving overseas. More than 61 000 Canadians died and another 134 000 were wounded in battle, some of them maimed for life. In addition, 34 000 military personnel were injured in accidents of various kinds and another 5000 died within three years of war's end, many as a result of their wounds, both mental and physical. At home, nearly everyone grieved the loss of a relative or friend, bore the brunt of restrictive wartime regulations, and experienced the soul-searching that accompanied the imposition of conscription for military service in 1917. The war also marked a major turning point in the political history of the nation and served as a catalyst for many of the trends gaining momentum in the industrial age.

PREPARING FOR WAR

The assassination of Austrian archduke Franz Ferdinand and his wife in Sarajevo by a Serb nationalist in June 1914 seemed at first to be a remote tragedy. What led to war was not so much the murder of a future head of state as the system of military alliances among European nations, which produced a domino effect when efforts were made to redress the outrage. Looking for revenge after the assassination, Austria-Hungary declared war on Serbia, and turned to its German ally for support. Germany, jealous of the power of France and Great Britain, embraced the crisis as an opportunity to show the world its military prowess. This, in turn, led Russia, an ally of Serbia, to mobilize its army; France, an ally of Russia, shortly did the same. As Germany prepared to invade neutral Belgium en route to an attack on France, Great Britain felt compelled to intervene. The British declaration of war on Germany also meant that Austria-Hungary was aligned against Great Britain. Italy and Romania eventually joined the effort to stop the German alliance, as did the United States in April 1917. The Ottoman Empire entered the war on the side of Germany in 1915.

As a member of the British Empire, Canada was automatically at war when Great Britain was. Canadians nevertheless had a choice about how to participate in the fighting in Europe, or, indeed, whether to participate at all. In August 1914, most people, including Wilfrid Laurier and Henri Bourassa, saw Germany as the aggressor and thought it prudent to support Great Britain. Neither the Canadian state nor individual citizens were prepared for what this decision meant.

Struggling to deal with the demands of war, Conservatives and Liberals in the House of Commons united to pass the War Measures Act early in August 1914. This act gave the federal government authority to do everything it deemed "necessary for the security, defence, peace, order and welfare of Canada." Under the provisions of the act, Ottawa imposed tough censorship laws, intervened in the marketplace, stripped many people of their democratic rights, and overrode provincial claims to jurisdiction.

Canada entered the war with a standing army of just 3110 men and a navy consisting of two aging vessels, the *Niobe* and the *Rainbow*. Since the end of the nineteenth century, most of Canada's defence expenditures had been channelled to the militia, whose budget had risen from $1.6 million in 1898 to $11 million in 1914. Militia strength stood at more than 74 000 in the summer of 1914, and it was from these part-time soldiers that Canada would draw many of its first eager recruits. Instead of staying in their militia units, volunteers were grouped in numbered battalions of about 1000 men. Battalions, in turn, were organized into regiments, brigades, and divisions for what became known as the Canadian Expeditionary Force (CEF).

Upon the declaration of war, Borden's minister of militia, Sam Hughes, telegraphed his 226 unit commanders, appealing for volunteers for a division of 25 000 men. He was swamped with replies. When the volunteers arrived at the army's new military base at Valcartier a few kilometres outside Quebec City, they found construction and confusion all around. More by good luck than good management, 31 000 men, 8000 horses, and sundry equipment, much of it useless, were

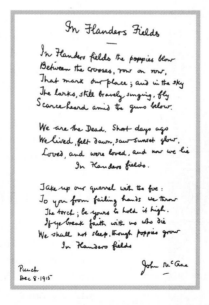

It was the battle of Ypres that inspired Lieutenant-Colonel John McCrae, a Canadian doctor, to write the poem "In Flanders Fields," a moving call to keep faith with the soldiers who had given up their lives.
Courtesy of Guelph Museums, McCrae House

loaded onto transports and dispatched to Europe on 3 October. Among those travelling with the First Division were 101 nurses under the direction of Matron Margaret MacDonald, all full-fledged members of the CEF.

Because no Canadian had sufficient military experience, a British officer, Major-General E.A.H. Alderson, took command. Under Alderson's leadership, soldiers were organized into the 1st Canadian Infantry Division and were drilled into fighting form in England. The division moved to France in February 1915. At Ypres, Belgium, in mid-April, they had their first real test when they experienced a chlorine gas attack. The Canadians refused to break lines when others around them, who had taken the brunt of the attack, fell back. It soon became clear that the war would be long and that Great Britain needed all the help it could get from the empire. Great Britain's Lord Kitchener, who was in charge of the War Office, had shocked his cabinet colleagues in the early days of the war by calling for a million soldiers. In the end, Great Britain needed five times that number.

While men and matériel continued to move across the Atlantic, there were difficulties at every turn. Many of the problems, such as inadequate facilities and bottlenecks in military supplies, would have occurred no matter who was in charge, but Hughes had the unfortunate knack of making even the smallest problem a major crisis. Patronage and corruption riddled the Militia Department's massive purchasing program, and confusion reigned in the command structure of the Canadian forces. Hughes was a stout defender of Canadian-made Ross rifles, even though the gun had a tendency to jam in the heat of battle. In 1916, they were replaced by British-made Lee-Enfields, but in the meantime Canadian soldiers often took Lee-Enfield rifles off their dead British comrades because the Ross rifle was so unreliable. Although he was knighted in 1915, Hughes was finally dismissed from his portfolio in 1916. By that time, his administrative incompetence had brought an avalanche of criticism against the government's mishandling of the war effort.

Even before Hughes's dismissal, Borden had begun the process of bringing efficiency to the war effort. A variety of committees, including the Imperial Munitions Board (IMB), War Purchasing Board, National Service Board, and Ministry of Overseas Military Forces, were established and staffed by people with administrative experience. Since the government lacked professional civil servants capable of managing an economy suddenly on a war footing, Ottawa was critically dependent on the expertise and good will of businessmen such as Joseph Flavelle, general manager of the William Davies Packing Company, who became chair of the IMB. Flavelle spurred private firms to new levels of productivity, enticed American companies to locate in Canada, and, when all else failed, created government-run factories to produce everything from acetone to airplanes. By 1917, the IMB was the biggest business in Canada with 600 factories, 150 000 workers, and a turnover of $2 million a day.

THE WARTIME ECONOMY

Although it did not change the direction of the Canadian economy in any major way, the First World War sped Canadians a little faster down the road to industrial maturity. Markets expanded, at least temporarily, and the value of Canadian exports doubled in the first three years of the war and doubled again by 1919. In 1913, only 7 percent of Canadian manufactures were sold overseas, a figure that rose to 40 percent during

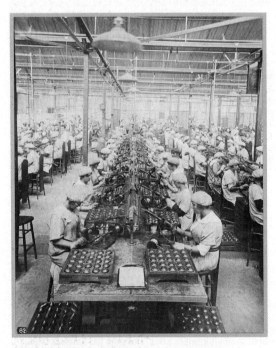

Women working in a wartime munitions factory.
Library and Archives Canada, C-018734

the final two years of the war. Factories ran full-tilt producing for the war effort, and grain acreage soared.

Canada's wartime economy, like that of peacetime, depended on private initiative, but the government found it necessary to intervene in a variety of ways. In addition to setting up the IMB and related committees to ensure that the army was properly equipped, the government brought a wide range of supplies and services under its control. The Board of Grain Supervisors became the sole agent for Canadian wheat sales; the Fuel Controller decided the price and use of coal, wood, and gas; and the Food Board determined policy relating to the cost and distribution of food. In an effort to increase agricultural efficiency, the Food Board purchased 100 tractors from the Henry Ford Motor Company to distribute at cost to farmers. The same board urged Canadians to eat more fish so that beef and bacon could be released for overseas armies. Children were encouraged to grow "victory gardens" as their contribution to the war effort.

Inevitably there were complaints about government policy. The Food Board's "anti-loafing law," threatening punishment for any man or boy not gainfully employed, was understandably not very popular, and no one enjoyed the discomfort that resulted from the "fuelless days" mandated by the Fuel Controller. The IMB's pattern of granting contracts sparked accusations from western Canada that Flavelle and his associates favoured central Canadian firms over those from the less industrialized regions of the nation. When companies producing war supplies recorded huge profits, Canadians became increasingly skeptical about the patriotic claims of corporations. People like Flavelle prospered while servicemen's families, without any resources to sustain them, were often forced to rely on charity.

By 1916, the Canadian economy was fully geared for war. Hostilities rejuvenated the Canadian shipbuilding industry, but in the industrial heartland rather than the Maritime ports. During the war, the British-owned Vickers Company employed more than 15 000 people in its shipyards near Montreal, while Davie Shipbuilding of Lauzon, Quebec, produced anti-submarine vessels and steel barges. Between 1914 and 1918, Canada's steel mills doubled their capacity to meet British demands for shells, supplying as much as a third of British artillery needs. Supplemented by the

domestic labours of women and children who knit socks, preserved jam, and rolled bandages for the men at the front, farm and factory production increased to meet the demand for food, clothing, and footwear.

Notwithstanding the enhanced role of government and industry, voluntary activities remained essential to the war effort. The 1200 branches of the Red Cross in Canada served as a virtual auxiliary of the Army Medical Corps. In many communities, the Imperial Order Daughters of the Empire and the Women's Institutes collected money, knit socks, and packed parcels for men overseas. A range of other organizations—the Great War Veterans' Association, the War Veterans' Next-of-Kin Association, the YMCA and YWCA, Consumers' Leagues, Women's Patriotic Leagues, Vacant Lot Garden Clubs, and the Women's Volunteer Army Division—all "did their bit."

Much of the work of caring for the families of soldiers and men who returned wounded to Canada was managed by volunteer groups. In the early days of the war, the federal government established a Canadian Patriotic Fund, an organization staffed largely by volunteers whose role was to help the families of soldiers overseas, a growing number of which were dependent on charity. An enlisted man was required to sign over a portion of his pay to his wife or dependent mother, but this did not always happen. Volunteers in the Patriotic Fund helped dependants apply for financial assistance—as much as $50 a month by the end of the war—and also arranged services for veterans who returned sick, wounded, insane, or addicted to alcohol.

The twin demand for workers and soldiers resulted in a labour shortage by 1916. To address the problem, the federal government created the National Service Board to more efficiently mobilize the nation's resources, and women were recruited into transportation and metal trades that were previously held only by men. More than 30 000 women were hired in munitions factories during the war and many more positions temporarily opened to women because of the conditions created by the conflict. Women were paid less than the men they replaced and were fired from their "untraditional" jobs at the end of the hostilities, but they got a sense of what they could do when given a chance.

As the economy moved into high gear, Canadians confronted inflation and a soaring cost of living. Wages, controlled by wartime regulation, failed to follow the upward spiral of prices, and many people got caught in the financial squeeze. In the last two years of the war, Canada's productive capacity was threatened by rising levels of strike activity and political unrest. Canada's War Labour Policy, which was proclaimed in 1918, prohibited strikes and lockouts while affirming the right to organize and receive fair wages and equal pay for equal work. Nevertheless, labour shortages blunted the efforts by governments and employers to prevent strikes and protests. There was no desperate reserve army of labour willing to take the jobs of striking workers, who recognized their potential power in bringing employers to heel. Union membership increased dramatically, and support for labour parties grew.

FINANCING THE WAR

The federal government, under the sweeping provisions of the War Measures Act, took a variety of economic initiatives that would have been unthinkable prior to the outbreak of hostilities. It suspended the gold standard, expanded the money supply, and engaged in deficit financing. When British financial markets closed, Ottawa floated loans in the New York bond market for the first time. Canadians also extended credit to Great Britain for the purchase of the necessities of war.

In an effort to raise money domestically, the government sold Victory Bonds, War Savings Certificates,

The Newfoundland Regiment, D Company, near St. John's, 1915.
Courtesy of the Provincial Archives of Newfoundland and Labrador/E22-45

and, for children, War Savings Stamps. The Canadian economy proved capable of generating nearly $2 billion in loans, and at no time during the war did government expenditures exceed 10 percent of the gross national product (GNP). In 1917, the federal government began the process of nationalizing half the country's railway capacity by taking control of the Grand Trunk Pacific and Canadian Northern and amalgamating them with other government-controlled railways, such as the Intercolonial, to create the Canadian National Railways system. The government also used the wartime emergency to build a more effective civil service. In 1918, Ottawa placed some 40 000 government workers under the Civil Service Commission, which was responsible for ensuring that people were hired on the basis of merit rather than patronage.

In response to farmer and labour demands that wealth be conscripted along with manpower, Ottawa implemented a war profits tax in 1916. It was pegged at 25 percent on all profits greater than 7 percent of capital for corporations and 10 percent of capital for other businesses with a capitalization of $50 000 or more. In 1917, the federal government imposed personal income taxes for the first time. The tax was a mere 2 percent on annual incomes up to $6000, a substantial sum at the time; single persons earning less than $1500 and married men with family incomes of less than $3000 were exempted. Tax rates rose progressively to reach a maximum of 25 percent on income over $100 000. Difficult to collect, the new taxes played a negligible role in paying for the war effort. Eighty-four percent of wartime revenues were raised through customs and excise duties while less than 1 percent came from personal income taxes. The "temporary" income and corporate taxes imposed during the war outlived the crisis that sparked them and by 1939 were generating nearly a third of the federal government's revenues.

THE WAR IN EUROPE

Canadian men enlisted in the armed forces for a variety of reasons. Patriotism motivated many young men. Others went overseas for adventure. As Larry Nelson, a Toronto enlistee in 1914, recalled, "[m]ost of us were young and saw it as a wonderful opportunity to throw off the shackles of working in an office or a factory or

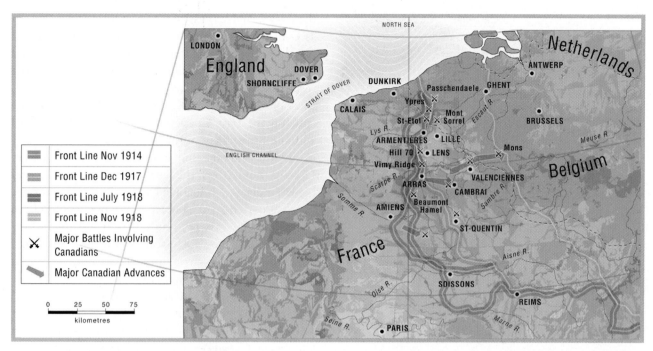

MAP 9.1 **The European front, 1914–1918.**

on a farm or what-have-you."[2] Still others, victims of the recession, enlisted to secure a steady job. Cultural background played a major role in determining who volunteered for overseas service. Over 65 percent of the first wave of volunteers were recent British immigrants, and one-half of all enlistees in Canadian forces in the First World War were British born. All were unprepared for a protracted war of unspeakable horror.

The 6000 Canadians who were killed or injured in the April 1915 battle at Ypres were only the first in a long list of casualties that horrified even the most hard-bitten soldier. On 1 July 1916, the first day of the Allied offensive on the Somme, 21 000 British soldiers were slaughtered, among them more than 700 of the Newfoundland Regiment, who were killed or wounded in the battle at Beaumont Hamel. Over four months of fighting on the Somme left 600 000 British and French soldiers dead or wounded. The Canadian Corps, now a full four divisions strong, had been brought in to sustain the failing offensive and suffered more than 24 000 casualties. But the worst was not over. With the Russian front crumbling, the Dardanelles taken by the Turks, and the Germans holding the line in Europe, there was every reason to believe that the Allies might lose the war. There were mutinies in the French army, and some Canadians were being shot for desertion as a warning to anyone else contemplating such a move.

In April 1917, the Canadian Corps took Vimy Ridge after a fiercely fought battle with more than 10 000 Canadian casualties. They did not know it at the time, but it was a turning point for Canadians in the war. Until 1917, the soldiers of the CEF fought as "imperials" under Great Britain's Army Act, and even the commanders of the Canadian Corps were British. Canadian soldiers fought well under British command, but they regularly complained about what seemed to them to be second-class treatment by the British military administration in everything from the quarters they were allocated to their place in line as cannon fodder.

By the fall of 1916, Borden was convinced that something had to be done to give Canadians more control over their own war effort. He began by creating a ministry of overseas military forces under the

Commander Arthur Currie directs a practice attack near the Canadian front in June 1917.
Library and Archives of Canada

control of Sir George Perley, the Canadian high commissioner in London, and redefining the CEF as an overseas contingent of the Canadian militia. Gradually, many of the British officers were replaced by Canadians until on 9 June 1917, Arthur Currie, the Canadian commander of the 1st Canadian Infantry Division, was made commander of the entire Canadian Corps. Under the methodical Currie, Canadians continued to see some of the worst fighting of the war, but they fought with their own maple leaf insignia on their badges. They also developed their own unique reputation for bravery and determination. In October 1917, the Canadians were summoned to Passchendaele, in Belgium, where the British Fifth Army had lost 68 000 men. In October and November, the Canadian Corps broke through the German lines, but the price— 15 000 men—was high.

While the vast majority of Canadian military personnel were in the land forces, significant numbers also served at sea and in the air. The British had advised Canada to concentrate their resources on the CEF, but

the unexpected success of German submarines (known as U-boats) in sinking the merchant ships that carried North American war supplies to Great Britain and Europe brought a new dimension to naval warfare. As a result, nearly 10 000 Canadians served in the navy. Most of them operated Canadian-built anti-submarine craft on the East Coast, but more than 1000 served with the British fleet in European waters.

In the summer and fall of 1918, three German U-boats hunted off the coasts of Nova Scotia and Newfoundland. Canadian anti-submarine vessels, which escorted merchant ship convoys, helped keep losses of major vessels to only two. It was more difficult to protect the widely scattered fishing fleets, and more than 30 schooners and trawlers were destroyed in Canadian and Newfoundland waters.

More than 20 000 Canadians served in the Royal Flying Corps, the Royal Naval Air Service, or, after 1 April 1918, the Royal Air Force. One of the most famous of Canada's fighting pilots was Lieutenant-Colonel W.A. "Billy" Bishop, who shot down 72 enemy planes and, unlike the more than 1500 other Canadians who pioneered the use of the "aeroplane" in wartime, lived to tell about it. The achievements of Canadian airmen such as Bishop, combined with the expertise Canadians gained in the British flying services and the tremendous growth of aircraft technology, helped ensure national aviation development after the war, including the establishment of the Royal Canadian Air Force as a third armed service.

THE HORRORS OF WAR

The realities of war bore heavily on the soldiers at the front. Not only was their courage tested in the heat of battle, they were obliged to live in conditions that were unpleasant in the extreme. While on duty, they lived in trenches that stretched from Switzerland to the English Channel. Their dugouts were pits of thick mud infested with fleas, lice, rats, and germs. Although soldiers devoured their rations of corned beef, biscuits, bread, and tea, it was not a healthy diet and left them constantly hungry and susceptible to diseases. If the enemy missed his mark, dysentery, pneumonia, and "trench fever" might be just as deadly. Chemical warfare was an entirely new and horrifying experience. To survive their first attack of chlorine gas at Ypres in April 1915, men urinated in their handkerchiefs and held them to their noses. Rats nibbled the corpses of fallen comrades while those who were still alive dug new trenches and maintained existing ones, moved supplies, and tried not to think of their hunger and fear.

Fear was justified. More than 61 000 Canadians died in the First World War, and they may have been the lucky ones. Those who survived often returned home so severely wounded, physically or mentally, that they were unable to resume normal lives. The mentally wounded—or "shell shocked," as they came to be known—returned to a society that was ill-prepared for such casualties. While a soldier whose wounds put him in a wheelchair received a government pension and the sympathy of other Canadians, there was little comfort for the emotionally disabled, who remained unfit to resume their work and family lives and who stared vacantly into space or sought comfort in the bottle.

Following the war, Canadians tried to find ways of justifying the sacrifice of so many men in the prime of their lives. Historian Jonathan Vance, in his book *Death So Noble*, shows that, as the memory of the war receded, the death and dismemberment of the ordinary soldier were idealized through monuments in town squares and reflections on the war that highlighted its role in fostering a national spirit. Such views conveniently glossed over the horror of war and the divisions it created among Canadians.[3]

Jack Turner and Lee Allan from Prince Edward Island taking a break from battle in 1917. Lee reads the *Island Patriot* while Jack holds *Jack Canuck*, a comic strip showing the heroics of soldier life.
Courtesy of Prince Edward Island Public Archives and Records Office Acc. 2767/107

Canadian men between the ages of 15 and 54, or nearly 233 000, had volunteered for the infantry by 1917. Canadians had also joined other branches of the CEF, such as the artillery, engineer, medical, and army service corps, or had responded to appeals to join British forestry and railway units, the Royal Navy, and the Royal Flying Corps, bringing the numbers almost up to the half-million demanded by Borden.

THE WAR AT HOME

The slaughter on the European front spread panic in the British War Office and led to a demand for more troops. Borden had pushed the approved strength of the CEF up to 250 000 in the fall of 1915 and then raised it again, to 500 000, in his New Year's message for 1916. But where would the soldiers come from?

In the early months of the war, it had looked as if voluntary enlistment would sustain the Canadian war effort. One in six

***Canadian Gunners in the Mud*, Passchendaele, 1917, by Alfred Bastien.**
Beaverbrook Collection of War Art © Canadian War Museum

While most men of military age never volunteered, preferring to stay at home, raise their families, and participate in the opportunities made available by the war, the proportion of recruits varied dramatically by region and culture. Only 13 000 were French-speaking, and men in Ontario and the West were more likely to sign up than those from the Maritimes and Quebec. The attachment of recent immigrants to their European homelands explains to some extent the lower recruitment rates in the longer-settled eastern provinces, but there were also other reasons.

French Canadians were initially sympathetic to the Allied cause, but the feeling waned as the war progressed. During the first year, they were dispersed among various units, creating language difficulties. The first and the last entirely French unit, the Royal 22nd Battalion, was established in October 1914. Anger at Ontario's 1912 legislation restricting French-language instruction in public schools and at the military's reluctance to create French-speaking regiments reinforced feelings of estrangement from a cause that was identified with Great Britain and English Canada. As wartime tensions mounted, provincial governments outside Quebec intensified their efforts to suppress French-language education in their jurisdictions, and English Canadians began accusing French Canadians of shirking their duty. Neither

approach made French Canadians more favourably disposed to fighting overseas.

Borden tried to maintain volunteer strength by stepping up recruitment efforts, conducting a national registration of all able-bodied men, and creating a Canadian defence force that would relieve soldiers stationed in Canada for European service. None of these measures worked. Few volunteers were forthcoming from the national registration program and recruitment efforts were largely ignored.

In May 1917, a month after the United States had entered the war, Borden announced his intention to impose conscription, or compulsory military service, on a war-weary nation. Opposition to his Military Service Act, which drafted single men between the ages of 20 and 35, was high, especially in Quebec and among farmers and labourers. Although Borden had postponed calling an election in wartime, he now changed his mind. An election would clear the air on the conscription issue and give the government a mandate to carry on.

Before dissolving parliament on 6 October, Borden approached Laurier to join him in a coalition to support an all-out war effort. The 78-year-old Liberal chief rejected the proposal, fearing the loss of Quebec to Bourassa's nationalists. In making this decision, Laurier was deserted by many party supporters in Ontario and the West. A rump of Liberals joined with the Conservatives to create a Union government that campaigned on a platform of conscription, prohibition, and the abolition of party patronage.

To ensure a victory for his unstable coalition, Borden passed the Military Voters Act, which enfranchised every man and woman in the CEF. The Wartime Elections Act, meanwhile, gave the vote to mothers, wives, and sisters of soldiers—dead or alive—and took it away from citizens of enemy origin naturalized after 1902. Although some women got the franchise for the first time, not all suffrage leaders were pleased about the conditions under which it had been granted. The only compensation for those

Canadian nurses at a hospital in France vote in the 1917 election.
Library and Archives Canada/PA2279

who were disenfranchised was that they would be exempt from conscription. Even these draconian measures failed to convince Unionists that they would carry the day. Running scared during the election campaign, they promised the sons of farmers that they would not be conscripted, a promise that was later broken.

The results of the election held on 17 December surprised few people: the Union government won 153 seats while the Liberals won 82. Sixty-two of Quebec's 65 seats went to Laurier, but the Liberals carried only 10 of 28 seats in the Maritimes, 8 of 82 in Ontario, and 2 of 57 in the West. While the distribution of seats made the Union victory look impressive, the popular vote told another story. Civilian voters in the Maritimes gave a slight majority of their votes to anti-conscription candidates; even in Ontario, anti-conscriptionists, though winning only 10 percent of the seats, won almost 40 percent of the civilian vote.

If anti-conscriptionists constituted a substantial part of the electorate in English Canada, they were the overwhelming majority in Quebec, where anti-conscription—and thus anti-government—feeling continued to run high after the election. In 1918, the Quebec legislature even debated a secessionist resolution. When conscription tribunals began hearing applications for military exemptions, violence erupted in the province. The worst incident occurred in late March 1918 in Quebec City, where furious crowds attacked the military service registry and trashed English businesses. When the police refused to intervene, Ottawa sent in troops from Toronto who, when provoked, opened fire, killing four people and injuring many more.

Whether conscription served its military purpose has been much debated, not only at the time, but also by subsequent generations of historians. Defaults and desertions were common, and tribunals were often sympathetic to local boys. Of the more than 400 000 men who registered under the legislation, fewer than 100 000 were successfully drafted and only 24 000 went to France. Because of the difficulty of raising conscripts, the Fifth Division in Great Britain was dissolved and its soldiers distributed among the thinning ranks of other divisions. The war ended a year after conscription had been imposed, but its effects were felt for a long time, not least in national politics, where the Liberal Party could claim that it had been Quebec's champion in a time of need.

ENEMIES WITHIN

The Wartime Elections Act revealed another source of tension for a nation at war: the people whose former homeland was in enemy territory. In 1914, there were about half a million people in Canada who had been born in, or traced their origins to, Germany, Austria-Hungary, or the Ottoman Empire. Many of the 100 000 enemy aliens—that is, people who still held citizenship in enemy countries—had arrived in the decade before the outbreak of war. Pre-war apprehension about the number of immigrants pouring into Canada in the early years of the twentieth century turned into outright hostility under wartime pressures. Shortly after war was declared, rumours began to fly about an invasion of Canada by German Americans, and newspaper editors cried sabotage at the slightest provocation.

Enemy aliens soon felt the impact of Ottawa's concern for military security. In urban centres, they were forced to register with police authorities and were forbidden to carry arms. Those who lacked the means to remain in Canada were required to perform menial work. Ultimately, more than 8579 enemy aliens were interned, including more than 3000 Canadian citizens. Major-General Sir William Otter, a legendary veteran of the Fenian engagements of 1866, the Northwest Resistance of 1885, and the South African War, was appointed director of Canadian internment operations.

In the early months of the war, efforts to intern enemy aliens were directed less at potential saboteurs than at unemployed men, many of them Ukrainian labourers, whose presence in Canadian cities was profoundly resented by long-time inhabitants. Otter initially established internment camps in northern Ontario and Quebec—Petawawa, Kapuskasing, and Spirit Lake—out of the way of nervous civilians. Between 1915 and 1917, some 900 men worked for six days a week at 25 cents a day, clearing land and building roads in several national parks. Others were contracted to private corporations to work as miners or farm labourers, but only after labour shortages put an end to the policy of giving preference to Canadians in hiring practices.

The facilities varied considerably. In Amherst, Nova Scotia, the Malleable Iron Works building

Internees at their compound located at Castle Mountain, Banff, July 1915.
Glenbow Archives, Millican Collection/NA1870-6

housed a cosmopolitan group drawn from captures made in Bermuda, the West Indies, and Newfoundland and from foreign vessels that docked at Halifax. Its most famous inmate was the Russian communist leader Leon Trotsky, who apparently spent a short time there in 1917 trying to radicalize his fellow inmates. Elsewhere, old forts, immigrant sheds, and exhibition buildings were commandeered into service to house internees. In Vernon, British Columbia, a comparatively well-appointed camp catered largely to the German immigrants who were living on the West Coast at the outbreak of the war.

Inevitably, tensions developed over disciplinary codes and labour demands imposed on prisoners. In the fall of 1917, the inmates at Kapuskasing refused an order to chop wood for the winter, resulting in an investigation of the conditions prevailing in the camp. The prisoners were eventually forced to comply not only because authorities in Germany wrote a note approving of such tasks as chopping wood, but also because guards at the camp became more vigilant in their pursuit of those who violated the rules. In all the camps, a total of six prisoners were killed by gunshot and four wounded in the course of their internment. More than 100 others were confined to mental institutions and another 100 died in confinement, mostly of tuberculosis and pneumonia.

While it could be argued that the treatment of internees fell well within the standards set by the 1907 Hague Convention, the reality was that men in camps

such as Kapuskasing and Banff were discriminated against on the basis of class and culture. Wealthy German officers and civilians, who were interned in camps such as the one in Vernon, had lived under much better conditions, with families, servants, and a rich social life. For the men who were required to work in national parks, as historian Bill Waiser points out, there was a real sense that prisoners were ineligible for the rights and privileges set aside for "real" Canadians.[4]

In some respects, harassment of people who traced their origins to enemy countries was even worse than official sanctions and internment. Universities fired German professors, judges threw cases brought by alien plaintiffs out of court, and angry mobs attacked businesses owned by Germans and Austro-Hungarians. Even people whose families were deeply rooted in Canada, such as the Germans of Lunenburg County, Nova Scotia, and Waterloo County, Ontario, felt the wrath of wartime prejudice. In an effort to demonstrate their patriotism, the citizens of Berlin, Ontario, changed the name of their city to Kitchener in 1916, while many people in Lunenburg County claimed their origins were Dutch (Anglicization of *Deutsch*) rather than German in the 1921 census.

Following the Bolshevik Revolution in the fall of 1917, radicals became the focus of attention in Canada. Pushed by an increasingly hysterical public and led by organizations such as the Toronto Anti-German League, the Union government cracked down on groups suspected of harbouring political dissidents. It issued an order-in-council making it an offence to print or possess any publication in an enemy language without a licence from the secretary of state. "Foreign" organizations, including the Industrial Workers of the World, were banned, as were meetings in which enemy languages were used. In British Columbia, tensions ran high when socialist labour leader "Ginger" Goodwin was shot by police constable Dan Campbell in 1918, ostensibly because Goodwin was evading the draft.

People who espoused pacifist views also found themselves subject to harassment by those who resented anyone who refused to fight. Because she clung to her pacifist views during the war, Francis Marion Beynon lost her job as a columnist for the *Grain Growers' Guide*. She was not alone in being driven from her comfortable pre-war existence. In 1918, J.S. Woodsworth resigned from the Methodist Church because it could no longer tolerate his pacifist stance and social gospel views that leaned too far to the left. Groups such as the Mennonites and Hutterites, whose religious convictions included a rigorous pacifism, found themselves subject to official and unofficial sanctions in a country that increasingly defined citizenship by the extent of one's military participation.

Acrimonious debates over commitment to the war effort tore apart friendships, families, and organizations. Suffragist and novelist Nellie McClung recalled in 1945:

> The fall of 1914 blurs in my memory like a troubled dream. The war dominated everything. Some of my friends were pacifists and resented Canada's participation in the war of which we knew so little. . . . Chief among the Empire's defenders among the women was Miss Cora Hind. Her views were clear cut and definite. We were British and we must follow the tradition of our fathers. She would have gone herself if women were accepted. Miss Hind saw only one side of the question and there were times when I envied her, though I resented her denunciations of those who thought otherwise. The old crowd began to break up, and the good times were over.[5]

A WHITE MAN'S WAR

In large measure, prejudices based on gender and race determined who could participate in the fighting. Although women might keep the home fires burning and serve behind the lines as nurses, there was never any real thought given to allowing them to be combatants. Women, it was believed, were too weak and emotional to stand the rigours of battle and, in any event, it was men's role to protect them. Nor were many women, despite their pre-war struggles to gain access to public life, eager to become soldiers. The wives, girlfriends, and relatives of men serving in the forces were often keen to go overseas, but they were systematically turned down by military authorities.

A few women, such as the Yukon's Martha Black, managed to get to Great Britain at their own expense.

While they waited for word of their loved ones at the front, these women worked as volunteers in British hospitals and other service institutions. Most of the more than 3000 women who joined the Canadian Army Nursing Service went overseas. Forty-seven died on duty, and many received distinguished service awards, including Matron Ethel Ridley, who was invested as Commander of the Order of the British Empire for her work as principal matron in France.

The reasons for excluding "visible" minorities from military service were more complex. For many people, the notion of a racial hierarchy of intelligence and ability led to the view that non-whites would make inadequate soldiers. Others were more paranoid in their thinking. If "the races" got a taste of killing white men, where might their martial energies ultimately focus? Still others felt uncomfortable fighting next to people unlike themselves, and commanders argued that the efficiency of their units would be compromised if racial minorities were admitted.

Like other aspects of decision-making, it took some time for policy to be set with respect to the recruitment of racial minorities. Only Aboriginal peoples were specifically denied admission to the army from the outset, on the spurious grounds that Germans might not extend to them the privileges of civilized warfare. Not widely publicized, the directive was ignored by some militia officers, who had discretion over whom to accept into their units. Throughout the war, officials repeatedly insisted that there was no "colour line," but when visible minorities offered their services, they were invariably turned down by militia officers. Fifty blacks from Sydney, Nova Scotia, who arrived at the recruitment office were advised: "This is not for you fellows, this is a white man's war."[6]

The crisis in recruitment helped to crack the wall of racial prejudice. In the fall of 1915, the directive against Native Canadians was lifted, and thereafter they were recruited for the 114th Battalion and accepted into other units. African Canadians faced a more difficult battle, but they had champions in Conservative Party MPs from the Maritimes, including the prime minister. In April 1916, with Borden presiding, the Militia Council decided to form a black battalion—the No. 2 Construction Battalion—headquartered in Nova Scotia. By the summer of 1916, Japanese men who had received basic training were admitted to

11 different battalions. Chinese men were also grudgingly accepted. When conscription was imposed, Natives and Asians were exempted because they were disenfranchised, and little effort was made to recruit black conscripts. In all, about 3500 Natives, 1000 African Canadians, and several hundred Chinese and Japanese Canadians served in the Canadian forces.

Prejudice did not stop once minorities were in the army. Units comprising of visible minorities were likely to be shunted into forestry and construction activities and were segregated from whites whenever possible. African Canadians were segregated on ships and in camps, and even had to wait for the creation of a separate "coloured" YMCA for their evening entertainment. Nor did their service in the war change their status once they returned home. It remained a white man's war to the end, and the service of visible minorities was largely forgotten in accounts of the war effort.

The Halifax Explosion

For all their problems at home and their losses on the front, Canadians were relatively lucky. Canada was not invaded, and German submarines inflicted only limited damage in Canadian waters. Only once were Canadians offered a taste of what it was like to have their world devastated by the horrors of war. Shortly after 9:00 a.m. on the morning of 6 December 1917, the French munitions ship *Mont Blanc*, laden with explosives, collided with the Belgian relief ship *Imo* in Halifax harbour,

producing one of the largest explosions in human history up to that time. More than 1600 people were killed outright, another 9000 were injured—including 200 blinded by flying glass—and 20 000 were left without adequate shelter for the coming winter. Homes, factories, train stations, churches, and a great sweep of harbour facilities disappeared in the blast or the subsequent fires and tidal wave that engulfed the city.

Already stretched to the limits by the demands placed on a busy wartime port, the citizens of Halifax were overwhelmed by the disaster. As soon as word of the tragedy got out, help poured in from surrounding communities, other provinces, Ottawa, Newfoundland, and eventually from around the world. The people of Massachusetts, where many Maritime-born Canadians lived and worked, established a Massachusetts-Halifax Relief Commission to raise donations and, in conjunction with the American Red Cross, dispatched a train equipped with medical personnel and supplies to the crippled city. Sir John Eaton, president of the T. Eaton Company, arrived in Halifax with his own train, food, sleeping car, staff, medical unit, clothing store, and supply depot, all made available at his own expense. Some $30 million, over half of it from the federal government, was provided to help Halifax and its sister town Dartmouth, which had also suffered from the blast, recover from the devastation.

Once people were sorted out and the debris cleared away, officials settled down to impose order on the chaos caused by the blast. The progressive impulse was implicit in much of what was done. In January 1918, under the War Measures Act, the federal government established the Halifax Relief Commission to take charge of relief, medical care, and reconstruction. The commission decided to create a new town in the north end of the city, designed by urban planner Thomas Adams, who was in the employ of the Canadian Commission of Conservation. To the marvel of visitors and residents, 10 parallel blocks containing 326 houses, shopping facilities, boulevards, and green spaces rose out of the ashes of the explosion in the north-end suburb of Richmond Hill. The homes were built of hydrostone, a type of cement block moulded under pressure,

Women from Africville walking to downtown Halifax after the Halifax Explosion.
City of Toronto Archives, Fonds 1244, Item 2451

which was manufactured in a factory built especially for the purpose. Known thereafter as the Hydrostone district, the neighbourhood proved to be the only enduring monument to the garden city dreams of the Halifax Relief Commission. Other development projects fell victim to dwindling resources and flagging idealism.

The tension between labour and capital in Halifax was heightened in the aftermath of the explosion. As part of its mandate, the Halifax Relief Commission had extraordinary powers to determine wages and working conditions for the projects it sponsored. The commission refused to recognize unions or to enter into collective bargaining, claiming that it was important to act quickly. Organized building trades in the city watched with growing concern as the commission paid more than the going rate for building materials and professional services and then violated its own wage rates.

After the explosion, there was widespread pressure to lay the blame on someone. People of German and French extraction were the most likely scapegoats in wartime Canada. In the days immediately following the disaster, unfounded rumour spread that the collision in the harbour had been the work of German saboteurs. By the time a commission of inquiry, known as the Wreck Commission, began its work under Justice Arthur Drysdale, most people in Halifax, including Drysdale, were disposed to lay blame on the captain and pilot of the French ship, *Mont Blanc*, who had miraculously escaped injury, rather than the dead captain of the Belgian relief ship. Despite evidence that the harbour commission's safety regulations left much to be desired and that the *Imo* was as much to blame as the *Mont Blanc*, the Wreck Commission concluded that the pilot and master of the steamship *Mont Blanc* were wholly responsible for the disaster. Drysdale also sat in judgment in the case filed by the owners of the *Mont Blanc* against the owners of the *Imo*, but, not surprisingly, he handed down a similar verdict. When the case was appealed to the Judicial Committee of the Privy Council, blame was assigned equally for the collision.

CANADA ON THE WORLD STAGE

Borden's willingness to pursue an all-out war effort despite the opposition in Quebec owed much to his faith that Canada would emerge from the First World War

with new international status. From the beginning, he pressed British authorities to give the dominion a voice in war planning. Borden argued passionately that Canadians would be unwilling to make greater sacrifices if they were not given a chance to affect policy at the highest level, but the British coalition government under H.H. Asquith continued to treat Canada as a colony.

Throughout the war, Canada had a London-based champion in Max Aitken, who had been elected as a Conservative to the British House of Commons in 1910. Aitken was a leading figure in the political manoeuvring that made David Lloyd George prime minister in late 1916 and, for his efforts, Lloyd George had Aitken elevated to the peerage. Under the new prime minister, who knew that the war was going badly and wanted Canadian help, the attitude in the British cabinet changed instantly with respect to military policy and consultation with Canada and the other dominions of the empire. In 1917, he called the Imperial War Conference and created the Imperial War Cabinet—the British War Cabinet with dominion representation. These bodies met again in 1918, elevating Canada's status in the empire and giving Borden more information and the opportunity to express his views. Nonetheless, the British remained firmly in control of their empire's war effort.

The United States entered the war against Germany in 1917. Canada had been instrumental in defending British policies to Americans, who were suspicious of British imperialism and angered by the violation of the freedom of the seas represented by the British blockade of Germany. In 1918, with Great Britain otherwise preoccupied, Canadians turned to the Americans for help in defending the East Coast of Canada from German raids. This first North American joint defence initiative was short lived, designed solely to meet a specific emergency. According to historians J.L. Granatstein and Norman Hilmer, the "Americans had appeared to give grudgingly; the Canadians accepted the help, but cautiously."[7]

The presence of fresh American troops provided a shot in the arm for war-weary Allied forces and by August 1918, the tide had turned. The final Hundred Days leading to the armistice on 11 November 1918 began with the battle of Amiens, spearheaded by Canadian troops. The Canadian Corps played a major role in bringing Germany to its knees in the last days of the fighting, but the cost was great: almost 20 percent of the casualties sustained by the Canadian Expeditionary Force during the war.

Canada was represented in the British Empire delegation to the Paris Peace Conference and separately signed the Treaty of Versailles with Germany—the first time Canadians signed a multilateral treaty. There would also be membership for Canada and other dominions in the new League of Nations, established to keep the peace, and the International Labour Organization, designed to maintain international labour standards. Despite these accomplishments, Canada had a long way to go before it would fully emerge as a nation in its own right.

Divided on how to pursue the war they had naively joined, Canadians were equally divided on the meaning of their commitment to the international security system embodied in the League covenant. In a curious about-face, the United States refused to become a member of the League of Nations, even though it was American president Woodrow Wilson who had proposed the idea. Canada responded to the new body awkwardly—enjoying the international prestige that membership brought and playing a valuable role in the League's social and humanitarian work but rejecting the idea that the security of one member was the responsibility of all other members.

DEMOBILIZATION AND RECONSTRUCTION

In October 1917, the government formed a cabinet committee on reconstruction and a few months later created the Department of Soldiers' Civil Re-establishment to oversee the problems of demobilization. Its minister, Senator James Lougheed, was charged with responsibility for the Board of Pension Commissioners, the Soldiers' Land Settlement Scheme, hospital treatment and vocational training for returned men, and the re-employment of munitions workers. Under Lougheed, the new department began building hospitals, nursing homes, and sanatoria and helped establish programs to retrain the disabled. In 1919, the new Department of Health took over many of the responsibilities formerly handled by the provinces and volunteers.

Health reform came too late to ward off yet another disaster. In the final months of the war, an influenza pandemic swept across the world. It killed as many as 50 000 Canadians—almost as many as died in the trenches—leaving citizens everywhere reeling with shock. Canadians and their government, already stretched to the limit by the war effort, had few resources with which to fight this new enemy. Although the epidemic finally receded, it contributed to the rising tide of discontent that swept the nation when the war ended.

What the cabinet did not predict, though it should have, was the rising tempers of soldiers when they were left hanging around Europe and Great Britain following the signing of the armistice. The lack of suitable transport and the inability of Canada's rail lines to carry more than 20 000 troops a month from the nation's only major ice-free winter ports—Halifax and Saint John—created an explosive situation. In March, discontent among Canadian soldiers stationed in Wales burst into violent protest when a black guard arrested a white soldier and placed him under a "coloured" escort. White soldiers attacked their black compatriots, and in the ensuing mêlée five people were killed and 27 injured. More riots followed in May. Determined to rid themselves of the troublesome Canadians, the British managed to find extra shipping capacity, and most Canadians were home by July.

The Great War Veterans' Association (GWVA), founded in Winnipeg in 1917, emerged as the voice of the former members of the CEF. At the war's end, the organization was dominated by able-bodied men who demanded their rights and would brook no opposition from Conservative ministers. By 1925, the GWVA was amalgamated with a number of other smaller organizations into the Canadian Legion, which was more cautious and non-partisan in its approach.

The long-term costs of helping returned men and their families were immense. In 1920, more than 6500 men were still in hospital. Over 20 000 parents, wives, and children of dead soldiers qualified for pensions in 1925. As health problems surfaced, the number of people qualifying for disability pensions rose from nearly 28 000 in 1919 to 43 000 in 1933. In the interwar period, the total cost of these and other programs for veterans ranked second after the national debt in government expenditures, with accumulated costs of over $1 billion by 1935.

The Influenza Pandemic of 1918

When a significant proportion of the world's population becomes infected with a virus at roughly the same time, the result is called a pandemic. The influenza pandemic of 1918 was particularly deadly, killing as many as 100 000 000 people worldwide. Why the influenza virus was so deadly remains a mystery and the origins of the virus are difficult to determine. At the time, it was called the "Spanish Flu," but only because the press in Spain, which was not a combatant in the war, was the first to publish accounts of the disease. One seemingly logical explanation, and the one usually given by Canadian scholars, is that the virus originated in the European trenches and quickly spread around the world as troops returned home.

By carefully tracking the progress of the disease, historian Mark Osborne Humphries provides convincing evidence to support another source of the deadly virus.[8] He argues that the flu arrived in Canada from the United States in the second and third weeks of September 1918 primarily with American soldiers on their way overseas to the battlefields of Europe. Although the virus seems to have originated in Kansas in the winter of 1918, it was not until the end of August that it reached pandemic proportions in the eastern United States. In mid-September, it appeared in Canada almost simultaneously in four separate locations. At Niagara-on-the-Lake, Ontario, St. Jean, Quebec, and Sydney, Nova Scotia, it arrived with recruits from the United States en route to the Allied offence in Europe. It was spread to Victoriaville, Quebec, at the same time by American visitors to a Eucharist congress.

The disease was then efficiently dispersed throughout the country by the Siberian Expeditionary Force (SEP) that had been assembled to support the "White" Russian forces against the Bolsheviks, who had seized power in 1917. Recruits for the 2700-man force were drawn from across Canada and converged on Vancouver in late September and early October. As soldiers travelling from points east fell ill, they were removed from the troop trains and deposited in local hospitals.

Thus, influenza was not spread by soldiers returning home from the battlefields of Europe but by recruits bound for a new front in Asia. Since the government was more focused on the war effort than on public health, it made little effort to contain the disease, which killed at least 50 000 Canadians before it ran its course in 1919.

Canadian Bank of Commerce staff during the influenza pandemic in 1918.
Glenbow Archives, NA-964-22

The costs of reconstruction helped to convince the government to demobilize its armed forces as quickly as possible. Only three warships, two submarines, and the Royal Naval College survived from the larger wartime military establishment. The infant airforce was reborn in 1920 but only because of assistance from Great Britain and the United States. As before 1914, the militia absorbed the bulk of the defence budget. There would be no massive standing army in Canada as a testament to the nation's role in the Great War.

FEMALE SUFFRAGE

In 1918, the Union government followed up the Wartime Elections Act with legislation that gave the federal franchise to women on the same basis as men. During the war, the wall of opposition to female suffrage in the provinces also began to collapse. In 1916, the three Prairie provinces adopted female suffrage, followed by Ontario and British Columbia in 1917 and Nova Scotia in 1918. Although New Brunswick extended the vote to women in 1919, they were not allowed to hold public office in that province until 1935. Prince Edward Island granted women the vote in 1922, and Newfoundland in 1925, but the latter based its legislation on British policy, which gave the vote to women over the age of 25—not, as for men, 21. By 1920, most of the property and income restrictions on voting rights had also been swept away. After 1922, only Status Indians, Asians in British Columbia, women in Quebec, and conscientious objectors, including Mennonites and Hutterites, were denied the right to vote.

Women's suffrage advocates had the pleasure not female only of seeing the franchise question largely resolved, but also of witnessing the implementation of programs that were specifically designated "women's issues," such as prohibition, mother's allowances, and female minimum-wage legislation. Under the provisions of the War Measures Act, the federal government legislated full prohibition in 1918, and following the war all provinces except Quebec and British Columbia maintained the policy, at least for a few years. In 1917, Alberta was the first jurisdiction to pass a minimum-wage law for women, a policy adopted during the 1920s by all provinces except New Brunswick and Prince Edward Island.

For many women, the franchise served primarily as a means of pressing politicians to pass reform legislation. The National Council of Women developed a policy of adopting a Canadian women's platform to identify issues to be pursued through the established political parties. In 1920, the platform included demands for equal pay for equal work, the female minimum wage, and political equality of the sexes. Party organizations successfully resisted attempts to integrate women fully into their activities, much to the disappointment of some suffrage leaders, who had hoped that the vote would transform Canadian political life.

LABOUR REVOLT

Suffragists were not alone in being disillusioned by the failure of the war to usher in a major transformation in society. Higher profits for a few were accompanied by low wages, repressive working conditions, and a spiralling cost of living for many. Desperate to mobilize resources for war, and with few close ties to labour,

governments did little to rectify abuses. This failure set the groundwork for a level of class conflict unprecedented in Canadian history.

Domestic conflicts may have developed in response to specific Canadian conditions, but they did not develop in isolation. The Bolshevik Revolution in Russia and the rising tide of socialist and communist protest in Europe and the United States inspired many Canadians, just as it terrified Canadian politicians and capitalists. When Borden dispatched Canadian troops in 1918–19 as part of a combined Allied endeavour to put an end to the Russian Revolution, the labour movement was, not surprisingly, highly critical of the move.

Unhappy as it might be with the Union government, the labour movement was also deeply divided. Conservative eastern craft unionism took control of the Trades and Labour Congress at the 1918 convention, but the Western Labour Conference held shortly thereafter in Calgary broke with TLC policies of conciliation and restraint. Those attending the conference resolved to create a single industrial union, the One Big Union (OBU), to challenge conservative unionists, hostile employers, and unsympathetic governments. Before the fledgling OBU could hold its founding convention, its strike philosophy had an unanticipated dry run.

On 15 May 1919, the Winnipeg Trades and Labour Council called a general strike following the breakdown of negotiations between management and labour in the metal and building trades in the city. At stake were the principles of collective bargaining and better wages and working conditions. Although only 12 000 of Winnipeg's workers belonged to a union of any kind, about 30 000 joined the strike within hours of the call for action. They included telephone operators and department store clerks who had waged successful wartime strikes and hoped to consolidate their gains by working to strengthen the labour movement as a whole.

Winnipeg's strike sparked a series of general strikes of varying lengths across the country. While these strikes were ostensibly held in support of the Winnipeg workers, local grievances came to the fore everywhere. Some Canadian leaders were convinced that they had a revolution on their hands, but they were wrong. Internal divisions and lack of resources caused most of the strikes to come to an end within a

Bloody Saturday

Labour and capital viewed the events of 21 June 1919 in Winnipeg in entirely different ways. Following is the official strikers' view of the events of that afternoon as reported in *Strike Bulletin*, the newspaper published by the Strike Committee.

> One is dead and a number injured, probably thirty or more, as a result of the forcible prevention of the "silent parade" which had been planned by returned men to start at 2:30 o'clock last Saturday afternoon. Apparently the bloody business was carefully planned, for Mayor Gray issued a proclamation in the morning stating that "Any women taking part in a parade do so at their own risk." Nevertheless a vast crowd of men, women and children assembled to witness the "silent parade."
>
> On Saturday, about 2:30 p.m., just the time when the parade was scheduled to start, some 50 mounted men swinging baseball bats rode down Main Street. Half were red-coated R.N.W.M.P., the others wore khaki. They quickened pace as they passed the Union Bank. The crowd opened, let them through and closed in behind them. They turned and charged through the crowd again, greeted by hisses and boos, and some stones. There were two riderless horses with the squad when it emerged and galloped up Main Street. The men in khaki disappeared at this juncture, but the red-coats reined their horses and reformed opposite the old post office.

> Then, with revolvers drawn, they galloped down Main Street, turned, and charged right into the crowd on William Avenue, firing as they charged. One man, standing on the sidewalk, thought the mounties were firing blank cartridges until a spectator standing beside him dropped with a bullet through the head. We have no exact information about the total number of casualties, but these were not less than thirty. The crowd dispersed as quickly as possible when the shooting began.

Demonstrations during the Winnipeg General Strike, June 1919.
Provincial Archives of Manitoba, N 12299

month. The Winnipeg strike was the longest, stretching from 15 May to 26 June. Although its leaders made every effort to keep it orderly, agreeing to have essential services such as milk delivery continue throughout the strike, it faced formidable obstacles. Opponents, drawn mainly from employer and professional groups in the city, organized a committee to crush the strike and discredit its leadership. Insisting that the strike was Bolshevik-inspired, the Citizens' Committee of One Thousand refused to let the issue of employees' right to collective bargaining become the sole focus of the debate.

With encouragement from the anti-strike forces, the federal government sent the Royal North-West Mounted Police to Winnipeg, allegedly to maintain order. On 21 June—a day that became known as Bloody Saturday—the Mounties attempted to disperse war veterans holding an illegal demonstration in support of the strike. The demonstrators refused to leave and police fired a volley of shots into the crowd. By the end of the day, two men were dead and many other protesters were injured. Following the confrontation, strikers were arrested by the score. Among those jailed were two Winnipeg aldermen and a member of the Manitoba legislature. Recognizing the state's determination to crush the strike, those leaders who had not yet been imprisoned capitulated on 26 June. Winnipeg would remain a class-divided city for generations to come.

The federal government moved quickly to make radical protest difficult, if not impossible. Section 98 of the Criminal Code, passed in the House on 7 July, outlawed any organization whose professed purpose was to bring about "governmental, industrial or economic change" by force. Penalties for membership in such an organization included a maximum 20-year jail sentence. Even attending a meeting, advocating the principles, or distributing the literature of such an organization could result in charges under section 98.

EXPANDING POLITICAL HORIZONS

Like the differences that increasingly separated French and English Canada, a heightened awareness of class division was a long-term legacy of the First World War. Left-wing parties benefited from such divisions. In 1921, J.S. Woodsworth, who had been imprisoned for his role as editor of the strike newspaper in the latter days of the Winnipeg General Strike, was elected to represent Winnipeg's working-class north end in parliament as a member of the Independent Labour Party. Some veterans of the strike would join the Communist Party of Canada when it was clandestinely formed in 1921.

The Labour and Communist parties were not the only expression of political diversity that followed in the wake of the war. In 1916, the Canadian Council of Agriculture developed the Farmers' Platform, which included a call for free trade; graduated income, inheritance, and corporation taxes; nationalization of railway, telegraph, and express companies; and reform of the political process to eliminate the problems created by patronage, corruption, and centralized party discipline. Farmer candidates ran in the 1917 election on the Union ticket, but they were not converted to the Conservative cause. When exemption from conscription for farmers' sons was cancelled in 1918, some 5000 farmers marched on Ottawa in protest. In the same year, the Farmers' Platform was fleshed out and rechristened the New National Policy. Soon, provincial farmers' parties and the National Progressive Party would challenge the old-line parties for the support of the nation's farmers.

In Newfoundland, as in Canada, politics lost its pre-war simplicity. Labour shortages led to a spread of industrial unionism, with the Newfoundland Industrial Workers' Association organizing railway shops, longshoremen, street railway workers, and factory workers. In the outports, fishing families got better prices for their fish but felt that the war effort was very much a St. John's affair. When Fishermen's Protective Union leader William Coaker supported the government's efforts to form a coalition and impose military conscription, outport families felt betrayed. The collapse of the economy following the war resulted in a wave of bankruptcies and escalating unemployment, but the cash-strapped government had difficulty responding to the mounting crisis. In 1919, the National Government collapsed. It was replaced by a Liberal-Fishermen's Protective Union (FPU) alliance led by Richard Squires, but it, too, failed to find a solution to the post-war crisis. Demonstrations in St. John's underscored the social tensions that were unlikely to be resolved by any government.

In Canada, the Liberal and Conservative parties came out of the war much altered but not entirely obliterated by the experience of Union government. When Laurier died in 1919, he was replaced as party leader by William Lyon Mackenzie King, a former minister of Labour who claimed to personify the progressive spirit of the age. King was determined to win back the alienated Progressives—"Liberals in a hurry," he would come to call them—while retaining the party's strength in Quebec. Borden, exhausted by the war, withdrew from politics, leaving his successor, Arthur Meighen, the impossible tasks of running the divided country and pulling the Conservative Party together to fight a post-war election.

CONCLUSION

Anyone surveying the Canadian scene in 1921 must have wondered if the nation could survive the challenges it faced. Much had changed since 1911, the last time that Canadians had voted in a peacetime election. Rather than bringing people together, the war had widened the gulf between Quebec and the rest of Canada and exposed deep regional and class divisions. A generation of young men had been wasted in the trenches, and even those who survived were often scarred for life. With the enfranchisement of women, the potential electorate had doubled; so, too, had the number of political parties. Canada's status as an independent nation had been further advanced by its

Conscription

Why was conscription introduced? Was it a military necessity? Did its introduction signal Canada's desire to assert itself in international affairs or did it reflect subservience to Great Britain? Did its proponents carry the 1917 election by deliberately employing anti–French-Canadian messages? Was it effective in producing the soldiers that leaders claimed were necessary? Historians of conscription have offered varied answers to these questions and, perhaps not surprisingly, much of the division has been between Francophone and Anglophone historians.

According to one perspective, political pressure from English Canada forced the government's hand. Borden was "responding to the will of the English-speaking majority," write the authors of an influential history of Quebec in this period.[9] English-Canadian historians agree that there was pressure on the government for conscription, but note that the government was aware that English Canadians were divided on the issue and feared that conscription might lose votes for a government already in difficulties.[10] Borden and his key ministers, they argue, imposed conscription because of British pressure for a greater Canadian commitment to the war effort. Moreover, Borden's own conviction that Canada should do more left few options when voluntary recruitment failed to meet the government's targets for fighting men.

From this viewpoint, conscription was a military necessity. Military historian A.M. Willms claims that, proportionate to its population, Canada before 1917 had contributed fewer military recruits than the other white-settler dominions. More recruits were necessary because of the heavy casualties of war.[11] French-Canadian historians have argued that this interpretation accepts the Allied view that a peace treaty was not negotiable. Robert Rumilly's biography of Henri Bourassa stresses the view that negotiations would have been possible if both sides had given up the idea that there had to be a clear victor.[12]

Rumilly and other French-Canadian historians generally accept Bourassa's view that no great principles were at stake in the war, but English-Canadian historians have rejected the idea that Canada simply subordinated itself to British imperialism. Ramsay Cook, explaining the support for conscription by *Winnipeg Free Press* editor John W. Dafoe, suggests that many English Canadians who fought for greater Canadian autonomy from Great Britain believed the war was being fought over "cherished values" of democracy and not from motives of "sycophantic colonialism or aggressive imperialism."[13] In their history of the First World War, published in 1989, J.L. Granatstein and Desmond Morton maintain that the members of Borden's cabinet did indeed believe they were fighting a battle for "Canadian liberty and autonomy."[14]

How did the government win the election that allowed it to impose a measure it deemed necessary in this battle for "liberty"? Most historians agree that the Wartime Elections Act did not respect the liberty of all citizens, but there is less agreement about the extent to which the government resorted to ethnocentric appeals in its attempts to overcome Anglophone divisions about the fairness of imposing conscription. Roger Graham, who wrote a biography on the influential cabinet minister and later prime minister Arthur Meighen, claims that the government attempted to avoid having the election contribute to national disunity.[15]

French-Canadian historians dismiss this claim, noting that the whole purpose of conscription was to assuage English-Canadian opinion that French Canadians were not doing their share.[16] Some Anglophone historians also disagree with Graham's suggestion that the government took the high road in the election of 1917. Note J.L. Granatstein and J.M. Hitsman: "The Union Government campaign, founded on the Military Service Act and the Wartime Elections Act, deliberately set out to create an English-Canadian nationalism, separate from and opposed to both French Canada and naturalized Canadians. No other conclusion can be drawn from this election campaign, one of the few in Canadian history deliberately conducted on racist grounds."[17]

In 2005, J.L. Granatstein, writing as Canadians were debating their military contribution to the war against the Taliban in Afghanistan, acknowledged that he had underplayed the military side of the equation in his earlier publications. He argues that there was, indeed, a need for more soldiers to replace the casualties of the fierce fighting on the European front and that military concerns were central to the federal government's difficult decision to introduce the Military Service Act. Moreover, he maintains, his earlier conclusion that "[C]onscription had not worked in Canada" was wrong.[18] The more than 24 000 soldiers who fought overseas as a result of the act "kept the units up to strength, allowed for the Canadian Corps to function with great effectiveness and efficiency in the final decisive battles of the Great War and helped to minimize casualties."[19]

involvement in the war but decisions made in Great Britain and the United States still determined the nation's well-being. Would Canada, like many nation-states cobbled together in the nineteenth century, simply dissolve into chaos? Or would the sacrifices and conflicts generated by the Great War inspire Canadians to work harder to develop a sense of national purpose? Only time would tell.

NOTES

1 Tim Cook, *At the Sharp End: Canadians Fighting the Great War, 1914–1916*, vol. 1 (Toronto: Viking Canada, 2007), 129.

2 Daphne Read, ed., *The Great War and Canadian Society: An Oral History* (Toronto: New Hogtown Press, 1978), 100.

3 Jonathan Vance, *Death So Noble: Memory, Meaning, and the First World War* (Vancouver: UBC Press, 1997).

4 Bill Waiser, *Parks Prisoners: The Untold Story of Western Canada's National Parks, 1915–1946* (Saskatoon: Fifth House, 1995), 47.

5 Alison Prentice et al., *Canadian Women: A History* (Toronto: Harcourt, Brace Jovanovich, 1988), 207.

6 Cited in James W. St. G. Walker, "Race and Recruitment in World War I: Enlistment of Visible Minorities in the Canadian Expeditionary Force," *Canadian Historical Review* 70, no. 1 (March 1989), 1–26.

7 J.L. Granatstein and Norman Hillmer, *For Better or for Worse: Canada and the United States to the 1990s* (Toronto: Copp Clark Pitman, 1991), 69.

8 Mark Osborne Humphries, "The Horror at Home: The Canadian Military and the "Great" Influenza Pandemic of 1918," *Journal of the Canadian Historical Association*, New Series, vol. 16 (Ottawa 2005), 235–261.

9 Paul-André Linteau, René Durocher, and Jean-Claude Robert, *Quebec: A History, 1867–1929* (Toronto: Lorimer, 1983), 524.

10 See, for example, J.L. Granatstein and J.M. Hitsman, *Broken Promises: A History of Conscription in Canada* (Toronto: Oxford University Press, 1977), 67.

11 A.M. Willms, "Conscription 1917: A Brief for the Defence," in *Conscription 1917*, ed. Ramsay Cook, Craig Brown, and Carl Berger (Toronto: University of Toronto Press, 1969), 1–14.

12 Robert Rumilly, *Henri Bourassa: La vie publique d'un grand canadien* (Montreal: Les Éditions Chantecler, 1953), 544.

13 Ramsay Cook, "Dafoe, Laurier and the Formation of the Union Government," in *Conscription 1917* (see note 11), 15–38.

14 Quoted in Desmond Morton and J.L. Granatstein, *Marching to Armageddon: Canadians and the Great War, 1914–1919* (Toronto: Lester and Orpen Dennys, 1989), 145.

15 Roger Graham, *Arthur Meighen*, vol. 1, *The Door of Opportunity* (Toronto: Clark, Irwin, 1960), 194–95.

16 Linteau, Durocher, and Robert, *Quebec: A History, 1867–1929* (Toronto: Lorimer, 1983), 524.

17 Granatstein and Hitsman, *Broken Promises*, 78.

18 Granatstein and Hitsman, *Broken Promises*, 269.

19 J.L. Granatstein, "Conscription in the Great War," in *Canada and the First World War: Essays in Honour of Robert Craig Brown*, ed. David Mackenzie (Toronto: University of Toronto Press, 2005), 74.

RELATED READINGS IN THIS SERIES

SELECTED READING

A variety of topics relating to the First World War are explored in Briton C. Busch, ed., *Canada and the Great War: Western Front Association Papers* (Montreal: McGill-Queen's University Press, 2003) and David Mackenzie, ed., *Canada and the First World War: Essays in Honour of Robert Craig Brown* (Toronto: University of Toronto Press, 2005). On the historiography relating to the war, see Tim Cook, *Clio's Wars: Canadian Historians and the Writing of the World Wars* (Vancouver: University of British Columbia Press, 2006) and Geoffrey Hayes, Andrew Iarocci, and Mike Bechthold, eds., *Vimy Ridge: A Canadian Reassessment* (Waterloo: Wilfrid Laurier University Press, 2007).

The military experience of the First World War is described in Tim Cook, *At the Sharp End: Canadians Fighting the Great War, 1914–1916*, vol. 1 (Toronto: Viking Canada, 2007); Andrew Iarocci, *Shoestring Soldiers: The First Canadian Division at War, 1914–1915* (Toronto: University of Toronto Press, 2008); G.W.L. Nicholson, *Canadian Expeditionary Force, 1914–1919* (Ottawa: Queen's Printer, 1964) and *Canada's Nursing Sisters* (Toronto: S. Stevens, 1975); Desmond Morton and J.L. Granatstein, *Marching to Armageddon: Canadians and the Great War, 1914–1918* (Toronto: Lester and Orpen Dennys, 1989); Desmond Morton, *When Your Number's Up: The Canadian Soldier in the First World War* (Toronto: Random House, 1993); Michael L. Hadley and Roger Sarty, *Tin-Pots and Pirate Ships: Canadian Naval Forces and German Sea Raiders, 1880–1918* (Montreal: McGill-Queen's University Press, 1991); S.F. Wise, *Canadian Airmen and the First World War* (Toronto: University of Toronto Press, 1980); Stephen Harris, *Canadian Brass: The Making of a Professional Army, 1860–1939* (Toronto: University of Toronto Press, 1988); Bill Rawling, *Surviving Trench Warfare: Technology and the Canadian Corps, 1914–1918* (Toronto: University of Toronto Press, 1992); and Duff Crerar, *Padres in No Man's Country: Canadian Chaplains and the Great War* (Montreal: McGill-Queen's University Press, 1995). Arthur Currie's career is the subject of A.J.M. Hyatt, *General Sir Arthur Currie: A Military Biography* (Toronto: University of Toronto Press, 1987). The war experiences of two soldiers who fought on the European front is engagingly described in R.B. Fleming, ed., *The Wartime Letters of Leslie and Cecil Frost, 1915–1919* (Waterloo: Wilfrid Laurier Press, 2007).

External affairs are the subject of Norman Hillmer and J.L. Granatstein, *Empire to Umpire: Canada and the World to the 1990s* (Toronto: Copp Clark Longman, 1994). On changing views of the war, see Jonathan F. Vance, *Death So Noble: Meaning, Memory and the First World War* (Vancouver: UBC Press, 1997). On war artists, see Dean Oliver and

Laura Brandon, *Canvas of War: Painting the Canadian Experience, 1914–1945* (Vancouver: Douglas and McIntyre/ Canadian War Museum, 2000); and Heather Robertson, *A Terrible Beauty: The Art of Canada at War* (Toronto: James Lorimer, 1977). Larger contexts are explored in J.L. Granatstein, *Canada's Army: Waging War and Keeping the Peace* (Toronto: University of Toronto Press, 2002); Mark Moss, *Manliness and Militarism: Educating Young Boys in Ontario for War* (New York: Oxford University Press, 2001); and Chris Madsen, *Another Kind of Justice: Canadian Military Law from Confederation to Somalia* (Vancouver: University of British Columbia Press, 1999).

On the war at home, see the works by Brown, Brown and Cook, and English cited in Chapter 4, and Desmond Morton, *Fight or Pay: Soldiers' Families in the Great War* (Vancouver: UBC Press, 2004); Robert Rutherdale, *Hometown Horizons: Local Responses to Canada's Great War* (Vancouver: UBC Press, 2004); Daphne Read, ed., *The Great War and Canadian Society: An Oral History* (Toronto: New Hogtown, 1978); Barbara M. Wilson, *Ontario and the First World War* (Toronto: University of Toronto Press, 1977); Ian Hugh MacLean Miller, *Our Glory and Our Grief: Torontonians and the Great War* (Toronto: University of Toronto Press, 2002); Frances Swyripa and John Thompson, eds., *Loyalties in Conflict: Ukrainians in Canada During the Great War* (Edmonton: University of Alberta Press, 1983); Jeffrey A. Keshen, *Propaganda and Censorship During Canada's Great War* (Edmonton: University of Alberta Press, 1996); and John Herd Thompson, *The Harvests of War: The Prairie West, 1914–1918* (Toronto: McClelland & Stewart, 1978). John Herd Thompson provides a useful summary of the treatment of ethnic minorities in both the First and Second World Wars in *Ethnic Minorities During Two World Wars* (Ottawa: Canadian Historical Association, 1991). See also L. James Dempsey, *Warriors of the King: Prairie Indians in World War I* (Regina: Canadian Plains Research Center, 1999) and James W. St. G. Walker, "Race and Recruitment in World War I: Enlistment of Visible Minorities in the Canadian Expeditionary Force," *Canadian Historical Review* 70, no. 1 (March 1989), 1–26.

Women's experience during the war is described in Alison Prentice et al., *Canadian Women: A History*, 2nd ed. (Toronto: Harcourt Brace, 1996). See also Susan Mann, ed., *The War Diary of Clare Gass* (Montreal: McGill-Queen's University Press, 2000) for the diary of a nurse behind the front lines in France and Mann's biography of Canada's premier nursing sister, *Margaret Macdonald: Imperial Daughter* (Montreal: McGill-Queen's University Press, 2005).

Works dealing with conscription include J.L. Granatstein and J.M. Hitsman, *Broken Promises: A History of*

Conscription in Canada (Toronto: Oxford University Press, 1977); Ramsay Cook, Craig Brown, and Carl Berger, eds., Conscription 1917 (Toronto: University of Toronto Press, 1969); Paul-André Linteau, René Durocher, and Jean-Claude Robert, Quebec: A History, 1867–1929 (Toronto: Lorimer, 1983); and Andrew Theobald, The Bitter Harvest of War: New Brunswick and the Conscription Crisis of 1917 (Fredericton: Goose Lane Editions, 2008).

Internment camps are discussed in Bohdan S. Kordan, Enemy Aliens, Prisoners of War: Internment in Canada During the Great War (Montreal: McGill-Queen's University Press, 2002); Bill Waiser, Parks Prisoners: The Untold Story of Western Canada's National Parks, 1915–1946 (Saskatoon: Fifth House Limited, 1995).

The Halifax Explosion is explored in Janet F. Kitz, Shattered City: The Halifax Explosion and the Road to Recovery (Halifax: Nimbus, 1989); John Griffith Armstrong, The Halifax Explosion and the Royal Canadian Navy: Inquiry and Intrigue (Vancouver: UBC Press, 2003); and Alan Ruffman and Colin D. Howell, eds., Ground Zero: A Reassessment of the 1917 Explosion in Halifax Harbour (Halifax: Nimbus, 1994). Suzanne Morton discusses the Hydrostone development in Ideal Surroundings: Domestic Life in a Working-Class Suburb (Toronto: University of Toronto Press, 1995).

Problems relating to demobilization are discussed in Desmond Morton and Glenn Wright, Winning the Second Battle: Canadian Veterans and the Return to Civilian Life, 1915–1930 (Toronto: University of Toronto Press, 1987). On pacifists, see Thomas Socknat, Witness Against War: Pacifism in Canada, 1900–1945 (Toronto: University of Toronto Press, 1987). On the influenza epidemic, see Esyllt W. Jones, Influenza 1918: Disease, Death and Struggle in Winnipeg (Toronto: University of Toronto Press, 2007); Janice P. Dickin McGinnis, "The Impact of Epidemic Influenza, 1918–1919," Canadian Historical Association Historical Papers (1977), 121–40; and Mark Osborne Humphries, "The Horror at Home: The Canadian Military and the "Great" Influenza Pandemic of 1918," Journal of the Canadian Historical Association, New Series, vol. 16 (Ottawa 2005), 235–261.

Political mobilization in rural Ontario is discussed in the early chapters of Kerry Badgley, Ringing in the Common Love of Good: The United Farmers of Ontario, 1914–1926 (Montreal: McGill-Queen's University Press, 2000).

On worker radicalism during and after the war, see A. Ross McCormack, Reformers, Rebels, and Revolutionaries (Toronto: University of Toronto Press, 1977); David Bercuson, Fools and Wise Men: The Rise and Fall of One Big Union (Toronto: McGraw-Hill Ryerson, 1978); and James Naylor, The New Democracy: Challenging the Social Order in Industrial Ontario, 1914–1925 (Toronto: University of Toronto Press, 1991). On the 1919 strikes, see Harry Gutkin and Mildred Gutkin, Profiles in Dissent: The Shaping of Radical Thought in the Canadian West (Edmonton: NeWest, 1997) and David Bercuson, Confrontation at Winnipeg: Labour, Industrial Relations, and the General Strike (Montreal: McGill-Queen's University Press, 1990). Works on post-war repression include Larry Hannant, The Infernal Machine: Investigating the Loyalty of Canada's Citizens (Toronto: University of Toronto Press, 1995); Barbara Roberts, Whence They Came: Deportation from Canada, 1900–1935 (Ottawa: University of Ottawa Press, 1988); and Donald Avery, Dangerous Foreigners: European Immigrant Workers and Labour Radicalism in Canada (Toronto: McClelland & Stewart, 1979).

Transitional Years:
Canada, 1919–1945

T he Great War accelerated the movement of people from rural areas to cities and laid the foundation for a more secular world view. During the 1920s, many Canadians embraced mass consumer culture, defining their success by the extent to which they could purchase the cars, radios, household appliances, and fashions that poured out of Canadian factories. While mass production seemed to promise a greater abundance for all, many people were left behind in the rush for material well-being. The problem of poverty in the midst of plenty was exposed during the post-war recession that prevailed until 1924 and even more starkly during the Great Depression of the 1930s. Although movements to create a "welfare state" or usher in a socialist transformation of the economic system failed in the inter-war years, the federal government's success in mobilizing the nation's resources in the Second World War between 1939 and 1945 paved the way for dramatic changes in Canadian government and society following the war.

Photo: Glenbow Archives/ND 3-6742

CHAPTER 10

The Turbulent Twenties

TIMELINE

1920–24 Recession grips Canada

1921 William Lyon Mackenzie King's Liberals form minority government; Progressive Party wins second-largest block of seats in the House of Commons; United Farmers of Alberta form provincial government

1922 United Farmers of Manitoba form provincial government

1923 United Farmers of Ontario are defeated in a provincial election

1925 Coal miners strike in Cape Breton; Maritime Rights dominate the election in Nova Scotia

1926 Arthur Meighen forms three-day government; Mackenzie King wins the federal election; Royal Commission on Maritime Claims (Duncan Commission) appointed

1927 Federal government introduces program for means-tested old-age pensions

1929 Persons case decided; New York stock market crash

Government "experts" on children's health joined appliance manufacturers and utility companies to convince Canadian mothers to make purchases that would protect their families from harmful organisms. Dr. Laura S. Hamilton boasted in the *Grain Growers' Guide* in 1920 that "[From] the provincial governments down to the daily papers inquirers can get directions as to the best literature on the subject, and in many cases that literature will be supplied free."[1] Electric stoves and mechanical refrigerators would allow women to pasteurize milk and keep it cold. Electric heating and boiled running water would provide babies with well-heated rooms, sterilized baby bottles, and germ-free laundered clothing. While most Canadians heard these promising messages, few had the money to heed the advice. Urban workers might get jobs manufacturing some of the miraculous new inventions, but those jobs rarely paid enough for them to purchase these innovations. Farm families were even less likely to make such purchases. A survey of Manitoba farm homes in 1922 suggested that 60 percent had wood-burning or coal-burning stoves, making proper pasteurization problematic. Few had mechanical refrigerators or even iceboxes. A decade later, only 2 percent of the province's farm homes had running water.

The discrepancy between industrial production and purchasing power suggests that the "Roaring Twenties" roared for industrialists and a growing middle class but largely bypassed the majority of the population. Indeed, from 1920 to 1924, a persistent recession gripped the country. That was followed by significant economic growth for five years. But the gap between production and consumption led to a spectacular collapse of international capitalism in late 1929. This chapter explores the winners and losers in the 1920s and traces the turbulent politics of class, region, gender, and race that resulted from popular anger with social injustices.

Year	Primary	Secondary	Tertiary	Other
1920	26.6	29.7	35.3	8.4
1930	15.9	26.1	52.3	5.7

TABLE 10.1 Percentage Sectoral Distribution of the GNP, 1920–1930

Source: William L. Marr and Donald Paterson, *Canada: An Economic History* (Toronto: Gage, 1980), 22.

A CHANGING ECONOMIC LANDSCAPE

Where Canadians lived and what kinds of jobs they did changed dramatically during the 1920s. Particularly after the economy picked up in 1924, Canadians found their lives reshaped by the acceleration of a second industrial revolution based on the internal combustion engine, resource development, electrical power, and new chemical processes. As Table 10.1 indicates, the long-term tendency away from primary industries continued, and secondary industry held its own. Employment and investment growth was concentrated in the tertiary, or service, sector. These trends resulted in continued migration from rural to urban areas and transformed the lives of many Canadians.

Automobiles, the symbol of the modern age, offer a good example of how the economic sectors evolved. By the 1920s, a few Ontario cities had cornered the lion's share of the employment created in the manufacture of automobiles, but every city and most towns across Canada had car dealerships, gas stations, repair shops, auto insurance firms, and tire shops. Since Canada's roads were still too primitive to make a cross-country tour anything more than a gruelling marathon, the public demand for better roads led provincial governments to construct hard-surfaced highways along much-travelled routes. Taxes levied on gasoline and cars helped finance the ribbons of asphalt that cost even more to build and maintain than railway lines. No longer tied to train routes, entrepreneurs built restaurants and cabins along busy highways to cater to the motoring public. Tourism developed to new levels and required more service workers, many of them on a seasonal basis. As cars increased in horsepower and highway accidents took an increasing toll in Canadian lives, a larger police force was required to enforce highway regulations.

The phenomenon of new technologies creating more service than manufacturing jobs was repeated in many sectors. While a small number of workers were required to produce radios, many more were employed selling radios, working for radio stations, or producing advertising for this popular medium. Motion picture technology created few manufacturing jobs in Canada, but movie houses sprang up even in small towns, employing projectionists, popcorn sellers, ushers, and piano players. In the late 1920s, the arrival of sound in movies created unemployment for piano players but raised the number of movie houses and moviegoers to new heights.

The selling of products also created employment, even if the growth of department stores and the arrival of supermarkets reduced the number of corner stores. Along with bigger stores came bigger advertising budgets. Advertising not only employed people directly, but also made possible the expansion of the staffs of radio

Clerical employment expanded in the post-war period as the service sector grew. As this photograph (ca. 1919) of the main office of the Great-West Life Assurance Company in Winnipeg illustrates, some of the new clerical employees were women. While office hierarchies reserved senior administrative posts and better salaries for men, an increasing number of women found employment as secretaries, stenographers, and file clerks.
Courtesy of The Great-West Life Assurance Company Corporate Archives

and newspaper offices. Department stores and other large retailers such as People's Credit Jewellers made extensive use of credit to lure customers.

RIDING THE ECONOMIC ROLLER COASTER

Canada, like many other nations involved in the First World War, had trouble adjusting its economy to peacetime production. After the armistice, the Union government moved quickly to reduce state involvement in the economy. Defence spending was slashed and pressures to create welfare programs were largely resisted. Although veterans received some consideration, the government took the position that it was up to market forces to make up for the slack resulting from the transition to peacetime conditions. When the Liberals came to power in 1921, they, like their predecessors, focused on reducing the deficit accumulated during the war rather than on stimulating the economy.

Between 1920 and 1924, a persistent recession, marked by double-digit unemployment rates, gripped the country. Eventually the market turned around in most regions and occupations and the recovery over the next five years was sufficiently robust that the Canadian economy in the 1920s recorded a higher rate of growth than in the previous decade. The roaring success of the American economy, which was increasingly dependent on foreign markets and resources in this period, encouraged investment in Canada. As in the first two decades of the twentieth century, much of the growth in the Canadian economy came from the staples of wheat, pulp and paper, minerals, and hydro-electric power. Automobiles and electrical appliances were the leading manufactured products, while the service sector continued its steady rise to undisputed dominance, accounting for over half of the gross national product (GNP) by 1930.

Apart from government indifference, several factors made the transition from wartime to peacetime economy a difficult one for Canadians. Export markets, which absorbed over a third of the value of Canadian output between 1916 and 1918, contracted sharply. In 1920, near-drought conditions in the southern Prairies and a precipitous drop in wheat prices spelled disaster for the wheat economy. Protectionist sentiment in the United States led to increased tariffs, which were particularly hard-felt in Canada. In 1921, the manufacturing, construction, and transportation industries stagnated and the GNP dipped an ominous 20.1 percent.

As the effects of the slump reverberated throughout the economy, companies went bankrupt at an unprecedented rate, unemployment rose sharply, and migration to the United States increased dramatically. Even banks were brought to their knees, resulting in desperate mergers and the messy collapse in August 1923 of the Home Bank with its 70 branches. Besieged by angry petitioners, Ottawa agreed to pay $3 million in compensation to depositors of the Home Bank. In 1924, the federal government created the Office of the Inspector General of Banks as a step toward restoring confidence in the badly shaken banking system.

From its trough in 1922, the economic barometer began to rise, and by 1924 the clouds of recession in most regions had lifted. Massive investment in old and new staple industries in response to foreign demand, often with foreign capital, helped spur the recovery. The long-established tendency toward North American economic integration accelerated. By 1924, American capital investment in Canada had exceeded British investment. Trade with the United States was greater than that with Great Britain, though trade with the entire British Empire still exceeded American trade. Surpluses in trade with Great Britain served to offset Canada's deficit in trade with the United States.

PRIMARY PRODUCTS

As markets for wheat in Great Britain and Europe began to return to their earlier buoyancy, Prairie farmers expanded their acreage and immigration to the West resumed. Between 1925 and 1929, the Prairie provinces brought nearly 24 million hectares under cultivation, produced an average of more than 400 million bushels of wheat annually, and supplied 40 percent of the world's export market. After three decades of expansion, the wheat economy was a complex network of growing, harvesting, and marketing mechanisms. Farmer-owned cooperatives competed with private corporations to market the grain and secure the best prices on volatile world markets.

Vancouver was a major beneficiary of the expanding grain economy. With the opening of the Panama

Marketing Potatoes in Prince Edward Island

The frustration of Prince Edward Island farmers with complex marketing systems in the interwar years is revealed in the following tongue-in-cheek account, published in the *Charlottetown Patriot* in March 1928:

> Potatoes are seeds that are planted and grown in Prince Edward Island to keep the producer broke and the buyer crazy. The tuber varies in colour and weight, and the man who can guess the nearest to the size of the crop while it is growing is called the "Potato Man" by the public, a "Fool" by the farmer, and a "Poor Businessman" by his creditors.

> The price of potatoes is determined by the man who has to eat them, and goes up when you have sold and down when you have bought. A dealer working for a group of shippers was sent to Boston to watch the potato market, and after a few days' deliberation, he wired his employers to this effect: "Some think they will go up and some think they will go down. I do too. Whatever you do will be wrong. Act at once."[2]

Canal in 1914, which connected the Pacific and Atlantic oceans for shipping, Vancouver became a major port for selling goods to Europe. Not content to limit its new markets to the products of British Columbia forests and mines, the Pacific coastal metropolis challenged the pre-war practice of sending all Western grain to Europe via eastern Canada. From 1921 to 1928, Vancouver's annual shipments of grain leaped from 1 million to 100 million bushels. In 1929, 40 percent of Canadian grain shipped abroad left from British Columbia ports. Prince Rupert began a modest effort to compete with Vancouver for some of the West Coast market in 1926. Vancouver's gain was costly to the Winnipeg economy, which stagnated as the city lost its status as the warehouse for all the grain going to Europe.

Encouraged by orderly marketing procedures established during the war, western farmers experimented with a system of wheat pools in the 1920s. Producers agreed to sell their wheat to a common pool and share the returns rather than gamble individually on the Winnipeg Grain Exchange. With high prices in the late 1920s, the system worked well, and just over half of the wheat crop in 1929 was sold through co-ops. When markets glutted and prices fell during the Great Depression, neither pools nor private companies could save farmers from ruin.

The most spectacular new staple industry of the 1920s was pulp and paper. Following the abolition of the American tariff on imported newsprint in 1913, Canadian output grew from 402 000 tons in 1913 to 2 985 000 in 1930, making Canada the world's largest producer of newsprint. The meteoric rise of the industry was capped during the 1920s when pulp and newsprint began to rival King Wheat as Canada's most valuable export. Much of the investment in pulp and paper came from the United States, which continued to absorb the bulk of the output. Although pulp and paper operations were scattered from Nova Scotia to British Columbia, over half of the productive capacity was located in Quebec, where abundant and accessible forest resources, cheap labour, and attractive power rates attracted capital. The demand for pulp and paper breathed new life into the forestry industry of the Ottawa, St. Maurice, Saguenay, Miramichi, and Humber rivers and animated declining communities such as Liverpool, Nova Scotia, and Kapuskasing, Ontario.

Unplanned growth in the newsprint industry resulted in cut-throat competition and unstable market conditions. Six companies controlled 86 percent of Canada's newsprint industry, but were unable to bring order to the market. Between 1920 and 1926, the price of newsprint dropped from $136 to $65 a ton. In 1927–1928, newsprint producers tried to control output, allocate tonnage, and set prices, but the huge American-based International Paper Company defied such efforts, offering to supply the Hearst newspaper interests at $7 to $10 per ton below cartel prices.

Efforts by Quebec premier Louis-Alexandre Taschereau to encourage price fixing proved futile because the big American publishers, demanding low prices for the paper that they purchased, proved more than a match for the newsprint producers.

As in pulp and paper development, Quebec also surged ahead in electrical generating capacity. By the early 1930s, Quebec accounted for nearly 50 percent of Canada's electrical energy. Private capitalists in Quebec developed power primarily for industrial purposes: in 1933, 96.5 percent of the province's capacity was devoted to industry, compared with 82.6 percent in Ontario. Other provinces lagged far behind Quebec and Ontario, although British Columbia had huge hydro potential and, together with the Yukon, produced nearly 10 percent of Canada's hydro-electric power. Because of the availability of abundant hydro-electric resources, Canada became the site of aluminum manufacture. Bauxite from the West Indies was imported to Quebec, where intensive electrolysis isolated aluminum for industrial use. By the 1930s, the Aluminum Company of Canada, originally established in 1902 as a subsidiary of an American corporation, had emerged as the world's second-largest aluminum producer. Its new reduction plant in Arvida, Quebec, was one of the marvels of Canada's industrial age.

During the 1920s, Canada's mining frontier continued to attract investment. The rich gold and copper ores in the Abitibi region of Quebec around Rouyn-Noranda were developed by a Toronto-based corporation, Noranda Mines. In 1927, Hudson Bay Mining and Smelting, a creation of the Whitney syndicate of New York, began to work the copper-zinc ores near Flin Flon, Manitoba. New uses for nickel in the appliance and automobile industries and in the Canadian five-cent piece kept Sudbury booming. In 1928, a merger ensured that Inco (Canada) controlled 90 percent of the world nickel market. Demand for British Columbia's silver, copper, lead, and zinc more than replaced slumping demand for its coal, with the value of provincial production of minerals up from $37 million to $68 million between 1922 and 1929.

Demand for gasoline and oil products rose quickly with growing sales of automobiles and the gradual move from coal to oil to power locomotives and heat homes. Canada's largest petroleum company, Imperial Oil, a subsidiary of the American corporate giant Standard Oil, expanded its operations in Turner Valley, Alberta. By 1925, Alberta oil fields accounted for over 90 percent of Canada's petroleum output, but only 5 percent of Canadian consumption was supplied by Canadian wells. The rest was imported from the United States, the Caribbean, Latin America, and Borneo.

SECONDARY INDUSTRY

In the manufacturing sector, consumer durables—automobiles, radios, household appliances, and furniture—were the big success story of the 1920s. Most of these companies were located in Ontario, home to the largest concentration of consumers.

Most of Canada's independent automobile manufacturers were left in the dust by the Big Three American firms—Ford, General Motors, and Chrysler—which controlled two-thirds of the Canadian market. High tariffs on imported cars encouraged the American giants to establish branch plants to supply the Canadian market and the British Empire, in which Canada had a tariff advantage. By the 1920s, Canada's automobile industry was the second-largest in the world, and exports accounted for over a third of its output. The spectacular growth of Oshawa, Windsor, and Walkerville, where the assembly plants of the big automobile manufacturers were located, was proof enough of the significance of "the great god Car." Between 1920 and 1930, the number of cars jumped from one for every 22 Canadians to one for every 8.5. Ford's economical Model T was particularly popular until GM's Chevrolet managed to capture the fancy of consumers in the late 1920s.

At its pre-Depression height in 1928, automobile manufacturing employed more than 16 000 people directly, and many more in parts and service. The burgeoning industry gobbled up iron, rubber, plate glass, leather, aluminum, lead, nickel, tin, and, of course, gasoline. In 1926–1927, the federal government reduced tariffs on automobiles in an effort to bring down prices and introduced Canadian content rules to encourage more parts manufacturing in Canada.

The electrical appliance industry was another area of post-war growth. Radios were particularly popular, but so, too, were washing machines, toasters, electric ranges, and vacuum cleaners. Like the automobile, household appliances fell in price during the 1920s, coming increasingly within reach of the middle-class consumer. Canadian General Electric and Westinghouse were the giants of appliance manufacturing, and during the decade, Hoover, Philco, and Phillips became household names. Only a few Canadian-owned companies, such as Moffatt and Rogers Majestic, managed to carve out a niche for themselves in the rapidly expanding appliance market. Whether they were wholly Canadian-owned or American branch plants, Canadian companies drew most of their product designs and production technologies from the United States. A notable exception was the "batteryless" radio, capable of running on alternating current, developed by Toronto-born Edward Samuel Rogers in 1927.

In the new age of consumerism, wholesaling, retailing, banking, and insurance expanded dramatically, while the paperwork associated with corporate enterprise kept offices growing. Spurred by the power of advertising and by low prices achieved through mass purchases, chain operations had grabbed over 20 percent of the Canadian retail market by the end of the 1920s. In the variety-store business, chains accounted for an astounding 90 percent of sales. Indeed, chains became the symbol of consumer society, promoting mass taste and uniformity in culture. Eaton's invested in chain operations, and outlets of such American companies as Woolworth, Kresge, and Metropolitan stores could be found on the main streets of most Canadian towns. In the grocery business, Dominion and Safeway became prominent names. Direct sales by such companies as Imperial Oil, Kodak, and Singer also became a feature of the retailing scene in the 1920s.

WINNERS AND LOSERS

The impressive growth in some consumer durable, service, and staple industries masked problems in other areas of the Canadian economy. In the Atlantic provinces, farming and fishing were crippled by falling prices. Market gardening remained a lucrative activity near large urban centres, but farmers and fishers who depended on international trade faced stiff competition, soft markets, and the constant threat of exclusionary

It is easy to overestimate the distribution of new labour-saving devices for the home in the interwar period. Mary Tidd had neither running water nor electricity in her home in Ross River, Yukon. For her, wash day continued to involve a great deal of physical labour, particularly the constant hauling of water from a well and arduous scrubbing on a washboard.
Yukon Archives, Claude B. Tidd Collection, 8533

tariffs. Primary producers across the country experimented with cooperative marketing organizations and attempted to improve their efficiency by investing in new machinery, but they were always at the mercy of market forces over which they had little control.

Having invested labour and capital in an attempt to improve their efficiency, farmers and fishers could no longer retreat into comfortable subsistence to ride out hard times. Nor did they want to. Like everyone else in the modern age, they longed for the comforts and advantages offered by the new consumer society. If they could not get them by farming and fishing, they would become part of the stream of labour moving into the cities. Nearly a million Canadians moved to the United States in the turbulent twenties. In Alberta, 100 000 new immigrants to the province were offset by nearly the same number of migrants to the United States.

Primary producers were not the only ones who faced uncertainty in the 1920s. In many of the industries that defined the first phase of the Industrial Revolution, including railways, coal, and iron and steel, atrophy had set in. Canada's two national railways embarked on an orgy of spending on branch lines, steamships, and hotels, piling up debts when they should have been retrenching to meet the fast-developing competition from automobiles. When retrenchment finally came and the demand for rails and rolling stock decreased, the iron and steel industry languished.

Only the Hamilton-based companies Stelco and Dofasco, fattened by the demands of the nearby automobile industry, survived the 1920s unscathed. Algoma and BESCO (British Empire Steel Corporation), the new Montreal-based holding company for the Maritime iron and steel industries, were dependent on railway orders and faced trying times. Their managers failed to make the investments necessary to retool their operations for the second industrial revolution. At the same time, over half of the rolled steel used in the manufacture of consumer durables in the 1920s was imported. The crisis in iron and steel, in turn, reduced demand for coal. With Ontario-based companies increasingly purchasing their coal from the United States, the share of the market held by Canadian coal producers fell from 50 to 40 percent.

It was a measure of the limited number of high-paying jobs available in the 1920s that workers used pull or bribes to find work in a steel plant. Second to landing an automobile industry job, working in steel represented one of the best prospects for good industrial wages in the 1920s, with average annual wages reaching $1325 by 1925.

Foremen and superintendents were invariably Anglo-Saxons and often members of particular fraternities. In Sydney, Masons, Oddfellows, and Knights of Columbus dominated particular areas of the steel mill. Central and southern Europeans managed to find and keep jobs in the mills in Hamilton, Sault Ste. Marie, and Sydney, but at considerable cost to themselves. A retired Ukrainian steelworker in Sydney explained: "Well, if you wanted to work steady in Sydney, you had to give the boss a bottle every week. . . . There even was an agent in the open hearth and the mixer, he collected two dollars from each one there and gave it to the boss, so those fellows could stay on the job."[3]

A few Canadians made fortunes by riding the waves of opportunity in the interwar years, but the economic transition brought only hardship to many. Historian Michiel Horn suggests that during the interwar period, "it is likely that more than half of the Canadian people were never anything but poor."[4] In 1929, the average wage of $1200 per year was $230 below what social workers estimated a family required to live above poverty level. The "Roaring Twenties" did not even purr for many Canadians, but worse was yet to come.

ECONOMIC COLLAPSE

By the end of 1929, it was clear that the problems experienced in a few industries and in some regions throughout the 1920s were becoming nationwide. The crash of the New York stock market on 29 October 1929 signalled the beginning, but was not the cause, of the Great Depression. Advanced capitalist economies depend on investors' willingness to invest in stocks. When almost all stocks are losing value, investors are "spooked," and reduce their investment in all companies. Anxious to sell their stocks at any price, investors deprived firms of the capital needed to sustain their operations at optimal levels. Financial institutions refused to issue new loans to make up the difference. A symbol of the underlying problems in the international economy, the crash reflected the shaky foundations upon which the prosperity of the period from 1924 to 1929 had been based.

That foundation was the unprecedented productivity made possible by new technologies and continuing reorganization of corporate practices. Since investment in the production of more commodities only made sense if there were people to buy them, the purchasing power of consumers was of critical importance to the success of the industrial sector. Studies now show that in most countries, the income of the working class lagged far behind the availability of new goods. Moneys not distributed as profits often went into new investments and, for a time, before inventories piled up, speculators bid up the price of stocks in expectation of continued economic growth. With stock issues largely unregulated by the state, many countries witnessed gigantic sales of stocks that had been pushed far beyond their real worth by profit-seeking speculators. Such business practices, when they became publicly known in 1929, scared many investors away from the stock market.

Although Americans led the way in the speculative frenzy, Canadians were not far behind. The country's richest capitalist, Sir Herbert Holt, had made an attempt in 1928 and 1929 to effect a merger of all the Canadian-owned pulp and paper companies in the country. The resulting company, Canada Power and Pulp, with assets of $60 million, issued debentures of $160 million, confident of its ability to turn around the slump in newsprint prices and thereby substantially increase the value of its assets. Even before the Great Depression began, holdout companies ruined Holt's plans to monopolize the industry. The company was insolvent by the early 1930s.

Trade with other countries offered the possibility of finding consumers abroad for items that home markets could not afford, but the 1920s was a period of global overproduction. There were no international bodies that could orchestrate a slowdown in production in that decade or ease the fall in production in the 1930s. The United States, the one country with the economic clout to assume a leadership role in the international economy, was unwilling to do so. As panic set in, the United States followed tight-money policies that squeezed not only its own borrowers, but also international borrowers dependent on American loans. Canadian politicians had less ability to affect the course of international events, but Canadians were very divided regarding what governments should do to promote prosperity and economic stability.

KING AND CANADA

The career of William Lyon Mackenzie King illustrates how political leaders tried to manage the contradictory demands placed on them. When Laurier died early in 1919, the Liberal Party decided to hold a leadership convention in Ottawa to secure maximum publicity. In response to post-war labour and farmer radicalism, the Liberals pledged state-funded old-age pensions, unemployment insurance, and health care to guarantee all citizens a minimum level of security.

Liberal power-brokers viewed King as a logical candidate to convince Canadians of the party's reformist intentions while reassuring vested interests that they would not be unduly disrupted. The grandson of the leader of the Upper Canada Rebellion of 1837, King had been a prominent civil servant and served as Canada's first minister of labour in the final years of the Laurier regime. He then amassed a fortune as a consultant for American corporations attempting to dampen labour radicalism, beginning with John D. Rockefeller's coal-mining interests in Colorado. When he agreed to run for the Liberal Party leadership, wealthy Canadians, headed by the heir to the Salada Tea fortune, assembled a trust fund to ensure that King's decision to enter political life would not affect his standard of living.

King's blueprint for social reform could be found in his book *Industry and Humanity* (1918). Amid a welter of platitudes, he announced that the long-term interests of capital and labour were one and that the two sides should work together to find solutions. The state could contribute by mediating between labour and capital and by guaranteeing a minimum economic standard to all.

Once in power, King found excuses to move slowly with a reform agenda. He acted on social policy only when convinced that popular pressure gave him no other choice. Most of the time, he felt constrained by the combined pressures of big corporations, conservative elements in his party, and provincial premiers determined to protect their constitutional jurisdictions. Nonetheless, by 1945, King's government had legislated a variety of reforms, including means-tested old-age pensions, national unemployment insurance, and family allowances. These policies served as the foundation for Canada's relatively conservative version of the modern welfare state.

King's caution in domestic policy was more than equalled on the international front. He believed firmly that national unity and Liberal Party unity—King usually confused the two—depended on placating Quebec's anger over the imposition of conscription in 1917. Though he supported membership in the League of Nations and ties with Great Britain, he emphasized Canada's North American character and its unwillingness to participate in European wars. He joined the leaders of Ireland and South Africa in pressing Great Britain for recognition of the white dominions as independent nations. An independent Canada might choose to join Great Britain if the latter went to war, but it would not be automatically considered at war if Great Britain was. For King, the League was a place where the world's nations could discuss contentious issues rather than a body to impose collective action against individual nations that it deemed to have acted aggressively against other members.

William Lyon Mackenzie King governed the country from 1921 to 1930 and again from 1935 to 1948.
Library and Archives Canada/C9062

King's contemporaries had difficulty following the twists and turns of his political thought. After his death, he became even more of an enigma when his diaries revealed a side of the prime minister known only to his closest friends. In the pages of these intensely intimate documents, King is shown as a mystic, a believer in numerology, and a devoté of seances and fortune-tellers.

King was a bundle of contradictions: a prudish bachelor who had close relations with married women, a hard-headed realist who talked to his dog and his dead mother, an opponent of privilege who gave important cabinet and patronage posts to businessmen and party funders. Ultimately, the contradictions in his thoughts and actions revealed much about the ambiguities that characterized many Canadians. An incident recorded in King's diaries illustrates the point.

One winter day, as the prime minister was walking near his home in Ottawa, he saw an old man who had fallen on the ice. He helped the man up and walked him home. Unaware that he was walking with the prime minister, the man told King that he was a Russian Jew who had fled persecution and poverty at home and had become a wealthy department-store owner in Canada. When they arrived at the man's door, King disclosed his identity. The old man's eyes lit up with surprise, the

prime minister noted in his diary. King went on to praise Canada as a country where a persecuted Russian Jew could make a fortune and be walked home by the prime minister. As an afterthought, he added that it was troubling to think that Jews like this old man had moved into the Sandy Hill area of Ottawa, and he worried that the area would be overrun with Jews.

THE CHANGING POLITICAL LANDSCAPE

The 1921 federal election set the stage for a new era in Canadian political life. Not only were there new political parties to contend with, but the result also produced a minority government, the first in the nation's history. The Conservatives were the big losers. The Union government had begun to disintegrate shortly after the armistice, with its Liberal members either returning to their old political home or joining the new Progressive Party. While Arthur Meighen brought new leadership to the Conservative Party in 1920, he was not a popular prime minister. He had been involved in drafting the legislation to impose conscription in 1917 and had made the decision to use the Mounties against the Winnipeg strikers. Although he represented Portage la Prairie, Manitoba, in the House of Commons, Meighen was an arch-defender of Tory high tariff policies, which were unpopular in the West. He was an easy target for all those who believed that the Borden government had allowed profiteers to benefit from the war while ordinary people suffered.

The Conservatives won only 50 seats to 116 for the Liberals. The success of the Liberals in Quebec, where they won all of the province's 65 ridings, was a foregone conclusion, given the lingering hostility of Quebecers to conscription. The real surprise on election night was the success of the Progressive Party, which had come second to the Liberals with 65 seats in parliament. Calling for the public ownership of utilities and a speedy elimination of all tariffs, the Progressives apparently struck a responsive chord among rural residents in English Canada.

The result followed a provincial trend that began in 1919 with the election of a minority United Farmers of Ontario government supported by the province's Independent Labour Party. The following year, a Farmer-Labour coalition emerged as the opposition party in Nova Scotia. In 1921, the United Farmers of Alberta headed a majority government even though they had run candidates only in rural seats and had won just 28 percent of the popular vote. In 1922, it was Manitoba's turn to elect a government run by farmers. In all three farmer-run provinces, a healthy labour component in the legislature suggested that old-party dominance in urban and industrial areas was as unsteady as it was in the countryside. Yet by 1929, the national Progressive Party was on life support and would be swept away entirely by the Great Depression. The United Farmers of Ontario was a spent political force, while the Manitoba Progressives were en route to a merger with the Liberals, formally achieved in 1932. How had a movement that showed so much promise in the opening years of the 1920s lost so much support by 1929?

THE PROGRESSIVE PARTY

The Progressive Party arose as an attempt by the organized farm movement to unite farmers around a political program and elect members of parliament who would speak for farmers' interests. Frustrated by their declining political power and business dominance in the Liberal and Conservative parties, many farmers found the idea of a new political party attractive.

Despite the widespread discontent in most farming communities, the Progressive Party faced real obstacles in becoming a truly national party. Its first leader, Thomas A. Crerar, had been a conscriptionist Liberal and a cabinet minister in Borden's Union government, which limited his appeal in rural Quebec. Like Canadians generally, the Progressives were divided on questions of economic restructuring. Opposition to tariffs held party supporters together, but there were strong disagreements on the merits of public control of railways, utilities, and the marketing of grain. While Crerar was a strong free enterpriser, many Progressives had won elections by promising their constituents to press for nationalization of the Canadian Pacific Railway (CPR) and the restoration of the wartime policy of orderly grain marketing through the government-run Canadian Wheat Board.

The grassroots character of the Progressives made it impossible to establish a national organization with control over local constituencies. At best, Progressives were a loose coalition of provincial organizations, a coalition within which the split between the radical and conservative wings made it difficult to come to an agreement on policy. On the conservative side, disenchanted imperialist Liberals, mostly from Ontario and Manitoba, focused on the party's reform agenda and rejected any notion of transforming the economic and political system.

A more radical wing, based primarily in Alberta, was relatively small but highly influential within the farmers' movement. Led by Henry Wise Wood, the United Farmers of Alberta rejected the party system altogether and claimed that elected representatives should be free to vote as their constituents wished rather than forced to support the party line. The radical wing of the farmers' movement emphasized cooperation among individuals as an alternative to domination by capitalist monopolies. While the radicals believed that the state could play a positive role in implementing social justice, they initially regarded the cooperative movement rather than the state as the key to creating a more egalitarian society.

Although Progressive MPs from Alberta on the whole remained committed to more democratic participatory politics, they had little influence over the majority of Progressives, who simply wanted the Liberal Party to get rid of tariffs. First Crerar, and then his successor as party leader, Robert Forke, accepted the wily King's invitations to join his party and cabinet when the radicals had frustrated their attempts to create a traditional party machine. In an effort to lure moderate Progressives into the Liberal fold, King lowered tariffs on farm machinery and equipment and acceded to Prairie demands to complete a rail link to the port of Churchill. King also restored the Crow rate (the favourable freight rates on grain imposed on the CPR in 1897 and later applied to all railways), which had been suspended in wartime. In the late 1920s, he capped his concessions to westerners by negotiating the surrender of federal control over the natural resources of the Prairie provinces.

Such concessions proved sufficient to remove the Progressives from contention in most federal ridings. In the 1930 election, the Progressive Party won only 12 seats, nine of them from the radical stronghold of Alberta. The movement that had begun with much promise in the early 1920s had run out of steam.

THE KING-BYNG AFFAIR

Prime Minister King's political manoeuvring also played a role in reducing the impact of the Progressive Party. In the 1925 election, the Liberals were reduced to 101 seats, with the resurgent Conservatives taking 116, thanks to Maritime discontent and solid support from Ontario. King managed to form a new minority government by wooing the low-tariff Progressives, who had been reduced to 24 seats, almost all in western Canada, and conceding a means-tested old-age pension (introduced in 1927) for the support of the two Labour MPs.

The Progressives and Labour joined the Conservatives in defeating the government in June 1926 with a motion of censure relating to widespread corruption in the Customs Department. When King asked Governor General Byng to dissolve parliament and call another election, Byng refused. Instead he asked Arthur Meighen to form a government. As governor general, Byng had the right to determine whether any party leader could form a government that could command a working majority in the House of Commons, and he believed that Meighen, leading the party with the most seats, deserved an opportunity to test his strength before the House was dissolved. Meighen's ministry lasted less than three days, making it the shortest-lived government in Canadian history, but it gave King the opportunity he needed to shift the emphasis of the 1926 election away from the customs scandal.

During the campaign, King made political hay out of Byng's refusal to accept his advice to dissolve parliament, claiming that the governor general had violated the principle of responsible government. In the end, the customs issue and the King-Byng disagreement may have cancelled each other out, allowing King to aim specific promises to the West and the Maritimes, conceding only tariff-hungry Ontario to the Conservatives. Westerners seemed particularly prepared to believe King's promises of lower tariffs and freight rates and to abandon the Progressives to keep Arthur Meighen, viewed as the high priest of protection, out of office. On 14 September 1926, the Liberals won enough seats to give Mackenzie King his first of four majority governments.

POLITICAL WOMEN

For women, who were newly enfranchised, the interwar period failed to produce the results that suffrage leaders had hoped for. Only nine women sat in provincial legislatures before 1940, all of them in the western provinces, and only two won seats in the House of Commons. The reasons for this unimpressive showing are complex. Following the granting of suffrage, the women's movement lost its single focus, and women sorted themselves according to class, regional, and cultural interests. Professional women on the edge of the male-dominated public world continued to argue for equality of opportunity, especially in the context of blatantly discriminatory hiring practices, but they framed their arguments in the language of human, not women's, rights. In the interwar years, feminism and women's rights became equated with "man-hating" and the promotion of "sex wars" to such an extent that virtually every woman in public life was quick to deny any association with feminist doctrines. To embrace sexual politics was to court further exclusion from the bastions of male power and frustrate efforts to secure the equality in the public sphere that professional women sought.

Women attempting to break into formal political structures also took care not to appear too assertive. A feminist agenda had to be disguised as an effort to strengthen the family or the nation in order to avoid immediate condemnation from the men who headed the country's political organizations. Even in left-wing parties where women had greater access to organizational hierarchies and women's issues were frequently addressed, women were under-represented in the leadership and often found their concerns discounted.

The women's sections of farm organizations demonstrated the strengths and weaknesses of 1920s feminism. Having won the battle for the vote, women's organizations used their political influence to convince governments to spend money to improve community services. Irene Parlby, president of the United Farm Women of Alberta (UFWA) from 1917 to 1921 and later the first female member of the Alberta cabinet, argued that rural homes could be strong only if their residents worked together to provide health, educational, and recreational facilities in their communities.

Saskatchewan farm women, led by Violet McNaughton, spearheaded a movement to have municipalities hire salaried doctors and work together to create "union hospitals" that served a large agricultural district. This constituted the first step in Saskatchewan's march toward becoming the first jurisdiction in North America to provide public hospital insurance (1947) and medical insurance (1962). Farm women's organizations took up the battle for better protection of women's property rights both within marriage and during divorce. The UFWA also attempted to persuade the provincial government to establish family planning clinics, but it made little headway on "women's issues" with the largely male United Farmers of Alberta cabinet.

Excluded from the inner circle of male-dominated political parties, women maintained their pre-suffrage practices of education and lobbying through their voluntary organizations and separate party committees. Apart from women's rights, they pressed for policies relating to child welfare, prison reform, and world peace, which were still identified as women's issues. Safely tucked away in their auxiliaries, women were rarely put forward as candidates for political office.

One concession won by the women's movement in most provinces was mothers' allowances. Beginning in Manitoba in 1916, mothers' allowances had been instituted in all the western provinces and Ontario by 1920, and in Nova Scotia by 1930. The other provinces held out until the 1940s. While this social program provided funds to women desperately in need of them, its detailed regulations reflected a conservative gender ideology. There was close surveillance of recipients to ensure that they lived chaste lives and spent the allowances on necessities. Only "virtuous" mothers were eligible in the first place—that is, widows and, in some provinces, wives of men unable to support their families for medical reasons. Never-married, single mothers needed not apply. Even deserted wives were initially excluded on the grounds that it might encourage men to leave their families if they knew that the state would lend a helping hand to those they had abandoned. Governments, particularly the Ontario government, stressed that the purpose of the allowance was to reinforce gender roles that required respectable mothers to remain home with their children. But the

allowances were too small in all provinces to keep a woman-headed family with no other income out of poverty.

While women achieved little in the way of electoral representation in the 1920s, they did make progress toward political equality. In 1929, five Alberta women were instrumental in convincing the Judicial Committee of the Privy Council that women were "persons" under the law. This right was theoretically denied them by nineteenth-century legislation and in practice meant that women were excluded from appointment to the Senate and a variety of other privileged bodies. The five women who pursued the so-called Persons case through its long battle in the courts were Nellie McClung, suffrage activist, writer, and former Liberal MLA; Emily Murphy, writer and, in 1916, the first woman magistrate in the British Empire; Irene Parlby; former Alberta MLA Louise McKinney; and Henrietta Muir Edwards, who had

Agnes Macphail.
Library and Archives Canada/C21562

helped found the National Council of Women of Canada and the Victorian Order of Nurses. Despite considerable feeling that Judge Murphy should have been rewarded with the post, Mackenzie King appointed Cairine Wilson, a mother of nine children and a prominent Liberal Party organizer, as the first woman senator in Canada in 1930.

Canada's first female MP, elected in 1921, was Agnes Macphail. A teacher from Grey County, Ontario, she sat as a Progressive and soon made her mark as a defender of farmers, workers, women, and prisoners. She advocated bringing more women into political life, championed peaceful solutions to international conflicts, and won the hearts of her constituents and Canadians generally with her feisty interventions in House of Commons debates. Her long career in federal politics came to an end when she was defeated in the election of 1940. By then an activist in the socialist Co-operative Commonwealth Federation, she served as a CCF member in the Ontario legislature from 1943 to 1945 and 1948 to 1951, during which time she was responsible for the enactment of the first equal pay legislation in Canada.

FIRST NATIONS IN THE AGE OF DEMOCRACY

In the 1920s, Canada's Aboriginal peoples began to organize more systematically to reform the political structures that kept them dependent on white authorities. They faced an uphill battle. Status Indians, except those who had joined the armed forces, were still denied the franchise, and amendments to the Indian Act in 1920 gave the Department of Indian Affairs the explicit right to ban hereditary chiefdoms and other forms of Native governance.

Interference with Native political practices was a long-standing grievance among Status Indians. Prior to the First World War, Chief Deskaheh, a Cayuga, had begun a movement to achieve independence for the Six Nations of Grand River, Ontario. His campaign gained international attention in the early 1920s when he appealed for intervention from both the British government and the League of Nations, where several small nations supported his petition. Chief Deskaheh's campaign caused the Canadian government considerable embarrassment, but in the end it

was unsuccessful. In 1924, Indian Affairs imposed an elective council on the Six Nations and banned the hereditary council. Women, who had hitherto preserved their traditional veto in the selection of chiefs, had no vote on the elected council.

Another member of the Six Nations, Fred O. Loft, played a key role in the first successful effort to establish a Canada-wide Aboriginal organization. The League of Indians of Canada, established in December 1918, included representatives from the three Prairie provinces, Ontario, and Quebec. Loft was a well-educated Mohawk who spent 40 years in the Ontario civil service, mostly as an accountant. Unlike the traditionalists of Grand River, he did not support independence from Canada or a total retreat from European ways. The League, under Loft's guidance, stressed the importance of improved educational opportunities on reserves and greater cooperation among Native peoples. As Loft observed, "The day is past when one band or a few bands can successfully . . . free themselves from officialdom and from being ever the prey and victims of unscrupulous means of depriving us of our lands and homes and even deny[ing] us the rights we are entitled to as free men under the British flag."[5]

Despite Loft's relative moderation, the Department of Indian Affairs regarded his league as a subversive organization. Government harassment, police surveillance, and accusations of communism weakened the group, which suffered from internal divisions. By the time Loft died in 1934, the League's Ontario and Quebec wings had already collapsed, and the Prairie branches soon succumbed. Nevertheless, the foundations for a pan-Canadian Native organization had been laid.

In the Northwest Territories, the discovery of oil at Norman Wells in 1920 led to greater southern interest in the region. The federal government quickly signed a treaty, number 11, with representatives of the Dene and the Métis in the region and established a council to support the Northwest Territories commissioner in his efforts to impose southern control. In the North, as elsewhere, Aboriginal peoples would eventually claim that treaty guarantees of Native rights to hunt, fish, and trap had been violated, that they failed to receive the reserve lands promised by the treaty, and that they had been misled at the time of the original negotiations. Treaty 11 was unlike the previous 10 in that a few of the people who signed it lived long enough to see their claims bear fruit. In 1976, the federal government conceded that their treaty obligations had not been fulfilled, thereby opening the door to new land claims negotiations in the Mackenzie Valley.

The federal government was slow to take responsibility for the Inuit, whose contact with southern society was mediated largely through the Hudson's Bay Company. When times were hard, the company frequently made provision for their Native trappers. There was little altruism in such a gesture, as the comments of one area manager reveal: "We must keep them alive for future profits even though we carry them at a loss till such time shall come."[6] The company continued to make decisions and implement programs for the Inuit, often with the help of federal funds, until a 1939 court decision confirmed that the welfare of the Inuit was a federal responsibility.

LABOUR POLITICS

During the 1920s, labour parties steered an uneasy course between socialism and reform. Several provincial labour parties espoused gradual nationalization of major industries and greater labour control of the workplace, but the struggle for immediate reforms for workers—minimum wages for women, improved workers' compensation, federal unemployment insurance—absorbed most of the time of elected Labour representatives. At the national level, the Labour Party elected few candidates during the 1920s, and only the popular J.S. Woodsworth was able to hold his seat for the entire decade.

Within the labour movement, craft union leaders reasserted their supremacy and forestalled the advance of industrial unions. The increased conservatism of labour was partly a result of state repression following the Winnipeg General Strike, but it was also reinforced by the post-war recession. The major industrial unions that survived, such as the United Mine Workers (UMW) and the Amalgamated Clothing Workers, became increasingly cautious in their practices. In the case of the UMW, this conservatism resulted in temporary breakaway movements in the Cape Breton and Alberta coal fields, but produced no major shift in mainstream labour politics.

A marked contrast to this trend was the Communist Party of Canada (CPC). Organized furtively in a

Women's Labour League members in Winnipeg sew dresses for the children of striking Cape Breton coal miners.
Provincial Archives of Manitoba/N13141

barn outside Guelph in 1921, the CPC included many of the nation's most committed labour radicals. Although the party never enrolled more than 30 000 members at any time in its history, Communist leadership in the coal fields, garment shops, hard-rock mining, and among northern Ontario bushworkers brought a spirit of militancy to groups either ignored or poorly represented by established unions. Immigrant unskilled labour, particularly Ukrainians, Finns, and Jews, formed the backbone of Canada's Communist Party. Recognizing that women in the workforce were potentially important to the movement, the CPC established the Women's Labour Leagues to educate and organize women.

Communist doctrines appealed to a few labour leaders, such as J.B. McLachlan, whose organizational work among the coal miners of Cape Breton during a 1909–1910 strike led management to blacklist him. When he urged coal miners to conduct a sympathy strike in support of Sydney steelworkers in 1923, he was removed from his position as district president of the UMW by John L. Lewis, the American president of the UMW. Convicted in court of seditious libel, McLachlan spent a few months in prison before returning to Cape Breton in 1924 to edit the *Maritime Labour Herald*.

In the 1920s, the coal and steel industries in the Maritimes reeled under the pressures of declining markets, incompetent management, and labour unrest. A protracted and bitter strike among Cape Breton coal miners in 1925 focused widespread attention on the troubled island. Following the First World War, British and Canadian capitalists had merged the steel and coal plants in Cape Breton with other Nova Scotia companies to create BESCO. The company's owners issued stocks far in excess of the value of the merged firms and then tried to squeeze profits from the flimsy structure by firing employees or reducing their wages rather than restructuring the industry to meet the demands of the new post-war economy.

As the appalling living conditions of miners and their families became more widely known, there was a great outpouring of sympathy across the country. Even miners in the Soviet Union sent assistance, adding fuel to the rumours that Cape Breton miners were influenced by communism. When Agnes Macphail visited the conflict-ridden area, she found a situation, she claimed, that would make her adopt more radical views than any she detected among the starving miners. Before the strike ended, one miner, William Davis, had been killed by company police, and Cape Breton miners had become renowned throughout Canada and around the world for their resistance to capitalist exploitation.

THE MARITIME RIGHTS MOVEMENT

Labour unrest in Cape Breton was only one chapter in a large volume of woes facing people in the Maritime provinces. In the post-war period, the region faced a crisis of tragic proportions. Manufacturing declined by 40 percent between 1917 and 1921, and the recession that gripped the national economy in the early 1920s never entirely lifted from the region. In the 1920s, nearly 150 000 people drifted to greener pastures to find work.

Meanwhile, Maritimers watched with dismay as national leaders ignored their problems—too busy, they bitterly concluded, catering to central Canada and the West. Maritimers resented the Crow rates and comparatively generous provincial subsidies to the western provinces. When Ottawa made huge territorial grants to Manitoba, Quebec, and Ontario in 1912, Maritime premiers opposed the policy, claiming that the wealth of these territories ought to belong to the dominion as a whole. Even more galling was the wartime policy of railway consolidation that merged the Intercolonial into the Canadian National Railways and moved its head office to Toronto. Not only were jobs lost and freight rates dramatically increased, but Saint John and Halifax were abandoned as major terminals of international trade.

The hope of redressing grievances seemed remote. As the population of the Maritimes declined relative to the rest of the nation, the political power of the region plummeted. Maritimers occupied 31 seats in the House of Commons in 1921, down from 43 seats in 1882. Convinced that their interests, already largely ignored, would be shunted aside completely, Maritimers of all classes and interests came together to fight for "Maritime rights."

The Maritime Rights Movement was led by business and professional interests who used the Maritime Board of Trade as a vehicle to bring a regional rather than a provincial perspective on the problems they faced. Within the movement, Maritimers demanded larger federal subsidies, national transportation policies that took the region's needs into account, and tariff policies that offered protection for the Maritime coal and steel industries. The federal Liberal Party was the first beneficiary of Maritime discontent, taking all but six constituencies in the 1921 election. When King subsequently dismissed the concerns of his Maritime backbenchers, the region turned to the Conservative Party to champion its interests.

Nova Scotia, with its long history of protest against confederation, took the lead in advancing the regional cause. The Tories, campaigning under the banner of Maritime Rights, won all but three seats in the provincial election of 1925. Premier E.N. Rhodes teamed up with Conservative premiers in New Brunswick and Prince Edward Island to bring pressure on Ottawa.

Once King had won his majority in 1926 and was confident of having largely pacified western and Ontario farmers, he at last turned his attention to the Maritimes. He set up the Royal Commission on Maritime Claims in 1926, naming as its head the British lawyer-industrialist Sir Andrew Rae Duncan. Recognizing that Maritime governments were forced to tax their citizens more than other provincial governments to maintain a minimal level of services, Duncan called for provincial subsidies based on need. He also recommended a revision of freight rates, assistance to the region's coal and steel industries, better ferry connections to Prince Edward Island, and improvements to port facilities at Halifax and Saint John to encourage international trade through the region.

While King appeared to embrace the Duncan Report, his government refused to fully implement its recommendations. The Maritime Freight Rates Act of 1927 helped the region's producers compete more effectively in central Canadian markets, but provincial subsidies based on need proved too hot a concept for the government to handle. So, too, was the plight of the region's fisheries, which became the subject for yet

Lawren Harris (1885–1970), *Miners' Houses, Glace Bay*, ca. 1925. This grim representation of life in Glace Bay depicts miners' lives and work as one. The pollution over the town and the rows of identical, stark-looking homes combine to make the miners' town look much like a cemetery or the underground of a coal mine.
Oil on canvas; 107.3 x 127 cm. Art Gallery of Ontario, Toronto. Bequest of Charles S. Band, Toronto, 1970

another commission of inquiry. Some assistance was provided to move Maritime coal to Quebec markets, but further aid to the coal and steel industries was deferred. As historian Ernest Forbes observes: "Unfortunately for the Maritimes, the King government turned [The Duncan Report] into a program for political pacification; only gradually would Maritimers realize how much of the substance of Sir Andrew Rae Duncan's program had been removed in its supposed implementation."[7]

NEWFOUNDLAND'S DILEMMA

Newfoundland, like the Maritimes, saw little prosperity in the 1920s and sought political solutions to the dilemma of poverty in the midst of plenty. When Richard Anderson Squires became premier in November 1919, he headed a coalition government made up of members of the Liberal Reform Party allied with William Coaker's Fishermen's Protective Union. As minister responsible for the fisheries, Coaker was in a position to make Newfoundland's greatest resource work for the benefit of the people who fished rather than the merchants who exported their catch. He set minimum market prices for cod and penalties for exporters who attempted to undersell. He also established a government-controlled fish-culling system, with trade agents hired in foreign markets. In 1921, the regulations were repealed because exporters simply ignored them. The fisheries failed to make the transition to an industrial economy, with results that would prove disastrous.

Although Newfoundland already carried a heavy debt load from earlier railway construction and the financing of the war effort, Squires borrowed more money. He used it for projects designed to make Newfoundland a more attractive site for investors and to oil his party's patronage machine. Though the Squires government reached agreement with the International Power and Pulp Company of Newfoundland to develop a paper mill at Corner Brook in 1923, the government collapsed in scandal that year. The next five years were mainly years of retrenchment, fuelling public dissatisfaction that returned Squires to power in 1928. In 1927, the Judicial Committee of the Privy Council decided in Newfoundland's favour in the

MORE TO THE STORY

The Liquor Trade

Liquor was big business in the interwar period. Both large-scale and mom-and-pop bootlegging operations sprouted everywhere during prohibition to serve the illicit alcohol trade at home and the lucrative American market, fuelled by a rigorous policy of prohibition south of the border from 1920 to 1933. As Canadian jurisdictions eased their restrictions against alcohol, the larger bootleggers often became legitimate big business operators in Canada while continuing their illegal operations in the United States.

Liquor empires could be found in all regions. In New Brunswick's Madawaska County, Albenie Violette, also known as Joe Walnut, assembled gun-toting groups of former lumberjacks and sailors to staff large-scale interests in distilling, rum-running, and bootlegging. Maritime rum runners purchased booze legally produced in Montreal, Toronto, and the Caribbean for export to tiny Saint-Pierre and Miquelon. From there, Maritime fishing vessels carried it legally to "rum row," just outside the American 12-mile limit, where it awaited fast motor launches of the American crime syndicates who smuggled it into the country.

The Bronfman family made their early fortune with an illegal distillery in Saskatchewan that similarly cooperated with American crime syndicates to smuggle booze into the United States. In 1924 they used their profits to open up the Distillers' Corporation in Montreal, and in 1926, with Ontario about to end prohibition, they bought control of Seagram in Waterloo.

While bootleggers were mainly men, a minority were women. Women were even more prominent as the operators

This young woman with a liquor flask in her garter epitomized the happy-go-lucky "flapper" of the 1920s.
Glenbow Archives/NA-3217-2

of "blind pigs," illegal drinking establishments whose owners were generally known by a combination of "Ma" and their surnames.

long-standing border dispute between Labrador and Quebec, but it was one of only a few bright spots in a difficult decade.

ONTARIO AND QUEBEC POLITICS

The Farmer-Labour government of Ontario, formed after the 1919 election, lasted only one term. Unlucky to have had their entire period in office marked by recession, this government alienated urban residents with its puritanical stances on liquor, gambling, and Sunday entertainments. George H. Ferguson's Conservatives roared back to power in 1923 and, buoyed by a reviving economy, succeeded in marginalizing the upstart class-based parties that had forcefully emerged after the war. Ferguson invested public funds in a provincial highway system, promoting in particular northern development with roads linking the region's forestry and mining communities with southern Ontario. He established the Liquor Control Board of Ontario to replace prohibition with state regulation and profit from liquor traffic and the Department of Public Welfare to increase the state's presence in the lives of the poor. A lifelong member of the Orange Order, Ferguson was able to repeal the contentious Regulation 17 and legislate a limited right to French-language education in elementary grades. While continuing Ontario's long-standing efforts to limit federal intervention in areas of provincial jurisdiction, he brought Ontario into the federal means-tested old-age pension plan.

Quebec remained a Liberal fiefdom, with Louis-Alexandre Taschereau, premier from 1920 to 1936, emulating Ontario in building roads and encouraging foreign investors. Taschereau proposed education and welfare reforms that drew on Ontario models but relented in the face of church opposition to any weakening of its traditional monopoly in the areas of education and social services for Roman Catholics. A member of the board of directors of an array of large corporations even as he served as premier, Taschereau had little sympathy for either clerical or labour critiques of the practices of increasingly powerful companies in the province.

CONCLUSION

The 1920s ended as they had begun in Canada, with the country mired in recession. To be sure, the decade had provided a glimpse of technology-induced prosperity. By the late twenties, middle-class Canadians drove cars, listened to radios, and bought electrical appliances for their homes. Canadians who could not afford such luxuries often joined political parties, trade unions, and cooperative organizations that promised to spread the wealth more equitably. However, ordinary Canadians had little effect on economic and political policy, which remained in the hands of free market supporters—people who had a lot of explaining to do when the Great Depression descended in 1929.

NOTES

1 Quoted in Nadine Koziak, "Advice Ideas and Rural Prairie Realities: National and Prairie Scientific Motherhood Advice, 1920–29," in *Unsettled Pasts: Reconceiving the West Through Women's History*, ed. Sarah Carter, Lesley Erickson, Patricia Roome, and Char Smith (Calgary: University of Calgary Press, 2005), 182–183.

2 *Charlottetown Patriot*, 26 March 1928, cited in Ruth A. Freeman and Jennifer Callaghan, "A History of Potato Marketing in Prince Edward Island, 1920–1987" (prepared for the Royal Commission on the PEI Potato Industry, April 1987).

3 Craig Heron, *Working in Steel: The Early Years in Canada, 1883–1935* (Toronto: McClelland & Stewart, 1988), 95.

4 Michiel Horn, ed., *The Dirty Thirties: Canadians in the Great Depression* (Toronto: Copp Clark Pitman, 1972), 14.

5 Donald B. Smith, "Fred Loft and the Future of the First Nations: A Report on Work in Progress" (unpublished paper).

6 Arthur J. Ray, "Periodic Shortages, Native Welfare, and the Hudson's Bay Company, 1670–1930," in *Out of the Background: Readings on Canadian Native History*, 2nd ed., ed. Ken S. Coates and Robin Fisher (Toronto: Copp Clark, 1996), 97.

7 Ernest R. Forbes, *Maritime Rights: The Maritime Rights Movement, 1919–1927: A Study in Canadian Regionalism* (Montreal: McGill-Queen's University Press, 1979), 181.

RELATED READINGS IN THIS SERIES

From *Nation and Society: Readings in Post-Confederation Canadian History*

Andrew Parnaby, "The Best Men That Ever Worked the Lumber: Aboriginal Longshoremen on Burrard Inlet, BC, 1863–1939," 238–56.

From Primary Documents CD-ROM, Volume II

Mackenzie King: Liberal Convention, 1919
Arthur Meighen
The Farmers' Platform, 1918
Edwards et al. *v.* Attorney-General for Canada et al.

The Impact of War and the Social Gospel
Iroquois Indian Chief in Geneva Colourful Figure
Indian High Chief Stalks Geneva Streets
Forward for Maritime Rights!
The Fight Goes On
Justice for Nova Scotia
Petition of August 27, 1927
Reviving Virility
Holding Up Progress

SELECTED READING

On the economy in the 1920s, see Tom Traves, *The State and Enterprise: Canadian Manufacturers and the Federal Government, 1917–1931* (Toronto: University of Toronto Press, 1979); Ian Macpherson, *Each for All: A History of the Cooperative Movement in English Canada, 1900–1945* (Ottawa: Carleton University Press, 1979); and Trevor J. Dick, "Canadian Newsprint, 1913–1930: National Policies and the North American Economy," in *Perspectives on Canadian Economic History*, ed. Douglas McCalla (Toronto: Copp Clark Pitman, 1987).

On the labour movement, see the works cited in Chapter 7 and Judy Fudge and Eric Tucker, *Labour Before the Law: The Regulation of Workers' Collective Action in Canada, 1900–1940* (Toronto: Oxford University Press, 2001); Ian Radforth, *Bushworkers and Bosses* (Toronto: University of Toronto Press, 1987); Craig Heron, *Working in Steel* (Toronto: McClelland & Stewart, 1988); Ruth A. Frager and Carmela K. Patrias, *Discounted Labour: Women Workers in Canada, 1870–1939* (Toronto: University of Toronto Press, 2005); Joan Sangster, *Earning Respect: The Lives of Working Women in Small-Town Ontario, 1920–1960* (Toronto: University of Toronto Press, 1995); David Frank, *J.B. McLachlan: A Biography* (Toronto: James Lorimer, 1999); Bryan D. Palmer, *Working-Class Experience: Rethinking the History of Canadian Labour, 1800–1991* (Toronto: McClelland & Stewart, 1992); and Michael Earle, ed., *Workers and the State in Twentieth-Century Nova Scotia* (Fredericton: Acadiensis Press, 1989). On working-class socialists, see Peter Campbell, *Canadian Marxists and the Search for a Third Way* (Montreal: McGill-Queen's University Press, 1999). See also Margaret Hobbs and Joan Sangster, eds., *The Woman Worker, 1926–1929* (St. John's: Canadian Committee on Labour History, 1999) for information on the Women's Labour League newspaper that was published between 1926 and 1929.

The political history of the 1920s is covered in John Thompson and Alan Seager, *Canada, 1922–1939: Decades of Discord* (Toronto: McClelland & Stewart, 1985); Ian Drummond, Robert Bothwell, and John English, *Canada, 1900–1945* (Toronto: University of Toronto Press, 1987); Douglas Owram, *The Government Generation: Canadian Intellectuals and the State, 1900–1945* (Toronto: University of Toronto Press, 1986); Robert A. Wardhaugh, *Mackenzie King and the Prairie West* (Toronto: University of Toronto Press, 2000); and J.W. Pickersgill, ed., *The Mackenzie King Record*, vols. 1–3 (Toronto: University of Toronto Press, 1960–1970).

On Ontario politics, see Kerry Badgley, *Ringing in the Common Love of Good: The United Farmers of Ontario, 1914–26* (Montreal: McGill-Queen's University Press, 2000); Peter Oliver, *G. Howard Ferguson: Ontario Tory* (Toronto: University of Toronto Press, 1977); and James Naylor, *The New Democracy: Challenging the Social Order in Industrial Ontario, 1914–1925* (Toronto: University of Toronto Press, 1991).

Quebec politics in the 1920s are discussed in Bernard L. Vigod, *Quebec Before Duplessis: The Political Career of Louis-Alexandre Taschereau* (Montreal: McGill-Queen's University Press, 1986).

On Western protest, see David Laycock, *Populism and Democratic Thought in the Canadian Prairies, 1910–1945* (Toronto: University of Toronto Press, 1990); W.L. Morton, *The Progressive Party in Canada* (Toronto: University of Toronto Press, 1989); Kenneth McNaught, *A Prophet in Politics: A Biography of J.S. Woodsworth* (Toronto: University of Toronto Press, 1959); and Allen Mills, *Fool for Christ: The Political Thought of J.S. Woodsworth* (Toronto: University of Toronto Press, 1991).

On political developments in the Atlantic region, important works include Ernest R. Forbes, *Maritime Rights: The Maritime Rights Movement, 1919–1927* (Montreal:

McGill-Queen's University Press, 1979); E.R. Forbes and D.A. Muise, eds., *The Atlantic Provinces in Confederation* (Toronto: University of Toronto Press, 1993); David Frank, ed., *Industrialization and Underdevelopment in the Maritimes 1880–1930* (Montreal: McGill-Queen's University Press, 1979); Robert J. Brym and R. James Sacouman, eds., *Underdevelopment and Social Movements in Atlantic Canada* (Toronto: New Hogtown, 1979); and Gary Burrill and Ian McKay, eds., *People, Resources and Power: Critical Perspectives on Underdevelopment and Primary Industries in the Atlantic Region* (Fredericton: Acadiensis Press, 1987).

Women's political activities in the 1920s are discussed in Robert J. Sharpe and Patricia McMahon, *The Persons Case: The Origins and the Legacy of the Fight for Legal Personhood* (Toronto: University of Toronto Press, 2007); Veronica Strong-Boag, *The New Day Recalled: Lives of Girls and Women in English Canada, 1919–1939* (Toronto: Copp Clark Pitman, 1988); Terry Crowley, *Agnes Macphail and the Politics of Equality* (Toronto: James Lorimer, 1990); and Catherine A. Cavanaugh, "Irene Marryat Parlby: An 'Imperial Daughter' in the Canadian West, 1896–1934," in *Telling Tales: Essays in Western Women's History*, ed. Catherine A. Cavanaugh and Randi R. Warne (Vancouver: UBC Press, 2000).

On social welfare developments in the 1920s, see Nancy Christie, *Engendering the State: Family, Work and Welfare in Canada* (Toronto: University of Toronto Press, 2000); James Struthers, *The Limits of Affluence: Welfare in Ontario, 1920–1970* (Toronto: University of Toronto Press, 1994); and Gerard William Boychuk, *Patchworks of Purpose: The Development of Provincial Social Assistance Regimes in Canada* (Montreal: McGill-Queen's University Press, 1998).

CHAPTER 11

The Great Depression

1930–39	Great Depression
1930–35	Richard Bedford Bennett serves as prime minister
1931	Statute of Westminster; Pope Pius XI issues encyclical *Quadragesimo Anno*
1932	Imperial Economic Conference in Ottawa; federal relief camps established; Co-operative Commonwealth Federation founded
1934	British-appointed Commission of Government replaces parliamentary government in Newfoundland; Bank of Canada Act
1935	Bennett's New Deal; Canadian Wheat Board established; On-to-Ottawa Trek; Social Credit elected in Alberta; Canada–United States trade agreement
1935–48	Third William Lyon Mackenzie King administration
1936	Union Nationale government elected in Quebec
1937	Royal Commission on Dominion-Provincial Relations established

As the 1930s Great Depression descended, Ed Bates, a butcher in Glidden, Saskatchewan, found it impossible to make ends meet, so he moved his family and business to Vancouver. There, too, work was difficult to find and the Bates family was forced to seek relief. Denied welfare by the Vancouver authorities because of their recent arrival, Ed and his wife Rose attempted to get social assistance in Saskatoon, only to be told they must return to Glidden to apply for help. Too proud to return home to live on welfare, they rented a car and tried to kill themselves by carbon monoxide poisoning. Ed and Rose survived the suicide attempt, but their son Jack did not, and they were charged with his murder. While there was no doubt that their actions had caused Jack's death, local citizens blamed the politicians, rather than the parents, for the tragedy. A defence committee was formed and a coroner's jury found Ed and Rose Bates not guilty in the death of their son.[1]

The Bates family tragedy occurred during the Great Depression, an economic catastrophe unprecedented in its intensity. With many people facing destitution, it became common to blame the political and economic system, rather than the individual, for widespread poverty. Demands for reform and even revolution led to the creation of new political parties and brought to the forefront of national politics such issues as social insurance and state regulation of industries so that ordinary people would never again be reduced to desperate measures because they could not find work.

Nevertheless, the continued conservatism of many Canadians, particularly politicians at all levels, cannot be overlooked. In the rural municipality of Montcalm, Manitoba, as in many municipalities across the country, unemployed single men were expected to board with area farmers, with the municipality providing money for their food to the farmer, not the unemployed individual. Families requiring assistance received no direct money, their relief instead being given to a grocer. Montcalm, like many other municipalities, only provided relief to long-time residents, denying any responsibility to recent arrivals.[2]

In remote areas, particularly Aboriginal communities, many people starved to death. After the Hudson's Bay Company cut off credit when its markets and profits sagged in the 1930s, communities where neither the company nor the federal government had practiced wildlife conservation were unable to feed themselves. Ralph Pearson, fur trade commissioner for the company, reported that "a score" of people died of starvation at Great Whale River in 1931. Their diet had consisted of roots, tree bark, and water. In Rupert's House, an entire Cree family of 13 children died of malnutrition while 10 of the 12 children in another family perished.[3]

THE DIRTY THIRTIES

The panic that began with the New York stock market crash of October 1929 produced a virtual halt in new investments in the Western world that endured through most of the next decade. Once the global downward spiral started, it took on a life of its own. Prices dropped dramatically and then dropped again and again as producers tried to convince someone to buy their products. Scholars still debate why this depression proved more devastating and enduring than earlier depressions that had, with some regularity, plagued capitalist economies. In part, it would appear that the nature of capitalism had changed. Greater links among the various local and national economies meant that when New York, London, and a few other large centres of capital sneezed, most of the world got a cold. The tendency toward larger companies and monopolization of various sectors had reduced economic flexibility. So had growing urbanization, which made the working class, rather than farmers, the majority in many countries. Farmers could support themselves through subsistence production and barter when commercial markets temporarily vanished, but workers had to depend on government and charities to survive when work was unavailable. That, in turn, sapped the financial strength of governments.

Politicians and business leaders in most capitalist countries in 1930 believed that the marketplace, not governments, must solve economic problems. They viewed public debt as a threat to the solvency of a nation, and feared that if banks were required to lend their money to public borrowers, they would have too little money left over to loan to the private sector. With government revenues shrinking because of the decline in private economic activity, most governments focused on cutting expenditures to avoid going into debt. Only as the Great Depression progressed were those who proposed that governments consciously go into debt to create employment and social programs able to receive an audience with the broad public.

Canada was hit especially hard by the Great Depression. Its small and open economy was buoyed by exports of primary products, which the world now decided it could no longer afford. Because the American market had played such an important role in the expansion of the 1920s, the collapse of the American economy could only mean disaster for its major trading partner. To make matters worse, in 1930 the American congress legislated the highest tariff barriers in the country's history. But that was only the beginning. Competition from Argentinian and Australian wheat, a problem throughout the 1920s, became increasingly serious in the 1930s as wheat prices dropped to their lowest in over a century. As the price of basic foods eroded, the market for fresh and salt fish collapsed. Automobile sales dropped to less than a quarter of their 1929 level, with the contraction of the British Empire market compounding a shrinking domestic demand. By 1933, the value of Canada's exports was less than half of what it had been in 1929. Although export volumes resumed their earlier levels by the late 1930s, values remained below the 1929 figure (see Table 11.1).

With some companies collapsing and others slashing their workforces, unemployment reached unprecedented levels. The two national railways laid off 65 000 employees in the first four years of the Great Depression. Although unemployment figures are elusive for this period, nearly 20 percent of the labour force was officially classified as unemployed in 1933, the worst year of the Great Depression. Many more Canadians were underemployed, working part-time and in menial jobs that did not use their skills and training. Since rural poverty and underemployment were never measured by statistical analyses, it is impossible to quantify the exact level of misery that prevailed outside the cities.

A destitute family in Saskatchewan, 1934.
Glenbow Archives/ND 3-6742

As had always been the case in Canada, seasonal unemployment added greatly to the poverty of working people. Hidden unemployment was rife in the 1930s as women were forced into unwanted retirement, and, in the case of married women, fired from their jobs, ostensibly to provide more work for men supporting families. Those remaining employed were increasingly concentrated in the clerical "pink-collar" sector, where wages were far below the male-dominated "blue-collar" sector. In manufacturing, women workers earned about 60 percent of men's wages in 1939.

Minimum wages for women workers in various economic sectors had been legislated in most provinces during the 1920s. The wage floors were generally well below the minimum level required for a woman to support herself, reflecting the reigning patriarchal view that women in the workforce ought to be living in their parents' homes and biding their time until marriage, when they would leave the labour force and be financially supported by their husbands. Even the minimum wage was not always enforced: waitresses in Edmonton restaurants had to strike in 1935 to force their employers to pay the modest minimum wages prescribed for their jobs by Alberta law.

During the Great Depression, some people profited while others suffered. For example, Gray Miller, chief executive officer of Imperial Tobacco, earned $25 000 a year at the same time that clerks in the company's United Cigar Stores earned as little as $1300 a year working 54-hour weeks. Prices fell more rapidly than hourly wages, but it was no mean feat to get enough hours of work to make this differential meaningful. In the manufacturing sector, administrative and supervisory staff did well, receiving salary reductions substantially below the reduction in the cost of living.

The tax system did little to alleviate the income imbalance in the marketplace. Only about 300 000 Canadians in a population of more than 11 million earned enough to pay income tax in 1939. At the time, tax was paid by married individuals earning over $2000 and singles earning over $1000. Income and corporate income taxes were nominal, and indirect taxes collected from both rich and poor, such as the tariff and

TABLE 11.1 Percentage Sectoral Distribution of the GNP, 1926–1939

	1926	1929	1933	1937	1939
GNP*	5152	6134	3510	5257	5636
Exports*	1261	1152	529	997	925
Farm income*	609	392	66	280	362
Gross fixed capital formation*	808	1344	319	809	746
Automobile sales (thousands)	159	205	45	149	126
Common stock prices (1935–39 = 100)	200.6	203.4	97.3	122.4	86.1
Unemployment (thousands)	108	116	826	411	529
Unemployment (percentage of labour force)	3.0	2.8	19.3	9.1	11.4
Cost of living index (1935–39 = 100)	121.7	121.6	94.3	101.2	101.5
Wage rates (1949 = 100)	46.1	48.5	41.6	47.3	48.9
Corporation profits ($millions pre-tax)	325	396	73	280	362

*millions, current dollars

Source: Adapted from Michael Bliss, *Northern Enterprise: Five Centuries of Canadian Business* (Toronto: McClelland & Stewart, 1987), 418–19.

Environmental Catastrophe

The misery of the farmers of the southern Prairies during the Great Depression provides one of the enduring images of the decade. Southern Saskatchewan, southeastern Alberta, and southwestern Manitoba turned into a dust bowl where farmers' attempts to grow cereal crops were mocked by drought, dust, and wind. "The Wind Our Enemy," by Anne Marriott, gave poetic voice to the farmers' disillusionment with nature's attack on their livelihood.

Prairie farmers liked to think of themselves as husbanders of the soil. Arguably, though, at the root of the farmers' problems was a futile attempt to dominate the natural environment rather than to respect its limitations. Dryland farmers ignored warnings from government experts about the dangers of one-crop farming, presuming that science and new technologies could conquer all obstacles. With wheat prices rising in the 1920s, farmers opted for short-term financial gains rather than the longer-term security that might have come from diversification of crops and animal husbandry.

A disastrous drought from 1917 to 1921, accompanied by an invasion of grasshoppers, was followed by frequent and devastating attacks of rust and smut. Sawflies, cutworms, and wireworms caused millions of dollars of damage annually to repeatedly sown cropland. In Saskatchewan alone, 57 percent of all homesteaders were forced to abandon their land between 1911 and 1931. By that time, there were few traces of the buffalo landscape that had characterized the region in the mid-nineteenth century. Natural predators had been eliminated or reduced to small populations, and the vegetation composition had been changed by cattle and horses overgrazing on fenced-in ranches.

The monoculture of wheat had transformed the environment and farmers' language testified to their view that this transformation represented "progress." As historian Barry Potyondi notes: "The everyday terminology of the farmers depreciated the value of the natural world and hinted at the artificiality of their intrusion: 'cultivated' crops and 'tame' grass replaced 'wild' hay; machinery replaced horsepower; 'correction' lines replaced ancient trails that followed natural contours. This was a collision of natural and human forces on a grand scale, legislated into being and mediated by science and technology."[4]

Dust storm of the 1930s.
Glenbow Archives/NA-2496-1

sales taxes, accounted for over two-thirds of federal tax revenues by the end of the 1930s. The provinces, starved for cash, began to introduce modest personal and corporate income taxes.

In cities, the unemployed depended on social assistance, or "relief," from the municipal authorities. Rates varied across the country but were low everywhere, and dozens of regulations existed to restrict funds to recipients deemed morally worthy. Reflecting long-standing beliefs that the destitute were responsible for their own plight, municipal councils tended to adopt the view that the unemployed could not budget for themselves. Most municipalities gave vouchers for food and rent to married men, usually with strict rules about what food could be purchased. Single men, if they were deemed eligible at all, were usually required to use their vouchers to get food in communal feeding halls and shelter in hostels.

The low rates of relief and demeaning regulations provoked mass demonstrations and relief strikes across the country, which often convinced councils to treat the unemployed less parsimoniously. For example, in Saskatoon in 1932, a sit-down strike by 48 women and their children at city hall ended after two days when

Making Ends Meet[5]

For Canadians of all ages, the poverty and unemployment of the 1930s often meant puzzlement and anger. People spent their savings, if they had any, and then were forced to make ends meet as best they could. Letters written to Prime Minister Richard Bedford Bennett provided a flavour of the challenges that were faced. A Saskatchewan teenager reminded him of the meaning of destitution for many children.

> Dear Sir
>
> I am a girl thirteen years old, and I have to go to school every day its very cold now already and I haven't got a coat to put on. My parents can't afford to buy me anything this winter. I have to walk to school four and a half mile every morning and night and I'm awfully cold every day. Would you be so kind as to send me enough money . . . so that I could get one.
>
> My name is
>
> Edwina Abbott

Working-age adults in the province felt the cold and the pressures of poverty in their own way. Housewives, who had little recourse once the family breadwinner was out of work, also sometimes turned to the prime minister. As one Saskatchewan woman explained to Bennett in 1933: "I really dont know what to do. We have never asked for anything of anybody before, We seem to be shut out of the world altogether we have no telephone Radio or newspaper. For this last couple of years we have felt we could not afford to have them."

Nor could this woman afford underwear for her husband, who worked outside in the cold Saskatchewan winter: "I have patched and darned his old underwear for the last two years, but they are completely done now." As a last resort, she wrote to ask the prime minister to "send for the underwear in the Eaton order made out and enclosed in this letter," a request to which he acceded.

Even old age offered little relief. The means-tested old-age pension was cost-shared by the provinces with the federal government on a 50-50 basis, causing poorer provinces to set rates well below the $20 maximum and establish tough conditions that deprived all but the poorest or best connected politically from collecting. This letter, written by a man from New Brunswick to Bennett in 1935, suggests the precarious lives of many elderly Canadians forced to rely on stringent poor relief.

> Dear Sir
>
> I am writing you a few lines to ask if you will be kind enough to let me know the Law of the Direct Relieved, I am an Old man of 73 years old cant hardly help myself nearly cripple of both hands and my wife 68 years old I went to see the man who is appointed to give the Relieved this morning and I had a hard time to get $3.00 worth I got a bag of flour and a gallon of Paraphine oil I couldn't not get no tea or anything else long as we cant get no tea we will have to eat that bag of flour with cold water indeed it is a hard way to live so long in the party conservative and to be used that way.

the council agreed to their demands: to reduce the reimbursement from relief recipients when they found work; to close the relief store, where social assistance recipients were segregated as shoppers; and to limit the powers of bureaucrats regulating relief.

While the lives of all unemployed people were grim, gender and race determined how grim. Most cities made no provision for single unemployed women without dependants or for never-married women with dependants. In November 1930, the Vancouver relief rolls included 4513 married men and 5244 single men. Only 155 women were on city relief, and they appear to have been mainly widows and deserted wives with dependants. It was left to the Women's Division of the Vancouver Police Department, along with other civic groups, to establish Dunromin, a shelter for single transient women. Reforms came gradually, mainly in response to a concerted campaign by the Women's Labour League and the Unemployed Women and Girls Club. At various times in 1933, the city provided milk to women with babies, relief for ill single women, medical care for pregnant women, clothing allowances for married women and their children, and assistance to needy Japanese and Chinese families. Asian and

African Canadians were more likely to be denied relief than their European-origin counterparts among the unemployed. In British Columbia, the relief rates for Asian-origin recipients were set at half the rate for whites. In Calgary, only a spirited campaign by the Communist Party of Canada resulted in the city's destitute Chinese citizens becoming eligible for social assistance.

In the first four years of the Great Depression, per capita income dropped sharply (see Table 11.2). Saskatchewan, staggering under the double assault of the collapse of the wheat economy and massive crop failures, experienced the greatest fall in income. Drought plagued the southern Prairies for most of the decade and raised fears that the region might swirl away with the dust storms that characterized the hot, dry summers. Gophers, which flourished in this climate, became food for many poor families. Government bounties on gopher tails also provided many children with pocket money. In every western province, the decline in staple exports had devastating consequences. Saskatchewan's net farm income—that is, receipts minus costs of operation—was a negative figure from 1931 to 1933. Without federal relief, there would have been mass starvation or mass migration away from rural western Canada during the Great Depression. Even with federal aid, approximately 250 000 people left the Prairies between 1931 and 1941.

The Maritime provinces could ill afford to sink any lower than they had in the 1920s, but they did. Dependent on primary industries and international trade, the region was devastated by the Great Depression. Even their major source of relief—outmigration—was closed as Maritimers who had fallen on hard times elsewhere returned home in the 1930s, reversing a trend that had dominated the region for half a century. The Great Depression highlighted the underdeveloped state of municipal and social services in the Maritimes and the utter inadequacy of the region's rapidly shrinking tax base.

Unable to find the money to participate in federal cost-sharing programs to help the destitute, the region's governments were responsible for some of the

The decline in prosperity of Western farmers was symbolized by the "Bennett buggy," a motor car that a farm family could no longer afford to operate in the conventional way. Hitched to a horse, it became an old-fashioned wagon.
Saskatchewan Archives Board/R-A19945

most mean-spirited relief policies in the nation. Unemployed miners in Cape Breton received less than a dollar a week to feed their families, and in New Brunswick, officials prosecuted relief recipients who produced children out of wedlock. Without the aid of relatives, neighbours, and charitable organizations, many of the region's dependent citizens—estimated at more than 12 percent of the population in 1933—would have succumbed to starvation. As it was, an untold number of people on relief died because hospital services were denied them until they were too far gone to be cured.

TABLE 11.2 Per Capita Income by Province, 1928–1929, 1933

Province	1928–29	1933	Average decrease (%)
British Columbia	$594	$314	47
Ontario	549	310	44
Alberta	548	212	61
Saskatchewan	478	135	72
Manitoba	466	240	49
Quebec	391	220	44
Nova Scotia	322	207	36
New Brunswick	292	180	39
Prince Edward Island	278	154	45

Source: *Rowell-Sirois Report*, Book 1, Canada: 1868–1939.

NEWFOUNDLAND ON THE ROCKS

The impact of the loss of external markets, which was devastating for Canada's resource-extracting regions, was even more dramatic in Newfoundland. The colony's long-standing efforts to preserve its relative political independence collapsed with its economy. With 98 percent of its exports coming from the fish, forestry, and mineral sectors, Newfoundland was unable to keep up payments to its mainly British creditors and at the same time provide minimal social assistance to a growing population of destitute citizens. In August 1932, a demonstration of unemployed workers in St. John's deteriorated into a riot that gutted the legislature and forced Premier Richard Squires to call an election. The United Newfoundland Party, led by Frederick Alderdice, won an overwhelming victory, but it had no solutions to the financial crisis. In desperation, the government turned to Great Britain for help.

Great Britain established the Newfoundland Royal Commission to assess the colony's future. Headed by Lord Amulree, the commission recommended the suspension of Newfoundland democracy and the handing over of power to the British-appointed Commission of Government headed by a governor. While humiliated, the members of the House of Assembly felt they had no choice but to acquiesce. The Commission of Government, which came into operation in February 1934, brought an injection of British funds to pay off interest on debts and began programs to encourage co-operatives and a cottage hospital system in the outports. Nevertheless, the loss of local responsible government demonstrated the vulnerability of the once-proud colony to the ravages of economic depression.

HANGING ON BY THE FINGERNAILS

The path to economic recovery in Canada proved to be long and difficult. By 1934, in tandem with the United States, the economic cycle had begun to edge upward, and most economic indicators showed a slow but steady rise until 1938, when the spillover of a sharp recession brought them tumbling down again. Unemployment still hovered around 11 percent in 1939, although the gross national product (GNP) had almost regained the levels of the late 1920s. Rearmament in Great Britain, which created a market for Canadian minerals, aided the process of recovery. Only with the economic demand created by the Second World War did the economic clouds finally lift entirely.

Some industries recovered relatively quickly from depression conditions after 1934. While most entrepreneurs were slow to gamble on new investment, the automobile industry rebounded quickly, injecting new life into the industries that had benefited from the automobile boom of the 1920s. Radio stations, cinemas, and oil and gas companies showed steady growth. When the price of gold was artificially raised from $20 to $35 during the Great Depression, mining companies had little difficulty attracting investors. Ontario and British Columbia were the main beneficiaries of the gold-mining boom, but many provinces—and the territories—experienced their own gold rushes in the 1930s. Discoveries of the mineral pitchblende near Great Bear Lake made Eldorado Gold Mines one of the success stories of the Great Depression. The source of radium used in the treatment of cancer, pitchblende also

The Newfoundland Royal Commission recommended in 1933 that Newfoundland relinquish its self-governing status and submit to a commission of government. Here, Newfoundland governor Sir David Murray Anderson signs in the commission at the Newfoundland Hotel.
PANL B 16-36

contains uranium, initially considered a useless by-product of the mining process.

As British war production increased, the demand for gold, nickel, zinc, copper, and other minerals strengthened the mining industry in northern Ontario, producing growth and a degree of prosperity in Sudbury and Timmins, among other centres. Mining wages, unlike manufacturing wages, permitted workers to live well in the Dirty Thirties. Toronto was the financial capital of this mining expansion, and in the late 1930s, Toronto surpassed Montreal as the major source of financial capital in the nation for the first time.

TRADE UNIONS AND HARD TIMES

Not everyone was content to try to deal individually with Great Depression–imposed hardships. Huge demonstrations by the unemployed and violent strikes by workers trying to limit wage cuts rocked many communities in the 1930s. Canada's union movement, bolstered by the labour surplus in the First World War, had suffered during the post-war recession, dropping from an estimated 378 000 workers to fewer than 250 000. With courts recognizing the rights of employers to use blacklists against union "agitators" and force workers to sign pledges not to join unions, recovery in membership in the "roaring" half of the 1920s was slow and there were more losses in the early 1930s. As the economy picked up in the late 1930s, the number of unionists began to return to wartime figures, but as late as 1939, union members represented only 17.3 percent of the labour force. But numbers tell only part of the story.

During the Great Depression, a new militancy developed among Canadian workers. Under the leadership of the Communist Party, the Workers Unity League (WUL), dedicated to the creation of militant industrial unions, was founded in 1929 and soon took root among miners, loggers, and garment workers. Defying the logic that in times of unemployment, employers can dictate conditions since workers fear job loss, WUL unions struck frequently to prevent wage cuts. Although the WUL was small in relation to the Trades and Labour Congress, the major Canadian union federation, it is estimated that strikes inspired by the League leadership accounted for half the labour stoppages of the early 1930s.

In the United States, meanwhile, workers began to join a brash new federation of industrial unions, the Congress of Industrial Organizations (CIO), which soon also had branches in Canada. Many of the early CIO organizers in Canada were activists in the WUL, which folded its tent in accordance with orders from the international organization of communist unions for radicals to work inside the mainstream union movement.

The CIO played a role in convincing Nova Scotia's Liberal premier, Angus L. Macdonald, to pass Canada's first provincial law establishing rules for state recognition of a union in a particular firm or industry and forcing employers to engage in collective bargaining with certified unions. When the CIO and local union organizations in Cape Breton signed 90 percent of the employees at the Sydney steel plant in 1936, management refused to bargain. Union leaders lobbied Macdonald and other members of the Nova Scotia cabinet. With an election approaching, the government passed the legislation, permitting a flurry of organizing activity throughout the province.

Mitch Hepburn, Ontario's Liberal premier from 1934 to 1943, was not as open to accommodation as his Nova Scotia counterpart. When the CIO-inspired United Auto Workers (UAW) called a strike in 1937 against General Motors in Oshawa, the union brought 4000 workers into the streets. Hepburn organized a special police force to protect strikebreakers that was quickly dubbed "Hepburn's hussars" or "the sons of Mitches." Afraid that things would get out of hand, General Motors instructed its Canadian managers to negotiate an agreement with the UAW.

In the same year, violence erupted in Peterborough when men and women employed by the city's two Dominion Woollens plants participated in a CIO-led strike. The determination of the police, particularly the Ontario Provincial Police, to help the employer keep the plants running with strikebreakers led to clashes with the striking workers. "Dorothy," one of the women arrested during the conflict, was surprised by the state's vilification and repression of people who were simply struggling for better pay. Interviewed a half-century later, she recalled:

> I remember being on picket line. That's all I was doing, I was really surprised how wild [the police] were. . . . The chief of police came and grabbed me

from behind with fingernails in my neck—you could see the marks. I was trying to kick out at him: I couldn't figure out why he was picking on me. He shoved me under the gate. . . . By that time I was crying and . . . started to run out. . . . Another girl came to rescue me from Chief Newall, and they threw her in [to the paddywagon] too. They made us go to city jail and we had "a bit of a trial." . . . The chief of police charged me with throwing pepper in his face, and I never even had any pepper.[6]

In 1939, on orders from the American Federation of Labor, CIO affiliates were expelled from the crafts-dominated Trades and Labour Congress. Undeterred, they joined a group of Canadian-controlled unions to form the Canadian Congress of Labour (CCL). The unions were biding their time. Only the high rate of unemployment gave employers and the state power to prevent willing workers from unionizing. When and if the economy turned around, the unions would be ready to assert themselves.

In Quebec, the Confédération des travailleurs catholiques du Canada (CTCC), formed in the 1920s, continued to be a strong force within the trade union movement. Associating strikes with socialism, church leaders believed that international unions were promoting an adversarial model that pitted class against class. In practice, the Roman Catholic unions and many of the priests associated with their operations soon came to the view that workers needed the weapon of the strike to deal with intransigent employers who could not otherwise be persuaded to treat their workers fairly. Equally important in influencing the outlook of the CTCC was the reluctance of Roman Catholic workers to leave strong international unions to join a local Roman Catholic union. Only concrete successes in extracting good contracts from employers could convince them to give the Roman Catholic union a try.

In the Roman Catholic and international union movements in the province, male organizers and workers dominated. There were some significant exceptions. During the Great Depression, Madeleine Parent and Lea Roback began lifelong careers as dedicated union organizers and political activists. Parent was a middle-class Francophone Roman Catholic who was denounced by her church for her "unladylike" profession. Roback, the daughter of Jewish storekeepers, was moved by communist convictions and braved anti-Semitism and sexism to fight for social justice for Montreal workers.

In Newfoundland, as in Canada, the Great Depression provided a spur to union organization. The Newfoundland Lumbermen's Association was formed in 1935 by 12 000 loggers to fight for a just piece rate for the wood that they cut. Railway clerks unionized, and when both their employer and the Commission of Government refused to recognize the union they took their case to Great Britain, which granted recognition of their rights as workers. In 1937, the Newfoundland and Labrador Federation of Labour (NLFL) was formed. It campaigned for an end to child labour, the implementation of a five-day, forty-hour week, and improvements in mine inspection and workers' compensation.

Western Canadian workers continued to prove receptive to radical labour leadership during the Great Depression. The WUL spearheaded strikes among New Westminster sawmill workers, Vancouver Island loggers, and fishers on the Skeena and Nass rivers. But repression limited labour's gains in the region. The Royal Canadian Mounted Police (RCMP) were used to suppress strikes such as the Estevan coal miners' strike in 1931, during which three miners were killed. Such repression highlighted the apparent league of the state with employers against workers.

THE BENNETT YEARS, 1930–1935

In the 1930s, even more than in the early 1920s, Canadians began to question whether the Conservatives and Liberals were anything more than the political henchmen of big business. Antipathy to the old-line parties led to the formation of several new national and regional parties while forcing the two main parties to concede some of the demands for reform to maintain their credibility with average Canadians.

Slow to grasp the seriousness of the situation as Canada faced its first Great Depression winter, Mackenzie King was an easy target for Labour MPs J.S. Woodsworth and A.A. Heaps, who demanded in the House that the government "take immediate action to deal with the question of unemployment." The Conservatives joined in the attack, causing King to lose his temper. He might, he said, be prepared to give some support to Progressive governments in Manitoba and Alberta, but he would not give any Tory government so much as "a five-cent piece."

The "five-cent piece speech" became the theme of Conservative candidates stumping the country in the July 1930 campaign. Under their new leader, R.B. Bennett, the Conservatives won a resounding victory, carrying 137 seats to 91 for the Liberals, 12 for the Progressives, and three for Labour. King was luckier than he realized at the time. With the nation sinking under the weight of the Great Depression, it was the Conservatives who would become associated with hard times, and the Liberals would be waiting in the wings to pick up the pieces in 1935.

Born in 1870 in Albert County, New Brunswick, Bennett was a Tory's Tory. He was proud of his alleged Loyalist roots, Methodist values, and rise to prominence from humble origins. After teaching to put himself through Dalhousie Law School, he moved west to take a position in the Calgary law office of Senator James A. Lougheed. He made his fortune through real estate deals, wise investments, and powerful clients such as the Canadian Pacific Railway. In 1911, he won the Calgary seat in the House of Commons and was one of a small number of Conservatives able to win a seat in the West in the 1925 and 1926 elections. This helped to make him an appealing candidate at the Conservative Party's first leadership convention, held in Winnipeg in 1927. Prior to this time, party leaders had simply been seconded by the parliamentary caucus.

Like King, Bennett was a bachelor and a self-made man and was prone to delivering boring speeches, but the similarities stopped there. Bennett had enormous energy and, unlike King, could never be accused of inaction. Eager to make good on his election promise to address the problems created by the Great Depression, he called a special session of parliament soon after taking power. The government introduced the Unemployment Relief Act to provide $20 million—an unprecedented sum—to help people get back to work and also embarked on a program of tariff increases designed to protect languishing Canadian industries from foreign competition.

It was not enough. Bread lines lengthened, prices continued to plummet, and municipal and charitable organizations collapsed under the weight of the demands placed upon them. At a loss as to how to stem the crisis, Bennett resorted to desperate measures and soon found his party embattled from without and divided within.

Prime Minister R.B. Bennett (left) in a somewhat contrived picture of political friendship with opposition leader W.L. Mackenzie King.
Library and Archives Canada/PA-148532

Bennett recognized that the municipalities, which had handled relief in the past, often by financing public works such as the construction of roads, auditoria, and museums, were too broke to finance relief on their own. They depended on property taxes that proved hard to collect when many property owners were unemployed or underemployed. Rather than municipalities or provinces, the federal government controlled banking and currency and had access to any form of taxation that it deemed advisable. Bennett feared that if he expanded the role of the federal government in addressing the crisis, he could bankrupt the country and drive private investors out of the economy for good. Only the persistence of the Great Depression and the growing impatience of Canadians with the view that the economy would eventually self-correct caused him gradually to shift his views regarding the role of government in the operation of the economy.

PROTEST FROM THE LEFT

In 1932, the Bennett government established relief camps under military control to house the single unemployed men who had been travelling from city to city in search of work. Single able-bodied men faced dismal prospects: employers preferred to hire married men, and many municipalities denied single people relief. From the government's perspective, these unfortunate people were a potentially explosive group that needed to be segregated from society until the economy improved. The transients were to be denied welfare unless they moved to remote camps where they would work for their board and receive an allowance of 20 cents a day. The camps offered many single unemployed men nutritious meals and medical care. Since governments were offering no other alternatives, many young men chose relief camps over life in the hobo tent jungles that sprang up in some cities or a life of begging and riding the rails.

Although the men performed useful work such as the construction of highways, airfields, and barracks, the isolation and lack of pay bred considerable anger. As Irene Baird's powerful novel *Waste Heritage* (1939) vividly illustrated, Communist Party organizers had little difficulty convincing camp workers to organize to demand "work and wages" and the closing of the camps.

Boredom was a common complaint in most camps, but the men often made the most of their meagre resources. In some Ontario camps that were close to towns, camp residents organized boxing and wrestling matches that townsfolk paid to watch. Funds collected from these events and occasional charitable donations were used to provide radios, reading material, and sports equipment. The men made their own checkerboards and asked local farmers to lend them sets of horseshoes. Living in primitive bunkhouses, the reliefers ate three ample military-style meals a day but complained bitterly about the monotony of the food.

Over 1500 mourners lined the streets of Bienfait, Saskatchewan, for the funeral procession of Peter Markunas, Nick Nargan, and Julian Gryshko, three miners gunned down by the RCMP during a strikers' demonstration in Estevan in 1931.
Saskatchewan Archives Board/R-A19508

While the Communist Party found eager recruits in many camps, protest was not always politically inspired. Camp conditions were sometimes intolerable, and, with no other recourse, the men resorted to direct action. In Ontario's largest camp, Lac Seul, for example, men clearing timber along the shoreline suffered from blackflies in the summer, extreme cold in the winter, and isolation and poor food much of the time. The men knew their rights and refused to work during a snowstorm and struck when camp administrators gave them less tobacco than the rules allowed. Chinese workers, who were segregated from others in the camp, struck in 1934 when they had their food rations cut.

Communism had attracted little support during the 1920s in Canada, but it thrived in the appalling conditions of the Great Depression. In the cities, communist organizers were active in efforts to protest injustice in welfare and housing. Bennett moved quickly to suppress dissent. In 1931, he declared the Communist Party illegal and imprisoned seven of its members, including its leader, Tim Buck. The party was legalized in 1936, only to be banned in Quebec in 1937. Banned yet again by Ottawa in 1940, the Communist Party reorganized as the Labour Progressive Party. The use of state violence to protect the established order was not new in Canada, but the intensity of the repression, which included jail sentences, beatings, and, for those who were not Canadian citizens, deportation, reached a new level in the hysteria fostered by the Great Depression.

While there were several instances in the 1930s of strikers being killed by police, the clash between the authorities and the victims of the Great Depression that gained the most national attention occurred in Regina in 1935. Relief camp workers, fed up with their lot, were enthusiastic recruits to the Relief Camp Workers Union (RCWU) organized by the Workers Unity League. In April 1935, the RCWU led nearly half of the 7000 relief camp residents in British Columbia on a strike for work and wages. The strikers converged on Vancouver, where they conducted orderly demonstrations that brought much sympathy from the public but little concrete action from authorities. Early in June, 1200 strikers boarded freight trains heading east.

Picking up support along the way, they planned to travel to Ottawa to put their demands directly to the prime minister.

The "On-to-Ottawa Trek" quickly attracted the nation's attention. Bennett responded by calling on the RCMP to stop the demonstrators in Regina. One constable was killed and hundreds of strikers and constables were injured in the mêlée that ensued as the strikers resisted RCMP orders to disperse. The next year, Mackenzie King abolished the relief camps, which by that time had provided temporary homes and education in radical politics to about 170 000 Canadians.

Communist effectiveness in organizing the unemployed and industrial workers during the Great Depression failed to translate into electoral success. Most Canadians remained cool to socialist alternatives, and even many workers who were impressed by the dedication of Canadian communists saw the repressive Soviet Union, the model state espoused by the Communist Party, as a society that Canada should not emulate. Fewer still wished to emulate fascist Italy or Nazi Germany, where dictators Benito Mussolini and Adolf Hitler were producing another kind of revolution.

THE EXTREME RIGHT

National pride led many German and Italian Canadians to support the dictators who had seized power in their native countries. While few people supported the use of violence to bring fascism to Canada, coteries of fascists came together in most major Canadian cities and some small towns. Their leaders were primarily of British or French descent, and their followers were drawn from all classes and cultures.

Hitler's glorification of violence, white supremacy, and hatred of Jews, communists, and homosexuals inspired Canadian Nazis to fight pitched battles with communists and union groups and make efforts to keep Jews off beaches and away from other public places. Their intended victims sometimes fought back. On 16 August 1933, as a mainly Jewish softball team played a wholly gentile team in Toronto's Christie Pits, Nazis from the Balmy Beach Swastika Club unfurled a swastika. The result was a race riot, with Jewish players and spectators and their supporters battling the racists through the night. Toronto police proved helpless in

efforts to restore order as thousands of teenagers joined one side or the other in the conflict.

In western Canada, anti-communist Ukrainian nationalist organizations sympathized with the racial exclusiveness and militarism of the Nazis, conveniently ignoring Hitler's estimation of the Slavs as an inferior people fit only to be slaves to the "Aryan" race. In Quebec, the Nazis claimed to represent the last stand of Roman Catholicism against the forces of decadence, and conservative religious leaders in the province turned a blind eye to fascist attempts to use the church to promote racism and anti-Semitism.

The ambivalence of Quebec's Roman Catholic leaders toward fascism reflected international trends. Alarmed by rising secularism, the militancy of labour movements, and the strength of parties on the left, many Roman Catholics found comfort in the state repression and heightened sense of nationalism advocated by the fascists. Abbé Lionel Groulx tapped into this trend, calling for Quebec to become an independent state where the Roman Catholic clergy would rule over a purified race of French Canadians. He and his followers urged people to reject secular pursuits such as gambling, drinking, and watching Hollywood

This bilingual anti-Semitic sign on telephone poles in the village of Ste-Agathe, Quebec, in 1939 was an indication of the virulent anti-Semitism in many parts of Canada in the 1930s. The English words on the poster are not a direct translation of the French. A closer translation is "Jews are not wanted here. Ste-Agathe is a French-Canadian village and we will keep it that way."
Library and Archives Canada/PA-107943

movies, to boycott Jewish stores, and to refuse to read liberal-leaning newspapers such as Montreal's *La Presse*. While Groulx's ideas attracted some support from the Francophone middle class, the majority ignored the nationalist and fascist campaigns, blending their Roman Catholic beliefs with secular practices and support for reformist currents within Roman Catholicism.

The racism of the extreme right was the ultimate expression of a heritage of several centuries of European imperialism in which claims of racial superiority played an important role in justifying the conquest of non-Europeans. In North America, no organization has been more identified with racism than the Ku Klux Klan (KKK), the secretive, violent brotherhood of hooded white men who took up the cause of white supremacy in the American South after the Civil War. The KKK was active in Canada in the 1920s and early 1930s, though details of its operations remain sketchy. With few blacks to terrorize, the Canadian KKK became a Protestant extremist organization with Roman Catholics as its target. The group called for an end to non-Protestant immigration and deportation of Roman Catholics born outside Canada. In targeting Roman Catholics, the KKK echoed the traditional concern of the Orange Order, which continued to be the major organization of Protestant pride in Canada.

With a membership of between 10 000 and 15 000 in Saskatchewan in the late 1920s, the KKK exercised influence within the provincial Conservative Party, which led a coalition government from 1929 to 1934. KKK pressures contributed to the government's decision to end French-language instruction in the early grades of school and dismiss nuns teaching in public schools. In 1931, E.E. Perley, a Conservative MP from Saskatchewan, informed Bennett that only Protestants from Saskatchewan should be appointed to the Senate. He wrote to Bennett in 1931: "Possibly you are aware that the Ku Klux Klan is very strong in this province and no doubt was a great silent factor both in the provincial and in the last federal election, in favour of the Conservatives. They are very much worked up over the fact that one of the first major appointments is to go to the Roman Catholic Church, and it certainly will do us a great deal of harm."[7] Fortunately, only a minority of Canadians believed that the Great Depression could be ended, and further economic crises averted, by deporting or persecuting Roman Catholics, Jews, and communists.

THIRD PARTIES

With as much as a third of the nation facing destitution by 1932, many Canadians looked to new political parties to find a solution to their problems. The Co-operative Commonwealth Federation (CCF), Social Credit, and the Union Nationale were born in the Dirty Thirties, each with its own formula for preventing capitalist boom-bust economic cycles.

The CCF

The CCF, formed in 1932 in Calgary, enjoyed only modest success in the 1930s. It formed no governments during the decade of the Great Depression, and

J.S. Woodsworth in 1935. While the CCF leader won a great deal of respect from Canadians, his party was vilified by the mainstream media and made only minor electoral inroads before the Second World War.
Library and Archives Canada/C3940

fewer than one voter in 10 cast a ballot for the CCF in the 1935 federal election. Yet the CCF ultimately proved influential. Forerunner of the New Democratic Party, the federation provided the first democratic socialist government in North America when Tommy Douglas was elected premier of Saskatchewan in 1944.

The CCF was formed as the result of a decision by a small contingent of Labour and Progressive MPs to capitalize on grassroots pressure to unite the disparate left-wing labour and farm organizations in the country. It inherited the often contradictory traditions of labourism, socialism, social gospelism, and farm radicalism. Early election results demonstrated that, outside industrial Cape Breton, the CCF had taken root mainly in the West. By 1939, it formed the opposition in British Columbia, Saskatchewan, and Manitoba, and was poised for greater successes in the future.

Led by J.S. Woodsworth, a Winnipeg Labour MP, the federation rejected both capitalism and the revolutionary rhetoric of the communists. The CCF's manifesto, adopted at the party's Regina convention in 1933, proclaimed the possibility of a parliamentary road to socialism and recommended state planning as the best route to social justice. Like other political platforms, the Regina Manifesto reflected a compromise among the party's constituents. It called for government or cooperative control of major industries and state intervention in the marketplace, but also promised not to nationalize land, and, indeed, would have as a goal the preservation of family farms. At the same time, socialists were assured that the CCF's ultimate goal was an egalitarian nation. After outlining a set of public-spending measures to get the unemployed back to work, the manifesto ended on a radical note: "No C.C.F. Government will rest content until it has eradicated capitalism and put into operation the full programme of socialized planning which will lead to the establishment in Canada of the Co-operative Commonwealth."[8]

Social Credit

Not all western Canadians who rejected the mainstream political parties turned to socialism for a solution to economic ills. When popular Alberta radio evangelist William "Bible Bill" Aberhart began in 1932 to inject "social credit" into his weekly radio

broadcasts, he found a receptive audience. Aberhart adapted doctrines espoused by a British engineer and fanatic anti-Semite, Major C.H. Douglas, to Alberta conditions and built on the traditional provincial suspicion of central Canadian financial institutions. Claiming that the Great Depression had been caused by the failure of the banks to print enough money so that consumer spending could match industrial production, Aberhart offered a blueprint for getting monetary policy back on track. To many free enterprisers, disillusioned by the severity of the Great Depression, Aberhart's nostrums proved appealing. If only the banks could be forced to supply consumers with money, they believed, prosperity could be restored.

Social credit meant that governments would replace financial institutions as the vehicle for deciding how much money should be in circulation and in whose hands. It claimed to offer a scientific formula to determine the shortfall in purchasing power, advocating that the government simply credit all citizens equally with a share of the shortfall to keep the economy healthy. Aberhart attempted unsuccessfully to convince the United Farmers of Alberta government to embrace social credit ideas such as the social dividend and the just price. Under the former, the state would boost purchasing power by issuing money to all adults, while the state's regulation of prices would ensure that social dividends were not eaten away by price-gouging business people.

Aberhart turned the social credit study clubs spawned by his radio appeals into a political movement that won 56 of 63 seats in the provincial election of 1935. Once in power, he failed to deliver on his promises to issue social dividends or control prices, and only attempted to regulate banks and currency when a revolt by backbenchers in the party forced him to stop procrastinating. Legislation to this end in 1937 and 1938 was disallowed by the federal government and ultimately by the courts, which upheld federal jurisdiction over banking and currency. Aberhart was thus able to blame the federal government for his failure to implement his election promises and could maintain provincial support for his party with his strong stand against Ottawa.

The political leanings of Social Credit shifted over time. In 1935, many Social Credit supporters in Alberta regarded the party as quasi-socialist, promising not only money for nothing but also a new deal for the unemployed and protection of citizens against money lenders. The government legislated moratoria on debts, earning it the eternal gratitude of many farmers. Beyond this achievement, its record was spotty. Aberhart was a prickly authoritarian who ignored popular pressure for better treatment of welfare recipients and improved workers' compensation. Although his attempt to legislate the press to print government propaganda was struck down by the courts, it revealed the anti-civil-libertarian tendencies of the Social Credit movement.

By the time of Aberhart's death in 1943, the Social Credit Party had become a right-wing organization with a relatively restricted membership in which religious fundamentalists and monetary cranks loomed large. The party leaders, always receptive to conspiracy theories, began to believe that bankers, communists, socialists, and unionists were all part of an international conspiracy to suppress the human freedom that only Social Credit philosophy could create and protect. A section of the party was convinced that, as Major Douglas had always argued, the Jews were the glue that stuck this strange alliance together. Under Ernest Manning, the premier of Alberta from 1943 to 1968, the party rejected such bigotry and purged itself of influential anti-Semites. The Manning government, flush with oil royalties, built schools and roads while practising fiscal conservatism with little hint of the party's early radicalism.

Union Nationale

In Quebec, the reform movement resulted less from popular pressure than from clerical responses to the 1931 papal encyclical *Quadragesimo Anno*, which supported state intervention to achieve social justice. The Jesuit-sponsored École sociale populaire, an organization that propagated church teachings, assembled representatives of lay Roman Catholic organizations, including unions, caisses populaires (credit unions), and professional groups, to produce a document on desirable social reforms in line with the pope's thinking. In 1933, they published *Le Programme de restauration sociale*, a program of reforms including government regulation of monopolies, improved working conditions in industry, a system of farm credits, and a variety of social insurance measures. The program suggested that, if regulation proved insufficient to lower prices, the state might have to set up companies in certain sectors in competition with private industry.

The business-oriented Liberal regime of Louis-Alexandre Taschereau proved resistant to reform. In frustration, more progressive Liberals, led by Paul Gouin, formed a breakaway party, the Action libérale nationale. Gouin, like many liberal Roman Catholics, believed that *Quadragesimo Anno* pointed the way to a progressive society in which the church regarded the state as an ally in improving the lives of ordinary people rather than as a competitor in the provision of services. Maurice Duplessis, a Trois-Rivières lawyer who led the province's moribund Conservative Party, sensed a political opportunity and formed an electoral alliance with the renegade Liberals. The alliance was termed the Union Nationale and in 1935 contested the provincial election with *Le Programme de restauration sociale* as its platform and with its two component parties maintaining organizational autonomy.

Disillusionment with the long-governing Liberals produced a close result: 48 Liberal and 42 Union Nationale seats. Shortly after the election, the Union Nationale was able to capitalize on evidence of government corruption and nepotism to force Taschereau's resignation. The hastily formed new government, forced to call an election in 1936, was badly mauled by the Union Nationale, which made corruption rather than reform the theme of its campaign. Duplessis outmanoeuvred Gouin to take full control of the Union Nationale, submerging its two founding parties into a new organization under his personal control and becoming the new political chief of the province.

In power, the Union Nationale delivered only on its promises to help farmers with cheap loans and programs to settle the unemployed in remote (and generally infertile) areas of the province. The coal, gasoline, and bread companies, whose prices the 1935 Union Nationale program promised to control, faced no regulation, while the power companies, which the Union Nationale suggested might be socialized, remained in private hands and without additional regulation. Employers, not labour, received a sympathetic ear from the government. In 1937, Duplessis demonstrated how far he would go in repressing dissent when he passed the Padlock Act. Designed to suppress communism, the act

Maurice Duplessis and Mitchell Hepburn, the two central Canadian premiers, worked together for several years, resisting federal social programs and economic regulation. While both men were economic conservatives, their motives for opposing the federal government differed in important respects. Hepburn wanted to avoid a redistribution of wealth away from the country's richest province, while Duplessis was leery of any proposals that might threaten the French-speaking, Roman Catholic character of Quebec.
Library and Archives Canada/C19518

was frequently invoked to intimidate any labour organization considered undesirable by the government.

Duplessis attempted to win popular support with a strong rhetorical assertion of Quebec nationalism and opposition to federal interference in the province. Rejecting the view that the federal government must expand its programs to cope with an increasingly industrial society, he clung tightly to the provincial compact view of confederation. Duplessis told the Royal Commission on Dominion-Provincial Relations established in 1937, "Under our federal system, each province, within its own jurisdictions, constitutes an autonomous state, enjoying all the prerogatives of a sovereign state without any subjection to the federal power."[9]

Such views echoed the perspective of Ontario's Liberal premier, Mitchell Hepburn. Although he and Duplessis ultimately parted ways on the question of how Canada should react to the outbreak of war in

Europe, the two men collaborated closely on several issues. These included an unsuccessful attempt to convince Ottawa to allow hydro-electric exports and a successful bid to prevent Mackenzie King from introducing a national unemployment insurance bill after Bennett's legislation for such a program had been overturned by the courts.

The emergence of third parties demanding reform and the explosion of militancy on the part of the unemployed in Canada in the 1930s made reform necessary if the capitalist system were to be preserved. Prime Minister R.B. Bennett gave backhanded credit to the Canadian Communist Party's general secretary for influencing the Conservative government to initiate its ill-fated New Deal reforms of 1935: "Tim Buck has today a very strong position in the province of Ontario and he openly demands the abolition of the capitalist system. A good deal of pruning is sometimes necessary to save a tree and it would be well for us in

Canada to remember that there is considerable pruning to be done if we are to save the fabric of the capitalist system."[10]

BENNETT'S NEW DEAL

Bennett only reluctantly embraced policies that defied the private enterprise values that he and his party's backers shared. His first instinct was to turn to the traditional Tory nostrum: the tariff. Bennett promised to create jobs by raising tariffs as a means of forcing Canada's trading partners to sue for mercy. While "blasting" his way into foreign markets proved an inadequate response to the immediate crisis, the policy had some redeeming features.

Great Britain was the first country to respond to Bennett's initiative. Long a proponent of free trade, Great Britain began to restore protectionism in the 1920s, finally abandoning free trade ideas altogether when the Great Depression threatened its agricultural population with destitution. It was, therefore, a policy coup for Bennett when Great Britain agreed to preferential treatment for Canadian apples, lumber, wheat, and a variety of meat and dairy products at the Imperial Economic Conference held in Ottawa in 1932. The agreement did little to help Canada's floundering manufacturing sector or the devastated wheat economy, but it was welcome news to apple growers in Nova Scotia, lumbermen in British Columbia, and Ontario's beef and dairy farmers. In 1935, the United States began its retreat from high tariffs when it signed a comprehensive trade treaty with Canada, the first since 1854.

There was also pressure on the government to manipulate the money supply as a means of stimulating the economy. Bennett resisted most of the "soft money" proposals that circulated during the decade but did provide relief to hard-pressed farmers through the Farmers' Creditors Arrangement Act. As banking practices became increasingly restrictive, there was widespread agreement that Canada needed a central bank, like the Bank of England or the Federal Reserve Bank in the United States, to convince the public that someone was in control. In 1934, the Bank of Canada Act established a central bank "to regulate credit and currency in the best interests of the economic life of the nation."

The bank's first governor, Graham Towers, was recruited from the Royal Bank at an astounding salary of $30 000 a year (about 20 times the average industrial wage). Towers pursued a policy of modest growth in the money supply in order to cut interest rates and stimulate the economy. Bankers' commitment to "sound money" was too strong for him to undertake bolder efforts to make credit available to most Canadians. Although the economy was experiencing deflation—that is, falling prices—conservative economists and bankers worried that an increase in the money supply would result in an unacceptable level of inflation.

Responding to pressing problems relating to wheat exports, municipal funding, and housing, Ottawa pumped money into the economy through programs established under the Prairie Farm Rehabilitation Act, the Municipal Improvement Assistance Act, and the Dominion Housing Act. The federal government also passed the Natural Products Marketing Act, providing a legal framework for marketing boards, and created the Canadian Wheat Board to manage the sale of Canada's most troubled staple. Given the magnitude of the crisis, it no longer seemed wrong to fix prices and regulate output in the farming sector.

The notion of a government-sponsored social security system was also becoming more acceptable. In 1935, Bennett, facing widespread criticism and an imminent election, introduced legislation for maximum hours of work and minimum wages and to provide unemployment insurance. Many voters were less than impressed with Bennett's proposals. What good was unemployment insurance to the already jobless, who were therefore ineligible to make claims? And would the courts uphold the legislation? Since provinces had constitutional control over matters of civil rights and property, the courts would surely declare unconstitutional unilateral federal legislation that violated provincial rights.

THE 1935 ELECTION

Whatever his motives, Bennett received few benefits from his conversion to social security. He not only lost the 1935 election, but also watched his party split into warring factions. One revolt was led by trade and commerce minister H.H. Stevens in response to public outrage against the apparent callousness of big corporations in the face of widespread human misery. In 1934, Stevens headed a parliamentary committee established by the government to investigate the gap between what producers were receiving and what consumers were required to pay for food, clothing, and other necessities of life. Testimony in the committee hearings revealed damning evidence that big meat-packing companies such as Canada Packers made huge profits while the farmers who raised the cattle and hogs had been paid "ruinous" prices. Similarly, seamstresses who did piecework for big department stores were paid a few pennies for dresses that sold for $1.59 at Eaton's or Simpsons. When Bennett resisted taking the captains of industry to task for their exploitative policies, Stevens resigned and established the Reconstruction Party. While the party of "the little man" won only one seat—its leader won his Vancouver riding—it split the Conservative vote in constituencies across the country. King, also resisting pressure to adopt new policies for new times, campaigned under the slogan "King or chaos" and won the largest majority of his political career.

As had been predicted, much of Bennett's New Deal was declared unconstitutional, and even marketing boards were deemed by the courts to be a matter for provincial rather than national legislation. King resisted appeals for dramatic action. In typical King fashion, he had the situation studied, appointing the National Employment Commission to investigate and recommend policy on unemployment and relief and in 1937 announced the establishment of the Royal Commission on Dominion-Provincial Relations as a means of resolving the constitutional impasse.

THE KEYNESIAN REVOLUTION

The general drift of economic thinking during the 1930s was toward economic planning and government intervention as a means of solving the problem of boom-and-bust cycles. Although a variety of experts came forward with solutions to the economic crisis, the most influential was British economist John Maynard Keynes. His book *The General Theory of Employment, Interest, and Money* (1936) became the bible of a new generation of academics, politicians, and bureaucrats attempting to understand the causes of, and solutions for, the Great Depression. Arguing that rigidities in the capitalist system prevented the laws of supply and demand from functioning in practice as they were

outlined in classical theory, he advised that the state should play a stabilizing role by increasing expenditures, lowering taxes, and inflating the money supply during the downside of the business cycle. In this way, he maintained, depressions would be less severe and recovery more immediate. If the policies were reversed once the economy was moving again, he argued, there was no need to fear that such actions would produce either runaway inflation or an intolerable level of public debt.

During the Great Depression, Keynes was read by only a few Canadians and understood by even fewer. One of his Canadian disciples was W.A. Mackintosh of the Department of Finance, who embraced a conservative version of Keynesian ideas that emphasized the timing of public works to coincide with economic downturns. For most Canadians, however, "pump-priming" activities had credibility not because of economic theories but because of the tangible successes of Franklin D. Roosevelt, the flamboyant president of the United States. His New Deal, introduced during his first administration (1933–1937), captured the imagination of people all over the world. Impressed by New Deal programs to encourage public works, cultural development, and a more humane workplace for Americans, Canadians demanded that their government spend its way out of the Great Depression too.

CANADA AND THE WORLD

Mackenzie King, along with leaders of other self-governing dominions, had urged the British government to recognize their sovereignty. By the Statute of Westminster, passed by the British Parliament in 1931, Canada and the other dominions were given full legal freedom to exercise their independence in domestic and foreign affairs. While Canada chose not to exercise its full autonomy immediately—amendments to the BNA Act still had to be approved by the British parliament, and the Judicial Committee of the Privy Council remained the final court of appeal—the Statute of Westminster paved the way to complete independence in foreign affairs for Canada.

Canada proved cautious in its approach to world events, unwilling to do much to defend either sovereignty or democracy for other nations. It was hardly alone. The ambivalence of League of Nations

Public Health before Medicare

In the two decades before the First World War, Canadian municipalities and charitable groups dramatically expanded the number of hospitals in Canada. Hospitals in the nineteenth century had largely become refuges for destitute ill people. Sick people with money preferred to be attended by physicians in their homes, aware that hospitals were dangerous places where diseases seemed to spread rapidly. As hospitals adopted strategies for destroying germs in their buildings and on operating tables by the turn of the twentieth century, they were able to persuade Canadians with means to make use of them when they required operations or a long period of medical attention. Municipalities could open new hospitals by using the income from paying patients to subsidize services for destitute patients. The result was a "two-tiered" system of medicine, with paying patients enjoying comfortable surroundings and charity patients in overcrowded, poorly ventilated public wards, which, in the case of the pre-war Hamilton Sanitorium, often meant tents and wooden shacks on hospital grounds. Provincial governments provided token support to hospitals, but fee-paying patients and charitable donations provided the bulk of the funds required for operation.

By the interwar period, governments began to see hospitals as only part of the answer in dealing with health issues. In the wake of the Spanish Flu epidemic of 1918–1919 and wartime concerns about the fitness of potential troops, the scope of public health activities was expanded. The federal Department of Health was established in 1919 to work with the provinces in such areas as tuberculosis, sexually transmitted diseases, "feeblemindedness," and child welfare. Its main achievements in the 1920s were a national network of venereal disease clinics and a national educational program on child care.

Provincial public health programs were expanded and public health nurses were appointed in many provinces to deal with the medical health concerns of outlying areas where there were few doctors. Such programs made a difference. In Quebec, in the first two months of 1937, rural counties with health units reported an infant mortality rate of 86.2 per thousand while counties without health units had a rate of 118.6 per thousand. The overall death rate was similarly higher in counties without public health units. Even in Ontario, the wealthiest province, only a third of the provincial population in the 1930s lived in areas with well-organized public health services. Reports from visiting public health nurses often portrayed a hopeless state of affairs. In 1921, the provincial nurse's report on the eastern Ontario town of Rockland, population 3000, noted:

> The town was in an unsanitary condition, there being no sewage system, no water filtration, no clean or adequate milk supply, no paved streets, no street lighting. Public health teachings were unknown and under these conditions there could be little else than sickness, distress and high death rates. Employment was provided for the majority of men in the town by the lumber mills but the families in all homes were so large that one wage earner had difficulty in providing proper food and clothes for the children.[11]

Not surprisingly, 75 of the 160 children born in Rockland in 1920 died before their first birthdays. As cities provided safe water supplies, better sanitation services, and medical facilities that rural and small-town governments could not afford, the gap between town and country widened. It was hardly surprising, then, that rural dwellers complained about the minimal government provision of medical services to citizens. Via the Farm Radio Forum, farm people discussed the question of a national health scheme, noting in 1943, "The government sponsors the TB testing of cattle, pays for loss and has blood testing every year free of charge. What about humans?"[12]

Saskatchewan, the province with the lowest infant mortality rate in rural areas in 1943, had had the country's highest rate before the First World War. The explanation for the change appears to be that, in the interwar period, much of rural Saskatchewan had implemented a "municipal doctor" scheme in which the municipality hired and paid physicians. With medical care prepaid through property taxes, people were less constrained from seeking medical attention by economic considerations. Doctors, who in other provinces often left rural areas when they realized how few of their patients could afford to pay medical bills, were attracted by the stability of income provided by the municipal-doctor plan.

A HISTORIOGRAPHICAL DEBATE

Populism, Right and Left

The Co-operative Commonwealth Federation (CCF) and Social Credit are sometimes seen as polar opposites, but not all scholars view them in this manner. Some point to the similarity in origin of these movements: both had urban roots but found a mass audience among Prairie farmers; both claimed a national platform but focused on regional and provincial strategies for political change; neither had an important base outside western Canada in the 1930s. Both parties were populist—that is, they claimed to be people's movements against the interests of the entrenched political and economic elites who dominated the country.

The CCF's populism was directed against all big capitalists, while Social Credit's populist attack targeted only financial institutions. The CCF may therefore be described as a "left-wing populist" movement because it *identified* farmers' interests with workers' interests against the interests of big business. Social Credit may be described as "right-wing populist" because it was suspicious of unions and suggested that workers and farmers had interests in common with capitalists other than bankers.

But were these two parties very different in practice? Some scholars say yes.[13] When the CCF assumed office in Saskatchewan in 1944, it nationalized auto insurance and the distribution of natural gas and established a provincial intercity bus company. By contrast, the Alberta government denounced all state ventures in the economy. The CCF pioneered universal free hospital and medical care insurance in Saskatchewan; the Social Credit regime in Alberta insisted that medical care schemes must be voluntary and must involve some direct payment for services by subscribers to prevent abuse of the program. The CCF passed labour legislation that favoured union organization in Saskatchewan, while Social Credit produced a labour code that made unionization difficult. Welfare recipients were subjected to mean-spirited treatment in Alberta, but received some sympathy in Saskatchewan.

Despite these contrasts, many scholars believe that the gap in performance between the CCF in Saskatchewan and Social Credit in Alberta has been exaggerated.[14] They claim that the farm programs of the two governments were similar and that whatever philosophical differences existed between them, both governments spent lavishly on health, education, and roads. The provincial takeovers in Saskatchewan are held to have had a negligible impact on overall private ownership and the direction of the provincial economy.

The claims of the two sides are difficult to adjudicate in part because the Alberta government, awash in oil revenues by the 1950s, had a vastly superior financial base compared with that of its Saskatchewan counterpart. It could afford to spend extravagantly, all the while deploring the tendencies of governments generally to spend more than they earned. Nonetheless, left-wing critics of Alberta Social Credit suggest that the poor in Alberta were largely passed over in the orgy of public spending. Their point of comparison is usually Saskatchewan, which they allege had more humanitarian social policies. Left-wing critics of the Saskatchewan CCF suggest that, in office, that party attempted to appease powerful elite interests at the ultimate expense of the poor.

members ensured an ineffectual response to the aggressive behaviour of Japan, Germany, and Italy in the 1930s. When Walter Riddell, Canada's representative at the League, called for stronger measures against Italy after its invasion of Ethiopia in 1935, he was told by Ottawa to change his position: Canada had no interest in the fate of Ethiopia.

Canada was equally unwilling to provide any formal aid to the Spanish republic when its armed forces, led by General Francisco Franco, who was supported by German and Italian arms, overthrew the country's elected government during a bloody civil war (1936–1939). More than 1200 Canadians fought as volunteers for the republic under the collective name of the Mackenzie-Papineau Battalion, but their government regarded them with suspicion and the Roman Catholic hierarchy in Quebec was openly sympathetic to Franco and the fascists. Canada made no official protest when Hitler annexed Austria or invaded and dismembered Czechoslovakia. Even after Germany invaded Poland and imposed a murderous regime, Mackenzie King suggested to the British government that he try to mediate between the Allies and Nazi Germany.

Though King's main goal in pursuing isolationist policies was to maintain Canadian unity, he was, like many British and French politicians, also motivated by anti-communism. Hitler's anti-communism appealed to capitalists and aristocrats throughout the world who were terrified by the level of frustration and anger expressed by workers and the unemployed during the Great Depression and thought that repression rather than reform was the solution to preserving ruling class privileges.

Isolationism also reflected Canada's military unpreparedness, itself exacerbated by Depression frugality. While the Royal Canadian Navy had ordered its first two destroyers in 1929, no more were purchased until 1937–1938, when four ships were added. The Royal Canadian Air Force (RCAF), mainly engaged in forest protection, aerial surveys, and other civilian work in the 1920s, suffered a 75 percent budget cut in 1931. The RCAF had more of a military emphasis by the late 1930s, but, with 400 personnel and 195 mostly decrepit aircraft, was largely a token force. Only 184

pilots graduated in advanced training by the Air Corps in 1937. Even the Canadian militia experienced deep cuts and resulting shrinkage in the Dirty Thirties.

CONCLUSION

Canadians emerged from the Great Depression with few political illusions. Although Canada had become a player in its own right on the international stage, the game of global politics was a dangerous one that threatened to engulf Canadians in another world war. Canada's new international status also did nothing to inspire a new national identity. Canadians were divided as never before along class, regional, and cultural lines, and many had abandoned the old two-party system to support new political parties that promised to address these interests. If there was cause for hope, it was that all parties professed to seek a solution to the problem of poverty in the midst of plenty and make Canada a better place for all Canadians. Time would tell whether such democratic idealism would survive the new values of the age of mass consumerism.

NOTES

1 James Struthers, *No Fault of Their Own: Unemployment and the Canadian Welfare State, 1914–1941* (Toronto: University of Toronto Press, 1983), 83–84.

2 Kenneth Michael Sylvester, *The Limits of Rural Capitalism: Family, Culture, and Markets in Montcalm, Manitoba, 1870–1940* (Toronto: University of Toronto Press, 2001), 128–29.

3 Tina Loo, *States of Nature: Conserving Canada's Wildlife in the Twentieth Century* (Vancouver: UBC Press, 2006), 103.

4 Barry Potyondi, "Loss and Substitution: The Ecology of Production in Southwestern Saskatchewan, 1860–1930," *Journal of the Canadian Historical Association*, n.s., no. 5 (1994), 235.

5 L.M. Grayson and Michael Bliss, eds., *The Wretched of Canada: Letters to R.B. Bennett, 1930–1935* (Toronto: University of Toronto Press, 1971), 53–56, 111.

6 Joan Sangster, *Earning Respect: The Lives of Working Women in Small-Town Ontario, 1920–1960* (Toronto: University of Toronto Press, 1995), 178.

7 E.E. Perley to R.B. Bennett, 6 January 1931. R.B. Bennett Papers, Library and Archives Canada.

8 Programme of the Co-operative Commonwealth Federation adopted at the First National Convention held at Regina, Sask., July 1933.

9 Canada, Royal Commission on Dominion-Provincial Relations, *Hearings* (1938), 8129.

10 Alvin Finkel, *Business and Social Reform in the Thirties* (Toronto: Lorimer, 1979), 92.

11 Cynthia R. Comacchio, *"Nations Are Built of Babies": Saving Ontario's Mothers and Children, 1900–1940* (Montreal: McGill-Queen's University Press, 1993), 166.

12 Health Study Bureau, Toronto, *Review of Canada's Health Needs and Health-Insurance Proposals* (Toronto, 1945), 41.

13 The view that there are sharp differences between Social Credit's performance in Alberta and the CCF performance in Saskatchewan is defended in Alvin Finkel,

The Social Credit Phenomenon in Alberta (Toronto: University of Toronto Press, 1989), 202–13, and Walter D. Young, *Democracy and Discontent: Progressivism, Socialism and Social Credit in the Canadian West* (Toronto: McGraw-Hill Ryerson, 1978). On the general distinction between left and right variants of populism, see John Richards, "Populism: A Qualified Defence," *Studies in Political Economy* 5 (Spring 1981), 5–27.

14 The best case for the convergence in the behaviour of the two parties in office is made in John F. Conway, "To Seek a Goodly Heritage: The Prairie Populist Responses to the National Policy" (PhD diss., Simon Fraser University, 1978). Peter R. Sinclair argues that the Saskatchewan CCF had lost its early radicalism before winning office in "The Saskatchewan CCF: Ascent to Power and the Decline of Socialism," *Canadian Historical Review* 54, no. 4 (December 1973), 419–33. An opposite view is found in Lewis H. Thomas, "The CCF Victory in Saskatchewan, 1944," *Saskatchewan History* 28, no. 2 (Spring 1975), 52–64.

RELATED READINGS IN THIS SERIES

From *Nation and Society: Readings in Post-Confederation Canadian History*

Denyse Baillargeon, "Indispensable But Not a Citizen: The Housewife in the Great Depression," 257–71.

From Primary Documents CD-ROM, Volume II

William Aberhart
The Regina Manifesto
The Original Platform of the Union Nationale
Statute of Westminster, 1931
After the Quebec Elections
Another Recruit

SELECTED READING

For an overview of the Great Depression in Canada, see John Thompson and Alan Seager, *Canada, 1922–1939: Decades of Discord* (Toronto: McClelland & Stewart, 1985). The Canadian economy during this dismal decade is discussed in Douglas Owram, "Economic Thought in the 1930s: The Prelude to Keynesianism," *Canadian Historical Review* 66, no. 3 (September 1985), 344–77; A.E. Safarian, *The Canadian Economy in the Great Depression* (Ottawa: Carleton University Press, 1970); Ian M. Drummond, *British Economic Policy and the Empire, 1919–1939* (London: Allen and Unwin, 1972); Ian M. Drummond and Norman Hillmer, *Negotiating Freer Trade* (Waterloo, ON: Wilfrid Laurier University Press, 1989); Gillian Creese, "The Politics of Dependence: Women, Work and Unemployment in the Vancouver Labour Movement before World War II," in *British Columbia Reconsidered: Essays on Women*, ed. Gillian Creese and Veronica Strong-Boag (Vancouver: Press Gang, 1992), 364–90; and E.R. Forbes, "Cutting the Pie into Smaller Pieces: Matching Grants and Relief in the Maritime Provinces during the 1930s," in his *Challenging the Regional Stereotype: Essays on the Twentieth-Century Maritimes* (Fredericton: Acadiensis Press, 1989). The background to the environmental debacle that produced "dust bowl" conditions on the southern Prairies is traced in Barry Potyondi, *In Palliser's Triangle: Living in the Grasslands, 1850–1930* (Saskatoon: Purich Publishing, 1995).

On mainstream politics during this period, see the works on W.L. Mackenzie King cited in Chapter 10 and Larry A. Glassford, *Reaction and Reform: The Politics of the Conservative Party Under R.B. Bennett, 1927–1938* (Toronto: University of Toronto Press, 1992).

On protest in western Canada, see Bob Hesketh, *Major Douglas and Alberta Social Credit* (Toronto: University of Toronto Press, 1997); Alvin Finkel, *The Social Credit Phenomenon in Alberta* (Toronto: University of Toronto Press, 1989); David R. Elliott and Iris Miller, *Bible Bill: A Biography of William Aberhart* (Edmonton: Reidmore, 1987); L.H. Thomas, ed., *The Making of a Socialist: The Recollections of T.C. Douglas* (Edmonton: University of Alberta Press, 1982); Seymour Martin Lipset, *Agrarian Socialism: The Co-operative Commonwealth Federation in Saskatchewan* (Berkeley: University of California Press, 1971); Kenneth McNaught, *A Prophet in Politics: A Biography of J.S. Woodsworth* (Toronto: University of Toronto Press, 1959); Allen Mills, *Fool for Christ: The Political Thought of J.S. Woodsworth* (Toronto: University of Toronto Press, 1991); and Ronald Liversedge, *Recollections of the On-to-Ottawa Trek* (Ottawa: Carleton University Press, 1973).

On the relief camps and relief workers' radicalism, see Bill Waiser, *All Hell Can't Stop Us: The On-to-Ottawa Trek and the Regina Riot* (Calgary: Fifth House, 2003); Laurel Sefton MacDowell, "Relief Camp Workers in Ontario During the Great Depression of the 1930s," *Canadian Historical Review* 76, no. 2 (June 1995), 205–28; and Lorne Brown, *When Freedom Was Lost: The Unemployed, the Agitator, and the State* (Montreal: Black Rose, 1987).

The struggle for human rights is discussed in Ross Lambertson, *Repression and Resistance: Canadian Human Rights Activists, 1930–1960* (Toronto: University of Toronto Press, 2004) and Christopher MacLennan, *Toward the Charter: Canadians and the Demand for a National Bill of Rights, 1929–1960* (Montreal: McGill-Queen's University Press, 2003).

On Canadian communists, see Ian Angus, *Canadian Bolsheviks* (Montreal: Vanguard, 1981); Ivan Avakumovic, *The Communist Party in Canada: A History* (Toronto: McClelland & Stewart, 1975); and William Beeching and Phyllis Clarke, eds., *Yours in the Struggle: The Reminiscences of Tim Buck* (Toronto: NC Press, 1977). Labour struggles and the role of communists within the labour movement are explored in Stephen L. Endicott, *Bienfait: The Saskatchewan Miners' Struggle of '31* (Toronto: University of Toronto Press, 2002).

There is a vast literature on the CCF. See Walter Young, *Anatomy of a Party: The National CCF, 1932–61* (Toronto: University of Toronto Press, 1969); Norman Penner, *From Protest to Power: Social Democracy in Canada, 1900–Present* (Toronto: Lorimer, 1992); and William Brennan, ed., *Building the Co-operative Commonwealth: Essays on the Social Democratic Tradition in Canada* (Regina: Canadian Plains Research Center, 1984). On women in the CCF and the Communist Party, see Joan Sangster, *Dreams of Equality: Women on the Canadian Left, 1920–1950* (Toronto: McClelland & Stewart, 1989). A biography of Canada's first female member of parliament and a founder of the CCF is Terry Crowley, *Agnes Macphail and the Politics of Equality* (Toronto: Lorimer, 1990). Provincial CCF histories include Nelson Wiseman, *Social Democracy in Manitoba: A History of the CCF-NDP* (Winnipeg: University of Manitoba Press, 1983) and Gerald L. Caplan, *The Dilemma of Canadian Socialism: The CCF in Ontario, 1932–1945* (Toronto: McClelland & Stewart, 1973). On intellectuals and the left, see Michiel Horn, *The League for Social Reconstruction* (Toronto: University of Toronto Press, 1980).

On the extreme right, see Janine Stingel, *Social Discredit: Anti-Semitism, Social Credit and the Jewish Response* (Montreal: McGill-Queen's University Press, 2000); Martin Robin, *Shades of Right: Nativist and Fascist Politics in Canada, 1920–1940* (Toronto: University of Toronto Press, 1991); and Esther Delisle, *The Traitor and the Jew: Anti-Semitism and Extreme Right-Wing Nationalism in Quebec from 1929 to 1939* (Montreal: R. Davies Publishing, 1993).

On Quebec political developments, see Paul-André Linteau, René Durocher, Jean-Claude Robert, and François Rocard, *Quebec Since 1930* (Toronto: Lorimer, 1991); Andrée Lévesque, *Virage à gauche interdit: les communistes, les socialistes, et leurs ennemis au Québec* (Montreal: Boréal, 1984); Conrad Black, *Duplessis* (Toronto: McClelland & Stewart, 1979); Bernard L. Vigod, *Quebec Before Duplessis: The Political Career of Louis-Alexandre Taschereau* (Montreal: McGill-Queen's University Press, 1986); and Herbert F. Quinn, *The Union Nationale* (Toronto: University of Toronto Press, 1979).

On the development of the welfare state, see Georges Campeau, *From UI to EI: Waging War on the Welfare State* (Vancouver: UBC Press, 2005); David Gagan and Rosemary Gagan, *For Patients of Moderate Means: A Social History of the Voluntary Public General Hospital in Canada, 1890–1950* (Montreal: McGill-Queen's University Press, 2002); James M. Wishart, "Class Difference and the Reformation of Ontario Public Hospitals, 1900–1935: 'Make Every Effort to Satisfy the Tastes of the Well-to-Do,'" *Labour/Le Travail* 48 (Fall 2001), 27–62; James Struthers, *The Limits of Affluence: Welfare in Ontario, 1920–1970* (Toronto: University of Toronto Press, 1994) and *No Fault of Their Own: Unemployment and the Canadian Welfare State, 1914–1941* (Toronto: University of Toronto Press, 1981); Raymond B. Blake and Jeff Keshen, eds., *Social Welfare Policy in Canada: Historical Readings* (Toronto: Copp Clark, 1995); James G. Snell, *The Citizen's Wage: The State and the Elderly in Canada, 1900–1951* (Toronto: University of Toronto Press, 1995); Cynthia R. Comacchio, *"Nations Are Built of Babies": Saving Ontario's Mothers and Children, 1900–1940* (Montreal: McGill-Queen's University Press, 1993); Alvin Finkel, *Business and Social Reform in the Thirties* (Toronto: Lorimer, 1979); and Alvin Finkel, *Social Policy and Practice in Canada: A History* (Waterloo, ON: Wilfrid Laurier University Press, 2006).

On foreign policy developments, see John Herd Thompson and Stephen J. Randall, *Canada and the United States: Ambivalent Allies*, 3rd ed. (Athens: University of Georgia Press, 2002); Norman Hillmer and J.L. Granatstein, *Empire to Umpire: Canada and the World to the 1990s* (Toronto: Copp Clark, 1994); and B.J.C. McKercher and Lawrence Aronson, eds., *The North Atlantic Triangle in a Changing World: Anglo-American-Canadian Relations, 1902–1956* (Toronto: University of Toronto Press, 1996).

CHAPTER 12

Mass Consumer Society and the Search for Identity, 1919–1939

TIMELINE

1921–41 — More than a million immigrants arrive in Canada

1923 — Federal legislation bans immigration from China

1928 — Rex v Syliboy court decision finds treaties with Mi'kmaq invalid in the Maritimes; opening of Pier 21 in Halifax

1930–35 — 28 000 immigrants deported from Canada

1937 — Court decision provides limited right to distribute birth-control information

1939 — Canada refuses permission for the *St. Louis*, a ship carrying German Jews fleeing from the Nazis, to land in Canada

During the Depression, an Eaton's saleswoman witnessed throngs of little girls admiring Shirley Temple dolls on display during the Christmas season. Priced at between nine and 16 dollars, the dolls, which were designed to take commercial advantage of the popularity of a child movie star, cost a month's income for a family on welfare.

> Some used to come at opening time and just stand there looking at those pink-cheeked, golden-haired lovely Shirley Temples. Little faces, they needed food. You could see a lot who needed a pint of milk a day a thousand times more than they needed a Shirley doll. They'd stare for hours. We tried to shush them away, but it didn't do any good. . . . This, mind you, went on day after day, day after day, and some of the [sales] girls thought they would go crazy. One [clerk] had a crying fit over just that, those hundreds of poor kids who would never own a Shirley Temple in a hundred years. They were lucky if they had breakfast that morning, or soup and bread that night.[1]

This moving account of would-be juvenile consumers speaks volumes about Canada in the interwar years. By creating desire through advertising, corporate capitalism touched most people, including children. The commercial media focused on the good life and encouraged people to indulge in the whims of the moment. Defying the sexual and social taboos of the pre-war period, many women wore shorter skirts, bobbed their hair, and displayed a devil-may-care attitude. Men returning from the war set the tone for a more cynical and worldly view of life than had prevailed in pre-war Canada. Having faced death in the trenches of Europe, they were unwilling to put up with the petty conventions that had characterized polite society in the pre-war years.

Notwithstanding the new trends, social values for many people remained as conservative as in an earlier age, when most Canadians lived in rural areas and tried to follow the injunctions laid down by priests and parsons. It is important to remember that prohibition, poverty, and a domestic ideal in which gender roles were rigidly prescribed also characterized the interwar years. If nothing else, the period from 1919 to 1939 was fraught with contradictions. The clash of old and new values created tensions and sparked debates about many issues, including how families should raise their children and what it meant to be a man or woman in the modern age.

POPULATION

By 1941, Canada's population was more than 11 500 000. Immigration had reached a high point during the late 1920s, but was reduced to a trickle during the Great Depression (see Table 12.1). Government efforts to sift and accommodate new entrants were signified by the opening of immigrant facilities at Pier 21 in Halifax in 1928. Before it closed in 1971, Pier 21 had welcomed more than a million new Canadians. The immigration facilities at Grosse Isle closed in 1937, but Quebec City and Montreal remained major entry points for immigrants from Great Britain and continental Europe.

In the interwar years, Canada still gave preferential treatment to immigrants from Great Britain and the United States. The federal government bowed to pressure from railway companies, manufacturers, and farmers—all facing labour shortages—and opened the doors to wider European immigration when the postwar recession began to ease. During the 1930s, the doors were firmly closed again. Even those trying to help Jewish refugees flee Hitler's genocide could not convince the administrators of immigration policy to pry them open. Only 4000 Jews were admitted to Canada between 1933 and 1939. Canada was not alone in its exclusionary policies. In 1939, the *St. Louis*, a ship bearing 907 German Jews, was refused permission to land anywhere in North or South America. "The line must be drawn somewhere,"[2] a senior official in the Canadian Immigration Department declared as the *St. Louis* returned its desperate cargo to the death camps of the Third Reich.

Most of the population growth in the 1930s came from natural increase and from Canadians returning home from the United States. As the Great Depression settled over the North American economy, many Canadians working south of the border lost their jobs. Those who had not taken out American citizenship were subject to deportation. Canada adopted a similar policy, with the result that 28 000 immigrants were officially deported between 1930 and 1935. Immigrants could be expelled for a number of stated reasons: criminality, medical causes, being a public charge, or "other civil causes," a euphemism for radicals and union organizers.

In the interwar years, Canadians were generally healthier than they had been in earlier generations and life expectancy was on the rise. The average Canadian boy born in 1931 could expect to live 60 years; the average girl 62.1 years. Better nutrition, preventive medicine, and reduced infant mortality helped increase life expectancy over the course of the twentieth century. Native peoples, however, had a much lower average life expectancy than other Canadians, testimony to the dire poverty in which they continued to live.

Most provinces saw little change in their ethnic distribution during this period. Despite its significant Acadian minority, the Maritimes continued to be dominated by people of British origin. Saskatchewan and Manitoba saw significant immigration from southern and eastern Europe, as they had before the First World War. Southern Ontario, by contrast, largely an Anglo-Celtic preserve before 1920, became home to tens of thousands of southern and eastern

TABLE 12.1 Canada's Population (in thousands), 1911–1941

Year	Natural increase	Immigration	Emigration	Net migration	Population
1911–21	1 349	1 592	1 360	233	8 788
1921–31	1 486	1 198	1 095	103	10 377
1931–41	1 242	149	262	−112	11 507

Source: David D. Corbett, *Canada's Immigration Policy: A Critique* (Toronto: University of Toronto Press, 1957), 121.

 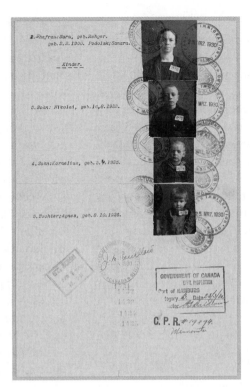

CPR card for Mennonite immigrants.
Courtesy of Barbara Tessman

European immigrants, whose numbers would grow even more dramatically in the decades following the Second World War.

Some of those entering Canada in the 1920s were fleeing religious persecution at home. Between 1922 and 1930, more than 20 000 Mennonites arrived from the Soviet Union, sponsored by the Canadian Mennonite Board of Colonization in cooperation with the Canadian Pacific Railway (CPR). Most of them settled on farms in Saskatchewan and Manitoba. By 1941, there were more than 100 000 Mennonites in Canada. Not all were pleased with their new homeland. In the 1920s, almost 8000 Mennonites moved to Latin America to protest the imposition of unilingual education in the Prairie provinces. Mennonites, who resisted the secular influences of the industrial age, feared that failure to educate their children in German would expose them to unwanted influences from the larger Canadian society.

For some new Canadians, the ties to their former homelands remained strong. Ukrainian-Canadian politics of the interwar period were strongly influenced by debate about the future of the Ukraine. While radicals supported the Soviet Union, conservative Ukrainians demanded the release of their homeland from the clutches of the communists. Rival nationalist groups battled the communists and one another as they fought over which dictator would make the best leader for an independent Ukraine.

Racism continued to dog many new Canadians. In 1923, federal legislation was passed to exclude Chinese nationals from immigrating to Canada. This policy made it impossible for men working in Canada to bring their families from China, and unemployment, especially during the Great Depression, often meant that they could not afford to send money to their families in their homeland. Many decided to return home, some accepting Vancouver City Council's offer of a free one-way ticket to China on condition that they agreed never to return to Canada. The Japanese invasion of China in 1937 resulted in a cessation of shipments of foodstuffs from China to Canada, making preparation of traditional meals in Chinatowns extremely difficult. Worse, communications between

China and Canada were cut off, leaving Chinese Canadians without knowledge of the fate of their loved ones back home.

The Japanese in Canada were also caught up in the web of international developments. Since most were second-generation Canadians, known as *Nisei*, they spoke English and shared the liberal democratic outlook of their white contemporaries. Nevertheless, they continued to face discrimination in educational and job opportunities and were subject to growing hostility as Japan began its military assault in Asia. An articulate minority among the *Nisei* formed voluntary associations to discuss their mutual problems and founded English-language newspapers such as *The New Canadian*, which was established in 1938. In doing so, they drove a wedge between themselves and their elders, who clung to the language and traditions of their Japanese homeland.

CANADA'S NATIVE PEOPLES

In the interwar years, the living conditions in most Native communities continued to deteriorate, and the provisions of the Indian Act remained harsh and unyielding. Courts, dominated by whites, rejected Native efforts to establish land claims. A 1928 decision in the case of *Rex* v *Syliboy* found that eighteenth-century treaties in the Maritimes had no validity because the Mi'kmaq were not competent to sign them. After the federal government transferred jurisdiction over their natural resources to the Prairie provinces in 1930, thousands of Native peoples were arrested for

These Métis trappers at their winter camp in the foothills of the Rockies eked out a bare living for their efforts.
Glenbow Archives, Brady Collection/PA2218-985

violating provincial fish and game laws. In their efforts to consolidate control over the land, the provinces ignored treaties with the federal government that had granted hunting and fishing rights in traditional Native territories.

In British Columbia, the infant mortality rate for Native peoples was 10 times the rate for the rest of the population. Artist Emily Carr's Squamish friend Sophie was the mother of 21 children who had died before reaching adulthood. In the late 1930s, while 10 percent of non-Native British Columbians died of tuberculosis, the comparable figure for Natives was 40 percent. Measles, whooping cough, and pneumonia also ended a disproportionate number of Native lives. Malnutrition, poor sanitation, and a lack of safe drinking water were endemic on reserves, the latter often the result of governments allowing companies to discharge industrial wastes into the streams that supplied the First Nations with water.

Improved communication meant that no region of Canada was immune from the influence of the dominant culture. Native peoples in the North, once protected by their remote location, now found themselves increasingly integrated into the new industrial order. As elsewhere, integration was fraught with difficulties. Trappers from the south ignored Native rights to hunt in certain territories, and overtrapping led to resource depletion. The Inuit who were drawn into the whaling industry off Herschel Island in the western Arctic suffered massive epidemics. The population began to rise only in the 1930s, as Inuit began to develop immunities to European diseases. Ultimately a new northern society emerged, which, according to historian Kenneth Coates, was characterized by "limited growth, federal government neglect, dependence on a small number of mines, a vibrant fur trade and a bicultural society."[3]

While Natives might find their treaty rights ignored by federal and provincial jurisdictions, the Métis had no treaty rights and lived in appalling conditions. In Alberta, a provincial commission established in 1934 to investigate conditions among the Métis heard shocking medical evidence suggesting that the Métis, still victims of intense discrimination, were facing extinction. As much as 90 percent of the Métis population was infected with tuberculosis; paralysis, blindness, and syphilis were also rampant. The province responded in 1939 by establishing six Métis colonies where schools and health care were provided, but no attempt was made to give these colonies a real economic base. In Saskatchewan and Manitoba, the Métis were almost completely ignored by their provincial governments.

ENVIRONMENTAL ATTITUDES

Government interference with Aboriginal trapping and hunting practices was often justified on the grounds of conservation of game. Wood Buffalo National Park, for example, was established after the First World War on the traditional hunting territory of the Chipewyan with a mandate to increase buffalo numbers. Park managers ordered the Chipewyan, who used the bison to supply most of their food, clothing, and trade needs, to drastically reduce their kill of buffalo. The Chipewyan balked at the notion that the government that had allowed the virtual extinction of the buffalo in the South now expected First Nations of the North to suffer so that buffalo numbers could be gradually increased. First Nations were hardly alone in resisting the interference of game wardens. Rural residents generally regarded the wardens as pesky and often threatened them with violence, occasionally murdering wardens who persisted in enforcing conservation measures.

Natives were not above taking advantage of the desire of wealthy Canadian and American sportsmen to have wilderness experiences. Seeing an opportunity to earn some much-needed income, they offered their services as hunting and fishing guides. For example, Johnnie Johns, a successful Yukon entrepreneur of Tagish and Tlingit heritage, began a long guiding career in the 1920s. Along the way he accepted "enfranchisement"—that is, he relinquished his Indian status, likely to improve his chances of being licensed as a chief guide.

It took the threat of extinction of a species or resource before governments thought to intervene to enforce conservation measures. For example, there had been little government response to the soil-destroying practices of Prairie farmers before the 1930s. Only when drought aggravated the problem to the point that wheat cultivation on the southern Prairies seemed

Mrs. Luke and caribou (1900).
Jewish Historical Society of British Columbia, LF.1A.262.P9

to be in jeopardy was action taken. Beginning in 1935, the federal government's new Prairie Farm Rehabilitation Administration (PFRA) organized Agricultural Improvement Associations to encourage better farming practices. Community pasture programs and water development projects soon followed. The PFRA also worked with Ducks Unlimited to establish wildlife conservation areas. Established in 1938, Ducks Unlimited Canada consisted mainly of wealthy business people who were also sportsmen, whose efforts were focused on preserving wetlands without challenging private property rights.

SEXUALITY AND RESPECTABILITY

As Canadians increasingly moved to cities, and movies and radio vied with churches and schools for the minds of the masses, fears were widely expressed of the risk of a moral breakdown in society. Church leaders in particular found modern culture, with its hedonism, violence, and secular values, profoundly disturbing. In an effort to counter these trends, traditionalists began to reaffirm the long-standing moral conventions that sex was only acceptable if it was heterosexual, confined to married couples, and infrequent. They also railed against drinking, smoking, swearing, and gambling, all

BIOGRAPHY

Grey Owl

In 1935, *Pilgrims of the Wild* by Grey Owl proved a runaway best-seller in Canada, retailing 5000 copies a month despite the depressed economy. The book was a ringing plea for protection of the beaver, their numbers depleted by centuries of fashion-conscious consumerism. A children's book by Grey Owl proved equally popular and more than 500 000 Canadians attended his public appearances over the next three years. When he died in 1938, a tribute book sold 100 000 copies in three days.

While Grey Owl claimed to have Aboriginal heritage, he was in fact English-born Archie Belaney. He assumed a Native identity in an effort to reinforce the respect that he believed First Nations demonstrated toward the natural world, a respect at odds with prevailing European values of humans' God-given right to dominion over nature. In his efforts to promote protection of fur-bearing animals, Belaney not only gave himself a new identity but "anthropomorphized" the beaver; that is, he gave them a human persona. Grey Owl attracted huge audiences with his pleas not to turn animals into commodities and to revive the links between humans and other species that he believed had characterized pre-modern times, but there is more than a little irony in the commercialization of his beliefs.

Grey Owl
Library and Archives Canada, C-036186

popular activities on the screen and in the trendy nightspots of interwar Canada.

While there were few penalties for heterosexual men who violated this moral code, women risked their reputations if they became sexually available "flappers." The "working girl" was increasingly accepted as a permanent feature of the economic system, but women in the public sphere were expected to maintain their "respectability" at all costs. In the interwar years, the courts in some jurisdictions still acceded to the requests of families to place "promiscuous" daughters in mental institutions or reformatories. A single woman who became pregnant continued to face dismal prospects. If they could afford to do so, pregnant unwed women tried to conceal their condition, and public and private institutions were prepared to exploit them for their own ends.

In Chester, Nova Scotia, the Ideal Maternity Home took in unwed pregnant women—for a hefty fee. Once registered in the home, a mother was pressured to give up her child for adoption, for which the owners of the home extracted a handsome sum from wealthy would-be parents eager to adopt a healthy white baby. Despite the profit that could be made from the adoption service, many of the babies born in the Ideal Maternity Home died. Their bodies were packed in empty butter boxes and hastily buried behind the home. Although the "butterbox babies" eventually became the subject of scandal, the desperation surrounding modern motherhood symbolized by the home was experienced by many Canadian women.

In Montreal or Quebec City, unmarried pregnant women could give birth at homes for unwed mothers run by the Sisters of Miséricorde. Women who took this option were hidden from society and were required, after giving birth, to work in the home for several months as penance and as a way of paying for their care. Few could afford to raise their children, and most left them to be adopted. Over a third of the children died in the home during their first year, mostly from preventable diseases. Both the mothers and the nuns who operated the homes knew that "illegitimacy" would haunt these children for as long as they lived. A sister wrote to the grandfather of one of the children left to the hospital's care in 1934: "Dear Sir: We regret to say that the baby born to E.C. is dead. Thank God for this great favour."[4]

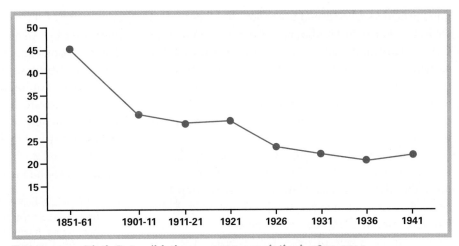

FIGURE 12.1 Birth Rates (births per 1000 population), 1851–1941
Source: Wayne W. McVey Jr. and Warren E. Kalbach, *Canadian Population* (Toronto: Nelson, 1995), 268, 170.

In the interwar period, birth-control information became more readily available to much of the population and the birth rate continued its steady decline (see Figure 12.1). Defying the 1892 law that forbade the provision of birth-control information, advocacy groups and a few birth-control clinics, beginning with one in Hamilton in 1932, let people know how to avoid unwanted pregnancies. Women's organizations such as the United Farm Women of Alberta argued that having smaller families would allow women to have more satisfying lives and to devote more time and resources to each child. In most families and cultures in Canada, this view became widely accepted.

In 1937, birth-control advocates won an important legal victory in an Ottawa courtroom. Dorothea Palmer, a field worker for the Parents' Information Bureau (PIB), was found not guilty of violating the law because her provision of birth-control information to working-class people in Ottawa was clearly done for the public good. The PIB was a birth-control advocacy organization sponsored by Kitchener-based industrialist A.R. Kaufman, who hired nurses to provide birth-control information and arrange for the distribution of contraceptives to women in many parts of the country. Although his goal seems to have been specifically to limit the fertility of the "lower classes"—the PIB began as a service to workers laid off from Kaufman's own factory—he was a key figure in the birth-control

movement in Canada. Largely because of the resolute resistance of Quebec and the Roman Catholic Church, the federal government declined to make birth-control devices legal.

A darker side of the birth-control movement was the idea that the human race would be improved if people who were physically and mentally inferior to some defined standard were sterilized to prevent them from reproducing. The extreme lengths to which this policy was taken in Nazi Germany eventually discredited such ideas, but in the interwar years eugenics was widely debated and viewed as an acceptable practice by many Canadians.

Women who were victims of sexual assaults were often wary of using the courts to have their assailants punished. If there was any suggestion of sexual impropriety in her life, the trial could easily be turned against the victim rather than the rapist. Women who laid complaints against rapists risked disbelief and ostracism within their communities.

THE BURDEN OF RESPECTABILITY

The desire to be seen as respectable rather than rough and ill-mannered encouraged most women to accept the view that sex should be confined within marriage and to condemn those who transgressed this norm as immoral women. Yet respectability had more than just a sexual dimension. Women wished to be seen as good mothers and frugal housekeepers who maintained clean homes for their families and attended to their husbands' needs. Similarly, men wanted to be seen as good providers who turned over enough wages to their wives to allow their families to live decently. When the Great Depression made it impossible for many men to sustain their breadwinning roles, it caused great distress. Some men in this position became hopelessly depressed, others committed suicide, and a great many deserted the families they no longer had the money to maintain.

Even during the Roaring Twenties, perhaps half of the population would have been hard-put financially to meet the ideal of respectability. A letter written by a Mrs. Richards to her landlord, the Halifax Relief Commission, in 1926, illustrates the efforts of women to cling to an image of respectability even when extreme poverty was the central fact of their lives. In begging for time to make up back rent, she argued that her husband's limited income made it "pretty hard to be respectable a[nd] to keep up under the conditions we are living." This family of six had one bed where the father and three of the children slept while the mother and baby slept on a mattress with a broken spring. There was too little money for food or fuel, but Mrs. Richards made plain: "I'm not going on the streets to earn money to pay back rent. I'll go to prison first." Her father-in-law had offered to help only if she put the older children in an orphanage and threw out her husband to live common-law with him. "I'm an Englishwoman and I'd not touch one cent of money belonging to that man," wrote Mrs. Richards. Her concluding sentence described the lives of many women in Canada in the interwar period: "I'm trying to live a[nd] pay my way a[nd] keep respectable a[nd] I cannot do any more."[5]

Not every man or woman made respectability his or her first goal. Many young people gave their elders cause for concern by engaging in premarital sex, drinking to excess, and cruising their parents' automobiles down the main streets of town with little regard for speed limits. Middle-class parents were shocked to find that some of their own children were adopting a live-fast, love-hard, die-young philosophy that they associated with the working class. Ironically, it was generally members of the working class who desperately tried to stake their claim to respectability in the interwar years.

For those without pretensions to respectability, there were ways to get by that often involved the complicity of their social betters, who were clients for their services. An ambitious young man might turn to making moonshine, running gambling dens, or pimping for prostitutes. For women, almost the only alternative to destitution was prostitution. Emily Murphy, a police magistrate in Edmonton from 1916 to 1931, regularly encountered destitute women who sold their bodies and risked their lives in the process. Writing to reformer Nellie McClung in 1930, she described one tragic end to the life of a prostitute:

> I have just been trying to identify a young half-breed girl at the undertaker's who died in a store here from haemorrhage. . . . She had been round the city, I believe, serving the taxis, and here she is at the end of the road, and no one knows her name. She had a heart—a lovely crimson heart—and some roses tattooed on her arm. Poor child! "Only a half-breed." I'd like to tell the world some of the things I know about "superior men"—but I've just got to keep the heartbreak of it all to myself.[6]

Although Murphy used this case to demonstrate the unfairness of the double standard, most women accepted this aspect of patriarchal society and social values in general, protesting only when they faced desperate straits.

Divorce remained uncommon in the interwar period. According to the 1931 census, fewer than 8000 people were legally divorced in Canada. Most desertions of homes involved men leaving their wives. While some women left abusive husbands, sometimes taking their children with them, most accepted the economic logic that fleeing simply plunged the family into permanent poverty. The judicial system continued to be unsympathetic to most women's accusations of battering and was even more unsympathetic to claims from children that their fathers or other relatives had abused them.

The most celebrated case of child abuse in this period occurred in Quebec. On 12 February 1920, Aurore Gagnon of Fortierville, Quebec, died at the age of 10, a victim of neglect and physical abuse by her father, Télesphore Gagnon, and her stepmother, Marie-Anne Houde. The parents were brought to trial and convicted of murder. While the father was sentenced to life in prison, the stepmother was condemned to hang because testimony from neighbours and family members suggested that she had been instrumental in the beating and torture of the child. The Prisoners' Welfare Association took up Houde's case and succeeded in having her sentence commuted to life in prison. While Gagnon was released within five years of being sentenced, Houde spent most of the rest of her life in the Kingston Penitentiary and was released just a year before her death from cancer in 1935.

Meanwhile, the story of *l'enfant martyre* became the subject of gossip, books, plays, and films, and in the 1990s was the subject of a documentary aired on the Quebec network TVA. As historian Peter Gossage points out, the story served to transmit negative stereotypes about women who married widowers and took on the task of raising their children. Like the fairy stories of an earlier time, these stories exploited widely held prejudices about stepmothers. In so doing they articulated dominant ideologies of family life, essentially by holding up for public condemnation an inverted example of the prescribed maternal role.[7]

MOTHERHOOD IN THE MODERN AGE

Mothers in the interwar years became the particular focus of a campaign to reform child-rearing practices, which hitherto had differed widely depending on family, class, and cultural standards. With the advent of mass-circulation magazines and government-sponsored child welfare departments, "scientific" advice on how to be a better mother proliferated. "Old-fashioned" methods and "maternal instinct" came under harsh criticism. In 1932, the *Canadian Home Journal* noted: "The trouble is that the home today is the poorest run, most mismanaged and bungled of all human industries. . . . Many women running homes haven't even the fundamentals of house management and dietetics. They raise children in the average by a rule of thumb that hasn't altered since Abraham was a child."[8]

Experts increasingly intruded in the nursery, with middle-class families leading the way in embracing new methods of bringing up baby. In the mid-1920s, Montreal and Toronto became the centres for research on children. Funded by the Laura Spellman Rockefeller Foundation and the Metropolitan Life Insurance Company, two nursery schools were established to study children. McGill University's Day Nursery

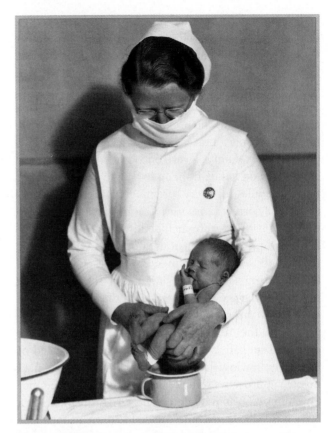

Child-care experts opined that regimentation was best for mother and baby. Such advice was reflected in attempts to "toilet train" infants almost immediately after birth.
Library and Archives Canada/PA 803178

closed in 1930, but St. George's School for Child Study (later the University of Toronto Institute of Child Study) became world-famous under Dr. William Blatz for its pioneering work on child development. By the late 1920s, St. George's School accepted a select group of students into a three-year program of child study. They, in turn, spread the new scientific approach to mothering across the nation.

While one of the major goals of the reformers was to reduce infant mortality through better hygiene, dietary practices, and prenatal care, there was also a tendency to medicalize motherhood. Women were encouraged to consult doctors once they became pregnant, have their babies in hospitals rather than at home, and submit their children to a strict disciplinary regimen monitored by doctors. In an age before state-funded medical care, such a route to motherhood was too costly for many women to pursue and was not always in the best interest of mother and child. Nevertheless, more and more women accepted professional advice on how to bear and raise their children. In 1926, the first year for which statistics are available, only 17.6 percent of births took place in hospitals; by 1960, that figure had increased to 94.6 percent.

Views about raising children departed dramatically from those of the pre-war period. Reflecting new notions of behavioural science pioneered by American psychologists, families were encouraged to teach their children good habits from an early age by establishing fixed schedules for every activity. Detailed charts indicating the correct times for feeding, sleeping, elimination, and bathing were included in most of the advice literature pressed on anxious mothers. At its height, the trend toward regimentation reached absurd lengths that included the injunction to begin toilet training at the age of two weeks. "If the time and place are always the same and the mother shows her approval of the first successes," one 1943 pamphlet opined, "the baby will soon learn what is expected of him."[9] Following the Second World War, more permissive approaches to child rearing were adopted, but for children born in the interwar period, the idea that a baby was "a little machine" made life difficult for those whose parents subscribed to the advice of experts.

HOUSING CANADIANS

By international standards of the period, Canadians were relatively well housed. They enjoyed better sanitation standards and sewage and drainage facilities than Europeans and experienced less overcrowding. Toronto in 1921 had the highest rate of home ownership of the 20 largest cities in North America. Although the middle class usually aspired to own their own homes, many renters lived well. About two-thirds of all urban households were renters, and in Montreal four families in five rented their lodgings. These statistics, of course, hid vast differences in the living arrangements of Canada's increasingly urbanized population.

During the Second World War, a committee headed by Queen's University economics professor C.A. Curtis produced a detailed picture of the shelter available to Canadians. Curtis concluded that 10 percent of existing dwellings in Canada were beyond repair and should be demolished. Another 25 percent

required major repairs. Using the assumption that a four-person nuclear family ought to have at least two bedrooms and a kitchenette, Curtis concluded that one dwelling in five was overcrowded. Most Canadians, he noted, paid too much rent relative to their incomes and the poorer they were, the more likely they were to be getting little value for their rent money.

The poor and the wealthy continued to live in different areas of the same cities, with the wealthy enjoying better sewage and drainage and access to municipal parks. Substantial differences in infant birth weight and mortality bore witness to the unequal prospects. In 1921, the infant mortality rate for Montreal's well-to-do suburbs of Outremont and Westmount was less than 6 percent. In contrast, that of west-end working-class districts was over 20 percent. Tuberculosis claimed hundreds of lives in that year, with the working-class districts predictably suffering the highest death rates.

Although Curtis ignored ethnicity as a factor in determining housing conditions, it had a bearing on the issue. Land titles often had restrictions that kept non-whites, Jews, and eastern Europeans out of new developments. French Canadians and eastern European immigrants were far more likely than Anglo-Canadians to be living in overcrowded conditions. In terms of accommodations, visible minorities fared the worst, being easy targets for prejudiced realtors. Natives on reserves lived in unheated shacks without sanitation or sewage and suffered from high rates of preventable diseases as a consequence. The Vancouver Housing Association, a community organization pressing for public housing, observed that families in the Chinese business quarters east of Dewdney Street had poor accommodation and that single Chinese males lived in crowded, poorly lit, poorly ventilated boarding houses. This reality should have come as no surprise since the British Columbia government gave unemployed Chinese men an accommodation voucher worth 20 cents while white men's vouchers were worth 60 cents. More affluent members of the Chinese community often took in their destitute countrymen. The Yip family, for example, even leased a large building on Canton Avenue from the city and converted it into a shelter for homeless older Chinese men.

In the early 1920s, the urban middle class largely lived in the heart of the cities, but in greener areas with larger lots than in working-class areas. Many workers chose to escape the pollution, noise, and squalor of urban neighbourhoods where they could afford to rent by building homes on the urban fringes. Working-class suburbs sprang up in places such as East York outside Toronto and West Kildonan outside Winnipeg. Municipal regulations did not extend to such areas and developers still focused on the central city. Working people often built their own homes in these early suburbs, sometimes little more than one-room shacks without utilities next to a dirt road. Though it might mean a long walk to workplaces and schools, such homes often seemed a pleasant alternative to renting in the city. Wives could contribute to the family economy by growing gardens and raising a few animals, possibilities that were denied to urban renters.

By the mid-1920s, however, urban planners and the middle class had their eye on the suburbs. Their vision clashed with the dreams of workers, who saw the suburbs as modest escapes from the cityscapes of their employers. Pressed by their planners and by developers, city councils began to implement regulations requiring that suburban homes meet certain building standards. While this alone caused many owner-built homes to be bulldozed, the imposition of municipal taxes also forced many poor people out of their homes. The suburbs of the late 1920s were mainly middle class, though a few, such as Hamilton's Westdale, also offered affordable homes for skilled workers.

Following planners' models, the new suburbs were residential oases separated from commercial and industrial life and characterized by curved streets, large parks, and generous-sized lots. The homes, largely built by developers, were generally modest, but mock masonry veneers in the Tudor style demonstrated a degree of pretension while large living rooms and formal dining rooms were common interior features. Pleasant middle-class suburbs caused their working-class predecessors to disappear almost without a trace by the 1950s, leaving the deceptive image that suburban living had always been associated with middle-class escape from cities. The automobile, the most coveted new possession for middle-class families, made previously unattractive urban fringes appear the ideal place to raise a family. With substantial citizens replacing the former poor residents in the

Tenants being evicted in Montreal during the Great Depression.
Library and Archives Canada/C30811

suburbs, city councils gladly ensured that these areas enjoyed connections to city utilities and extended streetcar and bus lines.

The Great Depression temporarily interrupted suburban expansion and the drive toward private home ownership, but many families persisted in trying to achieve freedom from landlords. Sweat-equity cooperatives, in which a group of individuals worked collectively to build homes for their members' private ownership, rose up in Quebec, Ontario, and the Maritimes. In 1936, Campus Co-operative Residence Incorporated was established in Toronto, becoming the country's first tenants' cooperative and first student housing cooperative.

Whether they lived in suburbs, the inner city, or in farmhouses, Canadians of the interwar period were influenced by the new domestic ideal propagated in the media. This ideal suggested that the home, rather than institutions such as the church and community hall, should be the major centre for entertainment. Radios, gramophones, and fine furnishings were necessary accoutrements for the ideal home. As "labour-saving devices" such as electric stoves, vacuum cleaners, and washing machines began to replace servants, wives increasingly did all their own housework, often in isolation from other women. Men were expected to spend less time at public places than they once had and more time with their families. Some Canadians paid outrageous rents because they placed so great an emphasis on having an accommodation that could approximate the goals of the new cult of domesticity.

WOMEN, WORK, AND THE FAMILY

Work did not always mean the same thing to men and women. Aside from the obvious distinction industrial society makes between unpaid work in the home, done largely by women, and work in the paid labour force, there were different attitudes toward waged work itself. These attitudes, notes historian Joy Parr, were reinforced by the different socialization received by girls and boys:

> Through waged work, boys learned manliness; they mastered disciplines and discriminations, ways of appraising their work and one another, which they would practice through their adult lives; varied though these ways of being manly were, they shared one trait: they were lessons males alone might learn. Girls did not learn womanliness through their paid employment. Their experience of waged work . . . was important in their growing into womanhood because it became them to remain under the protection of male kin while they waited for their life's work, in marriage and outside the market, to begin.[10]

Many young women from rural areas enjoyed the escape to the city. As their diaries and letters attest, they went to movies, dances, and shops with friends they had met at work and in boarding houses. However, their work lives were rarely glamorous. Before the Second World War, most were primarily underpaid store clerks, office workers, and domestics. Immigrant women whose first language was not English fared worse than their English-speaking counterparts. They were clustered in occupations such as sewing for extremely low piece rates and in minimum-wage jobs as cleaners and launderers.

Women's work was central in establishing a sense of community in small towns or local neighbourhoods of larger cities. New single-industry towns, such as Powell River, British Columbia, and Gagnon, Quebec, were springing up as "suburbs in the wilderness" designed to attract a core group of stable family men as employees. Management believed that such workers would be less prone to mobility and strikes than an earlier generation of single male workers. While most of the men worked in the town's main industry, their wives took up the challenge of establishing community facilities. A woman who arrived in Flin Flon, Manitoba, in 1926 when the town was still a bush camp, later recalled, "Without women this town would be nothing. Women organized the community centre, the schools, the hospital. . . . But most important, women were wives and mothers. They kept the house, raised the children right. . . . Women looked after the home and that's what makes this town great. It's a family town."[11]

In cities such as Halifax, Moncton, Hamilton, and Ottawa, female single parents headed one home in six. Most of these women were widows, although many were deserted and a few had never been married. Without husbands, women had little alternative but to join the paid labour force. If their children were young, this often meant placing them in orphanages, since there were few day-care facilities and reliable, affordable child-minders were not easy to find. In many orphanages, over half the children had at least one parent, but work lives and strict orphanage rules limited the time that a single mother was able to spend with her children.

Rose and Edith Biscun were nine and six respectively when their widowed mother, a Russian immigrant, placed them in the Winnipeg Jewish Orphanage in 1931. For the next five years, until their mother remarried and they went to live with her and their stepfather, they saw their mother only a half-day each week. She worked in a *shmata* (clothing) factory six days a week. Only Sundays and occasional holidays afforded the possibility of a family get-together. Children in single-parent families enjoyed fewer educational opportunities than in two-parent families because income from their labour was needed to help the family get by. In Halifax in 1931, 25 percent of children aged 15 to 19 were in school; for children of widows, the corresponding figure was 12 percent.

RURAL LIFE

In the interwar period, Canada is best described as half urban, half rural. As late as 1921, a majority of Canadians lived in communities of fewer than 20 000 people, and even in 1941, over 44 percent of Canadians were rural residents (see Table 12.2). During the Great Depression, three of every 10 Canadians lived on a farm. Most farmers depended on the sale of their produce to buy farm implements and consumer goods. When hard times descended, they were proud of their ability to survive by subsistence farming, an option not available to most city-dwellers. This was particularly true for farmers in the fertile belts of southern Ontario,

Montreal Housewives and the Great Depression

In the 1980s, historian Denyse Baillargeon interviewed working-class Montreal women who had married between 1919 and 1934 about their Great Depression experiences. While these women described incredible hardships, they also revealed a great deal about how they had managed to survive long periods when their husbands could find no work, and about the dreams they had held for their future.

One woman recollected how relatives helped to tide her family over during hard times.

They helped us out a lot because they brought us lots of vegetables from the country. One of my sisters was married to a farmer, so she could bring me lots of vegetables . . . We used to walk to my mother's place sometimes for weeks at a time. When we didn't go, she sent for us. She said: "Come on over, I was worried." . . . Then when we were at her place, we made many little things. Sewing, knitting . . . we were fortunate because we always had my mother-in-law . . . if we were lacking food, we went to eat there, and that was the end of that . . . as soon as my little girl ate, I knew that everything would work out. Sometimes she kept her for three or four days.

When family aid was not available or was insufficient, families had recourse to charitable organizations such as La Société de Saint-Vincent de Paul or the Salvation Army for food, clothing, and furniture. The completely destitute qualified for relief from the city, but it was minimal. Credit with the grocer, doctor, and small shopkeepers was available to some, but those who could avoid indebtedness often chose simply to go without. As a housewife explained:

We never had debts. I never bought anything on credit because I told myself that if I had no money today, I would have no more tomorrow. . . . If we had had debts, I do not know how we would have paid them. In those days, we always thought that the day after we might have no wages. There was nothing then, you know (no social measures). It was necessary not to rely on anyone. It was necessary to rely on ourselves. That is why many times we went without many things we would have liked to have. But you couldn't, you didn't, that was it.

Some women violated the taboo against married women working outside the home in order to supplement family income, but only if their families were small—one or two children—and baby-sitting could be arranged. One recalled:

He earned ten bucks a week. We couldn't get by. So I worked. I sewed for people, I knit, I did everything to make ends meet . . . 15 cents for knitted mittens, 35 cents for stockings . . . it was no fortune. But for me, it helped a lot.

Since most of these women had been poor before the Great Depression, the Depression seemed only an intensification of the poverty they largely took for granted. But they were not all fatalistic. Some women talked, for example, about how they ignored Roman Catholic teachings favouring large families and resorted to contraception. They believed that with fewer mouths to feed, they and their children would be better off. A housewife summed up her feelings at the time:

I told myself that the Good Lord sent me children but I did not want them to suffer later on. The big families always had miseries . . . So I said that my kids, if they wanted to study, they were going to study and I was going to help them and that is what I did. You have to plan. I said I prefer to have a small family and to be able to give them what they want. It was the education that I was looking to for later on.[12]

Quebec, and the Maritimes. Although farmers on the southern Prairies sometimes moved to cities and towns to seek work or relief, many farmers' sons and daughters, who had been able to find work during the late twenties, returned to farms during the 1930s to wait out the Great Depression.

More than ever before in Canadian history, Canadians in rural areas were connected to metropolitan centres. By the late 1920s, 40 percent of Alberta farmers owned an automobile, and many made use of it to shop in larger towns and cities. Automobiles and catalogue shopping restricted the ability of local merchants to corner the business of farmers. As larger centres grew and offered bigger and better services, many small towns began to languish, a trend that would continue throughout the twentieth century.

In the interwar period, the farm population of Ontario and Quebec declined, but it remained stable in

TABLE 12.2 Urban Percentages of Population for Regions and Provinces, 1901–1941 (people in cities of 20 000 or more)

	1901	1911	1921	1931	1941
Canada	34.9	41.8	47.4	52.5	55.7
Quebec	36.1	44.5	51.8	59.5	61.2
Ontario	40.3	49.5	58.8	63.1	67.5
Prairies	19.3	27.9	28.7	31.3	32.4
British Columbia	46.4	50.9	50.9	62.3	64.0
Maritimes	24.5	30.9	38.8	39.7	44.1

Source: Wayne W. McVey, Jr. and Warren E. Kalbach, *Canadian Population* (Toronto: Nelson, 1995), 149.

During the 1930s, provincial governments settled landless families who had no incomes on infertile lands where it was hoped that they could eke out a subsistence. Many of these families moved off their new lands when wartime employment made it possible for them to relocate to cities and towns. The "back-to-the-land" movement of the 1930s suggested the strength of agrarian ideology in Canada, which held that it was still possible in an industrial age for families to be rugged individualists, living off the land without the help of the state.

In the agricultural colleges attached to the universities, professors preached a new view of farming that had a growing appeal. The farmer, it was argued, was an intelligent businessman who studied all the relevant market factors and then decided what crops to grow, what animals to buy and sell, and what machinery he needed. Meanwhile, the farmer's wife, apart from her important work on the farm, was to provide the volunteer labour needed to ensure that a rich and wholesome social life was available to farm communities. Under the influence of such ideas, successful farmers increasingly viewed themselves as independent commodity producers more akin to small businessmen than to wage labourers.

In the interwar years, an alternative perspective rejected the notion that the farm family was the rural equivalent of an urban middle-class household. Farmers who joined the Co-operative Commonwealth Federation (CCF) or laboured in the cooperative movement blamed the market rather than the farmer when farm families faced bankruptcy. Radicals suggested that banks, farm implement companies, and speculators exploited farmers in much the same way that employers exploited workers. Many farm women were also active in the CCF and cooperative movements, campaigning for equal ownership of farm property by husband and wife and legalization of birth control. For these farm men and women, working-class people were more likely urban allies than were middle-class professionals and business owners.

the Maritime provinces and increased in the Prairies. More farms were created in northern Saskatchewan and Alberta and in the foothills of the Rocky Mountains. These provided an alternative to unproductive areas on the southern Prairies, the driest of which were abandoned after homesteaders had made heartbreaking efforts to turn deserts into productive farmlands. Despite farm expansion in the West, the opportunity to move up the social ladder from farm labourer to farm owner was declining. Farming was becoming more technologically intensive, with the result that larger farms were necessary to make agriculture profitable. As the number of farms declined and the costs of farming increased, many farm labourers, often unmarried male immigrants, found their dreams of owning their own land dashed.

The lot of farm labourers was mixed. John Grossman was a German émigré to Jansen, Saskatchewan, in the mid-1920s. As a farm labourer, he did such unpleasant work as hauling stones and pitching hay from sunrise to sunset, complaining that his employer and the employer's sons avoided the heaviest physical labour. He also was displeased that the farm owner was so rigid that he would not let him go to Saskatoon to attend an exhibition. Other farm labourers had a happier experience. Jens Skinberg of Dalum, Alberta, a Danish immigrant in the late 1920s, was, like Grossman, disappointed when he realized that he would not be able to afford his own farm. Instead, he spent his life as a farm labourer. The Danish cultural community of Dalum, including his employer, made him feel at home, and he chose not to seek urban or industrial employment opportunities.

A HISTORIOGRAPHICAL DEBATE

The Farming Community

The farming community of the interwar years was anything but unified. While some farmers saw themselves as allies of the working class, others increasingly viewed themselves as middle-class business people. Historians also take opposing sides on the issue. In the classic work *The National Policy and the Wheat Economy* by economist Vernon Fowke, Prairie farmers are presented as a rather uniform group of individuals oppressed by national tariff and railway policies.[13] C.B. Macpherson's study of the Social Credit movement, *Democracy in Alberta,* presents a similar though less sympathetic view of the farmers of that province. Macpherson portrays farmers as "independent commodity producers" who were, in fact, dependent on market forces over which they exercised little control. Still, as individuals who owned modest farmsteads and employed few labourers, their self-image did not allow them to identify with the cause of working people.[14]

Other historians present the farming community as more diversified and call into question the notion of "independent commodity producers." David McGinnis indicates that off-farm labour was required by most farmers in the interwar period to make ends meet; they might have viewed themselves as independent commodity producers, but this perspective was largely an illusion.[15]

Jeffery Taylor argues that false views of farmers' true position were not accidental but in large part were the creation of agricultural colleges and other institutions in Canadian society that shaped the view that farmers held of themselves.[16] The Manitoba Agricultural College, for example, rejected the older language of agrarianism in which farmers joined workers as an exploited producing class whose problems were the result of greedy monopolists. Instead, its professors encouraged farmers to see themselves as scientific managers of a producing property who could, if they behaved intelligently, make market forces work to their advantage.

John Herd Thompson notes that many farmers employed labourers on a seasonal basis and that they often proved to be very harsh employers.[17] In a study that focuses on farm labourers, Cecilia Danysk details the increasing stratification of the farm community in the interwar period. As the costs of farming soared, only the farmers who developed large land holdings could survive. The lifestyles of these farmers were quite different from those of farmers who eked out a living from small homesteads. They were even more at variance with the lives of farm labourers. While farm labourers had once been a group comprising men saving money to buy their own farms and transients who did not remain on the Prairies for long, the number of permanent farm labourers was on the rise in the interwar period because the cost of getting into farming had become prohibitive.[18]

CONCLUSION

If the First World War occasioned a degree of reflection on traditional gender roles and notions of respectability, the post-war period, on the surface, marked a return to conservative values. New self-styled experts on raising children added a facade of scientific methods to the enterprise that tied women ever closer to the home and prescribed rigid schedules for their children. Middle-class suburbs promised space and clean air where ideal family environments could be created, all the while creating an urban geography that ensured that legions of automobiles would descend on the inner city and make it less livable than ever. Beneath the surface, however, challenges to conventional ideas percolated. The birth-control movement gained ground and brought into question whether women had the right to do more with their lives than bear and raise children. Public housing advocates fought the deterioration of established neighbourhoods, and some farmers worked toward creating more equality between town and country through state intervention. Entrenched notions of individual responsibility and patriarchy still comprised most of what passed for common sense in this period, but often co-existed with newer notions of collective responsibility and a degree of openness regarding gender.

Notes

1 Cited in Veronica Strong-Boag, *The New Day Recalled: Lives of Girls and Women in English Canada, 1919–1939* (Toronto: Copp Clark Pitman, 1988), 13.

2 Irving Abella and Harold Troper, "The Line Must Be Drawn Somewhere: Canada and Jewish Refugees, 1933–1939," *A Nation of Immigrants: Women, Workers, and Communities in Canadian History, 1840s-1960s*, eds. Franca Iacovetta, Paula Draper, and Robert Ventresca (Toronto: University of Toronto Press, 1998).

3 Kenneth Coates, *Canada's Colonies: A History of the Yukon and Northwest Territories* (Toronto: Lorimer, 1985), 100.

4 Andrée Lévesque, "Deviants Anonymous: Single Mothers at the Hôpital de la Miséricorde in Montreal, 1929–1939," *Historical Papers/Communications Historiques* (1984), 178.

5 Suzanne Morton, *Ideal Surroundings: Domestic Life in a Working-Class Suburb in the 1920s* (Toronto: University of Toronto Press, 1995), 41–42.

6 Faye Reineberg Holt, "Magistrate Emily Ferguson Murphy," in *Edmonton: The Life of a City*, eds. Bob Hesketh and Frances Swyripa (Edmonton: NeWest Press, 1995), 148.

7 Peter Gossage, "La marâtre: Marie-Anne Houde and the Myth of the Wicked Stepmother in Quebec," *Canadian Historical Review* 76, no. 4 (December 1995), 596.

8 Cited in Katherine Arnup, *Education for Motherhood: Advice for Mothers in Twentieth-Century Canada* (Toronto: University of Toronto Press, 1994), 32.

9 Ibid., 92.

10 Joy Parr, *The Gender of Breadwinners: Women, Men, and Change in Two Industrial Towns, 1880–1960* (Toronto: University of Toronto Press, 1990), 186.

11 Cited in Meg Luxton, *More Than a Labour of Love: Three Generations of Women's Work in the Home* (Toronto: Women's Press, 1980), 29.

12 Translated from Denyse Baillargeon, "La Crise ordinaire: les ménagères montréalaises et la crise des années trentes," *Labour/Le Travail* 30 (Autumn 1992), 156, 158, 144, 146–47.

13 Vernon C. Fowke, *The National Policy and the Wheat Economy* (Toronto: University of Toronto Press, 1957).

14 C.B. Macpherson, *Democracy in Alberta: Social Credit and the Party System* (Toronto: University of Toronto Press, 1962).

15 David McGinnis, "Farm Labour in Transition: Occupational Structure and Economic Dependency in Alberta, 1921–1951," in *The Settlement of the West*, ed. Howard Palmer (Calgary: University of Calgary, 1977), 174–86.

16 Jeffery Taylor, *Fashioning Farmers: Ideology, Agricultural Knowledge and the Manitoba Farm Movement, 1890–1925* (Regina: Canadian Plains Research Center, 1994).

17 John Herd Thompson, "Bringing in the Sheaves: The Harvest Excursionists, 1890–1929," *Canadian Historical Review* 59, no. 4 (December 1978), 467–89.

18 Cecilia Danysk, *Hired Hands: Labour and the Development of Prairie Agriculture, 1880–1930* (Toronto: McClelland & Stewart, 1995).

Related Readings in This Series

From *Nation and Society: Readings in Post-Confederation Canadian History*
Denyse Baillargeon, "Indispensable but Not a Citizen: The Housewife in the Great Depression," 257–71.

From *Primary Documents CD-ROM*, Volume II
How to Take Care of the Family
The Canadian Mothers' Book
Indian Amendment Act, 1927
Church Report Urges Both Sterilization and Birth Control

Selected Reading

On immigrant experiences, see Donald H. Avery, *Reluctant Host: Canada's Response to Immigrant Workers, 1896–1994* (Toronto: McClelland & Stewart, 1995); Denise Chong, *The Concubine's Children: Portrait of a Family Divided* (Toronto: Viking, 1994); John E. Zucchi, *Italians in Toronto: Development of a National Identity, 1875–1935* (Montreal: McGill-Queen's University Press, 1990); Paul Voisey, *Vulcan: The Making of a Prairie Community* (Toronto:

University of Toronto Press, 1988); and Lubomir Luciuk and Stella Hryniuk, eds., *Canada's Ukrainians: Negotiating an Identity* (Toronto: University of Toronto Press, 1991).

Government policies that kept First Nations in poverty are explored in Hugh Shewell, *"Enough to Keep Them Alive": Indian Welfare in Canada, 1873–1965* (Toronto: University of Toronto Press, 2004). Compelling provincial and regional histories include Robin Jarvis Brownlie, *A Fatherly Eye: Indian Agents, Government Power, and Aboriginal Resistance in Ontario, 1918–1939* (Toronto: Oxford University Press, 2003); Maureen K. Lux, *Medicine That Walks: Disease, Medicine, and Canadian Plains Native People, 1880–1940* (Toronto: University of Toronto Press, 2001); and Mary-Ellen Kelm, *Colonizing Bodies: Aboriginal Healing in British Columbia, 1900–1950* (Vancouver: UBC Press, 1998). The impact of colonization on the Inuit is explored in Shelagh D. Grant, *Arctic Justice: On Trial for Murder, Pond Inlet, 1923* (Montreal: McGill-Queen's University Press, 2002). For the Métis, see Murray Dobbin, *The One-and-a-Half Men: The Story of Jim Brady and Malcolm Norris, Métis Patriots of the Twentieth Century* (Vancouver: New Star Books, 1981). On environmental issues that involved First Nations, see Tina Loo, *States of Nature: Conserving Canada's Wildlife in the Twentieth Century* (Vancouver: UBC Press, 2006) and John Sandlos, *Hunters at the Margin: Native People and Wildlife Conservation in the Northwest Territories* (Vancouver: UBC Press, 2007).

For a longer-term context on interwar family life, see Cynthia Comacchio, *The Infinite Bonds of Family: Domesticity in Canada, 1850–1940* (Toronto: University of Toronto Press, 1999). For farm families, see Kenneth Michael Sylvester, *The Limits of Rural Capitalism: Family, Culture and Markets in Montcalm, Manitoba, 1870–1940* (Toronto: University of Toronto Press, 2001). The interwar period for women is studied in detail in Veronica Strong-Boag, *The New Day Recalled: Lives of Girls and Women in English Canada, 1919–1939* (Toronto: Copp Clark Pitman, 1988); Andrée Lévesque, *Making and Breaking the Rules: Women in Quebec, 1919–1939* (Toronto: McClelland & Stewart, 1994); Denyse Baillargeon, *Making Do: Women, Family and Home in Montreal During the Great Depression* (Waterloo, ON: Wilfrid Laurier University Press, 1999); Joan Sangster, *Earning Respect: The Lives of Working Women in Small-Town Ontario, 1920–1960* (Toronto: University of Toronto Press, 1995), *Regulating Girls and Women: Sexuality, Family and the Law in Ontario, 1920–1960* (Toronto: Oxford University Press, 2001), and *Girl Trouble: Female Delinquency in English Canada* (Toronto: Between the Lines, 2002); Suzanne Morton, *Ideal Surroundings: Domestic Life in a Working-Class Suburb in the 1920s* (Toronto: University of Toronto Press, 1995); Frances

Swyripa, *Wedded to the Cause: Ukrainian Canadian Women and Ethnic Identity, 1891–1991* (Toronto: University of Toronto Press, 1993); Ruth A. Frager, *Sweatshop Strife: Class, Ethnicity, and Gender in the Jewish Labour Movement of Toronto, 1900–1939* (Toronto: University of Toronto Press, 1992); Karen Dubinsky, *Improper Advances: Rape and Heterosexual Conflict in Ontario, 1889–1929* (Chicago: University of Chicago Press, 1993); Margaret Little, *"No Car, No Radio, No Liquor Permit": The Moral Regulation of Single Mothers in Ontario, 1920–1997* (Toronto: Oxford University Press, 1998); and Cynthia R. Comacchio, *"Nations Are Built of Babies": Saving Ontario's Mothers and Children, 1900–1940* (Montreal: McGill-Queen's University Press, 1993). Changes in the experience of giving birth are the subject of Wendy Mitchinson, *Giving Birth in Canada, 1900–1950* (Toronto: University of Toronto Press, 2002). On children's health and the "national issue" in Quebec, see Denyse Baillargeon, "Entre la 'Revanche' et la 'Veillée des Berceaux': Les Médecins québécois francophones, la mortalité infantile, et la question nationale, 1910–1940" in Cheryl Krasnick Warsh and Veronica Strong-Boag, eds., *Children's Health Issues in Historical Perspective* (Waterloo, ON: Wilfrid Laurier University Press, 2005), 101–128.

On youth, see Louise Bienvenue, *Quand la jeunesse entre en scène: L'Action catholique avant la Révolution tranquille* (Montreal: Boréal, 2003). Varying experiences of men and women in the workforce and the home are discussed in Mary Kinnear, *In Subordination: Professional Women, 1870–1970* (Montreal: McGill-Queen's University Press, 1995); Joy Parr, *The Gender of Breadwinners: Women, Men, and Change in Two Industrial Towns, 1880–1950* (Toronto: University of Toronto Press, 1990); and Thomas Dunk, *It's a Working Man's Town: Male Working-Class Culture in Northwestern Ontario* (Montreal: McGill-Queen's University Press, 1991). On housing, see Peter Ward, *A History of Domestic Space: Privacy and the Canadian Home* (Vancouver: UBC Press, 1999); Michael Doucet and John Weaver, *Housing the North American City* (Montreal: McGill-Queen's University Press, 1991); Richard Harris, *Unplanned Suburbs: Toronto's American Tragedy, 1900 to 1950* (Baltimore: Johns Hopkins University Press, 1996), and his *Creeping Conformity: How Canada Became Suburban, 1900–1960* (Toronto: University of Toronto Press, 2004); and Jill Wade, *Houses for All: The Struggle for Social Housing in Vancouver, 1919–1950* (Vancouver: UBC Press, 1994).

On social developments in the Atlantic provinces, see the chapters on the 1920s and 1930s in E.R. Forbes and D.A. Muise, eds., *The Atlantic Provinces in Confederation* (Toronto and Fredericton: University of Toronto and Acadiensis Press, 1993) and Edward MacDonald, *If You're Stronghearted: Prince*

Edward Island in the Twentieth Century (Charlottetown: Museum and Heritage Foundation, 2000). On social developments in British Columbia, see Patricia E. Roy, *A History of British Columbia: Selected Readings* (Toronto: Copp Clark Pitman, 1989) and R.W. Sandwell, ed., *Beyond City Limits: Rural History in British Columbia* (Vancouver: UBC Press, 1999). On the Prairies, social histories of the period include Cecilia Danysk, *Hired Hands: Labour and the Development of Prairie Agriculture, 1880–1930* (Toronto: McClelland & Stewart, 1995); Jeffery Taylor, *Fashioning Farmers: Ideology, Agricultural Knowledge and the Manitoba Farm Movement, 1890–1925* (Regina: Canadian Plains Research Center, 1994); and Don Wetherell and Irene Kmet, *Useful Pleasures: The Shaping of Leisure in Alberta,* *1896–1945* (Regina: Canadian Plains Research Center, 1990). Quebec's social and cultural evolution is detailed in Paul-André Linteau, René Durocher, and Jean-Claude Robert, *Quebec Since 1930* (Toronto: Lorimer, 1983) and Susan Mann Trofimenkoff, *Action Française: French-Canadian Nationalism in Quebec in the 1920s* (Toronto: University of Toronto Press, 1975). The Canadian North is analyzed in Kenneth Coates, *Canada's Colonies: A History of the Yukon and Northwest Territories* (Toronto: Lorimer, 1985); William R. Morrison, *True North: The Yukon and the Northwest Territories* (Toronto: Oxford University Press, 1998); and Morris Zaslow, *The Northward Expansion of Canada, 1914–1967* (Toronto: McClelland & Stewart, 1988).

CHAPTER 13

Interwar Culture

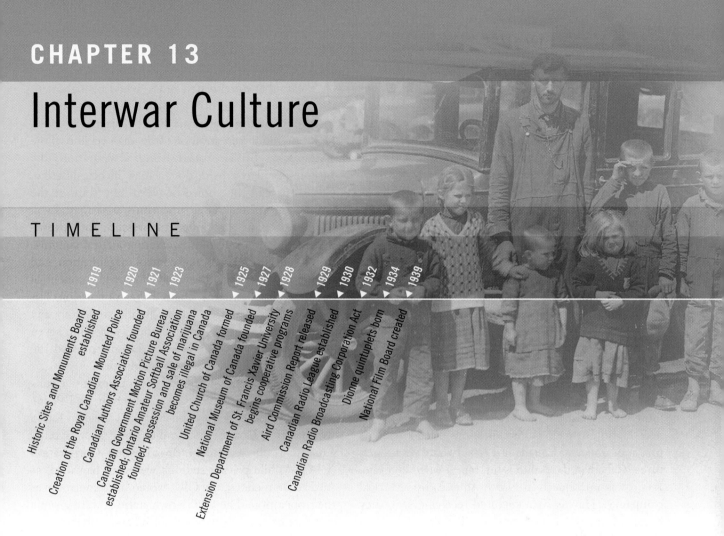

TIMELINE

Now, she messed around with a bloke named Smoky
  She loved him though he was cokie
He took her down to Chinatown
He showed her how to kick the gong around.[1]

This excerpt from the 1931 radio hit "Minnie the Moocher" by American jazz legend Cab Calloway demonstrates why many Canadians denounced interwar popular culture as immoral. Smoky, a cocaine and opium user (kicking the gong around is an allusion to opium use), and his good-time girlfriend, Minnie, were stock characters in Calloway's songs and films, which remained popular despite what traditionalists might think about a subculture that promoted sex, drugs, and jazz.

The demand for legislation to prevent the sale and use of "narcotic" drugs gained momentum in the interwar years. In British Columbia, opponents of Asian immigration campaigned hysterically against the supposed degeneracy of the Chinese, for which opium use was allegedly emblematic. Responding to the general moral panic about drug use, the federal government increased the penalties for "trafficking" and possession of opium and banned the use of marijuana in 1923, making a moral rather than a medical judgment of its harmfulness. The Royal Canadian Mounted Police (RCMP) quickly earned a reputation for its vigilance in cracking down on drug users and political radicals, both of whom conservatives regarded as violators of Christian morality. Formed in 1920 by a merger of the Royal North-West Mounted Police and the Dominion Police, the RCMP cultivated an image of moral rectitude and efficient policing that limited debates about its often high-handed interference with Canadians' civil rights.

The use of "narcotic" drugs was one of a litany of complaints from conservatives, which also included a rise in youth crime and in pregnancies among young unmarried women. They noted the increasing popularity of pool halls, dance halls, cinemas featuring Hollywood films, sensational newspapers, detective novels, and other "American" influences. While the phrase "culture war" was coined only recently, there is little doubt that there were bitter conflicts throughout the interwar years about the direction of society and especially its youth. No matter where one stood on cultural trends, almost everyone had an opinion on jazz, the flapper, and the Model T Ford, all harbingers of a new age of mass culture. This chapter traces the varied responses of citizens and the state to the challenges posed to older conceptions of community, based on religion and hard work, by new technologies and entertainments that celebrated secular pleasures and fun.

THE COMMUNICATIONS REVOLUTION

In the interwar years, the isolation of even the remotest rural regions of the nation was shattered by new developments in communications. Radio made its first appearance in Canada in 1920. Twenty years later, three Canadian households in four owned a radio. Radio was introduced in North America by electrical companies. Having manufactured receiving sets, they began to broadcast programs to sell them. Ten years after radio's introduction, Canada had more than 60 stations, many owned by electrical retailers or newspapers, which depended on advertisers for revenue. In this way, radio, like other media in the interwar years, became the handmaiden of corporate enterprise, selling its products and dreams to a largely uncritical and unsuspecting audience.

In the early days of radio, the United States dominated the North American airwaves. Most of the early Canadian radio stations had weak signals that were easily drowned out by stronger American programming beamed across the border. A decade after the advent of radio, over 40 percent of Canadians still had access only to American stations. Since Canadian stations were often affiliates of the major U.S. radio networks, they, too, aired popular American shows. Only a few Canadian programs, most notably religious shows, were cheap enough to produce profitably. With his *Back to the Bible Hour*, Alberta premier "Bible Bill" Aberhart was one of many radio preachers with a large audience in Canada.

Fears that unregulated radio would contribute to the Americanization of Canadian culture sparked the formation of the Canadian Radio League in 1930. Dedicated to the creation of a Canadian version of the state-owned British Broadcasting Corporation, the League popularized the slogan that, in broadcasting, Canadians had the choice between "the state or the United States." In 1928, Prime Minister William Lyon Mackenzie King responded to pressure for government regulation of radio by creating a royal commission to advise on the future control, organization, and financing of broadcasting. Sir John Aird, president of the Bank of Commerce, chaired the commission. His 1929 report called for a public broadcasting company to own and operate all radio stations and build seven stations across the country. The League pressed the government to follow his recommendation.

In 1932, the Privy Council awarded exclusive control over radio to the federal government, and Prime Minister R.B. Bennett established the Canadian Radio Broadcasting Commission, which in 1936 was reorganized as the Canadian Broadcasting Corporation (CBC). While private stations were not banished, as Aird recommended, the CBC would have control over their operation. The CBC's own stations were given a mandate to foster "a national spirit" and "interpret national citizenship." Like the railways, radio communication was seen by the government as a vehicle for strengthening national unity. The early years of CBC broadcasting were disappointing to those who supported state-controlled radio. Due to limited funding, CBC producers had difficulty creating programs that would lure Canadian radio listeners away from such popular American shows as *Amos 'n' Andy*, *The Jack Benny Show*, and *Burns and Allen*. Radio also strengthened the hold of the American recording industry, which had taken root in Canada before the war. New York's Tin Pan Alley and Nashville's Grand Ole Opry became the centres of production for popular music.

Canadians also watched American movies. After the First World War, movies became a favourite pastime for Canadians of all social classes. The average Canadian went to 12 movies a year in 1936. For children and teenagers in urban centres, the number was much higher. A 1933 study in Edmonton and Calgary suggested that over a third of all students in grades 6 to 10 watched at least one movie a week, with another

The Dionne Quintuplets

The five girls born to a poor rural Francophone couple on 28 May 1934 in Corbeil, Ontario, illustrate the impact of show business on Canadian society. They also reveal the increasing power of the state and medical experts over the lives of Canadian families. From the moment they were born, Annette, Emilie, Yvonne, Cecile, and Marie Dionne were famous. The media immediately focused on what was indeed a remarkable event—the birth and survival of quintuplets. Almost as quickly, the state removed the infants from the care of their parents, who were already raising five older children. Two months after their birth, the Ontario government placed the girls under the control of a local board of guardians and moved the babies to a specially equipped hospital so their upbringing could be overseen by Dr. Allan Roy Dafoe, who had helped deliver them. He and other medical practitioners monitored the babies' every activity. Only after a long battle, which enlisted the aid of the Roman Catholic Church and Franco-Ontarian nationalists, were the girls restored to their outraged parents.

It was little wonder that everyone wanted custody of "the quints." The girls were a major economic asset: they had endorsements of more than $1 million, were the subjects of Hollywood films, and became a major tourist attraction—3 million curiosity-seekers flocked to view them from behind a one-way screen. The girls never recovered from their first traumatic years and felt little bond with their parents or older siblings after their return to the family home. Emilie died in a convent in 1954, and the four survivors recorded their unhappy stories in *We Were Five* (1965). In 1995, the survivors charged that their father had sexually abused them, offering yet another wrinkle to their tragic story.

Much energy has been expended studying the lives of the quints. In recent years, the scholarly focus has been less on the complicated facts of the case than on the broader ramifications of public interest in the products of this "freak" event. The willingness of the state, the media, the medical profession, and even their own family to exploit the girls provides a fascinating glimpse into the values of the modern age, as do the more recent revelations by the surviving quints of their own private hell growing up in mid-twentieth-century Canada.

"The Quints" with Ontario premier Mitchell Hepburn (far right), Dr. Allan Roy Dafoe (middle), and Ontario cabinet minister David Croll (far left).
Archives of Ontario, S801

one in five seeing at least two movies a month. Most of these films were made in Hollywood. Even newsreels and cartoons, which theatres screened before the main attraction, tended to be American imports.

Marginalization of the Canadian film industry was apparent by the early 1920s as major American studios came to dominate the distribution and production of films. In 1923, Famous Players bought out the Allen company, the major chain of Canadian theatres that had started with a cinema in Brantford, Ontario, in 1906. When a Combines Investigation Act report on the film industry was released in 1930, it revealed that Famous Players distributed about 90 percent of all feature films shown in Canada. Nonetheless, the report concluded that the studio was not a "combine" under Canadian law: it did not collude with others to forestall competition in its industry because it controlled too much of the industry to combine with anyone.

Without a major feature film industry in Canada, talented actors flocked south. Oscar-winning Canadian actors Mary Pickford, Marie Dressler, Norma Shearer, and Walter Huston were acclaimed for their Hollywood careers. Fabulous incomes and glamorous lifestyles were the reward for success in Hollywood, and few could resist the dream of becoming a movie star. One young Canadian actor was an exception to this rule. In the 1930s, Deanna Durbin of St. Boniface, Manitoba, became a child star second in popularity only to Shirley Temple. Rejecting the artificiality of Hollywood, she left show business in her late teens to live in France, shunning requests from journalists to discuss her post-celebrity life.

More than any other cultural medium, movies defined the material desires of mass consumer society. The silver screen shaped individual fantasies, established clothing and hair styles, and encouraged new patterns of leisure and recreation. Because many movie plots centred on romance, they also educated people on sex roles and sexuality. Until his sudden death in 1926 at the age of 31, Rudolph Valentino was the screen's first great romantic hero. The lines of loyal fans at his funeral stretched for 11 blocks, indicating that movie stars commanded the attention of people in much the same way that monarchs and political leaders had in an earlier age.

Canadian politicians recognized that film was a powerful medium. In 1923, the federal government established the Canadian Government Motion Picture Bureau to coordinate the film activities of its various departments. In the late 1930s, King asked British film producer John Grierson to investigate the government's film policy. His report led to the creation of the National Film Board (NFB) in May 1939, with a mandate to interpret Canada to Canadians and the larger world. Quickly swept up in producing wartime propaganda, the NFB thrived under Grierson, who was appointed its first commissioner in October 1939. The NFB emerged from the war as one of the largest film studios in the world, with a staff of nearly 800 people and more than 500 films to its credit.

Magazines also helped establish Canadian standards of taste and behaviour, which were increasingly being defined in the United States. In 1925, it was estimated that American magazines outsold their Canadian counterparts by eight to one. Prime Minister Bennett responded to pressure from Canadian publishers for protection from foreign competition by slapping a hefty tariff on American magazines in 1931. Within four years, Canadian magazine sales had risen 64 percent, while American magazine sales in Canada had fallen 62 percent. General interest magazines such as *Maclean's*, *Liberty*, and *Chatelaine* were major benefactors, along with magazines aimed at rural Canada. After King returned to power, tariff protection fell victim to trade agreements and American magazines regained their former market share.

Although newspapers remained largely Canadian-owned, most of the foreign news in all but a few dailies was produced by American press services. There were a few bright spots in this grim press picture. *Canadian Forum*, a magazine founded in 1920 in Toronto, offered a Canadian and progressive perspective on national issues, though it did not have a wide circulation. In the 1930s, the *Winnipeg Free Press*, owned by the Sifton family and edited by John Dafoe, fought a lonely but consistent battle to awaken western Canadian readers to the horrors of Nazi Germany.

Except for establishing the CBC, interwar governments made little attempt to ensure greater Canadian content in the popular media. Their focus instead was on censoring what they felt was unsuitable material, particularly in the movies. Following the prompting of the Roman Catholic Church, Quebec's censorship board snipped not only sexual scenes but also depictions of burglaries, gambling, divorce, suicide, and unpatriotic behaviour. Other provincial boards were scarcely more liberal. Alberta's board would not allow the screening of pictures that depicted the seduction of women, adultery, abortion, venereal disease, or too much violence or drunkenness. In 1922, it condemned movies for "being 'too sensuous,' 'grossly suggestive,' 'immoral,' 'very offensive,' and 'vulgar' as well as for portraying a 'suggestive sex story,' 'a story of a vampire,' 'the life of an immoral woman,' 'a burlesque on clergymen,' and 'a burlesque on missions.'"[2]

A prime reason for much of the censoriousness was the concern that the new mass culture was corrupting the younger generation. If young people spent too much time listening to the radio, watching movies, and going to dance halls, it was argued, they might reject the moral values and religious convictions of their elders. Conservatives expected radio stations and movie houses to avoid content that was morally degrading. Because youth in the interwar years had relatively little purchasing power, filmmakers and recording studios did not yet target them as a special group as they would following the Second World War, but it was clear that mass consumer culture was preoccupied by youth and the values it embodied.

CANADIANS IN SEARCH OF FUN

The pre-war battles between Canadians who mainly wanted to have fun and those who wanted to impose their Christian discipline on the body politic intensified after the war. The magazine *Saturday Night* summed up the views of many secular-minded Canadians, including many church-goers, when it editorialized in 1919: "The people are getting a little fed up with the anti-horse race, anti-smoke, anti-drink, anti-anything movements, as well as the sin hounds who keep people from enjoying themselves in a legitimate manner on the Sabbath day."[3]

Alcohol provided a major industry, even during state-sanctioned prohibition. Bootleggers were not the only ones to profit from the public's unwillingness to respect laws banning liquor traffic. Pharmacists took advantage of the provisions in prohibition legislation that allowed them to prescribe liquor for medicinal purposes to gain extra business. Quarter-mile queues for prescriptions in Vancouver and the 50 percent increase in prescriptions for alcohol in Ontario each

December told the story of public-pharmacist collusion to make use of this loophole in anti-liquor laws.

Canadians had always gambled, but organized betting was on the increase in interwar Canada. The usual gender, class, and race divisions in the country also applied to gambling. Operators of male-only lunch counter operations, pool halls, barbershops, and bowling allies did double duty as "bookies," taking their patrons' illegal bets and selling them smokes and drinks while they waited to hear the results of horse races. Better-off gambling men, who did not patronize such low dives, might find their bookies in bridge clubs. Chinese gamblers, segregated from whites, established their own gambling operations and were far more likely to face repercussions from the police for their unauthorized betting.

Women became the major patrons of bingo games. Bingo had first been introduced to Canadians by troops who had learned the game while serving overseas in the First World War. By the 1930s, bingo games operated legally in Roman Catholic parish halls, urban charities, and small-town agricultural fairs, while dance halls and private homes hosted illegal games. Complaints that women were ignoring their children or blowing the family income on bingo were common. Halifax even tried to shut down all of its bingo operators in 1938. But nowhere in the country were juries willing to convict bingo operators. While the issue of problem gamblers concerned many Canadians, they were increasingly unwilling to abide by the Criminal Code's rigid restrictions on such activity. In 1932, for example, a Vancouver plebiscite approved a provincial lottery to raise revenues for hospitals; however, because of Criminal Code restrictions, the city could not act on the plebiscite results. Such increased openness to gambling and alcohol, along with racy images in the media, worried the traditional churches.

PROTESTANTISM IN A SECULAR SOCIETY

In the 1920s, this grace was said before meals in the home of J.S. Woodsworth, Labour politician and former Methodist minister:

> We are thankful for these and all the good things of life. We recognize that they are a part of our common heritage and come to us through the efforts of

our brothers and sisters the world over. What we desire for ourselves we wish for all. To this end may we take our share in the world's work and the world's struggles.[4]

While he remained a deeply committed Christian, Woodsworth and others like him had become estranged from the mainstream churches, whose thrust following the First World War was essentially conservative.

In the interwar years, many middle-class Protestant ministers and activists turned away from the social gospel's emphasis on reform to focus instead on the improvement of individual behaviour. Some church leaders, particularly Methodists, believed that churches should do more to create a united Canada whose values reflected British traditions. They looked with alarm at regional protest movements and efforts by minority immigrants to maintain their cultural heritage. In December 1923, Dr. W.B. Creighton, the Methodist editor of the *Christian Guardian*, told his readers that the church "do[es] not desire to have Canada filled with an unassimilated mass of people of different races and tongues and religions who would possess no common bond of union and whose presence in large numbers would undo all the work that has already been done in trying to build up the Canadian nation."[5] For Creighton and other church leaders, church union would contribute to a mighty Protestant effort to create a unified, British-inspired Canadian people embodying Protestant virtues of thrift and sobriety.

The merger of the Methodist, Presbyterian, and Congregationalist churches into the United Church of Canada in 1925 was motivated by lofty notions of the Christian mission in Canada, but the reality was quite different. For 14 years, the United Church and the Presbyterian Church struggled to sort out their jurisdictional disputes, as a large element of the lay Presbyterian population, particularly in Ontario and the Maritimes, was more concerned with preserving its Scots and Scots-Irish cultural traditions than with pursuing the exalted goals of its ministers. Refusing to accept the merger, many Presbyterians insisted that they had the right to remain a separate denomination and use the churches that their ancestors had built. A particularly galling point for Presbyterians was the removal of their name by the Act of Union that incorporated the new United Church. Finally, in 1939, the United Church relented and agreed to ask parliament

to recognize the reality that the Presbyterian Church had not disappeared.

The founders of the United Church hoped that a united Protestantism could influence legislators in such areas as temperance, censorship, Sunday observance, and gambling, but their success was limited. The prohibition issue offers a good example of the uphill battles faced by church leaders in the interwar years. After the First World War, the federal government yielded to distiller pressure, dispensed with federal prohibition legislation, and left the provinces to decide the fate of "demon rum" within their own borders. It was not long before the prohibition front began to crumble. British Columbians voted in 1920 for a government monopoly on hard liquor sales, with beer to be sold in grocery stores. Within four years, Quebec and the three Prairie provinces had restored liquor sales, though the Prairies chose to ban bar rooms and restrict liquor consumption to private homes. In Ontario, the puritanism of the Farmer government on the temperance issue and questions such as legalizing horse racing proved an important factor in its humiliating election defeat in 1923. Nova Scotia maintained prohibition until 1929. Only Prince Edward Island held out, finally abandoning prohibition in 1948.

Apart from attempting to influence legislators, Protestant churches tried to maintain their hold over their congregations by providing leisure activities such as picnics, plays, and exhibitions. By the 1930s, most mainstream churches sponsored dances, though 10 years earlier many had denounced men and women dancing cheek-to-cheek as immoral. Observing the limited number of young people in their pews, church leaders were prepared to modify their views in the hope of attracting adolescents to organized religion. Women continued to constitute the majority of active church members, but most churches resisted feminist efforts to have women ordained and elected as church elders. The United Church accepted its first female minister, Lydia Gruchy, in the 1930s, but it would be years before churches accepted more than a handful of women into their pulpits.

A growing minority of Canadians were unhappy with what they perceived as the decreased fervour of the established churches. Interested in neither the social gospel nor moral reform, they wanted their ministers to focus exclusively on the individual's relationship with God. The Pentecostals and the millennialist Jehovah's Witnesses were among religious sects that grew in the interwar period. Charismatic ministers such as Canadian-born Aimee Semple McPherson, who preached from her California temple, won the hearts of those who missed the energy and conviction of old-time religion.

ROMAN CATHOLICISM IN THE MODERN AGE

The Roman Catholic Church was as conservative as the major Protestant denominations on most issues of individual behaviour. While Roman Catholics refused to join in the campaign for prohibition, they were as keen as any Protestant denomination to control what Canadians could read, watch at the movies, hear on radio, or do in their spare time. Mainstream Protestant denominations cautiously endorsed the use of mechanical contraceptives to limit family size in the 1930s, but the Roman Catholic Church would endorse only the use of the unreliable rhythm method. It was also implacably against divorce.

On some political and economic issues, there was evidence of growing Roman Catholic liberalism. Cooperatives were particularly favoured by Roman Catholic reformers. Under Father Moses Coady, the founding director of the Extension Department of St. Francis Xavier University in Antigonish, Nova Scotia, attempts were made from 1928 onward to spread cooperatives through communities dependent on farming, fishing, coal mining, and steel production. Concentrating on the Atlantic region, Coady's achievements included the United Maritime Fishermen's Co-operative (UMFC), which challenged merchant exploitation by using cooperatives to provide supplies, process fish, and market the final product. Acadians in the region proved particularly receptive to the call for cooperatives. By the 1940s, the UMFC counted about 4500 members and was a force to be reckoned with politically and economically. The Pêcheurs unis du Québec, founded in

In July 1939, 105 French-Canadian couples, having received formal instruction in the church's doctrines regarding married life, were wed en masse in Delormier baseball stadium.
Archives Nationales du Québec/Conrad Poirier/P48, S1, P3711

1939, followed the same principles as its Maritime counterpart.

Many leaders of the Roman Catholic Church in Quebec were beginning to recognize that the church's position was increasingly removed from that of their Francophone parishioners, who were embracing North American secular values. The birth rate continued to fall in the interwar period, the percentage of workers enrolled in international unions vastly exceeded those who chose to join confessional unions, and blasphemous expressions were common in the Quebec vernacular. Church-sponsored newspapers and the independent but very Roman Catholic *Le Devoir* had a combined readership greatly inferior to secular newspapers such as *La Presse*. Although rural Quebec parishes might remain under the sway of the priests and nuns, six out of 10 Quebecers, including a majority of Francophones, lived in cities in the 1930s. They respected church leaders, but apparently listened to their views only when it suited them.

EDUCATION

By the 1920s, parents who could afford to delay their children's entry into the workforce generally encouraged them to complete as many years of secondary schooling as possible. The number of jobs for which high school matriculation was a qualification increased dramatically as employers demanded a more literate workforce. The national increase in school attendance illustrates the change. In 1921, 27 percent of girls and 22 percent of boys between the ages of 15 and 19 attended school; two decades later, the respective figures were 37 and 35 percent. In Ontario, the secondary school population quadrupled over the previous decade in the 1920s, though the provincial population had grown only 17 percent. Part of the explanation was that in 1921 Ontario became the first province to extend the school-leaving age to 16. Schools reinforced gender stereotyping in society and the workforce, with boys who were not academically minded streamed into programs training them for trades while girls received commercial or domestic training.

Quebec Francophones, and indeed Francophones generally, did not share in the trend toward increased schooling. As late as 1926, only 6 percent of Quebec Francophones attended school beyond the elementary level. While public schools across the country increasingly emphasized science and mathematics along with literature and grammar in a curriculum that responded to employers' notions of a useful education, Roman Catholic secondary schools in Quebec taught Thomist philosophy, Latin, religion, and humanities. The church regarded instruction in religious doctrines and religious values as more important than utilitarian, secular knowledge. It believed that too much education in non-religious subjects would lead young people away from the paths of righteousness into the murky waters of North American agnostic materialism. In the view of church leaders, elementary school was sufficient for those whose lives would be spent in honest toil as farmers, labourers, and housewives. Higher education was needed only for future priests, teachers, church administrators, and other professionals. Since the labour of older children was often necessary to ensure a sufficient income for many households or to help mothers of large families with the raising of younger children, many Quebecers were pleased that schooling was not compulsory.

By the early 1940s, reformist elements within the church had joined trade unions and liberal women's organizations in recognizing the need for a better-educated citizenry. In 1943, the Liberal government of Adélard Godbout passed legislation making education compulsory for children from ages six to 15. By then, the wartime economic situation had created full employment for adult males, and parents were more willing than in the past to accept state intervention in an area of parental authority.

French-language instruction in public schools continued to be resisted in the predominantly Anglophone provinces. Although Ontario permitted French instruction in elementary schools after 1927, the province did not extend to French-language schools any of the planning or coordination enjoyed by English-language schools. The provincial Department of Education provided no curricular materials in French, and the normal schools, which trained teachers, operated solely in English. Most western provinces either forbade or made little provision for French-language education. Only in New Brunswick was French-language education accepted without restrictions, but the province put little money into curriculum planning for Francophone schools, and the small tax base in Francophone communities guaranteed an inferior French-language school system.

Poor educational opportunities and recognition that people who spoke French were often condemned to poverty caused many Francophones outside Quebec to assimilate to Anglophone culture. This did not mean simply learning English, which would have been necessary in areas where the Francophone population was small, but abandoning French as the home language. In 1931, the number of Ontarians whose first language was French but who later became primarily English speakers was reported as 22.1 percent. The rate was even higher in provinces with small Francophone populations, such as British Columbia. Only in New Brunswick, with its concentrated Acadian community, was assimilation successfully resisted.

While schooling was regarded as important by nearly everyone, teaching, particularly at the elementary level, was still deprecated as a "woman's profession." Elementary school teachers in urban areas required only a year of normal school, which could be taken after high school matriculation, to be eligible to teach. In rural areas, they might be even less qualified for the classroom. Their limited training and poor salaries distinguished them from high school teachers, who were predominantly male and were more likely to have university degrees. During the Great Depression, as school boards ran short of cash, teachers faced not only pay cuts, but also sometimes months without any salary at all.

The problem was particularly severe in rural areas where the tax base was small. Rural teachers were usually single women who taught in one-room schools and boarded with local families or lived in rooms attached to the schools. In frontier areas, the living and working conditions were primitive. Still, many teachers enjoyed their work, appreciated the hospitality of local folk, and felt that they had more autonomy and independence than their urban counterparts of this period. Lillian Gates's description of her experience in the Cariboo in British Columbia was fairly typical: "I loved to be alone in my teacher's residence at Willow River, even if, in the winter months, sometimes at -45 degrees, I had to get up every 2–3 hours all night to keep my little wooden heater going. I loved to walk along the old logging trails, through the silent forests. . . . I learned to shoot, without success. The parents of my pupils supplied me with moose meat, caribou, grouse, ptarmigan and wild mushrooms."[6]

The enthusiasm for more schooling slowly extended to the post-secondary sector, but with university education generally still confined to an elite minority, provincial governments were reluctant to increase spending on universities. While University of Toronto students demonstrated in the late 1930s against spending cuts by Mitchell Hepburn's government, few ordinary people

MORE TO THE STORY

Medical Research in Canada

Canadian universities were not only teaching institutions; they also sponsored research. At the University of Toronto, Canadians made headlines in the field of medicine when a team headed by Frederick Banting discovered insulin, a life-saving therapy for diabetes mellitus. Banting and one of his co-researchers, J.J.R. McLeod, shared the 1923 Nobel Prize for their efforts. Banting gave half of his prize money to C.H. Best, a key researcher on the investigative team.

At McGill University's Medical Museum, Maude Abbott's authoritative cataloguing of the types of congenital heart disease led to the eventual development of surgical therapies for its treatment. Surgical intervention saved the lives of countless "blue babies," whose fate in earlier years had been almost certain death. Although Abbott was recognized as one of the world's leading authorities in her field, McGill never promoted her beyond the level of assistant professor.

In 1934, Wilder Penfield established the Montreal Neurological Institute, which rapidly became internationally renowned for its research, teaching, and treatment related to diseases of the nervous system. Penfield established the "Montreal procedure" for the treatment of epilepsy and was a tireless student of the brain, which he argued was the most important unexplored field of scientific inquiry.

C.H. Best (left) with Dr. Frederick Banting (right), co-discoverers of insulin.
Library and Archives Canada/C-001350

sympathized with the students' plight. More helpful than governments were private, mainly American foundations such as Carnegie, Ford, and Rockefeller, which poured money into major universities and helped fund the Canadian Social Science Research Council, whose grants allowed scholars outside professional faculties to conduct research.

Between 1929 and 1940, Canadian university enrolments increased from 23 418 to 37 225. Women's participation jumped from 16 to 24 percent of all enrolments, but their increase was concentrated in areas stereotyped as women's professions: nursing, household science, library science, and physical and occupational therapy. No males were enrolled in any of these areas in the 1940–1941 academic year. Men dominated in professional areas, such as engineering, medicine, and law, that promised higher salaries and greater independence.

Women were rarely hired as professors outside the departments offering training in "women's professions." Moreover, the positions of female faculty were never as secure as those of men. When the University of Alberta had to lay off a classicist during the Second World War, they chose to force the retirement of a distinguished scholar, Geneva Misener, rather than dismiss any of her junior colleagues, who were all "family men."

In the interwar years, women seeking educational challenges or career training became an important part of the audience for adult education programs. Several universities established extension programs aimed first at rural areas and eventually at the non-university population of the cities. E.A. Corbett, who led the University of Alberta's Faculty of Extension in the 1920s and 1930s, felt that his mission was to promote high culture in rural areas. He encouraged local drama productions, and his department lent films, classical music recordings, and books to groups and individuals. Under his leadership, the Faculty of Extension established a radio station to provide educational and cultural programs throughout the province and a summer drama program that later evolved into the Banff School of Fine Arts. McGill and the University of British Columbia established programs according to Corbett's model in the 1920s and 1930s.

Adult education was not restricted to universities. At the turn of the century, Frontier College had been founded by Alfred Fitzpatrick, a Nova Scotia–born Presbyterian minister, to provide basic education to workers, particularly immigrants. It flourished in the interwar years as university students flocked to work sites on the industrial frontier to teach those who otherwise would have had little hope of receiving any formal education. Trade unions and political parties of the left also ran schools for their activists in an attempt to counter information dispensed by the media, which the left viewed as tools of the capitalist class.

LITERATURE AND ART

A better-educated public provided an increasing market for Canadian literature, art, drama, and music, despite the overweening influence of American popular culture. With the support of voluntary groups, churches, universities, and corporations, Canadians produced a vibrant, if fragile, culture and a critical audience. Debates in the media about issues such as the relative merits of the Group of Seven, the growing American control of radio programming, and the necessity for censorship brought the politics of culture to a wide audience.

The creation of the Canadian Authors Association (CAA) in 1921 testified to a new sense of national identity among Canadian writers. At its largest, it had 800 members and a French-Canadian branch. It sponsored an annual book week and encouraged sales of the works of Canadian authors. As in the pre-war period, Canadian writers produced little that was genuinely innovative. Montreal poet F.R. Scott was highly critical of the uninspired outpourings of national sentiment by members of the CAA, satirizing them in his poem "The Canadian Authors Meet," first published in 1927:

> O Canada, O Canada, Oh can
> A day go by without new authors springing
> To paint the native maple, and to plan
> More ways to set the self-same welkin ringing.[7]

In the interwar years, many Canadian painters were in revolt against conventional subject matter and styles. Emily Carr, who by 1914 had largely given up painting due to lack of moral and financial support, resurfaced in the late 1920s to become one of Canada's most renowned artists. Her work was enriched by Native art forms and themes. Abstract and non-objective painting made tentative, if not particularly popular, debuts in Canada prior to the Second World War. Inspired by American and French artists, abstract painters used objects or natural scenes as a base for producing paintings that often bore no direct resemblance to the original objects. Non-objective painters began not with objects but with pure imagination to produce their art. Russian-born painter Paraskeva Clark of Toronto raised eyebrows with her cubist-inspired paintings, which owed a debt to experiments by Soviet artists in the early years after the revolution. Paris continued to have a great influence, particularly among artists in Montreal. Returning from Paris in 1940, Alfred Pellan became the first of many Francophone artists to demonstrate the influence of Picasso and other cubists.

During the Great Depression years, realism crept back into art. Works such as Leonard Hutchinson's woodcut *Protest*, Miller Brittain's paintings of unemployed longshoremen in Saint John, and Carl Schaefer's watercolours of rusting agricultural machinery in the fallow fields of southern Ontario are poignant reminders of the economic dislocation facing many people in this difficult decade. Following the policies set by Franklin Roosevelt's government in the United States, business and government commissioned work from Canadian artists.

The success of Carr and Clark, among other women artists, demonstrated that in artistic areas where their entry was not explicitly barred, some determined women could penetrate the barriers of social prejudice. In other fields, such as architecture, women were excluded completely. Esther Marjorie Hill, Canada's first female architect, earned her architecture degree from the University of Toronto in 1920. Returning to her native Edmonton, she was denied the

Emily Carr (1871–1945), *A Haida Village*, ca. 1929.
Oil on canvas; 82.7 x 60.7 cm. McMichael Canadian Art Collection; Gift of Dr. and Mrs. Stern, Dominion Gallery, Montreal; 1974.18.1/SRC

right to register by the Alberta Association of Architects. The Farmers' government, influenced by Canada's first female cabinet minister, Irene Parlby, finally passed legislation in 1925 making registration automatic for any graduate of a recognized faculty of architecture. This meant that Hill was theoretically able to practise her craft, but the hostility of the architects' professional body made it difficult for her to find clients. During the Great Depression, she was simply unable to make a living and moved to Victoria with her parents.

Many of the works of sculptor Frances Loring were architectural in nature. In the interwar years, she was commissioned to design public monuments and several war memorials across the country, including one for the Law Society of Upper Canada in Osgoode Hall in Toronto. Along with her lifelong companion, fellow sculptor Florence Wyle, Loring was a founding member of the Sculptors Society of Canada and worked to promote the acceptance of women within the artistic community.

Perhaps the most deeply influential art of the period was produced by the Group of Seven. More popular than the new experimental art, it contributed to a nature-based Canadian nationalism. Painting scenes all over the country, A.Y. Jackson remained particularly faithful to the group's original work. Arthur Lismer became educational supervisor of the Art Gallery of Ontario and built upon his earlier landscapes. Lawren Harris's work became more abstract and experimental. Fred Varley was named head of the Department of Drawing and Painting at the Vancouver School of Art in 1926. He was drawn to Asian art, and, through Emily Carr, also discovered Native art. Anthropomorphism permeated later Varley works, such as *Snow People*, and in 1938 he went north to sketch the landscapes and people of the Arctic. Despite the fact that individual members of the group went their separate ways, the impact of their original project was enormous.

MUSIC AND THEATRE IN THE INTERWAR YEARS

Film and radio reduced the audience for the vaudeville shows that had been popular before the First World War, and many of the old music halls were turned into cinemas. Although movies posed a major threat to touring theatre troupes, community theatre groups flourished. In 1933, the first Canadian Drama Festival was held, in which community theatre groups competed for prizes in acting, directing, design, and production after a series of regional run-offs. This remarkably successful annual event stimulated amateur theatre across the country.

Radio and records increased the audience for live bands, particularly dance bands, and a variety of night clubs sprang up in Canadian cities between the wars.

While visiting "hit parade" artists attracted the largest audiences, there was a market for full-time and part-time jazz and "swing" musicians in every city. Guy Lombardo and His Royal Canadians became famous in the United States in the 1930s for their broadcasts from New York's Roosevelt Grill on New Year's Eve. The United States also offered opportunities to those who shared the growing passion for country music. Wilf Carter drifted across the border in the 1930s, and, as Montana Slim, was soon being beamed into Canadian homes on American airwaves.

North American trends also influenced Francophone Quebec, where Marie Travers, known as La Bolduc, became Quebec's first successful recording artist. A gifted child born to English parents in the Gaspé town of Newport, she played a number of musical instruments and composed songs, the first of which were recorded in 1927. Her songs, such as "La Cuisinière," "La Servante," and "La Grocerie du coin," focused on themes of daily life and the material difficulties faced by ordinary people. Although her witty and, for the times, naughty lyrics earned her the disapproval of the church, she was wildly popular among Francophone Quebecers, who listened to her on the radio and flocked to buy her records.

The classical music tradition was strengthened in Canada by the creation of schools of music at the University of Toronto (1918), McGill (1920), and Laval (1922). With the founding of symphony orchestras in Toronto, Montreal, and Vancouver, professional classical musicians had an outlet for their talents. As with popular music, imported music dominated the radio waves, but some Canadian composers managed to gain an audience for their work. A few musicians struggled to give expression to unique Canadian images and motifs in their work. Claude Champagne's "Suite Canadienne" and Ernest MacMillan's "Two Sketches for Canadian Strings," which incorporate themes from folk music, have become Canadian classics.

THE INVENTION OF TRADITION

In the 1920s, Canadians began reflecting on the rapid changes that had occurred in the post-confederation period. In doing so, they often viewed the past through a romantic haze, inventing traditions, imagining

Guy Lombardo and His Royal Canadians

North Americans were swept off their feet in this period by a dance band featuring the talents of a tightly knit Italian-Canadian family from London, Ontario. Guy Lombardo and His Royal Canadians were North America's third-best-selling recording act of the first half of the twentieth century (behind Bing Crosby and the Paul Whiteman Orchestra), selling more than 100 million records in a career that spanned three decades and nosedived only when rock and roll eclipsed earlier popular music styles in the mid-1950s.

Guy Lombardo (1902–1977), the band leader, and his brother Carmen (1903–1971), singer, songwriter, and alto saxophonist, were the core of the Lombardos' entourage. Two other brothers also performed in the band at various times, and Guy's sister Rosemarie was a featured singer for several years in the 1940s. The children of Italian immigrants, the Lombardos were part of an ethnic community in London that trained many musicians. They began performing in the town while still teenagers and were soon in demand for performances throughout southern Ontario. Moving to the United States in 1924 and adopting the name Guy Lombardo and His Royal Canadians, they began a recording career that took them 26 times to the number one spot on *Billboard* magazine's hit parade from 1927 to 1950. As the band became popular, Guy Lombardo added more musicians to create the most successful "big band" of the Great Depression era. Composers assiduously courted the Lombardos, and the band introduced some of the major English-language standards of the twentieth century, including "Red Sails in the Sunset," "September in the Rain," and "Managua, Nicaragua." Their radio performances from the Roosevelt Grill in New York, beginning in 1929, were a top draw for two decades, and they also enjoyed some success in the early years of television.

Starting with "Many Happy Returns" in 1934, the Lombardo boys were featured in a number of popular movies. Guy also won trophies as a speedboat racer and invested heavily in oil and uranium properties in the United States.

The Lombardo band advertised its music as "the sweetest music this side of heaven," and critics often panned them as a formula orchestra that failed to innovate. Record-buyers, however, liked their sound, and their legion of fans included major jazz figures such as Louis Armstrong and Ella Fitzgerald.

Guy Lombardo and His Royal Canadians.
Friends of Lombardo/Guy Lombardo Music Centre

golden ages, and creating identities that may never have existed quite as they came to be described. The National Museum of Canada, created by an act of parliament in 1927, symbolized this new interest in the past, as did the establishment of the Historic Sites and Monuments Board of Canada in 1919. Upon the advice of the board, the government began to designate national historic sites across the country. Most of the sites recognized in the interwar years related to military and

political developments in the nation's past. Strongly influenced by the reconstruction of colonial Williamsburg in Virginia in the 1920s, the government embarked on its own reconstruction projects, beginning with a replica of Champlain's habitation at Port Royal, Nova Scotia, in 1939.

With a long recorded history of European settlement, Maritimers and Quebecers eagerly embraced historical approaches to identity creation. Pioneers in the pre-confederation period were increasingly depicted as happy folk, living in farming and fishing communities untouched by the materialism of the industrial age. In the 1920s, researchers began seeking out the descendants of people still living in the "traditional" way, claiming to find in them the essence of regional identities.

The "cult of the folk" sold well to consumers of culture and tourism in the modern age. In Nova Scotia, many of the symbols of provincial identity—Peggy's Cove, the *Bluenose*, and the Scottish bagpiper at the border—emerged in the interwar years. Meanwhile, a coterie of creative writers, calling themselves the "song fishermen," idealized the rural values of the past, which they felt were fast slipping away in a tide of modern values. Since many of the song fishermen were

One tradition quickly invented after the war was the honouring of war dead. How best to commemorate the fallen and what images of the war should be presented caused considerable debate. Trois-Rivières followed a typical strategy, erecting a cenotaph that depicted a solemn-looking warrior and listed those from the city and area who had lost their lives during the war.
Archives du Seminaire de Trois-Rivieres Fonds, Trois-Rivieres Photographies/FN-0064-65a-28

highly educated and actually lived and worked in the United States much of the time, their view of Nova Scotia "folk" was highly modern in its conceptualization and shaped to appeal to contemporary consumers. Historian Ian McKay underlines the contradictions embodied in the cult of the folk: in upholding their pre-modern, quaint, therapeutic otherness, he argues, it was simultaneously drawing them into the commercial and political webs of modern society.[8]

As a result of this new interest in the pre-industrial past, folklore became a subject of systematic study. Helen Creighton embarked on a lifelong career collecting Nova Scotia folk songs and stories in the 1920s. At the National Museum of Canada, Rhodes scholar Marius Barbeau collected traditional songs, texts, and artifacts of French Canadians and Native peoples. His first loyalty was to his Quebec homeland, which he concluded had preserved folk traditions reaching back to the Middle Ages. In his work with the Tsimshian in British Columbia, Barbeau collected stories about an ancient migration from a distant homeland, convincing him that they had journeyed from Asia. Barbeau founded the Archives de folklore at Laval University and helped make ethnology and folklore an academic pursuit in twentieth-century Canada.

THE "FOLK" IN QUEBEC

In Quebec, clerical-nationalists continued to cultivate their particular vision of the folk: pious, rural, and wedded to the communities of their birth. But there was a twist. In the pre-war period, Henri Bourassa and *Le Devoir* had championed a pan-Canadian clerical-nationalist vision for Francophones. Conscription and anti-French language legislation in several provinces soured many Quebec intellectuals on this vision, and in the post-war period the focus was on Quebec alone as the homeland of Francophone Roman Catholic culture. Abbé Lionel Groulx emerged as the new leader of clerical-nationalism, founding a newspaper, *L'Action Française*, and inspiring a new youth group, Association Catholique de la Jeunesse. *L'Action Française* firmly fixed its gaze on the past, insisting that only the preservation of the French language and the strictest adherence to the dictates of the church hierarchy could protect Quebec from being absorbed into the North American secular materialist culture that was seducing English Canadians. For a time in 1922, the paper flirted with the idea of formal Quebec sovereignty. But for the most part, Groulx's concern was the creation of a Quebec spirit of independence that would wall the province off intellectually from the rest of North America.

Groulx was a much-published historian of Francophone life in North America who encouraged others to follow his example of close analysis of documents and attention to small details in the history of French Canada. But his professionalism as a historian tended to clash with his desire to create heroes and mythologies that would inspire "the folk" to preserve social values that he argued were the true heritage of Quebec's founders. For example, Groulx turned Dollard des Ormeaux, a young victim of French-Iroquois warfare in 1660, into a champion of Francophone Roman Catholic virtues, even though the historical record was unclear about his motives as he attempted to circumvent an Iroquois blockade of Quebec's fur trade with rival Native groups. Similarly, religious-minded nationalists revised the history of the 1837 rebellion in Lower Canada to make it appear that the rebel leaders, who were generally secular-minded liberals, had been defenders of the faith. St. Jean Baptiste Day, a secular nationalist event of the 1830s, was revived by the church in a new form in Montreal in the 1920s as part of its campaign against secularism and materialism.

Despite clerical efforts to defend rural life, Quebec was rapidly urbanizing. Nationalists worried about the lack of Francophone participation at the apex of the emerging capitalist economy. For some, this meant little more than raging against Anglophones and Jews, for whom English was the language of business and who were allegedly reducing the French-speaking majority to ill-paid proletarians. More progressive nationalists, however, embraced the more liberal teachings of the Roman Catholic Church and formed the École sociale populaire to study and propagate ways in which Catholicism and the new industrial order could be reconciled. Increasingly, they viewed the Quebec state not only as the defender of church powers over social services and education, but also as a potential regulator of the new capitalism in the people's interest.

One of Canada's outstanding sports stories was supplied by a female basketball team, the Edmonton Grads, comprising students and alumnae of that city's Commercial High School. Beginning in 1915 and continuing for 25 years, the Grads put together an unrivalled record of wins over domestic and international opponents.
Provincial Archives of Alberta/A-11428

SPORTS IN THE MODERN AGE

In the interwar years, enthusiasm for professional sporting events increased among all social classes. Hockey's claim to be the national sport was cemented, as indoor stadiums, artificial ice, and the expansion of the National Hockey League (NHL) to American cities gave the game new prominence. The Montreal Forum opened in 1924, followed by Maple Leaf Gardens in Toronto in 1931. Not only sports stars but also sports commentators became household names, most notably Foster Hewitt, whose play-by-play during radio (and later television) hockey broadcasts, starting in 1931, entertained generations of Canadians. Although a few hockey superstars earned a sensational $10 000 a year during the 1920s, the average wage in the NHL was $900, a poverty wage if it was the only income a hockey player could claim. After the legendary Ottawa Senators, winners of four Stanley Cups, were forced to fold in 1934 as unemployment reduced the potential audience for professional hockey, the only Canadian teams in the NHL were the Montreal Canadiens and the Toronto Maple Leafs. Still, all four American teams in the league had a majority of Canadian-born players. Although the NHL dominated the hockey world, smaller-city leagues with semi-professional players continued to draw crowds throughout the period.

Baseball remained a popular participant sport. In Halifax, six teams from working-class neighbourhoods composed the Twilight League, which held games three days a week. As many as 2000 spectators attended some games. Softball was also popular. In 1923, the Ontario Amateur Softball Association was formed, the first association in the world for this increasingly popular sport. There was also professional baseball in Canada: Quebec had a semi-professional provincial baseball league and both Montreal and Toronto had teams in the International League, headquartered in the United States.

The sports world was still a largely male preserve, but women continued to make inroads. In 1928, Fanny (Bobbie) Rosenfeld, a Russian-born Canadian Jew, returned from the Amsterdam Olympics with a silver medal in the 100-metre dash. She had also been lead runner for the gold-medal relay team and was Canada's leading woman broad jumper and discus thrower. Ethel Catherwood won the gold medal in the high jump in 1928, setting an Olympic record in the process. Restrictions against women in sport, however, soon ended her athletic career. Since married women were forced out of sports, unlike married men, Catherwood married privately shortly after the Olympics. Her secret was exposed to the public when she divorced a few years later, and the newspapers revealed that she was living with a married man.

In the 1930s, champion swimmer Phyllis Dewar won four gold medals at the British Empire Games, a feat that was not surpassed by another Canadian until 1978. While hockey and football were regarded as inappropriate sports for "ladies," softball was acceptable for women as long as they remained in the amateur leagues. In basketball, the Edmonton Grads pursued a remarkable career throughout the interwar period. When the Grads disbanded in 1941, they left a record that has yet to be equalled, winning 93 percent of their games and 49 out of a possible 51 domestic titles.

The Women's Amateur Athletic Federation (WAAF), formed in 1925, acted as a national voice to encourage women to participate in organized sports. Trying to contend with opponents of women's sporting activities without challenging dominant notions of a woman's social role, they had little success. Montreal sportswriter Elmer Ferguson commented in *Maclean's*

in 1938 that "the violent sports are no good for your looks, dignity or health. Sorry but I like a little delicacy." WAAF's Ontario secretary Rosy Atkins was quick to reply: "A temporarily strained face doesn't permanently destroy beauty, nor does it reduce a woman's social charm or her ability to bake a pie. You don't understand us girls [and] you don't even know your men. The girls who play the sports you deplore are gilt-edged securities in the marriage market."[9]

SERVICE ORGANIZATIONS

Spurred by increased urbanization and a shorter work week, voluntary organizations proliferated in the interwar years. Churches, fraternal associations, and the militia continued to provide Canadian men with opportunities to bond on the basis of religious, ethnic, or patriotic inclinations. While trade unions also organized their own class-related social activities, middle-class businessmen were increasingly involved in community-service organizations such as the Rotary Club, Kiwanis, Gyros, and the Elks, which had no official ethnic or religious affiliations. These clubs raised funds for local facilities such as libraries, swimming pools, community halls, and parks; participated in parades to boost community spirit; and supported community groups such as the Boy Scouts.

Women remained active in both mixed-sex and women's church groups and continued their enthusiasm for secular voluntary organization in the interwar years. In 1919, women with university degrees founded the Canadian Federation of University Women (CFUW). Initially focused on women's role in social reform and the prevention of war, the CFUW became involved in a wide range of charitable activities and supported, through their scholarship program, the next generation of female scholars. In 1930, the Canadian Federation of Business and Professional Women's Clubs was organized to convince the business community's leaders that better training and fairer treatment for women were ultimately in the interest of business. In Ontario and Nova Scotia, black women established clubs that organized cultural programs, studied African-Canadian history, and worked for better local race relations. Women also generally led the Canadian Home and School (or Parent-Teacher) Associations that mushroomed in the 1920s.

CONCLUSION

With hindsight, it is easy to see that interwar Canada was a society in transition. Older lifestyles rubbed uneasily against the new mass culture and its commercially oriented values. Attracted by American movies, records, magazines, and radio programs, Canadians struggled to establish their own national culture, but it was an uphill battle. The threat of a larger North American culture was balanced by regional, local, and political identities. For cultural minorities, the sense of belonging to smaller groups was equal to or greater than their identification with Canada as a whole. The Great Depression exposed class and gender differences that had been easier to minimize in the better economic times of the 1920s. With the outbreak of the Second World War in September 1939, Canada's fragile unity would again be tested. Could the nation rise above its internal divisions to fight a common enemy?

NOTES

1 Transcribed from Cab Calloway and his Orchestra, recorded 23 December 1930, http://www.heptune.com/minnieth.html.

2 Rebecca Priegert Coulter, "Patrolling the Passions of Youth," in *Edmonton: The Life of a City*, ed. Bob Hesketh and Frances Swyripa (Edmonton: NeWest Press, 1995), 160.

3 Craig Heron, *Booze: A Distilled History* (Toronto: Between the Lines, 2003), 213.

4 Quoted in Vera Fast, "The Labor Church in Winnipeg," in *Prairie Spirit: Perspectives on the Heritage of the United Church of Canada in the West*, ed. Dennis L. Butcher et al. (Winnipeg: University of Manitoba Press, 1985), 242.

5 Cited in Mary Vipond, "Canadian National Consciousness and the Formation of the United Church of Canada," in *Prophets, Priests, and Prodigals: Readings in Canadian Religious History, 1608 to the Present*, ed. Mark G. McGowan and David B. Marshall (Toronto: McGraw-Hill Ryerson, 1992), 169.

6 Cited in Paul J. Stortz and J. Donald Wilson, "Schools, Teachers and Community Influence in North-Central British Columbia," *Histoire sociale/Social History* 26, no. 52 (November 1993), 267.

7 F.R. Scott, *Overture* (Toronto: Ryerson Press, 1945).

8 Ian McKay, "Helen Creighton and the Politics of Antimodernism," in *Myth and Milieu: Atlantic Literature and Culture, 1918–1939*, ed. Gwendolyn Davies (Fredericton: Acadiensis Press, 1993), 16.

9 Bruce Kidd, *The Struggle for Canadian Sport* (Toronto: University of Toronto Press, 1996).

RELATED READINGS IN THIS SERIES

From Primary Documents CD-ROM, Volume II
Restriction of Immigration
History as a Guardian of Living Traditions
Radio Commissioner Manager

SELECTED READING

On the media in Canada during the interwar years, see Mary Vipond, *The Mass Media in Canada* (Toronto: Lorimer, 1989) and *Listening In: The First Decade of Canadian Broadcasting* (Montreal: McGill-Queen's University Press, 1992). On the Dionne quintuplets, see the articles in the special issue of *Journal of Canadian Studies* 29, no. 4 (Winter 1995). Rival views of the survival of the social gospel movement in the interwar period can be found in David B. Marshall, *Secularising the Faith: Canadian Protestant Clergy and the Crisis of Belief, 1850–1940* (Toronto: University of Toronto Press, 1992) and Nancy Christie and Michael Gauvreau, *A Full-Orbed Christianity. The Protestant Churches and Social Welfare in Canada, 1900–1940* (Montreal: McGill-Queen's University Press, 1996).

On interwar missions and the beginnings of doubt about the churches' "civilizing mission," an interesting work is Robert Wright, *A World Mission: Canadian Protestantism and the Quest for a New International Order, 1918–1939* (Montreal: McGill-Queen's University Press, 1991). Works dealing with women missionaries include Myra Rutherdale, *Women and the White Man's God: Gender and Race in the Canadian Mission Field* (Vancouver: UBC Press, 2002); Ruth Compton Brouwer, *Modern Women Modernizing Men: The Changing Missions of Three Professional Women in Asia and Africa, 1902–1969* (Vancouver: UBC Press, 2002); and Shirley James Endicott, *China Diary: The Life of Mary Austin Endicott* (Waterloo, ON: Wilfrid Laurier University Press, 2003). Other useful works on religious developments in this period are Alan L. Hayes, *Anglicans in Canada: Controversies and Identity in Historical Perspective* (Champaign, IL: University of Illinois Press, 2004); Robert K. Burkinshaw, *Pilgrims in Lotus Land: Conservative Protestantism in British Columbia, 1917–1981* (Montreal: McGill-Queen's University Press, 1995); Royden K. Loewen, *Family, Church, and Market: A Mennonite Community in the Old and New Worlds, 1850–1930* (Toronto: University of Toronto Press, 1995); Michael Gauvreau, *The Evangelical Century: College and Creed in English Canada from the Great Revival to the Great Depression* (Montreal: McGill-Queen's University Press, 1991); Terrence Murphy and Gerald Stortz, eds., *Creed and Culture: The Place of English-Speaking Catholics in Canadian Society, 1750–1930* (Montreal: McGill-Queen's University Press, 1993); and Neil Semple, *The Lord's Dominion: The History of Canadian Methodism* (Montreal: McGill-Queen's University Press, 1996). On issues that caused endless difficulties for churches, see Craig Heron, *Booze: A Distilled History* (Toronto: Between the Lines, 2003); Robert A. Campbell, *Sit Down and Drink: Regulating Vancouver's Beer Parlours, 1925–1954* (Toronto: University of Toronto Press, 2000); Suzanne Morton, *At Odds: Gambling and Canadians, 1919–1969* (Toronto: University of Toronto Press, 2003); and Angus McLaren and Arlene Tigar McLaren, *The Bedroom and the State: The Changing Practices and Politics of Contraception and Abortion in Canada, 1890–1980*, 2nd ed. (Toronto: Oxford University Press, 1997). On the debates about "narcotic" drugs in this period, see Catherine Carstairs, *Jailed for Possession: Illegal Drug Use, Regulation, and Power in Canada, 1920–1961* (Toronto: University of Toronto Press, 2006). The role of the RCMP in moral surveillance is explored in Steve Hewitt, *Riding to the Rescue: The Transformation of the RCMP in Alberta and Saskatchewan, 1914–1939* (Toronto: University of Toronto Press, 2006).

Children's experiences during this period are described in Neil Sutherland, "'We Always Had Things to Do': The Paid and Unpaid Work of Anglophone Children Between the 1920s and the 1960s," *Labour/Le Travail* 25 (Spring 1990), 105–41. The changing world of adolescents is discussed in Cynthia Comacchio, *The Dominion of Youth: Adolescence and the Making of Modern Canada* (Waterloo: Wilfrid Laurier University Press, 2006). On higher education, important works include A.B. McKillop, *Matters of Mind: The University in Ontario, 1791–1951* (Toronto: University of Toronto Press, 1994); Paul Axelrod, *Making a Middle Class: Student Life in English Canada During the Thirties* (Montreal: McGill-Queen's University Press, 1990); Paul Axelrod and John G. Reid, eds., *Youth, University and Canadian Society: Essays in the Social History of Higher Education* (Montreal: McGill-Queen's University Press, 1989); and G.A. Rawlyk, ed., *Canadian Baptists and Higher Education* (Montreal: McGill-Queen's University Press, 1988). On youth as a social force in Quebec, see Louise Bienvenue, *Quand la jeunesse entre en scène: l'Action catholique avant la Révolution tranquille* (Montreal: Boréal, 2003).

The emergence of a radical tradition in Canadian literature during the interwar period is discussed in James Doyle, *Progressive Heritage: The Evolution of a Politically Radical Literary Tradition in Canada* (Waterloo, ON: Wilfrid Laurier University Press, 2002). On art history for the period, see J. Russell Harper, *Painting in Canada: A History*, 2nd ed. (Toronto: University of Toronto Press, 1977) and Ann Davis, *The Logic of Ecstasy: Canadian Mystical Painting, 1920–1940* (Toronto: University of Toronto Press, 1992).

On sports, excellent overviews are Colin D. Howell, *Blood, Sweat, and Cheers: Sport and the Making of Modern Canada* (Toronto: University of Toronto Press, 2001); Bruce Kidd, *The Struggle for Canadian Sport* (Toronto: University of Toronto Press, 1996); and M. Ann Hall, *The Girl and the Game: A History of Women's Sport in Canada* (Peterborough, ON: Broadview Press, 2002). Also see Colin Howell, *Northern Sandlots: A Social History of Maritime Baseball* (Toronto: University of Toronto Press, 1995) and Ron Hotchkiss, "'The Matchless Six': Canadian Women at the Olympics, 1928," *The Beaver* 73, no. 5 (October–November 1993), 23–42.

In addition to the works on regional social developments cited in Chapter 12, see Ian McKay, *The Quest of the Folk: Antimodernism and Cultural Selection in Twentieth-Century Nova Scotia* (Montreal: McGill-Queen's University Press, 1994) and Gwendolyn Davies, ed., *Myth and Milieu: Atlantic Literature and Culture, 1918–1939* (Fredericton: Acadiensis Press, 1993).

CHAPTER 14

Canada's World War, 1939–1945

TIMELINE

1939 — Second World War begins; Liberals under Adélard Godbout win Quebec election

1940 — Fall of France; Liberal government re-elected; National Resources Mobilization Act passed; federal unemployment insurance plan established; Permanent Joint Board on Defence created

1941 — Battle of Hong Kong; Canadian Women's Army Corps and RCAF Women's Division established

1942 — Dieppe landing; national plebiscite on conscription; Japanese evacuated from coastal areas of British Columbia; Kirkland Lake gold miners' strike; national campaign launched to recruit women for war work; Women's Royal Canadian Naval Service established

1943 — Invasion of Sicily

1944 — Liberation of France; Canada's first nuclear reactor facility established at Chalk River; PC 1003 recognizes right to collective bargaining; parliament passes legislation to implement family allowances

1945 — Second World War ends; United Nations established; Liberals re-elected; major strike at Ford Motor Company

On 3 March 1943, Joseph Goebbels, Adolph Hitler's minister of propaganda, noted in his diary: "It drives one mad to think that any old Canadian boor, who probably can't even find Europe on the globe, flies to Europe from his super-rich country which his people don't know how to exploit, and here bombards a continent with a crowded population."[1] Goebbels had reason to be concerned. By 1943, Canada was turning out fighter planes, pilots, and bombs at a rate few could have imagined in 1939. The sad irony of war was recognized by people other than Goebbels. What Canadians seemed unable to do in peacetime they did with surprising ease during the Second World War: they produced their way out of the Great Depression.

Canadians had hoped that the Great War would be the war to end all wars, but it was not to be. In 1939, Canadians were again fighting in Europe against Germany and its allies. There seemed little choice but to try to stop Adolf Hitler, who appeared to be determined to create a new world order in which he and his Nazi followers would reign supreme over peoples they deemed inferior. As in the First World War, Canadians were allied with Great Britain, France, and the United States, but this time Canadians declared war in their own right and emerged from it as a nation to be reckoned with on the world stage.

HITLER'S WAR

When Hitler came to power in 1933, he moved quickly to pursue a fascist program for the reconstitution of a German "homeland," which included destroying other nations and cultures. Italy's fascist leader, Benito Mussolini, gravitated toward Hitler, especially after Great Britain and France tried to thwart plans for an Italian empire in Africa. In 1938, Germany annexed Austria and then gobbled up Czechoslovakia.

Hitler Youth rally in Nuremberg Stadium on National Socialist Party Day, 1933.
© Stapleton Collection/Corbis

Italy annexed Albania in the spring of 1939, while in August Hitler signed a non-aggression pact with the Soviet Union under Joseph Stalin, freeing the way for the depredation of their mutual neighbour, Poland. In the Pacific, the Japanese had long been running roughshod over China. On 3 September, two days after Hitler had invaded Poland, Great Britain and France declared war on Germany. One week later, on 10 September, Canada joined the war against the Nazis.

Even more than the First World War, this war was easy for most Canadians to see as a struggle between good and evil. It was also a difficult war to avoid. With submarines, fast surface warships, and long-range aircraft capable of spanning great distances in a short time, every country in the world was vulnerable. Indeed, the Japanese bombing of Pearl Harbor in Hawaii on 7 December 1941 jarred the United States out of its own isolationism and into the war.

Although the Canadian government invoked the War Measures Act to ensure that it had all the powers it needed to fight an all-out war, it was initially slow to mobilize the nation's military and economic might. This policy earned Prime Minister William Lyon Mackenzie King harsh criticism from Premier Mitchell Hepburn of Ontario, among others, but it helped reassure Quebecers that this would be Canada's war, not one in which Canada's wartime policy would be dictated by Great Britain. Early in 1939, prompted by his Quebec lieutenant, Ernest Lapointe, and by the

Conservative Party's similar pledge, King had promised Quebec that his government would not impose conscription for overseas service in the event of war. It was a pledge that he would have occasion to repeat in two elections held during the early months of the conflict.

CONSCRIPTION, ROUND TWO

After war was declared, Quebec premier Maurice Duplessis hoped to gain an easy victory for his government by calling a snap election and making Canada's involvement in the war the major issue in the campaign. Quebec's ministers in King's cabinet threatened to resign if Duplessis won. Fearing that without its Quebec contingent, the cabinet might renege on King's promise not to impose conscription, a majority of Quebecers elected the provincial Liberal Party, led by Adélard Godbout, to office.

Hepburn's stinging criticisms of Ottawa's failure to pursue an all-out war effort prompted King to dissolve parliament in January and call a national election for March 1940. Campaigning on a policy of voluntary enlistment, the Liberals won a resounding victory, taking over 51 percent of the popular vote and 184 out of 245 seats in the House of Commons.

King was shrewd or just plain lucky to have called an election when he did. In April 1940, Hitler's forces struck down Denmark and Norway and then conducted a blitzkrieg—literally a lightning war—through the Netherlands, Belgium, and France. The surrender of France early in June and the evacuation of the British Expeditionary Force from Dunkirk raised fears that Great Britain might also have been defeated. As Great Britain's largest surviving ally, Canada was suddenly forced to consider a much larger contribution to the war effort than King and his cabinet had originally envisaged. The government moved swiftly to enact the National Resources Mobilization Act (NRMA), which provided for the conscription of soldiers for home defence and state control of economic resources.

As the war dragged on, pressures from army commanders, from within cabinet, from opposition members, and from many Canadians caused King to re-evaluate his position on conscription. He decided to call a national plebiscite on 27 April 1942, which asked Canadians for a "yes" or "no" vote on whether the government should be released from its pledge not to impose conscription for overseas service. While overall,

64 percent of Canadians voted "yes," at least 85 percent of Quebec Francophones demanded that King honour his original promise. King continued to resist imposing conscription, but even the threat of it was enough to spark the formation of the Bloc populaire canadien, a new nationalist political party in Quebec, and to return the ardently anti-conscriptionist Union Nationale to power in a 1944 provincial election.

King did his best to avoid conscription, including firing pro-conscription defence minister J.C. Ralston. In November 1944, Ralston was replaced by General A.G.L. McNaughton, King's choice in 1939 to command the army overseas. When McNaughton failed to secure the necessary voluntary enlistments, the government passed an order-in-council in late November 1944 allowing the armed forces to dispatch 16 000 NRMA men to overseas duty.

Commonly called "Zombies"—a word made fashionable in Hollywood as an African-Caribbean reference to men who had no souls—NRMA men were not pleased about this turn of events. In Terrace, British Columbia, they seized an anti-tank gun to defend themselves against officers trying to send them overseas; in London, Ontario, 600 men of the Oxford Rifles went absent without leave; and in Drummond, Quebec, 2000 civilians attacked RCMP and military police sent to hunt down deserters. These outbursts of violence went undisclosed in the media, whose war reporting was subject to censorship. In the end, only 13 000 NRMA men were sent overseas.

As in the First World War, conscription strengthened the credibility of Quebec nationalists and added to feelings of betrayal among French Canadians. Unlike Borden and the Conservative Party in the First World War, King avoided a backlash from Quebec in the subsequent election because it seemed clear that he had done nearly everything humanly possible to avoid conscription.

ENLISTMENTS

Overall Canadian participation in the war was impressive. Nearly 1.1 million men and women joined the forces, including 100 000 through the NRMA, from a

The provincial wing of the Bloc populaire canadien was led by André Laurendeau, a young journalist shown here speaking in Montreal before the 1944 election.
Centre de Recherche Lionel Groulx/P2/T1, 53.4

population estimated at 11.5 million in 1941. Most served in the army, although about 250 000 joined the Royal Canadian Air Force (RCAF) and nearly 100 000 joined the Royal Canadian Navy (RCN). More than 42 000 died in service, including more than 17 000 members of the RCAF, which suffered the highest proportion of casualties. More than 54 000 others were wounded or injured.

French-Canadian enlistment in the Second World War was significantly higher than in the First World War. Nineteen percent of the volunteers for overseas service were French Canadians, compared with 12 percent in the earlier war, and about 37 percent of the men called up for home defence were French Canadians. Like their English-Canadian counterparts, French Canadians who enlisted in the early stages of the war often did so to seek adventure. Others simply wanted employment. Eventually, the wartime economy led to a labour shortage, and recruitment became more difficult.

As in the First World War, Canadians were relatively lucky. The total dead and wounded in the Second World War reached a staggering 55 million. Many

A member of the WRCNs (Wrens) operating direction-finding equipment in New Brunswick, 1945.
Library and Archives Canada/PA142540

stretcher bearers, and cooks, women gradually took on less traditional roles such as mechanics, truck drivers, technicians, and spies. Margaret Eaton achieved the highest rank of any woman in the services when she was made acting colonel and director-general of the CWAC in April 1944.

While women's usefulness was never really questioned, their morality was. Rumours were rife about their lax morals, especially in the CWAC, where, it was alleged, women had a high incidence of "illegitimate" children and venereal disease. Men were allowed, and indeed encouraged, to vent their sexual energies; women, quite clearly, were not. Nor did women receive the same pay and benefits as men, even when they performed the same job. Women complained about their unequal status and the National Council of Women took up their cause, but the pay gap, while narrowed, was never completely eliminated. When the war ended, all three women's services were abandoned.

DESCENT INTO WAR

Just before the surrender of France in June 1940, Italy entered the war, greatly increasing the pressure on British armed forces in the Mediterranean and North Africa. With the benefit of French air bases, Hitler's Luftwaffe conducted a destructive blitz on London and other British cities beginning in the summer of 1940 and launched a devastating U-boat campaign against Allied shipping in the Atlantic. Instead of invading Great Britain, as was expected, Hitler turned his army on the Soviet Union in June 1941, ignoring his non-aggression pact with Stalin. The United States entered the war against Germany and Japan at the end of the year, but it took time for its presence to be felt. Meanwhile, Japan destroyed the Far East fleets of the United States and Great Britain, defeated the British and Australians in Malaya and Singapore, and captured the American army in the Philippines. In June 1942, Japanese forces occupied islands in the Aleutian chain of Alaska.

It is in this context that two incidents in the war, one in Hong Kong and the other in British Columbia, must be understood. In December 1941, two battalions of Canadian troops, totalling nearly 2000 men, were involved in an effort to defend the British colony of Hong Kong against the Japanese. Almost 300

were civilians, killed by bombs, invading armies, or concentration camp personnel. The Soviet Union alone lost 20 million people; and 6 million Jews were slaughtered by the Nazis.

Although only men participated in combat, some 50 000 women served in the Canadian armed forces. Women began volunteering their services as soon as war was declared. The military establishment was reluctant to accept them, but, in the face of manpower shortages and the British example, it finally relented to the extent of creating separate female auxiliaries in the various branches of the armed services. In 1941, the army created the Canadian Women's Army Corps (CWAC) and the air force organized the RCAF Women's Division. The navy followed suit in 1942 with the Women's Royal Canadian Naval Service. In all, the navy enlisted 7126 women, the army 21 642, and the air force 17 467. There were also 4439 nurses in the Canadian Nursing Service. One nurse and three members of the RCAF (WD) were killed in action.[2]

The military was careful to keep women's divisions separate and subordinate to those of men. Initially slotted into jobs as nurses, clerks, secretaries, drivers,

Japanese-Canadian internees packing to leave for camps in the interior of British Columbia.
Tak Toyota/Library and Archives Canada/C046350

Canadians lost their lives and another 1700 were taken prisoner. Mistreatment in prison camps in Hong Kong and as forced labour in Japanese mines killed nearly 300 before the end of the war. At the time and later, there was much criticism of political and military leaders for allowing Canadians to get involved in such a hopeless campaign.

In February 1942, two months after Japan's attack on American territory at Pearl Harbor, President Franklin Roosevelt announced that, by reason of military necessity, persons of Japanese ancestry were to be removed from the Pacific coast of the United States. A few days later, the Canadian government decided it would remove nearly 22 000 people of Japanese ancestry—nearly three-quarters of whom had been born in Canada or were naturalized Canadians—from the coastal areas of British Columbia. Their homes, businesses, and personal property, initially placed under the "protection" of the federal government, were auctioned to the highest bidders in 1943. Other than suspicions about a few individuals who were

already well known to the local RCMP, Ottawa had no evidence of any disloyalty of Japanese Canadians and no one was ever charged with treason, yet Mackenzie King's government suspended the civil liberties of the entire Japanese-Canadian population until 1949.

Coupled with hysteria created by the war, the long-standing racist attitudes of many British Columbians toward Japanese Canadians made it difficult for the federal government to pursue a more humane policy. About 700 men who had expressed support for a Japanese victory or had protested too vigorously against Ottawa's repressive policies were legally interned in a prisoner-of-war camp in Angler, Ontario. Women, children, the old, and the sick were unofficially interned in abandoned mining towns in the interior of British Columbia. Able-bodied men were separated from their families and sent to work in road camps in the province. Families who wished to remain together were shipped to sugar beet farms in Alberta and Manitoba. Among the children removed from their homes in 1942 were David Suzuki, the future scientist, and Joy Kogawa, whose 1981 novel, *Obasan*, dealt with her family's internment.

Beginning in May 1945, all Japanese Canadians were forced to choose between deportation to war-devastated Japan or relocation east of the Rockies. To make deportation a more attractive option, Ottawa offered money and free passage to those who were destitute or too elderly or infirm to begin life again in eastern Canada. Nearly 4000 people were shipped to Japan between May and December 1946. Starving and desperate in post-war Japan, some of the deportees tried to return to Canada, but found a mountain of bureaucratic red tape blocking their re-entry. It was not until the 1980s that the Canadian government officially acknowledged its mistreatment of Japanese Canadians during the war and provided compensation to surviving members of the community in recognition of their suffering.

THE WAR ON LAND

In Europe, the war continued to go badly for the Allies. Although the German army was stalled in its drive to Moscow, Allied efforts to create a division in France ended in dismal failure. An ill-conceived landing on French beaches at Dieppe in August 1942 left 907 Canadians dead and almost 2000 as prisoners. Only in the Middle East was there good news. In November, at El Alamein, the British Eighth Army finally broke through the German and Italian lines, forcing Field Marshal Erwin Rommel and his hitherto seemingly invincible Afrika Korps into retreat. At the same time, the Russians were fighting the Germans to a standstill at Stalingrad. A staggering 850 000 Germans and their Italian, Hungarian, and Romanian allies lost their lives in the campaign. In December, the 80 000 survivors surrendered. The war had reached a turning point.

By 1943, the Canadian Army Overseas had expanded into a full field army, the 1st Canadian Army, with two corps, three infantry and two armoured (tank) divisions, and a wide array of additional formations and support units. Aside from the disastrous Dieppe raid and some smaller operations, the army stood guard in Great Britain until the liberation of western Europe began with the Allied invasion of Sicily and then mainland Italy in the summer of 1943. The 1st Canadian Infantry Division took part in these operations, which became increasingly difficult as the Allies pushed up the boot of Italy against fortified lines the Germans had established in the mountainous terrain. During December 1943, in appalling conditions amid winter rains, more than 23 000 men from the 1st Division were killed or wounded in bitter fighting for the town of Ortona, on the Adriatic coast. In early 1944, the Canadian presence in Italy expanded, playing a key role in breaking through the strongly defended approaches to Rome.

Meanwhile, there had been a massive build-up of forces in Great Britain for the invasion of France at Normandy on 6 June 1944. Among the initial assault force was the 3rd Canadian Infantry Division. More than 100 warships of the RCN formed part of the naval forces that cleared mines, kept enemy warships and submarines at bay, landed troops, and provided artillery support to the soldiers struggling ashore. The huge air armada that forced back the Luftwaffe and saturated the German defences with bombs included many squadrons of the RCAF. During the following weeks, the 1st Canadian Army, under the command of Lieutenant-General H.D.G. Crerar, crossed to France. The push inland from the beaches was a slow-moving, brutal campaign, with the Germans concentrating their strongest armoured forces in the British-Canadian sector. By the last week in August, two German armies had been destroyed, with some 400 000 casualties, but the Canadians also paid heavily, with 5000 dead and more than 13 000 wounded, representing some of the heaviest losses of any Allied formation.

After the defeat of the main German forces in Normandy, the 1st Canadian Army moved up the coast of the English Channel, clearing strongholds. The culmination of these operations was a bitter five-week battle in October and early November, which, in the end, opened the Belgian port of Antwerp. The port was essential to maintaining the supplies of all the Allied armies in northwest Europe, but was opened at the cost of more than 6000 killed or wounded Canadians.

THE WAR AT SEA

The Royal Canadian Navy played a significant role in the war effort. After a shaky start, the RCN provided most of the escorts for the North Atlantic convoys that sustained Britain and the invasion force. In addition, the navy participated in the Normandy campaign, helped protect British waters against German U-boats,

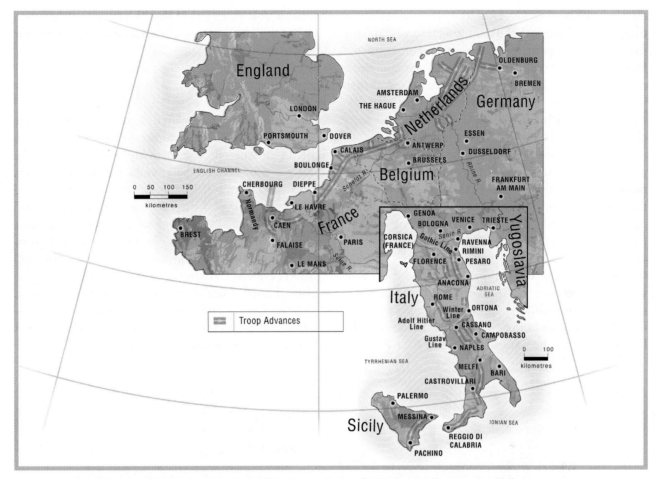

MAP 14.1 **The European front, 1944–1945–Italian Campaign and Northwest Europe Campaign.**

joined in offensive strikes at German naval bases in Norway, and contributed escort ships to convoys that supplied Russian forces through the Arctic port of Murmansk.

These achievements did not come easily. At the outbreak of the war, there were only six destroyers, a handful of small minesweepers, and no more than 3500 personnel in the RCN. The plan was to increase this force gradually, primarily for the protection of Canadian waters. The fall of France in 1940 necessitated a different strategy. With access to French ports, "wolf-packs" of German U-boats began to slaughter Allied merchant ship convoys. In response to Great Britain's urgent appeal in May 1941, the RCN rushed the small corvettes, intended for coastal defence, into high-seas service to provide anti-submarine escorts for convoys between Newfoundland and British waters. At the same time, programs to build corvettes and other anti-submarine vessels in Canada were expanded, and

recent recruits, ill-trained for their difficult mission, were pressed into service.

The entry of the United States into the war brought U-boats streaming into Canadian and American coastal waters in January 1942. Because the Americans were woefully short of anti-submarine vessels, the RCN was obliged to help the Americans on their east coast and in the Caribbean while maintaining its Newfoundland force and defending Canadian waters. The RCN faced a serious challenge in the Gulf of St. Lawrence, where deep waters gave advantage to the U-boats. During the war, two small warships and 19 merchant ships were sunk in the gulf and in the lower reaches of the St. Lawrence River. Among them was the Sydney–Port aux Basques ferry, which went down in October 1942 with a loss of 237 lives.

Convoys sailing under the protection of Canadian escorts from Newfoundland to Ireland suffered heavy losses in 1942. In early November, a convoy bound for the United Kingdom lost 15 of its 42 merchant ships, a tragedy that along with the mounting death toll finally sparked a new approach. The routes of three of the four Canadian mid-Atlantic escort groups were changed in early 1943 so that they could use British base facilities to get improved equipment and advanced training. In all, 12 000 Canadians in the merchant marine lost their lives on sunken ships.

Other measures to improve the RCN's escort organization gradually came into effect. The British turned over additional destroyers to the Canadians so that they could be used to reinforce the little corvettes. In April 1943, Rear-Admiral L.W. Murray, RCN, based at Halifax, became commander-in-chief of the Canadian Northwest Atlantic theatre. He was the only Canadian to command an Allied theatre of war. Soon thereafter, RCAF bombers were made responsible for providing support for the convoys across the whole breadth of the North Atlantic. During the last two years of the war, the RCN and RCAF played a major role in ensuring that thousands of ships and tens of millions of tonnes of cargo safely reached their destinations.

THE WAR IN THE AIR

Soon after war was declared, Canada agreed to play host to the British Commonwealth Air Training Plan (BCATP), whereby Canadian and other Allied pilots and air crews would be trained for the war effort. Canada was an ideal location for the program. It had ample space beyond the range of enemy aircraft and was close to vital American aircraft industries, upon which the success of the war in the air depended. At its height, the BCATP employed more than 100 000 ground crew at 231 sites across the country. The program trained more than 130 000 pilots, navigators, flight engineers, and other aviation specialists, representing almost half the total air crew supplied by Great Britain and the Commonwealth for the war effort.

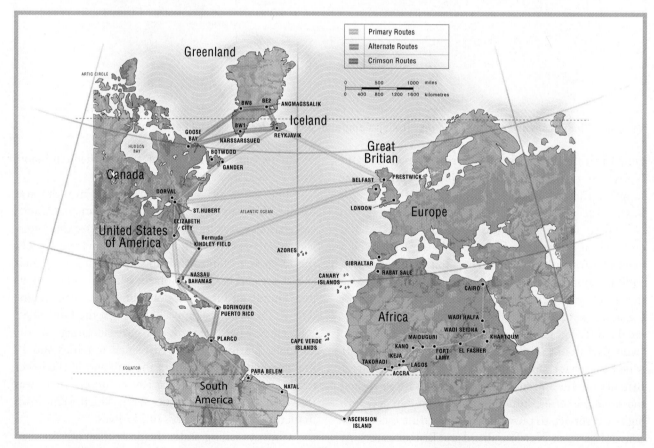

MAP 14.2 **Principal routes flown by Ferry Command, 1940–1945.**

An Enduring Controversy

Canada's participation in overseas wars has often sparked debate, but few topics have generated more controversy than the Allied bomber offensive against Germany. Twice—in 1993 and again in 2007—attempts to interpret Canada's involvement in the bombing campaign were the subject of a Senate committee investigation.[3]

In January 1992, the Canadian Broadcasting Corporation (CBC) and Société Radio-Canada (SRC) aired *Valour and the Horror*, a three part documentary on the Second World War, written by Brian and Terrance McKenna. The second episode, "Death by Moonlight: Bomber Command," emphasized the extraordinary risks to which air crews had been subjected and the questionable morality of targeting civilians.

In the weeks following the airing, the CBC was deluged with angry letters, many of them from veterans, who questioned the accuracy and tone of the series, especially the segment on Bomber Command. Critics demanded that the film be withdrawn from circulation, while its defenders argued that it was produced in the time-honoured documentary tradition of raising troubling questions and that suppressing it would be a violation of freedom of expression.

Hoping to gain political mileage, members of the Progressive Conservative government denounced the film in the House of Commons and in 1993 organized a Senate hearing as a platform for critics. Meanwhile, a group of air force veterans launched a $500-million class action defamation suit against the filmmakers and their associates, declaring that their case was "about right and wrong; good and evil; white and black; truth and falsehood."[4] Academic historians, long accustomed to debates about and reinterpretations of the past, were summoned to support both sides in the controversy, and thus were unable to establish a historical truth that might put an end to the matter. Although the case was eventually settled out of court, it put a "chill" on writers and filmmakers attempting to present revisionist history.

Shortly after the opening of the Canadian War Museum in Ottawa in 2005, a group of veterans, still smarting from the earlier confrontation, objected to the wording on a panel interpreting Bomber Command. The museum's curators had tried to head off controversy by entitling the panel "An Enduring Controversy" and directly raising the issues that sparked debate, but this approach was too much for some of the veterans, who felt that the heroism and sacrifice of the young men involved were somehow being called into question.

In an effort to blunt the escalating controversy, museum administrators submitted the issue to a blue ribbon committee made up of four historians—David Bercuson, Serge Bernier, Desmond Morton, and Margaret MacMillan. Although the academics were unanimous in their opinion that the panel was accurate and balanced in its interpretation, two of the four committee members—Bercuson and Bernier—suggested changes to the wording and images used in the panel that might assuage some of the veterans' concerns. Professor Desmond Morton, alarmed by the precedent that would be set in making the changes demanded by the veterans, argued, "A museum is not a monument to opinion. It is a place of learning, argument, and of struggling to understand the truth. Truth does not emerge from the suppression of facts."[5]

Since the museum was reluctant to be seen as caving in to one group or another on a matter of interpretation, it initially decided to maintain the panel as it was originally conceptualized. This time, a Senate committee convened by Liberal members of the Senate in May 2007 heard testimony from the aggrieved veterans and their supporters. Ultimately, the museum panel was expanded to provide more information on Bomber Command, but neither side was entirely happy with the outcome.

The controversy over the interpretation of the Allied bombing offensive against Germany raises the larger question of who has the authority to interpret the past and what role the public in general—and the actors in an event in particular—have in determining how public commemorations of the past are presented. Although the search for an elusive historical truth motivates many people, including academic historians, many are beginning to understand that history is never really past and that it will continue to generate new interpretations and controversy as long as humans have historical memory.

MORE TO THE STORY

War Artists

During the First World War, Lord Beaverbrook commissioned artists to record Canada's war effort. It was the first large official commission for Canadian artists. Men with well-established reputations, such as Maurice Cullen, and promising unknowns, such as David Milne, were hired for the task. So, too, were four men who would later be known as members of the Group of Seven: A.Y. Jackson, Frederick Varley, Arthur Lismer, and Frank Johnston.

In 1943, the war art program was reactivated, and artists were commissioned into the three divisions of the armed services. For the first time, female artists were included to document women's contribution: Molly Lamb eventually received a lieutenant's commission in the CWAC; Pegi Nicol MacLeod painted many aspects of the women's forces; Paraskeva Clark and Alma Duncan recorded women's work in the war industries.

Alex Colville, *Tragic Landscape*, 1945.
Beaverbrook Collection of War Art © Canadian War Museum

Paraskeva Clark, *Maintenance Jobs in the Hangar*, 1945.
Beaverbrook Collection of War Art © Canadian War Museum

Another successful joint venture with the British and the Americans was Ferry Command, which was responsible for delivering planes built in North America to Great Britain. In 1939, the idea of flying planes across the Atlantic rather than sending them by ship was denounced as visionary nonsense by most officials in the British Air Ministry. Fewer than 100 successful transatlantic flights had been made since the first one in 1919. To the surprise of many skeptics, both the idea and the planes flew. Based in Montreal, Ferry Command flew nearly 10 000 aircraft from enlarged or newly created air bases such as Gander and Goose Bay to Great Britain. At least 500 people lost their lives in Ferry Command, but

it was, in the words of historian Carl A. Christie, "one of the most spectacular achievements of the war."[6]

Far more controversial was the Allied bomber offensive against Germany. From its bases in northeastern England, the Royal Air Force's Bomber Command targeted German cities in an effort to disrupt industrial production and reduce German morale. Because the attacks were often on city centres or residential districts rather than industrial areas, critics claim that the campaign was immoral. The bomber offensive has also been judged by some scholars as ineffective and continued even when it became clear that the loss of lives among the air crews was unacceptably high.

Artists captured on canvas some of the worst horrors of the war. Charles Goldhamer painted RCAF flyers at a plastic surgery hospital in England; Aba Bayefsky and Alex Colville had the difficult job of documenting the Belsen concentration camp; Charles Comfort captured impressions of the Dieppe Raid and the Italian Campaign. Confronted with a larger-than-life situation, Canadian war artists produced some of their finest, if most disturbing, work during the war.

Charles Comfort, *Via Dolorosa, Ortona.*
Beaverbrook Collection of War Art © Canadian War Museum

Charles Goldhamer, *Burnt Airman with Wig,* 1945.
Beaverbrook Collection of War Art © Canadian War Museum

There is little doubt that the Allied bomber attacks were deadly. In all, some 560 000 Germans were killed and even more injured, most of them men over military age, women, and children. Although Bomber Command initially lacked the electronic and navigational aids to hit industrial sites with precision, even when more precise attacks became possible, the Royal Air Force chose to continue with area raids directed against German civilians. Historians Desmond Morton and J.L. Granatstein argue that Bomber Command was doing what it set out to do—hit back at Germany, whose Luftwaffe had killed more than 13 000 civilians in London and other British cities—but sinking to the level of the enemy in no way justifies the strategy.

On the question of efficiency, Allied bombing, at least initially, spurred the Nazis to greater productivity, just as the bombing of London in 1940 had made the British determined to carry on. Only in the final months of 1944 did German production of war materiel begin a rapid decline. Allied bombing seems to have made a contribution to this outcome. Germany was obliged to employ over half a million workers to repair bomb damage and almost a million men to operate the flak defences around their cities, personnel who could otherwise have been used in factories or on the battlefields.

As for the wisdom of the British air marshals who oversaw the bombing offensive, the evidence is mixed. There is little doubt that the head of Bomber Command, Sir Arthur Harris, was a single-minded individual, but his views on the strategic importance of air power to the war effort were shared by other Allied commanders. Nor is there any question that the bombing offensive was pressed in spite of the high casualty rates among the bomber crews themselves. Only one airman in three survived a 30-mission tour of duty in 1942.

Loss rates continued to rise the following year when the Canadian government convinced the Air Ministry to form an RCAF group—No. 6 Group—in Bomber Command. As a junior unit, 6 Group, which eventually totalled 14 squadrons, was assigned inferior aircraft and equipment and was stationed in the Vale of York, farther from their targets than any other group in England. The results were predictable. From 5 March to 24 June 1943, 6 Group lost 100 aircraft, morale sagged, and an increasing number of missions were aborted or failed to reach their objectives.

In February 1944, Air Vice-Marshal C.M. McEwan was appointed to bring his professional energy to bear on 6 Group. Better training, new aircraft, and a reprieve from missions in Germany while Bomber Command

An allied correspondent stands amid the rubble in the aftermath of the Hiroshima bombing of 1945
Stanley Troutman/CP Photo Archive

supported the Normandy invasion netted better results. By the end of 1944, 6 Group boasted the highest accuracy and the lowest casualty rate of any group in Bomber Command. Such achievements, however, do little to counter critics, who argue that the money and manpower committed to Bomber Command would have been much better spent on the understaffed and poorly equipped convoy service or in maintaining army ranks so that conscription could have been avoided. But fighting wars is always easier with hindsight.

VICTORY AT LAST

Early in 1945, the Canadians in Italy joined their comrades in the Netherlands for the final campaign. On the eastern front, the Red Army from the Soviet Union advanced on Germany, while the western front crumbled fast under Allied assault. Overrun from all sides, with their leader dead by his own hand, the Germans surrendered on 5 May.

The war in the Pacific dragged on for three more months and became the occasion for another embarrassing incident for the navy. When Canada agreed to provide support for a final drive against Japan, the crew members of the HMCS *Uganda*, already in Okinawa, refused to participate on the grounds that the war with Germany was over and they had not enlisted to fight Japan. Since only volunteers were authorized for the Pacific front, the men claimed they were not obliged to fight and had the right to come home. Before the *Uganda* reached Canadian shores, the war had come to an abrupt halt following the dropping of atomic bombs on Hiroshima and Nagasaki. On 14 August, the Japanese surrendered. Canada and the world had entered the atomic age.

Rich in uranium, a necessary ingredient of atomic energy, Canada played a major role in the production of the first atomic bomb. Early in the Second World War, a team of British, European, and Canadian scientists under the umbrella of the National Research Council had begun working on aspects of the atomic energy puzzle in laboratories based in Montreal. Canada also supplied the uranium for the Manhattan

Project, the code name for top-secret research, based in the United States, on the deadliest weapon ever produced. The Combined Policy Committee, consisting of three Americans, two British, and one Canadian—Minister of Munitions and Supply C.D. Howe—was established to oversee the project. In September 1945, Canada's first nuclear reactor facility was up and running at Chalk River, but, by that time, the military's use of atomic energy had already demonstrated its effectiveness.

THE BUSINESS OF WAR

On the surface, the Second World War had much the same impact on the Canadian economy as the First World War. It pulled the nation out of an economic slump, expanded production in all sectors of the economy, and dramatically increased export sales. On closer inspection, it was obvious that the country that had declared war on Germany in 1939 was vastly different from the one that had ridden to war on Great Britain's coattails in 1914.

Following a decade of increasing intervention in the economy, the government was better equipped in 1939 than it had been in 1914 to coordinate a major war effort. The system of planning, rationing, taxation, and wage and price controls imposed by the federal government early in the Second World War prevented the devastating inflation that had seriously disrupted the economy in the First World War. From April 1940, the Department of Munitions and Supply, under its energetic minister C.D. Howe, was given sweeping powers to bring wartime production to new heights of efficiency. With the help of members of Canada's business community, who were seconded to Ottawa, Howe expanded existing industries, created new ones, and focused the total resources of the country on the successful prosecution of the war.

The federal government's role in the war economy was pervasive. Its 28 Crown corporations produced everything from synthetic rubber to airplanes. In 1943, Ottawa made the Canadian Wheat Board the exclusive international sales agent for the nation's precious wheat crop. Under the auspices of the Wartime Prices and Trade Board, an army of controllers, regulators, and troubleshooters fanned out across the country allocating output, rationing consumer purchases, and

cutting through red tape. The federal civil service more than doubled, from 46 000 in 1939 to 116 000 in 1945. Ottawa would never return to its pre-war size and sleepy pace.

In the First World War, federal spending represented 10–15 percent of the GNP. By 1944, Ottawa's expenditures accounted for nearly 40 percent of GNP. Extensive taxation of corporate and personal incomes, the sale of Victory Bonds, and careful regulation of the money supply through the Bank of Canada enabled Canadians to finance their war without massive foreign borrowing.

Despite the impressive record, Canada's wartime economy encountered problems. Britain imposed exchange controls, including restrictions on the convertibility of sterling into dollars. As Britain's wartime purchases in Canada escalated and Canada came to depend on the United States for war supplies, Canadians faced the prospect of having a huge surplus of sterling and a crippling deficit in American currency. Ottawa responded with stringent exchange controls, monitored by the Foreign Exchange Control Board. Imports were permitted only under licence. By 1940, there were restrictions on travel to the United States and an embargo on the importation of many commodities from countries outside the sterling bloc. Still, the Canadian trade deficit with the United States mounted alarmingly.

Canada could do little to solve the problem. During the interwar years, Canadian and American industry had become so integrated that virtually everything Canada produced included American components. Parts for Canadian automobile factories, coal for Stelco's furnaces, and machinery for mining companies all came from the United States. The problem was eventually solved when the United States entered the war in 1941. By that time, North America already functioned as a unit in defence production, and the problem for Canada became too much, rather than too little, American exchange.

The Second World War tended to reinforce Canadian economic geography. Wartime production was initially expanded in existing industries, and virtually all plants built and operated by the government were located in the industrial heartland of the country. There were some notable exceptions. Winnipeg became a centre for munitions and communications

The Toronto Transit Commission offered women drivers full rates during wartime labour shortages.
TTC/14906

Day care was a problem for mothers who took jobs in the paid labour force. This Mi'kmaq woman brought her child with her to the Pictou shipyards in 1943.
Library and Archives Canada/PA116154

industries. Adjacent to Alberta's oil and natural gas reserves, Calgary was the obvious site for nitrogen and high-octane fuel production. Vancouver sprouted a Boeing aircraft factory and a modern shipbuilding industry. New military bases quickened the economic pace in communities from Summerside to Esquimalt, while such projects as Ferry Command brought development to the northern territories and Newfoundland and Labrador. Nevertheless, the bias in favour of central Canada was blatant in decisions relating to shipbuilding and repair. The ice-free ports of Halifax and Saint John were treated as secondary to Montreal, which was ice-bound during the winter and whose narrow access was infested with German U-boats. The failure to develop repair facilities in the Maritime provinces consolidated regional disparity and impeded the effectiveness of the Canadian navy.

Traditional attitudes toward labour were challenged during the war. By 1941, the labour pool had dried up and a shortage of workers loomed. In 1942, the government began a campaign to recruit women into the paid labour force. Before the war, only 21 percent of women between the ages of 15 and 65 worked outside the home, and of these, less than 13 percent were married. At first only unmarried women were recruited, but by 1943 even married women with children were strongly encouraged to do their patriotic duty. In Quebec and Ontario, a government-sponsored day-care system offered support for a handful of mothers. The number of women in the workforce increased from 638 000 in 1939 to over a million by 1944, some 255 000 of whom were engaged in what were defined as war industries. When the war ended, the pre-war sex-typing of jobs resumed.

THE ENEMY WITHIN

As in the First World War, the Canadian government took measures against enemy aliens and others perceived as potential troublemakers. The Defence of Canada Regulations included sweeping powers to curb freedom of expression and arrest anyone who might threaten public safety or recruitment efforts. Besides Japanese Canadians, several other groups also experienced the heavy hand of government control.

Among the first targets were members of political organizations associated with enemy nations. The RCMP, in charge of public security, arrested 358 known supporters of Nazi organizations and sent them to camps at Petawawa and Kananaskis. Another sweep after the fall of France and the entrance of Italy into the war netted over 850 more. Canada's official Nazi party was banned and its leaders interned.

On 4 July 1940, the government passed an order-in-council declaring the Jehovah's Witnesses illegal. The order made 7000 Canadian Jehovah's Witnesses subject to surveillance and arrest, while their meeting halls and property were handed over to the Custodian of Enemy Property. The treatment of the Jehovah's Witnesses, like the evacuation of the Japanese, demonstrates how pre-war prejudices are acted upon in wartime contexts. Because the Witnesses criticized the Roman Catholic Church, Cardinal Villeneuve loathed them and appealed to Justice Minister Ernest Lapointe to curb their activities. Lapointe, eager to maintain the Catholic hierarchy's support for the war effort, promptly had the ban issued and enforced. It lasted until 1943.

Even refugees were treated with suspicion. Canada accepted only about 3500 refugees from enemy countries between 1939 and 1945. Widespread opposition to Jewish immigration, especially in Quebec, contributed to Ottawa's minimal compliance with Britain's request to admit German and Austrian refugees, many of them Jews. Jewish refugees were initially put in prison camps with German prisoners of war. Although they were eventually housed separately, many remained under guard in rough internment camps. Not even reports of Nazi extermination camps, widespread by 1943, changed official or public sentiment.

The treatment of refugees became a major concern of the Canadian National Council on Refugees (CNCR), whose president was Senator Cairine Wilson. Under pressure from the CNCR, the government passed an order-in-council in December 1943 releasing enemy alien refugees from internment and granting them one-year permits to stay in Canada. The CNCR tried to find work for these unfortunate people, many of whom eventually made major contributions to their adopted country as scientists, university professors, and artists.

Anti-war dissidents also came under surveillance. Since the Communist Party spoke out against the war, it was outlawed in June 1940, and 133 of its leaders were arrested. Most Communist internees were released after Hitler invaded the Soviet Union in 1941. Apart from political dissidents, an estimated 12 000 Canadians, mainly Quakers, Mennonites, and Brethren in Christ, declared themselves conscientious objectors. Many were required to work in rural camps or factories, on pain of being interned in labour camps.

No internees were deported after the war. Although the Canadian government planned to deport the Japanese evacuees, the legality of the policy was soon called into question. By the time the courts handed down their decision, Canadians and much of the world were beginning to adopt a new attitude toward cultural minorities and refugee populations. The increasingly popular concept of human rights was reflected in the human rights codes banning discrimination in hiring and accommodation passed by the governments of Ontario and Saskatchewan in 1945.

THE WELFARE STATE

Almost as soon as the war started, Canadians began to worry about the nation's post-war agenda. Government planning of the economy during wartime had resulted in a higher standard of living for ordinary people. Why, they asked, could governments not continue such a role in peacetime?

The two major parties appeared at first to ignore such concerns, but they would soon change their tunes. In early 1942, Arthur Meighen, recently re-elected as the federal Conservative leader, sought a parliamentary seat in a by-election in the supposedly safe Conservative riding of York South. King, who feared Meighen's pro-conscription campaign, decided not to run a Liberal candidate, leaving the CCF to challenge Meighen. Throughout the by-election, Meighen talked of the need to impose conscription, while the previously unknown CCF candidate, Joseph Noseworthy, spoke of the need to plan employment and insurance programs for the post-war era. The majority of constituents liked Noseworthy's message. Meighen's defeat and subsequent resignation as Conservative leader had repercussions throughout the political system.

BIOGRAPHY

Tommy Douglas

Born in Scotland in 1904, Tommy Douglas immigrated with his family to Winnipeg in 1919, where he witnessed the General Strike. After serving as a printer's apprentice, he decided, in 1924, to enter the Baptist ministry. He attended Brandon College for six years, where he was exposed to social gospel teachings. Following his ordination in 1930, he moved to Weyburn, Saskatchewan, where he witnessed first-hand the suffering of farmers during the Depression. Douglas soon became deeply involved in politics, establishing a local association of the Independent Labour Party in 1931 and attending the founding convention of the CCF.

In 1935, Douglas was elected to the House of Commons and soon developed a reputation as a skillful and witty debater. He resigned his seat to lead the CCF to victory in Saskatchewan in 1944 and remained premier of the province until he resigned in 1961 to become leader of the federal New Democratic Party. Under his leadership, Saskatchewan earned a reputation for innovative and efficient government. Indeed, Douglas pioneered many of the social welfare programs that would eventually be implemented in other provinces of Canada.

Tommy Douglas.
Library and Archives Canada/C036 220

Reform-minded Conservatives argued that the country could not be allowed to fall to the socialists. In 1942, the Conservatives chose John Bracken, the Liberal-Progressive premier of Manitoba, as national leader. Convention delegates also adopted a platform that went beyond Bennett's New Deal to embrace universal pensions, medical insurance, equality for women, and union rights. At Bracken's insistence, the party changed its name to "Progressive Conservative" in the hope of shedding its reactionary image.

Despite attempts to steal its thunder, the CCF advance continued. In 1943, the party captured 34 of the 89 seats in the Ontario legislature and became the official opposition. Provincial Conservative leader George Drew was obliged to promise a comprehensive social security program in an attempt to blunt the CCF advance. Meanwhile, in Saskatchewan, the CCF under the leadership of the dynamic Tommy Douglas won the 1944 provincial election. Douglas capitalized on the popular policies of the CCF and the widespread

disenchantment among Saskatchewan farmers with Ottawa's price controls on grain. The shift in public opinion toward the left was not unique to Canada. In Great Britain, voters elected a Labour government in 1945 to preside over post-war reconstruction. A report published in Britain in 1942 by Sir William Beveridge, a distinguished social planner, argued for a government-sponsored social security system from the cradle to the grave.

Ever vigilant of trends that might undermine his power, King decided the time had come to implement major reforms. The government had introduced a national unemployment insurance program in 1940, but it was a cautious initiative. An insurance plan rather than a welfare scheme, the program required earners and employers to make contributions to a fund from which employees could draw if they were laid off work. As it was initially designed, unemployment insurance covered only a small proportion of the labour force, and even that unequally. Some exemptions, such as farm labourers, were testimony to the influence of special interest groups. Other exemptions reflected patriarchal notions of women's place in the economy. Married women were excluded from coverage as were domestic workers. Benefits were tied to wages and weeks of continuous work, provisions that discriminated against low-wage and part-time workers.

Many Canadians felt that Ottawa's plans to stabilize the economy should go beyond insurance policies for a small proportion of the labour force. Their perspective was supported in a report prepared for government by a committee but generally known by the name of its principal author, Leonard Marsh. A McGill economist, Marsh brought his CCF sensibilities and the insights of the Beveridge Report to the problems of reconstruction. The Marsh Report argued that full employment should be a major goal of the post-war industrial state; to that end, the government and the whole society should play a role in ensuring that people found work, remained healthy, and were properly fed, housed, and educated. Although the cost of programs such as universal old-age pensions and family allowances was high, Marsh argued that such spending constituted a necessary investment for human well-being and economic efficiency.

Conservative critics were appalled by such thinking. Charlotte Whitton, one of Canada's leading social workers, claimed that Marsh's schemes would make Canadians dependent on the state, destroy initiative, and encourage the "feeble-minded" to procreate. Finance minister J.L. Ilsley was also reluctant to embrace the Marsh proposals, which were costly to implement. Proponents of new social programs responded that maintaining the high taxes of the war period would be the key to financing peacetime social schemes.

Provincial cooperation would be necessary because the courts had ruled that provinces had jurisdiction over social policy. To proceed with national unemployment insurance, the federal government had been obliged to secure an amendment to the BNA Act. The King government had established a Royal Commission on Dominion-Provincial Relations in 1937 to explore ways of reforming the constitution to permit the federal government to intervene directly in the field of social welfare. When the proposals of the royal commission were unveiled in 1940, they were strongly opposed by the premiers of Ontario, Alberta, and British Columbia, who refused to concede their taxation powers so that the federal government could establish a national policy to create full employment and social services.

Most Canadians were unconcerned about constitutional niceties. They wanted reform and they wanted it right away. At a meeting of the National Liberal Federation in September 1943, the party followed the CCF and the Progressive Conservatives in adopting a platform supporting social security. King moved quickly to establish three new departments—Reconstruction, National Health and Welfare, and Veterans Affairs—to preside over government post-war planning. His administration introduced family allowance legislation by which mothers of children under 16 received a monthly stipend. The first cheques, amounting to between five and eight dollars per child, were mailed in 1945.

In the last two years of the war, the government focused on policies that would help cushion the shock of returning to peace. It passed the National Housing Act to generate construction, established the Industrial Development Board to help companies retool for peacetime production, created the Veterans' Charter to provide benefits for those who served in the war, and developed policies to help primary producers survive the transition to peacetime markets. In all, the government appropriated $3.12 billion for reconstruction, a remarkable sum even in today's dollars. These policies went some distance in helping the Liberals ward off the CCF threat and win the 1945 election.

LABOUR AND THE STATE

Another reason for the Liberal government's success in fending off socialism was its change of heart on trade union rights. King's initial wartime response to labour alienated the unions. The Industrial Disputes Investigation Act was vastly extended under the War Measures Act to allow the government to use conciliation to avoid strikes. If managers fired workers attempting to form unions, the government looked the other way.

Under wartime conditions, workers were no longer forced to submit silently to the dictates of government and hostile managers. Recognizing that labour shortages prevented employers from firing them for union activities, workers joined industrial and craft unions in droves and resorted to strikes and work slowdowns when companies refused to accept the unions formed by the democratic votes of their employees. In 1943, there were over 400 strikes involving more than 200 000 workers.

Eager to keep war industries functioning smoothly and his political popularity high, King felt compelled to act. In February 1944, Order-in-Council PC 1003 ushered in a new era of labour policy in Canada. The order guaranteed workers the right to organize and bargain collectively, established procedures for the certification and compulsory recognition of trade unions, defined unfair labour practices, and created an administrative apparatus to enforce the order.

The move to accommodate labour and a massive anti-socialist campaign by business interests reduced support for left-wing parties. In 1945, the Ontario Conservatives decisively won a provincial election that reduced the CCF to third place in the legislature. On 11 June, the CCF won only 28 of 245 seats in the federal election, with 15 percent of the popular vote. Although they received a reduced parliamentary majority, the Liberals were given a mandate to govern the country in peacetime. King had proven his ability to stay in the middle of the political road, no matter what direction that road took.

THE NEW WORLD ORDER

King also presided over a government that took a new road in international affairs. Even more obvious in retrospect than at the time, the Second World War reinforced Great Britain's long decline from its dominant role in world affairs. Its mantle passed to the United States. During the Second World War, Canada moved closer to the Americans economically, politically, and militarily. Critics such as the distinguished scholar Harold Innis, who taught political economy at the University of Toronto, would later claim that in this period Canada moved from "colony to nation to colony" in its efforts to maintain good relations with the superpower next door—that is, that it had achieved independence from Great Britain only to lose it to the United States.

As Hitler's armies erased national borders with ease, King recognized that Canada was increasingly dependent on the United States for its defence. American president Franklin Roosevelt was equally conscious of this fact and was afraid that Canada's involvement in the war made the whole North American continent vulnerable to the fascist dictators. In August 1940, Roosevelt invited King to meet him at Ogdensburg, New York. As a result of their meeting, the Permanent Joint Board on Defence was established to prepare for mutual assistance in defence of North America. The notion of permanency gave King few qualms and the board was established without prior reference to parliament. In the crisis atmosphere of the late summer of 1940, few people in Canada voiced any objection.

The United States also made adjustments to its wartime policies to ensure that Canada's economy would not suffer unduly. In March 1941, Great Britain and the United States concluded a lend-lease arrangement whereby $7 billion was made available to Great Britain for the purchase of equipment and supplies from the United States. Canada was initially excluded from the agreement, an "oversight" that was rectified at another meeting between Roosevelt and King at Hyde Park, New York, in April 1941. The Americans would increase purchases in Canada and would charge many of the components bought by Canada in the United States to the British account, thereby helping solve the balance of payment difficulties.

King told parliament that the Hyde Park declaration "involves nothing less than a common plan for the economic defence of the western hemisphere" and "the enduring foundation of a new world order."[7] King was given to rhetorical exaggeration, but in this instance he was strikingly prophetic. Valuable wartime arrangements as they were, Ogdensburg and Hyde Park were less important in themselves than as symbols of an intimate Canada–United States relationship that was becoming a dominant fact of life for Canada.

Once the United States had officially entered the war, Canada no longer figured very prominently in American calculations. King hated to be taken for granted, but he had to accept that Canada was a minor player in a world of superpowers. Notwithstanding diplomatic rhetoric about their close alliance, the United States resisted Canadian efforts to have a military mission in Washington to learn more about American military strategy. The United States also protested loudly when Canada quietly supported the successful efforts of Charles de Gaulle's Free French forces to seize Saint-Pierre and Miquelon—two French islands off the coast of Newfoundland—from the Vichy government. King refused to dislodge de Gaulle's forces because he suspected Vichy—the pro-German government in that part of France unoccupied by the Nazis—of using the islands as a base from which to report to the Germans on Allied convoy movements.

Canadians took the practical route and developed what became known as the "functional principle" in wartime planning. When Canadian interests were at stake, they would insist on having a voice in determining international policy. This approach was most clearly expressed in the words of Hume Wrong, a senior officer in the Department of External Affairs in 1942: "The principle . . . is that each member of the grand alliance should have a voice in the conduct of the war proportionate to its contribution to the general war effort. A subsidiary principle is that the influence of the various countries should be greatest in connection with those matters with which they are most directly concerned."[8] Canadians used such arguments to win a seat on the Allied Combined Food Board, which allocated food resources for the war effort, and with less success in organizations established to manage international relations in peacetime.

The American presence loomed ever larger as the war dragged on. Roosevelt had arranged for American bases in Newfoundland, still a dependency of Great Britain but one in which Canada had a considerable interest and had agreed to protect for the duration of the war. When the Japanese occupied the Aleutian Islands in the summer of 1942, the United States, with Canada's permission, built an overland route through Canada to Alaska. The Alaska Highway was a marvel of American efficiency. Between March and October 1942, civilian workers and seven engineer regiments, together totalling 11 000 people, began carving a highway from Alaska, a total of more than 2 000 kilometres, at a cost of nearly $150 million. To ensure oil supplies, the Americans built the Canol pipeline from Whitehorse in the Yukon to Norman Wells in the Northwest Territories. The Americans also developed northern staging routes of rough airstrips to transport bombers and fighter planes to Europe and the Soviet Union. By 1943, there were 33 000 Americans working in the Canadian North.

King and officials in the Department of External Affairs were troubled by the American invasion of

When British prime minister Winston Churchill (right) and American president Franklin Roosevelt (left) met in Quebec City in 1943, William Lyon Mackenzie King (centre) was on hand for a photo opportunity.
Library and Archives Canada/C31186

Canada's northern territories. In an effort to establish sovereignty over the area and reduce Canada's balance of American dollars, the government announced in December 1943 that the United States was to be paid in full for all permanent military installations they built in Canada. Canada ultimately paid $123.5 million for 28 airfields, 56 weather stations, and a variety of other facilities.

In 1943, the Canadian government decided to upgrade its diplomatic presence in Washington. The Canadian legation took on embassy status, and Leighton McCarthy, the Canadian minister to the United States, became an ambassador, the first Canadian diplomat to hold that rank.

Cooperation, more than conflict, characterized Canadian-American relations throughout the war. At American request, Canadians agreed to participate in an expedition to dislodge the Japanese from the Aleutians in 1943, and Canadians adopted American army organization for the 16 000 Canadian Army Pacific Forces assembled for the final campaign against the Japanese in 1945.

The new world order that was put in place after the Second World War was also largely dominated by American policy. In the spring of 1945, meetings were held in San Francisco to establish the United Nations, an organization designed to replace war with negotiation as a vehicle for settling international disputes. Although Canadian diplomats had their own ideas

Waving "the flag" to celebrate victory over Japan, 14 August 1945.
Alberta Provincial Archives/G 1293

about the economic structures that should govern the post-war world, they went along with American plans for the International Monetary Fund and the World Bank. Only time would tell whether this blueprint for peace and prosperity would be any more successful than the one put in place by the League of Nations following the Great War.

The prospects for a peaceful post-war world were not encouraging. When the war in Europe came to an end, the leaders of the Soviet Union, Great Britain, and the United States met in Potsdam, Germany, in July 1945 to discuss how to manage the peace process. It was a different group of leaders than had met to plot strategy during the war. Joseph Stalin was the only constant player. Roosevelt had died in April 1945, succeeded by his vice-president, Harry Truman. Great Britain was in the process of holding an election even as the Potsdam conference was in progress. A Labour victory meant that Clement Attlee replaced Winston Churchill at the bargaining table. The conference revealed the growing tension between the Soviet Union and the West, tension that ultimately led to the partition of Germany and the Cold War that was to characterize international relations for decades to come.

DEMOBILIZATION AND POST-WAR RECONSTRUCTION

In Canada, the people planning demobilization during the Second World War were determined not to repeat the mistakes that had created the unrest among veterans following the Great War. In January 1940, the government created the General Advisory Committee on Demobilization and Reconstruction under Great War veteran H.F. McDonald. A new department of Veterans Affairs was established in 1944 to help soldiers make a successful transition to civilian life. The Veterans' Charter of the same year offered veterans more generous benefits than those available in 1919, including gratuities totalling $752.3 million to help them get re-established. In 1942, the government passed an act requiring companies to rehire veterans in their former jobs under conditions "not less favourable" than if they had never enlisted. Nearly 200 000 veterans benefited from this injunction, and only four charges were brought against uncooperative employers under the Reinstatement Act. A slightly smaller number, about 150 000, had their re-entry into the labour market postponed for several years by a provision that helped veterans attend university or college. Others took up land offered by the Veterans' Land Act and settled into farming.

While it was all well and good to plan for the end of the war, victory in Europe brought the predictable problem of getting the forces home. Repatriation went faster than expected, but nothing could solve the problem of too few ships for too many soldiers. In theory, repatriation followed a point system allowing those with the longest service and who were married to come back first, with ex-prisoners of war, the wounded, and service women being given top priority. In practice, there were problems and unrest. The worst disorder took place in Aldershot, England, in July 1945, when Canadian forces erupted in a two-night riot. By the end of 1945, only half of the nearly 350 000 Canadians in Europe were home. A division of 25 000 troops and 11 air force squadrons was committed to the occupation of Germany. When few Canadians volunteered for this tour of duty, Canada informed the Allied command that it would pull its forces out of Germany by the spring of 1946.

Most of the ships arriving from Europe docked at Halifax, which did its best, under difficult circumstances, to welcome "the boys" home, but not before VE day (victory in Europe) celebrations blew the city apart. As news of the German surrender spread, Haligonians closed their offices, stores, and restaurants while throngs of service people and civilians celebrated in downtown streets. Seamen were free to come and go, but there was nothing for them to do. Even their canteen at the naval base closed at 9:00 p.m. With the city closed down, the inevitable occurred. Liquor stores were looted, a tram trashed, and chaos reigned in the streets of Halifax.

This should have been the end of the affair, but it was not. As a victory parade was forming up the next morning, more than 3000 sailors and a contingent from other services poured into the city to continue their looting rampage. Neither the naval patrols nor the city police were strong enough to keep the peace, and Rear-Admiral Murray was at a loss as to how to restore order among his men. The two-day riot caused $5 million worth of damage and left civilians and military authorities pointing fingers at each other for causing the fracas. In the inquiry following the riot, 41 soldiers, 34 sailors, and 19 airmen were among the 211 indicted for offences. Murray was relieved of his command because of the affair, and the navy took most of the blame for the damage.

While officials professed surprise at the extent of the rampage, conditions had been ripe for just such an incident. The population of Halifax had doubled during the war, although goods were still rationed on the basis of the 65 000 people counted in the 1941 census. With the shortage of consumer goods, living space, and recreational facilities, tensions between civilians and service personnel mounted. Halifax's problems were discussed several times in the war cabinet and plans were formulated to move out people who were not essential to the war effort, but no action had been taken. The pent-up frustrations were unleashed on VE day.

Among those returning on the big ships from Europe were more than 47 500 war brides (and a few war husbands) and their children, numbering nearly 22 000. The vast majority of war brides were British (44 886), although Canadian soldiers also married Dutch, Belgian, French, Danish, Italian, and German women. Once in Canada, war brides faced a difficult adjustment: to new families, new communities, and a new country. Some, such as Betty Oliphant, divorced their husbands but ended up staying in Canada anyway. Oliphant became the founder of the National Ballet School.

Canadian soldiers left behind an estimated 23 000 so-called war children, the result of relationships—some brief, others longer term, some even bigamous—with local women. These children and their mothers were abandoned by their Canadian fathers and faced a post-war world where having children "out of wedlock" and being an "illegitimate" child carried a debilitating social stigma. Although 414 child maintenance orders were served on Canadians by authorities in Great Britain, most women received no assistance other than from family and friends. Many war children were given up for adoption. In the post-war period, the plight of the war children was conveniently forgotten. Canadians were reminded of this aspect of the Second World War in 1998, when it was revealed that guitarist

TABLE 14.1 Marriages, Divorces, and Births in Canada, 1939–1948

Year	Marriages	Divorces	Births
1939	106 266	2073	237 991
1940	125 797	2416	252 577
1941	124 644	2462	263 993
1942	130 786	3091	281 569
1943	113 827	3398	292 943
1944	104 656	3827	293 967
1945	111 376	5101	300 587
1946	137 398	7757	343 504
1947	130 400	8213	372 589
1948	126 118	6978	359 860

Source: Adapted from F.H. Leacy, ed., *Historical Statistics of Canada* (Ottawa: Minister of Supply and Service, 1983), cited in Desmond Morton and J.L. Granatstein, *Victory 1945* (Toronto: HarperCollins, 1995), 119.

Eric Clapton had learned that his father was a soldier from Montreal. Like many other war children, Clapton had spent considerable energy searching for his lost father and his much-publicized experience helped further the efforts of others like him tracing their family roots.[9]

As in the First World War, the re-establishment of family life was difficult for many veterans. The number of marriages and births increased after the war, but so, too, did divorces (see Table 14.1). For many veterans, it was impossible to pick up the threads of civilian life. Some women resented being pushed out of civilian jobs and encouraged to stay at home. Others responded enthusiastically to state and business propaganda to establish homes in the suburbs and raise children in one of the world's luckiest democracies.

Much of the responsibility for establishing Canada's post-war economy on a peacetime footing fell on the shoulders of C.D. Howe, who was appointed minister for reconstruction in 1944. With his usual energy, he set about reducing rationing, converting war industries to peacetime purposes, and re-establishing Canada's export sales. Canada's merchant marine was scrapped, and most Crown corporations were sold or closed down. To meet 15 years of pent-up civilian demand, companies were given tax breaks to get their factories producing consumer goods. The loss of overseas markets was in part compensated for by sales made possible under the Marshall Plan.

When it looked as if communism might sweep war-torn European countries, the United States agreed in 1947 to a generous aid program, named after American Secretary of State George C. Marshall, who proposed it to help them restore their capitalist economies. Funds were initially tied to purchases in the United States, but soon Canada was included and sold a billion dollars' worth of its products overseas by 1950. With policies such as these, Canada managed to weather the adjustment to peacetime production reasonably well. Instead of the post-war slump predicted by many economists, Canada experienced growth, its GNP rising from $11.8 billion in 1945 to $18.4 billion in 1950.

Canada was not spared the wave of strikes that followed the First World War. In 1945 and 1946, proportionately more time was lost in strike activity than in 1919. A major strike was conducted at the Ford Motor Company plant in Windsor in 1945, and a national steel strike shut down plants in Sault Ste. Marie, Hamilton, and Sydney in 1946. The results of arbitration at Ford and the willingness of federal and provincial governments to enshrine the principles of PC 1003 in post-war legislation helped prevent the stand-off between labour and capital that had characterized the aftermath of the Great War. With the legal and administrative apparatus in place, the way was paved for organized labour to join big business and big government in the three-cornered power structure of modern corporate capitalism.

CONCLUSION

Canada came out of the war a different country from the one that went into it in 1939. With a stronger federal state and the beginnings of a social welfare system, the nation was in a position to avoid returning to the misery experienced during the Great Depression. The booming economy seemed to be holding its own in a peacetime context. In comparison to the devastated cities and countrysides of Europe and Asia, Canada was an untouched utopia and the destination of choice for many European refugees. Canadians were also assuming a new place among the nations of the world. Although not a major player like Great Britain or the United States, Canada began to embrace the term "middle power," a small nation no more, and one with

Origins of the Welfare State

Social scientists generally agree on the various factors contributing to the evolution of the welfare state in Canada, but the relative weight of these factors is in dispute. In identifying the groups pressing for the creation of federal social insurance programs, scholars list the following: the unemployed; business groups; municipalities and provinces; liberal churches; and elements within the state bureaucracy. They also note the support of key politicians. Is there evidence to suggest that one group more than another left its mark on the kind of welfare state that emerged in Canada? The contours of the debate can be understood by looking at how scholars explain the emergence of the unemployment insurance program in 1940.

Alvin Finkel suggests that pressure from big business was largely responsible for producing an unemployment insurance program.[10] According to Finkel, business people felt that unemployment insurance would help prevent public finances from being besieged by unplanned expenditures when unemployment rose. Business leaders wanted the scale of payments to be modest so that people would be encouraged to find work. They also wanted the cost to be borne by working people themselves rather than by companies or the government. To a considerable degree, their views prevailed in the program that was introduced in 1940.

James Struthers argues that this scenario is too one-sided, suggesting that popular pressures, both from the unemployed and from liberal-minded citizens, generally played a role in securing unemployment insurance.[11] Some argue that the business community, though divided, was largely opposed to the idea. According to sociologist Carl Cuneo, unemployment insurance was an example of the state implementing reforms to save capitalism from itself. By providing a social safety net for workers, the state was helping prevent widespread social unrest that might lead to revolution and the total destruction of the market economy.[12]

Still others stress the role of specific politicians. R.B. Bennett's need to appear reform-minded before the 1935 election is often mentioned.[13] Since Bennett had promised unemployment insurance as early as 1931, it is not surprising that it emerged as an item in his "New Deal" package of reforms in 1935. J.L. Granatstein attributes William Lyon Mackenzie King's reintroduction of unemployment insurance in 1940 to his desire to plan for expected post-war unemployment.[14] Struthers also sees the war as the major catalyst for the welfare state.

"When King finally pushed for speedy passage of the Unemployment Insurance Act, it was out of his own fear of postwar unrest," Struthers argues. "No one expected that veterans or unemployed war workers would queue up meekly in front of local relief offices. In the final analysis it was war and not the depression which destroyed the poor-law heritage."[15]

Most scholars concede the degree to which the state bureaucracy shaped the character of Canada's unemployment insurance program. While admitting that a variety of forces caused politicians to accept the need for some form of social insurance, political scientist Leslie Pal suggests that a state-centred, rather than a society-centred, perspective explains the character of the program itself. In its formative years, he argues, unemployment insurance became grounded in administrative logic when it came to determining contributions, benefits, duration, and coverage. Whereas employee groups tended to view unemployment insurance in terms of rights and employers saw it in terms of costs and the effect on the labour supply, officials were preoccupied with administrative feasibility, actuarial soundness, and strict insurance principles. This led to a similarity of views between employers and officials, particularly on the abuse question, but the similarity was coincidental in that the official view was arrived at independently. It was not the result of "pressure."[16]

When examined from the perspective of gender, there is also a remarkable coincidence of views between state bureaucrats, businessmen, and union leaders on the treatment of female workers under the unemployment insurance program.[17] Indeed, as Ruth Roach Pierson points out, neither progressives nor conservatives, labour nor management, organized to defend the right of married women workers to receive fair compensation when they lost jobs.

The return of the veterans to their old jobs generally meant the dismissal of women who had been recruited to non-traditional jobs in the workforce during the war. In her recent study, Jennifer A. Stephen documents the policies put in place by the federal government to discourage married women who had lost their wartime jobs from seeking new employment. Ottawa coordinated a massive campaign to persuade women that their place was in the home, closed day cares, and changed wartime tax rules to penalize two-income families. Meanwhile, the new family allowance was promoted as a program that made it unnecessary for married women to seek an income in the labour force.[18]

an expanding role to play in international affairs. It was also a country in the process of creating its own identity independent from the British Commonwealth. In 1946, Secretary of State Paul Martin introduced a bill, passed the next year, to establish a distinct Canadian citizenship, since up to that point Canadians still carried British passports. There was some discussion in the media about adopting a Canadian flag—Canadians still waved the Red Ensign, the Union Jack, or the Stars and Stripes during victory celebrations. Clearly issues of Canadian identity were on the agenda as Canada entered the atomic age.

Notes

1 Joseph Goebbels, Diary, 3 March 1943, cited in *Challenge and Survival: A History of Canada*, ed. H.H. Herstein, L.J. Hughes, and R.C. Kerbyson (Scarborough: Prentice Hall, 1970), 376.

2 Enlistment and casualty figures vary widely. The figures cited in this chapter are taken from Desmond Morton and J.L. Granatstein, *Victory 1945: Canadians from War to Peace* (Toronto: HarperCollins, 1995), 19.

3 For an analysis of the controversy around *The Valour and the Horror*, see David J. Becuson and S.F. Wise, eds., *The Valour and the Horror Revisited* (Montreal: McGill-Queen's University Press, 1994) and Graham Carr, "Rules of Engagement: Public History and the Drama of Legitimation," *Canadian Historical Review* 86, 2 (June 2005), 317–354.

4 Carr, "Rules of Engagement," 320.

5 Desmond Morton, "Comments on the Controversy over the Bombing Offensive," typescript, 5.

6 Carl A. Christie, *Ocean Bridge: The History of RAF Ferry Command* (Toronto: University of Toronto Press, 1995), 3.

7 J.L. Granatstein and Norman Hillmer, *For Better or for Worse: Canada and the United States to the 1990s* (Toronto: Copp Clark Pitman, 1991), 147.

8 Cited in Morton and Granatstein, *Victory 1945*, 234.

9 Olga Rains, Lloyd Rains, and Melynda Jarratt, *Voices of the Left Behind: Project Roots and the Canadian War Children of World War Two* (Fredericton: Project Roots, 2004), 1–3.

10 Alvin Finkel, *Business and Social Reform in the Thirties* (Toronto: Lorimer, 1979).

11 James Struthers, *No Fault of Their Own: Unemployment and the Canadian Welfare State, 1914–1941* (Toronto: University of Toronto Press, 1981).

12 Carl J. Cuneo, "State, Class and Reserve Labour: The Case of the 1941 Canadian Unemployment Insurance Act," *Canadian Review of Sociology and Anthropology* 16 (May 1979), 147–70.

13 See, for example, Larry A. Glassford, *Reaction and Reform: The Politics of the Conservative Party under R.B. Bennett, 1927–1938* (Toronto: University of Toronto Press, 1992).

14 J.L. Granatstein, *Canada's War: The Politics of the Mackenzie King Government, 1939–1945* (Toronto: Oxford University Press, 1975).

15 Struthers, *No Fault of Their Own*, 213.

16 Leslie Pal, *State, Class and Bureaucracy: Canadian Unemployment Insurance and Public Policy* (Montreal: McGill-Queen's University Press, 1975), 109.

17 Ruth Roach Pierson, "Gender and the Unemployment Insurance Debate in Canada, 1934–1940," *Labour/Le Travail* 25 (Spring 1990), 77–103.

18 Jennifer A. Stephen, *Pick One Intelligent Girl: Employability, Domesticity, and the Gendering of Canada's Welfare State, 1939–1947* (Toronto: University of Toronto Press, 2007).

Related Readings in This Series

From *Nation and Society: Readings in Post-Confederation Canadian History*

Esther Delisle, "Introduction" to *Myths, Memories, and Lies: Quebec's Intelligentsia and the Fascist Temptation, 1939–1960*, 272–80.

J.L. Granatstein, "Staring into the Abyss," 281–94.

From *Primary Documents CD-ROM, Volume II*

Don't Buy It

We're in the Army Now

King Explains the Introduction of Conscription

French Canadians on Conscription

Report and Recommendations of the Special Committee on Orientals in British Columbia, 1940

Women's Army Corps Stationed in a German Town
CWACs Stationed in England

SELECTED READING

On Canada's wartime experience, see Norman Hillmer, Robert Bothwell, Roger Sarty, and Claude Beauregard, eds., *A Country of Limitations: Canada and the World in 1939* (Ottawa: Canadian Committee for the History of the Second World War, 1996); J.L. Granatstein and Desmond Morton, *A Nation Forged in Fire: Canadians in the Second World War* (Toronto: Lester and Orpen Dennys, 1989); J.L. Granatstein and Peter Neary, eds., *The Good Fight: Canadians and World War II* (Toronto: Copp Clark, 1995); and Brereton Greenhous et al., *The Crucible of War, 1939–1945* (Toronto: University of Toronto Press, 1994). Recruitment issues are addressed in J.L. Granatstein and J.M. Hitsman, *Broken Promises: A History of Conscription in Canada* (Toronto: Oxford University Press, 1977) and Michael D. Stevenson, *Canada's Greatest Wartime Muddle: National Selective Service and the Mobilization of Human Resources during World War II* (Montreal: McGill-Queen's University Press, 2001). The various branches of the forces are the focus of W.A.B. Douglas, ed., *The RCN in Retrospect, 1910–1968* (Vancouver: UBC Press, 1982) and his *The Creation of a National Airforce* (Toronto: University of Toronto Press, 1968); W.A.B. Douglas, Roger Sarty, and Michael Whitby, *No Higher Purpose: The Official Operational History of the Royal Canadian Navy in the Second World War, 1939–1943*, vol. 2, part 1 (St. Catharines, ON: Vanwell Publishing, 2003); David Zimmerman, *The Great Naval Battle of Ottawa* (Toronto: University of Toronto Press, 1989); Marc Milner, *North Atlantic Run: The Royal Canadian Navy and the Battle for the Convoys* (Toronto: University of Toronto Press, 1982) and *The U-Boat Hunters: The Royal Canadian Navy and the Offensive Against Germany's Submarines* (Toronto: University of Toronto Press, 1994); Roger Sarty, *The Maritime Defence of Canada* (Toronto: Canadian Institute for Strategic Studies, 1997). The military aspects of the war are discussed in C.P. Stacey, *Six Years of War* (Ottawa: Queen's Printer, 1955), *The Victory Campaign* (Ottawa: Queen's Printer, 1960), and *Arms, Men and Governments: The War Policies of Canada, 1939–1945* (Ottawa: Queen's Printer, 1970); G.W.L. Nicholson, *The Canadians in Italy, 1943–1945* (Ottawa: Queen's Printer, 1957); Terry Copp, *Fields of Fire: The Canadians in Normandy* (Toronto: University of Toronto Press, 2003); Terry Copp and Bill McAndrew, *Battle Exhaustion: Soldiers and Psychiatrists in the Canadian Army, 1939–1945* (Montreal: McGill-Queen's University Press, 1990); Daniel Dancocks, *The D-Day Dodgers: The Canadians in Italy, 1943–1945* (Toronto: McClelland & Stewart, 1992); J.L. Granatstein,

The Generals: The Canadian Army's Senior Commanders in the Second World War (Don Mills, ON: Stoddart, 1993); Carl A. Christie, *Ocean Bridge: The History of RAF Ferry Command* (Toronto: University of Toronto Press, 1995); and Donald Avery, *The Science of War: Scientists and Allied Military Technology During the Second World War* (Toronto: University of Toronto Press, 1998). On women's participation at home and abroad, see Ruth Roach Pierson, *"They're Still Women After All": The Second World War and Canadian Womanhood* (Toronto: McClelland & Stewart, 1986) and Cynthia Toman, *An Officer and a Lady: Canadian Military Nursing and the Second World War* (Vancouver: University of British Columbia Press, 2007). On Native participation, see R. Scott Sheffield, *The Image of the "Indian" and the Second World War* (Vancouver: UBC Press, 2004). War artists are discussed in Dean Oliver and Laura Brandon, *Canvas of War: Painting the Canadian Experience, 1914–1945* (Vancouver: Douglas and McIntrye/Canadian War Museum, 2000) and Heather Robertson, *A Terrible Beauty: The Art of Canada at War* (Toronto: James Lorimer, 1977).

The controversy relating to Bomber Command is analyzed in David J. Becuson and S.F. Wise, eds., *The Valour and the Horror Revisited* (Montreal: McGill-Queen's University Press, 1994); Graham Carr, "Rules of Engagement: Public History and the Drama of Legitimation," *Canadian Historical Review* 86, 2(June 2005): 317–354; and Chapter 6 of Tim Cook, *Clio's Warriors* (Vancouver: UBC Press, 2006), 227–233.

On political developments at home during the war, see J.W. Pickersgill and D.F. Foster, *The Mackenzie King Record*, vols. 1 and 2 (Toronto: University of Toronto Press, 1960, 1968); Reg Whitaker, *The Government Party* (Toronto: University of Toronto Press, 1977); Douglas Owram, *The Government Generation: Canadian Intellectuals and the State, 1900–1945* (Toronto: University of Toronto Press, 1986); J.L. Granatstein, *Canada's War: The Politics of the Mackenzie King Government, 1939–1945* (Toronto: Oxford University Press, 1974); Robert Bothwell and William Kilbourn, *C.D. Howe* (Toronto: McClelland & Stewart, 1979); Lita-Rose Betcherman, *Ernest Lapointe: Mackenzie King's Great Quebec Lieutenant* (Toronto: University of Toronto Press, 2002); Leonard Marsh, *Report on Social Security for Canada, 1943* (Toronto: University of Toronto Press, 1945); Gary Evans, *John Grierson and the National Film Board, 1939–1945* (Toronto: University of Toronto Press, 1984); Malek Khouri, *Filming Politics: Communism and the Portrayal of the Working*

Class at the National Film Board of Canada, 1939–1946 (Calgary: University of Calgary Press, 2007); Claude Beauregard, *Guerre et Censure au Canada, 1939–1945* (Quebec: Septentrion, 1998); and E.R. Forbes, "Consolidating Disparity: The Maritimes and the Industrialization of Canada during the Second World War," *Acadiensis* 15, no. 2 (Spring 1986).

Three short studies published in 2000 by Enid Barnett provide some insight on the impact of Keynesian thinking during the war years: *The Keynesian Arithmetic in War-time Canada: Development of the National Accounts, 1939–1945*; *The War Budget of September 1939: Keynes Comes to Canada*; and *Keynes's 'How to Pay for the War' in Canada: The Story of Compulsory Savings, 1939–1945* (Kingston: Harbinger House Press, 2000).

For a discussion of labour policy during the war, see Jennifer A. Stephen, *Pick One Intelligent Girl: Employability, Domesticity, and the Gendering of Canada's Welfare State, 1939–1947* (Toronto: University of Toronto Press, 2007); Bryan Palmer, *Working-Class Experience: Rethinking the History of Canadian Labour, 1800–1991*, 2nd ed. (Toronto: McClelland & Stewart, 1992); Irving Abella, *Nationalism, Communism and Canadian Labour* (Toronto: University of Toronto Press, 1973); and Laurel Sefton MacDowell, "The Formation of the Canadian Industrial Relations System during World War II," *Labour/Le Travailleur* 3 (1978).

The treatment of minorities is the subject of Norman Hillmer, Bohdan Kordan, and Lubomyr Luciuk, eds., *On Guard for Thee: War, Ethnicity, and the Canadian State, 1939–1945* (Ottawa: Canadian Committee for the History of the Second World War, 1988); Bohdan S. Kordan, *Canada and the Ukrainian Question, 1939–1945* (Montreal: McGill-Queen's University Press, 2001); Irving Abella and Harold Troper, *None Is Too Many* (Toronto: Lester and Orpen Dennys, 1982); Daniel Dancocks, *In Enemy Hands: Canada's Prisoners of War, 1939–1945* (Edmonton: Hurtig, 1983); Marjorie Wrong, *The Dragon and the Maple Leaf: Chinese Canadians in World War II* (Toronto: Dundurn Press, 1994); and Tom Socknat, *Witness Against War: Pacifism in Canada, 1900–1945* (Toronto: University of Toronto Press, 1987).

Security and intelligence are the subject of John Bryden, *Best-Kept Secret: Canadian Secret Intelligence in the Second World War* (Toronto: Lester, 1993); Gregory S. Kealey and Reg Whitaker, eds., *RCMP Security Bulletins: The War Series*, 2 vols. (St. John's: Canadian Committee on Labour History, 1989, 1993); and Larry Hannant, *The Infernal Machine: Investigating the Loyalties of Canada's Citizens* (Toronto: University of Toronto Press, 1995).

On Newfoundland in this period, see Peter Neary, *Newfoundland and the North Atlantic World, 1929–1949* (Montreal: McGill-Queen's University Press, 1988) and the useful synthesis by James K. Hiller, "Newfoundland Confronts Canada, 1867–1949," in *The Atlantic Provinces in Confederation*, ed. E.R. Forbes and D.A. Muise (Toronto: University of Toronto Press, 1993).

On the Japanese evacuation, see Ken Adachi, *The Enemy That Never Was* (Toronto: McClelland & Stewart, 1976); Ann Gomer Sunahara, *The Politics of Racism* (Toronto: Lorimer, 1981); W. Peter Ward, *White Canada Forever: Popular Attitudes and Public Policy Toward Orientals in British Columbia* (Montreal: McGill-Queen's University Press, 1978); Patricia Roy et al., *Mutual Hostages: Canadians and Japanese During the Second World War* (Toronto: University of Toronto Press, 1989); and Greg Donaghy and Patricia E. Roy, eds., *Contradictory Impulses: Canada and Japan in the Twentieth Century* (Vancouver: UBC Press, 2008).

On foreign policy during the war, see James Eayrs, *In Defence of Canada*, vol. 2: *Appeasement and Rearmament* (Toronto: University of Toronto Press, 1965); Stanley Dziuban, *Military Relations Between Canada and the United States, 1939–1945* (Washington: Office of the Chief of Military History, Dept. of the Army, 1959); and two books by J.L. Granatstein and Norman Hillmer, *For Better or for Worse: Canada and the United States to the 1990s* (Toronto: Copp Clark Pitman, 1991) and *Empire to Umpire: Canada and the World to the 1990s* (Toronto: Copp Clark Longman, 1994).

War's end is described in Desmond Morton and J.L. Granatstein, *Victory 1945: Canadians from War to Peace* (Toronto: HarperCollins, 1995). On the Halifax riots of 1945, see Graham Metson, *An East Coast Port: Halifax at War, 1939–1945* (Scarborough, ON: McGraw-Hill Ryerson, 1981) and Stanley Redman, *Open Gangway: The (Real) Story of the Halifax Navy Riot* (Hantsport, NS: Lancelot Press, 1981). The experience of war brides is described in Joyce Hibbert, *The War Brides* (Toronto: Peter Martin Associates, 1978). On abandoned war children and their mothers, see Olga Rains, Lloyd Rains, and Melynda Jarratt, *Voices of the Left Behind: Project Roots and the Canadian War Children of World War Two* (Fredericton: Project Roots, 2004), 1–3.

Farley Mowat has produced two evocative memoirs of his wartime experience: *The Regiment* (Toronto: McClelland & Stewart, 1973) and *And No Birds Sang* (Toronto: McClelland & Stewart, 1979). See also Barry Broadfoot, *The Veterans' Years* (Toronto: Douglas and McIntyre, 1985); Murray Peden, *A Thousand Shall Fall* (Stittsville, ON: Canada's Wings, 1979); and E.L.M. Burns, *General Mud* (Toronto: Clarke Irwin, 1970). Heather Robertson offers a fine sampling of Canada's war art in *A Terrible Beauty: The Art of Canada at War* (Toronto: Lorimer, 1977).

Reinventing Canada, 1945–1975

I n the 30 years following the Second World War, Canada emerged as one of the world's great industrial nations, with all the benefits and problems associated with its new status. Wealth continued to be unequally distributed, but the state assumed increasing responsibility for ensuring the basic welfare of all Canadians. No longer tied to the apron strings of Great Britain, Canadians developed a stronger sense of their own identity. The arts flourished, buoyed by the new prosperity and government grants. As the centennial of confederation approached, many Canadians felt that at long last, they had something to celebrate, and Ottawa hosted a birthday party worthy of a great nation. Yet the country's survival remained at risk, threatened by internal divisions and the overwhelming impact of the United States on Canadian economic, political, and cultural life. The Cold War, which periodically threatened to become hot, helped impress the American view of the world on the consciousness of Canadians. Regional fissures made the assertion of a "Canadian identity" elusive, and the expansion of the state at all levels prompted conflicts between provincial and federal governments. Nowhere were tensions more bitter than between Ottawa and the province of Quebec, where a growing sovereignty movement raised the prospect of a breakup of Canada.

CHAPTER 15

Redefining Liberalism: The Canadian State, 1945–1975

TIMELINE

- **1948–57** Louis St. Laurent's Liberals form the government in Ottawa
- **1949** Newfoundland enters the Canadian confederation as the tenth province
- **1951** Universal old-age pension approved by parliament
- **1957** Equalization grants implemented
- **1957–63** John Diefenbaker's Progressive Conservatives form the federal government
- **1958** Hospital insurance and Atlantic Provinces Adjustment Grants approved by parliament
- **1960** Jean Lesage's Liberals win the Quebec election
- **1961** New Democratic Party created
- **1962** Medicare implemented in Saskatchewan
- **1963–68** Lester Pearson leads a minority Liberal government in Ottawa
- **1965** Canada and Quebec Pension plans established; Canada's new flag proclaimed
- **1966** Canada Assistance Plan introduced
- **1967** Centennial celebrations
- **1968** Parti Québécois formed; national medicare implemented; Canadian International Development Agency established
- **1968–79** Pierre Elliott Trudeau serves as prime minister
- **1969** Official Languages Act passed
- **1970** Report of the Royal Commission on the Status of Women; October Crisis; War Measures Act proclaimed
- **1971** First secretary of state for multiculturalism appointed
- **1975** Alberta Heritage Trust Fund established
- **1980–84**

An exchange of letters between a prominent Canadian businessman and a socialist feminist member of parliament in 1972 demonstrated the poles of political debate in post-war Canada. Taking exception to a speech in parliament by Grace MacInnis, New Democrat MP for Vancouver-Kingsway, Eric Harrington, president of Canada Vickers Ltd., wrote, in part:

> Could you please tell me what on earth "day centres" of which you claim we need 130 000 and "family planning centres" of which you claim we need 700 have to do with "equal rights for women"?
>
> Surely family planning and day-care centres for children are purely a family responsibility and a personal matter and don't have a damn thing to do with equal rights.
>
> Please all of you, stay out of our family affairs and our bedrooms, leave our children alone and do some planning that might help the economy, the

unemployment situation and a hundred other more important problems on which to date you have been ineffectual.

MacInnis replied pointedly:

> The fact that you can believe that family planning and day-care centres for children are purely a family responsibility and a personal matter indicates very clearly that you enjoy an income standard where you and those who surround you are well able to handle such matters from your own resources. Such, I regret to have to tell you, is not the case for a very large percentage of the Canadian people.[1]

The economic devastation of the 1930s, followed by successful government wartime economic planning, caused many Canadians to agree with MacInnis that goals that individuals had once set for themselves should become rights of citizenship. This chapter examines the post-war debates about what services Canadians were entitled to receive from government.

THE POST-WAR LIBERAL CONSENSUS

In the period from 1945 to 1975, Canadians embraced what is often described as a "post-war liberal consensus." It diverged from earlier conceptions of liberalism—which emphasized freedom from state intervention and endorsed such principles as freedom of trade, freedom of speech, and freedom of worship—by emphasizing freedom from want. Recognizing that the marketplace created inequalities in the distribution of wealth, the post-war consensus held that state intervention, rather than being the enemy of liberalism, was its essence, provided that the state limited its intervention to the economic sphere. The term "welfare state" is often used in the Canadian context to describe government programs designed to give cradle-to-grave security to citizens.

Supporters of the new liberalism defined the welfare state as the broad set of programs by which the state ensured a guaranteed minimum income and social opportunities for all citizens as a matter of right. Minimum wages and programs for employment creation, farm subsidies, and public education were included in the definition; so, too, were universal programs such as medical insurance and narrower programs that targeted certain groups, such as social assistance and old-age pensions.

Opponents of state intervention for the purpose of redistributing wealth put a different spin on the welfare state. Although they rarely attacked spending on education or pensions, they derided social assistance and unemployment insurance as programs that robbed people of initiative and cost too much money. These arguments tended to fall on deaf ears in times of prosperity, but they were never completely put to rest. When economic clouds appeared on the horizon in the 1970s, those advocating less ambitious welfare state policies began to gain more influence in policy circles.

FEDERAL PARTIES AND LEADERS

Recognizing the widespread appeal of new social programs, both the Liberals and the Progressive Conservatives embraced the welfare state in the federal election of 1945. With the established parties promising full employment and an array of new social programs, most

Canadians saw no need to take a chance on the radical and inexperienced Co-operative Commonwealth Federation (CCF). The CCF's wartime support was also undermined by a well-financed campaign of major banks and businesses in Canada, supported by most of the Canadian media, to scare off potential socialist voters. After the CCF had formed the official opposition in Ontario in 1943 and the government in Saskatchewan in 1944, every Canadian household received pamphlets warning of the dire consequences of electing a government pledged to gradual socialization of the major corporations in the country. Workers in large companies received similar attack ads against the CCF with their pay packets. The CCF lacked either the funds or the media clout to respond fully to these ads, which, party leaders charged, were filled with lies and distortions.

Before the Second World War, the Liberal and Conservative parties were patronage machines controlled by business interests and elite professional groups, but their programs had different emphases. The Liberals were continentalists, and, however marginally in practice, were disposed to support free trade and a foreign policy independent of Great Britain. The Conservatives were imperialists who, at least in theory, distrusted the Americans and sought greater empire trade and imperial unity in foreign policy. After the war, the empire quickly dissolved and Great Britain became a minor player in international affairs while international trade agreements largely removed the tariff as an issue in Canadian politics.

The result was that for a generation, there was little to differentiate the two major political parties in Canada. Both supported the basic premises of the Cold War, which led to closer continental ties in foreign and defence policy. Both favoured the cautious addition of social programs to appease public demands for social security. Neither condoned a degree of state intervention that might alarm private investors. Personalities and regional interests, rather than overarching ideologies, determined the public image of the main parties. As first radio and later television became the major source of information for voters, party leaders attempted to project themselves as good economic managers rather than as spokespersons for particular ideologies or cohesive programs.

The Liberal victory in the 1945 election demonstrated that most Canadians judged the government's war effort favourably and put their faith in William Lyon Mackenzie King's programs to prevent a postwar depression. But the victory was narrow. Ontario, which had been the province least happy with King's half-hearted policies regarding conscription, gave a majority of its seats to the Conservatives. Alberta favoured the Social Credit Party and Saskatchewan the CCF. British Columbia, meanwhile, virtually provided a three-way split among Liberals, Conservatives, and the CCF. Quebec gave 55 of its 65 seats to the government, though a clutch of Independent and Bloc populaire canadien seats illustrated that many French Canadians remained unhappy with King's conscription compromise. Atlantic Canada and Manitoba, along with Quebec, provided King with his victory. Over the next four years, King, despite the mandate for change that he received, demonstrated that he remained a fiscal conservative, unwilling to sponsor a great deal of social experimentation. In 1948, King stepped down as prime minister and was succeeded by Louis St. Laurent.

Born in 1882 to a poor family in Compton, Quebec, St. Laurent became a successful lawyer and by the 1940s held a string of corporate directorships. King had recruited St. Laurent to his cabinet as minister of Justice in 1941. He had quickly emerged as King's chief Quebec minister and chosen successor to the leadership of the Liberal party. Pleased with their increased prosperity through much of the 1940s and 1950s, Canadians gave St. Laurent resounding election victories in 1949 and 1953. His avuncular style earned him the affectionate nickname "Uncle Louis." Less suspicious than his predecessor of Canadian entanglements in foreign affairs, St. Laurent generally shared the American view of international events.

Support for the Liberals was sagging by 1956 when debate over the Trans-Canada Pipeline bill put it into free fall. Although the decision to provide federal assistance to the pipeline project, which was designed to bring Alberta's natural gas to Ontario and Quebec, was controversial, the issue was compounded by the government's decision to cut off debate in the House of Commons by invoking closure. Tiring of Liberal arrogance after 22 years in power, an increasing number of Canadians shifted their allegiance to the Conservatives. John Diefenbaker formed a minority Progressive Conservative government in 1957 and the following year won the biggest electoral majority held by any government to date—208 out of 265 seats.

Diefenbaker was a successful Saskatchewan lawyer with a burning ambition to succeed in politics. As a member of parliament since 1940, he had become one of the more prominent figures in his party but was twice rejected in national party leadership contests. After Conservative leaders John Bracken and George Drew had failed to defeat the Liberals, the party turned to the ambitious Saskatchewan MP. Sixty-one when he assumed his party's leadership in 1956, Diefenbaker was a powerful orator and liked to champion the cause of the underdog. His denunciation of the Liberal old-age pension as too small, his call for a huge spending program to open up Canada's North, and his willingness to grant subsidies to the economically challenged Atlantic provinces demonstrated that

John F. Kennedy, Governor General Georges Vanier, John Diefenbaker, Jacqueline Kennedy, and Olive Diefenbaker, Ottawa, 1961.
Library and Archives Canada/PA154665

the post-war Conservatives were not necessarily fiscally conservative.

Diefenbaker's pursuit of closer trade and foreign policy ties between Canada and Great Britain harkened to old-style Tory imperialism, but in practice he could do little to divert trade to Great Britain. Despite his eventual defiance of the Americans on nuclear weapons policy, Diefenbaker and his cabinet were forced, like their Liberal predecessors, to govern in a world dominated by the political and economic power of the United States. Their options blunted by the context in which they operated and their largely unexamined liberal values, Diefenbaker and his cabinet appeared to waffle on most issues and to represent little ideological difference from the Liberals they had defeated.

Lester Pearson became Liberal leader shortly before the 1958 election that so humbled his party. A long-time bureaucrat in the Department of External Affairs, Pearson was deputy minister when his old boss, St. Laurent, became prime minister and asked him to join the government as minister of External Affairs. Pearson remained at that post until the defeat of the Liberals in 1957. In that year, he won the Nobel Peace Prize for his role in defusing the Suez Crisis in 1956.

As leader of the opposition, Pearson recommitted his party to implementing the social programs it had promised in 1945 but never fully delivered. Pearson formed minority governments in 1963 and 1965, dependent on support from the New Democratic Party (NDP), the successor of the CCF. The brief Pearson period represented the heyday of social reform in twentieth-century Canada, with medicare capping a series of new programs designed to provide Canadians with a social safety net. By the time he left office, Pearson could boast that he had taken the reins of power in a country whose social programs were similar to those of the United States and in five short years had left the Americans in the dust.

Pierre Elliott Trudeau, elected Liberal leader and then prime minister in 1968, had the image of a reformer. The son of a Montreal millionaire, Trudeau

Pierre Elliott Trudeau.
Library and Archives Canada/C25000

was an intellectual and world traveller who had few real jobs on his résumé before he entered politics in the 1965 federal election. As a youth, Trudeau had embraced the fascist and anti-Semitic ideology that was common in nationalist Catholic intellectual circles in Quebec at the time. He later rejected his earlier nationalist and racist views, and became associated with progressive causes in his home province. He maintained this image in the federal arena. As minister of Justice from 1965 to 1968, he was responsible for legislation that legalized homosexual relations, liberalized divorce laws, and made abortion legal under some circumstances.

Largely unknown to the Canadian public before he faced a Liberal leadership convention in 1968, Trudeau captured the public imagination with his promise to create a "just society." Cosmopolitan and debonair by Canadian political standards, he projected an image of a vigorous, trendy, forward-looking leader. The spellbound media lapped it up, and Trudeaumania was born. In his 16 years of government, Trudeau consolidated existing social and regulatory programs and proved responsive to new social forces within Canadian society. Nevertheless, the wave of reform that had characterized the Pearson years ebbed as the economy slowed in the early 1970s.

THIRD PARTIES IN POST-WAR CANADA

Between 1945 and 1975, third parties continued to play a role in the nation's politics. The post-war liberal consensus failed to attract the allegiance of people on the left and right of the centrist mainline parties, which nevertheless were often forced to adopt some of the polices of their frequently perceptive critics.

The CCF, at the top of the polls for part of the Second World War, failed to translate that support into votes at war's end. Reduced to an eight-member rump in parliament in the Diefenbaker sweep of 1958, the CCF joined forces with organized labour in 1961 to create the NDP. Both the post-war CCF and the NDP were more moderate versions of the CCF that had been born in the Great Depression. In an attempt to shake off paranoid Cold War allegations that linked the party with communism, the CCF largely abandoned its commitment to public ownership. Instead, it proposed private enterprise regulated by a strong state that would control the direction of the economy and implement extensive social programs and progressive taxation to redistribute wealth. Despite its third-party status, the CCF-NDP had a significant impact on policy. The Liberals and Conservatives assumed that if they did not implement the social programs demanded by the CCF-NDP, they could lose votes to the socialist upstart.

On the right of the political spectrum, Ernest Manning, Social Credit premier of Alberta from 1944 to 1968, called in the 1960s for the Conservatives and Social Credit to merge to provide a truly conservative alternative. The unpopularity of such an idea was obvious during the 1967 Conservative leadership race to replace John Diefenbaker. The two leading candidates, Robert Stanfield and Duff Roblin, the former premiers of Nova Scotia and Manitoba, respectively, were both liberal-minded and had expanded the role of the state

in the lives of the residents of their respective provinces. Stanfield's early championing of the idea of a guaranteed annual income made him at least as liberal as most of the Liberal ministers he faced as leader of the opposition in the federal parliament from 1967 to 1976.

Social Credit had faded as a force in federal politics in English Canada by the 1960s, but the Créditistes, the Quebec wing of the party, carried 26 of 74 federal seats in that province in the 1962 election. Many working-class and rural Quebecers, dissatisfied with the traditional parties, regarded the Créditistes as a legitimate avenue of protest. The charismatic leadership of Réal Caouette, resentment against the power of the big banks over people's lives, and the Diefenbaker government's failure to integrate Francophone Quebecers into national policy-making helped the Créditistes make their breakthrough.

PROVINCIAL POLITICS

Social Credit's power base was essentially provincial. Its Alberta bastion was impregnable until 1971, when Peter Lougheed's Conservatives upset 36 years of continuous rule. British Columbia also expressed its conservative political values through the Social Credit Party rather than the Progressive Conservatives. In 1952, Social Credit, led by the charismatic W.A.C. Bennett, began a 20-year reign in British Columbia. Although the governments of Alberta and British Columbia embraced the new state interventionism in practice, their leaders denounced Canada's drift to the left.

The West also provided a provincial stronghold for democratic socialism. In Saskatchewan, the CCF-NDP governed from 1944 to 1964 and pioneered provincially based hospital insurance and medicare. NDP governments elected in Manitoba in 1969, Saskatchewan in 1971, and British Columbia in 1972 were responsible for a degree of social experimentation well exceeding that in the other provinces. The record of CCF-NDP governments in the western provinces made it more difficult for mainline parties at the national level to ignore the practicality and popularity of many social programs.

In Quebec provincial politics, Maurice Duplessis's Union Nationale provided a conservative administration until the death of *le chef* in 1959. Despite attempts by his successors to provide a more progressive face for the Union Nationale, Quebec voters elected the Liberals in 1960 and 1962. That party proved both reformist and nationalist, but the pace of reforms left many behind, and the Union Nationale was returned to office one last time in 1966. Thereafter, Quebec politics polarized between the federalist Liberals and the Parti Québécois (PQ), a new party created in 1968 under the leadership of René Lévesque. The PQ was devoted not only to achieving sovereignty for Quebec but also to increased levels of social planning.

Politics in the Atlantic provinces mirrored national politics: indistinguishable reform-minded Liberal and Conservative parties were differentiated in the public mind by the personalities of their leaders. With the lowest standard of living in the country and a shrinking proportion of seats in the House of Commons, Atlantic Canadians felt that they had little choice other than to be allied to a national party that could throw some policy and patronage crumbs their way. Even in industrial Cape Breton, where CCF candidates had a significant following, politics took a conservative turn in the 1950s. Meanwhile, the region's political leaders began cooperating across party lines to pressure Ottawa for policies that would lift the region from its economic doldrums. Atlantic premiers lobbied for special regional subsidies and development projects that would jumpstart their economies. Although their tactics brought some concessions, the region continued to lag behind the rest of the nation.

Ontario politics seemed the most predictable, with the Progressive Conservatives in power without interruption from 1943 to 1985, usually with a comfortable majority of seats in the legislature. The Conservatives were sometimes called "Red Tories" because of their willingness to spend lavishly on education and health in an effort to maintain public support. While the Ontario government was no more eager than administrations in poorer provinces to increase social assistance to the poor and was slow to move on minimum wage legislation and environmental regulation, the level of state intervention seemed to satisfy a voting majority. The well-funded, efficiently run party, commonly known as "the Big Blue Machine," was a force to be reckoned with throughout the post-war decades, not only in Canada's largest and wealthiest province but also in Ottawa, where it exercised enormous influence on the direction of national policy.

NEWFOUNDLAND AND LABRADOR ENTERS CONFEDERATION

Newfoundland and Labrador's entry into confederation in 1949 serves to illustrate the impact of the welfare state and the Cold War on post-war developments. While Canada's social programs proved enticing to many people in the dominion, the demands

---

Symbols of Independence

After 1945, Canada moved quickly to break many ties that smacked of colonial subordination. The Canadian Citizenship Act of 1947 enabled immigrants, for the first time, to become citizens of Canada as opposed to "British subjects." Shortly afterward, Canada's Supreme Court became indeed supreme in legal matters, as appeals to the Judicial Committee of the Privy Council in Great Britain were abolished. In 1952, Vincent Massey became the first governor general to be named by the government of Canada rather than by the British government. He was also the first native-born Canadian to hold the post.

The flag debate of 1964 showed that some Canadians, particularly former prime minister Diefenbaker, were unhappy with the severing of symbolic ties with Great Britain. The Pearson government proposed a distinctive Canadian flag with the maple leaf as the symbol of the nation. Diefenbaker's unsuccessful counter-proposal was a new flag that incorporated the Union Jack and the fleur-de-lys as a way of paying tribute to Canada's two founding peoples. Such a proposal ignored not only Native peoples, but also the increasing numbers of Canadians whose origins were neither British nor French.

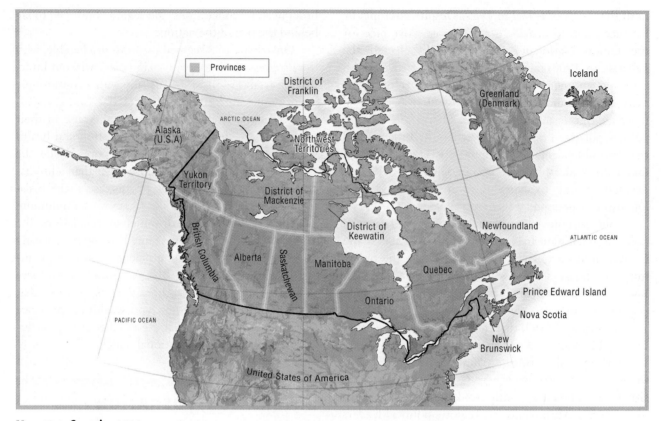

MAP 15.1 **Canada, 1949.**

of the Cold War made Canada more eager than ever to accept it as a new province. Great Britain wanted to rid itself of what might become a liability once the post-war economic boom ended, and Canada wanted to ensure that it controlled Newfoundland and Labrador's vast resources and strategically located territory, which sat astride the sea lanes of the North Atlantic, and therefore played an important role in Cold War strategy.

Newfoundlanders and Labradorians themselves were divided as to what, if anything, should replace the Commission of Government that had ruled them since 1934. In June 1946, they elected delegates to a national convention to recommend future forms of government. While some people, especially in the outports, favoured confederation with Canada, others, including many leaders of the Roman Catholic Church, wanted a return to the status of a separate dominion with responsible government.

Through radio broadcasts of the convention, Joseph Smallwood emerged as the principal proponent of joining Canada. Journalist, trade unionist, and farmer, the colourful Smallwood promised escape from the old dominion politics and a better material life within confederation. He argued that economic uncertainty would be forever banished by the social safety net provided by family allowances, unemployment insurance, and old-age pensions. Anti-confederates countered that closer economic ties to the United States would make a self-governing dominion prosperous.

The majority in the convention recommended against putting confederation on the ballot in the referendum, but the British did so anyway. Newfoundlanders and Labradorians, like their convention delegates, remained divided, casting 44.6 percent of their votes in the 3 June 1948 referendum for responsible government, 41.1 percent for confederation, and 14.3 percent for retaining the commission government. A second referendum on 2 July removed the Commission of Government option and resulted in 52.4 percent in favour of confederation with Canada. Soon afterward, the terms of union were finalized, and on 31 March 1949, Newfoundland

and Labrador became the tenth province of Canada, rounding out the nation from the Atlantic to the Pacific. Smallwood's Liberals won the first provincial elections in May 1949, and he remained premier of the province until forced to resign in January 1972 after the Conservatives, under the leadership of Frank Moores, finally toppled "the only living Father of Confederation."

POLITICS AND REPRESENTATION

The federal parliament and provincial legislatures remained largely the privileged arena of wealthy white males of British and, in the case of Quebec, French extraction. The upper levels of the public service were staffed with men from the same backgrounds. As the period progressed, there were slight gains for groups outside this dominant circle. In 1951, Thérèse Casgrain became leader of the Quebec CCF. Grace MacInnis was the only woman in parliament from 1968 to 1972, but five women were elected in 1972 and eight in 1974. A few women held cabinet posts, beginning with Ellen Fairclough, who was appointed secretary of state by John Diefenbaker in 1957, and Judy LaMarsh, who held major portfolios in the Pearson administration and was a key figure in the appointment of the Royal Commission on the Status of Women in 1967.

Not all politicians came from French or English backgrounds. Diefenbaker was partly of German-Canadian extraction, as was Ed Schreyer, who became Manitoba's first NDP premier in 1969. Herb Gray was appointed by Pierre Trudeau to cabinet, becoming the first Jew to hold such a position; Dave Barrett, the first NDP premier of British Columbia, was also of Jewish descent. The successes of ethnic immigrants were especially noticeable at the civic level. Steven Juba served as mayor of Winnipeg for two decades, William Hawrelak was mayor of Edmonton for several terms between the 1950s and the 1970s, and Nathan Phillips, who was Jewish, served as mayor of Toronto. Visible-minority Canadians fared less well and were rarely elected to legislatures or parliament. Dave Barrett's cabinet included one Native, and his caucus included two African Canadians. One of these was Rosemary Brown, who won 37 percent of the ballots for the NDP federal leadership in 1974 in a contest with Ed Broadbent.

Ellen Fairclough was MP for Hamilton West from 1950 to 1963 and, in 1957, became the first woman to serve in the federal cabinet.
City of Ottawa Archives/CA19893

SHAPING THE WELFARE STATE

The post-war welfare state had an inauspicious start. Shortly after the 1945 election, Mackenzie King called the Dominion-Provincial Conference on Reconstruction. The federal government's Green Book of proposals prepared for the conference called for comprehensive national programs to take care of the old, the sick, and the unemployed and support for public works to coincide with economic downturns. To fund these costly endeavours, Ottawa suggested it would require exclusive rights to income and corporate taxes and to succession duties. The provinces, led by Ontario and Quebec, argued that they could not surrender all major taxes and still fulfill their responsibilities. After meeting with the provinces over a period of nine months, the federal government announced that the talks had collapsed.

By this time, conservative forces in Canadian society were urging caution with respect to welfare state

Elsie Gregory MacGill

One of the strong voices within the Royal Commission on the Status of Women for a welfare state more attuned to women's needs was Elsie Gregory MacGill (1905–1980). MacGill was the daughter of British Columbia's first woman judge, Helen Gregory MacGill, a lifelong campaigner for women's rights. Refusing to be held back by a bout of childhood polio, MacGill embarked on a brilliant career as an aircraft designer. After becoming the University of Toronto's first woman graduate in engineering, she earned a master's degree in aeronautical engineering at MIT in 1929, a North American first for a woman. From 1938 to 1943, MacGill was chief aeronautical engineer at the Fort William plant of Canadian Car and Foundry. In this position, she designed Hawker Hurricane planes, the prize of the Allies' Second World War fighter aircraft. Responsible for the production of more than 2000 planes, she headed a staff of 4500 at the peak of Hawker fabrication.

After the war, MacGill set up her own consulting practice, continuing to design aircraft for most of her life. She became an activist in women's groups, serving for a time as president of the Canadian Federation of Business and Professional Women's Clubs. She fought for paid maternity leave, liberalized abortion laws, and publicly supported day care. Appointed as one of the members of the Royal Commission on the Status of Women, Elsie MacGill, as one of Canada's best-known feminists and scientists, was regarded by many as almost a co-chair to the official commission chair, broadcaster Florence Bird.

Elsie Gregory MacGill.
Library and Archives Canada/PA-148380

measures. The social radicalism of the Great Depression and the war had jarred many pro-business groups, such as the Canadian Chamber of Commerce, into supporting a degree of social reform, but they reverted to conservative positions once the predicted post-war depression failed to materialize. The country could not afford to implement a variety of social programs at once, critics argued, warning that if corporate taxation were to be the source of revenues for welfare, private investment would quickly dry up. The Canadian Medical Association, a wartime supporter of national prepaid medical insurance, recognized that a return to Depression conditions, in which even middle-class Canadians could not pay their doctors, was unlikely. It increasingly supported private, doctor-controlled medical insurance schemes and rejected a state medicare program.

THE ORIGINS OF MEDICARE

Although many physicians argued that doctor-controlled and voluntary private insurance schemes were preferable to a state program forcing all doctors and patients to enroll, national public opinion had long been against them. In 1944 and again in 1949, 80 percent of Canadians indicated their approval of a federal health plan that would cover complete medical and hospital care for a monthly flat rate. Governments initially rejected the call for universal medical and hospital insurance, but took steps to improve medical services. They put more money into hospitals, and most provinces paid medical bills for the poorest of the poor. In 1957, a hospital insurance program with costs shared by the provincial and federal governments was implemented.

Prosperity allowed more people to consult doctors and access hospitals, but health care services were uneven. The regional distribution of medical personnel paralleled regional patterns of wealth. Although Canadians collectively had one doctor to serve every 938 people in 1959, much more favourable ratios were found in Ontario, British Columbia, and Alberta. In Newfoundland, there was only one doctor for every 2190 residents. The gap in dental services, which were generally deemed inadequate everywhere in the country, was more extreme—one dentist to every 2400 British Columbians, but only one for every 11 000 in Newfoundland; if St. John's and Corner Brook were excluded, the figure for dental care in the province was one dentist for every 30 859 people.

The lack of local medical services caused the Newfoundland Federation of Labour to mock the slogans on the posters sent around to schools by Ontario public health organizations:

> "Brush your teeth three times a day and see your dentist twice a year," said posters in the school. The dentist was 150 miles away.

> "Fight cancer with a checkup and a cheque." The checkup meant a trip by coastal boat to a doctor with no training or equipment to diagnose cancer.

> "Prize your eyes," said the CNIB, but on the coast of Labrador or at the head of Bay d'Espoir, there had never been an eye specialist, not even in transit.[2]

By 1960, almost half of Canadians had purchased private medical insurance, but most plans covered only diagnostic and curative services and not dental care, prescription drugs, preventive services, or mental health care. Given the level of poverty in Atlantic Canada, it is not surprising that coverage in the region was 50 percent less than for the country as a whole. In the Prairie provinces, coverage was much lower in rural areas than in cities. People in the North often remained without professional medical services of any kind.

Diefenbaker established the Royal Commission on Health Services in 1961. Its report, submitted to the Pearson government in 1964, called for a universal medicare scheme embracing hospital, physician, dental, and prescription costs. The Liberals made medicare an issue in the 1965 election and, on their return to office, announced what was to be the first stage of a national health insurance program. While to some extent a response to the royal commission, the government's action also owed much to the province of Saskatchewan, which had introduced medicare in 1962. Saskatchewan had persisted with its legislation despite a strike by its

VOICES FROM THE PAST

A Plea for Medicare

Reverend Michael Di Stasi, minister of St. Paul's United Church in Toronto, told the Royal Commission on Health Services in April 1962 about the lives of unskilled Toronto workers from depressed parts of southern Italy and why they would benefit from a universal state-funded program of medical services.

> They have no assurance of steady employment, and many employers do nothing to make them eligible for unemployment insurance, so when they have no work they have no income. . . .

> Because they must live as cheaply as they can, the newly arrived immigrants crowd into a house where every

room is a bedroom. They don't want it this way. As soon as a man can, he buys or rents a house and sub-lets every spare room, trying to save towards having a real home. In times of low employment men may work for fifty or sixty cents an hour, walking miles to work to save carfare. Often the wife helps by earning a little at some menial job. . . .

Overcrowding, unemployment, lack of necessities, anxiety and depression have their effect on health so there is sickness in the immigrant families. And people at their income level cannot provide any pre-paid medical service.[3]

doctors. To encourage compliance, the government gave in to demands that physicians receive fees for service rather than salaries and that medical treatment continue to be dispensed from physicians' offices rather than from community health clinics integrating the services of a variety of health professionals.

The federal plan, implemented in 1968, added physician care and the services of some non-physician specialists to the earlier federal-provincial hospital insurance scheme. Ottawa would share costs with the provinces if provincial programs adhered to four principles: universality of coverage, coverage of most medical treatments, portability of benefits, and provincial administration. Although every province except Saskatchewan and British Columbia criticized the federal plan, by 1970 all provinces had established programs embodying the four federal principles.

Welfare Reform

While the jewel in the crown of the Pearson social programs was universal medicare, there were also other significant reforms, beginning with the introduction of the Canada Pension Plan (CPP), an earnings-related pension, in 1965. The CPP did not supplant the modest old-age pension that all seniors received regardless of income beginning in 1951. Recognizing that it was impossible to live on the old-age pension alone and that many pensioners had no other resources, Pearson introduced the Guaranteed Income Supplement in 1966. Low-interest loans for post-secondary students also made their appearance in 1966. The Canada Assistance Plan (CAP) of the same year built on the 1956 cost-sharing agreement on welfare and assured all Canadians of the right to receive social assistance. CAP established national guidelines that the provinces were obliged to incorporate into their welfare programs in order to receive federal assistance.

Canada's Welfare State in Perspective

How did Canadian efforts in the social policy arena compare with those of other countries? Critics of big government point to the rapid increase in Canadian social expenditures. According to the Organisation for Economic Co-operation and Development (OECD), the cost rose from 12.1 to 21.7 percent of gross domestic product (GDP) from 1960 to 1981. Less publicized was the modest extent of government spending on social programs relative to other OECD countries, including some of the world's most competitive trading nations. West Germany had the OECD's largest per capita social expenditures in 1960, yet it continued to post the greatest productivity gains of any OECD country. Sweden, Italy, Austria, and the Netherlands, all successful in global trade, also exceeded Canada in growth and volume of social expenditures.

Pensions are a case in point. By 1981, Canada devoted less of its GDP to public pensions than any other industrialized country. The CPP had, from the beginning, kept rates low to appease private insurance companies. Even with the Guaranteed Income Supplement, pensioners could not maintain a decent standard of living unless they had other income. Private pensions failed to make up the difference: among western democracies, only the United States had less private pension protection than Canada. In 1980, 44 percent of paid workers in Canada had private pension plan coverage. Lack of portability of most plans meant that many workers nominally covered by pension plans would never collect from them. It was not surprising, then, that Statistics Canada reported in 1980 that 27 percent of seniors lived on "limited incomes" and that the percentage for elderly women was even higher.

The Canadian version of the welfare state generally treated women less fairly than men. CPP pensions, which were calculated on the basis of individual earnings, penalized women on two fronts: first, women workers earned on average far less than men; second, many women withdrew completely from the labour force to raise their children. Unemployment insurance policy was also discriminatory. Men could leave jobs for any reason and, if they had worked the required number of weeks, collect unemployment insurance, provided they demonstrated that they were making reasonable efforts to find new work. Women who quit or were forced to leave a job during a pregnancy or after giving birth were deemed ineligible to collect unemployment insurance, even if they were looking for work. Women's organizations and the labour movement successfully campaigned to have this exclusion lifted.

The CAP was less discriminatory. It made state assistance, however modest, available to all women without male partners, including single and divorced mothers, rather than leaving provinces and municipalities the right to determine which "undeserving" women did not qualify for welfare. But "man-in-the-house" rules persisted in most jurisdictions, and a woman could be cut off social assistance if it was discovered that a man was spending the night at her home. In Ontario, volunteers from charitable organizations carried out surveillance of the moral behaviour of mothers' allowance recipients. Welfare rights groups protested the assumption that suggested that a man must be providing economic support to a woman who was his sexual partner, but the rules for assistance changed slowly.

Day-Care and the New Liberalism

The 1970 *Report of the Royal Commission on the Status of Women* argued that a major barrier to women's economic equality was the lack of affordable day care. Women were assigned the responsibility for child care, but had little government support except for family allowances, whose value over time had been eroded by Ottawa's failure to peg rates to inflation. If a mother of young children worked outside the home, she generally found that the costs of good private child care were prohibitive. The royal commission concluded: "Parents require supplementary help, and society may legitimately be called upon to contribute to community services for its younger generation. The equality of women means little without such a programme, which should include . . . day-care centres."[4]

In some countries, notably Sweden and France, state programs of free day care for all children had contributed to dramatic reductions in the rates of poverty for single mothers and fairer distribution of income between men and women. The royal commission recommended a more modest national program funded in part by user fees geared to income. Concern about rising social costs and a general indifference to gender equality led most governments to shelve this recommendation.

Public opinion on the day-care issue was divided because many Canadians continued to believe that a woman's place was in the home. Speaking to the Canadian Chamber of Commerce in October 1946, Laura Hardy, president of the National Council of Women of Canada, stated: "As women, we want to live in a Canada in which we can raise our children in our own homes and in the schools of our choice, not in public institutions under the guidance of the State."[5] Such phraseology reflected the Cold War rhetoric of opponents of reform: reformers, they often implied, were trying to impose a totalitarian communist state in which individual choice disappeared. A Gallup poll in 1960 indicated that 93 percent of Canadians opposed the idea of mothers of young children working outside the home; 10 years later, 80 percent remained opposed.

For both economic and personal reasons, many married women with children worked outside the home. The old liberalism dictated that the state should not intervene in a family's decision about how to care for children, but the new welfare-state liberalism suggested that the government had an obligation to ensure affordable, quality day care for the children of working parents. In practice, in the 1950s, only Ontario had developed systematic licensing of day-care centres; only Ontario and British Columbia had modest programs of subsidized day care. Even in these two provinces, most working parents relied on private arrangements for child care.

Studies by women's groups and social agencies pointed to the inadequacies of such haphazard arrangements. Forced by economic desperation to work yet unable to find affordable and reliable child-care centres, women sometimes left very young children with abusive, neglectful, or alcoholic caregivers. Social policy researchers documented a variety of cases of children warehoused in quarters infested with parasites, in facilities without toys or play areas, and in spaces so cramped that closets became sleep areas. Families often kept school-age children home to look after younger siblings. A disturbing number of children, including pre-schoolers, spent much of the day alone. Social workers and women's groups maintained that it was time to stop arguing about whether it was desirable that mothers work, recognize that many were working, and insist that the state help them to find quality, affordable day care.

By the end of the 1960s, several provincial governments had begun to provide child-care subsidies for the neediest families, but the provinces proved as unwilling as the federal government to fund universal public day care. While none of Canada's political parties made child care a priority, the NDP was more sympathetic than others to the issue. When Social Credit was voted out of office in British Columbia in September 1972, 2600 children received subsidized day care in the province. By the end of 1973, the new NDP administration was providing subsidies for 9500 children.

HOUSING POLICY

Discussions about the cost of state-sponsored social programs tended to assume that the poor were the main recipients, but this was not always the case. In 1954, the Canadian Mortgage and Housing Corporation (CMHC), a government body, hoping to encourage more private initiative, agreed to guarantee mortgages from private financial companies. To reduce the potential for default, the CMHC limited its loan guarantees to middle- and upper-income Canadians. Little government aid was available to renters, despite campaigns by trade unions, women's groups, and the Canadian Legion. Although the beginnings of state-subsidized senior citizens' housing were in evidence by the late 1950s, few public housing units were built for families before the 1960s.

Gradually and grudgingly, federal and provincial governments began to admit that the market economy would not adequately house all Canadians. The Ontario Housing Corporation was established in 1964; by 1972, it managed 50 000 units of public housing, including publicly and privately funded developments. Other provinces had similar, if less ambitious, programs. Federal funds made available to the provinces for social housing on a cost-sharing basis were not fully tapped, except by Ontario and Manitoba once the NDP came to power in that province. Most of the public-housing developments built in the 1960s and 1970s were notable for overcrowding, cheapness of construction, and lack of green space. Residents created committees to complain about pipes that froze every winter, inadequate heating systems, and cracking plaster. Their homes were a stark contrast to suburban

houses whose mortgages were guaranteed and subsidized by state funds. Yet only the homes of the poor were referred to as "welfare housing."

THE PROVINCES AND THE NEW LIBERALISM

The provinces extended their social welfare in areas other than social housing. In addition to providing funds for new schools, universities, hospitals, and highways, provinces established vocational programs to train young people in the skills demanded in the new economy and funded bursary programs to enable bright children from lower-income families to pursue post-secondary education. The new liberalism also motivated provincial governments to make social services and education opportunities available on a more equitable basis throughout provincial jurisdictions rather than allowing local councils and school boards to determine what services their area could afford. One of the most sweeping programs of municipal reform was undertaken in New Brunswick under the leadership of Louis J. Robichaud, who held office from 1960 to 1970. While his Program of Equal Opportunity brought howls of a "French takeover" from many Anglophones, it helped improve conditions in the poor, rural municipalities where most Acadians in the province lived.

The federal government aided poorer provinces in their efforts to improve social services. Beginning in 1957, Ottawa calculated the per capita revenues that various provinces could raise if they were taxing at the rates of the two wealthiest provinces, British Columbia and Ontario. It then provided per capita grants, called equalization grants, to provinces whose revenue potential fell short of the two wealthiest provinces. At least in theory, the size of these grants was meant to allow revenue-poor provinces to provide education, health, and social services comparable to those in the wealthier provinces. The percentage of federal corporate and personal income taxes that was rebated rose gradually from a mere 5 percent just after the Second World War to 24 percent by the early 1960s. Federal cost-sharing programs and grants enriched provincial coffers but created the threat of federal interference. Alberta's Social Credit government, for example, objected from the time that it joined the national hospital insurance program to federal insistence that it stop charging user fees for hospital care if it wished to be eligible for its full grant under the scheme.

At the same time, the Atlantic provinces, with their lagging economies, had little choice but to become dependent on federal largesse. In 1958, the federal government established subsidies in the form of Atlantic Provinces Adjustment Grants in recognition of the region's difficult position. The three Maritime provinces benefited absolutely from this transfer of moneys, but Newfoundland approached the grant from a different perspective. Having entered confederation in 1949 with a special subsidy to keep its services equal to those of the Maritime provinces, it soon became just one of four poor eastern provinces with claims on Ottawa.

Transfer payments were not the only federal schemes to help the have-not provinces. Ottawa also implemented a variety of targeted development programs. For example, in the early 1960s the government passed the Agriculture Rehabilitation and Development Act, which poured money into rural areas to improve efficiency in the development of local resources and create alternative employment in depressed regions. Because of its small size and largely rural-based economy, Prince Edward Island became the focus of a 15-year comprehensive development plan in 1969 that promised an investment of $725 million to help restructure farming and fishing activities, improve infrastructure, and diversify the economy, most notably in the area of tourism. Although there was some discussion about building a causeway to the mainland, this initiative was shelved for the time being as too costly and too controversial.

The federal and provincial governments attempted to lure industries into depressed provinces and the poorer regions of wealthy provinces. Unwilling to have the state itself take an entrepreneurial role, governments searched for private investors upon whom they could lavish government funds in return for promises to establish new industries. The major recipients of regional assistance grants were corporations. The 1960 federal budget allowed firms double the normal tax advantage for capital expenditures if they located in areas designated as slow growth. In the 1960s and 1970s, garment firms that set up what amounted to low-wage

sweatshops in rural areas of Manitoba, for instance, received a dizzying array of federal, provincial, and municipal subsidies. These included grants to introduce new technologies, "forgivable" loans from the federal government, federal wage subsidies, tax concessions, government-paid training for employees, subsidized hydro-electricity rates, and reduced tariffs on fabrics. Despite such programs, business leaders took great exception to federal NDP leader David Lewis's remarks criticizing "corporate welfare bums" in the 1972 federal election.

In the have-not provinces, the programs to lure corporate investment were equally wasteful, encouraging, it appeared, a take-the-money-and-run attitude on the part of investors. Manitoba threw away $150 million to attract mysterious foreign investors, who later proved to have Mafia connections, to develop a forestry complex. Saskatchewan developed a partnership with a multinational forestry company that siphoned off provincial money as efficiently as the Mafia did in Manitoba. In Nova Scotia, millions of dollars were lost in efforts to establish a heavy-water plant in Glace Bay and an electronics company in Stellarton. Both communities had been seriously affected by the decline in the coal industry that had previously sustained them, but the new industries failed to take root. Millions of dollars were poured into New Brunswick premier Richard Hatfield's pet project to build a luxury automobile, the Bricklin, but that company, too, went into receivership. In Newfoundland, Premier Smallwood attracted a variety of entrepreneurs willing to gamble with taxpayers' money, but few of his industrial ventures paid off. An oil refinery at Come-by-Chance that had been opened with great fanfare in October 1973—the *Queen Elizabeth II* was chartered at a reported fee of $97 000 a day for the occasion—went bankrupt within three years.

Regional assistance incentives generally failed in their stated objectives: they served to maintain rather than change the relative distribution of wealth in the country. State-subsidized private enterprise seemed no better a model for economic development in the peripheral regions of the country than unaided free enterprise. The Atlantic region, Manitoba, and Saskatchewan became dependent for much of their income on federal transfer payments. Fully half of the Atlantic region's income was derived from federal transfer payments by 1975.

The failure of regional development programs encouraged Atlantic Canadians to fight to at least hold on to what they already had. The citizens of Sydney, with help from Cape Bretoners generally, campaigned tirelessly to prevent their steel mill from closing down in the mid-1960s, when it was abandoned by the Dominion Steel and Coal Corporation (DOSCO). The provincial government agreed to operate the steel mill while the federal and provincial governments together established the Cape Breton Development Corporation (DEVCO) to keep the coal mines in operation and to seek to diversify Cape Breton's declining industrial base. But the governments' failure to modernize the steel mill demonstrated their attitude that the purpose of the takeovers was to save jobs in the short term rather than to build a strong industrial foundation for the area's future.

Public money was also wasted in central Canada as the federal government lavished funds on an unneeded second international airport for Montreal at Mirabel and on high-technology firms in the Ottawa region that failed to live up to their advance publicity. Among Canada's poorer provinces, Quebec seemed the most successful in using provincial subsidies to attract new industries. The investment arm of the Quebec Pension Plan offered competing incentives to companies thinking of building new plants or moving existing ones. Wealthier provinces had the luxury of focusing on indirect subsidies. Ontario simply stepped up existing infrastructure programs, ensuring that the transportation system and provincial training programs met industrial requirements. The Social Credit administrations in British Columbia and Alberta used low provincial taxes as a means of encouraging diversification. W.A.C. Bennett, the Social Credit premier in British Columbia from 1952 to 1972, proved somewhat less dogmatic in his reliance on private enterprise than Ernest Manning, the premier of Alberta from 1943 to 1968. He created a publicly owned ferry corporation, eliminating private operators, and placed the privately owned BC Electric under provincial government ownership in his drive to create an infrastructure that would attract more industry. Huge dams and new highways also attested to Bennett's ambition to turn British Columbia into an industrial powerhouse.

Despite incentive programs, secondary industry continued to concentrate in central Canada. In the mid-1970s,

Alberta made a highly publicized, though initially largely unsuccessful, effort to use its energy wealth to challenge this pattern. Conservative premier Lougheed warned that Alberta's oil and gas revenues must be used to diversify the economy to prepare for the era when these resources would be depleted. In 1975, his government created the Heritage Trust Fund, into which a portion of oil royalties was committed to provide moneys to stimulate new economic activity. Saskatchewan's NDP government followed a different tack, buying shares for the state in private companies in order to encourage economic development. It was responsible for establishing a steel-manufacturing firm in Regina, but the province's limited resources relative to the Heritage Trust Fund restricted achievements of this kind.

The energy-producing provinces responded bitterly when the federal government attempted to increase its revenues from oil and gas developments in the wake of the huge increases in oil prices imposed by the Organization of the Petroleum Exporting Countries (OPEC) after the Arab-Israeli war of October 1973. They were equally resistant to federal intervention to shield Canadian consumers from the price shocks, particularly when many of those consumers were businesses located in central Canada. Resource policy was added to a roster of western grievances against the federal government, which also included monetary policy, the promotion of bilingualism, the introduction of the metric system, and indifference to the plight of farmers.

The Prairie region had its dissenters. Saskatchewan sociologist John Conway noted that Alberta premier Lougheed "bash[ed] the 'feds' and [won] overwhelming mandates while ignoring the fact that his provincial economy is the near-private reserve of the multinational oil companies."[6] Whatever the complaints from the West and the Atlantic about central Canadian dominance in the federal government, the province most alienated from Ottawa was in central Canada: Quebec.

MODERNIZATION AND NATIONALISM IN QUEBEC

The new liberalism almost guaranteed a collision between Ottawa and Quebec City. With Ottawa insisting that the federal government play a large role in all areas of social and economic development, Quebec's long-standing resistance to federal involvement in areas of provincial jurisdiction became more pronounced. In the 1950s, Duplessis spurned more than $200 million in federal moneys earmarked for Quebec universities and refused to enter into any federal-provincial agreements that would give Ottawa the power to interfere in provincial affairs.

Determination to resist federal encroachments increased during the Quiet Revolution ushered in by the election of Lesage's Liberals in 1960. Following the Second World War, Francophones in Quebec, especially those living in the province's major cities, had experienced tremendous social change. They had embraced the secular values of the rest of North America and developed new ideas about the role of the state in their society. Nationalists in the province had expected their provincial government to follow policies that reflected a new liberal consensus and at the same time ensure that the national identity of Quebec's majority was preserved within the Canadian confederation.

Changes within the Roman Catholic Church helped precipitate a rising tide of reformism within Quebec. In the mid-1960s, Pope John XXIII convened the Second Vatican Council, which emphasized greater simplicity in church ceremonies and democratic participation in church governance. This new approach reinforced reformist approaches in Roman Catholicism and ensured that church leaders would not use their power to block the social reforms proposed by the Lesage government.

Although no conscious plan shaped the policies of the Lesage administration, its overall goal was to promote economic development in Quebec under Francophone control. This meant a significant expansion of the role of the state. One of the leading exponents of the new *étatisme* in Lesage's cabinet was René Lévesque. He waged a successful campaign for the province to nationalize all private hydro companies, making Hydro-Québec a monopoly. Ontario, after all, had nationalized hydro-electricity several generations earlier, and cheap electricity had helped fuel its industrialization. Surely, Quebec could imitate such success while creating positions for Francophone managers and engineers in massive power projects, breaking the cycle in which Anglophone entrepreneurs favoured their own for top jobs.

Another major provincial initiative was the establishment of the Quebec Pension Plan in 1965 in response to the creation of the Canada Pension Plan. Lesage argued that a separate plan was needed to provide Quebec with an investment fund to encourage secondary industries and build the infrastructure required to exploit natural resources. Over time, the fund would be used to give the province minority shares in companies, allowing it to push those companies to invest in Quebec and increase their Francophone representation.

Quebec's desire to run its own social programs soon led to confrontation with Ottawa. In their determination to prevent the federal government from using funding arrangements to control areas of provincial responsibility, provincial leaders in Quebec created a dilemma for the reform-minded Pearson Liberals. Their solution was to allow Quebec, or any other province for that matter, to opt out of a federal program, retaining its share of funding as long as it established a similar provincial program with the moneys. In practice, only Quebec availed itself of this option. When Trudeau became prime minister in 1968, he rejected the opting-out principle and announced that provinces that pulled out of future federal programs would not be reimbursed.

As the Quiet Revolution worked its way through the fabric of Quebec society, a growing number of Quebecers became sovereignists—supporters of a sovereign Quebec nation-state. While their opponents called them separatists, to emphasize that they wished to break up the country, the sovereignists or *indépendantistes* chose to emphasize the creative aspect of their goals. Resistance by the Trudeau government and most English Canadians to the de facto special status that Quebec had begun to develop in the Pearson period strengthened the hand of sovereignists in Quebec.

A major breakthrough for the sovereignty forces came in 1968 when René Lévesque left the Liberals and cobbled together an alliance of nationalist forces to create the Parti Québécois. By the mid-1970s, the PQ platform was sovereignty-association—the creation of a separate Quebec state with the maintenance of close economic links with Ottawa. Such a state, it was argued, could negotiate with Ottawa *égal à égal*. It was an interesting notion, but its flaw, as both federalists and supporters of complete sovereignty argued,

308 | Chapter 15

was that it assumed that the nine remaining provinces and two territories of Canada would be interested in establishing a special economic relationship with a sovereign Quebec and would be willing to let the federal government represent them in negotiations. The perception in the Atlantic and western provinces that Quebec, along with Ontario, already controlled the federal government made such a development improbable.

THE MOVE TO OFFICIAL BILINGUALISM

The federal government was not standing idly by as Quebec drifted outside the Canadian confederation. In 1963, the Pearson government established the Royal Commission on Bilingualism and Biculturalism under co-chairs André Laurendeau and Davidson Dunton. The commission confirmed that there was a strong relationship between poverty and French unilingualism in Canada. It also revealed that the rate of assimilation of French Canadians outside Quebec and northern New Brunswick was so alarming as to support Quebec nationalist claims that something had to be done to prevent the disappearance of French culture in North America. Trudeau, who distrusted Quebec nationalism, or "tribalism" as he called it, was determined to

Protest in Ottawa following proclamation of the War Measures Act, October 1970.
Library and Archives Canada/PA126347

make Francophones feel *chez nous* throughout the country.

In 1969, parliament passed the Official Languages Act, an attempt to put French on an equal footing with English throughout the federal government. The act created an official languages commissioner responsible for ensuring that federal departments served the public equally well in both languages. A significant percentage of new hirings required that successful applicants be functionally bilingual, and large numbers of existing unilingual civil servants (usually Anglophones) were given second-language instruction. In Trudeau's mind, one of the benefits of bilingualism in the public service was that it would advertise to young educated Quebecers that they need not look only to their own province for employment opportunities.

Through the 1970s, the federal government tried to expand the use of French across the country by providing funds to support French-language schools, French immersion programs for Anglophones, and organizations for Francophones outside Quebec. Even earlier, provincial governments had lifted long-established restrictions on the use of French as a language of instruction in schools. The success of these programs in strengthening either the French community or national unity was debatable. Although more Canadians than ever before were becoming bilingual, Francophones outside Quebec complained that economic realities in most of the country still forced them to become proficient in English to get well-paying jobs. Moreover, the lack of Francophone cultural facilities meant that they had to rely on English-language institutions.

Encouraged by developments in Quebec, federal support for bilingualism, and the momentum of the times, Acadians in the Atlantic region experienced their own quiet revolution. The number of Acadians continued to grow in the post-war period, but the rate of assimilation to Anglophone culture was high. It soon became clear that unless Acadians developed institutions and policies to address their needs, they would disappear as a cultural group. As in Quebec, education was identified as key to maintaining cultural identity. Acadians throughout the Maritimes pushed for more French-language instruction in their schools and for institutions of higher learning to prepare their children for the new opportunities of the service economy.

In New Brunswick, sheer numbers made these goals viable. Confrontations with Moncton's Anglophone mayor, student sit-ins at the Université de Moncton, and the well-attended Day of Concern over unemployment in January 1972 brought attention to Acadian demands for programs that would protect their culture and improve their economic condition. In the fall of 1972, New Brunswick Acadians founded the Parti Acadien, whose goal was to create a separate province of Acadie in the northeastern section of New Brunswick. New Brunswick became Canada's only officially bilingual province, its status declared in 1969 and confirmed in the constitution of 1982.

Opposition to official bilingualism ran deep in English Canada, though polls suggested majority support. While many middle-class families were placing their children in immersion programs, other Canadians resented the notion that they had to speak French in order to get federal jobs. In popular thinking, particularly in western Canada, all civil service jobs had become bilingual, the only people wanted for bilingual jobs were Francophones, and most federal grants were going to Quebec, the spoiled child of confederation. Canadians whose backgrounds were neither English nor French wondered where they fit into the Canadian mosaic. The Trudeau government established a secretary of state for Multiculturalism in 1971 to help stem criticism from this increasingly powerful segment of the Canadian population, but by that time Quebec had managed to grab headlines with acts of terrorism that called Canada's peaceable image sharply into question.

THE OCTOBER CRISIS

Resentment against Francophone militancy reached new heights during the October Crisis, which erupted in the fall of 1970. On 5 October, James Cross, the British trade commissioner in Montreal, was kidnapped by members of the Front de libération du Québec (FLQ). Five days later, Pierre Laporte, the Quebec minister of Labour and Immigration, was abducted by another cell of the FLQ. Although comprising only a few dozen members, the FLQ had been active since 1963 in pursuing its goals of revolutionary change in Quebec. Associated with more than 200 bombings between 1963 and 1970, the FLQ had targeted such bastions of privilege as McGill University, the home of

Montreal mayor Jean Drapeau, and the Montreal Stock Exchange.

In return for release of the hostages, the kidnappers demanded, among other things, the freeing of FLQ members who were imprisoned or detained and a broadcast of the group's manifesto. The manifesto was read on Radio-Canada following the Cross kidnapping, but when the FLQ struck a second time, politicians in Quebec City and Ottawa decided to take strong action. On 16 October, the federal government proclaimed the War Measures Act, under which it banned the FLQ, suspended civil rights, and imposed martial law on the nation. This was only the third time in the twentieth century that the War Measures Act had been invoked, and on the two previous occasions Canada had been at war with foreign powers.

The act played little, if any, role in the apprehension of the revolutionaries and the release of the trade commissioner in early December. It might have precipitated the murder of Laporte, whose body was found in the trunk of an abandoned car on the night of 17 October. Yet most English Canadians and, initially, most Francophones accepted claims by Prime Minister Pierre Trudeau and Quebec Liberal premier Robert Bourassa that the FLQ was planning a full-scale insurrection that had to be nipped in the bud. Ironically, the use of the act to detain more than 450 people, most of whom were never charged with any offence, became another example for Quebec nationalists of the injustice imposed by an English-dominated parliament. In reality, all the Francophone members of parliament had voted for the War Measures Act. The 16 MPs who had voted against it—15 New Democrats and 1 Conservative—were all Anglophones.

Opponents of the act, led by Tommy Douglas, the leader of the NDP, argued that the need to combat violent organizations and individuals did not justify providing governments with unlimited powers to curtail civil liberties. Civil libertarians charged that many of the arrests in Quebec were more of an effort to discredit peaceful separatists than to nab members of the FLQ. For example, Gerald Godin, editor of the popular separatist weekly newspaper *Québec-Presse*, and his wife, the popular *chanteuse* Pauline Julien, were among those who were arrested. So was labour leader Michel Chartrand, who quipped that it was absurd to think that he was part of the "apprehended insurrection" that Trudeau claimed the FLQ was planning. The media followed Chartrand everywhere, and he was lucky to be able to find enough privacy to make love to his wife, never mind meet with shadowy conspirators.

The "Special Status" Debate

Although Quebec premier Bourassa worked closely with the federal government to destroy the small revolutionary separatist movement, he and Trudeau often disagreed about how to react to the growing parliamentary movement for sovereignty. Trudeau defended the existing distribution of powers between the provinces and the federal government and rejected requests from Quebec for special status as the homeland of a French-Canadian nation. Wishing to appease nationalist sentiment, Bourassa emulated his predecessors in calling for Quebec City to have absolute control in a variety of areas increasingly dominated by Ottawa, particularly social programs, communications, and immigration.

Bourassa's determination to gain ground in the area of the constitutional division of powers frustrated Trudeau's attempts to achieve his most cherished objective. Like several of his predecessors, Trudeau wanted to patriate the Canadian constitution—that is, to end its life as a creature of the British parliament. In the past, the prime ministers who had supported patriation had had reason to believe that Great Britain would accept a request to hand control of the constitution to Canadians only if all the provinces had agreed with the central government on an amending formula. In 1964, Pearson had come close to success. Lesage, wishing to repay Pearson for agreeing to the "opting-out" principle, had indicated at a federal-provincial conference that Quebec would accept an amending formula that did not give the province a veto over constitutional changes. A storm of protest from nationalist intellectuals then convinced him to withdraw his support.

At a federal-provincial conference in Victoria in 1971, Trudeau offered Bourassa the veto that had eluded Lesage. Faced with an increasingly popular PQ, Bourassa spurned the prime minister, warning that Quebec would not support patriation until it was given extra powers. In particular, Bourassa wanted Pearson's "opt-out" principle to be applied to all social programs, present and future, for which federal funds were provided. Trudeau refused and was generally scathing in his comments about the Liberal premier of Quebec thereafter.

Bourassa's language legislation also appalled the prime minister. In 1974, the Quebec legislature passed Bill 22, a law that made French the only official language in Quebec and promoted its use in the workplace. All children were to be educated in French unless their parents were Canadian-born Anglophones. Immigrant children wishing to enroll in English-language schools would have to pass a language test. Unilingual English signs were banned. Quebec Anglophones criticized the bill for infringing on civil liberties. For nationalist Francophones, the legislation did not go far enough in restricting the use of English. They believed that the collective rights of a people—in this case, Francophone Quebecers—outweighed the individual rights of those who wished to choose their language of business and school without interference by the state.

Given the city's unique demography, Montreal was one of the centres of resistance to Bill 22. While over four-fifths of Quebecers had French as their first language, on Montreal Island the ethnic French constituted little more than 60 percent of the total population. This proportion had held fairly constant for over a century. It was the remaining 40 percent that had experienced the greatest change since confederation. In 1871, people of British origin had accounted for 38 percent of Montreal's population; only 2 percent of the population had been of neither French nor English extraction. By 1971, Allophones constituted 23 percent of Montrealers, and only 16 percent of the city's population was of British descent. These Allophones often resisted enrolling their children in French schools.

International Relations and the New Liberalism

If the new liberalism was reflected in federal social welfare programs and the Quiet Revolution in Quebec, it was also evident in international affairs. Most of Canada's leaders wanted the nation to play a role on the world stage. The image that Canada attempted to project was that of a peacekeeper and benevolent donor in the area of foreign aid. Like its

A HISTORIOGRAPHICAL DEBATE

The Development of Quebec Nationalism

What have been the causes of growing sentiment for sovereignty in Quebec since the 1960s? Political scientist Kenneth McRoberts offers one of several theories rooted in economics to explain this phenomenon. The Quiet Revolution, he argues, raised Francophone hopes that they would take over the levers of economic power in the province and experience a measurable increase in their standard of living. When this failed to occur, the upwardly mobile professional middle classes were particularly offended. They provided the impetus for the PQ and movements that preceded its founding.[7] A somewhat more radical view is provided by sociologist Marcel Rioux, who argues that Quebec Francophones identified with the movements for decolonization in the Third World and wished to end their own colonial status. According to Rioux, the Quebec Francophones were an ethnic group relegated to working-class status and therefore gradually began to develop the view of themselves as an ethnic class that must break free not only from the Canadian confederation, but also from the capitalist ethos that pervaded Anglophone North America.[8]

Several authors have challenged the view that the educated middle class and indeed Francophones generally failed to benefit from the reforms of the Quiet Revolution. Historian Ramsay Cook, comparing the incomes of male workers in Montreal, notes that the spread of average earnings between Francophones and Anglophones fell from 51 percent in 1961 to 32 percent in 1970 and 15 percent in 1977.[9] Economists François Vaillancourt and Pierre Saint-Laurent demonstrate that increased public employment for Francophones accounts for much of the decline in the income gap between the two linguistic groups.[10]

Political scientist Mary Beth Montcalm argues that the very economic success of the Francophone middle classes impelled them toward the creation of their own nation. Comparing Quebec separatism with similar breakaway nationalist movements in Belgium, France, Spain, and Great Britain, she argues that the rise of middle-class groups with distinct ethnic identities has been a common catalyst for modern separatist movements. It is not economic anxiety but rather the wish of such groups to establish an ethnic state in their own image that motivates such movements. Thus, Montcalm sees cultural goals rather than economic ones as the primary motivation of the Quebec sovereignty movement.[11]

Political scientist André Bernard goes further, suggesting that the struggle to preserve the French language united Quebec secessionists, regardless of social class:

> The French language . . . is a fundamental characteristic of the French-Canadian nation, but it is also more than that. It is the symbol of identity for French Canadians as a group, the rallying force among them, their pride and their wealth. It has an appeal which compares to no other group characteristic. In the last analysis, it is what French Canadians fight for. In this light, the idea of a unilingual French-speaking people in the territory populated and dominated by French Canadians is more a reflection of ideology than a formula prompted by narrow economic interests.[12]

American counterpart, the Canadian government subscribed to the view that poverty in countries outside North America and western Europe was the result of "underdevelopment" rather than the effects of colonialism and a vastly uneven distribution of wealth.

While the old liberalism might have argued that the untrammelled marketplace, left to its own devices, would bring development to these nations, the new liberalism recognized the need for non-market intervention to encourage the process. Foreign aid would allow the governments of these countries to build the infrastructure necessary to encourage industrial development and agricultural improvement, including transportation systems and schools. Like the poorer regions of Canada, these nations would gradually improve their standard of living and take on the values of the clearly "developed" regions of the world.

In 1950, Canada was one of the signatories of the Colombo Plan, meant to provide assistance to former British colonies in Asia as they gained their independence. Over the next two decades, aid was extended to Commonwealth nations in other parts of the world, to Francophone Africa, and, in 1970, to Latin America. The Canadian International Development Agency

(CIDA) was established in 1968 to coordinate the nation's foreign aid efforts. CIDA increased publicity and expenditures in the area of foreign aid, and reports of Canadians assisting Third World countries to build modern highways and improve crop yields became more common.

In the early 1970s, Canada committed itself to spending 0.7 percent of its gross domestic product on foreign aid, but by the end of the decade such expenditures had barely reached 0.4 percent. By then, the economic buoyancy that had led to the original promise had disappeared and the government was less willing to tax citizens or incur debts to support development in other nations. Critics of the foreign aid program questioned not only its lack of generosity but also its heavy reliance on "tied aid": countries received funds on condition that they spent specified amounts of their grants to acquire Canadian goods or services. This discouraged the development of indigenous technologies and competencies on the part of recipient nations.

Canada was perhaps more successful in its role as international peacekeeper, but even here there was mounting criticism. In 1956, Canadian diplomacy was responsible for finding a solution to the Suez Crisis when British and French troops attacked Egypt following its nationalization of the Suez Canal. Canadians were proud of the role they played in the Suez Crisis, particularly after Minister of External Affairs Lester Pearson won the Nobel Peace Prize for his efforts in defusing the potentially explosive situation. Canada was a member of the United Nations Emergency Force that kept the peace between Egypt and Israel from 1956 until 1967, when Egyptian president Gamal Abdel Nasser expelled the UN forces. Among other hot spots where Canadian peacekeepers served were the Congo (Democratic Republic of the Congo/Zaire), Yemen, and Cyprus.

The importance of peacekeeping as opposed to warfare was rarely in question in Canada, but the nation's tendency to follow the United States in many of its foreign policy decisions did not always find favour. As we will see in the next chapter, much of Canada's domestic and foreign policy in the post-1945 period reflected the influence of the United States, which had replaced Great Britain as the world's most powerful nation.

CONCLUSION

When the Second World War came to an end, the federal government took the responsibility of finding ways of balancing the ordinary citizen's sense of entitlement to social programs with the business community's sense of entitlement to low taxes. This was a dramatic departure for Canadians but one that was followed by many nations of the world. Between 1945 and 1975, there was sufficient economic growth in Canada to allow governments to provide general satisfaction to both groups. Indeed, the major opposition to the increasing role of the federal government in the lives of ordinary citizens came from provincial governments whose leaders pursued their own ambitious agendas. The state's expansion in the post-war period was not limited to social programs. As the next four chapters show, the state played an integral role in most areas of economic and social life in post-war Canada.

NOTES

1 Library and Archives Canada, MG 32, C 12, Grace MacInnis Papers, vol. 19, File "Women, Status of, 1972," J. Eric Harrington, president, Canada Vickers Ltd., to MacInnis, 9 May 1972; MacInnis to Harrington, 18 May 1972.

2 Canada, Royal Commission on Health Services, brief presented by the Newfoundland Federation of Labour, October 1961.

3 Canada, Royal Commission on Health Services, brief presented by Reverend Michael Di Stasi, April 1962.

4 *Report of the Royal Commission on the Status of Women in Canada* (Ottawa: Information Canada, 1970), 261.

5 Quoted in Alvin Finkel, "'Even the Little Children Cooperated': Family Strategies, Childcare Discourse, and Social Welfare Debates, 1945–1975," *Labour/Le Travail* 36 (Fall 1995), 105.

6 J.F. Conway, *The West: The History of a Region in Confederation* (Toronto: Lorimer, 1983), 228.

7   Kenneth McRoberts, *Quebec: Social Change and Political Crisis*, 3rd ed. (Toronto: McClelland & Stewart, 1988), 173–208.

8   Marcel Rioux, *Quebec in Question* (Toronto: Lorimer, 1971).

9   Ramsay Cook, "Quebec's New Quiet Revolutionaries," in *Canada, Quebec and the Uses of Nationalism* (Toronto: McClelland & Stewart, 1986), 87–104.

10 François Vaillancourt and Pierre Saint-Laurent, "Les déterminants de l'évolution de revenu entre Canadien

anglais et Canadien français," *Journal of Canadian Studies* 15, no. 4 (Winter 1980–1981), 69–74.

11 Mary Beth Montcalm, "Quebec Nationalism in a Comparative Perspective," in *Quebec: State and Society in Crisis*, ed. Alain Gagnon (Toronto: Methuen, 1984), 45–58.

12 André Bernard, *What Does Quebec Want?* (Toronto: Lorimer, 1978), 45.

Related Readings in This Series

From *Primary Documents CD-ROM, Volume II*

Too Late
Voters of Newfoundland
Boning Up
Trudeaumania

FLQ Manifesto, October 8, 1970 [translated]
Trudeau's "Just Watch Me" Interview
Reaction of René Lévesque, President of the Parti Québécois, to the Invocation of the War Measures Act, October 17, 1970

Selected Reading

Key works that deal broadly with post-war national political developments include Ian Drummond, Robert Bothwell, and John English, *Canada Since 1945: Power, Politics and Provincialism*, rev. ed. (Toronto: University of Toronto Press, 1989); José E. Igartua, *The Other Quiet Revolution: National Identities in English Canada, 1945–1971* (Vancouver: UBC Press, 2006); J.L. Granatstein, *Canada, 1957–1967: The Years of Uncertainty and Innovation* (Toronto: McClelland & Stewart, 1986); Robert Chodos, Rae Murphy, and Eric Hamovitch, *The Unmaking of Canada: The Hidden Theme in Canadian History Since 1945* (Toronto: Lorimer, 1991); Reginald Whitaker, *The Government Party: Organizing and Financing the Liberal Party of Canada, 1930–1958* (Toronto: University of Toronto Press, 1977); Norman Penner, *From Protest to Power: Social Democracy in Canada, 1900–Present* (Toronto: Lorimer, 1992); William Brennan, ed., *Building the Co-operative Commonwealth: Essays on the Social Democratic Tradition in Canada* (Regina: Canadian Plains Research Center, 1984); John English, *The Life of Lester Pearson*, vol. 2, *Worldly Years* (New York: Alfred A. Knopf, 1992); John G. Diefenbaker, *One Canada: Memoirs of the Right Honourable John G. Diefenbaker* (Toronto: Macmillan, 1975); Denis Smith, *Rogue Tory: The Life and Legend of John G. Diefenbaker* (Toronto: Macfarlane Walter & Ross, 1995); Lester B. Pearson, *Mike: The Memoirs of the Right Honourable Lester B. Pearson* (Toronto: University of Toronto Press, 1972); and John Boyko, *Into the Hurricane: Attacking Socialism and the CCF* (Winnipeg: J. Gordon Shillingford, 2006). An extensive

literature on Pierre Trudeau includes John English, *Citizen of the World: The Life of Pierre Elliott Trudeau, Volume One, 1919–1968* (Toronto: Knopf Canada, 2006); Max Nemni and Monique Nemni, *Young Trudeau: Son of Quebec, Father of Canada, 1919–1944* (Toronto: Douglas Gibson Books, 2006); Ramsay Cook, *The Teeth of Time: Remembering Pierre Elliott Trudeau* (Montreal: McGill-Queen's University Press, 2006); and Claude Couture, *Paddling with the Current: Pierre Elliott Trudeau, Étienne Parent, Liberalism and Nationalism in Canada* (Edmonton: University of Alberta Press, 1998).

On civil rights developments, see Christopher MacLennan, *Toward the Charter: Canadians and the Demand for a National Bill of Rights, 1929–1960* (Montreal: McGill-Queen's University Press, 2003); and Ross Lambertson, *Repression and Resistance: Canadian Human Rights Activists, 1930–1960* (Toronto: University of Toronto Press, 2004).

Provincial political histories dealing with this period include Roger Graham, *Old Man Ontario: Leslie Miscampbell Frost* (Toronto: University of Toronto Press, 1990); Allan Kerr McDougall, *John P. Robarts: His Life and Government* (Toronto: University of Toronto Press, 1986); Nelson Wiseman, *Social Democracy in Manitoba: A History of the CCF-NDP* (Winnipeg: University of Manitoba Press, 1983); Raymond B. Blake, *Canadian at Last: Canada Integrates Newfoundland as a Province* (Toronto: University of Toronto Press, 1994); James Hiller and Peter Neary, eds., *Twentieth-Century Newfoundland: Explorations* (St John's: Breakwater, 1994); David Mitchell, *W.A.C. Bennett and the Rise of British Columbia* (Vancouver:

Douglas and McIntyre, 1983); Alvin Finkel, *The Social Credit Phenomenon in Alberta* (Toronto: University of Toronto Press, 1989); Verner Smitheram et al., *The Garden Transformed: Prince Edward Island, 1945–1980* (Charlottetown: Ragweed Press, 1982); Margaret Conrad, "The Atlantic Revolution of the 1950s," in *Beyond Anger and Longing: Community and Development in Atlantic Canada*, ed. Berkeley Fleming (Fredericton: Acadiensis Press, 1988), 55–96; Thomas H. McLeod and Ian McLeod, *Tommy Douglas: The Road to Jerusalem* (Edmonton: Hurtig, 1987); and Della Stanley, *Louis Robichaud: A Decade of Power* (Halifax: Nimbus, 1984).

Studies of post-war Quebec include Michael Gauvreau, *The Catholic Origins of Quebec's Quiet Revolution, 1931–1970* (Montreal: McGill-Queen's University Press, 2005); Paul-André Linteau, René Durocher, and Jean-Claude Robert, *Quebec Since 1930* (Toronto: Lorimer, 1991); Kenneth McRoberts, *Quebec: Social Change and Political Crisis*, 3rd ed. (Toronto: McClelland & Stewart, 1988); René Lévesque, *Memoirs* (Toronto: McClelland & Stewart, 1986); Alain Gagnon, *Quebec: State and Society in Crisis* (Toronto: Methuen, 1984); John Saywell, *The Rise of the Parti Québécois, 1967–1976* (Toronto: University of Toronto Press, 1977); Dale C. Thomson, *Jean Lesage and the Quiet Revolution* (Toronto: Macmillan, 1984); William Coleman, *The Independence Movement in Quebec, 1945–1980* (Toronto: University of Toronto Press, 1984); and Michael Behiels, *Prelude to Quebec's Quiet Revolution: Liberalism versus Neo-Conservatism, 1945–1960* (Montreal: McGill-Queen's University Press, 1985).

Among useful works on Francophones outside Quebec are Matthew Hayday, *Bilingual Today, United Tomorrow: Official Languages in Education and Canadian Federalism* (Montreal: McGill-Queen's University Press, 2005); Michael Behiels, *Canada's Francophone Minority Communities: Constitutional Renewal and the Winning of School Governance* (Montreal: McGill-Queen's University Press, 2005); Richard Wilbur, *The Rise of French New Brunswick* (Halifax: Formac, 1989); Sally Ross and Alphonse Deveau, *The Acadians of Nova Scotia: Past and Present* (Halifax: Nimbus, 1992); and Georges Arsenault, *The Island Acadians, 1720–1980* (Charlottetown: Ragweed Press, 1989).

Federal-provincial relations are discussed in David Milne, *Tug of War: Ottawa and the Provinces Under Trudeau and Mulroney* (Toronto: Lorimer, 1986) and Garth Stevenson, *Unfulfilled Union: Canadian Federalism and National Unity*, 3rd ed. (Toronto: Gage, 1988). On federal-provincial relations in the social welfare area, see Keith Banting, *The Welfare State and Canadian Federalism*, rev. ed. (Montreal: McGill-Queen's University Press, 1987). Among useful works on the evolution of the welfare state more generally, see Alvin Finkel, *Social Policy and Practice in Canada: A History* (Waterloo, ON: Wilfrid Laurier University Press, 2006); Dennis Guest, *The Emergence of Social Security in Canada*, rev. ed. (Vancouver: UBC Press, 1997); Nancy Christie, *Engendering the State: Family, Work and Welfare in Canada* (Toronto: University of Toronto Press, 2000); John C. Bacher, *Keeping to the Marketplace: The Evolution of Canadian Housing Policy* (Montreal: McGill-Queen's University Press, 1993); James Struthers, *The Limits of Affluence: Welfare in Ontario, 1920–1970* (Toronto: University of Toronto Press, 1994); James Snell, *The Citizen's Wage: The State and the Elderly in Canada, 1900–1951* (Toronto: University of Toronto Press, 1996); Megan Davies, *Into the House of Old: A History of Residential Care in British Columbia* (Montreal: McGill-Queen's University Press, 2003); Jennifer Stephen, *Pick One Intelligent Girl: Employability, Domesticity, and the Gendering of Canada's Welfare State, 1939–1947* (Toronto: University of Toronto Press, 2007); and Raymond B. Blake and Jeff Keshen, eds., *Social Welfare Policy in Canada: Historical Readings* (Toronto: Copp Clark, 1995). On medicare and the Canada Pension Plan, see P.E. Bryden, *Planners and Politicians: Liberal Politics and Social Policy, 1957–1960* (Montreal: McGill-Queen's University Press, 1997). On unemployment insurance, see Ann Porter, *Gendered States: Women, Unemployment Insurance, and the Political Economy of the Welfare State in Canada, 1945–1997* (Toronto: University of Toronto Press, 2003); and Georges Campeau, *From UI to EI: Waging War on the Welfare State* (Vancouver: UBC Press, 2004). An excellent work on the welfare state in Quebec is Dominique Marshall, *The Social Origins of the Welfare State: Quebec Families, Compulsory Education, and Family Allowances, 1940–1955* (Waterloo, ON: Wilfrid Laurier University Press, 2004). On provincial welfare regimes more generally, a comprehensive overview is found in Gerald William Boychuk, *Patchworks of Purpose: The Development of Provincial Social Assistance Regimes in Canada* (Montreal: McGill-Queen's University Press, 1998). On day care, see Susan Prentice, ed., *Five Decades of Child Care Advocacy and Policy in Canada* (Halifax: Fernwood, 2001).

CHAPTER 16

The American Dream: Canada and Its Southern Neighbour, 1945–1975

TIMELINE

1946	Gouzenko revelations made public
1949	NATO created
1950–53	Korean War
1951	Massey Commission report
1952	Atomic Energy of Canada Limited created; first Canadian television stations begin operation
1954	Canada joins International Control Commission for Indochina; NATO proclaims a nuclear-centred strategy
1956	Canada signs Defence Production Sharing Agreement
1957	Canada Council created; suicide of Herbert Norman
1958	Canada signs NORAD agreement
1963	Nuclear weapons for Canada debated in federal election
1965	Lester Pearson criticizes American policy in Vietnam; Auto Pact signed
1974	Foreign Investment Review Agency created
1975	Petro-Canada created

Interviewed during Canada's centennial year, Prime Minister Lester Pearson spoke cautiously about Canada's relations with the United States. "We can't ignore the fact that the first result of any open breach with the United States over Vietnam, which their government considers to be unfair and unfriendly on our part, would be a more critical examination by Washington of certain special aspects of our relationship from which we, as well as they, get great benefit."[1] In other words, Canada's close economic relations with the United States had to be considered when the Canadian government set its foreign policy.

In the post-war years, the influence of the United States was paramount in trade and foreign policy and was also the source of many of Canada's cultural values. Canadians read American books, watched American-produced television programs, and listened to American popular music. The Vietnam War (1965–1975) and an increasing awareness of the downside of the American Dream eventually caused Canadians to develop a level of ambivalence about their powerful southern neighbour, but the United States continued to provide the benchmark against which Canadians, and many other western nations, measured their successes and failures.

THE COLD WAR

Canadian foreign policy, economic development, and cultural expression were all connected to some degree in the 30 years following the Second World War. This was the era of the Cold War, in which capitalist democracies were pitted against communist states, competing for resources, trade, and political allies throughout the world. Their fierce ideological battles tended to create a simplified view of the political and economic options available to nations on either side of the communist-capitalist divide. Increasingly enthralled by the American mass entertainment industry, most Canadians embraced the cultural values espoused by the United States as leader of the "free world" and the economic opportunities created by the expanding American military. The politics of the Cold War are therefore a good place to start examining the complex relations between Canada and the United States after 1945.

The Soviet Union had been a valued member of the anti-Nazi forces during the Second World War. Its troops did the lion's share of the front-line fighting and dying, and it lost almost as many citizens as all other combatants combined. After the war, Soviet leaders insisted on friendly governments in central and eastern Europe and maintained the presence of Soviet troops in the nations of the region, fearful of a third German invasion in the twentieth century.

The western countries, particularly the United States, rejected this reasoning and insisted on the right of the countries in central and eastern Europe to military and economic independence. Economic aid for the war-shattered Soviet Union was made dependent on Soviet willingness to withdraw troops from eastern Europe and open the markets of those countries, and of the Soviet Union itself, to western investment. The Soviets responded by tightening the screws on eastern Europe, replacing democratically elected post-war coalition governments with communist-dominated regimes subservient to the Soviet state. Each side then declared that the other was bent on world domination.

In dramatic contrast to its isolationism in the interwar years, the United States became a champion of international activism. Its chief policy goal, trumpeted in classrooms, from the pulpit, and in the media, was the containment of communism at home and abroad. Yet both sides tried to avoid a direct confrontation—a "hot war"—instead limiting themselves to virulent rhetoric and support for either pro-Soviet or pro-western forces in localized conflicts.

Soviet agents seemed to be everywhere, including Ottawa. In September 1945, Igor Gouzenko, a cipher clerk in the Soviet Embassy, revealed to the Canadian government that a Soviet spy ring had been in operation in Canada throughout the war. Given Canada's close involvement with research relating to the atomic bomb, this was perceived as a serious matter, and arrests were followed by increased security within the government—and increased mistrust of the Soviet Union. Despite the evidence of the spy ring, most External Affairs officials, while appalled by dictator Joseph Stalin and his police-state apparatus, regarded American claims concerning Soviet intentions in foreign policy as vastly exaggerated. Publicly, however, Canada supported American views, determining that a less partisan approach would not serve Canadian interests.

The Permanent Joint Board on Defence, established during the Second World War, remained in operation to coordinate the defence policies of the two nations. Although the Canadian government balked at the board's suggestion that the two countries integrate their defence forces, Canada was increasingly drawn into American defence strategy. In 1949, Canada became a founding member of the North Atlantic Treaty Organization (NATO), a military pact that included the United States, Great Britain, and continental western European nations. Canada had insisted on formal acknowledgement that NATO's goal was economic and military cooperation, but the organization soon became primarily an American instrument for coordinating the defence policies of its allies.

THE KOREAN WAR

In 1950, Canada agreed to contribute troops to the United Nations forces sent to hold the line against communism in Korea. Following the Second World War, Korea was divided into two zones: North Korea, under the supervision of the Soviet Union, and South Korea, under the control of the United States. The two zones were slated for amalgamation but were frozen in their antagonistic divisions by the Cold War. When troops from North Korea invaded South Korea in June 1950, the United States manoeuvred the United Nations into sending a peacekeeping force into the region. Canada worked behind the scenes to restrain its aggressive ally, but had little success. United Nations troops under American general Douglas MacArthur, having driven the communists out of South Korea, entered North Korean territory. This foray led to a military response from China, and the war grew in length and intensity.

The Korean War finally came to an end in 1953, with Korea seemingly permanently divided. In total, about 25 000 Canadians participated in the hostilities,

The Gouzenko Affair

The revelation that the Soviets had operated a spy network in Canada in which Canadians spirited classified information to the Soviet government created a sensation when it became public news in February 1946. By then, western-Soviet relations had deteriorated and many Canadians were prepared to view their wartime ally as a bogeyman. But how damaging were the leaks to the Soviets? In practice, both the Canadian and Soviet governments agreed that what the Soviets had gleaned from their Canadian spies was not particularly significant. Much of it was public information they could have obtained without resorting to espionage. The government's concern was less with the actual information that had been passed to the Soviets than with the potential for real secrets to fall into the hands of the "enemy." Canada had played an important role in the early research leading to the invention of the nuclear bomb, and any possibility that key scientific information could leave government labs and end up in the hands of the Soviet political and scientific establishment was unthinkable.

The government established a commission to investigate the Gouzenko files and determine what charges should be laid against the individuals fingered in them. The commission was allowed to detain individuals without formal accusations. It recommended charges against 22 individuals, but only half were found guilty, usually of lesser charges than the commission had made. The sensationalism of the commission's accusations, which often smacked of guilt by association, received far more publicity than the eventual court cases.

On the basis of the evidence provided by Gouzenko, Scientist Raymond Boyer and Fred Rose, Canada's only Communist MP, were found guilty of conspiracy for passing scientific information to the Soviets in 1943. Boyer had been involved in improving a chemical explosive and wanted to share the discovery with Canada's Soviet allies. But the Canadian government, after consultation with the Americans, decided to withhold this scientific advance from the Russians. Boyer, believing the Soviets needed to know about the discovery in order to strengthen their defence effort against the invading Nazis, gave the information to Fred Rose, who passed it on to Soviet embassy officials. Ironically, a year later, the Canadian government passed on the same information, unaware that the Soviets already knew.

Rose and Boyer's defence that they were aiding the anti-Nazi cause counted for nothing in the atmosphere of the Cold War. They had, after all, knowingly given the Soviets information their government wanted kept secret; therefore, they were traitors. But, as civil libertarians protested, the Canadian state seemed to want to crucify these men not for having consorted with an enemy but for lacking the foresight to realize that Canada's wartime friend would become its post-war enemy. Rose received a jail sentence. As a criminal, he was ejected from his parliamentary seat.

In the aftermath of the Gouzenko affair and the resulting court cases, a chill fell over political activity on the part of Canada's scientists. State authorities branded the Canadian Association of Scientific Workers, a pacifist-minded organization, as communist, prompting most of its members and supporters to leave. The organization collapsed and was not replaced.

Igor Gouzenko.
Library and Archives Canada/PA-129625. Reprinted by permission of the *Montreal Gazette*

Personnel of the 25th Canadian Infantry Brigade preparing a machine gun position in Korea, 1951.
Library and Archives Canada/NA112639

NORAD agreement was formally signed by the Progressive Conservative government in 1958, suggesting a wide consensus in Canada in support of close Canadian-American cooperation in defence matters.

America's exclusive possession of nuclear weapons from 1945 to 1949, followed by a decade of clear nuclear superiority over the Soviet Union, encouraged political leaders in the United States to enunciate a policy of "deterrence": the Americans threatened to use nuclear weapons against communist states if they intervened in other countries' affairs. In 1954, NATO members, hoping to avoid the expense of large conventional armed forces, adopted nuclear deterrence as the mainstay of their defence strategy. Although once begun, a nuclear war would be difficult to contain, NATO decided to build up stocks of "tactical" nuclear weaponry—intermediate-range weapons designed for battle in a particular region—as opposed to "strategic" weapons designed for a full-scale nuclear war.

and 300 lost their lives. As it had during the Second World War, Canada's economy boomed during the Korean conflict. By contrast, the two Koreas, both controlled by ruthless dictators, experienced economic devastation and lost millions of lives.

THE NUCLEAR ISSUE

Meanwhile, Canada and the United States were pouring billions of dollars into an elaborate defence program designed to protect North America from a Soviet air attack. Between 1949 and 1957, three radar defence systems were built, including the Distant Early Warning (DEW) Line. The DEW Line stretched from Alaska to Baffin Island and did much to open the Canadian North to southern influences. Cooperation on this project helped pave the way for the North American Air Defence Agreement (NORAD), which produced a unified air command for North America. Negotiated by the Liberals under St. Laurent, the

In December 1957, in line with NATO policy, Canada agreed to play a role in surveillance of possible military strike plans by the communists. In 1959 and 1960, Canada ordered a variety of aircraft and missiles meant to help serve this objective. Canada also agreed to permit storage of American nuclear weapons at Goose Bay and Harman air force bases, which, though on Canadian territory, were controlled by the Americans. In 1956, Canada received a reward for its close cooperation with American defence policies: the Defence Production Sharing Agreement, which guaranteed that Canadians would benefit from the industrial potential of military production for the Cold War.

SUPPORTING DEMOCRACY?

At the same time Canada was forging military alliances and profiting from war industries, its leaders were cultivating an image as peacemakers in a war-torn world.

Herbert Norman

When Herbert Norman committed suicide in Cairo in 1957, the veteran diplomat's death gave an individual's face to the victims of McCarthyism in Canada. Norman had been hounded by the House Un-American Activities Committee (HUAC) and the Senate Internal Security Subcommittee in the United States since the early 1950s and also investigated thoroughly by Canadian authorities. When it became clear, however, that McCarthyists in the United States were not going to leave him alone, he became depressed and ended his life. Lester Pearson, minister of External Affairs, denounced the American politicians whose relentless attacks had led to Norman's demise, well aware that many of them also considered Pearson a communist sympathizer.

Norman was the son of Canadian missionaries in Japan and had been involved in left-wing activities as a graduate student at Cambridge from 1933 to 1935. Upon graduation, he returned to Canada and, after a period as a professor of classics, joined the Department of External Affairs in 1939. He headed a unit that decoded Japanese wartime intelligence. After the war, he played a major role in the conversion of Japan from a military dictatorship to a democracy, and later was in charge of External Affairs' American and Far Eastern Division. Although Norman promoted policies that helped preserve capitalism in Japan—particularly the breakup of giant farms into small holdings—right-wingers in the United States were aghast when he asked for mediation between North and South Korea in the early months of the Korean War rather than supporting their efforts to wrest all of Korea from the control of communists. They exposed his radical political views from his student days, accusing him of remaining a tool of the communists.

Pearson, himself the target of McCarthyists because of his ambivalence about the benefits of nuclear weapons, responded by posting Norman to divisions of External Affairs that did not deal with the Far East. Neither American nor Canadian investigations of Norman provided any evidence that he still held left-wing views or had any connections with communists. When he was posted to Cairo as ambassador in 1956, his American opponents, already suspicious of Egyptian president Nasser's close dealings with the Soviet Union, strongly objected. They released Senate subcommittee testimony that included unsubstantiated allegations that Norman was a communist. The same testimony indicted Pearson as a Soviet agent.

A substantial book of essays edited by political scientist Roger Bowen in 1984 denounced the Cold Warriors, who the authors believed had caused the Norman tragedy in 1957. They accused "witch-hunters" in the United States of making life intolerable for an innocent man.[2] However, University of Toronto political scientist James Barros produced a Cold War–flavoured book that suggested there was substantial reason to believe that both Norman and Pearson were Soviet agents, though he thought Pearson more likely to be "an unconscious ideological sympathizer."[3] This was a constant refrain of Cold Warriors against those who opposed the worst excesses of Cold War militarism, even when the opponents were clearly anticommunists themselves.

The Brian Mulroney government of the 1980s decided to settle the issue of Norman's loyalty to Canada by appointing the conservative political scientist Peyton V. Lyon to do an exhaustive search of all the records pertaining to Norman, including those that had informed the Barros account. His conclusion was that Norman was neither a spy nor an agent of Soviet influence within Canada. "The Herbert Norman tragedy was largely caused by the crude, ideological intervention into Canadian affairs by a subcommittee of the United States Senate." As for Professor Barros's book, Lyon claimed that his so-called evidence largely amounted to guilt by association. "Its destructiveness is repugnant, its means often despicable."[4]

Canada's ability to play this role depended to a large extent on toeing the line drawn by the United States. If vital interests of the Americans were at stake, the Canadian peacekeeping role was invariably compromised. This was the case in policy relating to Vietnam, a tiny Asian nation that, like Korea, had the misfortune of becoming one of the hot spots in the Cold War.

A French colony since the nineteenth century, Vietnam emerged from the Second World War with a powerful nationalist movement led by French-educated communist Ho Chi Minh. In 1954, France was forced to recognize communist control over the northern half of Vietnam and ceded South Vietnam to anticommunist Vietnamese landlords and businessmen.

Negotiations in Geneva that year produced an accord calling for reunification of North and South Vietnam after elections to be held in 1956. An International Control Commission (ICC) with Canada, Poland, and India as its members was established to monitor the implementation of the provisions of the Geneva accord. The Americans, aware that the communists would win national elections, forced a delay to give the pro-American South Vietnamese regime a chance to establish its credentials. Such plans foundered as the regime unleashed a reign of terror, murdering suspected communist sympathizers and uprooting peasant villages. By the 1960s, the Americans' goal was to maintain the partition so that South Vietnam could remain non-communist.

The ICC members rarely proved neutral in their observations. Poland seemed able to see only South Vietnamese violations, while Canada focused exclusively on violations by the North Vietnamese. A report in 1962 prepared by Canada and co-signed by India, desperate for American goodwill because of border wars with China, was regularly brandished by American officials during their undeclared war in Indochina (1965–1975) to demonstrate North Vietnamese atrocities. Although Canada provided weapons to the Americans and "humanitarian" aid to the South Vietnamese, its leaders claimed to be neutral in the conflict. In 1981, however, documents released by two New Democrat MPs revealed that the Canadian and American defence departments collaborated to test chemical defoliants that the Americans used in Vietnam.

Canada made several efforts to negotiate a ceasefire between the United States and North Vietnam, but its efforts were not appreciated by the Americans. In April 1965, Prime Minister Lester Pearson, addressing students at Temple University in Philadelphia, cautiously advocated that the American government temporarily cease bombing North Vietnam in an effort to seek diplomatic solutions in Indochina. Meeting Pearson afterward, American president Lyndon Johnson grabbed him by the shirt collar and shouted, "You pissed on my rug!"

With this experience in mind, the Pearson government approved a report prepared by two veteran ambassadors—one American, one Canadian—calling on the two countries to avoid public criticism of one another. The Merchant-Heeney report, which appeared in July 1965, indicated that disagreements should be aired only through diplomatic channels. Pearson never uttered another indictment, however cautious, of American policy in Indochina.

Ottawa supported the general direction of American foreign relations, claiming that Canada wished to encourage the development of non-communist, democratic regimes around the world. In practice, it was not a government's democratic character but rather its support for western investment and trade that became the criterion for American and NATO approval. Fascist Spain and Portugal were included in NATO. In Asia and throughout Latin America, the United States supported a variety of thuggish regimes. To Canada's embarrassment, many of these regimes were installed with American support by overthrowing democratically elected governments that the United States deemed as too leftist or too nationalist. Yet there was silence from Ottawa as repressive military dictatorships overthrew a string of democratic governments, including those of Iran (1953), Guatemala (1954), Brazil (1964), Dominican Republic (1965), Greece (1967), and Chile (1973).

RED BAITING

The American impact on Canadian thinking was complex. Not only were imported messages increasingly filtered through nationalist lenses, but American society itself was dynamic. The messages that it transmitted through mass culture changed over time. One dramatic example is the shift from the repressive atmosphere of the early Cold War to the radicalism that prevailed during the student and anti-war movements of the late 1960s.

The Cold War was an ideological battle, and its participants, hoping to impose their values on other countries, were intolerant of dissenting views. The Soviets and their allies crushed dissent ruthlessly. Although western countries claimed that they were champions of freedom of expression and association, their behaviour often indicated otherwise. In the United States, the House Un-American Activities Committee had harassed communists since the 1930s, but the anti-communist campaign in 1950 became identified with one man—Senator Joseph R. McCarthy of Wisconsin. He used the HUAC to investigate a wide spectrum of American citizens, including government bureaucrats, university professors, writers, and popular entertainers. He finally overreached himself when he began launching an investigation into possible subversion in the American army in 1954. By that time, many institutions had begun their own witch-hunts, and many blacklisted people found themselves out of a job. In one of the most controversial court cases of the twentieth century, Americans Ethel and Julius Rosenberg were convicted of passing atomic secrets to the Soviet Union and hanged in 1953.

McCarthyism in Canada was less virulent than in the United States, but it infected Canadian institutions nonetheless. Anti-communism became a key ingredient in immigration policy. While restrictions on former Nazis were lifted to the point that the RCMP complained that war criminals were being admitted to Canada, no such tolerance was extended to communists and ex-communists. Communists were not only deported and kept out as permanent immigrants, they were prevented from even visiting Canada. There were consequences for simply being a disarmament advocate, even without connections to the Communist Party. *Toronto Star* journalist Ray Gardner was one of several journalists on a media blacklist during the 1950s and was unable to find work.

Following the Gouzenko affair, the federal government attempted to root radicals out of the civil service. After all, it was just such people who had handed information to Soviet embassy officials about nuclear research during the Second World War. A security panel was established with broad powers to determine which state employees might be a threat to national security, a charge that led to either firing or demotion with no chance of appeal. The RCMP infiltrated popular movements, including trade unions, to report on the activities of communist sympathizers. The National Film Board came under close scrutiny in this period, as did universities. Homosexuals, regardless of their political beliefs, were excluded from government employment on the grounds that Soviet agents might blackmail them into becoming spies by threatening to disclose their sexual orientation. In such an environment, the civil libertarian argument that individuals ought to be judged by their actions and not their beliefs or associations was rejected out of hand. The RCMP kept files on 800 000 individuals and organizations

from 1945 to 1980, with the Unitarian Church of Canada, the feminist movement, the National Gay Rights Coalition, organizations of Chilean immigrants, and the separatist Parti Québécois all facing infiltration of their organizations by the authorities.

Communists and communist sympathizers who had been democratically chosen to head unions were denounced so stridently in the media and by their non-communist union opponents that the state confidently persecuted them and, in some cases, destroyed their unions. In 1946, Maurice Duplessis jailed Kent Rowley and Madeleine Parent, organizers for the Trades and Labour Congress local of textile workers in Valleyfield, Quebec. In British Columbia, the Labour Relations Board refused to certify the communist-led Wood-workers Industrial Union of Canada as bargaining agent for locals wishing to secede from the American-dominated Industrial Woodworkers of America (IWA). The provincial police then joined with employers to break strikes by this "illegal" union. The breakaways were forced to rejoin the IWA, whose American leadership had purged communists from leadership roles in both the United States and Canada.

Anti-communist paranoia cost as many as 10 000 Canadian seamen their jobs between 1949 and 1962. The Canadian government, concerned that the democratically elected leaders of the Canadian Seamen's Union (CSU) were communists, brought Hal Banks into the country to organize a rival union. Although the American and Canadian governments were aware that Banks was ineligible for immigration to Canada because of a criminal record, they cooperated to destroy the CSU, which they feared would call strikes at the behest of the Soviets and interrupt shipments to North America's allies. The Canadian government, the shipping companies, and the Trades and Labour Congress were all aware that Banks was a thug who replaced the CSU with his own Seafarers International Union (SIU) by forcing CSU supporters out of work and replacing them with men who were sufficiently intimidated by Banks to join the SIU. The corrupt and violent leadership of Banks was only dealt with by the authorities in the 1960s, after the CSU had been eliminated. Until then, Banks's intimidation and fleecing of his members continued apace. Banks fled Canada, and American authorities refused to extradite him. They claimed that Banks had disappeared, but it took a

Toronto Star reporter little time to track him down in New York City.

Lives could be ruined if individuals were suspected of being communists or even of being soft on communism. Members of peace groups, such as the Women's International League for Peace and Freedom, founded in 1915, also suffered from red baiters, who smeared anyone who opposed them. In such an atmosphere, those leery of the Cold War philosophy or of particular actions that flowed from such a philosophy generally kept their mouths shut. In both Canada and the United States, fundamental criticism of foreign policy or of red baiting was rare.

This reticence changed dramatically in the 1960s. The civil rights and anti-war movements in the United States sparked an extensive student movement that questioned everything about American society. By the end of the decade, movements for black power, feminism, gay liberation, Native rights, and Third World liberation challenged fundamental notions about American society. Young Canadians were influenced by this awakening of dissent, to the dismay of many of their elders. Ironically, Canadian social critics, while borrowing ideas liberally from their American counterparts, were likely to assert the need for greater independence from the United States.

VOICES OF DISSENT

Many Canadians were concerned by the apparent contradictions that resulted from Canada's special relationship with the United States. Even at the height of the Cold War in the 1950s, campaigns for nuclear disarmament, human rights, and a more balanced assessment of various communist regimes were waged despite the threats to careers and reputations that involvement in such activities posed to individuals. They picked up steam in the 1960s, stimulated by the student rebellion that swept North America and western Europe. While a product of complex changes in Canadian society, student protest was, in part, directed toward American intervention against self-determination in Third World[5] nations and Canada's alleged complicity in these interventions. Pacifists, communists, socialists, feminists, and adherents of a return to Canada's one-time focus on British-Canadian relations also opposed Canada's embrace of the American vision of the world.

The voice of dissent in the 1960s was also fuelled by one of Canada's most purposeful immigrant groups: Americans evading the draft, military deserters, and others opposed to the Vietnam War. Estimates of the numbers of American war resisters who immigrated to Canada vary but range as high as 100 000. Most of them were young and well-educated. They settled all over the country but were concentrated in Montreal, Toronto, and Vancouver, where the peace movement was most vocal.

Students and draft dodgers joined a peace movement that had emerged with renewed vigour in the 1950s. Outraged by atmospheric testing of nuclear bombs and Cold War brinkmanship, the new generation of pacifists focused on dismantling nuclear weapons and establishing peaceful forums for settling international conflicts. James Minifie's *Peacemaker or Powder-Monkey: Canada's Role in a Revolutionary World* (1960), a Canadian best-seller, struck a responsive chord with many Canadians. A CBC correspondent in Washington, Minifie advocated Canadian withdrawal from NORAD and NATO so that Canada could more effectively play a peacemaker role in the world. The Quakers, a centuries-old pacifist religious sect, established a peace centre on Grindstone Island, Ontario, in 1960, to conduct research and plan action. That year also witnessed the creation of Voice of Women, a peace and social-justice activist group that conducted highly visible publicity and civil-disobedience campaigns against war and for a more humane social order.

THE RESPONSE FROM OTTAWA

In the early 1960s, there were indications that Canada might chart an independent course on defence rather than continue to offer unquestioning support to the Americans. Prime Minister John Diefenbaker appointed Howard Green, well known for his support of nuclear disarmament, to the position of secretary of state for External Affairs in 1959. Green convinced Diefenbaker to reconsider Canada's agreement to acquire nuclear warheads as part of its commitment to NATO and NORAD defence strategies.

The issue of nuclear weapons divided Canadians and caused dissension in the ranks of both the Liberal and Progressive Conservative parties. Under Pearson, the Liberals had initially opposed nuclear weapons, but not with unanimity. Diefenbaker's cabinet was also divided on the issue: Green's anti-nuclear stance was opposed by Defence Minister Douglas Harkness, who argued that Canada should adopt the most up-to-date military equipment. Diefenbaker himself vacillated on the issue, much to the annoyance of the Americans. Matters came to a head only after the Cuban missile crisis in October 1962 starkly raised the issue of the efficacy and morality of the nuclear deterrent.

In 1959, troops led by Fidel Castro toppled a corrupt military regime in Cuba and ushered in a socialist revolution. The overwrought Americans established a trade embargo against Cuba, but Canada refused to follow suit. Early in 1961, President John F. Kennedy authorized plans for an invasion of Cuba by 2000 CIA-trained Cuban exiles. The Bay of Pigs invasion failed miserably, but justified Castro's decision to accept Soviet missiles to defend his besieged country.

Kennedy demanded that the Soviet Union remove the missiles, calling upon his Canadian allies to put their NORAD forces on alert in the event that the Soviets refused to back down.

Concerned that Kennedy was being too belligerent, Diefenbaker waited three days before announcing that Canadian forces were on alert. Harkness, in defiance of a cabinet decision, had secretly put the forces on alert immediately after Kennedy's request. As events unfolded, Canada's half-hearted public response was of little immediate consequence: the Soviet Union agreed to withdraw the offending missiles in return for an American guarantee that they would respect Cuban independence. However, Diefenbaker's lack of cooperation infuriated the Americans, who became determined to topple the unpredictable prime minister.

In the months preceding the 1963 federal election, statements from the American State Department and a

Lester B. Pearson and John F. Kennedy, 1963.
AP/Wide World Photos/R61025

TABLE 16.1 Percentage of Foreign Control of Selected Canadian Industries, 1939–1973

Industry	1939	1948	1958	1968	1973
Manufacturing	38(32)*	43(39)	57(44)	58(46)	59(44)
Petroleum and natural gas**	–	–	73(67)	75(61)	76(59)
Mining and smelting	42(38)	40(37)	60(51)	68(58)	56(45)
Railways	3(3)	3(3)	2(2)	2(2)	2(2)
Other utilities	26(26)	24(24)	5(4)	5(4)	7(4)
Total†	21(19)	25(22)	32(26)	36(28)	35(26)

*Numbers in brackets indicate percentage controlled by American residents
**Petroleum and natural gas combined with mining and smelting to 1948
†Total includes merchandising, not shown separately

Sources: Adapted from F.H. Leacy, ed., *Historical Statistics of Canada*, 2nd ed. (Ottawa: Statistics Canada, 1983), Series G, 291–302; John Fayerweather, *Foreign Investment in Canada: Prospects for National Policy* (Toronto: Oxford University Press, 1974), 7.

retiring American NATO leader drew attention to Diefenbaker's about-face on defence policy. The Americans revealed that Diefenbaker's earlier agreement to purchase weapons systems associated with Canada's NATO and NORAD commitments necessitated acquisition of nuclear warheads. To drive home their point, they loudly rejected claims by Diefenbaker that the Bomarc missiles acquired by Canada to intercept Soviet missiles could make effective use of non-nuclear warheads.

Diefenbaker decried American interference in the Canadian election and finally decided to reject nuclear weapons for Canada. His unpopular government went down to defeat by Lester Pearson's Liberals, who had

TABLE 16.2 Destination of Domestic Exports (excluding gold), 1946–1975 (in millions of dollars)

Area	1946	1955	1965	1975
United States	884	2 548	4 840	21 074
United Kingdom	594	768	1 174	1 795
Japan	1	91	316	2 130
Other western European	189	261	626	2 347
Other American	202	216	433	1 583
Centrally planned (communist) economies	91	12	418	1 049
Other	312	363	717	2 571
Percentage of exports to U.S.	38.9	59.8	56.8	64.7

Source: F.H. Leacy, ed., *Historical Statistics of Canada*, 2nd ed. (Ottawa: Statistics Canada, 1983), Series G, 401–7.

abruptly changed their position on the nuclear question following the missile crisis. Once in office, the Liberals followed through on their commitment to the controversial nuclear warheads. Pearson's secretary of state for External Affairs, Paul Martin Sr., suggests in his memoirs that it was important for the Pearson government to restore harmonious relations between the governments of Canada and the United States. "One of the functions of Canadian diplomacy has been to ensure that the United States will always harbour a special regard for Canada."[6]

When Pierre Elliott Trudeau came to power in 1968, he initiated a reassessment of Canada's NATO and NORAD commitments, but the results were mixed. Plans were announced to gradually cut Canada's NATO troops in Europe by half, but its NORAD commitment remained unchanged. The obsolescence of the nuclear warheads available to the Canadian forces allowed Trudeau to return Canada to its earlier status as a nation without nuclear weapons. While Trudeau supported the campaign to slow down the arms race, he continued to support the policy of nuclear deterrence.

Trudeau also tried to move away from the Americans on foreign policy. In 1970, two years before the Americans took the same step, he recognized the People's Republic of China. This decision called into question the view that the defeated anti-communist forces compelled to retreat to Taiwan in 1949 remained the legitimate government of all of China. In addition to reflecting Trudeau's personal position on the Chinese question, the recognition of the People's Republic was popular among Canadians attracted by the prospect of increased trade with this poor but populous country.

CONTINENTAL ECONOMIC INTEGRATION

While these initiatives underscored the point that Canada could establish policy without the approval of the United States, no prime minister was prepared to go too far in defying the nation's chief trading partner. A shift in economic dependence from Great Britain to the United States had proceeded gradually since the time of confederation. By the turn of the twentieth century, the United States had overtaken Great Britain as Canada's major trading partner, and in the interwar period most Canadian companies controlled from outside the country were in American hands. Close wartime relations between the two countries simply accelerated long-term trends.

The post-war economic boom gave the United States a powerful incentive for ever-closer economic and political relations with Canada. The Paley Commission, established by President Harry S. Truman in 1951, noted in its report, tellingly entitled *Resources for Freedom*, that the United States was fast running out of the raw materials required to fuel its military and civilian economy. Where better to invest than in the vast, friendly hinterland to the north? During the 1950s and 1960s, American investment poured into Canada.

The nuclear industry is a good case in point. The development of the atomic bomb and nuclear reactor stimulated the Canadian uranium market. Because of the strategic importance of the element, the Canadian government had nationalized Canada's major uranium mining company, Eldorado Mining and Refining, in 1944. Following the war, Eldorado served as a marketing agency for all private Canadian uranium companies, selling most of the Canadian output to the United States Atomic Energy Commission at fabulous prices.

In 1952, another Crown corporation, Atomic Energy of Canada Limited (AECL), was created to develop peaceful uses for atomic energy. Its greatest success was the CANDU reactor, which was sold internationally. Ontario was the first province to enter an agreement with AECL to build nuclear power stations, and the first demonstration plant at Rolphston came into operation in 1962. With major finds at Beaverlodge and Blind River in Northern Ontario, Canada supplied a third of the world's military and civilian uranium requirements in the 1950s. Eldorado Nuclear, Rio Tinto–Rio Algom, and Dennison Mines became literally and figuratively

TABLE 16.3 Origin of Canadian Imports, 1946–1975 (in millions of dollars)

Area	1946	1955	1965	1975
United States	1 387	3 331	6 045	23 641
United Kingdom	137	393	619	1 222
Japan	–	37	230	1 205
Other west European	14	143	514	2 074
Other American	164	409	548	1 802
Centrally planned (communist) economies	5	8	59	234
Other	134	246	618	4 537
Percentage of imports from U.S.	75.3	72.9	70.0	68.1

Source: F.H. Leacy, ed., *Historical Statistics of Canada*, 2nd ed. (Ottawa: Statistics Canada, 1983), Series G, 408–14.

some of Canada's hottest companies, while Uranium City, Saskatchewan, and Elliot Lake, Ontario, were added to the pantheon of boom towns on Canada's resource frontier.

Defence production generally emerged as a major aspect of Canada's industrial development in the post-war period and further encouraged continental economic integration. Under the Defence Production Sharing Agreement of 1956, Canadians had the right to bid for military contracts on an equal basis with Americans. In the late 1960s, an estimated 125 000 Canadian jobs were tied to armaments production. Largely because of the Vietnam War, arms sales were 56 percent greater in 1965 than they had been in 1964; by 1972, American defence procurement in Canada included contracts for shells, military aircraft, and radio relay sets along with natural resources.

The impact of the war on Canada's economy went well beyond the sale of arms and minerals. With the American economy enjoying a war-induced boom, other exports to the United States, such as lumber for constructing homes and office buildings, also soared. The structure of trade as it emerged in the post-war period had one enduring characteristic. Exports, which made up a quarter of the gross national product, consisted largely of unprocessed and semi-processed goods. By contrast, Canada's imports were mainly manufactured products. While the Americans imported only 10 percent of the manufactured products they consumed, Canadians imported 36 percent.

THE GORDON REPORT

Canadians were ambivalent about this transformation in their economic relations. They had long courted American capital investment and had boasted about the success of the tariff in encouraging American companies to locate north of the forty-ninth parallel. Now, the degree of American control in Canada's economic destiny began to take on sinister overtones. (See Tables 16.1, 16.2, and 16.3.) In 1955, the Canadian government appointed the Royal Commission on Canada's Economic Prospects to inquire into and report on the long-term prospects of the Canadian economy. Chaired by Walter Gordon, a partner in one of Toronto's major accounting firms, the royal commission concluded that branch plants typically hired American managers, devoted little attention to research and development, and remitted a high percentage of their profits to foreign investors.

Built to serve only a Canadian market, branch plants often operated inefficiently and were restricted from export opportunities by head office. The high level of foreign investment in Canada contributed to its growing balance-of-payments problem as capital flowed out of the country in the form of interest and dividends. If Canadians hoped to create a balanced economy and let their manufacturing sector reach maturity, it would be necessary to curtail American influence. The commissioners urged the government to exercise closer control over the activities of foreign companies operating in Canada and suggested that foreign corporations be required to employ more Canadians in senior management positions, include Canadians on their boards, and sell an "appreciable interest" in their equity stocks to people in the country where they did their business.

While nationalists supported policies that limited American control of the Canadian economy, classical

Chrysler plant in Windsor, Ontario, 1954 (above), and an Esso station, ca. 1950. American corporations seemed omnipresent in the post-war Canadian economy.
Library and Archives Canada/NA112635 (above) and Provincial Archives of Alberta

economists, represented by University of Toronto economist Harry Johnson, argued that economic nationalism was a "narrow and garbage cluttered cul-de-sac."[7] Canada, and Canadian workers in particular, he maintained, would benefit from the removal of all restrictions on trade and foreign investment. Only by remaining open to global economic trends could the Canadian economy function at optimal efficiency and therefore provide the best jobs and highest incomes.

The free trade option elicited a considerable following among business people and politicians in the early 1960s, but the only tangible result was the Auto Pact of 1965. The pact, which created an integrated continental market for automobiles and automobile parts, included quotas for Canadian production, mak-

ing it more an example of "managed trade" than unfettered free trade.

Meanwhile, the Diefenbaker government took up the Gordon report's challenge to limit American influence on the Canadian economy. It introduced tax incentives for Canadian-based industries and incurred the wrath of the United States by trading with communist countries such as Cuba and the Soviet Union. The Pearson government appeared at first willing to go even further than its predecessors. Lester Pearson named his long-time friend Walter Gordon minister of Finance. Gordon's first budget included such nationalistic proposals as a 30 percent "take-over tax" on the sale of publicly held Canadian companies to foreigners. Although Gordon was forced by an angry business community and American government pressures to

Voices from the Past

Views of Foreign Ownership

In the 1950s and 1960s, Canada's political and business leaders expressed conflicting views regarding the benefits of foreign ownership of Canadian industries. The following excerpts provide a hint of the debate's flavour.

> With an enormous area still of almost virgin country to be opened, Canadians need and welcome foreign investments and with their own healthy stake in the national development they have no fears of any domination.
>
> –G.K. Sheils, president of the Canadian Manufacturers' Association, in the *Financial Post*, 1953

> The free and unhampered flow of foreign investment into Canada has brought so many benefits to this country that it certainly is entitled to a fair and unbiased hearing from the Canadian people.
> ... If one allows for Canadian investment abroad and the use of foreign resources as a percentage of net capital formation, it turns out that not more than 6 per cent of Canadian investment in the postwar world depended on foreign resources.
> ... Canada's economy has been growing at such a rapid rate that the role of foreign investment in relation to our productive capacity has diminished and will continue to do so.
>
> –C.D. Howe, minister of Trade and Commerce, in the House of Commons, 1956

> No other country in the world with something like our relative state of development has ever had such a degree of foreign domination, or even one half or one quarter the degree of foreign domination. Canada is being pushed down the road that leads to loss of any effective power to be masters in our own household and ultimate absorption in and by another.
>
> –James Coyne, president of the Bank of Canada, to the Canadian Chamber of Commerce, 1960

> During the two-and-one-half years I held that office [minister of Finance], the influence that financial and business interests in the United States had on Canadian policy was continually brought home to me. On occasion, this influence was reinforced by representations from the State Department and the American Administration as a whole. It was pressed by those who direct American businesses in Canada, by their professional advisors, by Canadian financiers whose interests were identified directly or indirectly with American investment in Canada, by influential members of the Canadian civil service, by some representatives of the university community, and by some sections of the press.
>
> –Walter Gordon, *A Choice for Canada*, 1966[8]

abandon the tax, his economic nationalism was gaining significant popular support.

In 1964–1965, Gordon introduced legislation to protect Canadian banks, insurance companies, and other financial services from foreign control, and steps were taken to reduce American dominance of the Canadian media. Gordon tweaked the beaks of too many powerful business people, and his cabinet influence had been reduced by the time he resigned as finance minister in late 1965. Nevertheless, Pearson agreed to Gordon's proposal to establish the Task Force on the Structure of Canadian Industry to examine whether it really mattered who owned industry in Canada. Gordon's choice for its head was a respected economist, Mel Watkins, of the University of Toronto.

THE WATKINS REPORT

Although Watkins was once a critic of economic nationalism, his investigation of Canada-U.S. economic relations converted him to a different view. His report, which appeared in 1968, was tougher than the Gordon report of 11 years earlier. Watkins attempted to torpedo the common view that whatever the impact on Canada's sovereignty, American investment was helping to create a more dynamic, efficient economy than Canadians could build on their own. He challenged the myth that Canada remained short of capital and needed foreign investment. If Canadians who invested abroad had kept their money at home, he argued, they would have reduced the need for foreign capital by half.

The task force painted a picture of a branch-plant manufacturing economy geared to serving the Canadian market alone, leaving international markets to plants headquartered in the United States. While defenders of American branch plants pointed with pride to the large number of corporations operating in Canada, Watkins charged that having a Canadian "miniature replica" of an American industry further minimized Canada's economic competitiveness. Watkins argued that a few firms working at full capacity, focusing on international and national markets and spending money to apply the latest technologies, would better serve the national interest.

A much debated document, the Watkins report was released at a time when nationalistic sentiment was strong and misgivings about the United States were growing. An organization calling itself the Committee for an Independent Canada was formed to rally support for the demands of the task force for legislation to encourage Canadian investment and research and to curb foreign ownership. At a 1969 party convention, the Waffle group within the New Democratic Party won a third of the votes for a resolution that called for public ownership of industry to replace foreign private ownership. Watkins became a leader of this socialist and nationalist group. He argued that private market forces left on their own had made Canada an economic colony of the United States and only a democratic socialist strategy could empower Canadians to determine their economic fate collectively.

ECONOMIC NATIONALISM IN THE 1970S

Despite Trudeau's skepticism about economic nationalism, his government enacted several of Watkins's recommendations. The Canada Development Corporation was created in 1971 to encourage Canadian ownership and management in vital sectors of the economy. In 1974, the Foreign Investment Review Agency, under the direction of Herb Gray, was established to screen proposals for foreign takeovers of existing Canadian businesses.

There was also federal intervention in one of the industries where the Americans exercised greatest control in Canada: petroleum. In late 1975, the federal government created Petro-Canada, a Crown corporation with a broad mandate to develop a Canadian presence in the petroleum industry. It was a task that earlier Canadian governments had shunned. There were campaigns in the 1950s by independent petroleum companies for an oil pipeline from Montreal to Alberta that would replace a developing north-south energy grid with an east-west one. But the industry's dominant company in Canada, Imperial Oil, was controlled by Standard Oil of New Jersey, which also had large investments in Venezuela and the Middle East. Standard Oil's marketing strategy collided with the nationalist goals of the independent producers. Lacking an infrastructure that could provide reliable data on the industry, the federal and Alberta governments relied on Imperial for information and advice and therefore rejected the independents' plans as impractical.

Not surprisingly, the federal government's tentative entry into the petroleum industry was greeted with hostility by the American oil giants. It was not the only source of friction between the United States and Canada over oil. American oil companies operating in Alaska claimed the right to have their supertankers travel across the Arctic passage to transport their product to eastern American markets. Canada argued that such voyages would violate Canadian sovereignty and adversely affect the fragile northern environment. Although the government decided not to publicly protest when the American tanker *Manhattan* carried several cargoes across the Arctic in 1969 and 1970, it passed the Arctic Waters Pollution Prevention Act to protect its northern coast.

By this time, Richard Nixon had been elected president of the United States. He was a Republican who escalated the war in Vietnam and championed a narrow national policy on matters of trade and defence. The Nixon administration's hostility to Canada's efforts to establish sovereignty in northern waters suggested that confrontation would occur if Canada attempted to push the point. In an effort to find another way to establish its position, the Canadian government campaigned at the United Nations for "law of the sea" legislation that would give northern countries greater control over their coastlines.

In August 1971, the Nixon administration made matters difficult for opponents of economic nationalism in Canada by establishing the Domestic International Sales Corporation (DISC). DISC used the tax system to further encourage American multi-national firms to export from their American facilities to the detriment of their branch plants. The legislation also imposed a temporary import surcharge of 10 percent. Although this was not the first time Americans had pursued a policy of economic nationalism, it was the first time since the Second World War that Canadians were not exempted from such measures. Trade policy in the United States, once largely made in the offices of the secretary of state with a sharp eye on Canada as a strategic ally, moved to economic departments concerned mainly with protecting American jobs.

Following Nixon's announcement, Trudeau's minister of External Affairs, Mitchell Sharp, issued a statement that committed Canada to what became known as the "Third Option" in Canadian foreign policy. Option one, maintaining Canada's present relationship with the United States, had been tried and found wanting. Option two, closer integration with the Americans, was clearly impossible in the age of Nixon. Option three, reduction of Canada's vulnerability to American actions by expanding global political and economic links, seemed the obvious choice. Diplomatic efforts to expand Canada's trade with other nations bore some fruit, but Canada remained overwhelmingly dependent on the American economy for its imports and exports.

CONTINENTALISM AND THE PROVINCES

Federal efforts to control American investment in Canada often met a hostile response from the provinces. In the post-war period, as American resource demands increased, north-south economic links became more important to several provinces than east-west links. Since the provinces had constitutional jurisdiction over resources and could earn much-needed income from their development, they increasingly resisted the use of the federal power over trade and taxation to shape patterns of resource exploitation. Alberta governments, both Social Credit and Conservative, were particularly resistant to any "discriminatory" treatment of foreign capital, arguing that the rise of their province from have-not to have status in the post-war period was largely the doing of the giant American energy corporations.

Before the war, the federal government had disallowed provincial efforts to secure long-term contracts to sell hydro-electricity to the Americans. In the post-war period, the combination of American and provincial pressures gradually led the federal government to abandon its policy that hydro should be harnessed mainly for national needs. The American Northwest could not meet its own power needs, and the United States negotiated a treaty with Canada to develop dams on the Canadian side of the Columbia River in British Columbia. These would provide flood control as the Americans produced more hydro-electricity on the American Columbia. The original treaty between the two countries agreed to return to Canada half of the power generated on the American side, but Premier W.A.C. Bennett of British Columbia preferred to sell that power to the United States and use the Peace River to satisfy British Columbia's power needs.

Yielding to pressure from British Columbia, the federal government negotiated a protocol that included commitments to sell power to the western American states. Canada ratified the Columbia River Treaty and Protocol in 1964. Soon Manitoba was signing long-term deals with the United States to deliver power from the province's North. Native peoples were removed from thriving communities along northern rivers so that giant power projects could meet the dual needs of American consumers and the provincial treasury. Cree and Inuit peoples of northern Quebec suffered the same fate in the 1970s when the Quebec government began its ambitious James Bay project to meet not only provincial power needs but also considerable demand from the state of New York.

THE AMERICANIZATION OF CANADIAN CULTURE

Although the Canadian government was slow off the mark in attempting to regulate American-dominated resource and manufacturing industries, it was quicker in recognizing the danger posed by American cultural industries. Concerns about the overwhelming American influence on Canadian culture, particularly in Anglophone Canada, led to the creation in 1949 of a royal commission to study national developments in the arts, letters, and sciences. Headed by Vincent Massey—scion of the farm-implements giant Massey-Harris, wealthy Liberal Party backer, former Canadian high commissioner to Great Britain, and in 1952 Canada's first native-born governor general—the royal commission recommended government programs to strengthen Canadian cultural production and resist the impact of American popular culture.

The recommendations of the Massey Commission encompassed a wide range of Canadian cultural life. Despite a powerful lobby by private broadcasters, the commission opposed calls to remove the CBC's control over private stations. Indeed, it called on the CBC, as the regulator of private broadcasters, to force such stations, many of which simply played American recorded music, to carry more live local performances. It also put the CBC in charge of licensing television stations and set national productions in the arts as a prime goal for CBC Television, which began broadcasting in 1952. Massey and his fellow commissioners called for federal grants to provinces for their universities on a per capita basis, and more funds for such national agencies as the National Film Board, the Historic Sites and Monuments Board, and the National Museum. Their most ambitious recommendation was for a Canada Council that they envisioned as the equivalent for the arts and letters of the National Research Council for science. It would enhance Canadian cultural production in such areas as music, drama, and ballet, provide funds for Canadian artists to perform abroad, and subsidize the volunteer groups that kept the arts alive throughout the country.

In 1957, the federal government responded by establishing the Canada Council with a mandate based on the Massey Commission's recommendations. The result was that, while profitable popular culture remained Americanized, there was a strengthening of the Canadian presence in literature, music, and art.

When television made its commercial appearance after the Second World War, the federal government decided to grant licensing power over the new medium to the CBC's board of governors. The CBC was to establish a television network and initially would be given a monopoly over Canadian TV. By 1960, nine CBC stations and 38 affiliates were on the air. The stations gave over much of their prime time to American shows, but CBC-TV also produced Canadian dramas and variety shows that provided an outlet for many Canadian actors, musicians, and entertainers.

Although American sitcoms and teleplays proved more popular than their Canadian equivalents, there were a number of successes in the early years of Canadian television programming. *Front Page Challenge*, a sedate guess-the-name-in-the-news show, was introduced in 1956 and remained on the air until 1995 with the same host, Fred Davis, and original panelist Pierre Berton still in harness. *Country Hoedown* introduced a generation of country music entertainers, notably Tommy Hunter, and *Don Messer's Jubilee*, which was first aired in 1959, earned a devoted following. *The Plouffe Family*, a sitcom focusing on the lives of a working-class Montreal family, was a huge success in both its French and English versions.

In 1958, the federal government responded to pressure from private broadcasters to end the CBC monopoly over television. Under new legislation, private channels became eligible for licences and the Board of Broadcast Governors (BBG) was set up to license radio and television stations. After the first private stations went on the air, featuring almost non-stop American entertainment, nationalist pressures forced the BBG to establish a 55 percent Canadian-content guideline in the 1960s. Cheaply produced game shows, modelled on American programs, were the private stations' answer to the rule, and hopes that content regulations would stimulate a viable Canadian television production industry were largely unrealized.

While most television shows, whether produced in Canada or the United States, constituted light entertainment, they also embodied a set of conservative social values and stereotypes. "Family shows," including *Father Knows Best* and *Leave It to Beaver*, extolled middle-class patriarchal families in which father earned the money while mother cared for the household. A woman's purpose in life was presented in innumerable commercials that explained how, by purchasing the advertised products, a housewife could fulfill herself and be the envy of her neighbours by staying young and attractive while keeping a spotless house with impeccably well-groomed and well-nourished inhabitants.

American content and American models were evident in other areas of mass culture besides television. In response to competition from "the tube," radio stations turned their attention from drama and comedy to music. Most of that music was recorded in the United States. Movies were overwhelmingly American. The average Canadian watched 18 movies per year in 1950 before television caused a drop in movie attendance. In 1953, 74.6 percent of the feature films that were distributed in Canada originated in the United States, 16.9 percent in France, and 5.8 percent in Great Britain. There was only one Canadian film in movie houses that year: *Tit-coq*, written by and starring Quebec playwright Gratien Gélinas. Nonetheless, the government resisted imposing quotas on Hollywood movies, instead entering an agreement with the major studios to include mentions of Canada in American feature films.

Canadian entertainers continued to seek success in the larger American market, and their reputations among the home folk were enhanced when they achieved it. Former CBC newsman Lorne Greene was lionized for his role as the patriarch of the Ponderosa ranch in television's *Bonanza*. A variety of Canadian recording artists, including the Crewcuts, Paul Anka, the Diamonds, the Guess Who, and Anne Murray, topped the American charts at various times. Johnny Wayne and Frank Shuster, about to lose their Canadian television series, were renewed after American audiences cheered their comic portrayal of Julius Caesar's murder on *The Ed Sullivan Show* in May 1958.

THE NATIONALIST RESPONSE

In an effort to help homegrown talent, the federal government provided assistance to Canadian filmmakers and recording artists. Tax breaks and subsidies were given to producers of Canadian films, and in 1970 the Canadian Radio-Television and Telecommunications Commission introduced regulations requiring radio stations to ensure that no fewer than 30 percent of the songs they played were of Canadian origin. While these measures were not without effect, the next several decades would confirm that Anglophone Canadians preferred to spend their money on American movies and American and British recordings. American culture's hold on the mass market would not easily be dislodged.

By the early 1970s, much of English Canada's artistic community had become ardent Canadian nationalists. Cultural icons such as authors Pierre Berton and Farley Mowat, poet Earle Birney, and artist Harold Town were prominent members of the Committee for an Independent Canada. Celebrated novelist and poet Margaret Atwood wrote *Survival* (1972), an outline of the development of Canadian literature that attempted to find a distinct Canadian identity in the resilient, if often cheerless, characters who peopled national writing.

Not every successful Canadian author applauded such developments. Mordecai Richler, one of Canada's best-known authors at home and abroad, argued that cultural nationalism would result in mediocre work and that Canadians should be willing to have their work judged by international standards. Like many Canadians who were not of British descent, Richler suspected that Canadian nationalism was a plot by white Anglo-Saxon Protestants to impose their version of a national identity on immigrant groups who had their own complex identities, of which being Canadian was but a component. The French-Canadian artistic community, particularly in Quebec, was largely estranged from the new assertive cultural nationalism of English Canada. As we shall see in Chapter 19, Québécois artists had, for the most part, joined in the movement for Quebec sovereignty, and felt that their language saved them from the onslaught of American culture visible in the rest of the country.

CULTURE IN QUESTION

The bombarding of Canadians with American messages disquieted some Canadian scholars. One of the first to voice his concern was the country's most celebrated political economist, Harold Adams Innis. In a number of essays, collected in *Empire and Communications* (1950) and *The Bias of Communications* (1951), Innis suggested that media empires in the United States were shaping the thinking of people the world over. Democratic discussion was being diverted by the limited number of individuals who controlled access to information. As historian Mary Vipond observes, Innis's "thesis has provided the theoretical groundwork for contemplation of one of the central paradoxes of Canadian history: how technology in general and communications technology in particular have acted as a double-edged sword that simultaneously facilitates the promotion of national unity and serves as the highway on which the culture of another nation rides into our homes."[9]

In 1965, George Grant wrote *Lament for a Nation*, in which he explored the career of John Diefenbaker, whose government, some people believed, had been brought down in 1963 by the hostility of the Kennedy regime. Grant pointed out the self-defeating character of the well-meaning nationalism of Diefenbaker. On the one hand, Diefenbaker genuinely wanted Canada to develop outside of the shadow of the Americans. He sought to focus on Canada's links with the British Commonwealth to provide a counterweight to the overwhelming influence of the United States in the nation's economic and political life.

More problematic, according to Grant, Diefenbaker, while sometimes defiant of the Americans, shared their fundamental values. He accepted the supremacy of the marketplace over the state and of individual acquisitiveness over collective goals. Canadians generally shared Diefenbaker's contradictions, lamented Grant. They had embraced American social values, all the time protesting that they wished to be a sovereign people. Yet their materialistic pursuits had turned them into a people who had integrated their economy and foreign policy with that of the Americans and who consumed what the American entertainment industry served them.

Writing in 1970, historian Donald Creighton, like Grant a conservative who lamented Canada's fascination with the United States and its break with British ties, had a withering description of the Canadians of the post-war period: "They had permitted their government to turn its back on their past and to repudiate their history; and in the bankruptcy of their own national philosophy, they turned instinctively to the nearest creditor, the United States. . . . Imitation and plagiarism had become deep-seated Canadian instincts; economic and political dependence had grown into a settled way of life."[10]

Universities came under criticism from Canadian nationalists in the 1960s for their policies to cope with the large enrolments of baby boomers. Most universities had hired a significant number of foreign, mainly American, academics, many of whom ignored Canadian topics in their teaching and research. In 1972, the Association of Universities and Colleges of Canada established a commission to study and make recommendations on the state of university scholarship and teaching relating to Canada. Chaired by Thomas H.B. Symons, the founding president of Trent University, the commission concluded in its two-volume report, entitled *To Know Ourselves*, that students were much more interested in learning about Canada than professors were in teaching about it. Indeed, the commissioners maintained that no country in the world spent so little time studying itself. The Symons report was hotly debated, but it ultimately helped convince the federal government to establish programs to encourage Canadian studies and to pass legislation giving preference to qualified Canadians in university hiring. Canadian universities in the late 1960s and early 1970s also acceded to student pressures to expand their offerings in the literature and history of the country.

A HISTORIOGRAPHICAL DEBATE

Vietnam: What Role Did Canada Play?

As we have seen, Canada prided itself on its image as a peacemaker in international relations. But in instances where American interests were at stake, how successful was Canada in fulfilling this role? Was Ottawa able to strike an independent course, or did it take its cue from the Americans?

There is considerable debate about Canada's role in the International Control Commission (ICC), which was originally established in the 1950s to monitor the Geneva Accord for the resolution of conflict in Indochina, and about its larger role in the war in Indochina.

Political scientist James Eayrs's *Indochina: Roots of Complicity*, as the title suggests, views Canada as "complicit" in pushing the American point of view within the ICC. Though he deals with only the first three years of the commission's existence (1954–1957), Eayrs demonstrates that Canada quickly established a partisan stance within the ICC. Apart from faithfully supporting American positions, Canada's commissioners developed the habit of reporting confidential information to the Americans. Put less delicately, Canada betrayed its trust and acted as a spy for the United States.[11]

Douglas Ross challenges Eayrs's interpretation. While conceding that Canada's focus in the ICC was on North Vietnamese violations, he points out that Canada was trying to counter Poland's one-sided attacks on South Vietnam. Ross argues that Canada joined the ICC in order to influence the course of events in Indochina and that Canadian diplomacy urged moderation on the Americans in their prosecution of the war, although the strength of militaristic forces in the United States limited the impact of such counsel.[12]

Political scientist Victor Levant disputes most of Ross's account. His *Quiet Complicity* emphasizes that in 1962, Canada joined India in preparing a report on North Vietnamese violations of the Geneva Accord, which the Americans used to justify increasing their scale of intervention in Indochina. Using American State and Defense Department records, he argues that Canada was well aware of American plans to bomb North Vietnam and was willing to use its diplomats as intermediaries for the Americans to deliver threats to the North Vietnamese government.

Levant, in contrast to Ross, focuses on the economic gains made by Canadian business from the war in Vietnam. He rejects the view that the Canadians were acting on orders from the United States government or out of fear of that government's retaliation if Canada behaved independently. Rather, he argues that the shared views of the elites of the two countries led Canada's political leaders to support the main lines of American policy. Canada's leaders were supporters of international capitalism and wanted to see the defeat of the Vietnamese communists at any cost.[13]

So Many Worlds, the second volume of Paul Martin Sr.'s autobiography, which Levant brands "a classic example of historical amnesia and political double-talk,"[14] denies that Canada's role in Vietnam was partisan. Martin maintains that Canada worked tirelessly to arrange for ceasefires and to have the two warring sides arrive at a compromise, but that ultimately, the Canadians were unable to achieve much due to the rigidity that characterized the two factions. While Martin's autobiography concedes that good political relations with the Americans could translate into special consideration on economic questions, he ignores this connection in his discussion of Canada's behaviour regarding Vietnam.[15]

CONCLUSION

The shadow of the United States cannot be ignored in any discussion of Canadian development following the Second World War. As the world's most powerful nation in the age of the atomic bomb and instantaneous communications, the United States exerted an influence even greater than that of France or Great Britain in earlier eras of Canadian history. Many Canadians accepted this reality without much concern, but others were troubled by the spectre of American domination and were prepared to battle for an independent economy, a made-in-Canada foreign policy, and a more assertive Canadian cultural nationalism. As we shall see in Chapter 18, this battle was joined with the efforts of ordinary Canadians in the 1960s to make their voices heard.

NOTES

1 Kari Levitt, *Silent Surrender: The Multinational Corporation in Canada* (Toronto: Macmillan, 1970), 2–3.

2 Roger W. Bowen, ed., *E.H. Norman: His Life and Scholarship* (Toronto: University of Toronto Press, 1984).

3 James Barros, *No Sense of Evil: Espionage, The Case of Herbert Norman* (Toronto: Deneau, 1986), 157.

4 Peyton V. Lyon, "The Loyalties of E. Herbert Norman," *Labour/Le Travail* 28 (Fall 1991), 249, 259.

5 The term "Third World" was coined in the 1950s to differentiate the poorer countries of the world from the wealthier industrialized nations. The First World consisted of the western powers plus Japan. The Second World comprised the Soviet Union and its satellites in eastern Europe. Self-determination suggested the right of the peoples of these poor nations to choose their own future without undue influence from outside powers. Though decolonization proceeded rapidly from 1945 on, most of the newly independent nations found that in practice they were forced to become economic vassals of either the West or the Soviets.

6 Paul Martin, *A Very Public Life*, vol. 2, *So Many Worlds* (Toronto: Deneau, 1985), 389.

7 Harry Johnson, *The Canadian Quandary* (Ottawa: Carleton University Press, 1963), 11–12.

8 Quoted in Philip Resnick, *The Land of Cain: Class and Nationalism in English Canada, 1945–1975* (Vancouver: New Star Books, 1977), 79, 102, 114, 115.

9 Mary Vipond, *The Mass Media in Canada* (Toronto: Lorimer, 1989), 131.

10 Donald Creighton, *Canada's First Century, 1867–1967* (Toronto: Macmillan, 1970), 356.

11 James Eayrs, *In Defence of Canada*, vol. 5, *Indochina: Roots of Complicity* (Toronto: University of Toronto Press, 1983).

12 Douglas Ross, *In the Interests of Peace: Canada and Vietnam, 1945–1973* (Toronto: University of Toronto Press, 1983).

13 Victor Levant, *Quiet Complicity: Canadian Involvement in the Vietnam War* (Toronto: Between the Lines, 1986).

14 Ibid., 297.

15 Martin, *A Very Public Life*, Chapter 13.

RELATED READINGS IN THIS SERIES

From *Nation and Society: Readings in Post-Confederation Canadian History*

Steven High, "'I'll Wrap the F*#@ Canadian Flag Around Me': A Nationalist Response to Plant Shutdowns, 1969–1984," 320–41

From Primary Documents CD-ROM, Volume II

The Forces of Geography
Education Only Weapon for Defense of Democracy
Documented Report Bares Red Hold on Smelters
Russian Roulette
Toronto Can Be a Good Scout Too

SELECTED READING

Surveys and books of essays dealing with a cross-section of the issues discussed in this unit include John Herd Thompson and Stephen J. Randall, *Ambivalent Allies*, 4th ed. (Montreal: McGill-Queen's University Press, 2008); Robert Bothwell, *Canada and the United States: The Politics of Partnership* (Toronto: University of Toronto Press, 1992) and *Alliance and Illusion: Canada and the World, 1945–1984* (Vancouver: UBC Press, 2007); Edelgard E. Mahant and Graeme S. Mount, *Invisible and Inaudible in Washington: American Policies Toward Canada* (Vancouver: UBC Press, 1999); Norman Hillmer, ed., *Partners Nevertheless: Canadian-American Relations in the Twentieth Century* (Toronto: Copp Clark Pitman, 1989); and Allan Smith, *Canada: An American Nation? Essays on Continentalism, Identity and the Canadian Frame of Mind* (Montreal: McGill-Queen's University Press, 1994).

Canada's aims and roles throughout the Cold War are discussed in Reginald Whitaker and Steve Hewitt, *Canada and the Cold War* (Toronto: James Lorimer, 2003); Norman Hillmer and J.L. Granatstein, *Empire to Umpire: Canada and the World to the 1990s* (Toronto: Copp Clark Longman, 1994); J.L. Granatstein and Norman Hillmer, *For Better or for Worse: Canada and the United States to the 1990s* (Toronto: Copp Clark Pitman, 1991); Denis Smith, *Politics of Fear: Canada and the Cold War, 1941–1948* (Toronto: University of Toronto Press, 1988); James Eayrs, *In Defence of Canada*, vols. 4 and 5 (Toronto: University of Toronto Press, 1980,

1983); George Ignatieff, *The Making of a Peacemonger* (Toronto: Penguin, 1985); and Ernie Regehr and Simon Rosenblum, eds., *Canada and the Nuclear Arms Race* (Toronto: Lorimer, 1983). On Canada in Korea, see Ted Barris, *Deadlock in Korea: Canadians at War, 1950–1953* (Toronto: Macmillan, 1999); David J. Bercuson, *Blood on the Hills: The Canadian Army in the Korean War* (Toronto: University of Toronto Press, 1999); and Brent Byron Watson, *Far Eastern Tour: The Canadian Infantry in Korea* (Montreal: McGill-Queen's University Press, 2002). Canada's role in Vietnam is discussed in Douglas Ross, *In the Interests of Peace: Canada and Vietnam, 1945–1973* (Toronto: University of Toronto Press, 1985); and Victor Levant, *Quiet Complicity: Canadian Involvement in the Vietnam War* (Toronto: Between the Lines, 1986). On the domestic Cold War, see Richard Cavell, ed., *Love, Hate, and Fear in Canada's Cold War* (Toronto: University of Toronto Press, 2004); Reginald Whitaker and Gary Marcuse, *Cold War Canada: The Making of a National Insecurity State, 1945–1957* (Toronto: University of Toronto Press, 1994); Steve Hewitt, *Spying 101: The RCMP's Secret Activities at Canadian Universities, 1917–1997* (Toronto: University of Toronto Press, 2002); Reginald Whitaker, *Double Standard: The Secret History of Canadian Immigration* (Toronto: Lester and Orpen Dennys, 1987); Len Scher, *The Un-Canadians: True Stories of the Blacklist Era* (Toronto: Lester, 1992); Roger Bowen, *Innocence Is Not Enough: The Life and Death of Herbert Norman* (Vancouver: Douglas and McIntyre, 1986); and Nicholas Fillmore, *Maritime Radical: The Life and Times of Roscoe Fillmore* (Toronto: Between the Lines, 1992). On Canadian financial aid to the Third World, see David R. Morrison, *Aid and Ebb Tide: A History of CIDA and Canadian Development Assistance* (Waterloo, ON: Wilfrid Laurier University Press, 1998). The changes in Canada's relations with Great Britain and the nations of the former British Empire in the post-war period are explored in the essays in Philip Buckner, ed., *Canada and the End of Empire* (Vancouver: UBC Press, 2004).

On the relationship between the Cold War and Canadian-American economic relations, see Melissa Clark Jones, *A Staple State: Canadian Industrial Resources in Cold War* (Toronto: University of Toronto Press, 1987); and J.L. Granatstein and Robert Cuff, *American Dollars and Canadian Prosperity* (Toronto: Samuel-Stevens, 1978). On Canadian-American economic relations from 1945 to 1975 more generally, useful sources include Dimitry Anastakis, *Auto Pact: Creating a Borderless North American Auto Industry, 1960–1971* (Toronto: University of Toronto Press, 2005); Steven High, *Industrial Sunset: The Making of North America's Rust Belt, 1969–1984* (Toronto: University of Toronto Press, 2003); Mel Watkins et al., *Foreign Ownership and the Structure of Canadian Industry: Report of the Task Force on the Structure of Canadian Industry* (Ottawa: Ministry of Supply and Services, 1968); Ian Wahn et al., *Eleventh Report of the Standing Committee on External Affairs and National Defence Respecting Canadian-American Relations* (Ottawa: Ministry of Supply and Services, 1970); Herb Gray et al., *Foreign Direct Investment in Canada* (Ottawa: Ministry of Supply and Services, 1972); Kari Levitt, *Silent Surrender: The Multinational Corporation in Canada* (Toronto: Gage, 1971); and H.G. Johnson, *The Canadian Quandary* (Ottawa: Carleton University Press, 1977). Walter Gordon, the politician most associated with Canadian economic nationalism of this period, is the subject of Denis Smith, *Gentle Patriot: A Political Biography of Walter Gordon* (Edmonton: Hurtig, 1973).

On American cultural impact on Canada, see George Grant, *Lament for a Nation* (Ottawa: Carleton University Press, 1983); Ian A. Angus, *A Border Within: National Identity, Cultural Plurality, and Wilderness* (Montreal: McGill-Queen's University Press, 1997); Mary Vipond, *The Mass Media in Canada* (Toronto: Lorimer, 1989); Paul Rutherford, *When Television Was Young: Primetime Canada, 1952–1967* (Toronto: University of Toronto Press, 1990); and Michael Dorland, *So Close to the States: The Emergence of Canadian Film Policy* (Toronto: University of Toronto Press, 1998). See also Gerald Friesen, *Citizens and Nation: An Essay on History, Communication and Canada* (Toronto: University of Toronto Press, 2000).

CHAPTER 17

Growth at All Costs: The Economy, 1945–1975

TIMELINE

▼ 1949 Asbestos strike; Newfoundland Loggers' Strike; St. Lawrence
▼ 1959 Seaway opens
▼ 1962 Canada launches Alouette 1
▼ 1963 Major powers sign nuclear test ban treaty
▼ 1972 United Nations Conference on the Human Environment
▼ 1973 OPEC oil embargo sparks an "energy crisis"

In 1964, Cominco began operating a lead-zinc mine in the Northwest Territories, creating an instant community that was named Pine Point. About $100 million of federal money was lavished on the project, which included not only developing a town, but also building new highways, hydro-electricity plants, and a railway to haul minerals to waiting markets. By 1975, about 1800 people, mostly white southerners, lived at Pine Point, about 500 of whom were employed by the mine. Their high wages and modern homes were evidence of the good lives that many Canadians were able to attain in the post-war period.

Forty miles west of this new town created by business and government was the long-established Native community of Fort Resolution. Its view of the economic benefits of the mine was rather different from Cominco's. Speaking to a federal inquiry established in 1974 to determine whether oil and gas pipelines should be built across the Mackenzie Valley, Mike Beaulieu of Fort Resolution indicated why many Native northerners resented the presence of development-minded resource companies in their midst:

> We, the Dene people, do a lot of hunting and trapping and fishing. Our hunting has decreased a lot due to the construction of the highway, the building of the mine, and the increase of the people from the South. . . . Our traditional grounds are slowly being overtaken by these [mine] employees. There is virtually no benefit to be spoken of from the mine.[1]

The impact of the Pine Point mine on the environment and on Native peoples provides an example of the other side of the equation of the unprecedented economic growth that characterized the period from 1945 to 1975. Dramatic improvements in overall living standards were accompanied by environmental degradation, uneven distribution of the new wealth, and destruction of many communities. This chapter traces the economic history of the period when the American dream of unlimited prosperity became a realistic goal for many Canadians, but an unattainable—even undesirable—illusion for others.

THE WELFARE AND WARFARE ECONOMY

At the end of the Second World War, the federal government rejected radical demands for public ownership and extensive state regulation of the economy. Led by the Department of Finance and the Bank of Canada, Ottawa proposed that another depression would be prevented if the government pursued a policy of expanding the money supply and incurring government deficits in times of unemployment.

Reconstruction Minister C.D. Howe's White Paper on post-war reconstruction, presented to parliament in April 1945, set the tone for the government's strategy: "The Government will be prepared in periods when unemployment threatens to incur the deficits and increases in the national debt resulting from its employment and income policy whether that policy in the circumstances is best applied through increased expenditures or reduced taxation."[2] The private sector would continue to operate companies, price goods, and make investment decisions.

Even this moderate Keynesianism shocked economic conservatives. Traditional economic theory held that large government deficits and accumulating debt would produce uncontrollable inflation because banks, having loaned most of their money to the state, would have little left over for private borrowers. In 1945, the federal debt alone was one-and-a-half times the nation's gross national product (GNP).

Despite skepticism on the part of Prime Minister William Lyon Mackenzie King, the government did not lose its nerve. Spending was increased rather than decreased, and the Bank of Canada expanded the money supply to finance much of the debt. The Canadian government moved quickly to rid the private sector of wartime price controls and to privatize most of the 28 public corporations that had been established to produce goods required for the war effort. Still, social policy commitments and, in the 1950s, military spending ensured growing state expenditures. Measured in

macroeconomic terms—that is, the performance of the economy as a whole, with special emphasis on growth in output and productivity—the government's new strategy worked well.

Immediately after the war, when production slowed, exports contracted, and inflation reared its ugly head, the federal government kept the economy moving with tax incentives to industry and programs targeted at veterans, the private-housing market, and municipalities. Soon, consumer demand, fuelled by a decade and a half of depression and denial—and a well-orchestrated advertising campaign honed on wartime propaganda techniques—picked up the slack. Industries geared for war hardly skipped a beat as plants were quickly converted from producing troop carriers, uniforms, bombs, and barracks to making cars, clothes, appliances, and housing materials. Emerging from the war with shiny new plants and equipment (some of them purchased at fire sale prices from the federal government), the Canadian business community continued its orgy of investment in capital stock until 1957.

Canadian officials might have been leery of wartime controls, but they were enthusiastic about the level of multilateral trade that had developed during the war. Since Canada's economic prosperity depended on a healthy export trade, trade liberalization became a cornerstone of Canadian post-war foreign policy. In November 1947, Canada signed the General Agreement on Tariffs and Trade (GATT), which bound its 23 signatories to consultation aimed at reducing trade barriers. Ironically, the intent of the agreement was immediately compromised in Canada by a series of restrictive trade measures announced by Finance Minister Douglas Abbott. Another exchange crisis precipitated by a binge of post-war spending on American products had forced the government to reimpose import controls. By 1949, controls were being lifted again, foreign investment resumed, and exports began to rise.

The cyclical upswing was reinforced by massive military spending, sparked by the escalating Cold War. Between 1949 and 1953, defence expenditures rose from 16 to 45 percent of the federal budget, and a new ministry was created to orchestrate the business of war. Howe became the minister of Defence Production, and in this guise continued to play godfather to the business community. With well over $1 billion spent annually on defence in the 1950s, every aspect of the Canadian economy was shaped by military considerations. As late as 1960, when defence had slipped back to a quarter of federal budgetary expenditures, military purchases accounted for 89 percent of the shipments in the aircraft industry, 41 percent in electronics, and 21 percent in shipbuilding.

Contrary to the philosophy espoused in Howe's White Paper in 1945, federal planners failed to tailor their policies to cyclical swings. Ottawa ran budget surpluses for most of the years between 1949 and 1956, but they were not sufficiently large to offset private investment or ambitious spending by provincial and municipal governments. In the heady atmosphere of post-war prosperity, politicians and the public came to believe that both welfare and warfare could be accommodated. Their treasuries fattened by higher personal and business taxes, governments at all levels spent money at an unprecedented rate, investing in infrastructure (roads and electrical power facilities) and building up social capital (schools and hospitals).

In cooperation with the provinces and private industry, the federal government became involved in several megaprojects, which also accelerated economic growth. The Trans-Canada Highway, the Trans-Canada Pipeline, and Beechwood Power absorbed huge amounts of labour and capital. So, too, did the St. Lawrence Seaway, a jointly-funded project with the United States, begun in 1954 and completed in 1959. Its purpose was to enlarge the canals and develop the power potential along the inland waterway. Nearly 3800 kilometres from Anticosti Island to Lake Superior, the seaway was an impressive engineering and construction feat that cost the Canadian government over $1 billion.

Owing to the booming economy, the unemployment rate for 1956 was only 3.2 percent, the lowest rate for the rest of the century. Wages increased faster than prices throughout the post-war decade while production increased by 5.3 percent a year and consumption by 5.1 percent. The government's debt as a proportion of GNP was cut in half from 1946 to 1956 because a wealthier population was paying enough taxes to cover both increased government spending and debt reduction. With unemployment low, the unemployment insurance fund bulged.

In 1957, the economic bubble burst. The American economy went into recession, and the Canadian economy, so closely integrated with that of its southern neighbour, followed suit. By 1958, the rate of unemployment was twice its 1956 level. The economy continued its sluggish performance for several years and then took off again in the early 1960s. It was not until the mid-1970s that Canadians again faced the prospect of hard economic times.

ECONOMIC GROWTH IN THE FABULOUS FIFTIES

Although the new economy was constrained by considerations of welfare and warfare, the direction of economic development in the 1950s bore a marked resemblance to the trends of the 1920s. Spectacular growth occurred in construction, consumer durable, staple, and service industries, while innovation and mass marketing sustained a high level of productivity.

Much of the productivity was stimulated by technological innovation leading to new product lines. Many new products, such as synthetic fibres, plastics, and pesticides, had been stimulated by wartime needs; others, including televisions, the self-propelled combine harvester, and the snowmobile, had been developed prior to the war but became commercially viable only in the improved post-war economic climate. In the iron and steel industry, the basic oxygen furnace, introduced in 1954, improved efficiency. Metropolitan Life installed elephantine computers in their offices in 1956, at the same time that the Department of National Revenue entered the electronic age. Developments in the chemical industry revolutionized agriculture and sparked massive forest-spraying programs. Homemakers even used DDT to rid their houses of annoying insects. The pharmaceutical industry could hardly keep up with the demand for new products, including such miracle drugs as penicillin, polio vaccines, and the birth-control pill.

Attempting to anticipate consumer demands and take advantage of government largesse, entrepreneurs darted from one opportunity to another, building up corporate empires at a dazzling rate, succeeding in one venture, failing in another, moving fast enough to avoid bankruptcy and public criticism. H.R. MacMillan graduated from his wartime duties to put together

The American Fast-Food Industry

The fast-food industry was one example of an American-dominated service industry that made its entry into Canada in the post-war period. Franchise operations, such as Colonel Sanders' Kentucky Fried Chicken, Burger King, and, after 1968, McDonald's, defined the eating-out experience for teenagers and two-income families seeking occasional relief from having to prepare a meal.

Sociologist Ester Reiter worked at a Toronto Burger King in the early 1980s and interviewed fellow employees as part of a thesis project. Each Burger King is operated by a franchisee, who pays Burger King's Miami headquarters a large fee for the right to operate a firm with the Burger King name, and every outlet is required by Miami to unswervingly follow the procedures laid out in the Manual of Operating Data. "Burger King University" in Miami trains managers to implement these procedures uniformly. Headquarters is linked by computer to each franchise and monitors performance daily. The result is that the "Burger King experience" is the same for workers and customers whether one is in New Orleans or Halifax. For employees, this means a rigid work schedule in which the time allowed to take an order, prepare a specific item, or deliver food to a customer is measured in seconds.

Reiter's fellow workers were teenagers, often working part-time, and immigrant women for whom better jobs were unavailable. Few liked the work, which paid minimum wage, and many felt like robots, waiting for their breaks in the "crew room" for a chance to listen to rock music and talk about plans for the weekend. On the job, "hamburgers are cooked as they pass through the broiler on a conveyor belt at a rate of 835 patties per hour. Furnished with a pair of tongs, the worker picks up the burgers as they drop off the conveyor belt, puts each on a toasted bun, and places the hamburgers and buns in a steamer. The jobs may be hot and boring, but they can be learned in a manner of minutes."[3]

TABLE 17.1 Canada's Economic Growth, 1945–1976

Year	GNP*	GNP in 1971 dollars*	GNP per capita in 1971 dollars*
1945	11 863	29 071	2 400.81
1951	21 640	35 450	2 530.52
1956	32 058	47 599	2 959.95
1961	39 646	54 741	3 001.48
1966	61 828	74 844	3 739.40
1971	94 450	94 450	4 379.17
1976	191 031	119 249	5 195.02

*millions of dollars

Source: F.H. Leacy, ed., *Historical Statistics of Canada,* 2nd ed. (Ottawa: Statistics Canada, 1983), tables A1, F 13, F 15.

MacMillan Bloedel in 1953, one of the largest forestry companies in the world, with integrated timber reserves, sawmills, and shipping operations. E.P. Taylor, another of Howe's wartime recruits, engineered his investment firm, Argus Corporation, into one of North America's major conglomerates, with controlling interest in everything from Canadian Breweries and Orange Crush to Massey-Ferguson and Domtar. The Bronfmans used their commanding position in the distilling industry to create their own investment companies. In New Brunswick, K.C. Irving constructed an empire based on oil, timber, and communications that would make him one of the richest men in the world.

FARMING AND FISHING

In the post-war period, "planning" was the watchword among farmers everywhere. Marketing boards revolutionized agricultural output in Canada by establishing quotas, setting prices, and defining market boundaries. A larger percentage of farm products was destined for canning and, increasingly, freezing. Such novelties as the potato chip and the TV dinner gobbled up the output of Canadian farms. Farms became larger and could increasingly be viewed as full-fledged business enterprises, part of a delicately balanced network of production, processing, and marketing required to feed an increasingly urbanized North American society. Giant American corporations such as Hostess Foods,

Stokely Van Camp, Swift's, and Swanson's competed with domestically based processors such as McCain Foods, Aylmer, E.D. Smith, and Schneider's for the produce of Canadian farms. Increasingly, corporations established vertically integrated operations by growing the crops required for their processing plants.

The crops in demand in the marketplace were changing. During the war, federal subsidies encouraged Prairie farmers to diversify their output. Oats, barley, and flax soon became as important as wheat to western producers. Although the volume of post-war wheat sales was maintained through special agreements with Great Britain, the price of wheat remained low on international markets throughout the 1950s, discouraging further expansion of the wheat economy. A similar transformation occurred in the Annapolis Valley, where farmers were paid to uproot their apple orchards and concentrate on other fruits, vegetables, poultry, and dairy products for a domestic rather than a British market.

The transformation of the East Coast fishing industry in the post-war decade paralleled that of agriculture. As European markets for saltfish disappeared, sales of fresh and frozen fish were increasingly geared to an oversupplied North American market. At the same time, technology revolutionized productivity in the fisheries. The stern trawler, introduced on the Grand Banks in the 1950s, could harvest 180 000 kilograms of fish in a two-week period. In 1953, Great Britain built the *Fairtry*, a factory freezer trawler with unsurpassed fishing power. Within a decade, there were 1400 trawlers of various shapes and sizes engaged in the Banks fishery, netting an unprecedented 2.6 million metric tonnes of fish.

The federal government seemed helpless to stop the uncoordinated exploitation of the Banks fishery, which was still defined as an international resource. In 1949, the International Commission for the Northwest Atlantic Fisheries was created, but it had no authority to bind its membership to comply with conservation measures. Nor was the law of the sea, formulated more than 300 years earlier, of much value in regulating the new uses of the ocean. Interest in resources in and under the ocean finally led the United Nations to institute the Law of the Sea Conference. At conference meetings in 1958 and 1960, Canadian officials demanded that nations be given the right to control ocean activities within 12 miles of their shores. In 1964, Canadians made a unilateral declaration of a nine-mile limit, which was soon extended to 12 miles. A 200-mile limit was established by the third Law of the Sea Conference in 1977, opening a new resource frontier of great potential—if it were managed well.

RESOURCE INDUSTRIES

Impressive growth also occurred in mining and hydro-electric power generation, benefiting from North American military requirements and the demands of the booming North American economies. Private companies developed copper deposits at Murdochville on the Gaspé Peninsula, lead-zinc-copper ores in the Dalhousie-Bathurst region of New Brunswick, and potash in Saskatchewan. In 1949, a consortium of six American steel companies and two Canadian resource groups formed the Iron Ore Company to bring the vast deposits on the Ungava-Labrador border into production. The company built a 570-kilometre railway in Quebec from Sept-Îles to the new resource town of Schefferville and was enthusiastic about improvements to the St. Lawrence–Great Lakes transportation system so that ores could easily be moved to mills in the industrial heartland of North America.

Canada's energy resources seemed to know no bounds in the post-war period. On 3 February 1947, Imperial Oil's Leduc No. 1 well, near Edmonton, struck oil, and energy discoveries in Alberta soon became regular fare. From 1945 to 1960, Alberta's annual production of crude petroleum increased by a factor of 16 while natural gas production increased tenfold. Saskatchewan also made promising finds of energy resources during this period. In the early 1950s, four corporate giants—Imperial, Shell, Texaco, and British American—dominated the Canadian oil and gas industry. Gulf Oil entered the picture when it bought out British American in 1956. The last integrated Canadian-owned oil company, Canadian Oil, which operated the White Rose chain of service stations, was taken over by Shell in 1952. Canadians remained active on the production side of the industry through such companies as Pacific Petroleums, Home Oil, Husky, and Hudson's Bay. With world oil and gas prices remaining low—less than $2 a barrel in the mid-1960s—the big problem for Canadian producers was finding a market for their abundant product.

By 1952, pipelines in which Imperial Oil was a major shareholder funneled oil from Alberta either to Vancouver or through Wisconsin to Sarnia, Ontario. Canadian-owned Westcoast Transmission Company's 1000-kilometre pipeline to Vancouver was completed in 1951. In 1956, the Canadian government entered an agreement with an American company, TransCanada PipeLines, to build a gas pipeline from Alberta to Montreal. In addition to a generous loan to the company, Ottawa agreed to create a Crown corporation to build the uneconomical section of the pipeline through northern Ontario. Predictably, it was Howe, as minister of Trade and Commerce, who backed the ambitious project and demonstrated his government's arrogance by having closure imposed on the vigorous parliamentary debate incited by the project. Although ownership of TransCanada gradually fell into Canadian hands, an American consortium including TransCanada eventually built a larger line south of the Great Lakes. The United States absorbed about half of the Canadian output of oil and gas, but cheap imports of crude oil from the Middle East kept the industry lean until the early 1970s.

Oil well at Leduc, Alberta, 1947.
Imperial Oil Archives

Ontario, with its state-owned hydro plants, seaway, and nuclear power stations, and Alberta, with its burgeoning energy industry, set a high standard for other provinces to follow. Yet follow they did. Newfoundland Premier Joey Smallwood convinced British and European capitalists to develop the mighty Churchill Falls in Labrador, while New Brunswick Premier Hugh John Flemming wrung $30 million out of the federal government to help him complete his Beechwood Power complex on the St. John River. Nova Scotia put its energies into developing coal-generated thermal power plants. In the early 1950s, Alcan built a huge generating station at Kemano, British Columbia, to supply its $450-million aluminum smelter at Kitimat. Social Credit Premier

W.A.C. Bennett was determined to make his province rich by developing the potential of the Rocky Mountain Trench and the Columbia River. Saskatchewan's socialist premier, Tommy Douglas, with generous subsidies from Ottawa, planned an ambitious power-generating project on the South Saskatchewan River.

THE POST-INDUSTRIAL ECONOMY

The increasing importance of communications in determining the pace of economic change in the second half of the twentieth century led analysts to coin the terms "information age" and "post-industrial age" to describe the phenomenon. While manufacturing and service industries remained significant players in the economy, communications technology, represented by computers and satellites, contributed to quantum leaps in productivity and subjected people to revolutionary changes. As new commodities, new production techniques, and new social values burst on the scene, products and

Founder of the Centre for Culture and Technology at the University of Toronto, Marshall McLuhan contended that communications technologies defined the shape and scope of institutions and values—in McLuhan's words, "the medium is the message."
© Bettmann/Corbis

in the early 1970s, permitting vast quantities of information to be sent over telecommunications networks. Marshall McLuhan's much-talked-about "global village" had become a reality, or so it seemed.

Canadians were among the first people in the world to experiment with the communication technologies that defined the information age. In 1958, Canada's television network, stretching from Victoria to Sydney, was the longest in the world. Canada also established cable-television systems more quickly than other nations. When the satellite Alouette 1 was launched on 29 September 1962, Canada became the third nation in space after the Soviet Union and the United States. With its Anik (the Inuit word for "brother") series launched in the 1970s, Canada led the world in the use of satellites for commercial communications, and was later the first nation to establish a digital data network for computer users.

COMPUTERS

Virtually every human activity has been altered in some way by computer technology. Computer technology has helped send people to the moon, revolutionized the office, and automated manufacturing processes. It also has changed the way people communicate with each other.

Canada's first entry into the computer age was UTEC, developed by scientists at the University of Toronto between 1947 and 1951. A massive structure that filled a whole room, UTEC was powered by electric tubes, overheated quickly, and experienced more downtime than computing time.

Had innovation stopped with the first generation of computers, the computer revolution would have been stillborn, but the invention of the transistor in 1949 transformed the whole field of electronics. Computers became smaller, more reliable, and less expensive to build and operate. Integrated circuitry, developed in 1958, led to further miniaturization. By

approaches considered crucial to the industrial age were regularly threatened with obsolescence. Constant adaptation became necessary for economic survival.

Since information was the key to diffusing and controlling technological innovation, communications technology—itself subject to breathtaking innovation—determined the pace and direction of the post-industrial economy. With the development of satellite and space communications in the late 1950s and 1960s, signals could be transmitted around the world in a split second. Computers were linked to telecommunications systems

1968, a single silicon chip could hold 256 bits of random access memory (RAM), more than the first generation of computers could cram into a large room. Within another decade, Apple, a microcomputer company based in California, was selling desktop computers to the technology-fixated consumer.

The vast quantities of capital invested in computer technology by the United States and Japan made it difficult for Canada to compete successfully in the latest race for economic supremacy. Eventually, however, Northern Telecom established a niche by producing telephone equipment and switching devices for the global telecommunications market.

While their labour force participation continued to expand, women, such as these typists at the Dominion Bureau of Statistics, worked in traditional, poorly paid occupations.
C. Lund/Library and Archives Canada/PA133212

THE SERVICE ECONOMY

In the post-industrial age, seven out of 10 Canadians in the labour force were employed in providing services rather than producing goods. Sectors such as transportation, communications, retail and wholesale trade, finance, real estate, education, health and welfare, recreation, personal services, food, and accommodation created new jobs that replaced employment in the goods-producing primary and secondary sectors of the economy.

One of the most obvious features of Canada's service economy was the growth of government spending. The expansion of government services meant a plethora of new jobs. Government spending, which had accounted for only 5 percent of the GNP in 1867, had risen to 30 percent by 1960 and increased still further as the major social programs of the 1960s were introduced. By 1985, it had reached an astounding 48.2 percent of the GNP. Nearly half of government expenditure was on goods and services; the rest involved transfer payments, which moved private income from one group of citizens to another. The federal share of the GNP rose only marginally after 1960, but the provinces' share doubled as their responsibilities rapidly grew.

The trend toward urban concentration, typical of the industrial age, was consolidated by the service economy. While goods-producing industries were often located near resources, most tertiary industries required a large pool of nearby clients for their services. Nevertheless, the trend to urbanization began to slow in the 1970s as people moved away from congested city cores and monotonous suburbs to rural "exurbia." Commuting to work in the cities from exurban homes became a way of life for an increasing number of Canadians. To improve their tax bases, many city councils expanded their boundaries into exurbia, becoming vast, sprawling administrative units. Metropolitan growth increased the size and power of Canada's major cities, making Canada little more than a cluster of city states and their economic hinterlands. In 1971, three out of four Canadians were classified as urban dwellers.

The growth of the service sector was one of the major factors contributing to the influx of women into the paid labour force. Prior to the Industrial Revolution, women performed many of the services essential to survival. As services moved from the domestic economy into the market economy, women often moved with them. Domestic work as a paid occupation declined under the impact of household appliances in the twentieth century, but teaching, nursing, secretarial, clerical, and cleaning jobs expanded dramatically and remained dominated by women. Overall, women's labour force participation in Canada increased from 23.4 percent in 1953 to 48.9 percent in 1979, while the male participation rate fell from 82.9 percent to 78.4 percent during the same period. Despite their increasing participation in the labour force, women with full-time jobs in 1971 made on average less than 60 percent of what men with full-time jobs earned. Women were also far more likely than men to be employed in part-time work.

END OF THE ECONOMIC MIRACLE

Spurred by government spending and technological innovation, the Canadian economy continued its spectacular rate of economic growth until the mid-1970s. Labour productivity had tripled since the end of the war, due largely to technological and administrative changes, and workers received some benefits from their increased output. While the cost of living had also tripled, wages and salaries had increased sixfold. Higher taxation ate up much of the increased income, but, because of new social programs, Canadians in 1975 had far less need than earlier generations to set aside money for health purposes and old age.

Despite the impressive growth, there were dark clouds on the horizon. The American government had been unwilling to raise taxes to offset expenses associated with the Vietnam War. Allowing the economy to overheat, it then made a fruitless attempt to reduce inflation by cutting spending and tightening credit. American unemployment increased, and the government responded with trade restrictions, which had repercussions for Canadian trade and therefore Canadian rates of employment and inflation.

As the debate raged over how Canada should respond to the twin evils of unemployment and inflation, the Organization of the Petroleum Exporting Countries (OPEC) oil-price shocks late in 1973 seemed to knock the stuffing out of western economies, which had relied throughout the post-war boom on cheap energy. In 1974, though unemployment was a manageable 5.3 percent, inflation stood at 14.5 percent. One year later, inflation was down to 9.9 percent, but unemployment had reached a post-war high of 6.9 percent. The combination of high unemployment and high inflation, unseen in the post-war period, was labelled "stagflation," a short form for stagnation plus inflation.

THE DEBATE OVER CONTROLS

A political debate ensued about how to combat this unsettling economic phenomenon. In the August 1974 federal election, Conservative leader Robert Stanfield called for wage and price controls. Prime Minister Pierre Trudeau won re-election after vigorously opposing such massive state intervention in the economy. In October 1975, Trudeau reversed his stance, announcing a three-year program of controls. Trudeau's economic policies to deal with stagflation proved contradictory. Government spending increased substantially in accordance with Keynesian prescriptions for a stagnating economy but, beginning in 1975, the money supply was severely restricted. Tight money policies were also implemented by the United States and most governments in Europe in an effort to control inflation.

If the three decades that followed the war had been characterized by a focus on maintaining high levels of employment and providing easy credit, the years that followed would be notable for the state's focus on price stability and decreasing interest in unemployment. The shift occurred in large part because the business community, concerned about profit margins, began to abandon the post-war consensus on economic policy. Owners and managers of major firms complained that unions, emboldened by low rates of unemployment and generous unemployment insurance benefits, were forcing employers to pay wage increases that hurt profits.

Recognizing that corporate complaints were rejected by the public as self-interested propaganda, Canada's largest firms sponsored a number of economic research institutes to promote their perspective. The Fraser Institute in British Columbia and the C.D. Howe Institute in Ontario, among others, presented a pro-employer line as the product of supposedly disinterested research. The media uncritically reported their claims that tight money policies were necessary to slow the Canadian economy in the short run to stop inflation and create long-term stability. In these reports, it was rarely stated that such policies would create a higher rate of unemployment.

THE COSTS OF GROWTH

Following the Second World War, government policy and economic activity was focused on bringing every Canadian into the modern age. Farming communities lost population at an alarming rate as the agriculture industry was restructured. (See Figure 17.1.) While the new corporate giants in the food industry prospered from the restructuring, farmers often did not. In Saskatchewan, the farm population fell from 514 677 to 233 792 between 1941 and 1971. Those who remained had larger farms that were more diversified, but federal farm subsidies and income from off-farm jobs provided the greater part of their livelihoods. Except in British Columbia, where the number of fruit and vegetable growers fell relatively modestly, similar patterns prevailed across the country. Prince Edward Island witnessed the most change as costs of production for its major farm products, particularly potatoes, increased well out of proportion to rising prices to consumers: between 1951 and 1981 the size of farms increased while the number of farms dropped from 10 137 to 3154. In 1981, only 10 percent of Islanders were engaged in farming, down from nearly 50 percent 30 years earlier. Overall, the nation lost a third of its farming population between 1951 and 1961 and then lost a third again by the 1971 census. More than one Canadian in four lived on a farm at the end of the Second World War. Thirty years later, fewer than one in 15 farmed.

The story was the same in the fisheries. The magnificent trawlers that came to dominate the ocean fishery sealed the fate of inshore fishers. By the 1950s, the real choice for most inshore fishers was between becoming a labourer on a corporate trawler or changing occupations. Not surprisingly, the number of Canadians in the Atlantic fishery declined by nearly 40 percent between 1951 and 1961.

As the fisheries developed into a modern industry, cooperative fishing organizations founded prior to the war lost control of processing and marketing structures. During the 1950s and 1960s, large domestic and foreign corporations emerged as integrated trawling and processing firms selling mainly through Boston, New York, and Chicago. The East Coast fishery, like its West Coast counterpart, became part of the continental corporate universe. Most fishers earned a wage

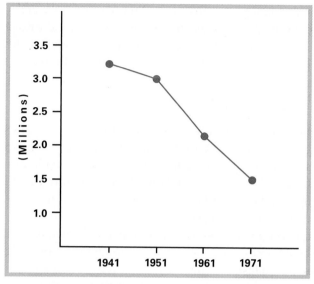

FIGURE 17.1 Farm Populations in Canada, 1941–1971 (in millions)

Source: F.H. Leacy, ed., *Historical Statistics of Canada*, 2nd ed. (Ottawa: Statistics Canada, 1983), Series M1-11.

rather than pursuing self-employment. In 1956, the remaining poverty-prone self-employed fishers became eligible for unemployment insurance.

Most Canadians moved voluntarily from their rural communities to urban centres, where they had better access to jobs and services, but there were exceptions. In Newfoundland and Labrador, families in outport communities had to be enticed by government grants to move to anticipated "growth centres." Inuit in the Arctic were also often reluctant to relocate from their traditional communities to "northern suburbs,"[4] where they were expected to live under government surveillance. In both cases, the moves failed to live up to their promise. The housing and sanitary conditions in communities created by the state for the Inuit were appalling. Even had they been better, the fact remained that people had been uprooted to live in communities where it was difficult to make a living. Similarly, outport Newfoundlanders found few jobs in the communities to which they had been encouraged to relocate.

The transformation from subsistence to consumer society was evident in every corner of the nation. In the North, the Inuit were incorporated into the North American economy through their painting and sculpture, which had become popular in the art market in southern climes. With factories turning out textiles and clothing at unprecedented rates, women throughout Canada no longer engaged in domestic production. A vacationing antique dealer in the late 1950s bought 1200 spinning wheels in rural areas of Cape Breton.

WORKING CONDITIONS

Industrial workers benefited more from the economic growth of the post-1945 period than farmers, fishers, and hunters. In some industries, working conditions improved noticeably. Ontario's lumber industry, finding it difficult to retain workers in an economy with low unemployment, replaced logging camps—once notorious for their crowded, cold, and poorly maintained bunkhouses—with suburb-like accommodations. In other industries, however, employers reckoned that highly paid workers would put up with unsafe or unhealthy conditions. In the mining industry, for example,

Workers in a fluorspar mine, St. Lawrence, Newfoundland.
Library and Archives Canada/PA130784

innovations such as scooptrams meant back injuries and respiratory problems for nickel miners. The remote-controlled vehicles could have been enclosed to prevent their operators from bouncing about and inhaling diesel fumes, but the mining companies resisted the expense that this would have entailed.

The United Steelworkers vividly described the work environment of the mines before an Ontario government commission on the mining industry in 1978. After noting the large numbers of accidents and deaths in mines, the Steelworkers pointed to such hazards as

immense pressures from underground rock that is frequently described as "solid" but which in fact is constantly in varying states of flux and change; total absence of natural light; working with heavy equipment which for the most part is designed for maximum efficiency, and not for the protection of workers using it; the use of high explosives, high noise levels, air concussions, etc. . . . hygiene, sanitary and health dangers arising from dusts, gases, fog, oils, deep holes, falling rocks (loose), runs of muck (broken ores), slippery and unsure footing, and in some instances (as in Elliot Lake) ionizing radiation.[5]

Machines that improved productivity posed problems not only for worker safety but also for the preservation of jobs. During the post-war boom, the proliferation of technology created more jobs than it made redundant, but by the 1970s, the net impact of technology on employment prospects appeared to be negative. Microprocessors, first introduced in 1971, displaced blue-collar workers by controlling systems that automatically cut boards, stitched seams, and assembled parts. White-collar jobs, particularly those dominated by women, were even more in jeopardy as file clerks, keypunch operators, and other low-paid workers found their jobs automated. "The chip" devalued the work of many women. As Heather Menzies argues, "Cashiers are deskilled by the transfer of price information and change calculation into the memory and processing components of the cash register. Like the weaver in the industrial factory, the cashier valued for good price memory and arithmetic efficiency is no longer needed; the cashier becomes a highly replaceable unskilled worker."[6]

Many workers who lost their jobs proved ill-equipped to take up the other jobs that were available, thus becoming victims of "structural unemployment." Most unemployed coal miners, for example, lacked the skills to be computer programmers, nor could farmers be readily transferred to jobs in health care industries. Although training programs were implemented to address the problem of structural unemployment, they failed to produce the skilled labour force required in Canada's post-industrial economy. Indeed, many of Canada's most highly trained workers were immigrants. After 1967, Canada's immigration laws substituted education and occupation biases for ethnic ones in an effort to attract skilled workers to the jobs expanding in the information age.

GROWTH AND THE ENVIRONMENT

Of all the costs of economic growth, its impact on the biosphere that supports life is no doubt of greatest importance in the long term. Considerations of the impact of uncontrolled economic development on the environment were far from uppermost in the minds of most Canadians in the period of post-war prosperity. While the development of the bomb caused many people to question the notions of science as neutral and scientists as servants of historical change, it did not translate into a general skepticism about scientific and industrial progress. The long-term consequences of industrial pollutants received little attention, even though polluted air, undrinkable water, and scorched landscapes had been associated with factory production since the early days of the Industrial Revolution.

The age of innocence came to an abrupt end in 1962 when American scientist Rachel Carson published *Silent Spring*. In her highly publicized book, Carson provided stunning revelations about the dangers posed by the "tide of chemicals born of the Industrial Age." Rivers and oceans, the air and soil, and animal and human species, she argued, were being rapidly destroyed. Lest Canadians should consider their pristine environment immune from such dangers, she singled out the "Rivers of Death" created in New Brunswick and other forested areas of Canada where aerial pesticide-spraying programs begun in the 1950s

were more effective in killing fish than their intended target, the spruce budworm. "We stand now where two roads diverge," Carson concluded. "The road we have long been travelling is deceptively easy, a smooth superhighway on which we progress with great speed, but at its end lies disaster. The other fork of the road offers our last, our only chance to reach a destination that assures the preservation of our earth."[7]

As the environmental movement gained momentum, public and private institutions began to alter their behaviour. The Soviet Union, Great Britain, and the United States signed a treaty to ban atmospheric testing of nuclear weapons in 1963, and industries built higher smokestacks to diffuse their polluting emissions. Consumers contributed to the environmental cause by avoiding the use of chemical-laden detergents, foods laced with pesticides, and leaded gasoline. Despite such well-meaning efforts, the environmental problem would not go away. Scientists discovered that polychlorinated biphenyls (PCBs), a family of highly toxic chemicals used in electrical equipment, continued to poison the food chain after their use had been discontinued. No one knew how to dispose of the hazardous waste from nuclear power plants. Even the emissions released into the atmosphere by tall smokestacks came back to earth hundreds of kilometres away as acid rain and snow, which ravaged lakes and forests.

The United Nations Conference on the Human Environment met in Stockholm in 1972 to discuss the decaying state of the planet. Chaired by a Canadian, Maurice Strong, the conference produced a declaration of environmental rights and established a program to fund and coordinate investigations into environmental problems. In the same year, the study *Limits to Growth* reported the findings of scientists who used sophisticated computer modelling techniques to investigate the "predicament of mankind." They maintained that accelerated industrialization, rapid population growth, increased agricultural consumption, depletion of renewable resources, and environmental deterioration threatened the very future of civilization. If the planet were to continue to support life, the report concluded, a "sustainable state of global equilibrium" must become an urgent priority. Canadian scientist David Suzuki helped focus public attention on environmental issues through his CBC television series *The Nature of Things*.

Suzuki worked and lived in British Columbia, a province that epitomized the triumph of economic growth over environmental concerns. Social Credit, which governed British Columbia from 1952 to 1972 and again from 1975 to 1991, did little to stop the environmental degradation wrought by resource companies. Preferring short-term prosperity, they seemed indifferent to lax reforestation policies and agricultural land lost to industrial development and urban sprawl. As late as the 1980s, only a third of logged land in British Columbia was being reforested. Studies of pulp mills in the province decried a record of poor control over effluents, which seeped into rivers and lakes. Waste coal from strip-mining operations in the East Kootenays fouled the Elk River Valley's creek system, and the stench in cities such as Prince George challenged company claims that they used the best pollution-dissipating equipment.

Perhaps the group of Canadians that suffered most from the "growth at all costs" philosophy were Aboriginal peoples. Although they fought in the courts to stop megaprojects that would harm the ecology of their traditional hunting and fishing territories, their concerns were largely brushed aside by the larger society. Hydro-electric projects, mines, pulp and paper mills, and new transportation systems displaced Native peoples or jeopardized their traditional ways of life. In the 1950s, Native settlements along the St. Lawrence were flooded when the seaway was built. Effluent from the Reed paper mill made it unsafe for Natives in the area to fish in the English-Wabigoon River system near Kenora. Not only was their major food supply affected, but the tourism that depended on good local fishing and had made the reserves outside Kenora relatively prosperous dried up. Moreover, mill operators rarely hired Native labour. Thus, for Native peoples in the area, chronic unemployment accompanied environmental degradation.

By the late 1960s, the public was increasingly concerned about protecting the environment, but governmental policy was slow in coming. Economic growth had been the liberal answer to the socialist call for a

MORE TO THE STORY

The Working Poor

The prosperity of the average Canadian in the early 1970s often hid from view the lives of millions who were just scraping by. Despite the common view that poverty was generally limited to people on social assistance, most poor households included one or more individuals who held a job.

Journalist Sheila Arnopolous provided a glimpse into the lives of some of these people in a series of articles in the *Montreal Star* in 1974. Her focus was on immigrants from the Caribbean, Latin America, India, Pakistan, Greece, Portugal, and Italy who worked in Montreal. Some were illegal immigrants—it was estimated in the late 1970s that 100 000 illegal immigrants worked in Canada, generally in sweatshops in Montreal and Toronto. Intimidated by the threat of discovery and deportation, they often had to accept work at less than the legislated minimum wage.

While legal immigrants did not share the fear of deportation, they often spoke little English or French and were desperate for work, so they rarely demanded that authorities enforce minimum wage laws. Many such workers laboured under conditions reminiscent of the nineteenth century, with subsistence pay and workdays of 12 hours. Noted Arnopolous, "They man the clanging textile and clothing factories which line St. Lawrence and Park. They clean toilets in glittering highrises, wash dishes in grimy restaurant kitchens, pull switches and operate machinery in fuming plastics and chemical factories, abattoirs, machine shops."[8]

Far from urban industrial sites, farmworkers also often laboured under conditions and rates of pay that few Canadians were aware existed in their prosperous society. Excluded from minimum-wage protection, immigrant orchard workers in British Columbia and Ontario and Native sugar-beet pickers in Manitoba worked long hours for negligible pay and slept in miserable accommodations provided by their employers. Many farmworkers were illegal immigrants; still others were contract workers for the growing season and were required to return home to Latin America or the Caribbean once the harvest was over. Canada apparently wanted their labour power, but did not want them as citizens.

more egalitarian distribution of wealth. If the pie kept getting bigger, even if there were no change in its distribution, the poor would be relatively better off and therefore unlikely to demand radical changes in the economic structure. How could the standard of living of the lowest people on the economic scale be improved if the economy remained static?

ECONOMIC DISPARITY

Notwithstanding the egalitarian rhetoric underlying the nation's democratic institutions, post-war Canada remained a highly stratified society. Economic cycles might come and go, but the structure of inequality remained hauntingly familiar. In post-industrial Canada, age, class, ethnicity, gender, and geography remained important factors in determining how one fared in the quest for economic well-being, but this reality was rarely acknowledged.

In 1965, John Porter published *The Vertical Mosaic*, an impressive analysis of stratification in Canadian society. He showed that ethnicity and class in Canada were closely interrelated and that an economic elite of fewer than 1000 men—most of them of British background, Protestant in their religious affiliation, and graduates of private schools such as Upper Canada College—dominated the Canadian economy. Even in Quebec, where over three-quarters of the population was French in origin, Anglophone elites controlled the economic structures.

Studies conducted for the Royal Commission on Bilingualism and Biculturalism confirmed Porter's

Native dwellings contrast sharply with houses in Fort George, Quebec, 1973.
John Flanders/Library and Archives Canada/PA130854

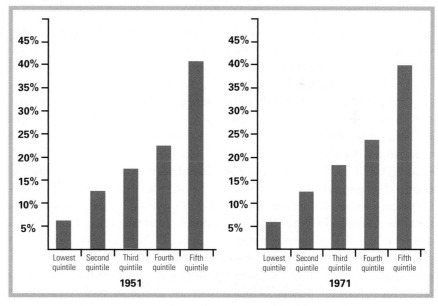

FIGURE 17.2 Percentage Distribution of Income of Families and Unattached Individuals, by Quintile, 1951 and 1971

Source: *The Canadian Encyclopedia*, 2nd ed., vol. 2 (Edmonton: Hurtig, 1988), 1051.

findings in Quebec, revealing an ethnic hierarchy that included Francophones among the poorest of Quebecers. Only Italians and Native peoples in Quebec had a lower per capita income than French Canadians in 1961. The Quiet Revolution did much to improve the status of Francophones both in Quebec and elsewhere in the country. In contrast, visible minorities, especially First Nations, Métis, Inuit, and African Canadians, remained at the bottom of the economic scale throughout the nation.

Women also figured prominently in the ranks of Canada's economically disadvantaged. Until the 1960s, it was perfectly legal to state a preference for either men or women in job advertisements. "Help Wanted, Male" and "Help Wanted, Female" did much to stream men and women into different occupations. Commonly, "women's jobs"—secretaries, sales clerks, food servers, child-care workers—were those with the lowest pay. Professional and technical occupations followed a similar pattern. Women dominated the relatively poorly paid occupations of dental assistant, occupational therapist, and librarian. By contrast, in 1971, less than 5 percent of dentists and lawyers and just over 10 percent of physicians were women. Even within the same occupation, women were paid less than men. In 1970, female janitors earned just 58.5 percent of the wages of male janitors; female secretaries earned 57.4 percent of the income of their male counterparts; and women who operated sewing machines could expect to make 63.6 percent of the wages of a male operator.

Despite growth and change in the Canadian economy since the Second World War, the overall distribution of income remained remarkably static, as Figure 17.2 indicates. Obviously, the welfare state did little to redistribute wealth. The Economic Council of Canada, an advisory group to the government on economic planning, calculated in 1961 that 27 percent of Canadians received incomes low enough to qualify them as poor. Eight years later, the federal government, using the same measures, announced that poverty had been cut in half. Academic studies suggested that the growth of the economy accounted directly for half of the decline, while an increase in the number of two-income families, indirectly also related to economic growth, accounted for much of the rest.

POVERTY AND THE REGIONS

Whether the national economy was booming or in recession, certain provinces and regions of provinces lagged well behind the national average. Southern Ontario generally prospered far more than the rest of the country, while northern Ontario suffered high rates of unemployment and poverty. Even within southern Ontario, there were large pockets of poverty in the southeast. Montreal had a vibrant mixed economy, but northern Quebec and the Gaspé experienced grinding poverty even during economic upswings. In wealthy Alberta and British Columbia, northern residents, especially Native peoples, had little to show for the resource boom that created high average incomes in their provinces.

The Atlantic region, Saskatchewan, and Manitoba constituted the country's have-not provinces. Dependent on equalization grants to provide reasonable levels of service to their citizens, they remained unable to provide the economic diversification that would create more jobs. The bias of federal fiscal and monetary policies toward the more populous and wealthy regions compounded the problem. How, for instance, could the bank rate be set to meet the needs of the lagging Atlantic region when the central Canadian economy was facing inflationary pressure?

TAXATION AND THE DISTRIBUTION OF WEALTH

If the distribution of wealth remained largely unchanged despite extensive welfare measures introduced in the post-war period, an assessment of the taxation system helps to explain why. Before the war, most working Canadians earned less than the minimum income required before personal income tax had to be paid. After the war, most workers became income taxpayers. Corporate taxes, once presented as a temporary wartime measure, were given permanent status in 1949. But taxes on profits were alleviated by generous capital cost (depreciation) allowances and, for many firms, by a variety of loopholes. Dividend holders received a 10 percent tax credit in recognition of dividends foregone because of corporate tax assessments, and in 1953 that credit was doubled.

The Diefenbaker government, criticized for overtaxation by ordinary Canadians and the business community, established the Royal Commission on Taxation in 1962. John Diefenbaker chose Kenneth Carter—former president of the widely respected tax-study organization, the Canadian Tax Foundation—to head the commission. Carter was a senior partner in one of Canada's leading firms of chartered accountants, a firm that had dealings with many of the country's largest companies. Yet his commission's report would bring little comfort to the corporate elite. Concluded the commissioners: "The present system does not afford fair treatment for all Canadians. People in essentially similar circumstances do not bear the same taxes. People in essentially different circumstances do not bear appropriately different tax burdens."[9]

Commission studies of the incidence of all forms of taxation revealed that the poorest Canadians paid proportionately more taxes than well-off citizens. Carter recommended that indirect taxation be substantially reduced and the base for personal and corporate income tax broadened by the removal of most loopholes. The poor would be compensated through the tax system by the institution of a "negative income tax"—that is, a payment from the government to individuals whose incomes were too low to support a decent standard of living.

The Carter recommendations, released in 1966, took the Pearson government by surprise. Faced with a barrage of lobbying by industry, the government proved unwilling to take major steps in the taxation arena. In the early 1970s, the Trudeau government made a half-hearted attempt at tax reform, taxing most capital gains at half the rate of other income and increasing income exemptions to remove the poorest citizens from the tax rolls. But negative income taxes were rejected and most of the exemptions of rich individuals and corporations remained on the books. Indeed, the federal government abandoned estate taxes in 1972, with provincial governments quickly following suit.

Meanwhile, provincial governments, desperate for new sources of revenue and unwilling to increase corporate taxes for fear that business would move away, began to introduce sales taxes, despite Carter's evidence of their disproportionate impact on the poor. The limited impact of Carter's recommendations demonstrated the overwhelming influence of the corporate elite in Canadian political and economic decision-making.

THE TRADE UNION MOVEMENT

The trade union movement was partially incorporated into the liberal consensus in the post-war period. Although legislation recognized the right of workers to organize, the Industrial Relations and Disputes Investigation Act of 1948, which applied to federal workers and their provincial equivalents, also attempted to co-opt union leaders into the planning mechanisms of corporations and governments.

Under the new labour laws, workers found their rights to negotiate limited to wages and narrowly defined working conditions. Unions were expected to enforce contracts and keep their members in line. Decisions to reduce the size of a workforce, speed up production, or use hazardous materials in the workplace were generally not covered by contracts, and union leaders were obliged to inform their members that strikes or slowdowns meant to force management to reconsider these issues would not be tolerated. Even when management appeared to violate a contract, workers were not allowed to strike. Instead they had to use often drawn-out grievance procedures to seek redress. Employers generally found that "management's right to manage" had been preserved.

When better wages and working conditions could not be won at the bargaining table, unionists could use the weapon of the strike. Wartime wage freezes created pent-up demands for increases at war's end. Many working-class families had fared well in wartime because of overtime pay and two salaries. A resurgence of patriarchal arguments that women should return to their homes so that men could find jobs, aided by discriminatory hiring and firing policies, caused the number of married women in paid work to decline precipitously. Their husbands, if they worked in the mass-production industries, then demanded "family wages," which they believed employers could afford to pay. In 1946 and 1947, about 240 000 workers struck for a total of almost seven million workdays. Automobile, steel, rubber, textile, packing, electrical manufacturing, forestry, and mining companies all felt the sting of such action. Average wages rose from 69.4 cents per hour in 1945 to 91.3 cents per hour in 1948.

Women, who were generally not members of unions, noticed little increase in their wages. In 1948, the Retail, Wholesale and Department Store Union (RWDSU), supported by the Canadian Congress of Labour (CCL), initiated a three-year drive, headed by Eileen Talman, to organize Toronto's Eaton's store. The company pulled out all the stops to oppose the union: linking unions with communism, raising wages just before the vote on unionizing took place, and warning part-time workers that unionism would cost them their jobs. When only 40 percent of the workers supported affiliation with the RWDSU, the CCL leadership, almost exclusively male, concluded that women were too passive to unionize and ceased its attempts to organize sectors dominated by female labour. Such stereotypical views were exploding in Quebec, where women endured a bitter and ultimately successful strike at Dupuis Frères department store in 1952 to win better pay and working conditions. Members of the increasingly secular Confédération des travailleurs catholiques du Canada, these women were a harbinger of things to come in post-war Quebec.

Quebec workers who struck were well aware that the provincial government often came to the armed defence of strike-bound employers. In 1949, workers in the town of Asbestos, unwilling to delay a strike until a government-appointed board of arbitration reported on their grievances, struck so that the company would not have time to stockpile asbestos before the inevitable walkout. During the five-month strike, the workers faced a large contingent of provincial police, who protected replacement workers hired by the company. Many strikers were arrested or beaten in clashes with officers.

The brutal state response to the strike galvanized considerable resistance to the Union Nationale. Liberal and liberal-nationalist intellectuals, including future prime minister Pierre Trudeau, were increasingly united on the need to defeat Maurice Duplessis and protect workers' interests. Even within the church, there were dissenters against Duplessis's heavy-handed tactics. Rank-and-file clergy who supported the Asbestos strikers briefly had a champion in Archbishop Charbonneau of Montreal, but his ecclesiastical superiors transferred him out of the province. The Roman Catholic Church had played a

VOICES FROM THE PAST

Factory Women on Strike

The predominantly young female labour force of Lanark Manufacturing Company, a firm making wire harnesses for the automobile companies, went on strike in August 1964. On strike for six months, their militancy countered popular stereotypes of women as passive workers. Here are some of their recollections about why they struck, what they faced during the strike, and what they gained by their action. Worker Rosemary Couisineau described factory conditions as follows:

just total exhaustion and stress. Sometimes you'd come home and the tightness in your back felt like you were all in knots . . . You had to work so hard and so fast. If you made a mistake, the verbal abuse you'd get . . . Predominantly young women were put on the rotary because, as one worker described it, "you had to hurry up. That's why we had more energy than the older girls, because we were young."

One young woman recounted the struggles on the picket line:

It broke our hearts when we saw people still going in . . . and they did everything they could to stop the scabs

from working. The police used to protect the scabs going in and out . . . So we'd fight back—even with the police. We'd do anything to get back at 'em. They're supposed to be protection for the public, right? They're not supposed to be biased. But they sure were . . . It was all one-sided . . . I was in court every week for something or other.

Striker Yvette Ward, sizing up the results of the strike years later, concluded:

A lot of times I sit and think about it. Lanark, to me, was a landmark in the history of labour because these kids weren't afraid. They went ahead and did it, even though they knew they might lose their jobs forever . . .

I can't help but remember the unity and the courage and the knowledge that all of the girls from that time had—and the few men that were working there. We were bound together so tight. These girls were working for peanuts, and didn't have much to fight for, but they did. They fought for six months steady without a stop and never gave up for one minute . . . It was the experience of a lifetime.[10]

long-standing role in mediating labour conflict in Quebec, but its rigidity during the Asbestos strike destroyed that role forever.

It was not only in Quebec that striking workers were confronted by police. In November 1945, the Ontario government sent provincial police and reinforcements from the RCMP through the gates of the Ford Motor Company plant at Windsor to end a five-week-old strike. The strikers responded by blockading the plant with cars. The federal government appointed Justice Ivan Rand to mediate the conflict. The major issue was the closed shop, or compulsory union membership, for employees. Rand successfully proposed a formula for union membership: in a bargaining unit where a majority voted to join a union, employers must collect union dues from all members of the unit, but individuals could formally apply to have their dues sent to a designated charity rather than the union. A less happy ending greeted the loggers of Newfoundland, who struck in 1959 only to have Premier Smallwood use the RCMP to enforce his decision to decertify the International Woodworkers' Association as the bargaining agent of the loggers.

Opposition by employers to unions meant that the rate of unionization of private sector workers stalled after the 1950s. By contrast, public sector workers were increasingly unionized. Because women were heavily concentrated in the lower echelons of the public service, four-fifths of Canada's new unionists from 1966 to 1976 were women. Women in the "caring" professions, such as nursing, social work, and teaching, also questioned the stereotype that "women's work" was mainly community service rather than remunerative professional labour.

At times consciously feminist, at times not, these women gradually recognized that their work was undervalued and that their working conditions required improvement. No longer deterred by arguments that it was unladylike to organize, women who had the opportunity to do so unionized at a rapid rate. Strikes of teachers, social workers, and civil servants, unheard of before the 1970s, began to become commonplace by the end of the decade. "We are not Florence Nightingales," the United Nurses of Alberta president, Margaret Ethier, proclaimed as Alberta's nurses "walked the bricks" during an illegal strike in 1979, the first of three such strikes by the province's nurses in an eight-year period.

Increasingly, the strike was also being used as a weapon in Quebec: in 1960, there were 38 strikes in the province; in 1975, there were 362. The province's Roman Catholic unions formally ended their affiliation with the church in 1960, organizing the Confédération des syndicats nationaux (CSN). The CSN played a major role in the Common Front formed by Quebec public sector unions in 1972, conducting general strikes to improve the position of the lowest-paid public sector workers, most of whom were women. The Common Front provoked much opposition. The Robert Bourassa government invoked legislation to end the labour disruption, jailing the heads of Quebec's three largest labour federations when they encouraged their members to defy back-to-work orders. Several conservative unions, alienated by the CSN's embrace of such militant tactics, broke away to form the Centrale des syndicats démocratiques.

CONCLUSION

The three decades of prosperity that followed the Second World War led many commentators to believe that a working compromise had been reached between private profit-making and a fair distribution of social wealth. In striking this balance, the state played an important role in the economy, directing funds toward companies and needy individuals to attract investment. Governments in Canada argued that they had sufficient economic powers to ensure that private economic decision-makers, foreign and national, were forced to respect the public interest.

Measured by purchasing power, most Canadians had never been so well off, yet millions remained on the outside of the new consumer society, looking in. Moreover, by the 1960s, it was becoming increasingly clear that uncontrolled economic growth was not only destroying communities but also the natural environment. Even those who ignored such problems watched in dismay as the illusory consensus that informed state policies regarding the economy began to come unstuck in the 1970s. With inflation, high unemployment, and labour unrest, Canadians would be forging their national policy in a very different atmosphere in the closing decades of the twentieth century.

Notes

1 Mr. Justice Thomas R. Berger, "Northern Frontier, Northern Homeland: The Report of the Mackenzie Valley Pipeline Inquiry" (Ottawa: Minister of Supply and Services Canada, 1977), 1:123.

2 Canada, Department of Reconstruction, "Employment and Income with Special Reference to the Initial Period of Reconstruction," Sessional Paper No. 90, 12 April 1945.

3 Ester Reiter, "Life in a Fast-Food Factory," in *On the Job: Confronting the Labour Process in Canada*, ed. Craig Heron and Robert Storey (Montreal: McGill-Queen's University Press, 1986), 317–18.

4 Frank James Tester and Peter Kulchyski, *Tammarniit (Mistakes): Inuit Relocation in the Eastern Arctic, 1939–1963* (Vancouver: UBC Press, 1994), 7.

5 Quoted in Wallace Clement, *Hardrock Mining: Industrial Relations and Technological Changes at Inco* (Toronto: McClelland & Stewart, 1981), 227–28.

6 Heather Menzies, *Computers on the Job: Surviving Canada's Microcomputer Revolution* (Toronto: Lorimer, 1982), 56.

7 Rachel Carson, *Silent Spring* (Boston: Houghton Mifflin, 1962), 244.

8 Sheila Arnopolous, "Immigrants and Women: Sweatshops of the 1970s," in *The Canadian Worker in the Twentieth Century*, ed. Irving Abella and David Millar (Toronto: Oxford University Press, 1978), 204.

9 Canada, *Report of the Royal Commission on Taxation*, vol. 1, *Introduction, Acknowledgements and Minority Reports* (Ottawa: Queen's Printer, 1966), 1.

10 Ester Reiter, "First-Class Workers Don't Want Second-Class Wages: The Lanark Strike in Dunnville," in *A Diversity of Women: Ontario, 1945–1980*, ed. Joy Parr (Toronto: University of Toronto Press, 1995), 179, 186, 194.

Related Readings in This Series

From *Nation and Society: Readings in Post-Confederation Canadian History*
Tina Loo, "People in the Way: Modernity, Environment, and Society on the Arrow Lakes," 362–89.

From Primary Documents CD-ROM, Volume II
Out of the Dust
Settlement Is Imperative in Asbestos
Fisheries Workers, Newfoundland, 1974
The St. Lawrence Seaway, July 1, 1958

Selected Reading

In addition to titles cited in Chapters 15 and 16, works covering post-war economic developments include Lawrence Robert Aronsen, *American National Security and Economic Relations with Canada, 1945–1954* (Westport, CT: Greenwood, 1997); Kenneth Norrie and Douglas Owram, *A History of the Canadian Economy* (Toronto: Harcourt Brace Jovanovich, 1991); Harold Chorney, *The Deficit and Debt Management: An Alternative to Monetarism* (Ottawa: Canadian Centre for Policy Alternatives, 1989); David A. Wolfe, "The Rise and Demise of the Keynesian Era in Canada: Economic Policy, 1930–1982," in *Modern Canada, 1930–1980s*, eds. Michael S. Cross and Gregory S. Kealey (Toronto: McClelland & Stewart, 1984); and Robert M. Campbell, *Grand Illusions: The Politics of the Keynesian Experience in Canada, 1945–1975* (Peterborough, ON: Broadview Press, 1987). The impact of economic and political developments on organized labour is discussed in Bryan Palmer and Joan Sangster, *Labouring Canada: Class, Race, and Gender in Canadian History* (Toronto: Oxford University Press, 2008); Peter S. McInnis, *Harnessing Labour Confrontation: Shaping the Postwar Settlement in Canada, 1943–1950* (Toronto: University of Toronto Press, 2002); and Steven High, *Industrial Sunset: The Making of North America's Rust Belt, 1969–1984* (Toronto: University of Toronto Press, 2003). On taxation debates, see Canada, *Report of the Royal Commission on Taxation* (Ottawa: Queen's Printer, 1966); John N. McDougall, *The Politics and Economics of Eric Kierans: A Man for all Canadians* (Montreal: McGill-Queen's University Press, 1993), Chapter 6; and J. Harvey Perry, *A Fiscal History of Canada: The Postwar Years* (Toronto: Canadian Tax Foundation, 1989).

Growing concern for the environment and uncontrolled technological innovation is discussed in Chad Gaffield and Pam Gaffield, eds., *Consuming Canada: Readings in Environmental History* (Toronto: Copp Clark, 1995); Tina Loo, *States of Nature: Conserving Canada's Wildlife in the Twentieth Century* (Vancouver: UBC Press, 2006); John Sandlos, *Hunters at the Margin: Native People and Wildlife*

Conservation in the Northwest Territories (Vancouver: UBC Press, 2007); Rachel Carson, *Silent Spring* (Boston: Houghton Mifflin, 1962); *Limits to Growth: A Report for the Club of Rome's Project for the Predicament of Mankind*, 2nd ed. (New York: Universe, 1974); and E.F. Schumacher, *Small Is Beautiful: The Study of Economics as if People Mattered* (New York: Harper and Row, 1975).

Thomas Berger's report for the Mackenzie Valley Pipeline Inquiry, *Northern Frontier, Northern Homeland*, rev. ed. (Vancouver: Douglas and McIntyre, 1988), offers a classic statement on Native dilemmas over the development ethic, as does Mel Watkins, ed., *Dene Nation: The Colony Within* (Toronto: University of Toronto Press, 1977). On the impact of hydro-electric projects on Native communities and the environment generally, see Jean L. Manore, *Cross Currents: Hydroelectricity and the Engineering of Northern Ontario* (Waterloo, ON: Wilfrid Laurier University, 1999); James Waldram, *As Long as the Rivers Run: Hydroelectric Development and Native Communities in Western Canada* (Winnipeg: University of Manitoba Press, 1988); and Sean McCutcheon, *Electric Rivers: The Story of the James Bay Project* (Montreal: Black Rose Books, 1991). On Native peoples and the economy, see also Dianne Newell, *Tangled Webs of History: Indians and the Law in Canada's Pacific Coast Fisheries* (Toronto: University of Toronto Press, 1993).

Donald Savoie discusses the economic implications of regionalism in *Regional Economic Development: Canada's Search for Solutions* (Toronto: University of Toronto Press, 1986). Works with extensive coverage of regional economic developments include Gerald Friesen, *The Canadian Prairies: A History*, 2nd ed. (Toronto: University of Toronto Press, 1987); Rennie Warburton and Donald Coburn, eds., *Workers, Capital and the State of British Columbia* (Vancouver: UBC Press, 1987); Patricia Marchak, *Green Gold: The Forest Industry in British Columbia* (Vancouver: UBC Press, 1983); and Gary Burrill and Ian McKay, eds., *People, Resources and Power in Atlantic Canada: Critical Perspectives on Underdevelopment and Primary Industries in the Atlantic Region* (Fredericton: Acadiensis Press, 1987).

CHAPTER 18

Community and Nation, 1945–1975

TIMELINE

1951 Major revisions to the Indian Act

Contraceptive pill first introduced; Les Insolences du Frère Untel published;
Status Indians entranchised in federal elections;
Diefenbaker government passes
Canadian Bill of Rights; birth control pill
1960 becomes widely available

Halifax decides to raze Africville

1961 Liberalization of Immigration Act

1962 Gerda Munsinger affair

1966 Further liberalization of Immigration Act;
centennial celebrations

1967 National Indian Brotherhood founded;
Black United Front established in Nova Scotia

1968 Federal legislation passed to encourage bilingualism
and biculturalism; White Paper on Indian Policy tabled

1969 Report of the Royal Commission on the Status of Women

1970 Secretary of state for Multiculturalism established

1971 National Action Committee on the Status of Women
created; Le Dain Commission Report on
Non-Medical Use of Drugs

1972

1974–77 Mackenzie Valley Pipeline Inquiry

Gerda Munsinger, born Gerda Hessler, was one of millions of victims of the chaos of the Second World War and early post-war years in Europe. Living in the eastern zone of occupied Germany after the war, she was a voluptuous teenager who was often raped by Soviet soldiers. When she moved to the western zones of the country, her life remained precarious. She married Mike Munsinger, an American soldier whom she had met while waitressing in Frankfurt, but she was denied entry into the United States and the marriage was annulled. Eventually she migrated to Canada as a domestic servant.

After she completed her required year in domestic service, Munsinger found work as a nightclub hostess and model. In 1959 and 1960, she had an affair with Pierre Sevigny, associate minister of Defence in the Diefenbaker government, and a brief fling with George Hees, another government minister. Munsinger innocently gave both ministers as references when she applied for Canadian citizenship in 1960. This led to an RCMP investigation and meeting with Diefenbaker to suggest to him that Munsinger was a spy and a common prostitute. Though they had no real evidence for either allegation, the RCMP successfully recommended deportation of this prospective Canadian in 1961.

In 1966, the Pearson Liberals, in response to withering Conservative attacks on a number of fronts, revealed the Munsinger affair to the Canadian public, rehashing the unproven claims that Munsinger was a spy and a prostitute. Oblivious to their impact on Munsinger, who was not a public figure and no longer lived in Canada, Pearson and his colleagues slung mud at will. More interesting than the frivolous charges is why the Liberals believed that they might stick. In part, they hoped Canadians would link the manufactured Munsinger affair with a sex scandal that had helped bring down a Conservative government in Britain a few years earlier. But more obviously, the Liberals were making opportunistic use of public images of appropriate behaviour for women and fears of how immigration might be affecting the social fabric of the country. Gerda Munsinger was neither a "housewife" nor a "spinster," the two respectable designations for women at the time, so it was easy to portray her as a prostitute, the non-respectable alternative. Notions of gender roles and sexuality changed gradually in the post-war years and particularly after the mid-1960s, but the depth of older beliefs about how a woman should comport herself throughout life were reflected in the Munsinger media blowout.[1]

This chapter examines the social values of the country that rejected Gerda Munsinger in the period of post-war economic growth. Many responded to their newfound prosperity with a sometimes contradictory mix of unbounded consumerism and cautious traditionalism. Others, either because they were denied their share of the expanding economic pie or because they found little satisfaction in the individualist consumerist world, campaigned for a reassertion of communitarian values and greater social equality.

This post-war float encouraged women to think of themselves as consumers and ornaments.
Provincial Archives of Alberta/BL2021/1

POPULATION

"Now we are 20 million," announced Bobby Gimby in his popular hit record "Ca-na-da," which was widely aired during the 1967 centennial. In the post-war period, the baby boom helped boost Canada's population from about 12 million in 1945 to 23 million in 1975. Women had limited their pregnancies during the Great Depression and the war, but the relative security of the post-war period encouraged couples to marry young and have more children. At the peak of the baby boom in 1959, the fertility rate of women in their childbearing years was about 50 percent greater than in 1941. The birth rate plummeted again after the birth control pill became available in 1960.

Immigration was the other major factor in Canada's population explosion. From 1946 to 1962, almost 1.8 million new immigrants came to Canada. Early post-war immigrants were primarily European; only 4 percent came from Asia and Africa, and many of these were white South Africans and Israelis. Overseas offices of the Department of Immigration were confined to Europe, as were visa offices, and the minister of Citizenship and Immigration enjoyed substantial discretionary power in keeping out people deemed undesirable. Initially, there was also some resistance to opening doors to immigrants from countries that had been Canada's enemies during the Second World War. About 10 000 Germans and 20 000 Italians were permitted entry from 1946 to 1950, but the explosion in labour needs led to the acceptance of 189 705 Germans and 166 397 Italians from 1951 to 1957.

As the economic boom of the 1960s began, it became clear that western Europe, back on its feet after post-war rebuilding, would no longer produce the steady stream of immigrants required to support Canada's expanding economy. To attract the well-educated technical and professional people that Canada most wanted,

TABLE 18.1 A Growing Population, 1941–1976*

Period	Population increase	Births	Population increase due to births (%)	Net immigration	Population increase due to immigration (%)	Population at the end of period
1941–51	2 141**	1 972	92.1	169	7.9	13 648
1951–56	2 072	1 473	71.1	594	28.9	16 081
1956–61	2 157	1 675	77.7	482	22.3	18 238
1961–66	1 777	1 518	85.4	259	14.6	20 015
1966–71	1 553	1 090	70.2	463	29.8	21 568
1971–76	1 425	934	65.5	491	34.5	22 993

*All population figures are in thousands
**Excludes Newfoundland

Source: *Canada Year Book*, 1994, 113.

immigration regulations were changed to open the door to skilled people from regions other than Europe and the United States. Domestic servants, always in short supply, were also granted entry to Canada, even if they came from non-European countries. Revisions to the Immigration Act in 1962 and again in 1967 reduced the colour bias that had once kept Canada's gates largely closed to non-whites. People from the Caribbean and Asia in particular took advantage of Canada's changing immigration policy.

As Table 18.1 suggests, immigration accounted for a dramatically larger proportion of the population increase in the early 1970s than in the late 1950s, when immigration levels were almost the same. This is explained by the huge decline in the birth rate from 28.3 newborns per 1000 population in 1959 to 15.7 in 1976.

The dramatic decline in infant deaths since the beginning of the century meant that in 1976, only 13.5 infants per 1000 failed to reach their first birthdays, compared with 88.1 in 1921. Better nutrition, preventive medicine, and the use of antibiotics increased not only infant survival but life expectancy generally. Children born in 1976 could expect to live 13 years longer than children born in 1931. By the 1970s, life expectancy had reached 70 years for men and 77 for women.

As always, these figures mask demographic differences within the larger Canadian population. Wealthy Canadians still tended to live longer than the poor, and Native peoples were the most likely to suffer early deaths. Although infectious diseases in Native communities were less common than in earlier periods and

medical care facilities and personnel were more accessible, poverty-related diseases such as tuberculosis continued to thrive. Despair produced disastrous rates of alcoholism and drug addiction, leading to an array of health problems. Natives between the ages of 20 and 39 had a risk almost four times that of the general population of dying a violent death, the result of either homicide, suicide, or accident.

CHANGING SOCIAL VALUES

For the majority of Canadians, education levels and income increased along with material expectations. The nuclear family, consisting of a husband, a wife, and several children, remained the ideal for most Canadians, but with each census, it accounted for a noticeably smaller proportion of households. Divorce laws were liberalized in 1969, allowing more unhappy marriages to be dissolved and increasing the number of single-parent households. The effectiveness of "the pill," which was widely prescribed in the 1960s, allowed women the option of delaying childbirth or not having children at all. Reflecting somewhat greater tolerance of homosexuality, same-sex couples "came out" in unprecedented numbers. Common-law marriages, once associated with the poorer classes, became popular across the economic spectrum, particularly among young adults. Divorce and remarriage substantially increased the number of "blended" families, which might include a couple's biological children and each partner's offspring from earlier marriages.

Marijuana and a New Generation

Illegal drug use in Canada before the Second World War was largely associated in the public mind with the lower classes and non-whites. Social prejudices, rather than scientific knowledge, often dictated the legislation that made some intoxicants illegal while others, such as alcohol, were legal but regulated after prohibition ended in various provinces. Marijuana was first included in legislation banning certain substances in 1923; in 1961, it was placed under the Narcotic Control Act, and stiffer penalties were introduced for possession and "trafficking."

During the 1960s, marijuana became the recreational drug of choice for many teenagers and young adults despite its illegality. Even at the conservative University of Alberta, where only 1 percent of students in residence had used drugs in 1965, fully a quarter of residence students in 1971 had experimented with illegal drugs, usually marijuana. Police arrested more than 1500 people in Alberta for cannabis possession in 1971, more than the number of arrests for this act in the entire country just four years earlier.

Police forces presented their arrests of marijuana sellers and users as a victory for the forces of social good. The RCMP commissioner warned in 1968 that "the lawless 'beat' generation will create a mounting fear of anarchy in Canada unless it is met firmly by police with massive public and governmental support."[2] They singled out hippies—mainly young people who had dropped out of society, condemning materialist social values that they regarded as empty, and whose use of marijuana to free minds stifled by social repression was well advertised.

Arrests for marijuana possession and threats by university administrations to expel students convicted on drug charges fuelled pressures from student groups to remove marijuana from the Narcotic Control Act or even get rid of the act altogether. Pierre Trudeau responded by establishing the Commission of Inquiry into the Non-Medical Use of Drugs, headed by Gerald Le Dain, Dean of York University's Osgoode Hall Law School.

The Canadian medical profession was not united in its response to the rise of marijuana use. While some physicians echoed the British Advisory Committee on Drug Dependence, which said that marijuana use was no more harmful physically than alcohol consumption, others were unwilling to advocate legalization because the long-term effects of its use were unknown. Supporters of legalization pointed out that studies of marijuana's effects were not possible until marijuana ceased to be an illegal substance.

The Le Dain Commission attempted to balance the conflicting voices regarding marijuana. In their 1972 report, the commissioners called for the removal of possession of marijuana from the Criminal Code and weaker penalties for producers and sellers of the substance. But the government, pressured by conservative forces within the country and abroad—particularly by the American government, which was increasing penalties for drug use and sales—was unwilling to change its narcotics legislation. Instead, the Department of Justice quietly instructed prosecutors in 1972 to seek an absolute discharge for anyone convicted of simple possession.

The baby boomers tended to embrace more liberal social values than their parents had. Children of a prosperous and media-dominated age, they fostered an ever-changing youth culture characterized at first by rock music and blue jeans and later by premarital sex, mind-altering drugs, unisex clothing and hairstyles, and political protest. The changes were most evident among middle-class teenagers enrolled in expanding liberal arts programs at universities, but they had an impact throughout the post-war generation.

Surveys among Canadian young people showed that by the mid-1960s, a majority of university students were sexually active; a decade later the same was true for high school students. The widespread availability of contraceptives meant that fear of pregnancy became a less important reason for unmarried people to avoid sex.

The "sexual revolution" was complex, especially for young women. To the extent that women were able to choose their partners, many experienced the new sexual morality as a form of liberation, freeing them from the compulsory heterosexual monogamy that had earlier characterized socially acceptable sexual relations. Others were not so positive, arguing that

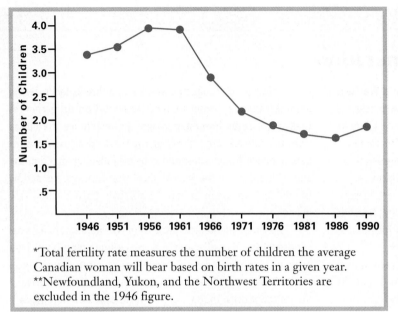

*Total fertility rate measures the number of children the average Canadian woman will bear based on birth rates in a given year.
**Newfoundland, Yukon, and the Northwest Territories are excluded in the 1946 figure.

FIGURE 18.1 Total Fertility Rates,* 1946–1990**
Sources: F.H. Leacy, ed., *Historical Statistics of Canada*, 2nd ed., (Ottawa: Statistics Canada, 1983), Series B1-14; *Canada Year Book*, various years.

changing values relating to sex—"scripted by men for men's benefit"—exploited women.[3] Many young women complained that they felt compelled by peer pressure to have sex with their boyfriends and were too often subject to physical force when they were reluctant to consent.

EDUCATION

Most young people in the post-war years received more schooling than their parents. Technology and the increased concentration of business ownership limited the opportunities of those who had simply learned a trade as an apprentice. In the 1950s, a high school diploma was essential for all but the least-skilled, lowest-paying jobs. By the 1970s, employers expected university degrees or college diplomas for many junior positions. Over half of Canadians had nine grades or fewer of schooling in 1951. Twenty-five years later, only a quarter of the population over 15 years of age had not completed at least nine grades. University degrees, once limited to a numerically negligible, if extremely influential, elite, became more common, with one in 10 Canadians aged 25 to 44 in 1976 holding at least one university degree. In the early post-war period, Quebec continued to lag behind the rest of the

country in the area of education with over two-thirds of its children in the labour force by age 16 in 1948, a figure that was far larger than in Anglophone communities. The impact of the Quiet Revolution had largely wiped out the gap between Quebec and Canada as a whole by 1975.

The gender balance in higher education also began to change. Although in the early years of the twentieth century women had been discouraged from attending university, they were increasingly found in undergraduate classrooms by the mid-1970s. Gender still governed what programs students pursued. Fields such as engineering, law, and medicine remained male bastions, while schools of social work and nursing had a largely female clientele. Men dominated graduate programs, outnumbering women 8.5 to 1 in receipt of doctorates in 1975, but these trends too were changing.

Responding to public pressure, governments made huge outlays on education between 1945 and 1975. Throughout rural areas, one-room schoolhouses where poorly paid, inadequately trained young women taught eight grades gave way to modern, centrally located facilities. For many rural residents, the creation of consolidated school divisions was a mixed blessing because it removed local control over schools and created the need for daily busing of children, sometimes over long distances.

By the 1970s, most public school boards across the country required that new teachers hold at least a university degree in education to be considered for a teaching position. Powerful teachers' associations in every province had won professional wages for teachers, sometimes using strikes or the threat of strikes to achieve their demands. Teachers, parents, politicians, and business people endlessly debated the best ways to educate children as citizens and future employees. For the most part, schools became more humane, as corporal punishment and rote learning gave way to child-centred education and attempts to encourage critical thinking. Critics charged that children graduated from 12 or more years of schooling less knowledgeable about the basics of reading, writing, and arithmetic than earlier generations of high school graduates.

Who Is Fit to Have a Baby?

While the high birth rate from 1945 to 1960 reflected both the prosperity of the period and the high value that most Canadians placed on the domestic ideal, society and the state continued to frown on women who had children out of wedlock. In Quebec, thousands of "illegitimate" Roman Catholic children were placed in homes for the "feeble-minded," regardless of their actual intelligence, to hide them from society. At least until the late 1950s, single mothers in Canada were denied mothers' allowances, thus virtually ensuring that they had to give their children up for adoption.

Single mothers were not the only Canadians deemed unworthy to have children. People labelled mentally unfit were also discouraged from reproducing. According to popular psychology of the period, the offspring of such people would grow up to become criminals. The province of Alberta has a particularly shameful history of enforcing eugenicist policies. From 1929 to 1972, the provincial Eugenics Board ordered the sterilization of 2822 "mentally defective" people. The board interpreted this category broadly: it included, among others, some adult sexual offenders, young women whom the board determined to be promiscuous or potentially promiscuous, and school-age children whose parents could not cope with them and whose intelligence appeared to be less than average. Such children, who were placed in the Provincial Training School for Mental Defectives in Red Deer, ranged from those requiring around-the-clock care to others quite able to feed and dress themselves but who scored poorly on the intelligence tests venerated by educational psychologists of the period.

Most of the men and boys ordered sterilized by the board were vasectomized, but some sexual offenders were castrated. Several boys with Down's syndrome had one testicle removed so that the medical director of the training school could have laboratory specimens for a study of the causes of the condition. Girls in the school were routinely sterilized at puberty. Among them was Leilani Muir, an inmate of the school from 1955 to 1965. An abused child at home, Muir suffered developmental delays and scored poorly on an IQ test. School officials told her that she was to have her appendix removed, but during the appendectomy, for which there were no medical grounds, her Fallopian tubes were tied. Muir left the school when she was 21 and later moved to Victoria, where she worked as a waitress and was twice married and divorced. At the age of 45, after her mother finally informed her of the sterilization, she sued the provincial government. In 1996, the Court of Queen's Bench awarded Muir $750 000 in compensation. Two years later the province agreed to substantial financial compensation for other living victims of the eugenics policy.

The enthusiasm for more schooling gradually extended to the post-secondary sector. Between 1944 and 1947, university enrolment doubled as a result of generous federal grants to veterans wishing to pursue university educations. Federal grants to universities, recommended by the Massey Commission in 1951 and quickly implemented by Ottawa, also gave a boost to institutions that were receiving only modest funding increases from the provinces. Demands from the growing numbers of high school graduates and their parents led the provinces to loosen their purse strings in the 1960s, and new universities such as York in Toronto, Simon Fraser in Burnaby, and the University of Regina were opened. Some affiliated colleges, such as United College in Winnipeg and Brandon College, became full-fledged universities. Church-affiliated universities throughout the country became more secular in their governing structures so that they could also become eligible for government grants. In Charlottetown, for example, Prince of Wales College and St. Dunstan's, which historically had catered to largely Protestant and Roman Catholic clienteles, were merged, amid much controversy, to become the state-supported non-denominational University of Prince Edward Island in 1968.

EDUCATION IN QUEBEC

Education changes were perhaps most dramatic in Quebec. In 1960, there were only 20 seminaries, 60 boys' secondary schools, and 20 girls' schools whose certificates permitted students to enter the Roman

Catholic universities. While 11 percent of Anglophones in the province between the ages of 20 and 24 attended university, only 2.9 percent of Francophones in the same age group did so. Not only was the number of graduates from Roman Catholic secondary schools poor in relation to graduates of the province's Protestant system, but critics persistently complained that the Roman Catholic curriculum was antiquated. For boys, education still focused on classical thought; for girls, the system taught above all else "preparation for family life, the beauty of the home, its virtues, and its unique position in society."[4] The teachers in Quebec's Roman Catholic schools were less educated than the teachers in the Protestant system.

Dissatisfaction with the conservative, clerically run educational institutions of Quebec revealed itself in the phenomenal success of *Les Insolences du Frère Untel* (*The Impertinences of Brother Anonymous*), which was published in 1960. Written by Brother Jean-Paul Desbiens, it was a stinging indictment of Quebec education by someone within the ranks of the Roman Catholic Church. The Jean Lesage government appointed a commission to examine the state of Quebec education and make recommendations for improvement. Although the commissioners decided that schools should remain organized along religious lines, they recommended that the state play a larger role in administration and curriculum development.

In 1964, for the first time since 1875, the provincial government established a ministry of Education, with Desbiens as one of the department's officials. Under the guiding hand of Education Minister Paul Gérin-Lajoie, new curricula were introduced to bring Quebec schools into line with education systems in the rest of North America. The ministry set up a network of secular junior colleges, or CEGEPs, to provide post-secondary vocational and academic training. Between 1960 and 1970, enrolment in Quebec's secondary schools rose 101 percent, college enrolments rose 82 percent, and university enrolments rose 169 percent.

The creation of the Centrale de l'enseignement du Québec, a militant teachers' union, out of the old Roman Catholic teachers' association reflected the continued secularization of education—and unions—in Quebec. Leaders of the new union issued manifestos inspired more by Marx than by Jesus and easily overwhelmed the rapidly declining numbers of priests and nuns in their ranks who clung to traditional Roman Catholic perspectives. Nevertheless, conservatives could still mobilize the support needed to win school board elections, for which voter turnout was notoriously low, and fought off attempts to formally secularize the school system. In this goal, they had the support of the Protestant boards, which believed that the dual system defended Anglophone rights and the superior schools developed by the wealthier non–Roman Catholic community. Despite its continued existence, few Roman Catholic teachers supported the confessional system, and most taught little differently than teachers in the public schools.

CITIES AND SUBURBS

Demands for more and better housing were common in a generation that had weathered the Great Depression by sharing living space and deferring the purchase of goods. With the help of government-guaranteed mortgages, veterans' housing grants, and consumer credit, people flocked to homes in the suburbs. The media, particularly in the advertising they carried, portrayed the suburbs as a world of quiet, privacy, modern appliances, and fine furnishings. Little consideration was given to European models of apartment buildings around central shopping and entertainment courts. Canada, it was believed, remained a relatively unpopulated country with great empty spaces on the outskirts of even its major cities.

The new suburbs increased the costs of urban administration. In addition to utility lines and sewers, new roads were needed for the cars and public transport that became indispensable to suburban life. More police and firefighters were required, and each new area had to be given its own schools, if pupils were not to be bused to large, centrally located institutions. In the prosperous 1950s, municipalities raised the funds for such developments from property taxes. They also successfully pressured provincial governments to establish grants to municipalities for construction projects, to increase school grants, and to take over all or most of the costs of social welfare.

In most cases, new suburbs initially lacked shopping areas, community centres, theatres, taverns, sport complexes, and other recreational areas. Residents found entertainment in the city centre and friendship via workplace, church, and community organizations that were only sometimes located within their new subdivisions. Many suburbanites, and, indeed, increasing numbers of Canadians generally, either sought privacy or had it thrust upon them in anonymous settings that brought the term "community" sharply into question. Instead of attending community events, people watched television, and even built their homes to accommodate a "TV room." Impersonal supermarkets, department stores, and malls eventually replaced neighbourhood shops where customers and merchants all knew each other.

Women experienced this new privatization most directly, sometimes with devastating psychological consequences. While most men spent time away from home and developed camaraderie with fellow workers, many women remained in the home all day and had little connection with a world beyond their families. Often well-educated and unenthusiastic about housework, suburban women suffered from what American feminist Betty Friedan, in her ground-breaking book *The Feminine Mystique* (1963), called "the problem that has no name." Some women, particularly if their children were older or if kin were available to act as child minders, sought refuge in paid work; others focused their energies on voluntary activities that sought to transform the suburban community into something approaching the richness of more established urban locations. A surprisingly large number developed various nervous disorders for which a male-dominated medical profession prescribed tranquilizers such as Valium that often created long-term addictions and left the underlying problems unresolved.

Older children, too, often fared poorly in suburban environments, where public recreational spaces were few. A report of the Social Planning Council of Metropolitan Toronto in the 1970s described the dilemma:

> Suburban youth are expected to act as adult consumers. . . . While the market influences youth to consume, it creates an environment which does not

This new suburb in Lethbridge in 1951 followed the model that was common in bigger cities. Planned as a neighbourhood of about 1500 homes around an elementary school (in the foreground), it featured curved streets and cul-de-sacs meant to break the monotony created by similar-looking boxy homes.
Glenbow Archives NA 5327-293

> enable them to meet some of their basic needs, needs for belonging, needs for social contact. . . . When young people transcend the framework of home and neighbourhood and move out into the larger suburban community they come up against the stark reality that they are almost alone in seeking public forms of community life.[5]

Not all women remember the suburbs in a negative way. For some, voluntary work in community leagues and church auxiliaries was a fulfilling experience. Many women formed close friendships with neighbours and shared shopping and child care. Toronto suburbanite Anne Lapp recalled fondly: "Nearly all of us had small children and it was a day-long job keeping them out of the mud and excavated house sites. . . . It was like a small village and we knew almost everyone."[6]

HOUSING STANDARDS

While middle-class ideals defined the suburban lifestyle, many post-war neighbourhoods on the urban fringe were shantytowns. Tarpaper shacks in Ville Jacques Cartier on Montreal Island, unserviced homes in Bridgeview on British Columbia's Lower Mainland, and shacks without water or sewer facilities, garbage collection, or street lighting outside St. John's demonstrated that many suburbs had greater problems than middle-class angst. Residents of these instant slums were unable to find accommodation in urban cores, where established housing disappeared as office towers and apartments for the middle class encroached upon residential neighbourhoods.

Although public housing programs developed slowly, it was not due to the failure of early experiments. Toronto's Regent Park, Canada's first large-scale public housing development, was completed in 1947 and, 11 years later, a study suggested that its 1200 families—low-income people whose former neighbourhoods were plagued by crime, alcoholism, poor health, and school absenteeism—had established a relatively peaceful, healthy neighbourhood. While residents complained of a lack of recreational facilities and about the bureaucratic management of the project, their lives had improved as a result of their relocation to roomy row houses with excellent sewage and sanitary services.

Opportunities to find decent housing varied particularly dramatically among regions. Atlantic Canadians, Native peoples, northerners, and Gaspésiens, for example, were far less likely to live as well as people in southern Ontario. While fewer than one in 10 new homes built in Ontario in the early 1960s lacked either a furnace or a flush toilet, more than four in 10 built in Atlantic Canada during that period lacked one or both of these amenities. Older people, even with their new old-age pensions, often had difficulty finding suitable housing.

By the 1970s, the core areas of many cities had become rundown. Slumlords refused to maintain their properties and city governments controlled by suburban councillors funnelled municipal funds away from the downtown areas. While tenants formed organizations to demand stricter implementation of municipal housing standards and more funding for public housing, homeowners called for improved municipal services. Some middle-class people had a different view of how conditions in the core areas could be improved. They supported programs for "redevelopment," which often meant little more than levelling existing homes and replacing them with fancier houses that only the well-off could afford.

Where the basic architectural structures were sound, as in Cabbagetown in downtown Toronto, slumlords renovated homes to meet the tastes of affluent Torontonians who preferred to live close to their offices and the city's night life. In other cities, poor districts were transformed into chic shopping areas, such as Osborne Village in Winnipeg. Increasingly, the poor were forced to live farther from the urban core.

THE IMMIGRANT EXPERIENCE

If the post-war suburbs often appeared colourless, the established areas of cities were often reinvigorated by the huge influx of immigrants. The majority of the post-war immigrants settled in cities, and by the 1970s the initial destinations of over half of all immigrants to Canada were Greater Toronto, Montreal Island, and Greater Vancouver. Although many would eventually move to the suburbs, newcomers initially concentrated in older areas of the cities, creating Little Italys, Little Portugals, Little Budapests, and Little Jerusalems. The colourful, multilingual storefronts, the smells of a variety of cuisines, and the preference for streets and cafés over privatized living transformed Vancouver, Montreal, and Toronto into cosmopolitan metropoles.

Male immigrants in the early post-war period were usually blue-collar workers, and the jobs they were able to obtain generally paid poorly. Their wives often had little choice but to seek work, even if they had young children. Maria Rossi's experience was typical. In November 1956, she and her daughter arrived in Toronto. Her husband had emigrated one year earlier from their peasant farm in southern Italy. The family rented a basement flat in the home of another Italian émigré family, and Maria spent her first few days in Canada buying cooking utensils and observing the annual Santa Claus parade. Four days after her arrival, she began work as a steam press operator at a local laundry. For the next 20 years she worked continuously in a variety of low-paying jobs including sewing, cooking, and cashiering.[7]

Poverty initially left many immigrants with little money or time for joining and participating in ethnic organizations. However, within a generation, most immigrant groups had spawned dozens of organizations, from community centres to businessmen's clubs and from sports teams to charities. In the meantime, the private cafés and clubs within an ethnic organization provided entertainment for immigrants, especially men. Women, when freed from housework, child care, and paid work, were generally active in community-based churches.

Political organizations also abounded in ethnic communities. Ukrainian-Canadian politics had long been dominated by the struggle between supporters of the Soviet Union and adherents of an independent Ukraine. With 80 000 Ukrainians—most of them fiercely anti-communist—arriving in Canada in the early post-war period, nationalists, who enjoyed financial and ideological support from the Canadian government, came to dominate Ukrainian-Canadian organizations. Their activities helped publicize the famines induced by Soviet collectivization policies in the 1930s that had taken the lives of millions.

Zionism, the movement to create a Jewish homeland in Israel, became a uniting cause for Canadian Jews in the aftermath of the Nazi Holocaust. Spurred by the horror of their treatment by the Nazis, Jews in Canada and elsewhere stepped up their campaign to put an end to anti-Semitism. The Canadian Jewish Congress, which before the war had moved cautiously in its efforts to counter discrimination, became more militant, linking with other civil liberties groups to demand that the force of law be used against open manifestations of religious and cultural intolerance in Canada. Not all efforts to eradicate anti-Semitism were successful. Although Ernest Manning managed to purge the quasi-Nazis from the Social Credit Party in Alberta in 1947, anti-Semitism, drawn from the twisted writings of Social Credit founder Major Douglas, remained integral to the national party, and particularly its Quebec wing under Réal Caouette.

Immigrants wanted their children to learn English and succeed in their new homeland, but they also hoped to preserve their home languages and cultural practices. By the 1960s, minority ethnic groups were more assertive about preserving their cultural heritage. They were encouraged in their endeavours by the federal government's determination, announced in 1969, to support programs to promote bilingualism and biculturalism in Canada. If the so-called founding communities could be supported by Ottawa, why not "other" Canadians? Minority ethnic groups lobbied for federal and provincial grants for what became known as

multiculturalism. In 1971, Prime Minister Pierre Trudeau appointed a secretary of state for Multiculturalism and began to fund ethnic organizations and festivals. Provinces with large ethnic minorities also introduced heritage-language instruction in schools.

Ethnic diversity helped mute the prejudices that had once been prevalent in Canada. By the 1960s, schools were making special efforts to teach students about the problems created by prejudice, and opinion surveys indicated a growth of tolerance among Canadians. Still, discrimination in employment, housing, and other areas of community life continued to face many non-whites. Human rights legislation in the 1970s ameliorated the situation somewhat, but it could not eliminate racism and bigotry from Canadian society.

ASIAN-CANADIAN COMMUNITIES

When Hing Chang, an exceptional student, decided to leave her Vancouver high school in the late 1940s to go to business college, her principal was supportive, but admitted that college training, a ticket to success for white Canadians, would not help Hing find a job. His top Chinese-Canadian graduates had faced discrimination in their job searches and had been unable to secure good positions.

Before the 1970s, Chinese Canadians had good reason to feel embattled in Canadian society. Their communities were close to downtown and viewed with contempt by urban redevelopers. Two-thirds of Toronto's Chinatown was bulldozed in the 1960s to build a new city hall. In Vancouver, city by-laws eroded the distinct character of Chinatown. As author Denise Chong, daughter of Hing Chang, recalled:

> Vancouver's city council enacted bylaws to sanitize the squalor and ordered commerce off the sidewalk—gone were the squawking chickens in cages, the barbecued pork and duck that once hung for the customer's perusal. The gambling dens that used to be my grandmother's livelihood and entertainment had also disappeared; the last one had been padlocked long ago by city police. Now when we went to Chinatown, I couldn't help but feel, as its walls seemed to close in, that we were walking through the debris of my mother's past.[8]

After Canadian recognition of the communist government in Mainland China, new Chinese immigrants began to arrive in Canada, reinvigorating the

Events such as the Chinese dragon parade celebrate the cultural diversity of Canadian society.
Vancouver Public Library/79795-A

Chinese-Canadian community and eventually giving it enough clout to resist redevelopers. Educational institutions and major employers gradually became less racist, opening new opportunities for more Chinese Canadians.

Immigration from India and Pakistan increased dramatically following the reform of immigration laws in the 1960s. As doctors, engineers, and teachers whose skills were much in demand, they settled in communities throughout Canada and managed to survive the prejudice of their white neighbours and co-workers. Those without university degrees were often ghettoized in low-wage, supposedly unskilled factory jobs. Sociologists found that South Asian women workers were confined to the lowest-paying and most difficult tasks on the worst shifts in many factories. South Asians also provided much of the farm labour force in British Columbia, picking pesticide-sprayed crops without protective clothing or masks and living in converted barns without running water or electricity.

AFRICAN CANADIANS

Because of Canada's restrictive immigration laws, few blacks were allowed to immigrate to Canada. In the 1950s, the door opened a crack to admit domestic servants from the Caribbean, but the overwhelming majority of African Canadians could trace their origins to migrations of the eighteenth or nineteenth century. Their deep roots in Canada counted little to the white majority. African Canadians, like their American counterparts, faced particularly deep-seated racism. And, also like their American counterparts, they began in the post-war period to organize resistance to their unjust treatment.

In Nova Scotia, home to 30 percent of Canada's black population in 1961, they fought for their rights through the Nova Scotia Association for the Advancement of Coloured People (NSAACP), founded in 1945. In 1946, the NSAACP raised money to help Viola Desmond fight segregation in movie theatres. Desmond, a Halifax beautician, was arrested in a New Glasgow theatre for sitting downstairs rather than in the balcony, to which blacks were usually restricted. She was thrown in jail and fined for attempting to defraud the government of one cent in amusement tax—seats in the balcony were less expensive than those downstairs. Sentenced to 30 days in jail or a $20 fine, she paid the money but appealed the decision. The case was thrown out on a technicality, but the incident resulted in so much negative publicity that such discriminatory laws were soon abandoned.

Elsewhere, discrimination on the basis of race was also common and was upheld by the courts. In 1949, the Appeal Court of Ontario ruled that there was nothing legally wrong with a clause in property deeds that barred Jews and blacks from buying property in Beach O'Pines near Sarnia. In Dresden, Ontario, where blacks made up 17 percent of the town's 2000 people in 1950, restaurants, pool rooms, and barber and beauty shops refused patronage from non-whites. Although black organizations, particularly in Nova Scotia, struggled against the most blatant forms of discrimination, especially segregated facilities, they were unable to break down the racist attitudes that kept many of them in the ranks of the underclass. Apart from discrimination in the job market, African Canadians could expect to live in poorer housing and receive less schooling than whites.

In theory, such victimization of minority groups should have abated considerably with the passage of the Canadian Bill of Rights by the Diefenbaker government in 1960. The bill declared parliament's commitment to equality of Canadians regardless of race, religion, colour, national origin, or sex. But provincial authority over civil rights and property meant that without a constitutional amendment, the Canadian Bill of Rights applied mainly in areas covered by federal laws. The provinces moved only slowly to protect minority rights, and only after considerable political protest from minorities.

Encouraged by the black power movement in the United States, African Canadians became more assertive in their struggle against discrimination in the 1960s. A new generation of black leaders, many of them recent immigrants from the West Indies and Africa, refused to accept second-class citizenship, challenging the moderate approach of the early post-war leaders, who were usually associated with African-Canadian church congregations.

Numbers contributed to a greater community confidence. From 1955 to 1961, only 4219 Caribbean immigrants were allowed to enter Canada. Some were professionals or skilled workers; almost half were domestics who entered under the Caribbean Domestic Scheme, which was meant to maintain Canada's imperial trade and investment ties with the region and supply wealthy households with a source of cheap domestic labour. Following the reform of immigration laws, the number of West Indian immigrants increased dramatically. More than 140 000 West Indian immigrants came to Canada between 1971 and 1981, with two-thirds settling in Ontario. Their concentration in southern Ontario allowed them to establish a rich institutional culture, including social clubs, newspapers, Toronto's annual Caribana festival, and anti-racist organizations. Nonetheless, a detailed study of race relations in Toronto published in 1985 suggested that at least 10 percent of the white population of Metro Toronto was deeply racist and that the colour bar to a variety of jobs remained firm.

The plight of blacks in Nova Scotia received international attention when the city of Halifax decided to demolish Africville. Located on the shores of Bedford Basin, Africville had been home to Halifax's black population since the middle of the nineteenth century. The community had been shamefully neglected by city authorities, who had provided no water, sewage facilities, or garbage collection to its homes and had located the municipal dump nearby. In 1961, city council decided to remove the 400 citizens of Africville to make way for an industrial development on the site. Residents' protests were ignored; most whites and even a few blacks argued that urban renewal was a necessary prelude to a better future for all Haligonians. Although many residents were compensated for their property and offered alternative housing, they resented not being fully consulted and feared the loss of community that would result from the relocation.

In the wake of the demolition of Africville, the Black United Front (BUF) was founded in 1968 to intensify the struggle for change. A visit to Halifax by Stokely Carmichael, a leading African-American militant, served as a catalyst for the new organization. In an effort to defuse what appeared to be a growing militancy among blacks in Canada—a student protest against racism at Sir George Williams University (now Concordia) ended in the destruction of the university's

Africville in the 1960s.
Nova Scotia Archives and Records Management (Bob Brooks, Negatives, Sleeve 6)

computer system—the federal government offered to fund BUF and other black organizations.

Beginning in the late 1960s, provincial human rights legislation, backed up by human rights commissions with powers to investigate and prosecute cases of clear discrimination on the basis of race, sex, or religion, demonstrated a greater desire on the part of authorities to reduce systemic racism in Canada. Canadians became quite complacent about racism, comparing their society favourably to that of their southern neighbours, where race relations often boiled over into violence. Minorities, particularly Canada's Native peoples, often had a different view.

NATIVE PEOPLES FIND A VOICE

Canada's first peoples probably felt the sting of intolerance even more than immigrant groups. From 1946 to 1948, a special joint committee of the House and Senate reviewed the Indian Act. Its report demonstrated that the old assimilation goals were to continue, although there would be some reforms. In 1951,

ineffectual bans on the potlatch and the Sun Dance were lifted. Elected band councils could make decisions in areas that traditionally concerned municipal governments, but Indian Affairs could overrule these decisions. Beginning in the 1950s, the provinces began to enfranchise Natives, and Status Indians were finally granted this token of citizenship by the federal government in 1960. By this time, Native peoples, like many other subordinate groups, were becoming increasingly militant in their pursuit of fairer treatment.

A catalyst for action by Treaty Indians was the unveiling of the Trudeau government's White Paper on Indian Policy in June 1969. Ottawa planned to relinquish Native lands while at the same time removing Indians' special status, dismantling the Department of Indian Affairs, and having the provinces assume responsibilities for services to Native peoples. The Native response to the White Paper was overwhelmingly negative. The National Indian Brotherhood (NIB), which was formed in 1968 to speak for Treaty Indians, led the resistance, claiming that Indians wanted self-government and not the assimilation implied in becoming ordinary citizens of the provinces.

MORE TO THE STORY

Recovering Community

In the early 1970s, almost every adult resident of Alkali Lake, a Shuswap community of 400 people in the British Columbia interior, was an alcoholic. Phyllis Chelsea and her husband, Andy, were typical. He had been in hospital on several occasions for kidney trouble after binge drinking, and Phyllis had required medical care twice after Andy had beaten her while in a drunken stupor. One evening, after again drinking heavily, Phyllis stopped to pick up her children at their grandmother's house. There she was confronted by her eldest daughter, then only seven, who refused to go home, accusing her parents of being violent drunks. Phyllis was shocked and resolved to stop drinking immediately. Andy was initially unwilling to follow her example, until one day he was deeply struck by the many bruised, hungry faces he saw among local children on their way to school, a reflection of the effects of alcohol on families in the community.

The Chelseas began to spread their anti-alcohol message zealously on the reserve. They persuaded the band council to

make treatment for alcoholism a condition for receiving financial help. They and their converts looked after the children of reserve residents who had enrolled in Native treatment programs. As people sobered up, it soon became clear that alcohol was a symptom, not the primary cause, of the degradation of many Native peoples. The extent of sexual abuse that had occurred at the Roman Catholic–run St. John's Mission residential school near Williams Lake gradually became public. Sexual abuse had, in turn, become common in the households of Alkali alcoholics. Healing circles became crucial in allowing people to overcome the shame that had caused generations of local residents to seek comfort in drunkenness. By the early 1980s, Phyllis Chelsea could point proudly to a community in which 95 percent of the adults were sober. The children attended a new school built by the band, where elders "came to share prayers, pipe ceremonies, and songs in Shuswap," thus renewing the traditional culture that had all but died out in the wake of poverty, abuse, and despair.[9]

Native groups argued that Aboriginal peoples had a right to reassert their cultures, which had long been suppressed by government and church policies. The White Paper, if implemented, would be a final nail in the coffin for Native peoples, a policy of cultural genocide. Surprised by the vehemence of Native reaction, the Trudeau government withdrew the White Paper but offered no framework for negotiating Native demands for self-government.

During the 1970s, pressures from the NIB—the name was changed to the Assembly of First Nations in 1982—and provincial associations led the government to gradually give Native peoples the responsibility for their own education. After 1973, it became increasingly common for Native children to attend local schools controlled by their band councils, particularly in the elementary grades, but many reserves had little success in convincing Ottawa to build high schools nearby so that their children were not forced to either bus several hours a day or live in towns away from their reserves. Although the residential education system was phased out in the 1960s and 1970s, its scars remain. In 1990, the head of the Manitoba Association of Chiefs, Phil Fontaine, made a public issue of claims that had frequently been heard privately: Native children in residential schools had been victims of violence, including sexual abuse, at the hands of lay teachers and members of religious orders.

Native peoples who left the reserves for towns and cities were rarely assimilated into the larger society. Undereducated and faced with discrimination, many succumbed to lives in urban ghettos marked by poor housing, poverty, and drunkenness. Indian and Métis Friendship Centres and Native-run addiction programs helped rescue some from the worst aspects of city life, but for the most part Aboriginal leaders reckoned that reserves offered their people a better opportunity to live in prosperity and preserve their cultural inheritance.

Berger Commission hearings in the Northwest Territories.
Northern News Services Ltd.

NORTHERN FIRST NATIONS

Not all Native peoples had the option of living on reserves. Despite having signed Treaty 11 in 1921, the Mackenzie Valley First Nations had no reserves. Other Yukon Indians and Inuit had never signed treaties with the federal government. Such a situation made northern Native peoples particularly vulnerable to the burgeoning development of the post-war North. Native peoples of the Yukon and Northwest Territories were particularly vocal in rejecting the oil and natural gas pipelines proposed in the 1970s to fuel southern Canada and the United States. While some Métis of the Northwest Territories supported a pipeline as a source of jobs, a large percentage joined the Indians of the region to declare the existence of a Dene nation seeking independence within the framework of Canadian confederation.

The Dene had supporters in the white community, particularly from sections of the Roman Catholic Church. By the 1960s, Canada's churches—Roman Catholic and Protestant—had begun to reverse their centuries-old position that Native cultures were inferior and that the goal of white missionaries ought to be assimilation of Native peoples into mainstream Canadian culture. The churches began to support Native demands for an end to residential schools and for schools on reserves to be run by Natives. In the North,

Oblate missionary René Fumoleau led an effective campaign to publicize the case of the Dene against pipeline advocates.

In 1974, the Trudeau government, which supported the proposed pipeline projects, appointed Justice Thomas Berger, a former leader of the New Democratic Party (NDP) in British Columbia, to study the impact of a pipeline in the Mackenzie Valley on local residents and the environment. In his report, Berger proved sympathetic to the Dene and Inuit, who stressed the extent to which they still subsisted on local resources. They made clear their desire to hold off major developments until their land claims had been settled and they were in a position to negotiate with potential investors rather than having the Canadian government impose projects upon them. Although the government accepted Berger's call for a halt to pipeline developments for a decade, it was slow in pursuing comprehensive land-claims settlements in the North and providing aid to bands seeking to establish local businesses under Native control.

THE WOMEN'S MOVEMENT

Native peoples were not alone in questioning their position in post-war Canadian society. Women from all regions, classes, and ethnic groups increasingly challenged sexual stereotypes and double standards. Some women, inspired by the feisty women's liberation movement in the United States, joined feminist organizations to fight for full equality.

Women were not passive during the early post-war period even if few protested the well-orchestrated cult of domesticity. Homemakers organized consumers' leagues that demanded state control of the price of necessities. Although Communist and CCF women often led these movements, in Quebec, Catholic women's organizations were prominent in calls for rent control. Throughout the country, married women responded to an improving job market and the high cost of living by rejoining the labour force.

While employers and families required women's paid work, social institutions adapted slowly. There were virtually no arrangements for child care outside the home, and both single and married women returned from work to find the housework waiting. The "double day" of housework and paid work often left

women with even less leisure time than their mothers had enjoyed, although their wages sometimes allowed them to purchase labour-saving devices, prepared foods, and off-the-rack clothing. Neither at home nor at work did women receive recognition for their contribution. Housework was not perceived as "real" work, while women who worked outside the home were confronted with low wages, paternalism, outright harassment, and lack of opportunity for advancement.

Individual reactions to the obstacles facing women slowly coalesced into political action. In Quebec in 1966, Thérèse Casgrain, a leading figure in the provincial NDP and the peace group Voice of Women, helped found the Fédération des femmes du Québec (FFQ), an umbrella group of women's organizations, to fight for women's rights. In English Canada, women's groups, galvanized by leaders such as Laura Sabia, president of the Canadian Federation of University Women, and *Chatelaine* magazine editor Doris Anderson, pressured Ottawa for action. Supported by the FFQ, English-Canadian women's groups formed the Committee for the Equality of Women, whose tactics convinced the Pearson government, spurred by outspoken cabinet minister Judy LaMarsh, to create the Royal Commission on the Status of Women. Established in 1967 and chaired by journalist Florence Bird, the commission served as a catalyst to focus complaints from women of every social class in Canada. The National Action Committee on the Status of Women, an umbrella organization for the many women's groups springing up across the country, was created in 1972. It lobbied governments to ensure that the recommendations from the commission's 1970 report—which included calls for reform in education, employment, immigration, criminal and family law, and child care—would not simply gather dust.

A CULTURE OF PROTEST AND GAY RIGHTS

The women's movement emerged in the context of increasing dissent within Canadian society in the 1960s.

Expanded university campuses spawned movements for greater democratization of society, beginning with universities themselves. In the 1960s, the "New Left," a loose grouping that embraced a socialist vision of society, was transplanted from the United

States to Canada. Students for a Democratic University and like-minded groups arose on most campuses to demand that students be more involved in university decision-making and that courses have a more "critical perspective" on social problems. Sizeable numbers of New Left adherents found political homes in the left-wing Waffle group of the NDP or, in Quebec, in the left wing of the Parti Québécois. Environmental and gay rights movements were well established by the early 1970s, though their major successes occurred after 1975.

Despite laws against homosexuality, gays and lesbians established their own bars and other social gathering spots in the post-war period. In 1964, Jane Rule published *Desert of the Heart*, a novel of lesbian love, while the Association for Social Knowledge, a same-sex organization, was formed in Vancouver and the tabloid *Gay* began publication in Toronto. The unwillingness of gays and lesbians to hide their sexual orientation forced the government to consider whether it should enforce anti-gay legislation or accept that sex between consenting adults should be legal, regardless of whether those adults were of the same or different sexes.

While homosexuality lost its criminality in 1969, it did not lose its stigma. In the post-war period, under the influence of psychology, the view that sex with someone of the same gender was conscious criminal behaviour gave way to the view that homosexuality was a pathology that psychotherapy could cure. If it was an advance for gays and lesbians to have their sexual orientation viewed as within the laws of the land, they still had to fight the view that their sexual preference violated the laws of nature. As long as they were regarded as mentally deranged, they remained the target of discrimination in employment and housing and were denied rights of adoption and spousal benefits available to opposite-sex couples. Fledgling gay rights organizations pressed for an end to such discrimination and for recognition of sexual orientation as largely biologically determined, rather than as the result of reversible mental traumas.

They had their work cut out for them. As late as 1963, the RCMP persuaded the Diefenbaker government, still convinced that homosexuality and communism were perversions and therefore related, to allow it to use a "fruit machine" to root out homosexual

applicants for civil service jobs. Only the apparent unreliability of the machine in measuring erotic responses resulted in this fruity idea's demise.

THE POOR ORGANIZE

The new culture of protest among the young middle class in the 1960s encouraged a revival of lobbying organizations among working people and the poor. By the 1970s, hundreds of groups representing tenants, welfare rights advocates, single mothers, the unemployed, and other categories of the poor and powerless were organized. These groups provided emotional support and empowered individuals to make collective demands upon government to improve their lot. Demonstrations at provincial legislatures, city halls, and sometimes the homes of slumlords brought increased media attention to those who lived destitute lives within a prosperous society.

Thousands attended a conference of poor people's organizations in Ottawa in 1971 that led to the creation of a national poverty organization to fight for a guaranteed annual income and other legislation that would benefit the country's poorest citizens. In Quebec, where nationalist sentiment and social grievances spurred tens of thousands to join community groups, there was a close alliance between grassroots movements and the powerful trade unions. "Social animators," often university-educated facilitators paid by the unions, mobilized citizens and provided a link between the protests of radical baby boomers, organized workers, and the poor.

Work in such organizations led many of the underprivileged to recognize their problems as public or social issues resulting from the operations of the economic system rather than primarily individual troubles resulting from personal inadequacies. So, for example, the Unemployed Citizens' Welfare Improvement Council of Greater Vancouver demonstrated against provincial legislation in 1970 that would have required welfare recipients to work for municipalities as a precondition for receiving welfare. They were hardly on the defensive as they made their views known to the government:

> We demand a recognition of the right to the necessities of life as being separate from the right to work.

We demand it be recognized that people must have the right to refuse jobs which have no future, which do not meet union conditions and which lack adequate pollution control devices—without fear of cut-offs and other punitive action.

We demand an immediate implementation of the guaranteed annual income tied to the fluctuations of the cost of living. For the present time we consider $200 per adult and $60 per dependent child to be the minimum adequate sum.[10]

None of the above demands were met, but the province quietly dropped the proposed legislation that had sparked the demonstration.

RELIGION IN A SECULAR AGE

Mainline Christian churches faced major challenges in the post-war period. While most Canadians continued to believe in God, there was a growing minority who were agnostics or atheists. Believers were increasingly unlikely to attend church, and told pollsters that they, not their ministers, made the moral decisions that shaped their lives. Many mainstream Christians could not distinguish between the beliefs of their church and those of other Christian denominations and saw their church merely as a Sunday social obligation.

While some people were abandoning organized religion, claiming their church was not addressing social issues, fundamentalist Protestant denominations, with an otherworldly orientation, were gaining in membership. In the 1950s and early 1960s, the mainstream Protestant denominations tried to strike a balance in their views, supporting social programs such as medicare while staking out more conservative ground on other issues, opposing homosexuality, abortion, divorce, and jobs for married women.

Ironically, while they opposed greater social opportunities for women, Protestant churches offered women opportunities to demonstrate leadership skills in social and charitable activities and missionary roles. The United Church, the largest Protestant church, reported 401 757 members in its Women's Auxiliary and Women's Missionary Society in 1955. In keeping with their notions of distinct gender roles, the churches generally reserved their paid positions and their senior decision-making bodies for men. The Presbyterian Church set up a committee on the role of women in the church in the 1950s and found little support for the ordination of women or even the election of women elders.

By the 1970s, the mainstream Protestant churches, influenced by the growing women's movement, which had a strong component within the churches, began to change their views on gender roles within society and within the church. While progress, particularly in the ordination of women, occurred slowly—the Anglican Church agreed to ordain women in 1976—the churches joined other social groups in calling for state-subsidized quality day care and greater economic equality between the sexes. Others supported community groups active in combating child abuse and violence against women.

At the same time, the Roman Catholic Church was undergoing its own struggles and soul-searching, as liberal trends in Rome played themselves out in an institution with an extremely conservative history. Liberal elements preached "the preferential option of the poor" and were likely to support the ordination of women and the relaxing of celibacy requirements. They offended conservatives who stressed the need for the church to concern itself with both the rich and the poor and to respect the God-given hierarchy of the church. Congregations increasingly failed to heed the pronouncements of that hierarchy on moral issues. Despite the church's frequently reaffirmed ban on the use of contraceptives, the birth rate among Roman Catholics failed to rise above the rate for non–Roman Catholics. Quebec, though nominally overwhelmingly Roman Catholic, had the country's lowest birth rate by the 1970s. Pollsters found that most Roman Catholics, like most Canadians generally, supported a woman's right to abortion, despite the official position of their church.

Fewer Roman Catholics were going to church at all. In Montreal, church attendance dropped by half in the 1960s. Despite reforms designed to appeal to the secular generation, the church had difficulty recruiting enough priests and nuns to minister to their congregations. In 1946, there were 2000 new priests in Quebec; in 1970, only 100. Convents, the mainstay of the religious workforce, were deserted as jobs in teaching, nursing, and social work opened up for women in the paid labour force and feminist ideology challenged the church's teachings on the role of women. Although Protestant churches gradually opened their ministries to women, the Roman Catholic Church successfully resisted movements from within to end its long-standing practice of maintaining an all-male celibate priesthood.

CONCLUSION

The post-war period witnessed an acceleration of the long-established shift in Canada from small-scale rural communities toward an urban, industrial society in which market forces shaped relations among individuals. In such a society, there was continuous tension between the marketplace ideology that defines citizens as consumers of products, interested mainly in individual and household accumulation, and human need for identity and contact with a broader community. For some, the extensive organization of community groups in the suburbs recreated a sense of belonging. Others sought a sense of community on the basis of ethnicity, gender, political perspectives, sexual orientation, or religious affiliation. While this search for community produced a Canadian society that was pluralistic, it also promoted fragmentation within and challenged efforts to create a national culture that could withstand the impact of New York and Hollywood.

NOTES

1 On Gerda Munsinger and her treatment by the Canadian authorities, see Franca Iacovetta, *Gatekeepers: Reshaping Immigrant Lives in Postwar Canada* (Toronto: Between the Lines, 2006) and Bryan D. Palmer, *Canada's 1960s: Historicizing the Ironies of Identity* (Toronto: University of Toronto Press, forthcoming).

2 Marcel Martel, *Not This Time: Canadians, Public Policy, and the Marijuana Question 1961–1975* (Toronto: University of Toronto Press, 2006), 168.

3 Myrna Kostash, "Dissing Feminist Sexuality," *Canadian Forum* (September 1996), 16.

4 Kenneth McRoberts and Dale Posgate, *Quebec: Social Change and Political Crisis*, 2nd ed. (Toronto: McClelland & Stewart, 1980), 53.

5 Cited in Harold Chorney, *City of Dreams: Social Theory and the Urban Experience* (Scarborough, ON: Nelson, 1990), 202.

6 Veronica Strong-Boag, "'Their Side of the Story': Women's Voices from Ontario Suburbs, 1945–1960," in *A Diversity of Women, 1945–1980*, ed. Joy Parr (Toronto: University of Toronto Press, 1995), 53.

7 Franca Iacovetta, *Such Hardworking People: Italian Immigrants in Postwar Toronto* (Montreal and Kingston: McGill-Queen's University Press, 1992), 77.

8 Denise Chong, *The Concubine's Children: Portrait of a Family Divided* (Toronto: Viking, 1994), 228.

9 Dan Smith, *The Seventh Fire: The Struggle for Aboriginal Government* (Toronto: Key Porter, 1993), 57.

10 Library and Archives Canada, Grace McInnis Papers, vol. 4, File "Citizen Participation, 1970."

RELATED READINGS IN THIS SERIES

From *Nation and Society: Readings in Post-Confederation Canadian History*

Mona Gleason, "Psychology and the Construction of the 'Normal' Family in Postwar Canada, 1945–60," 298–319.

Gary Kinsman, "'Character Weaknesses' and 'Fruit Machines': Towards an Analysis of the Anti-Homosexual Security Campaign in the Canadian Civil Service," 342–61.

James Overton, "A Newfoundland Culture?" 390–404.

James W. St. G. Walker, "Allegories and Orientations in African-Canadian Historiography: The Spirit of Africville," 405–15.

From Primary Documents CD-ROM, Volume II

Domestic Workers Need Your Support!
Remarks on Aboriginal Treaty Rights
International Women's Day, 1978
Colonialism in Our Backyard
Surviving Nuclear Threats

Selected Reading

The social history of the post-war period is explored broadly in Robert Rutherdale and Magda Fahrni, eds., *Creating Postwar Canada: Community, Diversity and Dissent, 1945–1975* (Vancouver: UBC Press, 2007) and Nancy Christie and Michael Gauvreau, eds., *Cultures of Citizenship in Post-war Canada, 1940–1955* (Montreal: McGill-Queen's University Press, 2004). A Quebec perspective is found in Magda Fahrni, *Household Politics: Montreal Families and Postwar Reconstruction* (Toronto: University of Toronto Press, 2005).

On baby boomers, see Douglas Owram, *Born at the Right Time: A History of the Baby Boom in Canada* (Toronto: University of Toronto Press, 1996). On post-war education, see Paul Axelrod, *Scholars and Dollars: Politics, Economics, and Universities of Ontario, 1945–1980* (Toronto: University of Toronto Press, 1982) and Henry Milner, *The Long Road to Reform: Restructuring Public Education in Quebec* (Montreal: McGill-Queen's University Press, 1986).

For a critical analysis of post-war social values, see Len Kuffert, *A Great Duty: Canadian Responses to Modern Life and Mass Culture, 1939–1967* (Montreal: McGill-Queen's University Press, 2003). Canadian suburbanization is addressed in Richard Harris, *Creeping Conformity: How Canada Became Suburban, 1900–1960* (Toronto: University of Toronto Press, 2004); Stanley R. Barrett, *Paradise: Class, Commuters, and Ethnicity in Rural Ontario* (Toronto: University of Toronto Press, 1994); Paul-André Linteau, "Canadian Suburbanization in a North American Context: Does the Border Make a Difference?" in *Cities and Urbanization: Canadian Historical Perspectives*, ed. Gilbert A. Stelter (Toronto: Copp Clark Pitman, 1990), 208–24; and Valerie Korinek, *Roughing It in the Suburbs: Reading Chatelaine in the Fifties and Sixties* (Toronto: University of Toronto Press, 2000).

Immigration policies are analyzed in Franca Iacovetta, *Gatekeepers: Reshaping Immigrant Lives in Postwar Canada* (Toronto: Between the Lines, 2006); Ninette Kelley and Michael Trebilcock, *The Making of the Mosaic: A History of Canadian Immigration Policy* (Toronto: University of Toronto Press, 1998); Donald H. Avery, *Reluctant Host: Canada's Response to Immigrant Workers, 1896–1994* (Toronto: McClelland & Stewart, 1995); Reginald Whitaker, *Double Standard: The Secret History of Canadian Immigration* (Toronto: Lester and Orpen Dennys, 1987); and Freda Hawkins, *Canada and Immigration: Public Policy and Public Concern* (Toronto: Institute of Public Administration of Canada, 1972). Among excellent works on immigrant and ethnic experiences are Franca Iacovetta, *Such Hardworking People: Italian Immigrants in Postwar Toronto* (Montreal: McGill-Queen's University Press, 1992); Frances Swyripa,

Wedded to the Cause: Ukrainian-Canadian Women and Ethnic Identity, 1891–1991 (Toronto: University of Toronto Press, 1993); Jean Burnet, ed., *Looking into My Sister's Eyes: An Exploration in Women's History* (Toronto: Multicultural History Society of Ontario, 1986); Bridglal Pachai, *Beneath the Clouds of the Promised Land: The Survival of Nova Scotia Blacks*, vol. 2, *1800–1989* (Halifax: Black Education Association, 1990); and Edgar Wickberg, ed., *From China to Canada: A History of the Chinese Communities in Canada* (Toronto: McClelland & Stewart, 1982). On the Canadian Jewish Congress and the struggle for religious tolerance, see Janine Stingel, *Social Discredit: Anti-Semitism, Social Credit and the Jewish Response* (Montreal: McGill-Queen's University Press, 2000).

The lives of Canada's Native peoples are explored in the works by Arthur J. Ray and J.R. Miller cited in earlier chapters and Kenneth Coates, *Canada's Colonies: A History of the Yukon and Northwest Territories* (Toronto: Lorimer, 1985); Boyce Richardson, *Strangers Devour the Land*, 2nd ed. (Vancouver: Douglas and McIntyre, 1991); Sally Weaver, *Making Canadian Indian Policy: The Hidden Agenda, 1968–1970* (Toronto: University of Toronto Press, 1980); J.R. Miller, *Shingwauk's Vision: A History of Native Residential Schools* (Toronto: University of Toronto Press, 1996); and Celia Haig-Brown, *Resistance and Renewal: Surviving the Indian Residential School* (Vancouver: Arsenal Pulp Press, 1988). Saskatchewan's Native policies are assessed in David M. Quiring, *CCF Colonialism in Northern Saskatchewan: Battling Parish Priests, Bootleggers, and Fur Sharks* (Vancouver: UBC Press, 2004).

On the post-war ideal of families and sexuality, see Elise Chenier, *Strangers in Our Midst: Sex, Psychiatry and the Law at Mid-Century* (Toronto: Canadian Scholars' Press, 2006); Mona Lee Gleason, *Normalizing the Ideal: Psychology, Schooling, and the Family in Postwar Canada* (Toronto: University of Toronto Press, 1999); Mary Louise Adams, *The Trouble with Normal: Postwar Youth and the Making of Heterosexuality* (Toronto: University of Toronto Press, 1997); Richard Cavell, ed., *Love, Hate, and Fear in Canada's Cold War* (Toronto: University of Toronto Press, 2004); and Amanda Glasbeek, *Moral Regulation and Governance in Canada: History, Context and Critical Issues* (Toronto: Canadian Scholars' Press, 2006). On the debates about narcotics use, see Michael Martel, *Not This Time: Canadians, Public Policy, and the Marijuana Question 1961–1975* (Toronto: University of Toronto Press, 2006).

Protest movements in this period are surveyed in Bryan D. Palmer, *Canada's 1960s: Historicizing the Ironies of Identity* (Toronto: University of Toronto Press, forthcoming).

On the women's movement, see Ruth Roach Pierson et al., eds., *Canadian Women's Issues*, vol. 1: *Strong Voices* (Toronto: Lorimer, 1993); Ruth Roach Pierson et al., eds., *Canadian Women's Issues*, vol. 2: *Bold Visions* (Toronto: Lorimer, 1995); Constance Backhouse and David Flaherty, eds., *Challenging Times: The Women's Movement in Canada and the United States* (Montreal: McGill-Queen's University Press, 1992); and Jeri Dawn Wine and Janice L. Ristock, eds., *Women and Social Change: Feminist Activism in Canada* (Toronto: Lorimer, 1991). On African-Canadian women, see Peggy Bristow, Dionne Brand, Linda Carty, Afua P. Cooper, Sylvia Hamilton, and Adrienne Shadd, *"We're Rooted Here and They Can't Pull Us Up": Essays in African Canadian Women's History* (Toronto: University of Toronto Press, 1994). On the changing position of women in Canada, important works include Angus McLaren and Arlene Tigar McLaren, *The Bedroom and the State: The Changing Practices and Politics of Contraception and Abortion in Canada* (Toronto: McClelland & Stewart, 1997); Pat Armstrong and Hugh Armstrong, *The Double Ghetto: Canadian Women and Their Segregated Work*, 3rd ed. (Toronto: McClelland & Stewart, 1994); and Mary Kinnear, *A Female Economy: Women's Work in a Prairie Province, 1870–1970* (Montreal: McGill-Queen's University Press, 1999).

The state campaign against homosexuals is discussed in Gary Kinsman and Patrizia Gentile, *The Canadian War on "Queers": National Security as Sexual Regulation* (Vancouver: UBC Press, 2005); Daniel J. Robinson and David Kemmel, "The Queer Career of Homosexual Vetting in Cold War Canada," *Canadian Historical Review* 75, no. 3 (September 1994), 319–45; and Gary Kinsman, "'Character Weaknesses' and 'Fruit Machines': Towards an Analysis of the Anti-Homosexual Security Campaign in the Canadian Civil Service," *Labour/Le Travail* 35 (Spring 1995), 133–61, and *Regulation of Desire*, 2nd ed. (Montreal: Black Rose, 1996). On lesbians, see Sharon Dale Stone, *Lesbians in Canada* (Toronto: Between the Lines, 1990); Becki Ross, "Down at the Whorehouse? Reflections on Christian Community Service and Female Sex Deviance at Toronto's Street Haven, 1965–1969," *Atlantis* 23, no. 1 (Fall 1998), 48–59; and Line Chamberland, "Remembering Lesbian Bars: Montreal, 1955–1975," in *Rethinking Canada: The Promise of Women's History*, 3rd ed., ed. Veronica Strong-Boag and Anita Clair Feldman (Toronto: Oxford University Press, 1997), 402–23. The beginnings of "queer" militancy are explored in Tom Warner, *Never Going Back: A History of Queer Activism in Canada* (Toronto: University of Toronto Press, 2002) and Donald W. Macleod, *A Brief History of Gay: Canada's First Gay Tabloid, 1964–1966* (Toronto: Homewood Books, 2003).

Religion in post-war Canada is discussed in Tony Clarke, *Behind the Mitre: The Moral Leadership Crisis in the Canadian Catholic Church* (Toronto: HarperCollins, 1995); Gregory Baum, *Compassion and Solidarity* (Toronto: CBC Enterprises, 1987); John Webster Grant, *The Church in the Canadian Era* (Toronto: Welch Publishing, 1988); Pierre Berton, *The Comfortable Pew: A Critical Look at Christianity and the Religious Establishment in the New Age* (Toronto: McClelland & Stewart, 1965); Alan L. Hayes, *Anglicans in Canada: Controversies and Identity in Historical Perspective* (Champaign: University of Illinois Press, 2004); and Reginald Bibby, *Fragmented Gods: The Poverty and Potential of Religion in Canada* (Toronto: Irwin, 1987).

CHAPTER 19

Creating a Canadian Culture, 1945–1975

TIMELINE

1948	Refus global published; Barbara Ann Scott wins Olympic figure-skating title
1953	Stratford Festival launched
1957	Canada Council created
1958	Willie O'Ree breaks colour barrier in National Hockey League
1961	Fitness and Amateur Sports Act passed
1969	Pierre Vallières publishes White Niggers of America
1970	CRTC rules require radio stations to devote 30 percent of airplay to Canadian records
1971	Mon Oncle Antoine released
1972	Canada wins first Canada-Soviet hockey series
1973	Maria Campbell publishes Halfbreed

In 1974, a movie directed by Michel Brault became the first Canadian film to win the prize for best director at the Cannes Film Festival. *Les ordres* was a film about the arrests that occurred in Quebec after the War Measures Act was declared in 1970. The five fictional characters arrested in the film include a socialist doctor who founded a medical clinic in a working-class area, a social worker whose clientele are disenfranchised citizens, a trade union militant in the textile industry and his homemaker wife, and an unemployed musician who is a social activist in municipal politics in Montreal. None has any links with the Front de Libération du Quebec (FLQ) or other terrorist groups. They are arrested because they are regarded as suspicious by the Canadian and Quebec governments owing to their work on behalf of the oppressed in Quebec society. Their protestations of innocence and efforts to compel the authorities to divulge the evidence that they are conspirators trying to create an independent Quebec through violent means are rebuffed. The political elite in Ottawa and Quebec City denounced the film, charging that it distorted the truth about Canadian politics and encouraged people to support the movement for an independent and socialist Quebec.

Quebecers were not alone in attempting to define a new identity for themselves in the period following the Second World War. Like Brault's social rebels, many Anglo-Canadians and ethnic minorities, including Canada's Native peoples, challenged the social values that had been associated with Canada in the past and criticized the mass consumer culture sweeping North America. Much of Canadian literature, theatre, film, art, and music reflected efforts to establish the collective identities of various groups within Canada. Some scholars argue that this approach differentiated between Canada's cultural production and that of the United States, whose heroes were involved mainly in establishing their personal identities and drawing the boundaries between themselves and larger society. This chapter describes some of the cultural developments of the post-war period and the popular entertainments that became an important form of recreation for Canadians.

QUEBEC'S CULTURAL REVOLUTION

Quebec's artists had begun to challenge the status quo well before the Quiet Revolution of the 1960s. Although the Duplessis years would later be characterized as *la grande noirceur*, or the Dark Age, they nonetheless witnessed important cultural developments. In 1948, painter Paul-Émile Borduas and other Quebec artists published

Paul-Émile Borduas, *Les carquois fleuris*, 1947. Borduas had an enormous influence on post-war Quebec painting. He studied at the École des Beaux-Arts in Montreal and later moved to Paris. Borduas opposed all formalism in art, arguing that each painter must experiment by letting individual feeling determine both the subject and style of their work.
The Montreal Museum of Fine Arts

Refus global, a rejection of the narrow world of religious and political orthodoxy within which artists and writers were expected to work in their province. The manifesto resulted in Borduas's exile from Quebec but inspired many poets and painters to become innovative in their choices of the form and content of their work.

Quebec's novelists of the immediate post-war years abandoned the pre-war focus on rural Quebec in favour of an urban setting, reflecting the lives of most Quebecers. Roger Lemelin, creator of *Les Plouffes* (*The Plouffe Family*) (1948), dealt frankly with issues of social class in several works. In *Alexandre Chevenant* (*The Cashier*) (1954), Gabrielle Roy used a portrayal of an unhappy Montreal cashier to depict the economic and cultural alienation of urban society. Roy, who grew up in St. Boniface, Manitoba, also wrote novels, short stories, and non-fiction articles about her childhood and years as a teacher in the West. Her realistic works are in sharp contrast to *La Belle Bête* (*Mad Shadows*), published in 1959 by a young Marie-Claire Blais, who blazed a trail with her surreal novel in which chronology and the boundary between the real and the imagined are deliberately left vague.

Culture and Sovereignty

The society-wide questioning of existing structures and social values unleashed by the Quiet Revolution resulted in a flowering of Quebec culture, and the climate of nationalist pride created a strong home market for artistic expressions of every kind. By the 1960s, political commitment, particularly support for sovereignty, marked much of the celebrated literature in Quebec. Hubert Aquin's *Prochain Épisode* (1965), a stream-of-consciousness account of an imprisoned sovereignist member of a group much like the FLQ, won widespread acclaim. Its general message was that as long as Quebec remained within confederation, it would be a colonized society in which individual Francophones could find no real identity. Such ideas echoed Jacques Godbout's *Le Couteau sur la table* (*Knife on the Table*), published two years earlier. Godbout's principal character is a young Francophone whose life is aimless and who becomes the lover of an equally aimless but wealthy Anglophone woman; he begins to discover himself and break from his shallow lover only after he reads of the exploits of the nascent FLQ.

Non-fiction best-sellers also often extolled Quebec's separation from Canada. FLQ activist Pierre Vallières's autobiographic account, *Nègres blancs d'Amérique* (*White Niggers of America*), published in 1969, claimed that Francophones in Quebec were treated as an underclass in the province much as African Americans were treated in the United States, and would continue to be oppressed until they achieved sovereignty.

Quebec nationalism and the view that Quebec would be better off as an independent nation rather than a province of Canada also became prevalent themes in Quebec plays and songs. Michel Tremblay, who emerged as the province's leading playwright, broke with Quebec's theatrical tradition to have his characters speak the language and intonation of the Quebec streets rather than standard Parisian French. The language of the street was often referred to as *joual*, a reference to the common pronunciation of *cheval*, the French word for horse. While nationalists generally defended *joual*'s richness of expression, some Quebec intellectuals regarded the street slang of the province as infected with anglicisms.

Quebec's popular music also reflected the new nationalism. In the 1950s, Francophone radio stations were largely limited to pop music from France, local attempts to copy the metropolitan sound, and standard North American English fare. Only Félix Leclerc, a Quebec nationalist whose traditional French-Canadian music also won him an audience in France, stood out as a distinctly Québécois talent. By the end of the 1960s, the airwaves were dominated by homegrown talents such as Robert Charlebois, Claude Dubois, and Pauline Julien, who drew on traditional French-Canadian folk music, rock and roll, and influences from France to create a new sound. Gilles Vigneault became the major songwriter of the sovereignist movement. His "Mon pays" helped define the yearning of many Quebecers for an independent national existence, while his "Gens du pays" became the anthem of the sovereignist movement.

Film and Broadcasting

State subsidies, both provincial and federal, were crucial to the creation of many new cultural groups and products in post-war Quebec. Without state support, many new theatre groups could not have performed,

and publishing houses would have been unable to take the risk of publishing new titles.

In no area was state funding more crucial than in film. The National Film Board (NFB) was the pivotal player in film financing before the late 1970s, when the Parti Québécois government established a provincial film board. Quebec Francophones wanted to see movies in their own language and about places and events familiar to them, and locally produced movies drew large audiences. An early success was Claude Jutra's *Mon Oncle Antoine* (1971), which also drew good crowds for its English-language version, though the play's depiction of small-town Quebec demonstrated the haughty control of the English over the French-Canadian majority.

Television in Quebec, as elsewhere in North America, became an important medium for cultural production and political awareness. In the early 1950s, Radio-Canada, the French-language CBC, joined its English-speaking counterpart in branching out from radio to television. During the Duplessis years, information programs on Radio-Canada became an important source of liberal viewpoints. With its funding coming from the federal government, Radio-Canada was largely impervious to Union Nationale bullying. By contrast, Quebec newspapers, fearful of losing provincial government advertising, offered little criticism of the Duplessis regime. Radio-Canada produced a number of celebrities, one of whom was René Lévesque, the future premier, who in the 1950s hosted a popular weekly information show on international events. By the late sixties, Quebec federalists accused Radio-Canada journalists of using the network to broadcast sovereignist propaganda.

Radio-Canada and Radio-Québec, the Quebec broadcasting service established by the provincial government in 1968, provided Quebec entertainers with important outlets for their creative talents. The massive outpouring of Francophone literature, movies, television shows, and recordings demonstrated the extent to which the French language insulated Francophones from North American culture, but such insulation could easily be exaggerated. Most of the major American television shows, movies, and best-selling novels were available in French versions. Young people snapped up copies of the latest recordings by the Beatles or Rolling Stones or whoever was currently in the top 10.

Denys Arcand

Quebec's most successful director and screenwriter to date had begun to make his mark by the early 1970s. Denys Arcand's life in many respects mirrored the larger social changes that were taking place in Quebec.

Born in 1941 in the village of Deschambault, Quebec, about 65 kilometres southwest of Quebec City, Arcand lived in a deeply Roman Catholic home in which his mother, who had trained as a nun, was particularly intent that her children should become devout followers of the faith. He spent his high school years in a Jesuit college, then studied history at the Université de Montréal, emerging with a master's degree in 1963. Like many young men of the Quiet Revolution period, he experienced a great deal of religious skepticism. His first post-university job was as a filmmaker for the National Film Board (NFB), producing historical films. In one of them, his thinly disguised depiction of the nuns of New France as fanatics was emblematic of the change that had occurred from one generation to the next in the fortunes of the church in Quebec.

In 1970, Arcand directed a three-hour documentary on textile workers in Quebec called *On est au coton*. The title had a double entendre, suggesting that it was not only about workers in the cotton trade, but also about people reduced to the level of sheep. The film's scathing indictment of capitalists' treatment of their workers caused the NFB, still reeling from Cold War purges, to halt release of the film after only a few showings. NFB intervention ironically gave Arcand a great deal of publicity in Quebec for what otherwise might have been dismissed as an overly long documentary. By 1976, Arcand's growing international reputation as a filmmaker forced the NFB to finally remove all restrictions on the viewing of the film.

Arcand's follow-up film to *On est au coton* was also a political documentary, *Québec: Duplessis et après* (1972). It interposed shots of recent developments in Quebec with footage of the Duplessis years to attempt to burst the bubble of politicians who pretended that the corruption and demagogy of the Duplessis years had evaporated in post–Quiet Revolution Quebec. A year later, Arcand released a feature film, *Rejeane Padovani*, that went further, presenting Quebec's politicians as the corrupt puppets of Mafia figures who really

Denys Arcand at the 2004 Academy Awards.
Laura Rauch/CP Photo Archive

ran the province. The radicalism of this Quebec director, which might have resulted in his being crushed by the combination of his state and church opponents a decade earlier, had proven by the mid-1970s to be an asset in his quest for artistic and commercial approval.

A committed separatist, Arcand supported Parti Québécois efforts during the referendum of 1980 to win sovereignty for Quebec. His 1982 film on the referendum, *Le confort et l'indifférence*, mocked both the "yes" and "no" sides of the referendum debate for their lack of vision about Quebec's future and their focus on such seeming trivia as whether the price of gasoline would go up or down in an independent Quebec.

Arcand's commercial achievements extended beyond the French-speaking world with the surprise success in 1986 of *The Decline of the American Empire*, a film of repartee in which a group of French-Canadian friends talk about sexual exploits and politics. The film won a number of important film prizes, but Arcand resisted pressures to make movies that focused less on Quebec and might win him broader appeal. His next film, *Jesus of Montreal* (1989), examined a world of actors who cobbled together a living in Montreal, portraying biblical figures part of the time while also starring in pornography flicks and beer commercials. It was a critical success but was of little interest to American audiences. Nonetheless, in 2004, Arcand's film, *The Barbarian Invasions,* a film in which one of the key characters in *The Decline of the American Empire* is dying, became a huge international success with its humorous dialogues about life, sex, and history. Though the film, like most of Arcand's efforts, focused on talk rather than action, Arcand won the Best Director award at the Oscars and the film was named the Best Foreign Film of that year.

Anglophone Culture in Quebec

Quebec Anglophones made significant contributions to Quebec and Canadian culture. From his base in Montreal, Nova Scotia–born novelist Hugh MacLennan examined conflicting social values in *Two Solitudes* (1945), which focused on English-French dualism, and in *The Precipice* (1948), which examined the impact of American culture on small-town values. Despite their didactic tone and Canadian content, MacLennan's books sold well internationally.

Mordecai Richler became the best known of the Jewish novelists of Montreal, gaining an international reputation with his novels, including *The Apprenticeship of Duddy Kravitz* (1959) and *St. Urbain's Horseman* (1971), which provided vivid portrayals of the Jewish experience in the city. Leonard Cohen, another product of Montreal's Jewish community, achieved national fame as a poet and novelist and international recognition as a composer of poetic popular-music lyrics. In his plays such as *On the Job* (1975) and *Balconville* (1979), playwright David Fennario spoke out for the working-class Anglophones. Fennario tried to promote solidarity of social class across the language divide as an alternative to ties based solely on language. His view was that just as the exploiters in Quebec spoke both languages, so did the exploited.

LITERARY DEVELOPMENTS OUTSIDE QUEBEC

For obvious reasons, English-speaking Canadians were more susceptible than Quebecers to the American media onslaught in the post-war period. There was much debate among intellectuals and artists about what, if anything, differentiated Canadian and American cultural identity. Like their Francophone counterparts, many Anglophone artists struggled to define regional and ethnic identities, and the rate of cultural production in many areas of the arts was impressive.

In the late 1940s and 1950s, writers from a number of regions—including Thomas Raddall and Ernest Buckler from the Maritimes, Ontario's Morley Callaghan and Hugh Garner, and the West's W.O. Mitchell, Sheila Watson, and Adele Wiseman—were gaining a national audience. Minority cultures brought a rich complexity to literary production that was hitherto dominated by the descendants of British immigrants. Although not prolific, Wiseman created a moving account of the experience of Jewish immigrants in the Prairies in her novel *The Sacrifice* (1956). John Marlyn, in *Under the Ribs of Death* (1957), dealt with the experiences of the son of Hungarian immigrants in the north end of Winnipeg and expressed the confusion of many newcomers as they faced an environment that reviled their native cultures yet denied them a firm place within the dominant Anglo-Canadian culture.

Female writers began to come into their own in the post-war period. In *The Swamp Angel* (1954), Ethel Wilson made a hero of a woman who leaves her husband and wealthy home for a life of adventure in remote areas. Although the book met a mixed critical reception at the time, Wilson's novel would be embraced by feminists in the 1960s. Margaret Laurence's novels and short stories, many peopled by the fictional characters of Manawaka, clearly a replica of her hometown of Neepawa, Manitoba, were best-sellers. Her small-town characters, searching for moral values that made more sense than the prudishness and bigotry that surrounded them, had resonance for many Canadians, and many women identified with the struggles of her female characters to defy society's stifling restraints. Not surprisingly, Laurence was influenced by Ethel Wilson, with whom she corresponded frequently. Alice Munro, whose short stories focused on rural Ontario, became a favourite with many Canadians. Like Laurence, she stripped away the veneer of conventional morality to look at the emotions that women experienced as they tried to find both meaning and passion in their lives. Margaret Atwood even more clearly identified with women's liberation and Canadian nationalism with her novels *The Edible Woman* (1969) and *Surfacing* (1972). Mavis Gallant, a Canadian expatriate in France, was internationally respected for her brilliant short stories, dealing sometimes with Canadian themes but more often with the lives of expatriates like herself.

Two male novelists also developed international reputations for their work. Timothy Findley's plays, novels, and short stories had political themes, including the horrors of war, the extent of state manipulation in people's lives, and the issue of how and why people are labelled as mad. When his novel *Famous Last Words* appeared in 1977, it became an instant classic. Findley was Canada's leading openly homosexual writer, and some of his short stories explored homosexual relationships. Less overtly political were the novels of Robertson Davies, which had a more psychological focus. His books, such as *Fifth Business* (1970), won huge audiences.

Among Francophone writers outside Quebec, the most distinguished was Antonine Maillet. In 1979, she won France's major literary prize, the Prix Goncourt, for *Pélagie-la-Charrette*, a fictional work examining the theme of Acadian expulsion. An earlier work, *La Sagouine*, had gained a wide audience and provided Canadians with a fictional character as enduring as Longfellow's *Evangeline*.

Few Native authors of fiction developed a national reputation before 1975. Occasionally, white authors made notable efforts to sensitively describe the lives of Canada's Aboriginal peoples. Playwright George Ryga's *The Ecstasy of Rita Joe* (1970) and novelist Rudy Wiebe's *The Temptations of Big Bear* (1973) played a role in drawing mainstream society's attention to the oppression that characterized Canada's treatment of the descendants of its original inhabitants. While fictional

works by Natives had yet to make best-seller lists, several non-fiction works were influential. Harold Cardinal's *The Unjust Society* (1969) and Shuswap chief George Manuel's *The Fourth World* (1974) placed before a broad public the perspectives of Natives clamouring for dramatic legislative changes in Canadian-Native relations.

Native autobiographical works also attracted attention. In her 1973 autobiography *Halfbreed*, Maria Campbell described the dire poverty of her childhood in northern Saskatchewan. While Métis traditions partly compensated for grim living conditions and racial discrimination, the death of Campbell's mother in 1952 put an end to this source of solace. Only 12 years old at the time, Maria struggled to hold together her family of seven brothers and sisters and her proud but discouraged father. She married at the age of 15, but the relationship quickly deteriorated. Campbell drifted across western Canada, becoming a prostitute and drug addict in Vancouver and later doing low-paid "women's work"—cooking, waitressing, and hairstyling. In the late 1960s, she became a militant Native activist in Alberta. The popularity of her account of her struggles as a Native person and a woman indicated a growing willingness of Canadians to listen to voices from the margins of society.

The increase in the production of serious literature in Canada in the post-war period was more than matched by skyrocketing sales for formula romances. In the 1950s, Harlequin was a struggling Winnipeg publisher. Its empire grew as it convinced booksellers of the vast popularity of its escapist plots, mainly among female consumers. By the late 1980s, Harlequin had sold more than 200 million books in more than 100 countries.

Despite the variety and quality of Canada's post-war literature, Canadian universities were slow to include Canadian publications in their course curricula. The upsurge of Canadian nationalism of the late 1960s and early 1970s changed this colonial attitude. "Can Lit" gradually became a mainstay of many English departments. At the same time, there was a massive increase in the production of academic works on the history, politics, and sociology of Canada, many of which were assisted by grants from the federally funded Canada Council or Social Sciences and Humanities Research Council, the latter established in

Margaret Atwood

Margaret Atwood was the best-selling Canadian author of the twentieth century. Born in Ottawa in 1939, Atwood spent her childhood between Toronto, where her father taught biology at the University of Toronto, and northern Ontario, where he conducted research. After completing a bachelor's degree in English at the University of Toronto, she studied in the United States, earning a master's degree at Harvard. Her publishing career began with her first book of poetry, *The Circle Game,* in 1966. It won the Governor General's Award for poetry, but poets in Canada cannot earn a living from their publications, and Atwood earned her keep by lecturing at the University of British Columbia, Sir George Williams University, the University of Alberta, and York University from 1964 to 1972. Her first novel, *The Edible Woman,* appeared in 1969, followed by *Surfacing* in 1972. That year, Atwood also published her first book of Canadian literary criticism, *Survival: A Thematic Guide to Canadian Literature.*

A prolific writer, Atwood became a public figure in Canada, defending causes raised in both her fictional and non-fictional writings. An ardent nationalist, feminist, and defender of civil liberties, she spoke out against Toronto police raids on gay bath houses in 1981 and the Canada–United States Free Trade Agreement in 1988.

Atwood's international reputation took off with the publication of *The Handmaid's Tale* in 1986, an eerie futuristic account of American society in which the subordination of women to men was total. As Atwood told interviewers, she simply pasted together historical accounts of the treatment of women to create the dystopia of *The Handmaid's Tale.* The book won the Governor General's Award for fiction in 1986 and Atwood's first of four nominations for Great Britain's prestigious Booker Prize, a prize she finally won for *The Blind Assassin* in 2000.

Margaret Atwood.
Courtesy of McClelland & Stewart. Photo by Nigel Dickson

Atwood's work covers a variety of themes and locales, but Canadian history is central to much of it. From her poetry collection *The Journals of Susanna Moodie* (1970) to her novel *Alias Grace* (1996), the latter dealing with the complexities surrounding a nineteenth-century Ontario murderer, Atwood demonstrates an abiding interest in uncovering the past of her country and particularly its women.

1977. The view that Canada was the "peaceable kingdom," once touted by historians who focused on the supposedly placid constitutional evolution of the country, was challenged by new social historians, who focused on the class, gender, and ethnic conflicts that shaped the nation.

THEATRE AND FILM

Since its founding in 1957, the Canada Council has played a major role in supporting theatre and film production in Canada. Provincial and sometimes municipal government grants also helped encourage cultural production. The town of Stratford, Ontario, demonstrated the potential for theatre in Canada when local business people launched the Stratford Festival in July 1953. Modelling their first theatre in part on Shakespearean designs, the festival's directors provided a blend of Shakespeare and other drama aimed at both the southern Ontario and tourist markets. Stratford was eventually joined by summer festivals in many communities across Canada.

Professional theatres opened in most urban centres, initially concentrating, like Stratford, on the classics. Unable to compete with better-financed theatres a short drive away, many small-town playhouses closed. Canadian playwrights had difficulty convincing theatre directors to consider using their plays before the nationalism of the 1960s produced a sea change in attitudes toward homegrown culture. In the lean years of the 1950s, only CBC radio and television offered playwrights such as John Coulter and Lister Sinclair an audience for their work.

By the 1970s, many Canadian playwrights were having their works staged at major theatres, which began to include Canadian fare among the classics and Broadway imports. Producing new Canadian drama became the raison d'être of many new alternative theatres, such as the Touchstone Theatre in Vancouver, the 25th Street Theatre in Saskatoon, and the Tarragon and Theatre Passe Muraille in Toronto. The Mummers' Troupe and the Mulgrave Road troupe were the most successful of the early alternative theatre groups in Atlantic Canada. Like the Company of Sirens in Ontario, the Mulgrave Road troupe used drama to raise public consciousness about child abuse, wife battery, and other little-discussed problems.

English-Canadian films were generally less successful than the country's theatrical productions. In the 1970s, the federal government began to provide tax concessions to financial backers of Canadian films. This policy resulted in a quantitative leap in the number of films produced in the country, but few of these films were well received by film critics or at the box office. There were some serious films with Canadian themes, including *Goin' Down the Road*, *The Grey Fox*, and *Wedding in White*. *The Apprenticeship of Duddy Kravitz*, a 1974 movie starring American actor Richard Dreyfuss, was a major financial success. Some actors protested the granting of starring roles to Hollywood

Chief Dan George of British Columbia played roles in several Hollywood movies, including *Little Big Man* in 1971. In this movie, his character challenged the Hollywood stereotypes that helped reinforce long-standing racist views of First Nations peoples.
© Bettmann/Corbis

actors in publicly subsidized films, but producers and directors argued that there was little chance of exporting a Canadian-made film or, for that matter, attracting Canadians to the theatre if established American stars did not appear in movies made in Canada.

ART

In art, as in theatre and literature, regional, ethnic, and gender sensibilities struggled to emerge. Native artistic expression, long ignored by mainstream art dealers and critics, finally received recognition. On the West Coast, Bill Reid earned an international reputation for his revival of traditional Haida carving. In the 1950s, Norval Morrisseau, an Ojibwa from Sand Point Reserve in Ontario, began to create paintings that incorporated the pictography of rock paintings and Ojibwa spiritual themes. This style, labelled Woodland Indian art, won applause in the white professional art community in the early 1960s and influenced the work of such celebrated artists of the 1970s as Daphne Odjig of Ontario and Jackson Beardy of Manitoba. Largely due to the promotional energy of Toronto artist James Houston, what is now known as Inuit art was introduced to southern buyers. Beginning in the late 1940s, he encouraged Inuit to produce their prints and ivory and soapstone carvings for market through Inuit cooperatives.

In the post-war period, artists increasingly turned to the land and its people for inspiration. Northwest Coast Native art and the British Columbia landscape influenced the work of Jack Shadbolt, a Vancouver surrealist painter. On the Prairies, the major landscape artists included Dorothy Knowles, Wynona Mulcaster, and Ernest Lindner. The paintings of Esther Warkow of Winnipeg recalled the pre-Holocaust life of Polish Jews. In a class by himself was William Kurelek, whose work reflected his attempts to deal with a difficult childhood as a Ukrainian Canadian growing up in rural Alberta and Manitoba. His lyrical work depicted Prairie life and dealt with a variety of spiritual themes. In Ontario, filmmaker and artist Joyce Wieland produced provocative works that reflected her nationalist and feminist values. Several artists from London, Ontario, among whom Greg Curnoe was best known, created regional art celebrating local identity and the Canadian struggle to be free of American control. With the Maritime environment as his context, Alex Colville became the founder of a school of art now called Atlantic Realism, which inspired a generation of artists, including Christopher Pratt, Mary Pratt, and Tom Forrestall. The Atlantic region also proved a fertile spawning ground for many of Canada's so-called folk artists, who, though largely untrained, produced paintings and sculpture that were quickly snapped up by sharp-eyed collectors.

RECORDING ARTISTS

Before the 1970s, Canadian radio stations mainly played American recording artists, and the profits from moneys Canadians paid for records mostly flowed south. A few Canadians managed to crack both the Canadian and American airwaves. Among them was Nova Scotia's Hank Snow, who eventually moved to the United States to pursue a successful career. His first major hit, "I'm Movin' On," remained number one on *Billboard*'s country chart for 21 weeks in 1950, an achievement as yet unequalled. In 1949, acclaimed Montreal jazz artist Oscar Peterson made his debut in the United States at Carnegie Hall, but he maintained a Canadian base, moving from Montreal to Toronto in 1958. The two biggest Canadian groups of the 1950s, the Crew Cuts and the Four Lads, consisted entirely of graduates of St. Michael's Choir School in Toronto. Turning from sacred music to covers of African American rhythm and blues songs, the Crew Cuts had the distinction of recording the first rock 'n' roll tune to reach number one on the American charts. "Sh-Boom (Life Could Be a Dream)" was the biggest selling record in North America in 1954. Paul Anka of Ottawa, whose popularity extended over several decades, also began his hit-making career in the 1950s.

Generally, however, there was a drought of Canadian artists on the radio. Major folk artists such as Gordon Lightfoot, Joni Mitchell, Ian and Sylvia, and the Travellers received much acclaim but little airplay other than on CBC Radio, which had loyal but small audiences. In 1969, the only Canadians with regular radio airplay nationally were Winnipeg's The Guess Who and Toronto's The Band. The Guess Who's "American Woman," which topped the *Billboard* chart in the United States in 1970, gave a Canadian spin to anti-war sentiments in the Vietnam War era, warning the "American Woman" to keep her "ghetto scenes" and "war machines" away from Canadian boys. In 1970, the Canadian Radio-television Commission (CRTC), which had been established as the regulatory agency for broadcasters, introduced regulations requiring radio stations to ensure that no fewer than 30 percent of the records they played were of Canadian origin. Within a year, artists such as Anne Murray, Neil Young, Gordon Lightfoot, and Joni Mitchell were common fare on the radio, and their Canadian success spilled over to the American airwaves.

CBC radio and television continued to be the main source of publicity for Canadian artists outside the formulaic world of pop music. Because of CBC exposure, a growing number of Canadian artists could fill concert halls nationally rather than just regionally. John Allan Cameron of Cape Breton, who performed folk music with Celtic roots, was an example. Another was Stompin' Tom Connors, who grew up in Skinners Pond, Prince Edward Island, and appealed to both folk and country audiences with his working-class perspective on Canadian themes. His trademark was a pounding foot, inspired by the need to be heard above noisy crowds. Although country and western music was often trivialized by cultural snobs in the 1960s, CBC programs such as *Don Messer's Jubilee* had a wide following across the country. Folk festivals, such as Toronto's Mariposa and the Winnipeg Folk Festival, which attracted an audience of 30 000 during its first year of operation in 1974, also provided showcases for a variety of musical artists.

There was a growing audience for dance in Canada in the post-war period. Canadian dance companies such as Les Grands Ballets Canadiens and the Danny Grossman Dance Company came into their own, and dancers such as Karen Kain and Frank Augustyn of the National Ballet and Evelyn Hart of the Royal Winnipeg Ballet won prestigious international competitions. With grants from the secretary of state for Multiculturalism, cultural groups began to revive dance traditions that had been pushed aside in the rush to conquer fleeting popular dance styles such as the twist, the monkey, and the mashed potato.

HERITAGE CONSERVATION

Heritage conservation became an important means by which national, regional, and ethnic identities could be preserved. Besides the work of the Historic Sites and Monuments Board and the National Museum, little attention had been paid before 1960 to preserving historic buildings and artifacts. An explosion of conservation and historical reconstruction activities accompanied the centennial celebrations in 1967 and continued thereafter.

Such activities involved all levels of government and were carried out for a variety of reasons. Sometimes the goal was job creation, as in the federally sponsored reconstruction of the fort of Louisbourg as a tourist attraction in Cape Breton in the early 1960s. Provincial projects such as the Acadian Historic Village in Caraquet, New Brunswick, and the Ukrainian

Frank Augustyn and Karen Kain dance in the National Ballet's production of *The Sleeping Beauty.*
National Ballet of Canada Archives

Willie O'Ree.
Courtesy of Willie O'Ree

Village outside Edmonton represented recognition by the government of the voting power of ethnic groups. At other times, projects involved attempts to invigorate decaying areas of cities, as in the conversion of dilapidated buildings on the Halifax waterfront and in Winnipeg's warehouse district into fancy shops. In some cases, such as the remains of a Viking settlement at l'Anse-aux-Meadows in Newfoundland and the well-preserved buildings in old Quebec City, historic sites received international recognition. Museums, like historic sites, mushroomed after 1960, most focusing on the history of Canada or its regions.

Preservation of historic sites, as many commentators pointed out, was not quite the same thing as preservation of history. While the object of much enthusiasm and capital investment, the history of preserved places and buildings was often presented in a romantic and simplified way to tourists. The thousands of visitors who parked their vehicles for a day at pretty-as-a-picture Peggy's Cove, near Halifax, learned little of the difficult lives of the fishers and their various battles with fish buyers or banks. For all its meticulous detail in reproducing the exteriors and interiors of buildings, the Ukrainian Village outside Edmonton gave little hint of the political divisions that were important to pioneer life for the early generations of Ukrainian immigrants to western Canada.

PROFESSIONAL SPORTS

Prosperity in the post-war period resulted in a larger potential audience of paying customers for professional sporting events. As in other nations, sports became increasingly identified in Canada with the "national identity." The cost of being an athlete also increased dramatically. In 1961, the Fitness and Amateur Sports Act was passed, which made federal funds available for sports activity. Amateur sports became more bureaucratized, presided over by paid administrators rather than enthusiastic volunteers.

Hockey remained the national passion, and fans were often quite demonstrative in their feelings for their teams. In March 1955, after the legendary Maurice "Rocket" Richard of the Montreal Canadiens was suspended for the balance of the season as a penalty for brawling, fans at the Forum pelted National Hockey League (NHL) president Clarence Campbell with food and then took to the streets, breaking windows and looting stores in what many saw as a demonstration of Quebec nationalism. In 1967, the size of the NHL doubled, but all the new teams were American. The Vancouver Canucks joined the league in 1970, and four Canadian teams, representing the cities of Ottawa, Winnipeg, Edmonton, and Quebec City, were included in the World Hockey Association, a rival to the NHL, founded in 1972.

Canada's victory in the first Soviet-Canada hockey series in 1972 was a cause of nationwide celebration. For years, Canadian coaches, players, promoters, and fans had insisted that Canadians were the best hockey players in the world and that their unimpressive showings at the Olympics and other international amateur

CBC Radio host Peter Gzowski became one of Canada's media celebrities. His morning radio shows from the 1970s onward were broadcast nationally and featured guests from all walks of Canadian life. Gzowski announced he was retiring in 1997 as federal cuts at the CBC contributed to the cancellation of his radio program *Morningside*. CP PHOTO/Jeff Chevrier

competitions were due to strict definitions of amateurism that excluded players in the NHL. Thus, when a series of games was arranged between the Soviets and the best Canadian players in the NHL in 1972, Canada's reputation was on the line. Paul Henderson's famous series-ending goal has come to be seen as one of the classic moments in Canadian sports history.

Although racial integration in North American sport advanced in the post-war period, the NHL remained virtually lily white until the late 1980s. Before 1986, only one black player, Willie O'Ree, had been allowed to play in NHL major-league games. A Fredericton-born left-winger and speed demon, O'Ree was legally blind in one eye after being struck by a puck at a time when players were not obliged to wear helmets. He had played hockey in New Brunswick growing up and later in the junior leagues in Kitchener and Quebec City. Recruited to a Boston Bruins farm team, O'Ree was asked to play in two Bruins games in 1958. Three years later, he played most of the Bruins' regular season games, but despite a strong performance was traded several times after the season and relegated back to the minors for the remaining 14 years of his hockey career.

Football was second to hockey as Canada's national sport. In 1956, the Western Interprovincial Football Union and the Interprovincial Rugby Football Union joined forces to form the Canadian Football Council, later renamed the Canadian Football League. All of the teams in the league were Canadian, and they played with rules different from those of their American counterparts, which helps account for the fact that football did not follow the path of hockey in becoming integrated on a North American scale.

While professional sports teams were almost exclusively male, both female and male Canadian athletes won international honours in individualized sports. Two women received particular media attention in the early post-war period. Barbara Ann Scott won the 1948 Olympic figure-skating title and skated professionally in ice shows. Marilyn Bell was hailed for her swimming achievements, beginning in 1954 with a 52-kilometre swim across Lake Ontario at the age of 16. She later went on to become the youngest swimmer to cross the English Channel and the Strait of Juan de Fuca.

THE PUBLIC BROADCASTER

The Canadian arts community faced many frustrations in trying to convince the networks, and often audiences, that they could provide worthwhile alternatives to the slick American products that dominated the weekly ratings that were so important in attracting advertisers. In the mid-1970s, the CBC drew a large audience for a series of Canadian plays directed by John Hirsch. In spite of this success, the network mysteriously refused to continue the series into a second year and gradually cut funding devoted to "serious" programming. The network occasionally stumbled onto a winning product such as *King of Kensington*, but on the whole Canadians turned to the public broadcaster for the sorts of programs they simply could not find on private television, Canadian or American: drama, dance, documentaries, and current affairs. How well Canadian broadcasters, including the public broadcaster, reflected the nation is debatable. CBC personality and media critic Nathan Cohen explained why a Hugh Garner script about a hydro lineman was turned down by five producers. "Finally, one of them said to me, 'What do we know about working people? You can't expect us to do plays about people we don't understand.'"[1]

The CBC did appear to understand children, and from its earliest days produced popular kids' shows. They began with *Let's See* in 1952, which featured the puppets Uncle Chichimus and Holly Hock. Later, *The Friendly Giant* greeted several generations of children in the mornings, eventually joined by *Mr. Dress-Up* and *Sharon, Lois, and Bram*. Canadian children's broadcasting was less frenetic than most of the popular American fare, such as *Captain Kangaroo* and *Sesame Street*, and eventually gained an audience in American public broadcasting.

CBC Radio had its own loyal following of about 10 percent of all radio listeners in Canada. After the 1970s, emphasis was placed on current affairs, with its new FM network concentrating largely on classical music. CBC Radio programs such as *This Country in the Morning* and *As It Happens* became the preferred means of learning about the country's political and cultural developments for many Canadians. Their respective hosts, Peter Gzowski and Barbara Frum, became media icons, with Frum departing for television in the

A Censored TV Producer Speaks

Noel Moore's television documentaries had won awards, and he had no reason to regard a CBC request to produce a feature on the life of Russian revolutionary leader V.I. Lenin as problematic. His version of Lenin's life, in many respects, challenged official Soviet propaganda, but it was not tame enough for some Canadian politicians. As Moore explained:

> When the film was due to be shown on CBC Television some reactionary guy on the back benches of the Conservative Party queried it. He stood up in the House and asked if it was true that a document of revolution was going to be shown tomorrow night? So the CBC cancelled my film in 1971 and showed two other films—one was about the life of Hitler and the other was a skiing film which showed you how to set off dynamite to blow up avalanches and in the process they showed in infinite detail how a bomb was made. And, at the same time, my harmless little film essay was denounced. That was when the whole October Crisis blew up. . . .

> The CBC pulled my film on the weakest of excuses. They claimed it was because of this Conservative backbencher, but the phone call came from the Prime Minister's Office—the PMO. . . .

> I was blackballed by the CBC after this film. I never did another job for them even though I had won national and international awards. . . .

> Ironically, the CBC had just shown an American documentary about the Hollywood Ten and said, "Look how normal we are in Canada. These kinds of things can't happen here." It was happening in Canada and it was cold-war hysteria. Anyway, my film about Lenin did go on the air eventually. It was aired about six months later. The CBC couldn't afford not to show it this time, there was too much at stake.[2]

1980s and Gzowski, after an unsuccessful attempt to launch a television career, returning to radio to host *Morningside*. While talk shows on privately owned radio stations focused on sensationalism, CBC Radio focused on current affairs and cultural production at regional and national levels. As the main venue for recording artists whose music did not fit the pigeonholes of mainstream radio, CBC was essential for the celebration of local cultures.

The Canadian Television Network (CTV), a privately owned English-language television service, was launched in 1961. Driven by the need for popularity and profits, it showed as many American programs on prime-time television as Canadian-content rulings would allow. CBC Television felt obliged to follow suit, with the result that Canadians were bombarded with American culture in the 1960s. Few Canadian programs were picked up by American networks.

CENSORSHIP

While some critics complained that the big money that controlled the private media for all practical purposes amounted to censorship over ideas and information displeasing to media owners, there was also formal state censorship of what Canadians could see and hear. Radicals such as the French feminist Simone de Beauvoir were barred from the CBC in the 1950s owing to government apprehension about their corrupting influence. During the same decade, books such as *Peyton Place*, *Lady Chatterley's Lover*, and *The Tropic of Cancer* were seized by customs officials at the border.

Censorship regulations were gradually relaxed but Canadians remained cautious about permitting free access to films and publications. Across the country, film censorship boards decided what films could be played in provincial theatres. In Alberta, a British Information Office film extolling the United Nations and condemning racism ran afoul of the anti-communist witchhunters, and popular American films *The Wild One* and *The Blackboard Jungle* were banned for not being uplifting. Municipal library boards and school boards also at various times banned books of clear literary merit, usually for having too much explicit sex or too many profane words. Campaigns by the religious right in Canada, influenced by the successes of the well-funded Christian right in the United States, led to book bannings as supposedly secular libraries and schools bowed to pressure from groups who claimed that certain books offended Christian sensibilities.

CONCLUSION

In the post-war period, Canadians developed cultural and sporting industries that brought worldwide attention and praise. Much of the success of these industries was owed to the efforts of governments to protect the Canadian market for homegrown products through subsidies and regulations. As Canadians began seeing themselves reflected in cultural productions, they also developed a sense of their own identity. This did not mean that national differences were erased. Indeed, quite the contrary. Francophone Canadians, especially in Quebec, developed their own separate cultural identity from English Canadians, and the language barrier meant that the two solitudes continued to move along different paths.

NOTES

1 Paul Rutherford, *When Television Was Young: Primetime Canada, 1952–1967* (Toronto: University of Toronto Press, 1990), 284.

2 Len Scher, *The Un-Canadians: True Stories of the Blacklist Era* (Toronto: Lester, 1992), 75–77.

RELATED READINGS IN THIS SERIES

From *Nation and Society: Readings in Post-Confederation Canadian History*

Howard Ramos and Kevin Gosine, "'The Rocket': Newspaper Coverage of a Quebec Cultural Icon, A Canadian Hockey Player," 416–34.

From *Primary Documents CD-ROM*, Volume II

Waiting
I Remember
Black Song Nova Scotia/The Call to Tea
Barbara Ann Scott

SELECTED READING

On cultural identities in Canada, see José Igartua, *The Other Quiet Revolution: National Identities in English Canada, 1945–1971* (Vancouver: UBC Press, 2006); William Dodge, ed., *Boundaries of Identity* (Toronto: Lester, 1992); and Neil Bissoondath, *Selling Illusions: The Cult of Multiculturalism in Canada* (Toronto: Penguin, 1994). On Quebec cultural developments, see Renate Usmiani, *Michel Tremblay* (Vancouver: Douglas and McIntyre, 1982); Gabrielle Roy, *Letters to Bernadette* (Toronto: Lester and Orpen Dennys, 1990); and Guy Bouthilier and Jean Meynaud, *Le choc des langues au Québec* (Montreal: Presses de l'Université du Québec, 1972).

On Canadian literature generally, see James Doyle, *Progressive Heritage: The Evolution of a Politically Radical Literary Tradition in Canada* (Waterloo, ON: Wilfrid Laurier University Press, 2002); Margaret Atwood, *Survival* (Toronto: Anansi, 1972); and Northrop Frye, *The Bush Garden: Essays on the Canadian Imagination* (Toronto: Anansi, 1971). On authors writing in English, see Judith S. Grant, *Robertson Davies: Man of Myth* (Toronto: Penguin, 1994); Janice Williamson, *Sounding Differences: Conversations with Seventeen Canadian Writers* (Toronto: University of Toronto Press, 1993); Ed Jewinski, *Michael Ondaatje: Express Yourself Beautifully* (Toronto: ECW Press, 1994); and Beverly Rasporich, *Dance of the Sexes: Art and Gender in the Fiction of Alice Munro* (Edmonton: University of Alberta Press, 1990).

On Native cultural assertion, see Arthur Ray, *I Have Lived Here Since the World Began: An Illustrated History of Canada's Native People*, rev. ed. (Toronto: Key Porter, 2005); Olive Dickason, *Canada's First Nations: A History of Founding Peoples from Earliest Times*, 4th ed. (Toronto: Oxford University Press, 2006); and J.R. Miller, *Skyscrapers Hide the Heavens: A History of Indian-White Relations in Canada*, 3rd ed. (Toronto: University of Toronto Press, 2000). See also G. Gottfriedson and R. Schneider, *In Honour of Our Grandmothers: Visions of Cultural Survival* (Penticton, BC: Theytus Books, 1994).

Histories of Canadian film include Michael Dorland, *So Close to the States: The Emergence of Canadian Feature Film Policy* (Toronto: University of Toronto Press, 1998); Gary Evans, *In the National Interest: A Chronicle of the National Film Board of Canada from 1949 to 1989* (Toronto: University of

Toronto Press, 1991); and R. Bruce Elder, *Image and Identity: Reflections on Canadian Film and Culture* (Waterloo, ON: Wilfrid Laurier University Press, 1989).

Key works on Canadian art include *Visual Arts in Canada: Painting, Drawing, and Sculpture* (Ottawa: Canadian Heritage, 1993); Dennis Reid, *A Concise History of Canadian Painting* (Toronto: Oxford University Press, 1988); and Elizabeth McLuhan and Tom Hill, *Norval Morrisseau and the Emergence of the Image Makers* (Toronto: Methuen, 1984).

On the media in Canada, see Paul Rutherford, *When Television Was Young: Primetime Canada, 1952–1967* (Toronto: University of Toronto Press, 1990); Mary Vipond, *The Mass Media in Canada* (Toronto: Lorimer, 1989); and Frank Peers, *The Public Eye: Television and the Politics of Canadian Broadcasting, 1952–1968* (Toronto: University of Toronto Press, 1979).

On heritage preservation, see C.J. Taylor, *Negotiating the Past: The Making of Canada's National Historic Parks and Sites* (Montreal: McGill-Queen's University Press, 1990); *Prairie Forum* 15, no. 2 (Fall 1990), special issue on Heritage Conservation; and Ian McKay, *The Quest of the Folk: Antimodernism and Cultural Selection in Twentieth-Century Nova Scotia* (Montreal: McGill-Queen's University Press, 1994).

On sports in Canada, see Bruce Kidd, *The Struggle for Canadian Sport* (Toronto: University of Toronto Press, 1996); Richard S. Gruneau and David Whitson, *Hockey Night in Canada: Sport, Identities and Cultural Politics* (Toronto: Garamond, 1993); Ann Hall, *Sports in Canadian Society* (Toronto: McClelland & Stewart, 1991); Donald Macintosh, *Sports and Politics in Canada: Federal Government Involvement Since 1961* (Montreal: McGill-Queen's University Press, 1987); and Colin Howell, *Blood, Sweat, and Cheers: Sport and the Making of Modern Canada* (Toronto: University of Toronto Press, 2001).

PART V

Post-Modern Canada, 1975–2008

I f the first three decades after the Second World War were years of bright hope for most Canadians, the quarter-century that followed had more sombre tones. Economic growth stalled, along with average incomes. The old liberal consensus cracked and neo-liberal perspectives took the reins in Canadian politics. In an era of economic globalization, it was argued, concern for economic competitiveness took precedence over efforts to improve the lives of disadvantaged members of society. The gap between the rich and poor yawned ever wider, and the disparity between have and have-not provinces increased. Not surprisingly, the new direction sparked angry responses. The poor rallied to demand better treatment, while women, gays, environmentalists, and Native peoples recorded some victories in a period when social justice seemed largely in retreat. Early in the new millennium, new challenges emerged when terrorist attacks against the United States produced consequences that once again raised issues of Canadian sovereignty and fundamental values.

CHAPTER 20

Canada in the Global Village, 1976–1999

TIMELINE

- 1981–82 Major global recession
- 1985 Macdonald Commission report
- 1988 Canada and United States sign the Free Trade Agreement
- 1990 North American Free Trade Agreement begins
- 1992 North American Free Trade Agreement signed; collapse of East Coast cod stocks
- 1997 APEC summit in Vancouver
- 1999 Confrontation in Seattle between World Trade Organization and its opponents

When Canadian general Roméo Dallaire was named force commander of the United Nations Assistance Mission for Rwanda (UNAMIR) in 1993, his assignment was to persuade the combatants to honour their pledges to accept a peace agreement. When it became clear that one side of the agreement, led by Hutu extremists, planned to slaughter the Tutsi minority in Rwanda, he tried to convince the United Nations to send the military support necessary to prevent genocide, but American and French opposition blocked this measure. Although he saved as many lives as he could, Dallaire witnessed the death of 800 000 Tutsis and Hutu moderates before the Tutsi-led armed opposition managed to overpower government forces. "What I have come to realize as the root of it all," he later wrote, "is the fundamental indifference of the world community to the plight of seven to eight million black Africans in a tiny country that had no strategic or resource value to any world power."[1]

Dallaire's painful awakening to the greed and callousness that underlay the foreign policies of most Western nations prompted him to call into question their claims to be promoting democracy and human rights. It also showed Canada at its finest in international affairs, because Canada, alone among developed nations, agreed to send reinforcements to UNAMIR once the slaughter had begun in April 1994.

Rwanda was an exception. Canada, like other nations in this period, largely pursued self-interest on the international stage. This chapter explores how Canada defined that self-interest and its impact on foreign and trade policies from 1975 to 1999. In turn, we look at how changing attitudes about Canada's role in the world, particularly in the economic sphere, helped shape so-called neo-liberal perspectives that jeopardized the welfare state consensus of the first three postwar decades.

GLOBALIZATION

By the closing decades of the twentieth century, few people disagreed with Canadian communications theorist Marshall McLuhan that human beings are living in a "global village." Events anywhere in the world can be communicated instantaneously through radio, television, and (beginning in 1990) the Internet. Globalization—defined as the compression of time and space through changes in communication technologies—is manifested in worldwide networks that call into question many of the institutions established in the Industrial Age, including geographically defined nation-states.

The global reach of giant corporations was one of the most obvious manifestations of accelerated globalization. Following the Second World War, Japan built an extremely efficient industrial sector that often produced cheaper and better-quality goods than those produced in North America and Europe. By the 1970s, Japanese radios, televisions, stereo equipment, appliances, computers, and cars were putting North American factories out of business. A close alliance between business and government had promoted Japan's industrial initiatives, and the "Four Tigers" of Asia—Hong Kong, South Korea, Taiwan, and Singapore—were soon benefiting from similar strategies to make important strides in industrial development.

Their well-being threatened by new competitors, the energy crisis, and the environmental movement, giant corporations in North America and Europe began moving their production facilities to off-shore locations around the world. Developing countries, desperate for capital investment, offered cheap labour, lower taxes, and fewer regulations that would eat into profits. Able to transfer assets instantaneously around the world, these "transnational" corporations could defy attempts by any government to control their activities. It was not long before corporate managers were extracting favourable conditions from the governments of western nations eager to prevent jobs from being exported to othercountries. Corporate taxes were cut, trade union protection reduced, environmentalregulations relaxed, and social programs pared back in an effort to convince corporateleaders that they were welcome.

The weakening commitment to environmental protection shattered ecologists' hopes that the world

Police used pepper spray to break up demonstrations at the site of the APEC Summit meetings in Vancouver in November 1997. Here, a demonstrator receives help after getting pepper spray in her eyes.
Dan Loh/CP Picture Archive

community would recognize that the future of the biosphere depended on collective action to reduce alarming trends. Disasters such as those that occurred at Three Mile Island in Pennsylvania (1979), Bhopal, India (1984), and Chernobyl, Ukraine (1986) underscored the difficulty of controlling technology. The destruction of the ozone layer by chlorofluorocarbons (CFCs), used in aerosols, foam insulation, and supercleaners for electronic equipment, and the rapid disappearance of tropical rain forests caused further deterioration of the atmosphere. Although the major world powers reduced their stocks of nuclear weapons in the aftermath of the Cold War, the weapons that remained were capable of wreaking irreparable environmental damage.

The collapse of East Coast cod stocks in 1992 brought home to Canadians the truth that environmentalists had espoused for decades: there were limits to growth. A spate of international conferences resolved little because the governments whose representatives were in attendance refused to challenge the power of multinational corporations, which did not attend.

TRADING BLOCS

While governments increasingly capitulated to the view that corporations rather than the state should set the rules for the economy, regional trading blocs were created or strengthened in an effort to secure elusive markets. The European Economic Community, created by six western European nations in 1957, expanded to include almost all of western Europe and in the 1990s much of eastern Europe in what became known as the European Union (EU). Members of the EU were expected to drop all trade barriers against fellow members and collectively determine protectionist trade policies with the rest of the world. Canada and the United States signed the Free Trade Agreement in 1988. Four years later, the North American Free Trade Agreement (NAFTA) brought Mexico into the North American trading bloc.

The spread of free trade seemed a logical consequence to the economic developments in the post-war period that had gradually made transnational corporations more powerful than most nation-states. When a recession began in late 1981, corporations undertook a massive program of "restructuring" for a leaner and meaner global economy. Automating production processes, reducing the number of workers, and offering a more flexible response to changing market conditions, it was argued, would allow the fittest to survive and triumph. A wave of mergers and takeovers followed, which further concentrated economic power. By 1986, 32 families and nine giant conglomerates controlled over a third of Canada's non-financial assets.

NEO-LIBERALISM

In the new climate of corporate concentration and "downsizing," the views of American economist Milton Friedman, whose views were not very popular during the age of prosperity gained ascendancy among western leaders. According to Friedman and his followers (sometimes called monetarists because of their emphasis on monetary policy), government intervention—deficit financing, tax incentives, and the expansion of the money supply—had led to rigidities and inefficiencies in western economies. The solution was to encourage efficient production to improve the supply of goods and services rather than to stimulate demand through government spending. If governments simply reduced taxes, controlled inflation, and let the private sector adjust to changing economic conditions, the global economy would right itself soon enough. Opponents of Friedman noted that such policies had been pursued before and during the Great Depression with disastrous results, but reminders of this kind, voiced eloquently by Canadian-born economist John Kenneth Galbraith, were increasingly ignored by political leaders.

Supply-side economics inspired the policies of conservative governments in Great Britain under Margaret Thatcher (1979–1990), in the United States under Ronald Reagan (1981–1988), and in Canada under Brian Mulroney (1984–1993). Although their economies were experiencing the worst dislocation since the 1930s, these leaders attempted to reduce spending on social programs, privatize government activities, cut back the civil service, and exercise tighter control over the money supply. All argued that they had no choice. With western economies growing at a fraction of the rates they had posted in the period of prosperity, government revenues were being outstripped by expenditures.

Since governments felt compelled to cut corporate taxes and generally resisted significant increases to the individual tax rate, annual deficits, the result of the imbalance between revenues and expenditures, became commonplace. Deficits compounded from year to year created large debt loads that had to be financed through loans from financiers. As a result, an increased portion of state expenditure went simply to repaying debts, leaving even less money to finance social programs. Many people accepted the argument that governments could not go on spending forever without taking their revenues into account. In this context, the view that it was necessary to increase marketplace control over the economy and reverse the extensive state interventionism of the post-1945 period gained growing support. The term "neo-liberalism" was used to describe this perspective because it harkened back to classical liberal economic theory, which regarded state intervention as harmful to the economy.

FEDERAL MANOEUVRES

The Liberal Party had been the chief political beneficiary of post-war prosperity. Given credit by Canadians for implementing welfare state policies, it governed the country for 32 of the 39 years from 1945 to 1984. It was weak in western Canada, where competition between the right-wing Progressive Conservatives and the left-wing New Democrats squeezed out the party that was seen not so much as centrist but as central Canadian. By contrast, the party was strong in Quebec, if only because the Progressive Conservatives and New Democrats were viewed as Anglophone. The selection of Francophone leaders from Wilfrid Laurier and Louis St. Laurent to Pierre Elliott Trudeau served to reinforce the view that the Liberal Party was the most sympathetic to the interests of Quebec and Francophones.

By the late 1970s, the Progressive Conservatives were beginning to tap into the resentment among middle-class Canadians against increasing taxes and state intervention. In the federal election of 1979, the Liberals were reduced to second place. Once in office, the willingness of Joe Clark's Progressive Conservative minority government to allow energy price increases met with little favour outside the energy-producing provinces of western Canada. The government's first budget was defeated by the opposition parties, forcing a second election in less than a year. In 1980, Trudeau's Liberals remained the safest bet for many Canadians. They were perceived as the party that balanced corporate and individual interests, promoted social welfare and full-employment policies, and resisted American control over the economy. After their humiliation nine months earlier, the Liberals once again formed a majority government.

By 1984, Trudeau was gone and the new Liberal leader, John Turner, had a different legacy with which to contend. After almost three years of a bruising recession and increasing government deficits, Canadians were ready to change governments. Brian Mulroney, the new Progressive Conservative leader, knew how to take advantage of the groundswell of support for change. He promised Canadians that he would restore employment and reduce deficits without touching Canada's social programs, which he labelled a "sacred trust." Mulroney took advantage of a televised forum on women's issues to announce that his party would implement a national day-care program if he won the election. While he did not deliver on the promise, his willingness to make it suggested that he did not believe the Progressive Conservatives could be elected on a program of cutting back the state's obligations.

THE MACDONALD COMMISSION

In 1984, Mulroney claimed to be opposed to free trade between Canada and the United States. That issue, he suggested, had been settled in the federal election of 1911. Contrary to Mulroney's claims, the idea had been revived by the Royal Commission on the Economic Union and Development Prospects for Canada. Appointed by Trudeau in 1982, with the country mired in recession, the commission was chaired by Donald Macdonald, a former Liberal finance minister. Its report, released in September 1985, argued that Canada had to maintain a flexible economy, capable of adjusting to global economic change and new technologies. Market mechanisms, rather than government intervention, the report maintained, provided the best means of ensuring a vibrant Canadian economy. To that end, free trade with the United States offered the only hope for continued economic prosperity.

The commission marshalled a broad array of evidence to support free trade. Despite attempts to pursue a "third option" of more diversified trade, especially through an arrangement with the European trading bloc, Canada's dependency on the United States had actually grown in the previous decade. Over three-quarters of Canada's exports were sold to the United States, and half of that trade was between the parent companies and branch plants of multinational corporations. With over a third of their gross national product (GNP) derived from foreign trade, Canadians would experience a crisis of unthinkable proportions if the flow of goods across the Canada–United States border was disrupted. The time had come, the commissioners claimed, to shake up the industries that remained sheltered behind the old National Policy and lay the foundations for a New Age economy that would serve Canadians in the twenty-first century.

THE FREE TRADE AGREEMENT

Ignoring his pre-election statements, Mulroney followed the advice of the Macdonald commission and initiated trade negotiations with the Americans. The Mulroney government had powerful backers in taking this step. The Business Council on National Issues, an organization comprising the chief executive officers of

When the Inglis Appliance Factory shut down its Toronto operation in 1989, most workers blamed the Free Trade Agreement for the loss of their jobs.
DavidSmileyPhotographer.com

150 leading Canadian corporations, most of them multinationals, was fully committed to free trade. The venerable Canadian Manufacturers' Association, once the bulwark of the National Policy, came on side. Even the Canadian Federation of Independent Business, which represented the increasingly powerful small business community in Canada, threw its weight behind the scheme.

The details of the Free Trade Agreement were ironed out in the fall of 1987. Canada's chief negotiator, along with Trade Minister Pat Carney, was Simon Reisman, a career civil servant who had been instrumental in negotiating the 1965 Auto Pact. Tariffs on primary and manufactured goods would be eliminated over a 10-year period, and free trade in services would gradually be implemented. Most non-tariff barriers to trade, such as quotas and content regulations, were also slated for elimination. Following a year of heated debate, Mulroney called an election on 25 November 1988 after the Liberal majority in the Senate made clear their unwillingness to ratify the Free Trade Agreement before the government had received an electoral mandate for its implementation. Leaders of the New Democratic Party (NDP), labour unions, feminists, some church groups, and a variety of nationalist coalitions opposed free trade in principle, while the Liberal Party, which waffled about the concept, rejected certain features of the actual proposal.

In taking a negative stand, opponents of the Free Trade Agreement maintained that it would allow multinational corporations to consolidate their North American operations in locations with better climates and lower wage levels than those prevailing in Canada. Jobs would be lost in the goods-producing sectors, and the wages of those remaining in the labour force would be substantially reduced. Moreover, they argued, Canada's cultural industries would be threatened and Canadians would be forced to tailor their welfare, environmental, and regional development policies to "harmonize" with the goals of the larger economic partner. Under such pressure, Canada as a nation would surely fall apart. Such a sweeping agreement was not necessary. Since American industry did not want to lose Canadian resources and markets, economic nationalists argued, there seemed little likelihood of the United States suddenly pulling the plug on trade with Canada.

Mulroney maintained that Canada would remain a sovereign nation once the agreement was in effect. Although the government's ability to levy tariffs to protect industries would gradually disappear, he claimed that the opening of the American market to more Canadian-produced goods and services would, overall, benefit workers in the manufacturing and service sectors. Moreover, the agreement merely furthered the work of the General Agreement on Tariffs and Trade (GATT), which had effectively removed tariffs on 80 percent of all goods produced in Canada. Mulroney accused his opponents of "scare-mongering" when they suggested that old-age pensions or medicare might be undermined by free trade. Since the details as to which subsidies would constitute unfair trade practices had yet to be negotiated, opponents of the agreement were left with little evidence to back up their claims that government policies in everything from agriculture to regional development might be undermined.

If the 1988 election is taken as a referendum on the issue of free trade, its opponents won, since the Liberals and New Democrats together received over 52 percent of the total votes cast. Supporters of the agreement, the Progressive Conservatives and the fledgling Reform Party, won about 46 percent of the vote, with the remaining vote going to parties whose campaigns were focused mainly on other issues. The

Liberals and the New Democrats had formed no alliance in the campaign, and the large plurality of Progressive Conservative voters returned a second Mulroney majority government. By the end of 1988, the Free Trade Agreement had been approved by both the Commons and the Senate. Canada was entering a new economic era.

THE FREE TRADE ERA

The ink was barely dry on the Free Trade Agreement when many firms, beginning with Gillette, announced that they were closing all or part of their Canadian operations and centralizing their manufacturing in the United States. In every case, they insisted that their plans to vacate Canada were unrelated to the agreement and had been in place prior to its enactment. After 1 January 1989, they could move without fear that Canada would use tariff or non-tariff barriers to restrict their penetration of Canadian markets. Supporters of free trade minimized the importance of the exodus, arguing that tariffs encouraged non-competitive operations with the limited horizon of a domestic market. Canadians, they argued, should turn the companies that remained into world-class firms with markets around the globe.

With the agreement securely in place, company executives began to go back on their claims that free trade would do little to jeopardize Canadian welfare and environmental programs. Instead they argued that welfare measures and state interventionism more generally were obstacles to attracting and retaining corporate investment. It could hardly be a surprise if firms, freed from the necessity of maintaining Canadian operations, chose to locate in the country where there was less corporate taxation, trade union protection, and industrial regulation.

A deep recession gripped Canada in 1990. Although it affected all western nations, the recession was more severe in Canada than in most other countries, lasting for three years and followed by a "jobless recovery." Mel Hurtig, a prominent Edmonton publisher responsible for the three-volume *Canadian Encyclopedia* and long-time champion of Canadian nationalism, charged in his best-selling book *The Betrayal of Canada* (1992) that, in its first two years, the Free Trade Agreement was responsible for the loss of 264 000 manufacturing jobs as branch plants closed and new operations

were located in Mexico and elsewhere. He claimed that the agreement had already brought "a big decline in the standard of living of Canadians," and predicted that "the future will be much worse . . . the destruction and disappearance of our country."[2]

Supporters of the agreement accused the nationalists of blaming free trade for job losses that were purely the result of the recession. Even without the Free Trade Agreement, they argued, Canadians would have been victims of the restructuring and downsizing policies that were part of global economic strategy. They had their own statistics to throw at the doomsayers, including a 16 percent increase in the volume of Canadian exports between 1989 and 1992, the continued success of the government in fighting inflation, and the drop in the value of the Canadian dollar, all of which suggested that the Canadian economy was making the necessary adjustments to survive in an increasingly competitive economic environment.

While free traders argued that nothing could stop this irresistible force toward global marketplace

Mel Hurtig was one of the leading opponents of the Free Trade Agreement in 1988. In the years that followed, he documented the agreement's negative impact on the Canadian economy and attempted in vain to lead a political struggle to force the Canadian government to tear it up.
Courtesy of Mel Hurtig

MORE TO THE STORY

Massey-Harris

The agricultural machinery company founded in 1847 by Daniel Massey went from strength to strength in the late nineteenth and early twentieth centuries. The company moved from Newcastle to Toronto in 1855 and in 1891 merged with its chief competitor to become Massey-Harris, the largest company of its kind in the British Empire. By the first decade of the twentieth century, it had captured a huge share of the rapidly expanding Prairie market for farm machinery and had established branch operations in the United States. When the company ran into difficulties following the Second World War, it was reorganized under the direction of its holding company, Argus Corporation, and continued to prosper. As Massey-Ferguson, it developed a global market and reached annual sales of more than $1 billion in the 1960s.

In the difficult economic climate of the late 1970s, Massey's fortunes again began to slip. Conrad Black, the ambitious young head of Argus, became chair of the troubled company in 1978, but the bottom fell out of the farm machinery market in 1980 and Argus wrote off its Massey-Ferguson shares as worthless. In an effort to save the capital and jobs that Massey represented, banks, governments, and shareholders poured $1.2 billion into the failing firm between 1978 and 1984. By 1987, when Massey-Ferguson changed its name to Varity Corp (after the Varity Plough Company, which had been acquired in 1892), it was a third of its former size, but nonetheless ranked as the 49th largest firm in Canada with sales and operating revenue of $1.8 billion. Following the signing of the Free Trade Agreement, it moved its head office to the United States.

decisions regulating everything, including social justice and the environment, their opponents took another perspective. By the end of the century, an equally global movement had developed that called into question the type of globalization being imposed on nation-states. Its leaders argued that there was no reason why globalization should be controlled exclusively by transnational corporations and by the governments of a few wealthy nations, led by the United States. Such an approach was nothing more than a new and vicious form of imperialism that was producing poverty in most countries and creating a race for the bottom in such areas as environmental standards and working conditions. This view appeared to be confirmed by the creation in 1995 of the World Trade Organization (WTO), whose sole purpose seemed to be to break down barriers to transnational trade. When the WTO met in Seattle in 1999, well-orchestrated protests publicized opposition to the brand of globalization endorsed and promoted by the WTO. The Canadian government was represented at the official WTO meetings, while other Canadians were among the tens of thousands in Seattle who were determined to expose what they regarded as the undemocratic activities of the governments and

In his 1992 cartoon "Oh please, Oh please," cartoonist Bruce MacKinnon offers an Atlantic Canada perspective on the North American Free Trade Agreement.
Reprinted with permission from The Halifax Herald Limited

corporations that ran the WTO and the corporations that pulled their strings.

Huge demonstrations and street theatre greeted international trade and finance organizations in the years following the Seattle confrontation, though the media tended to trivialize the opposition by focusing on a small sub-set of anarchists who glorified violence in their attack against the kingpins of the new global order.

THE JOBLESS RECOVERY

Although moderate economic growth had succeeded the recession, by 1995, Canada, like many western countries, could not find work for about a tenth of its labour force. Profitable businesses such as major banks, the energy giants, and Bell Canada joined less successful employers and governments in reducing their workforces. Business leaders justified cutbacks by asserting that trade liberalization was forcing companies to be more competitive. That meant mergers, factory shutdowns, and the introduction of technology, particularly computerization, all of which reduced the economy's demand for labour. Robots often replaced assembly-line workers; traditional "women's jobs" vanished as voice mail and electronic mail replaced many secretaries; and automated banking reduced the need for tellers. The unemployed remained out of work for longer periods of time than had their counterparts even a decade earlier.

Between 1990 and 1998, the after-tax income of Canadian families fell 7 percent in constant dollars. While the majority of households still had a comfortable income, a growing number of Canadians were living below the poverty line. Rates of poverty had dropped gradually during the era of prosperity, but climbed during the recessions of the early 1980s and early 1990s. While 3.5 million Canadians were classified as poor in 1987, a year of considerable economic growth, there were an additional 1.4 million impoverished Canadians just six years later. About 1.4 million children under the age of 18 were among the poor in 1993, representing 21 percent of all Canadian children. Sixty percent of poor children lived in homes headed by single mothers, whose ability to find work or day care, never mind both, had been undermined first by the recession and then by the jobless recovery.

Women's labour force participation nonetheless continued to rise. By 1994, women made up 45 percent of the workforce, an increase of 8 percent from 1976. Fewer women believed it was either desirable or likely that they could depend entirely on the income of a man to maintain them and their children. Men's wages and job security were on the decline, making it imperative in most families for women to seek paid work. Although women increasingly unionized and fought successfully for better wages, there was still a considerable degree of inequality in income. In 1994, women working full-time earned 72 percent of the incomes of men working the same number of hours. Far more women than men were trapped in part-time work, with the result that women's incomes overall were only 58 percent of men's. Apart from gender, colour was a factor in labour-force earnings. Members of visible minorities earned 30 percent less than other Canadians in the labour force in 1998, with African-Canadian males and most Aboriginal peoples encountering the greatest income disparities.

Demonstrations against the free trade version of globalization became common after the Seattle demonstration of 1999. Two years later, for example, tens of thousands demonstrated in Quebec City as the Summit of the Americas proposed erasing economic borders within North and South America.
Tom Hanson/CP Picture Archive

INFLATION VERSUS UNEMPLOYMENT

Federal economic policies, both under the Progressive Conservatives and their Liberal successors, elected in 1993, continued to emphasize the battle against inflation and government debt rather than the battle against unemployment. Yet high unemployment drained the federal treasury as unemployment insurance and social assistance costs mounted, and it deprived that treasury of the income taxes that would have resulted from more people working. Jean Chrétien's Liberals hinted in the 1993 election that there might be some return to employment creation as a priority, but shortly after the election, Finance Minister Paul Martin, a leading member of the corporate community, made clear that the new government would follow substantially the same financial policies as its predecessor. Social programs would be cut and the Bank of Canada's monetary policies would not be fundamentally altered. Unemployment insurance, rather than unemployment, became a target of government policy. It was made much harder to get and, in 1997–1998, only a third of the unemployed received unemployment insurance versus 80 percent in 1990–1991.

Young people were disproportionately the victims of the new unemployment. In an economy that was producing few new jobs, experienced workers were favoured over newcomers, making it difficult for young people to get a start in the labour market. In contrast to the generation of the 1960s, young people in the 1990s were unlikely to find well-paying manufacturing jobs after high school. They were in a somewhat better position to find employment if they had post-secondary education, but even this provided no guarantee. Life-long employment with a single company became increasingly uncommon, and young workers often had to be content with short-term contracts followed by new intensive job searches.

"McJobs" in the service industry appeared to be the fate of large numbers of people in their twenties, even if they had excellent qualifications for professional employment. While some young people beat the odds and either found good jobs in the profession for which they had trained or created their own fortunes through entrepreneurial ventures, it was clear that opportunities were limited. The term "Generation X" entered the language to denote a generation who some pessimists suggested could only live well if they remained in their parents' homes throughout their adult lives. In 1995, despite a large decline in the labour participation rate of young people owing to longer periods of study, fully 20 percent of those between the ages of 15 and 25 who were out of school and actively seeking work could not find even part-time jobs. The rate for high school graduates was the same as for dropouts.

TAXES AND A TURNAROUND

As the new millennium approached, rates of economic growth picked up and government deficits began to fall. Moreover, the federal and most provincial governments were well on their way to becoming deficit-free and making some progress in paying off their accumulated debts. With federal surpluses piling up in 2000, the policy focus of those with good incomes became tax reduction. Business-sponsored think tanks, supported by a compliant media, made it appear that wealthy Canadians, who paid the largest share of taxes, were being whacked by the taxman and were lining up for green cards to enter the United States. Evidence suggests that wealth in Canada was being redistributed in favour of the rich. In 1973, the wealthiest 10 percent of families had 6.77 times the income of the poorest 10 percent after the impact of taxes and social transfers was factored in. The comparable figure in 1998 was 7.24.

A HIGH-TECH ECONOMY

By the end of the twentieth century, Canadians were experiencing a robust export trade, most of it the result of a booming American economy and its demand for Canada's resources. Increases in resource prices, particularly for energy, were only part of the story. Canada's high-technology sectors, especially transportation and communications, were winning large contracts abroad. Bombardier of Valcourt, Quebec, was a prime example. Before the 1970s, Bombardier had both Canadian and international markets for its recreational equipment, led by snowmobiles. By the 1990s, it had established itself firmly as an international player in the aerospace, defence, and mass transit sectors. In the latter, it had large contracts in Turkey, New York, Malaysia, and Germany, among others, and with Vancouver's SkyTrain. With production facilities in 19 countries, Bombardier seemed the picture postcard for those arguing that Canada was a net beneficiary of globalization. Various federal and Quebec industry grant programs quietly aided this allegedly private-enterprise success story.

While the World Wide Web (WWW) and cell phones provided expanding global markets, Canada's fibre-optics firms, particularly Nortel, also performed well in the late 1990s. The WWW, which had become part of everyday life for many Canadians by the end of the millennium, had begun in December 1990 as a project in a physics laboratory in Geneva, Switzerland. Two computer scientists combined the concepts of the "internet" and hypertext to revolutionize communications with a new system of information storage and exchange. Soon governments, including Canada's, were talking about an "information highway" that would connect all citizens, and corporations were using "the net" to lure new customers for everything from books to stocks. While Canadians proved less willing than Americans to use the internet for more than retrieval of information, the WWW was touted as the wave of the future for everything from receiving information from governments to buying groceries.

CANADIAN FOREIGN POLICY AND THE ECONOMY

In the late twentieth century, the impact of economic concerns on foreign policy continued to be evident. Arms sales provide an example of economic activities with a foreign-policy overlay. Although Canada proclaimed its support of human rights and peace among nations, it cheerfully sold arms to Iraq and Iran as the two countries waged a territorial war in the 1980s. In 1985, Canada sold $1.9 billion in military commodities, a sixfold increase since 1970. Almost 90 percent of those arms were sold to the Americans. The federal government continued to subsidize defence industries, even though studies suggested that the expenditures would create more jobs in other areas of the economy.

In the 1990s, as the Soviet Union dissolved, it became clear that the end of the Cold War would not necessarily usher in an era of peace. Iraq's invasion of Kuwait, an American ally, in August 1990 marked the first major post–Cold War incident. Canada supported a tough United Nations embargo against Iraq, and then supported an American invasion of that country despite criticism from the peace movement that the embargo had not been given a chance to work. The Gulf War was enormously popular in the United States but less so in Canada, particularly in Quebec where a majority opposed Canadian participation. Nonetheless, Mulroney lent his full support to President George Bush, extending him a hero's welcome when he visited Ottawa after the war.

Canada's role in peacekeeping remained the aspect of foreign policy that made Canadians proudest. Although only 1149 Canadian military personnel served in United Nations peacekeeping missions in 1991, they accounted for more than 10 percent of all UN peacekeepers in the world. The nation's long record of service in Cyprus and the Middle East drew praise from many quarters of the globe. That record was supplemented by Canada's peacekeeping efforts in the chaotic and dangerous atmosphere of Yugoslavia, which had flown apart in the early 1990s, leaving a variety of competing ethnic-based groups to vie for territory in a series of bloody civil wars. The image of Canadian peacekeeping was tarnished by racist and murderous behaviour on the part of some of its peacekeepers in Somalia.

In this period, Prime Minister Chrétien and most of the provincial premiers conducted trade missions in the People's Republic of China, demonstrating an unwillingness to apply more than token pressures on China's government to respect human rights. The government also rejected calls to suspend defence orders for such countries as Turkey, Vietnam, and Thailand because of their questionable human rights records, and was slow to respond to concerns over the use of child labour by some of its Asian trading partners. In 1997, the Canadian government resisted pressures to exclude Indonesia's President Suharto, responsible for the murder of hundreds of thousands of his fellow citizens, from the Asia-Pacific Economic Cooperation (APEC) summit in Vancouver. Outside the meeting of the political and economic leaders of the Pacific Rim countries, protesters denounced Suharto's presence. RCMP officers pepper-sprayed protesters, and evidence suggested that the Prime Minister's Office had directed much of the security strategy for the conference. Although Canada's overall record in opposing dictators when trade was at stake was spotty, the government of Brian Mulroney played a leadership role in boycotting trade with South Africa's apartheid regime. The boycotts in turn caused an economic crisis in that country that forced its whites-only government to negotiate with liberation forces for a transition to a non-racial democracy.

CONCLUSION

Since 1975, Canadians have engaged in a protracted debate about the role of the state in the economy and the welfare of the nation's citizens. Neo-liberals maintain that the struggle to reduce government debts should be the country's first priority even if some people get hurt.

If Canada drowned in a sea of debt, it would have no future in a world where capital is global in its scope. Opponents counter that such arguments betray a lack of understanding of economic history, especially that of the 1930s, when lack of compassion brought misery to millions of Canadians. With a more redistributive taxation system and policies designed to meet the needs of the nation's most needy citizens and conserve its vast resources, Canada could serve as a model of what needs to be done if human beings are to survive on this planet. The jury is still out on this question, but one thing is clear. As we will see in the next chapter, the economy and the policies designed for its well-being have a major impact on Canadian political life.

NOTES

1 Roméo Dallaire, *Shake Hands with the Devil: The Failure of Humanity in Rwanda* (Toronto: Random House, 2003), 6.

2 Mel Hurtig, *The Betrayal of Canada*, rev. ed. (Toronto: Stoddart, 1992), 339.

RELATED READINGS IN THIS SERIES

From *Nation and Society: Readings in Post-Confederation Canadian History*
Michael J. Broadway, "'This Little Piggy Went to the Prairies': Growth and Opposition to the Prairie Hog Industry," 438–451.

From Primary Documents CD-ROM, Volume II
Restructuring: The Free Trade Agreement (FTA) to Women: Free Trade Ahead
Does Globalization Help the Poor?
Fortress Quebec: A Return to Tear Gas and Violence
No Sitting on the Fence

SELECTED READING

International economic and environmental developments are assessed in Robert Gilpin, *The Challenge of Global Capitalism: The World Economy in the 21st Century* (Princeton: Princeton University Press, 2000); M. Patricia Marchak, *The Integrated Circus: The New Right and the Restructuring of Global Markets* (Montreal: McGill-Queen's University Press, 1991); and Susan George, *A Fate Worse Than Debt* (New York: Grove Press, 1988). The implications for Canada are discussed in Stephen Clarkson, *Uncle Sam and Us: Globalization, Neoconservatism, and the Canadian State* (Toronto: University of Toronto Press, 2002). On the Canadian economy after 1975, directly opposed views are found in Harold Chorney, John Hotson, and Mario Seccarecia, *The Deficit Made Me Do It* (Ottawa: Canadian Centre for Policy Alternatives, 1992) and Linda McQuaig, *Shooting the Hippo: Death by Deficit and Other Canadian Myths* (Toronto: Viking, 1995), on the one hand, and David Laidler and William Robson, *The Great Canadian Disinflation: the Economics and Politics of Monetary Policy in Canada, 1988–1993* (Toronto: C.D. Howe Institute, 1993) and Kenneth Norrie and Douglas Owram, *A History of the Canadian Economy* (Toronto: Harcourt Brace Jovanovich, 1991) on the other. Focusing on threats to the welfare state are Gary Teeple, *Globalization and the Decline of Social Reform: Into the Twenty-First Century* (Toronto: Garamond, 2000) and such feminist readings of the changing socio-economic environment as Isabella Bakker, ed., *Rethinking Restructuring: Gender and Change in Canada* (Toronto: University of Toronto Press, 1996); Patricia M. Evans and Gerda R. Werkele, eds., *Women and the Canadian Welfare State: Challenges and Change* (Toronto: Oxford University Press, 1997); and Sylvia B. Bashevkin, *Women on the Defensive: Living Through*

Conservative Times (Chicago: University of Chicago Press, 1998). An attempt to place recent Canadian economic developments within the country's larger economic and intellectual history is Harold Chorney and Philip Hansen, *Toward a Humanist Political Economy* (Montreal: Black Rose, 1992). Maureen Baker, *Canadian Family Policies: Cross National Comparisons* (Toronto: University of Toronto Press, 1995) places changes in Canadian social policy in international perspective.

On Canadian-American economic relations before the Free Trade Agreement, useful works include Stephen Clarkson, *Canada and the Reagan Challenge*, 2nd ed. (Toronto: Lorimer, 1985) and G. Bruce Doern and Glen Toner, *The Politics of Energy* (Toronto: Nelson, 1985). The argument for free trade is put forward in the three-volume *Report of the Royal Commission on the Economic Union and Development Prospects for Canada* (Macdonald Report) of 1985. Views from the opposite side are found in James Laxer, *Leap of Faith: Free Trade and the Future of Canada* (Edmonton: Hurtig, 1986) and Marjorie Griffin Cohen, *Free Trade and the Future of Women's Work: Manufacturing and Service Industries* (Toronto: Garamond, 1987). On the impact of the Canadian-American Free Trade Agreement, see Duncan Cameron, Daniel Drache, and Mel Watkins, eds., *Canada Under Free Trade* (Toronto: Lorimer, 1993); Mel Hurtig, *The Betrayal of*

Canada, rev. ed. (Toronto: Stoddart, 1992); and Maude Barlow and Bruce Campbell, *Take Back the Nation* (Toronto: Key Porter, 1991). Works on NAFTA include Mario F. Bognanno and Kathryn J. Ready, eds., *The North American Free Trade Agreement: Labor, Industry and Government Perspectives* (Westport, CT: Praeger, 1993); Ricardo Grinspan and Maxwell A. Cameron, eds., *The Political Economy of North American Free Trade* (New York: St. Martin's Press, 1993); and Deborah Brandt, ed., *Women Working the NAFTA Food Chain: Women, Food and Globalization* (Toronto: Sumach, 2000). Opposing perspectives by Canadians are represented by Ian Robinson, *North American Trade as if Democracy Mattered: What's Wrong with NAFTA and What Are the Alternatives?* (Ottawa: Canadian Centre for Policy Alternatives, 1993) and Stelios Loizides and Gilles Rheaume, *The North American Free Trade Agreement: Implications for Canada* (Ottawa: Conference Board of Canada, 1993).

Canada's controversial involvement in peacekeeping in Somalia in the 1990s is explored in Sherene Razack, *Dark Threats and White Knights: The Somalia Affair, Peacekeeping and the New Imperialism* (Toronto: University of Toronto Press, 2004). On the Rwanda tragedy, see Roméo Dallaire, *Shake Hands with the Devil: The Failure of Humanity in Rwanda* (Toronto: Random House, 2003).

CHAPTER 21

The Politics of Uncertainty, 1976–1999

TIMELINE

1976	Parti Québécois forms Quebec government
	Established Programs Financing replaces block funding for medicare and post-secondary institutions
1977	Joe Clark heads federal government
1979–80	Pierre Trudeau serves as prime minister
1980–84	National Energy Program; Quebec referendum rejects sovereignty-association
1980	Quebec referendum
1982	Constitution Act proclaimed
1984	John Turner is prime minister from June to September
1984–93	Progressive Conservatives under Brian Mulroney form federal government
1987	Meech Lake Accord approved unanimously by premiers; Reform Party established
1990	Meech Lake Accord dies; Bloc Québécois formed
1992	Charlottetown Accord defeated in national referendum
1993	Kim Campbell is the first woman prime minister of Canada, for just over four months; Liberals under Jean Chrétien form federal government
1995	"No" side wins a narrow victory in a second Quebec referendum
2000	Federal Clarity Act passed

In 1995, Dr. Hubert Kammerer, an activist in Friends of Medicare (a group opposing the drift toward privatizing medical services), wrote to the *Edmonton Journal* about the unnecessary death of a patient he had recently discharged from hospital. The patient was a diabetic law professor who suffered from dementia and therefore needed home care to inject him with insulin twice a day. Following health care cuts in Alberta, the professor's home-care visits were reduced to twice weekly. One evening, left to take responsibility for his own insulin, he injected himself, forgot he had done so, then injected himself again. He died of irreversible brain damage. Dr. Kammerer wrote that this was an extreme example of what "can be found in a health care system that has had too much cut out of it too quickly and is in danger of falling apart."[1]

The "welfare state" consensus of the three postwar decades cracked in the last quarter of the twentieth century. Just as neo-liberals supported unfettered investment and trade, they opposed expensive social welfare programs. Both of the country's major political parties and their provincial counterparts embraced neo-liberal thinking. As they did so, the neo-liberals quickly discovered that many Canadians supported the goal of a generous welfare state and joined organizations to prevent what they saw as a deep and troubling transformation of their society. This chapter looks at the political struggles of the last quarter of the twentieth century with an emphasis on the ideological battle between egalitarians and free marketers.

QUEBEC SOVEREIGNTY

The success of the Parti Québécois (PQ) in the 1976 provincial election in Quebec ushered in a new era in Canadian political life. Although the PQ was defeated by the resurgent Liberals in 1985, they were returned to power in 1994. Two referenda—in 1980 and 1995—failed to achieve the PQ's stated goal of creating a sovereign Quebec, but in the 1995 referendum Quebecers came close to endorsing such a policy. Only a paper-thin majority—0.6 percent—voted to maintain the federation; moreover, for the first time, a decisive majority of Francophones—60 percent—expressed the desire to have Quebec form an independent nation.

Apart from high unemployment, the major impetus for sovereignty in Quebec came from the flowering of cultural nationalism. No longer protected by an omnipresent Roman Catholic Church and a high birth rate from assimilation into North American values, Francophone Quebecers attempted to create a distinct identity for themselves within a secular North American context. The more radical nationalists felt that the best way to nurture and protect a new identity was to make Quebec an independent nation with a seat in the United Nations, ambassadors abroad, and a central bank. They claimed that the federal government's efforts to exercise control over social programs and civil rights were not only intended to circumvent a constitution that promoted decentralization but also to erode the ability of the people of Quebec to determine their own future.

The rest of the country was skeptical about such claims. Wasn't the prime minister invariably a Quebecer? Wasn't Quebec benefiting handsomely from its membership in confederation? Quebec received more than its per capita share of transfer grants and federal government contracts. Ottawa's bureaucracy, once virtually closed to Francophones, especially at senior levels, came to reflect the linguistic balance in the nation. Sovereignists argued that the poverty that federal programs were trying to address was itself the product of a long history of colonialism. Only by seizing their destiny in their own hands could Quebecers become a prosperous, entrepreneurial people, no longer dependent on outsiders who, while handing them money, were trying to assimilate them.

Unlike the militants who had grabbed the headlines during the October Crisis of 1970, the PQ under René Lévesque wanted to secure independence through a democratic process. The PQ faced a powerful opponent in Pierre Trudeau, who vigorously championed Canadian federalism. In June 1979, the Liberals lost an election to the Progressive Conservatives led by Joe Clark, whose minority government lasted only

Claude Ryan and René Lévesque.
Library and Archives Canada/PA117480

10 months. The Liberals under Trudeau roared back to power in March 1980, just in time for the PQ-sponsored referendum on sovereignty-association. About 60 percent of Quebecers, including half of all Francophones and most Anglophones and Allophones, voted "non" to a question that asked for authorization for the Quebec government to negotiate political sovereignty with economic association. The outcome did not put an end to the question of Quebec's status in confederation: even federalists in Quebec were reluctant to defend the status quo in federal-provincial relations. Claude Ryan, leader of the Quebec Liberal Party and head of the "non" campaign, advocated a renewed federalism that would give Quebec control over social programs and most economic policies, leaving the federal government in charge of foreign affairs, defence, and monetary policy. This was a far cry from Trudeau's

advocacy of federal control in any area involving the national interest.

PATRIATING THE CONSTITUTION

Once the referendum was over, Trudeau announced that the federal government was tired of endless constitutional consultations with the provinces and Quebec's inevitable vetoes of attempts to patriate the constitution. The time was long overdue to end Great Britain's responsibilities for Canada's constitutional amendments and Trudeau was determined to go down in history as the prime minister who finally "brought the constitution home." With or without provincial approval, Ottawa would ask the British government to place the constitution in Canadian hands. The patriated constitution would include a charter of rights and freedoms and a new amending formula.

Most provinces resisted Trudeau's initiative, seeing it as a bid to weaken provincial rights. Only Ontario and New Brunswick, which had few grievances with Ottawa at the time, supported the plan. Lévesque had the support of seven other premiers in opposing Trudeau. The eight provinces agreed to stand together in challenging the procedure in the courts. The Supreme Court ruled in September 1981 that "substantial consent" of the provinces, but not unanimity, was needed for patriation.

Pierre Trudeau and Queen Elizabeth II completing the patriation of Canada's constitution.
Library and Archives Canada/PA141503

On 5 November 1981, nine premiers came to terms with Trudeau, fearing that the alternative was unilateral federal action with no concessions to provinces. The premiers of the three western-most provinces and Newfoundland and Labrador had been won over by Trudeau's agreement to strengthen provincial control over resources. In Quebec, which had lost its veto over constitutional change, Lévesque argued that he had been betrayed by the Anglophone premiers and that their actions, which he referred to as the "night of the long knives," demonstrated that Quebec would never receive justice in the federal system.

THE CHARTER OF RIGHTS AND FREEDOMS

The Constitution Act of 1982 resulted from the deal between Trudeau and the provincial premiers, and consisted of the renamed British North America Act, an amending formula, and the Charter of Rights and Freedoms. The amending formula allowed the federal government to change the constitution with the approval of the federal parliament plus two-thirds of the provinces representing a combined population of at least 50 percent of all Canadians. Unanimous consent of all provinces and both houses of parliament would continue to be required for amendments affecting representation in the House of Commons, Senate, and Supreme Court and for changes affecting the use of the French and English languages.

Furthermore, a province that believed that its legislative or proprietary rights were compromised by an amendment could declare that amendment null and void within its boundaries. A province would also have the right to opt out with full financial compensation from a program established by amendment that affected education or cultural matters. As a concession to Atlantic Canada, Saskatchewan, and Manitoba, section 36 of the constitution committed Canadian governments to the principle of equalization to "ensure that provincial governments have sufficient revenue to provide reasonably comparable levels of public services at reasonably comparable levels of taxation."

The Charter guaranteed Canadians freedom of speech, association, conscience, and religion and prohibited discrimination on the basis of colour, sex, or creed. Voting rights, rights to legal counsel, and protection against arbitrary arrest were also enshrined in the document. While the courts could be used to protect various rights that governments had at times infringed in the past, there were several restrictions on constitutional freedoms. Legislatures could place "reasonable limits" on citizens' enjoyment of their rights. Mobility rights were limited by giving provinces experiencing high unemployment the right to give existing residents preferential treatment in hiring. Provinces could also override constitutional rights by specifically exempting pieces of legislation from the Charter's reach. This clause, dubbed the "notwithstanding clause" because it allowed legislatures to assert that a law would apply notwithstanding Charter provisions, was used by Quebec to exempt all of its legislation from the Charter. The Quebec government claimed that its own human rights code protected citizens better than the federal version.

Section 28 declared that Charter rights "are guaranteed equally to male and female persons." This provision owed its existence to concerted pressure from women's groups, as the proposed Charter had originally said nothing about gender equality. Effective feminist lobbying also succeeded in exempting the section from the override provisions of the Charter. Although equality provisions fell short of the demands of some women's groups, feminists celebrated their success in overcoming government indifference and their own disagreements to secure section 28.

Native lobbies were likewise only partially successful in pressuring for changes to the constitution. Their attempts to win the right to self-determination failed, but the Charter acknowledged Aboriginal concerns by guaranteeing that nothing in the document would affect existing treaty rights or prejudice later land settlements. A constitutional conference on Native rights was to be called within one year of the proclamation of the constitution.

For women, the new constitution would prove a disappointment in practice. Early Charter decisions regarding gender rights suggested that the courts, dominated by men, were blind to the differences in social power between the sexes. In 1989, a study prepared for the Canadian Advisory Council on the Status of Women reported that "women are initiating few cases, and men are using the Charter to strike back at women's hard-won protection and benefits."[2]

Aboriginal peoples were no more successful. Three first ministers' conferences yielded nothing on attempts to win an amendment guaranteeing Native self-government. Seven provinces, including either Ontario or Quebec, had to be on side, and Quebec refused to consider constitutional amendments on the grounds that it had not signed the new constitution and therefore did not recognize its legitimacy. At the third conference, in 1987, British Columbia, Alberta, and Saskatchewan, all with Conservative or Social Credit governments, claimed that Native demands were imprecise. They feared that their provinces' rights to control resources would be compromised by a self-government amendment. In practice, the focus of constitutional talks after 1982 was far more on the rights of provinces, especially Quebec, than it was on social justice issues.

THE MEECH LAKE ACCORD

In the 1984 federal election, Brian Mulroney had swept Quebec and was determined to cement his party's new-found respect in the province. Robert Bourassa, returned to power as Quebec premier the following year, was equally eager to win constitutional concessions that could blunt the sovereignist thrust. He presented five demands that had to be fulfilled before Quebec would sign the constitution. The first was a clause recognizing Quebec as a distinct society. The second was a Quebec veto for constitutional amendments. The remaining three would give all provinces a greater role in immigration, allow them to remain outside any new cost-sharing programs without financial penalty, and have the federal government choose Supreme Court judges from lists of nominees provided by the premiers.

A first ministers' conference held at Meech Lake, near Ottawa, in April 1987, tentatively approved a package that met Quebec's demands and incorporated concerns expressed by other provinces. To win support from premiers who balked at the idea of Quebec having a veto over constitutional change, Mulroney granted all provinces a veto. The Meech Lake Accord would be the first test of whether an amendment could muster the consent of the federal parliament and all the provincial legislatures. The first ministers had given themselves a three-year deadline to achieve this consent, and, to close off public debate, Mulroney announced that not one word of the document could be changed.

To Mulroney's chagrin, there was considerable opposition to the deal. PQ leaders claimed that the "distinct society" clause was window dressing because it recognized no special powers for Quebec. Trudeau, by contrast, denounced the clause because it might lead to special powers for Quebec and, in his view, a kind of quasi-sovereignty for that province. How the courts would interpret the distinct society clause was hypothetical, but Meech opponents, both federalist and sovereignist, rejected a clause that appeared to abandon such an important question to the judiciary.

Elijah Harper.
CP Photo

Apart from the distinct society clause, the two aspects of the accord that drew the most fire were cost-sharing provisions and the unanimity required for constitutional amendments. Supporters of particular amendments believed that the unanimity clause would permanently dash hopes of reform. For the Aboriginal peoples, who had been one province short of a crucial amendment just months before Meech Lake was announced, the unanimity clause was a particularly bitter pill. Aboriginal self-government appeared to have been sacrificed on the altar of provincial rights.

Outside Quebec, a large majority of Canadians opposed the accord. Women's groups, trade unions, and anti-poverty groups criticized the provision that allowed provinces to exempt themselves from new federal shared-cost programs to set up their own programs. Groups working for new national policies, particularly in the child-care area, suspected that provincial opposition would block the establishment of new programs. After all, medicare had been legislated with popular support but limited enthusiasm from provincial governments. Similar opposition to a national child-care program would result in federal abandonment of the notion or a hodgepodge of "opt-out" programs with federal money but no national standards.

National women's groups demanded that women be included in a clause that exempted Aboriginal peoples and multicultural groups from the application of the distinct society clause. Quebec women's groups were divided on the issue. Many feminist nationalists decried the suggestion that a Quebec government might use the distinct society clause to limit women's abortion rights or to bar women from certain occupations. They claimed that Anglophone women who feared that Quebec might revert to Roman Catholic conservatism and roll back women's victories were out of touch with modern Quebec, which had the most progressive women's legislation in Canada.

Although northerners had no direct voice in the constitutional amendment process, most were relieved at the growing opposition to the accord. Residents of the Yukon and the Northwest Territories could hardly support an agreement that would virtually preclude them from becoming provinces. Without provincehood, they would have no right to nominate senators or Supreme Court judges, and they would have no say at constitutional conferences or regarding constitutional amendments.

Much of the Meech Lake debate might have become academic had several elections between 1987 and 1989 not changed the provincial arithmetic. Clyde Wells in Newfoundland and Labrador had the provincial legislature rescind its earlier ratification and a new Liberal government in New Brunswick under the leadership of Frank McKenna (whose party won every seat in the legislature in the 1987 election) dragged its feet on approving an agreement that seemed to isolate the province's Acadian population. A minority Progressive Conservative government, led by Gary Filmon, was elected in Manitoba in 1988. Both opposition parties in the province opposed Meech, with the NDP under a new leader reversing the position it had taken when in power. Filmon's party was divided on the issue, uniting against the accord only after Bourassa had used the notwithstanding clause to nullify a Supreme Court decision regarding Bill 101, which prohibited the use of languages other than French on store signs.

Elijah Harper, the lone Native member in the Manitoba legislature and a former minister in the provincial cabinet under the NDP, became a key player in the Meech Lake drama by using procedural methods to prevent the accord's passage in Manitoba before the deadline. The party leaders could have changed the procedures to force a vote on time, as Ottawa pressured them to do, but, responding to public opinion, they decided to let the agreement lapse. When it became clear that Manitoba could not pass the accord in time, Wells called off the vote in Newfoundland and Labrador.

Bourassa was furious, arguing that the accord had been designed to meet Quebec's demands and not to address the discontent of the other provinces. Quebec Francophones also reacted angrily to the defeat of the accord: for several months, polls suggested that a majority of Quebecers were prepared to vote in favour of sovereignty. A group of nationalist MPs from Quebec, mainly Progressive Conservatives, responded in 1990 by forming the Bloc Québécois, a federal party supporting an independent Quebec and attempting to defend Quebec rights in Ottawa until such time as independence was achieved. The party was headed by Lucien Bouchard, a renegade minister in Mulroney's cabinet. This was the first time since 1867 that a Quebec party dedicated to removing the province from confederation had a presence in Ottawa.

Although Bourassa continued to support federalism, his party adopted a tough constitutional policy demanding that Quebec have absolute jurisdiction in many areas of economic and social policy where the federal government had total or shared power. To appease sovereignists and put pressure on the rest of the country, the Quebec National Assembly passed legislation calling for a referendum on either sovereignty or an offer of constitutional renewal from the rest of Canada.

THE CHARLOTTETOWN ACCORD

As the clock ticked toward Bourassa's referendum deadline, Mulroney convened a marathon session of the premiers and some Native leaders, producing the Charlottetown Accord of 28 August 1992. The accord was a complex document that included concessions to each of the players in the room. Quebec was to receive much of what it had been promised during the Meech Lake discussions, but was denied important new powers. The federal government agreed to turn over certain areas, such as housing and forestry, to the provinces, but this fell far short of Quebec's demands.

To achieve agreement on special status for Quebec, Bourassa had to make a concession that was galling to most Quebec nationalists: equal provincial representation in the Senate. Quebec nationalists maintained that Canada was a partnership between two founding nations. They did not accept the implicit thrust of the proposed Senate reform: that Canada was a federation of 10 equal provinces.

The premiers recognized Native rights to self-government, but the perimeters were to be determined in subsequent negotiations. A social charter, the brainchild of Ontario's NDP government, committed governments to maintain existing social programs but made this commitment "non-justiciable": no one could take a government to court for failing to live up to the social commitments in the constitution.

Several provinces, including Quebec, agreed to test support for the constitutional proposals in binding referenda. The Mulroney government, despite its opposition to popular consultation on constitutional

Cartoonist's view of Brian Mulroney turning his attention from the constitution to the economy.
Reprinted with permission from the *Globe and Mail*

changes, therefore decided to hold a national referendum on the Charlottetown Accord. It was only the third national referendum in Canadian history and the results of the first two—on prohibition in 1898 and conscription in 1942—had not been binding.

Ultimately, the "yes" forces could not withstand the many-pronged "no" campaign. Some Canadians felt left out of the constitutional process; many more did not like certain features of the accord and resented being told that they had to accept the deal as a package. Weary of continued constitutional impasse, disillusioned by political dishonesty, incompetence, and scandal, and uneasy because of the long recession that showed no sign of lifting, many Canadians simply wanted to send their politicians a message. On 26 October 1992, three have-not provinces—Newfoundland and Labrador, Prince Edward Island, and New Brunswick—supported the accord in the hope that constitutional bickering could be put to an end. Ontario voters were split virtually down the middle. In the remaining six provinces, the accord suffered a clear defeat.

Popular disillusionment with the constitutional process and politics in general was directed primarily at Prime Minister Mulroney. When he announced his intention to resign as prime minister early in 1993, there was widespread rejoicing. Voters virtually obliterated his party in the federal election that year, with only two Conservatives elected across the country and the new party leader, Kim Campbell, Canada's first woman prime minister, soundly defeated in her own Vancouver riding. The Liberal Party under Jean Chrétien returned to power with a comfortable majority.

QUEBEC AFTER CHARLOTTETOWN

After a fiery campaign by leader Lucien Bouchard, the Bloc Québécois won 49 percent of the Quebec vote in the federal election, enough to give the party 54 of Quebec's 75 seats and make it the official opposition in parliament. The Bloc's promises to defend Quebec interests appealed to many Francophones who were reluctant to support Quebec's leaving confederation, but it was clear that the desire for independence and exasperation with the rest of the country's apparent inflexibility regarding Quebec were growing.

In the provincial election in 1994, the Parti Québécois, led by Jacques Parizeau, won an impressive majority of seats. The PQ enjoyed much greater support among Francophones than did the Liberals under their new leader, Daniel Johnson. Johnson's political pedigree was impressive—he was the son of former Union Nationale premier Daniel Johnson and the brother of former Parti Québécois premier Pierre Marc Johnson—but he was an uncharismatic leader. Nonetheless, the Liberals' overwhelming support from Anglophones and Allophones, in addition to support from Francophones on the Island of Montreal, meant that they virtually tied the PQ in the popular vote.

About 10 percent of the Francophone vote went to a new party, the Action démocratique du Québec, formed mainly by breakaway Liberals and led by the youthful former president of the Liberal youth wing, Mario Dumont. It was generally unclear to campaign observers whether Dumont was a sovereignist or a supporter of "special status" for Quebec within confederation. Dumont's supporters and PQ supporters who hesitated before the party's sovereignty option were called "soft nationalists" to distinguish them from hard-liners such as Jacques Parizeau, who wanted Quebec to become an independent nation-state first and worry about its relations with Canada afterward.

During the 1994 election, Parizeau promised a referendum on sovereignty during the PQ's mandate. There was a great deal of debate among sovereignist leaders about what the question should be. The eventual referendum question in October 1995 read: "Do you agree that Quebec should become sovereign, after having made a formal offer to Canada for a new economic and political partnership, within the scope of the bill respecting the future of Quebec and of the agreement signed on June 12, 1995?"

Voters were confused. Polls suggested that a third of committed "yes" voters believed that a sovereign Quebec would continue to have representatives in the Canadian parliament and that its citizens would keep Canadian citizenship and social benefits. Even more voters accepted the claim of the sovereignist forces that an independent Quebec could continue to use Canadian currency. The "no" side asserted that the sovereignists were telling lies to attract the support of

soft nationalists. They pointed out that the government of Canada, contrary to what the sovereignists said, could not negotiate sovereignty-association with Quebec. Canada's remaining nine provinces would not agree that Quebec, which had enjoyed just a tenth of the constitutional decision-making power allocated to provinces and a quarter of the representation in the federal parliament, should suddenly become an equal partner to the federal government of Canada. Quebec could leave confederation, but, if it did, it could not continue to enjoy the benefits that came with Canadian citizenship.

In the early stages of the referendum, such arguments seemed to sway a comfortable majority of the people of Quebec, but the campaign momentum took a swing in the other direction when Lucien Bouchard became its unofficial leader. Bouchard was popular in Quebec; for some, he became an almost saintly figure when he survived an attack of a rare and usually deadly disease in 1994. Publicly less strident than Parizeau, he seemed better able to convince Quebecers that Canada was bluffing when it claimed that it would not negotiate with Quebec.

Bouchard was also able to take advantage of the mean-spiritedness taking hold in much of the rest of the country to create pessimism about the advantages for Quebec of staying in Canada. The federal government had announced massive cuts in social spending. As most opinion surveys showed, Quebecers were far more egalitarian in their values than Canadians as a whole. Bouchard's attempts to portray a Canada that was no longer caring and sharing struck a responsive chord. With the province's unemployment rate seemingly stuck in permanent double digits well above the Canadian average, there was a great desire for change in Quebec.

Prime Minister Chrétien's decision not to offer Quebec any changes, constitutional or otherwise, should its citizens vote "non" alienated some soft nationalists and made life difficult for Johnson, the official leader of the "non" forces. Only in the last week before the vote, with polls suggesting the sovereignty forces were taking the lead, did Chrétien actively step into the campaign. On nationwide television, he made an emotional plea to Quebec not to throw away the benefits of confederation, promising recognition of the province as a distinct society and decentralization of power in Canada. Meanwhile, an estimated 100 000 Canadians from outside Quebec joined a last-minute rally in Montreal to plead with the province not to break up the country.

Referendum night was a nail-biter for both sides. The complete division within Quebec society was obvious. Premier Parizeau responded gracelessly to defeat, telling supporters, "It's true we have been defeated, but basically by what? By money and the ethnic vote." While the "ethnic" vote was solidly against leaving Canada, about 40 percent of Francophones also voted to reject the vague offer represented in the referendum question. Within months of the referendum defeat, Parizeau had resigned the premiership and Bouchard had moved from Ottawa to Quebec City to become the province's premier and the undisputed leader of the sovereignist forces.

Despite Bouchard's best efforts to keep sovereignty on the front-burner of Quebec politics, there was a growing antipathy in the province to placing constitutional issues ahead of economic ones on the public agenda. In 2000, the federal government, taking advantage of a decline in enthusiasm in the province for a referendum, passed the Clarity Act, which insisted that no referendum was valid unless its wording was clear and unambiguous. While the Bouchard government denounced the federal intervention in Quebec political life implied by the bill, few people in the province seemed very interested in the debate.

Nonetheless, in the aftermath of the second referendum, Canada's future seemed less assured than ever. Nor was it only Quebec that seemed restive and unsure about its political future. In every region of the country, economic slowdown had produced social and political instability and the search for scapegoats. It remained to be seen whether an economic upturn alone would be enough to end the disputes between provinces and Ottawa.

ONTARIO'S INTERRUPTED PROSPERITY

Southern Ontario, the country's traditional industrial heartland, was hardest hit by the economic uncertainty that had descended in the 1970s. Manufacturing jobs disappeared, particularly during the recessions of 1982–1985 and 1990–1993, and companies declared bankruptcy at an alarming rate. In the post-war years, high-paying jobs in such sectors as steel, automobiles and automobile parts, aerospace, and electrical appliances had been the sources of envy by much of the rest of the country. Now people working in these industries were being laid off with little prospect of finding jobs for which they were qualified.

The succession of Progressive Conservative administrations that had governed Ontario from 1943 to 1985 came around slowly to the business view that the state could no longer afford the full range of services it was providing. When the newly chosen premier, Frank Miller, put forth this message in 1985, the Conservative dynasty came crashing down. The Liberals formed a minority government with NDP support and won a big majority in 1987. By then, the Ontario economy was booming again and the Liberals, led by David Peterson, stood squarely against the federal Mulroney government's program of social spending cuts and free trade with the United States. The government eliminated so-called extra-billing by physicians and extended full funding to separate schools up to grade 13. But the Liberal bubble soon burst. A party fund-raising scandal weakened the Liberals and voters reacted angrily to an election call in 1990, just three years into the government's mandate. They replaced Peterson with the NDP, headed by Bob Rae.

The NDP proved unable to adopt a consistent policy. In their first budget in 1991, they defied the neoliberal logic that had gripped most governments in Canada, producing a stimulative budget with a $10-billion deficit. The business community and media condemned this return to Keynesianism, which would have looked perfectly respectable to all political parties in the 1950s, as socialist irresponsibility.

Over the next two years, the NDP largely recanted its first budget and cut social spending. After a frenzied campaign by the insurance industry, it also abandoned the popular election promise of public auto insurance, which had been introduced in the three other provinces where Co-operative Commonwealth Federation (CCF) or NDP governments had been elected. Rae attempted to maintain the general principles of the post-war social compromise, but alienated much of the union movement when he imposed an across-the-board wage cut of 5 percent on all public sector workers in provincial or municipal institutions.

Those whose salaries were under $30 000 were spared, and the government's "social contract" attempted to compensate for wage cuts with job security guarantees and greater worker involvement in implementing programs. Nevertheless, unionists were appalled by a supposedly pro-labour government violating union-negotiated contracts.

One area where the NDP government had considerable success was in bailouts of large private companies that had run into trouble either because of changing economic circumstances, poor management, or international corporate strategies. Spruce Falls Power and Paper, Algoma Steel, de Havilland Aircraft, Mitel Corp., Provincial Papers, St. Mary's Paper, Algoma Central Railway, Urban Transportation Development Corp., and Ontario Bus Industries, among others, rebounded with state aid, saving many jobs. Still, unemployment remained high.

In 1995, Ontario voters were in a mood to punish the hapless Bob Rae, who had the misfortune to govern during five years of economic stagnation. Pushed by Ottawa's cost-cutting measures, Rae asked for $2 billion in wage cuts from Ontario's public service. When the public sector unions boycotted talks on the matter, the NDP government imposed the "social contract"—a wage freeze and 12 unpaid days off—quickly dubbed "Rae Days." During the 1995 election campaign, Liberal leader Lyn McLeod, the first woman to lead a major party in Ontario, focused on the need to cut the deficit without raising taxes, but voters—particularly middle-age, middle-class white men—wanted an even sharper right turn. Mike Harris's Progressive Conservatives received 45 percent of the vote, almost double their previous total, running on a campaign of cutting the public service, slashing social assistance, privatizing government services, and cancelling employment equity programs.

In office, the Harris government cut taxes for the middle and upper classes while slashing health, education, and welfare expenditures to pay for it. The government cut programs to aid battered women, the disabled, and the mentally ill, closed dozens of hospitals throughout the province, and weakened environmental regulation. It initiated extensive reform at the municipal level, attempting to offload welfare expenditures onto the municipalities and initiating plans to create a "megacity" in Metro Toronto.

All of these policies provoked vocal resistance. The megacity plan was decisively rejected in local referenda, and ongoing "Days of Action" were organized by a coalition of labour and community groups. The Tories dismissed the opposition as "special interest groups" and continued to pursue their neo-liberal agenda. By the 1999 provincial election, the Ontario economy was booming and Harris was talking about reinvesting in the province, particularly in health and education. He was re-elected but with a decline in seats and the popular vote.

THE NEW WEST

Battles over control of natural resources in the early 1970s marked the return of western alienation as a major factor in national politics for the first time since the Second World War. Throughout the 1970s, the question of resource rents caused a considerable falling-out in Ottawa's relations with the three most westerly provinces. In 1980, the National Energy Program (NEP) brought matters to a head. Introduced by Trudeau, the main features of the NEP were a low "made-in-Canada" price for oil, larger federal revenue from energy production, and greater Canadian ownership of the energy industry.

The energy-producing provinces wanted Canadians to pay international prices for energy, claiming that the made-in-Canada price simply deprived them of revenues and drove away projects to develop the tar sands of northern Alberta. The costs of removing oil from the tar sands with existing technology could not be justified if the price of oil were kept artificially low. This debate pitted the three most westerly provinces and the oil-producing "wannabes" in the Atlantic provinces—Newfoundland and Nova Scotia—against energy-poor provinces and the federal government, at least while international oil prices were high. When prices began a steep decline in 1982, major oil-sands projects in Alberta came unglued. By the time the prices revived in the 1990s, cheaper processes for the extraction of oil from tar sands had become available.

Although the NEP was modified sufficiently to enable a truce between Trudeau and Alberta premier Peter Lougheed in 1981, it would be blamed by many westerners—perhaps most—for an economic downturn, beginning in 1982, in which many people lost their homes and savings. A separatist party, the Western Canada Concept (WCC), held huge rallies in Calgary and Edmonton in the wake of the announcement of the NEP and elected a rural MLA in a provincial by-election in 1982.

Trudeau claimed that the NEP was an instrument of nationalism, but if so, it was more central Canadian than pan-Canadian nationalism. Its goal to provide cheap energy meant that the energy-producing provinces, along with the multinationals that dominated the sector, had to sacrifice revenue to fuel the industries of central Canada. Since there was nothing in the policy that would help the western provinces use energy revenues to foster secondary industry, it had few long-term benefits. Ultimately the policy was a costly one for all Canadians: the grants and tax incentives offered to Canadianize the industry proved expensive for the public purse, particularly at a time when deficits were beginning to soar. Unlike transfer payments to individuals, these incentives had no obvious stimulative impact on the economy.

The NEP was not the only source of western alienation. Grain farmers were angry at the decision of the Trudeau government in the early 1980s to phase out the historic Crow rates, which had kept the cost of shipping grain competitive with American farmers' transportation costs. Another common complaint in the region was that the lion's share of federal contracts was awarded to Quebec. Western outrage greeted the announcement that Bombardier had received a large contract for maintenance of Canada's CF-18 military aircraft despite the fact that Winnipeg's Bristol Aerospace had submitted a lower and technically superior bid.

Such events combined with a resurgence of right-wing sentiments to help produce the Reform Party in 1987. Led by Preston Manning, son of Ernest Manning, Alberta's long-time Social Credit premier, the Reformers declared that the West did not want out of confederation: rather, it wanted in, and wished to reconstruct confederation to better reflect the regions. While they were anti-separatist, Reformers shared the WCC's right-wing agenda. They wanted the federal deficit slashed, even if it meant sacrificing subsidy programs to farmers and abandoning universality in social programs, and they wanted Canadian immigration policy to favour Europeans as it had before 1962.

Manning's iron grip over the party ensured that members of Canada's extreme right were excluded from membership and that the original racist immigration plank was partially modified.

By the 1993 federal election, the Reformers were wooing Ontario voters, appearing more like a Canadian version of the Republican Party in the United States than a regional protest party. The "New Canada" that Preston Manning and his colleagues promoted from the floor of parliament was one that was largely under the control of the provinces, with the federal government bowing out of social programs such as medicare.

Their pitch appealed to many traditional Progressive Conservative voters who believed that Mulroney's administration had been too awash in patronage and shady dealings, but they proved largely unable to win seats outside the three westernmost provinces.

British Columbia

Before the 1990s, the divide between right and left remained fairly wide in British Columbia. The NDP took between 39 and 46 percent of the vote in provincial elections, but repeatedly lost to Social Credit in what was essentially a two-party province. The Socreds, under William Bennett, demonstrated the shift away from the post-war consensus after the 1983 provincial election, when, despite their marginal victory in the popular vote, they implemented a program of massive cuts in education and social spending and the privatization of a large variety of government services.

In response, public servants and state employees such as teachers, nurses, and social workers joined with client groups to form Operation Solidarity. They shut down most state operations in the province for a week to protest the cuts. Leaders of the private sector unions shunned a request to make the shutdown a general strike, and in the end Solidarity had to be content with fairly minimal concessions on the part of Bennett's government.

Social Credit became a spent force after Bennett's successor, William Vander Zalm, a charismatic millionaire, resigned over allegations of conflict of interest in his sale of the family firm. Vander Zalm was replaced by Rita Johnson, Canada's first woman premier. In the election that followed, the NDP won a large majority without increasing their traditional vote. Much of the Social Credit vote had gone to the Liberals, who formed the official opposition. Mike Harcourt, the NDP premier, resigned in late 1995 after a flurry of criticism about his feeble attempts to deal with a party fund-raising scandal.

The Harcourt government had also had a difficult time trying to balance the demands of environmentalists and unionized forest workers, both traditional NDP supporters in the province. Clear-cutting at Clayoquot Sound on Vancouver Island became a defining issue for the organized environmental movement not only in British Columbia but across the country. Hundreds of protesters, including NDP MP Svend Robinson, were arrested as they tried to prevent loggers from clear-cutting. Forestry workers protested that the environmentalists were unconcerned about the economic devastation that would affect families and communities if logging stopped with nothing to replace it.

The triumph of the right wing in the Liberal Party gave Harcourt's replacement, Glen Clark, a chance to revive a government battered by scandal. Unlike voters in Ontario and some other provinces, British Columbia voters were not yet prepared to elect a party that focused on tax cuts and seemed suspect in its commitment to social spending. The NDP were re-elected in 1996.

Alberta

In Alberta, the Conservatives remained in office continuously after 1971, but underwent an ideological sea change as prosperity oozed away in the 1980s and 1990s. While the Conservatives had initially invested generously in social programs, they began to make cuts in social spending in the 1980s. The election of Ralph Klein as premier in 1993 escalated the shift toward less state responsibility for citizens. Klein slashed the costs of government, with social programs taking most of the punishment. Nurses, school teachers, welfare recipients, and the elderly suffered the most in a program that attracted national attention. Within the province, the most controversial move was the closing down of a large number of intensive care units in hospitals and encouraging private medical entrepreneurs

to make up for deficiencies in a slimmed-down public health system. As provincial energy revenues soared in the late 1990s, the "Klein Revolution" gave way to generous spending on health and education once again. But true to their new right-wing ideology, the Conservatives also passed legislation that permitted a degree of privatization of hospitals.

Saskatchewan and Manitoba

In the 1980s, Saskatchewan replaced the NDP administration of Allan Blakeney with a free-enterprise Conservative government under Grant Devine. The Tories privatized some Crown corporations and attempted unsuccessfully to lure businesses with subsidies and loans. Floundering in a sea of corruption, the Conservatives lost the 1991 election to the NDP, led by Roy Romanow, but much of its populist zeal was gone. Although the new government used a combination of taxes and cuts to deal with declining revenues and developed a reputation for prudent fiscal management, it had few ideas about how to diversify the Saskatchewan economy.

Manitoba's political parties were perhaps more sharply divided than Saskatchewan's. Following the NDP government led by Ed Schreyer in 1977, Sterling Lyon's Conservatives, unlike other Tory administrations of the prosperity era, were dedicated to cutting programs for the poor and health and education spending. In the 1980s, NDP premier Howard Pawley reversed directions again and, despite the province's relative poverty, ignored the growing neo-liberal campaign of the business classes. Tax increases necessary to maintain public expenditures eventually led to a tax revolt that deposed Pawley's government. The Conservatives under Gary Filmon, initially vague about the direction in which they would take the province, had clearly joined the neo-liberal camp by the mid-1990s. But in 1999, provincial voters, angry with health care cuts, put the NDP back into office, this time under Gary Doer.

ATLANTIC CANADA

During the era of post-war prosperity, the Atlantic provinces had depended on federal equalization grants and transfer payments to offset the poor economic performance of the region. Development programs, sponsored by federal and provincial governments, failed to usher in a period of sustained prosperity, and people continued to leave the region to find work. When the federal government began trying to rein in national deficits in the 1990s by cutting back on unemployment insurance and other forms of transfer payments, the four eastern provinces faced challenges at a level not seen since the 1920s.

Crisis in the Fisheries

In 1977, when Canada declared a 200-mile exclusive fishing zone in the Northwest Atlantic, it looked as if the fortunes of Atlantic Canadians were at last looking up. Rich in oil, natural gas, and fish, the offshore banks promised untold riches. From the beginning of the new era in the fishing industry, there were tensions between inshore fisheries and large corporations as to how to best manage the fisheries in light of Canada's weak efforts to prevent foreign overfishing within the 200-mile limit. Predictably, given the extent of overfishing by the North Atlantic nations, the fisheries boom of the 1970s quickly turned into a bust. By the early 1980s, East Coast processing companies were in trouble, and two corporate giants, Fishery Products International and National Sea, swallowed up their competitors. As fish stocks began to collapse in the late 1980s, Canadian quotas were cut, fish plants were shut down, and many fishing communities faced extinction.

In July 1992, the federal government announced that there would be a two-year moratorium on northern cod fishing. This meant unemployment for many Atlantic Canadians, but people from Newfoundland and Labrador were hit particularly hard. At least 19 000 fishers and plant workers in that province were thrown out of work, and the survival of dozens of communities on Newfoundland's east coast was threatened.

The Elusive Promise of Offshore Oil

Meanwhile, in the late 1970s, the large Hibernia oil field was discovered off Newfoundland. Brian Peckford, Newfoundland's Progressive Conservative premier, insisted that the province have equal control with Ottawa over offshore developments. Trudeau was reluctant to relinquish federal control of offshore resources, and in

1984 the Supreme Court upheld his view that Ottawa had exclusive jurisdiction.

The election of the Mulroney Progressive Conservatives in 1984 resulted in a victory for Peckford. With the assistance of John Crosbie, the colourful and outspoken Newfoundland member in the Mulroney cabinet, the Canada-Newfoundland Atlantic Accord was signed in 1985. While it offered fewer benefits from offshore developments than Crosbie had hoped, it seemed to signal a less rigid attitude in Ottawa toward accommodating the interests of have-not provinces.

Expectations in Newfoundland and Nova Scotia that they might follow Alberta's lead to become energy-rich provinces from an offshore oil bonanza proved slow to materialize. While stimulating economic growth, the Hibernia development provided few jobs after the construction phase ended, and the clawback provisions on equalization payments meant that the federal government rather than the provinces received the lion's share of the royalties.

Fighting Against Gravity

The tendency of capital investment to gravitate toward established centres of economic growth resulted in provincial governments resorting to desperate measures to accommodate corporate interests. When Michelin, the French-owned tire manufacturer in Nova Scotia, threatened to quit the province if one of its three sites was unionized, the province quickly passed legislation requiring that a majority of the workers from all three sites had to vote for the union before it could be legally recognized. Since two plants were in areas without a strong union tradition, the bill effectively killed chances for the union to gain a toehold. The government that was so willing to accommodate corporate concerns seemed deaf to complaints about rock slides, cave-ins, and dangerous levels of methane gas from miners at the Westray coal mine in Pictou County. When an explosion destroyed the mine in 1993, eight months into its operation, 26 men were left dead beneath the surface.

Economic uncertainty helped fuel political volatility. In New Brunswick, voters unhappy with flamboyant Conservative premier Richard Hatfield gave every seat in the province to Frank McKenna's Liberals in 1987. McKenna was particularly aggressive in trying to attract call centres to his province, but these low-paying operations did little to change the overall economic picture in New Brunswick. Following McKenna's resignation in 1997, his party collapsed and a reorganized Progressive Conservative Party swept back to power in 1999 under the youthful Bernard Lord.

Prince Edward Island experienced a similar swing from the Liberals to the Progressive Conservatives. Catherine Callbeck led the provincial Liberal Party to victory in the 1993 election, making history as the first woman in Canada to be elected to a provincial premiership. History would have been made in that election whatever the result, since the leaders of the other two major parties were also women. However, Callbeck's victory was short-lived. Forced to deal with drastic federal cutbacks, she was blamed for the pain they caused in a province where the small tax base gave finance ministers little room to manoeuvre. In 1996 Callbeck and the Liberals were turned out of office by the Progressive Conservatives led by Pat Binns. A native of Saskatchewan, Binns was a farmer who proved successful in maintaining voter confidence in the primarily rural province through two more provincial elections.

Nova Scotia's politics, dominated by the Conservatives from 1978 to 1990, entered a period of fierce three-party competition in the late 1990s. Disillusioned by the cutbacks of both Conservative and Liberal governments, a large number of provincial voters decided they had had enough of Tweedledum and Tweedledee and gave their votes to the New Democratic Party, though the NDP failed to form a government.

FEDERAL CUTBACKS

The combination of slow economic growth, increased taxes on ordinary income earners, and the return to the pre-war philosophy of business-government relations worked together to move many Canadians away from the social values that had marked the era of prosperity. Increasingly, poverty was seen not as a product of impersonal forces in the competitive marketplace but as the result of shiftlessness. "Welfare bums" who preferred government handouts to hard work, including new immigrants, were blamed for higher taxes and the appearance of increasing crime and violence, though statistics demonstrated it was not a reality.

Such views overlooked the composition of the poor. Single mothers of young children, many of whom lacked job training and most of whom lacked access to affordable quality day care, had become the largest group of poor householders. Moreover, many of the poor were not social assistance recipients; rather, they were "working poor," barely able to support themselves, let alone their families, on minimum wages that rose less quickly than inflation. Among the social welfare recipients, an increasing proportion were part-time and even full-time minimum-wage workers.

The inadequacy of minimum wages and the Canada Assistance Plan meant that many families ran out of money before their next pay cheques were due. Children whose parents were unable to afford even basic groceries regularly went hungry the last week of the month before welfare cheques arrived. Such families were forced to rely on private initiatives, such as food banks, to survive. Food banks started modestly in the early 1980s in some urban centres. By 1992, 150 000 people were served each month by the Daily Bread Food Bank in Toronto alone, and an estimated 2 million Canadians relied on food banks at some point that year.

Public funds had been important throughout the post-war period in placing a floor on poverty and guaranteeing citizens of all social classes improved access to quality education and health services. In the post-prosperity era, governments became less willing to provide these funds. Attempts by the federal government to limit growth in grants to the provinces had begun under Trudeau in 1977, when block funding replaced equal federal-provincial sharing of medicare and post-secondary education costs. The new arrangement was called "Established Programs Financing" and gave the provinces a percentage of federal income and corporate taxes plus a cash grant. While cash grants were initially increased by the annual rate of inflation, the Trudeau government set limits to increases in federal spending on post-secondary education for 1982 and 1983.

In 1986, the Mulroney government went further, announcing that federal cash grants for medicare and post-secondary education would be reduced by 2 percent annually. Four years later, it introduced a bill to speed up the federal withdrawal from Established Programs Financing so that by 2004 the government's

Poverty Activists

The poor did not stand idly by as governments reduced the "social minimum" that welfare state programs had once guaranteed. In Quebec, for example, the Fédération des femmes du Québec organized a women's march on Quebec City in June 1995 that forced Premier Jacques Parizeau to announce a few policy changes of benefit to women. About 4000 women, most of them living in poverty, completed a 10-day trek to Quebec City to demand that politicians act to address their dire circumstances. The women had walked 20 kilometres a day from three gathering points, staying with feminist sympathizers along the way. Together with poor women and children across the country, they represented the largest group of the victims of state policies that placed less and less emphasis on responsibility for those whose social conditions disadvantaged them in the marketplace.

When the women arrived in Quebec City, the opposition Liberals refused to have anything to do with them, alleging that they were part of a separatist conspiracy to discredit Canadian federalism. Sovereignist premier Parizeau told the women that their demand for a program of social infrastructure spending could be met only when Quebec was independent from Canada. He then announced an increase in Quebec's minimum wage from $6 to $6.45 an hour, 20 percent of the increase the marchers had demanded. Many of the protesters were understandably disappointed that their efforts to draw attention to the plight of the poor were being manipulated by politicians with their own agendas.

In Ontario, protests by the poor embarrassed governments that were dismantling welfare state programs. The Ontario Coalition Against Poverty, wrote one activist,

> mounts large collective actions, often with our union allies or the Mohawk warrior society of the Tyendanaga First Nation Reserve, around a specific economic issue such as the withdrawal of provincial and federal governments from public housing, or Toronto's policy, mimicking New York's, for the "social cleansing" of panhandlers and homeless from the downtown tourist areas. We have picketed and enforced semi-embargos on businesses investing in a re-development scheme which, by closing a hostel, threw homeless men back on the street. . . . And we have mobilized the larger actions. . . . in Ottawa, a march on Parliament Hill "to persuade the prime minister of the seriousness of the homelessness crisis," interrupted by arrests by the RCMP, whose line we broke; the occupation of a Toronto city park, designating it "safe" from police harassment for the homeless, and holding it for three days until we were violently removed, with arrests, by the police; and most recently, the second, more powerful march on Parliament in November 1999. Each of these was a small, but in our present situation, real victory.[3]

cash transfer for medical and education spending, which was $9 billion in the 1989–1990 fiscal year, would be zero. Campaigning in 1993, the Liberals promised to stop the cuts to the provinces, but once they were in office they announced they would actually speed up the Progressive Conservative timetable for getting rid of Established Programs Financing. The Liberals also cancelled one of the pillars of Lester Pearson's social reforms: the Canada Assistance Plan. Under it, there had been some federal control over provinces to ensure that legitimate social welfare recipients were not denied aid. By the 1990s, it was clear that federal governments were unwilling to take a stand against provincial governments that discriminated against certain groups of poor people.

The federal government made a commitment in 1989 to end child poverty. At the time, 14.4 percent of Canadian children were being raised in poverty. Though some programs were implemented to direct cash to the poorest households with children, cuts in social assistance and unemployment insurance, along with inflation, resulted in an increase in the child poverty rate to 21.1 percent by 1996.

THE TRADE UNION MOVEMENT

Canada's trade union movement was under attack in the age of neo-liberalism but fared much better than its American counterpart from 1976 to 1999. In the United States, southern and western states passed "right to work" legislation that banned the closed shop. As northern firms moved south to take advantage of cheap labour and poor environmental standards, workers in the northeast often abandoned their unions to preserve their jobs, albeit at a high cost in wages and working conditions. The central government, for both constitutional and ideological reasons, did nothing to stop a trend to roll back workers' gains. By the mid-1990s, only about 15 percent of American workers were unionized, about half the rate of 20 years earlier.

In Canada, by contrast, the fall-off was less steep. From a peak of 37.2 percent of the non-agricultural labour force in 1984, the rate of unionization in Canada had fallen to 32.5 percent in 1998. Nevertheless, in the era of free trade, Canadians were not immune to trends south of the border. As many Canadians were learning in the age of globalization, local governments had little ability to protect citizens against the often take-it-or-leave-it demands of mobile multinational corporations. In Quebec, governments

A HISTORIOGRAPHICAL DEBATE

If Quebec Leaves

Increasingly, social scientists—if not governments—have been prepared to speculate on the political and economic impact of Quebec sovereignty on Quebec and the remaining Canadian provinces. Historian David J. Bercuson and political scientist Barry Cooper have marshalled arguments as to why the rest of Canada would be better off without Quebec. They argue that Quebec nationalism is incompatible with the liberal democratic values that they believe are central to English-Canadian politics. Quebec nationalists, they maintain, place the rights of French Canadians above majority and individual rights. Bercuson and Cooper suggest that majority rule ought to be—and without Quebec would be—the essential principle of governance in Canada.[4]

Some authors point to liberal democracies that accommodate minority communities without losing their liberal character. Political scientist Alain Gagnon cites the examples of Switzerland and Belgium, where regional governments "have the right and the obligation to protect their respective linguistic community against any infringements." Gagnon labels this "a charter of rights and freedoms whose application varies according to specific regions."[5]

Bercuson and Cooper reject such regionalism and suggest that a Quebec-free Canada could avoid decentralization by giving each province equal representation in the Senate. Other scholars are skeptical that such a proposal would be acceptable to Ontario. They predict that if Quebec left confederation, Canada would begin to fall apart. Economist Tim O'Neill observes that Ontario's dominance in population and economic activity could lead the provinces to "forge separate regional and interregional alliances with other provinces and possibly with contiguous areas of the United States."[6]

Federal bilingual policy is a sore point for many scholars. Bercuson and Cooper scoff at those who claim that "what makes us great is official bilingualism and French on our cereal boxes."[7] While few other Anglophone scholars share this rejection of legislated bilingualism, many Quebec nationalists do. They argue that Quebec's government should operate only in French, while governments outside Quebec should offer services in French only in heavily Francophone areas. Sociologist Hubert Guindon, a sovereignist who supports unilingualism for Quebec, maintains that "the official bilingualism adopted by the Canadian state was politically irrelevant."[8]

Bercuson and Cooper argue that a Canada without Quebec would be more prosperous than today's Canada. Adopting the neo-liberal view that the federal government's spending has been out of control for several decades, they suggest that Quebec pressures have played a key role in preventing the government from trimming its programs. Although they provide no figures to corroborate this view, they conclude, "By ending the wasteful transaction costs of official bilingualism and especially the ongoing transfer of wealth from Canada to Quebec, the citizens of Canada would undoubtedly be more wealthy, not less."[9]

Quebec economists of a nationalist bent have rejected the view that Quebec is a net gainer from tax transfers in Canada. Georges Mathews produced "a balance sheet of federalism for Quebec," which claims that Quebec had a marginally favourable balance from 1973 to 1986 but afterward was a net loser.[10] Pierre Fortin also argues that confederation continues to have a negative economic impact on Quebec, claiming that the federal debt, failed federal development policies, and monetary instability in addition to the duplication of powers between the federal and provincial governments have hurt Quebec's economy.[11] Indeed, such policies hurt every province's economy, and Fortin suggests that radical decentralization might be of benefit to the whole country. If emotional attachments to Canada make residents of the other provinces reluctant to support decentralization, then Quebec must either receive special status or become sovereign.

Scholars in have-not provinces, especially Atlantic Canada, have been less sanguine about the economic prospects of their provinces should Quebec leave. Tim O'Neill notes that "neither extensive decentralization nor separation will have a positive impact on Atlantic Canada" because the region depends more on federal transfers than other areas do.[12] O'Neill also observes that notions that either Quebec or the rest of Canada will benefit economically from a breakup take as a given that the breakup would be amicable and would cause little short-term economic disruption. Yet there has already been an indication that the two sides would have difficulty determining how to divide the national debt.

Political scientist Peter Russell suggests that the aftermath of Quebec sovereignty might depend on how it is achieved. If it comes through a unilateral declaration of independence rather than through a long process of negotiations, "the climate of uncertainty and tension generated by such a move will reduce international confidence and put severe strain on the Canadian economy."[13] Opponents of independence, particularly Anglophones and First Nations peoples, "might insist on federal protection of their rights against a Quebec government operating outside Canadian law. Civil disobedience and violence cannot be ruled out."[14] While such views strike many as alarmist, some Quebec nationalist intellectuals readily concede that the sovereignty-association formula is probably impossible. There is no guarantee that the rest of Canada would negotiate a common market with a seceding province. Guindon, reflecting on the debate in the 1980 Quebec referendum, observes: "The common myth shared by both those opposed to sovereignty association and those in favour was that should the 'oui' forces have won decisively, it would have led automatically to the creation of a sovereign state with association with Canada. . . . Such naivete, in a sense, honours us. But it augurs poorly for the kind of sophistication that will be required to inch our way toward sovereignty."[15]

The accuracy of these analyses will become apparent only if Quebec actually leaves Canada. While the "constitution industry" and most Canadians, including most Quebecers, still hope that accommodation is possible, Quebec's leaving is no longer unthinkable. It is therefore only natural that scholars continue to paint scenarios of Canada without Quebec and Quebec without Canada.

often neglected to enforce the law against replacement workers that had been enacted by Lévesque in 1977. Ontario's NDP government passed similar legislation, but it was repealed by Harris in 1995. Both the PQ and the NDP, supposedly friends of organized labour, had at one time or another imposed wage rollbacks on public employees. Conditions were worse for organized labour in provinces where the social democratic parties had never been in power. Alberta, though a rich province, boasted of its American level of unionization to companies looking for a low-wage, no-union environment in which to establish.

The trend toward a greater feminization of the labour movement, apparent since the 1960s, continued after 1975, though mainly in the public sector. The huge retail and service sectors proved determined to resist attempts by their largely female workforce to organize. Eaton's workers in Ontario and Manitoba, who had unionized in the early 1980s, found that their employer did not accept their democratic decision to deal collectively with management. When Manitoba's Labour Relations Board imposed a first contract on a recalcitrant Eaton's in Brandon, the store responded by firing half of its workers and demanding concessions from the union for the workers who remained.

Some of the success of Canada's unions in the last quarter of the twentieth century might have resulted from Canadian sections of many American industrial unions breaking away to form national unions. The Canadian Auto Workers (CAW), for example, formed after a rupture between the Canadian wing of the United Auto Workers and the union's American headquarters. With only 120 000 members in 1984, the CAW doubled in size over the next 17 years, partly through mergers with smaller unions in other sectors and partly by organizing unorganized workers. The union included automobile workers, fishers, retail employees, office workers, shipbuilders, aerospace workers, and many others.

CONCLUSION

As Quebec faced its second referendum in 1995, industrialist and press magnate Conrad Black made a blunt speech in which he ridiculed attempts to distinguish Canada from the United States on the basis of its social programs. From his viewpoint, it was absurd to try to define Canada in terms of programs that merely made Canadian businesses less competitive than their American counterparts. If Canada is to be internationally competitive, he argued, it cannot afford to continue subsidizing a national railway passenger service, a national airline, or a national broadcaster such as the CBC. It cannot offer its citizens significantly more in the area of social programs or environmental protection than the Americans offer their citizens. Many Canadians found such arguments disturbing and maintained that with a relatively small population dispersed across a vast expanse of geography, a strong state is necessary to solve problems and create a degree of unity that market forces alone cannot guarantee. As the twentieth century came to an end, many hoped that the Canadian difference could be preserved despite economic pressures that seemed to militate against a distinctly "Canadian dream."

NOTES

1 *Edmonton Journal*, 9 November 1995.

2 Gwen Brodsky and Shelagh Day, *Canadian Charter Equality Rights for Women: One Step Forward or Two Steps Back?* (Ottawa: Canadian Advisory Council on the Status of Women, 1989), 3.

3 Norman Feltes, "The New Prince in a New Principality: OCAP and the Toronto Poor," *Labour/Le Travail* 48 (Fall 2001), 146.

4 David J. Bercuson and Barry Cooper, *Deconfederation: Canada without Quebec* (Toronto: Key Porter, 1991), 15–16.

5 Alain Gagnon, "Other Federal and Nonfederal Countries: Lessons for Canada," in *Options for a New Canada*, eds. Ronald L. Watts and Douglas M. Brown (Toronto: University of Toronto Press, 1991), 232.

6 Tim O'Neill, "Restructured Federalism and Its Impacts on Atlantic Canada," in *The Constitutional Future of the Prairie and Atlantic Regions of Canada*, eds. James N. McRorie and Martha L. Macdonald (Regina: Canadian Plains Research Center, 1992), 63.

7 Bercuson and Cooper, *Deconfederation*, 134–35.

8 Hubert Guindon, *Quebec Society: Tradition, Modernity, and Nationhood* (Toronto: University of Toronto Press, 1988), 143.

9 Bercuson and Cooper, *Deconfederation*, 140–41.

10 Georges Mathews, *Quiet Resolution: Quebec's Challenges to Canada* (Toronto: Summerhill Press, 1990), 139–40.

11 Pierre Fortin, "How Economics Is Shaping the Constitutional Debate in Quebec," in *Confederation in Crisis*, ed. Robert Young (Toronto: Lorimer, 1991), 3–44.

12 O'Neill, "Restructured Federalism," 63.

13 Peter H. Russell, "Towards a New Constitutional Process," in *Options for a New Canada*, eds. Ronald Watts and Douglas Brown (Toronto: University of Toronto Press, 1991), 148.

14 Ibid.

15 Guindon, *Quebec Society*, 166–67.

RELATED READINGS IN THIS SERIES

Selected Reading

On Quebec since 1975, see Paul-André Linteau et al., *Quebec Since 1930: A History* (Toronto: Lorimer, 1991); Kenneth McRoberts, *Quebec: Social Change and Political Crisis*, 3rd ed. (Toronto: McClelland & Stewart, 1988); René Lévesque, *Memoirs* (Toronto: McClelland & Stewart, 1986); Pierre Godin, *René Lévesque: Un enfant du siècle* (Montreal: Boréal, 1994); and Robert Chodos and Eric Hamovitch, *Quebec and the American Dream* (Toronto: Between the Lines, 1994). Ontario developments are discussed in Thomas L. Walkom, *Rae Days* (Toronto: Key Porter, 1994); Patrick Monahan, *Storming the Pink Palace: The NDP in Power, a Cautionary Tale* (Toronto: Lester, 1995); and Daniel Drache, ed., *Getting on Track: Social Democratic Strategies for Ontario* (Montreal: McGill-Queen's University Press, 1992).

On western Canada, see Gerald Friesen, *The Canadian Prairies*, rev. ed. (Toronto: University of Toronto Press, 1987); Bill Waiser, *Saskatchewan: A New History* (Calgary: Fifth House, 2005); Michael Payne, Donald Wetherell, and Catherine Cavanaugh, eds., *Alberta Formed, Alberta Transformed* (Edmonton: University of Alberta Press, and Calgary: University of Calgary Press, 2005); Patricia Marchak, *Green Gold: The Forest Industry in British Columbia* (Vancouver: UBC Press, 1983); Rennie Warburton and Donald Coburn, eds., *Workers, Capital, and the State of British Columbia: Selected Papers* (Vancouver: UBC Press, 1987); and Jim Silver and Jeremy Hull, eds., *The Political Economy of Manitoba* (Regina: Canadian Plains Research Center, 1990). On the Reform Party, see Trevor Harrison, *Of Passionate Intensity: Right-Wing Populism and the Reform Party of Canada* (Toronto: University of Toronto Press, 1995).

On the Atlantic provinces, see E.R. Forbes, "The Atlantic Provinces, Free Trade, and the Constitution," in *Challenging the Regional Stereotype* (Fredericton: Acadiensis Press, 1989), 200–16; Gary Burrill and Ian McKay, eds., *People, Resources, and Power in Atlantic Canada: Critical Perspectives on Underdevelopment and Primary Industries in the Atlantic Region* (Fredericton: Acadiensis, 1987); Wallace Clement, *The Struggle to Organize: Resistance in Canada's Fisheries* (Toronto: McClelland & Stewart, 1986); Shaun Cornish, *The Westray Tragedy: A Miner's Story* (Toronto: Fernwood, 1994); Donald J. Savoie, *Visiting Grandchildren: Economic Development in the Maritimes* (Toronto: University of Toronto Press, 2006) and *Pulling Against Gravity: Economic Development in New Brunswick During the McKenna Years* (Montreal: Institute for Research on Public Policy, 2001); and *Our Place in Canada: Main Report of the Royal Commission on Renewing and Strengthening Our Place in Canada* (St. John's: Government of Newfoundland and Labrador, 2003).

Useful works on the constitutional debates include David Milne, *The New Canadian Constitution* (Toronto: Lorimer, 1982); Keith Banting and Richard Simeon, eds., *And No One Cheered: Federalism, Democracy and the Constitution Act* (Scarborough, ON: Nelson, 1983); Michael D. Behiels, ed., *The Meech Lake Primer: Conflicting Views of the 1987 Constitutional Accord* (Ottawa: University of Ottawa Press, 1989); C.E.S. Franks, *The Myths and Symbols of the Constitutional Debate in Canada* (Kingston, ON: Institute of Intergovernmental Relations, 1993); and Deborah Coyne, *Roll of the Dice: Working with Clyde Wells During the Meech Lake Negotiations* (Toronto: Lorimer, 1992).

On the trade union movement, see Bryan D. Palmer, *Working-Class Experience: Rethinking the History of Canadian Labour, 1800–1991* (Toronto: McClelland & Stewart, 1992) and Leo Panitch, *The Assault on Trade Union Freedoms: From Wage Controls to Social Contract*, rev. ed. (Toronto: Garamond, 1994).

CHAPTER 22

Community and Culture, 1976–2008

TIMELINE

1970	Greenpeace formed
1980	Terry Fox's Marathon of Hope
1984	Edmonton Oilers win the first of five Stanley Cups in seven years
1985	Indian Act amended to remove discrimination against women marrying non-Indians
1988	Supreme Court rules that Canada's abortion law is discriminatory
1990	Standoff at Oka
1992	Canadian army ends discrimination against homosexuals
1996	Report of the Royal Commission on Aboriginal Peoples
1997	Supreme Court decision in the Delgamuukw case
1999	Nunavut becomes a territory; beginning of confrontations at Burnt Church

"Kids are expensive. If it were just my wife and I, she wouldn't have to work. But at one point when there was five in here . . . Your kids want everything now. You can't just buy them 'adventure' running shoes. They want Adidas or Reeboks. That's the killer . . . My parents didn't have much. To me, what I wanted and what I got were two different things. I just saw a kid walk by with a $150 starter coat. My son's got one too [laughs] and I'm thinking when does it end? I think I would have been satisfied growing up, to have a decent coat, never mind a starter coat with a Montreal Canadiens logo. Sure, I'd like my kids to have better than what I had or at least better than what my parents could give me, but then we put a gun to our head by doing this . . . When does it stop?"[1]

These comments by "Dom," a Niagara Falls man in his early forties in 1995, reflect the conflicting values of many Canadians as the twentieth century closed. While most adult Canadians worked outside the home, some people looked back nostalgically on earlier times when a single income had supported a family. Participating in the rampant materialism of society, many Canadians nonetheless also viewed consumerism more as a curse than a blessing. In this chapter we look broadly at the social and cultural developments in Canada as one millennium ended and another began, providing some context for the hopes and worries of people like Dom.

POPULATION

Canada's population increased from 23 550 000 in the census of 1976 to more than 31 million in 2002 (see Table 22.1). Population growth was hardly uniform across the country: Alberta's jumped 10.6 percent, Newfoundland and Labrador and Saskatchewan shrank slightly, and the three Maritime provinces experienced negligible growth (see Table 22.2).

TABLE 22.1 Growth of Canada's Population, 1971–2001

Period	Census population at end of period	Total population growth	Births	Deaths	Immigrants	Emigrants
1971–76	23 450	1 882	1 755	824	1 053	358
1976–81	24 820	1 371	1 820	843	771	278
1981–86	26 101	1 280	1 872	885	677	278
1986–91	28 031	1 930	1 933	946	1 199	213
1991–96	29 672	1 641	1 936	1 024	1 137	229
1996–01	31 021	1 410	1 705	1 089	1 217	376

All numbers are in thousands

Source: Statistics Canada, Matrices 6367-6378, 6408-6409

While a fertility rate of 2.1 was required to maintain the existing population, Canada's rate by the end of the century was 1.5. Canada would thus experience a drop in population unless it attracted enough immigrants to make up the declining birth rate. Between 1945 and 1975, only 4 percent of immigrants to Canada came from outside Europe or the United States. Increasing prosperity and mobility in Europe, along with a decline in fertility similar to Canada's, limited its potential contribution as a supplier of newcomers to Canada, and few Americans in this period saw Canada as their land of opportunity. So Canada looked

TABLE 22.2 Population in 2002, by Province and Territory

Area	Persons (thousands)
Canada	31 372
Newfoundland and Labrador	519.4
Prince Edward Island	136
Nova Scotia	934
New Brunswick	750.3
Quebec	7 445
Ontario	12 102
Manitoba	1 155.6
Saskatchewan	995.9
Alberta	3 116.3
British Columbia	4 115.4
Yukon Territory	30.1
Northwest Territories	41.5
Nunavut	28.7

Source: Statistics Canada, CANSIM; Statistics Canada, "The Daily," 27 September 2007.

elsewhere. By the turn of the century, immigrants were arriving at the rate of nearly 250 000 a year, over half from Asian countries. Most of the newcomers settled in Toronto, Vancouver, and Montreal.

More than ever, Canada's population was concentrated in a few cities. According to the 2006 census, 80 percent of Canadians lived in communities of over 1000 people and over a third of the population lived in the three megacities of Montreal, Toronto, and Vancouver. Two more cities, Calgary and Edmonton, surpassed the million population mark in the first few years of the twenty-first century. The other side of the growing urban concentration was the loss of population in many resource and manufacturing towns. Kitimat, Prince Rupert, and Terrace in northwestern British Columbia were examples. Alcan was running the Kitimat smelter at half capacity while the town lost a methanol plant. Forestry and fishing in Prince Rupert were in the doldrums. The Skeena-Cellulose pulp-mill complex closed in 2001, causing job losses, direct and indirect, of about 6000.

Wherever they lived, Canadians on average were far older than their counterparts in the past. Sagging birth rates and longer life expectancy explained the change. The median age of Canadians in 2006 was 39.5 years, compared to just under 26 years in 1966. In four decades, the percentage of Canadians over 65 had risen to 13.7 percent of the population from 7.7. This was the inverse of the change in the under-15 population, which had declined from 34 percent in 1961 to 17.7 percent in 2006. Life expectancy for Canadian women in 2007 reached 82.5, with the average man likely to live 77.7 years. The gap between the life expectancy for the sexes was narrowing. Still, women over 65 outnumbered men by 648 937 in 2006.

The low birth rate reflected the changing notions of Canadians about families and marriage that had begun in earnest in the 1960s. In 1973, the average age of Canadians marrying for the first time was 25.2 for men and 22.8 for women. By 2003, the figures rose to 30.6 and 28.5, respectively. Fewer Canadians were marrying. Cohabitation and singlehood were on the rise. The marriage rate in 2003 was 4.7 marriages for each 1000 of the population, compared to 10.9 in the late 1940s. In Quebec in 2003, the marriage rate was a mere 2.8 per 1000, reflecting the greater popularity of cohabition over marriage in Quebec.

EDUCATION

Formal education became more important than ever as a means to finding satisfying and high-paying work in the last quarter of the twentieth century. As secure blue-collar jobs with good union wages began to evaporate, the doors to young people with limited education shut tightly. In 1995, 20 percent of both high school dropouts and high school graduates looking for work were unable to find even part-time positions, and many of those able to find employment worked for the legal minimum wage.

Studies of the career paths of the baby boomers demonstrated that by the 1990s, almost half of university graduates who were in the labour force had reached high-level management or professional positions. Their earnings easily outstripped those of their high school classmates who had not gone beyond secondary school, with the income of community college graduates sitting in between those of university and high school graduates. University education proved particularly important to immigrant children as a means of improving their economic situation relative to their parents, though social class continued to be the major factor that determined which young people would go on to post-secondary education.

While education became more important, it also became less affordable. Government cutbacks in grants to post-secondary institutions resulted in higher tuition fees. In the 1960s, tuition paid about a fifth of the cost of a university education in most provinces. By 2005, it paid about half. The consequence, of course, was that students had to dig deeper to pay for their education. Part-time jobs helped but were hard to find in the high-unemployment 1990s. More and more students lived at home throughout their education years or relied on student loans.

Tales of recent graduates who had accumulated debts of as much as $50 000 but could only find modest jobs abounded in the 1990s. However, studies suggest that in 2000, university graduates of the early 1990s were out-earning people of their age who had not attended university. Still, the high cost of post-secondary education deterred many youth. Stagnating university and college enrolments told the story. Full-time university enrolment, having reached 575 713 in 1994–1995, had climbed only another 5000 by 1998–1999, while part-time enrolments plummeted by almost 40 000 to 246 000. Community college enrolments increased a bit more—from 380 000 full-timers to almost 404 000, with part-time enrolments steady at around 91 000.

By the 1996 census, women outnumbered men among university graduates, but this did not mean that they were bound, as a group, for better financial futures than men. In 2000, as in 1980, proportionately more women, in spite of generally superior academic performances, were tracked into sex-segregated occupations that led to lower incomes. Eighty percent of engineering graduates were men, and two-thirds of graduates in the physical sciences in 1996 were men. However, women made up two-thirds of the graduates in arts programs. In other high-paying areas such as law and medicine, significant advances had been made in gender parity.

If education in Canada was seen increasingly as a vehicle for providing highly trained workers for industry, it had yet another purpose for Quebec governments: maintaining French language and culture. Shortly after its election in 1976, the Parti Québécois government passed Bill 101, which, among other things, permitted only Quebec-born Anglophones to educate their children in English. The Supreme Court later extended that right to all Canadian-born Anglophones who lived in the province. Under this law, all immigrants, regardless of linguistic background, were obliged to send their children to French-language schools. Some Allophones initially resisted the French-Canadian majority's imposition of French as the only language of instruction. From their point of view, they had moved to Canada, or indeed just to North America, and did not see why they had to embrace the cultural aspirations of French Canadians.

Most immigrants, however, managed to adjust to the bilingual and bicultural structures that characterized Canada at the end of the twentieth century.

Immigrant Experiences

The federal government's commitment to multiculturalism helped make newcomers feel more at home in Canada but, as in the past, some Canadians felt that Canada's immigration laws were too liberal, especially when it came to admitting visible minorities. Also, as in the past, immigrant experiences differed greatly. In the 1980s and 1990s, for example, wealthy Hong Kong residents, skittish about the impending return of their city to the Chinese government in 1997 after a century of British control, were actively courted by the Canadian government because of the capital and expertise they promised to inject into the country.

Vietnamese and other Indochinese immigrants, many of them "boat people" fleeing either political repression or economic hardship, began arriving in Canada in the late 1970s and were often the brunt of racist attitudes. While many prospered in their new home, the rate of unemployment among Canadians of Vietnamese descent in the early 1990s was double the Canadian average. Violent youth gangs in the Vietnamese community reflected the presence of an underclass for whom racism made the future appear quite bleak. Middle-class Vietnamese resented the media spotlight on gangs and the limited attention paid both to those who were succeeding despite the odds and to the conditions that caused some youth to turn to gangs.

Immigrants from the Caribbean and Africa not only experienced a great deal of racism in employment and housing; they also regarded themselves as victims of police racism. A series of shootings of unarmed blacks in Montreal and Toronto led to accusations that many police officers were racists who stereotyped all blacks as criminals. Neo-Nazi skinheads—largely unemployed white male youths—attacked non-whites of Asian and African origin and desecrated Jewish cemeteries. Intolerance had its violent side, even in Canada.

Native Struggles

In the last quarter of the twentieth century, Native peoples increased their social activism to the point that politicians and the general public were finally forced to take notice. Efforts were made to restore traditional Native cultural practices and languages, both long under attack by government and churches bent on assimilationist goals. In their determination to have land claims settled, Aboriginal peoples sometimes became involved in violent conflicts with authorities.

Native militancy occurred in a context of continued desperate conditions on and off reserves. The low life expectancy in relation to the rest of the population, high rates of suicide, high unemployment, and poor living conditions testified to the slow rate of change experienced by Native peoples at the hands of the Canadian state and Canadian society more generally. Incarceration rates tell a startling tale: while Natives comprise 3 percent of the adult population of Canada (976 305 Canadians identified themselves as Aboriginal in the 2001 census), they constitute 15 percent of the prisoners in provincial and territorial prisons, and 17 percent of those in federal prisons. In Saskatchewan, where 11.4 percent of the population is Native, they constitute a full 72 percent of the inmate population.

Many northern Natives, in the wake of the Mackenzie Valley Pipeline Inquiry, eventually reached settlements with the federal government. In 1984, the Inuit of the Mackenzie Delta received a land settlement—242 000 square kilometres—and the Yukon First Nations also reached a land settlement with Ottawa in 1988. In November 1992, the Inuit of the eastern Arctic accepted a negotiated deal that provided them with 350 000 square kilometres of subsurface mineral rights. At the same time, they voted for the partition of the Northwest Territories, with the eastern Arctic to become a separately administered territory called Nunavut (meaning "the people's land" in the Inuktitut language). In March 1999, Nunavut officially became a territory and elected its own assembly. Nunavut's population in 2001 was 26 745, of whom about 80 percent were Inuit.

Land Claims and the Legal System

Outside the territories, the federal government proved even slower to settle land claims made by Native peoples who lacked treaties or reserves or by Treaty Indians who claimed more territory than the government had allotted them. Many Natives felt frustrated as their

British Columbia Native Peoples and the Struggle for Self-Determination

The history of British Columbia's dealings with its first peoples was perhaps the most egregious in the country. After British Columbia entered confederation, the non-Aboriginal minority who had deprived the First Nations of voting rights insisted to the federal government that treaties could not be signed with Natives in that province. For a century, Native lands were seized for industrialization and urban expansion without negotiating with the landowners. Gradually things began to change. Frank Calder, a Nisga'a leader, started the ball rolling for comprehensive land claims in Canada by taking to the Supreme Court a lower court decision that denied that Aboriginal title had ever existed in British Columbia. While the Supreme Court, in its 1973 decision, was divided on the issue of whether Aboriginal title had been extinguished, a majority of the justices agreed that it had existed before colonization began. This led Pierre Trudeau to accept the notion that comprehensive land claims had to be negotiated with First Nations that had never signed treaties.

In 1985, the Supreme Court of Canada awarded the small Musqueam Band $10 million in compensation for Indian Affairs' duping them into granting an unfair golf-course lease on their land. Increasingly, many Native peoples, rather than hoping for monetary compensation after their resources had been depleted and their traditional lifestyle destroyed, began to actively resist developers, even if it meant breaking Canadian law. In the late 1980s, in various parts of the province, Natives clashed with loggers whose activities despoiled traditional Aboriginal lands.

In 1990, the province finally agreed to negotiate land issues. A year later, however, Judge Allan McEachern of the British Columbia Supreme Court issued a verdict in the *Delgamuukw* case that suggested British Columbia's first people did not hold Aboriginal rights to the land. That ruling was invalidated in 1997 when the Supreme Court, hearing an appeal of this case involving the Gitskan-Wet'suwet'en Nation, rejected McEachern's logic. Not only did the first peoples have Aboriginal rights, but those rights went beyond hunting and fishing to the broader rights involved in determining what activities took place on their traditional lands.

The Supreme Court decision placed some pressure on British Columbia's New Democratic Party (NDP) government to negotiate agreements with Native nations if only to counter the economic uncertainty that business representatives claimed the court's decisions created for them. Perhaps fittingly, the first successful negotiations between the government and a First Nation were with the Nisga'a of the Nass Valley. The Nisga'a had fought their dispossession by non-Aboriginals for more than 100 years. Mainly relying on the courts and petitions to governments, they had persisted in their claims of ownership of their traditional lands even as the government of Canada, at British Columbia's request, kept handing away the lands to forestry and mineral companies.

In 1998, the governments of British Columbia and the Nisga'a people reached agreement on a treaty, which was subsequently ratified by a referendum of the Nisga'a and a vote of both the British Columbia legislature and the parliament of Canada. Finally, it was ratified by a Senate vote on 13 April, 2000, and became the law of the land.

The opposition parties in British Columbia made exaggerated claims about the treaty and played upon non-Aboriginal fears of being displaced by the original owners. Arguably, as many Nisga'a opponents of the treaty claimed, it was the Nisga'a that gave away the most in the negotiations. They were left with 1930 square kilometres of territory in which they would exercise law-making authority in such areas as land use, cultural practices, and employment policies. The various benefits and monetary grants that accompanied the treaty were deemed to be worth $487.1 million. But the Nisga'a also made major concessions. They had to give up all claims to 80 percent of their traditional territory and accept the Canadian Criminal Code and the Canadian Charter of Rights and Freedoms rather than exercising complete sovereignty within their lands. Moreover, the avalanche of criticism to the Nisga'a treaty emanating from right-wing parties and their supporters made it difficult for other Native groups to negotiate a similar or better deal.

claims to land and treaty rights to hunt and fish were bogged down in bureaucracy and the courts. In an effort to make Canadian authorities take notice, some First Nations resorted to direct action. One of the first confrontations occurred in 1974 when Natives occupied Anicinabe Park in Kenora, Ontario, claiming that the park, like much of Kenora, belonged to Aboriginal peoples.

Over the next two decades, pent-up frustrations erupted across the country. In northern Alberta, the Lubicon Cree, who had been waiting for a reserve for more than 50 years, forcibly kept out oil companies that

Ronald Cross, also known as Lasagna, was a prominent Native figure in the Oka crisis. The media suggested that he had ties with the Mafia and was a Vietnam War veteran fixated on violence. In fact, the Mohawk Warrior had no connections with organized crime and had never served in the armed forces of any nation. For his part in his people's resistance at Oka, Cross received a five-year sentence for criminal assault.
Tom Hanson/CP Photo Archive

wanted to drill on disputed territories. Supported by environmentalists, the Temagami in Ontario tried to prevent logging on their territories. The Cree of northern Quebec threatened both court action and sabotage if Quebec proceeded with a second James Bay hydroelectric project. The Nova Scotia Mi'kmaq pursued their hunting and fishing rights against an unsympathetic provincial government and used an investigation into the wrongful conviction of a young Mi'kmaq, Donald Marshall, to expose the racism they faced on a daily basis. In Manitoba, the Public Inquiry into the Administration of Justice and Aboriginal People was sparked by two tragic deaths: the conspiracy of silence that followed the murder of Helen Betty Osborne in The Pas in 1971 and the shooting of an unarmed Native leader, John Joseph Harper, in Winnipeg in 1988. The inquiries in Manitoba and Nova Scotia, in addition to a royal commission in Alberta, concluded that all components of the legal system, from the police through the judiciary, demonstrated prejudice against Native peoples.

There were many examples of leniency toward non-Aboriginals who murdered Aboriginals. In Saskatchewan, for example, a white supremacist shot Aborginal Leo Lachance in the back as he left a Prince Albert pawnshop and received a sentence of only four years, with eligibility for statutory release before the end of the third year. Pamela George was raped and murdered by two white Regina men in 1995, yet both murderers served only four years. Meanwhile, there were recurring allegations by Saskatoon Natives that the police routinely compelled inebriated Aboriginals into their cars and dropped them outside the city on so-called starlight tours that resulted in the deaths by freezing of several individuals. In 1990, Neil Stonechild was dropped on the outskirts of Saskatoon one evening when the temperature fell to minus 22 degrees Celsius. It was not until 2003 that two Saskatoon police officers were convicted of a crime related to this death: unlawful confinement for which each received eight months.

The most sensational conflict erupted in the summer of 1990 between the Quebec Provincial Police and the Mohawk Warriors at a reserve near Oka, Quebec. As the standoff escalated, one police officer was killed and the Canadian military was called to intervene. The Warriors, who ran gambling casinos and smuggling operations at other reserves, were controversial among the Mohawk, but the issue they chose was not: the town of Oka wished to develop a golf course on lands the Mohawk regarded as sacred. While denouncing the Warriors as terrorists, the federal government was forced to buy the disputed land to make it available to the Mohawk, but the solution appeared to be a pragmatic reaction to confrontation rather than magnanimity toward Native peoples.

Other confrontations followed: at Gustafsen Lake, British Columbia, and Ipperwash Park, Ontario, in 1995; at Shubenacadie Reserve, Nova Scotia, in 1999; and, most notably, at Burnt Church, New Brunswick, in 1999 and 2000.

The Burnt Church standoff was a particularly protracted one. In 2002, the Burnt Church band council accepted a deal with the Department of Fisheries and Oceans (DFO) that modestly increased the community's quota of traps. Atlantic Aboriginal leaders continue to press for co-management of the fishery by First Nations and the DFO rather than sole management by the latter with consultation of the former. Atlantic governments had severely limited the fishing and hunting activities of Natives in defiance of eighteenth-century treaties—most notably those drawn up in 1725 and 1752, which recognized the Native right to conduct these activities. Court rulings regarding these treaties and the 1760 treaty involving the Mi'kmaq, the Maliseet, and the Passamaquoddy led to a Supreme Court ruling in 1999 that declared the Mi'kmaq right to a portion of the fish catch that allowed them to make a "moderate livelihood . . . at present day standards . . . [to be] established by regulation."[2]

The Mi'kmaq, who maintained that they had never given up their rights to control their resources, responded by working out plans to regulate the fishery. In St. Mary's Bay, Nova Scotia, Native and non-Native fishers amicably worked out an agreement to jointly manage the lobster fishery. Elsewhere, this proved impossible. When the Mi'kmaq of Esgenoopetitj (Burnt Church), New Brunswick, laid a small number of lobster traps in the fall of 1999, non-Native fishers responded by destroying their traps, attacking the Mi'kmaq and their property, and vandalizing fish plants that accepted lobsters from Natives.

The following year, the federal government informed the Burnt Church Natives that they could lay 40 lobster traps collectively. This was hardly generous given that the average non-Native commercial fisher was allowed 300 traps. The Natives responded by indicating that they, not the DFO, had the right to regulate their fishery. They proposed that the band lay 6000 traps, which, if the number of traps in the area were to remain constant, would still allow the average non-Native fisher 294 traps. The DFO response was an armed campaign to sink Native boats and destroy their lobster traps in Miramichi Bay. In the federal government's view, this was a defence of their right to regulate the fishery, though they failed to explain how the court's requirement that Natives be allowed a "moderate living" could be met by a 40-trap limit for an entire reserve. In the Esgenoopetitj First Nation's view, the DFO had violated the laws of a sovereign people.

NATIVE WOMEN

Under the Indian Act, women who married white men lost their treaty status, as did their children, even though Native men could marry non-Native women without the same loss of status for themselves or their offspring. In the early 1970s, Native women formed two organizations—Indian Rights for Indian Women and the National Native Women's Association—to campaign against the discriminatory treatment. They were supported in their efforts by non-Native women's groups. Together they persuaded the federal government to remove the offending section from the act in 1985.

Although the 76 000 women and children who were potentially eligible to be reinstated as Status Indians had won a legal victory, they were not always welcomed back into reserve communities. Some band councils argued that these women and their children were not Indian enough, either culturally or in their bloodlines. More generally, they charged that the federal government had done nothing to add to the land base of overcrowded reserves to make the reintegration of these women and their families possible without creating hardship for existing residents.

Native women often charged that white imperialism had eroded women's traditional influence in Native communities. Men's power on reserves, they argued, had been buttressed by state assumptions that viewed men as the natural leaders of the community and the main source of family support. In an atmosphere of hopelessness, alcoholic or drug-dependent Native men struck out at their wives and children. Studies of remote reserves revealed a pattern of physical and sexual abuse in which girls and women were the main victims. Native women organized support groups and healing centres and demanded that elected band councils implement programs to counsel men who abused women and to protect their potential victims.

Native women experienced horrendous rates of violence at the hands of both Native and non-Native men. The police appeared to take little interest in their plight. More than 500 Aboriginal women were murdered or disappeared without a trace in Canada from 1974 to 2004, and it was only rarely that the police investigated these cases closely and made any arrests. The disappearance of more than 50 Vancouver-area women, the majority of them Natives and prostitutes, in the late 1990s and early 2000s occasioned little police interest for a number of years. When an arrest was finally made and bodies found on a Port Coquitlam pig farm in 2004, it was revealed that several individuals had brought their suspicions of the accused to police over the years, but the police had done little to follow up. In 2004, the Native Women's Association of Canada launched Sisters in Spirit, a campaign to inform Canadians about the levels of violence perpetrated against Native women.

Women's March Against Poverty, Ottawa, 1996.
Canadian Women's Movement Archives

THE WOMEN'S MOVEMENT

The women's movement continued to play an important role in Canadian society. While the movement had diversified and its goals had been increasingly deflected by government cutbacks, the continuing vulnerability of many women helped generate a female point of view on a wide variety of public policy issues. Indeed, surveys suggested that in Canada, as in other countries, there was a significant "gender gap" in voting intentions and political ideas between men and women. More men than women, for example, embraced neo-liberal thinking and voted for candidates who promoted neo-liberal agendas. Whether or not they were conscious feminists, many women identified with the feminist critique of institutions and legislation that limited their ability to achieve either greater equality with men or economic independence.

The liberalization of divorce laws and the flight of men from family obligations increased the number of self-supporting women. By 2008, 38 percent of marriages had ended in divorce before their 30th anniversaries. The number of single-parent families correspondingly jumped, rising from 477 525 to 714 005 from 1971 to 1981 alone, with 85 percent of such families in the latter year headed by women. A majority of women-headed families lived in poverty, with Statistics Canada reporting that in 1998, 59.5 percent of children raised by their mothers alone were growing up poor. By contrast, in France, the figure was 15 percent and in Sweden, 5 percent. In those countries, government policies focusing on retraining and finding work for single mothers, along with free day care, were clearly effective, but governments in Canada resisted pressure for such sweeping programs.

If the women's movement could point to only modest successes in its campaigns to end women's poverty, it had more success in its demands for a woman's right to choose to terminate a pregnancy. Pro-choice groups stressed a woman's right to control her own body, while anti-abortionists claimed that a fetus was a living person from the moment of conception and that its right to life outweighed a woman's right to reproductive self-determination. After the re-laxation of the abortion law in 1969, access to abortion was uneven across the country, leading the Supreme Court to rule in 1988 that the law, which required an abortion to be approved by a three-doctor panel, vio-lated the guarantees of equal rights for all Canadians in the Charter of Rights and Freedoms.

After the court decision, parliament grappled un-successfully with the divisive issue, leaving Canada with no law restricting rights to an abortion. Mean-while, anti-abortionists were becoming increasingly militant, picketing abortion clinics and harassing pa-tients. In 1992, a bomb blast destroyed a Toronto clinic run by Dr. Henry Morgentaler, a tireless cru-sader for women's right to safe abortion. Two years later, a Vancouver doctor who performed abortions was shot by an anti-abortionist.

As the women's movement evolved, it identified and brought to public attention problems that had been previously overlooked. One such subject, virtu-ally ignored by even the Royal Commission on the Status of Women, was violence against women. Sexual assaults, battering, the physical and sexual abuse of children, and sexual harassment in the workplace had generally been regarded as private problems and were often not taken very seriously by authorities. When NDP MP Margaret Mitchell rose in the House of Commons to speak on the issue of wife battering in May 1982, she was greeted with laughter and disparag-ing remarks from some of her fellow MPs.

The denigration of women fighting for equal rights came not only in the form of laughter and dismissal. On 6 December 1989, a deranged young man fatally shot 14 female engineering students at the École Polytech-nique de Montréal while shouting his hatred of femi-nists. In the wake of this tragedy—which became known in the media as the Montreal Massacre—women's groups continued to press for battered women's shelters, rape crisis centres, counselling for abusers and their vic-tims, and stronger court charges and convictions for rapists, batterers, and harassers. Government action proved slow in coming, and what few programs were available were often among the first victims of fiscal re-straint in the debt-conscious 1990s.

Also in that decade, the women's movement faced challenges from within. Women living in poverty and minority women called on the feminist movement,

whose roots were among white, middle-class women, to raise issues that affected less privileged women and to give women of colour important roles as decision-makers and spokespersons. Judy Rebick, president of the National Action Committee on the Status of Women (NAC), brought the language of class and race into the mainstream feminist movement. She insisted that the movement work to prevent the exploitation of domestics, who were largely visible-minority immi-grant women, and pursue not just equal pay for equal work, but equal pay for work of equal value—a concept that would weigh traditional female jobs against men's jobs that required about the same education and skills.

Some women vented their displeasure with the radical turn of the women's movement when Sunera Thobani was named Rebick's successor in 1993. Of East Asian background, Thobani was the first visible-minority president of NAC, and her election signalled both a continuation of the radicalism of the Rebick pe-riod and a symbolic commitment to the demands of visible-minority women in the organization. NAC's Women's March Against Poverty and the election of Joan Grant-Cummings, an African Canadian, to suc-ceed Thobani in 1996 indicated that the organization would continue to address issues affecting poor and minority women. Meanwhile, political leaders were less likely than they had been in the 1980s to respond to the NAC's demands for reforms relating to women, a reflection not only of the deep-seated racism and elitism of Canadian politics but also of the new neo-liberal agenda of the 1990s.

THE ENVIRONMENTAL MOVEMENT

Apart from the women's movement, the most visible popular movement against the status quo in late twentieth-century Canada was the environmental movement. Greenpeace was particularly astute at fo-cusing public attention and creating controversy. In 1970, a small group of American and Canadian ac-tivists in Vancouver created Greenpeace to protest nuclear testing at Amchitka in the Aleutian Islands. Publicity generated by the fledgling organization prompted the United States to abandon their tests. Buoyed by its initial success, Greenpeace conducted dramatic non-violent protests to raise the profile of other issues, among them French nuclear testing in the South Pacific, the slaughter of whales and dolphins, the clubbing of baby seals for fur coats, and the dumping of nuclear and other toxic wastes in lakes and oceans.

By the mid-1970s, branches of Greenpeace had mushroomed throughout the world, and Greenpeace protesters popped up everywhere, precipitating incidents for the television cameras. In 1985, a Greenpeace member was killed in New Zealand by a bomb planted on the Greenpeace flagship *Rainbow Warrior* by French agents attempting to stop a "peace flotilla" protesting nuclear tests on Mururoa Atoll. While many people were angered by Greenpeace's tactics, no one could deny the organization's effectiveness. The Newfoundland seal hunt was restricted, and the save-the-whales campaign brought reforms to the whaling industry. By the mid-1980s, Greenpeace was an international organization with its headquarters in Amsterdam, retaining a strong contingent of Canadian members, many of whom could remember when it had operated on a shoestring budget with one leaking boat.

Local and national networks on environmental issues were often as effective as Greenpeace in achieving their objectives, though they received less media attention. By 1994, the Canadian Environmental Network included 2250 groups organized to deal with a specific environmental problem or environmental issues generally. British Columbia was the most activist province and won an important victory in the mid-1990s after using civil disobedience to force the NDP government to end the cutting of trees in the old-growth forests of Clayoquot Sound.

Among the national successes of the environmental movement was an agreement with the United States to tackle the problem of "acid rain." It had been clear since the 1970s that emissions from coal-burning factories in the United States and Canada were killing many lakes and trees and contributing to respiratory ailments and the erosion of buildings. The Canadian Coalition on Acid Rain played a major role in persuading the Canadian government that this was a major issue and that it was necessary to pressure the Americans to take action. In 1990, the American congress finally passed legislation that placed caps on emissions of sulfur dioxide and nitrogen oxide, the principal culprits in acid rain production.

By the 1990s, a key focus for many environmental groups across the country was the reduction of greenhouse gases that were contributing to global warming and the potential havoc associated with rapid climate change. In 1998, the Canadian government signed the Kyoto Accord, an international agreement on greenhouse gas reduction. Canada agreed

Oil drilling protest in Victoria, BC, staged by Greenpeace.
Sean White/CP Photo Archive

to reduce its emissions to a level 6 percent below its emissions in 1990, but actually increased its emissions over the next decade.

The issue of toxins in the workplace received greater publicity during this period, but, as with Kyoto, government actions often contradicted claims of concern for workers' health. The Harris government in Ontario eliminated the Workplace Health and Safety Agency, the Occupational Health Laboratory and Library, the Occupational Diseases Panel, and the joint labour-employer toxic-substance determination process. Training requirements for health and safety representatives were relaxed, while budgets for Occupational Health Clinics were slashed. Lax safety inspection in workplaces was evident in the small number of health and safety inspectors employed by the provinces, ranging from one inspector for every 11 000 workers in British Columbia to one for every 32 000 workers in Alberta in 1995.

GAY RIGHTS

Gays and lesbians continued to struggle for acceptance in Canadian society and for legal protection from discrimination during this period. Although homophobia remained endemic in much of Canadian society, promoted by fundamentalist preachers and a masculine culture with strict gender definitions, there were a number of legislative victories. In 1977, sexual preference was removed as a criterion for immigration. The Parti Québécois added sexual orientation to

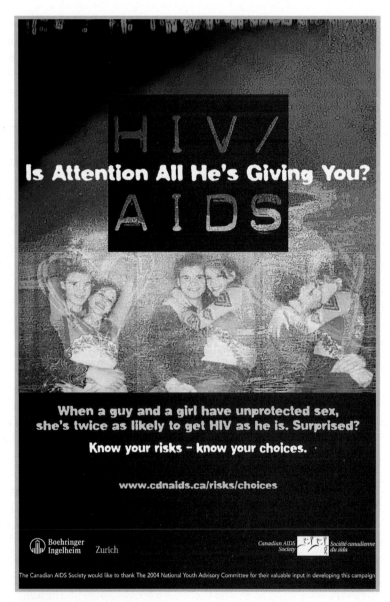

AIDS awareness campaign poster.
2005 Youth Campaign, Canadian AIDS Society

Quebec's human rights code, and most other provinces eventually followed suit. Activists won court battles that gave same-sex partners benefits similar to those for heterosexual spouses. After legal challenges, the Canadian army agreed in 1992 to end long-standing policies against homosexuals.

Other court decisions also defended gay rights. Alberta's Individual's Rights Protection Act (IRPA) failed to protect the rights of homosexuals, with the result that King's College in Edmonton fired Delwin Vriend, a laboratory coordinator, on the grounds that

his homosexuality made him unfit to be employed at a Christian college. In 1998, the Supreme Court ordered his reinstatement and implicitly added gay rights to the IRPA. In 1999, the court declared illegal an amendment to Ontario's Family Law Act that provided protections for common-law "spouses," defining spouses as members of the opposite sex.

There were setbacks as well. While gays won the right to be ordained as ministers in the United Church in 1988, the Roman Catholic Church joined evangelical Protestants in continuing to denounce homosexuality, along with abortion and divorce, as threats to the traditional family. In 2008, the Anglican Church faced secession by various congregations opposed to gay ordination. Intolerance against homosexuality sometimes manifested itself in violence. Homophobic thugs beat up and in some cases killed gay men. In the 1980s, Toronto's gay newspaper *The Body Politic* was slapped with obscenity charges, while police raids on gay bars and bathhouses indicated a continued willingness to harass gays in the name of public morality.

The spread of AIDS—Acquired Immune Deficiency Syndrome—constituted a daunting challenge to the gay community, whose male members initially formed the majority of the victims of the disease. AIDS organizers developed support systems for persons infected with AIDS and education campaigns to slow the spread of the disease. They also pressured governments to increase funding to community groups and medical research to fight AIDS.

Gay activists in the 1990s were often more militant than their counterparts of a generation earlier. In contrast to the repression of earlier days, activists celebrated gay culture. Gay Pride Days became annual events in many cities, with the gay pride parade in Toronto attracting more than 100 000 participants and

spectators annually. No longer confined to the closet, gays and lesbians published newspapers and magazines, founded bookstores, established theatre companies, made films, and wrote books dealing with gay lifestyles and concerns.

THE CHURCHES

The evangelical Protestants who trashed gays and "women libbers" enjoyed the greatest relative growth in members in the last quarter of the twentieth century. Still, the numbers of Canadians who claimed affiliation with the traditional denominations easily dwarfed the congregations of Pentecostal churches, Adventists, Churches of Christ, and other groups that tended to identify with the New Right because of its opposition to changing gender roles and notions of personal moral choice.

Churches continued to face the dilemma of the extent to which they should become involved in secular issues, and which ones. During the 1980s recession, the Social Affairs Commission of the Canadian Conference of Catholic Bishops issued a manifesto entitled *Ethical Reflections on the Economic Crisis.* The bishops set forth the ethical priorities they wanted governments to follow: "The needs of the poor have priority over the wants of the rich; the rights of workers are more important than the accumulation of machines or the maximization of profit; the participation of the marginalized takes precedence over an order that excludes them."[3] With unemployment in double digits, the bishops called on the government to focus on policies that would create jobs rather than continuing to emphasize the battle against inflation urged by the business community.

Although leaders of the Anglican and United churches praised the Roman Catholic bishops for their stand, voices were raised against economic radicalism as well. Much of the hierarchy identified with the business leaders, whose corporate sponsorship was essential to the churches' charitable work. In 1988, the limits of the churches' social justice movement were demonstrated by the decision of the Roman Catholic and Anglican churches to take no position on the Canada–United States free trade agreement and the mildness of the United Church's public opposition to the deal.

TABLE 22.3 Religious Affiliations of Canadians, 1911–2001 (in percentages)			
Religious organization	1911	1951	2001
Roman Catholic	39.4	44.7	43.2
United Church	–	20.5	9.6
Anglican	14.5	14.7	6.9
Presbyterian	15.6	5.6	1.4
Lutheran	3.2	3.2	2.0
Baptist	5.3	3.2	2.5
Christian Orthodox	1.2	1.2	1.6
Other Christians*	18.0	3.9	5.5
Jewish	1.0	1.5	1.1
No religion	0.4	0.4	16.2
Other	2.0	1.4	7.5**

*Includes Methodists and Congregationalists for 1911; Adventists, Churches of Christ, Disciples, Pentecostal, and Salvation Army for 1951 and 2001 along with smaller groups
**Includes Muslims, 2 percent; Hindus, 1 percent; Buddhists, 1 percent; and Sikh, 0.9 percent

Source: *Canada Year Book, 1994*, 123; Statistic Canada, 2001: Analysis Series, Religions in Canada, 18.

In this period most of the mainline Protestant churches were forced to grapple with declines in their membership. While the percentage of Canadians who identified themselves as Roman Catholic declined only slightly from 1951 to 2001, many Protestant denominations dropped dramatically in their percentage of adherents from 50 years earlier (see Table 22.3). Much of the decline was accounted for by two factors: the change in religious affiliation of immigrants (only 10.7 percent of immigrants arriving in the 1990s were Protestants compared to 39.2 prior to 1961) and an increased number of Canadians who followed no religion. Even among professed Christians, many people were attracted to New Age religions—spiritual movements with an affinity to Asian and ancient New World religions. Meanwhile, Muslims, Hindus, Buddhists, and Sikhs were growing in numbers.

For traditional Roman Catholics and Protestants, Canada's evolution as a multicultural country began to pose new issues. Was Canada really a "Christian" country? As new Canadians of non-Christian faiths protested that public schools required their children to participate in Christian ceremonies, many school boards agreed to take the religion out of Christmas and end such practices as prayers and Bible readings in schools. The growing number of atheists and agnostics applied similar pressures on other public institutions to end religious observances.

The trend toward greater secularism in Canada challenged all denominations. In 1961, only 1 percent of Canadians claimed no religion; in 2001, more than 16 percent made that claim, and in British Columbia the figure was 35 percent. While most Canadians believed in God, few felt the need to attend houses of worship. Fewer than 20 percent regularly attended a church, mosque, or synagogue, and there was a steep drop in infrequent attendance from the 1980s to the early 2000s. Church attendance was lowest in Quebec despite the nominal adhesion of 83 percent of the province's residents to the Roman Catholic faith. Baptisms, church marriages, and confirmations for young people had become less common. While Canadians still overwhelmingly described themselves as Christians, there was a drop from 80 percent of Canadians who styled themselves that way in 1991 to 72 percent in 2001. Among self-described Christians, there was a

doubling to 700 000 of those who indicated no affiliation with any particular Christian sect.

There was no simple explanation for the gradual alienation of Canadians from religious institutions even as most of them continued to believe in a divine presence. Sometimes, particularly in the case of the Roman Catholic Church, individual members disagreed with key doctrines and chose to avoid church attendance while remaining nominally adherent. In Quebec, for example, large majorities supported birth control, a woman's right to abortion, and gay marriage, all of which were anathema to the pope. In general, women, who had once been more likely to attend church regularly than men, were leaving the churches in droves. While women were striving to gain equality with men in all spheres, the churches continued, in many cases, to preach a return to patriarchal values.

CULTURAL INDUSTRIES

Trends from the 1960s and early 1970s in Canadian cultural development continued: Canadian literature blossomed, a respectable recording industry developed, and almost no one paid money to watch Canadian films except the rare one that achieved American acclaim. At the same time, Hollywood movie moguls, in an effort to take advantage of tax breaks and lower wage rates, increasingly made films in Canada, much to the annoyance of many Americans, who were beginning to understand what Canadians had felt when their industries drifted south of the border following the Free Trade Agreement.

A Canadian film, Denys Arcand's *Le Declin de l'empire americain* (*Decline of the American Empire*), made in 1986, attracted large audiences in French and English Canada and went on to become a huge international success. In 2004, Arcand enjoyed critical and commercial success with *Barbarian Invasions*, which garnered two Academy Awards, among other international honours. While Arcand and a few others continued to draw large audiences in the early 2000s, Quebec filmmakers complained that reduced government subsidies and the chain ownership of cinemas made it difficult to make French-Canadian films or find audiences for them. Increasingly, filmmakers had to be content with having their movies screened on television, where they often found large audiences, rather than in movie houses. Quebec-made films accounted for only 10 percent of box-office receipts in the province, just slightly higher than the national figure for box-office receipts that came from Canadian-made movies. The monies available for filmmaking in Canada told part of the story. In 2000, there were 1075 feature films made in the United States with a total budget of US$31 billion. By contrast, in Canada that year, only C$330 million, or less than 1 percent of the American total in US dollars, was spent making 30 feature films. Nonetheless, a number of Canadian filmmakers, including Cynthia Scott, Anne Wheeler, Atom Egoyan, and David Cronenberg, made bankable films.

While the situation for feature films was dismal, documentaries, mainly made by the National Film Board, continued to receive acclaim. Studio D, a feminist film unit within the NFB between 1994 and 1996, was particularly successful, producing *If You Love This Planet*, an Academy Award–winning anti-nuclear documentary; *Not a Love Story*, an anti-pornography film; and *Forbidden Love*, an examination of lesbian relationships. In the 1990s and early 2000s, the number of women and visible-minority film directors increased dramatically, with names such as Deepak Mehta, Mima Shuma, Alanis Obomsawin, and Patricia Rozema joining the list of critically acclaimed Canadian filmmakers.

English-Canadian television largely failed to thrive in an era of government cuts and the "200 channel universe" that allowed copious numbers of American programs into Canadian homes. There were exceptions. Canadians warmed to their political and social humorists, and shows such as *This Hour Has 22 Minutes* and *Royal Canadian Air Farce* drew audiences in the millions. Canadians also continued to watch news programs produced within the country, with the new Newsworld channel creating a staunch following. CBC's *People's History of Canada* series in 2000–2001, with its nation-building theme, was also a success. But Canadians seemed to find little difference between the sitcoms, dramas, and game shows produced at home and those beamed in from American channels, and devoted more of their time to the latter.

The French language assured Quebec's television producers of a larger audience. In the 1980s and 1990s, hundreds of thousands of Francophones watched Pierre

Gauvreau's *Le Temps d'une paix* (*Peacetime*), a dramatization of life in Quebec from 1918 to 1930, and *Cormoran*, which highlighted political and class struggles in Rimouski during the Great Depression. Among TV series focusing on modern Quebec, several by the feminist author, broadcaster, and former PQ cabinet minister Lise Payette have been particularly successful. Her *Marilyn*, which began a long TV run in 1991, had as its protagonist a charwoman whose experiences put her in contact with people from all walks of life in Quebec.

The increasing popularity of Canadian literature in the post-war period continued to grow late in the twentieth century, and international audiences became more interested in Canadians' work. Margaret Atwood, Michael Ondaatje, Carol Shields, Rohinton Mistry, Anne Michaels, and others won major international book awards, and a host of writers such as Wayne Johnston, Alice Munro, M.G. Vassanji, Anne-Marie MacDonald, Bonnie Burnard, Mordecai Richler, and Guy Vanderhaeghe also topped Canadian and international best-seller lists. The multicultural character of Canada's contribution to world literature was striking. Mistry and Vassanji are Indian expatriates, while Ondaatje was born in Sri Lanka.

Native authors were also beginning to be noticed by the broader society. Thomas King's portraits of Native life in works such as *Medicine River* (1990) and Tomson Highway's plays, including the critically acclaimed *Dry Lips Oughta Move to Kapuskasing* (1989), represent a few of the Native attempts to bring their stories to Canadians as a whole. The Mi'kmaq found a voice in the poetry of Rita Joe.

For many Canadians, books, films, and theatre were less important cultural activities than gambling. Most provinces, beginning with Quebec in 1970, had established lotteries by the mid-1970s, and in 1990 Manitoba became the first province to establish a government-operated casino. New Brunswick introduced Video Lottery Terminals in 1991 and was quickly followed by the other provinces. Gambling became a major source of revenue for provincial governments. While governments set aside some of the revenue for programs for gambling addicts, critics of the casinos, VLT machines, and lotteries that were ruining the lives of many Canadians complained that governments were addicted to gambling revenues.

RECORDING ARTISTS

Sales of "Canadian content" recordings increased from $53.6 million in 1990–1991 to $127.2 million by 1995–1996. By the latter date, 14.5 percent of sales in Canada, against 10.5 percent five years earlier, were of records whose artists, writers, or producers were Canadian citizens. In part, this was simply because Canada produced a number of international superstars in the 1990s, many of them women. Céline Dion, Alanis Morissette, Shania Twain, Sarah McLachlan, and Diana Krall were the world's best-selling female artists in pop, country, folk, and jazz. Among male artists, Bryan Adams, Barenaked Ladies and The Tragically Hip were Canada's best-known exports. They were joined in the early 2000s by Nickelback, whose first CD produced the biggest pop tune in the United States in 2002, "How You Remind Me."

Popular music was one of the few occupations by which a talented few could transform their economic prospects. Céline Dion, for example, was the fourteenth child of a working-class Quebec family before becoming Quebec's leading Francophone pop star and, in the 1990s, the world's best-selling female artist. Another rags-to-riches story is the career of Shania Twain, who grew up in poverty in Timmins, Ontario, in a Métis environment with her mother and Métis stepfather. When her parents died in a car crash, the teenage Twain raised her younger brothers and sisters with money she earned as a local singer. By 2000, she was country music's all-time best-selling artist and had recorded the biggest-selling CD in country music history. Folk-pop singer Sarah McLachlan was responsible for Lilith Fair, a female musicians' summer festival that for several years drew large numbers in the United States and Canada.

While some of these artists might have found success without the Canadian-content regulations, the rules encouraged more diversity in the types of music aired by radio stations and broadcast on the video channels that appeared in the 1980s. Political tunes such as Bruce Cockburn's "Rocket Launcher" and Parachute Club's "Rise Up," which might not have been played in Canada in the period before the "Can Con" rule, proved to be big sellers. Rita MacNeil's "Working Man" made every country-music station playlist though it bore little resemblance to the

Sarah McLachlan.
© Neal Preston/CORBIS

maudlin American country music that stations had played before the requirement to fill the airwaves with Canadian music 30 percent of the time forced a broadening of the genre's definition in Canada. "Working Man," which also became a chart-topper in Great Britain, featured Men of the Deeps, a coal miners' choir from Cape Breton, singing with MacNeil.

In the 1990s, some Native artists gained recognition. Kashtin, two Innu performers from northern Quebec who sang in their Native language, produced a hybrid of Native music and rock and roll and played to large audiences of both Francophones and Anglophones in the south. Susan Aglukark, although singing mainly in English, paid tribute to her Inuit heritage and dealt with social problems of the North.

Native dance troupes performed traditional dances in ceremonial costumes before their own people and increasingly before white audiences as well, attempting to reproduce the dances as they had been performed by their ancestors rather than refashioning them for commercial broadcasters.

MEDIA CONCENTRATION

The mass media, with its great impact on Canadian social values, has come to be controlled by fewer and fewer corporations and individuals. In 1980, the Royal Commission on Newspapers reported that three chains controlled 90 percent of French-language newspapers and another three conglomerates controlled over

Terry Fox during his Marathon of Hope.
The Canadian Press

Winnipeg entrepreneur and former Manitoba Liberal leader who had already built a television empire.

Such media concentration, which also occurred in other western democracies, raised questions about the degree to which the media could be counted on to provide a range of points of view. The need to lure corporate advertisers prevented groups such as trade unions from establishing their own papers or television stations.

Entry was easier in the book-publishing industry, but a small number of corporations made most of the money, and Canadian firms were increasingly absorbed by mega-corporations. Ryerson Press was taken over by the American firm McGraw-Hill in 1970; Copp Clark, Canada's oldest publisher, was bought first by the British firm Pitman in the 1950s and then by the conglomerate Pearson in 1995. In the 1980s, while Canadian-owned firms were responsible for most of the new textbooks that appeared in Canada, they garnered less than a third of the revenues from book sales. Only the continued presence of the Canada Council, which had been making grants to independent publishers since 1972, and the determination of many operators of small presses and their authors kept an independent Canadian book publishing sector alive in an age of transnational corporate transcendence.

PROFESSIONAL SPORTS

Hockey continued to be the major spectator sport in Canada. When the World Hockey Association (WHA) faced bankruptcy in 1979, all of the WHA teams but Ottawa joined the National Hockey League (NHL), and the transfer of the NHL's Atlanta franchise to Calgary increased the number of Canadian teams to seven. The Edmonton Oilers won five Stanley Cups from 1984 to 1990, and Oiler Wayne Gretzky became almost synonymous with the game. To the chagrin of most Edmontonians, Gretzky was sold to the Los Angeles Kings in 1988 by Oiler owner Peter Pocklington for $18 million. It was a reminder that hockey, like most professional sports, had become big business and that a franchise belonged to owners rather than a particular city. By the mid-1990s, the cost of signing star players had forced both Quebec City and Winnipeg to concede that they could not draw the home audiences

two-thirds of English-language newspapers in Canada. Since that time, concentration of ownership has increased. The Southam chain dominated most large Anglophone urban markets outside the Atlantic provinces, though it faced well-established competitors in Toronto. Once owned by the Southam family, the chain was controlled by magnate Conrad Black from 1996 to 2000, when it was bought by I.H. Asper, a

needed to sustain professional hockey teams, and their teams headed south of the border.

Football fans proved reluctant to pay the high ticket prices necessitated by the 1990s to finance lucrative players' contracts. Though the ownership of Ontario teams was private, the western teams were owned and operated by non-profit community organizations. An attempt to increase interest in the Canadian Football League (CFL) by expanding franchises to the United States in the mid-1990s flopped. American football fans proved uninterested in the Canadian version of the game. By 1996, the CFL was once again made up of only Canadian teams.

Professional baseball in Canada was represented by American major league teams in the two largest cities. The Montreal Expos had difficulties filling the stadium, and the team was relocated to Washington, D.C., in 2004. The Toronto Blue Jays attracted large crowds in their home town, even though no member of the team was a Torontonian or even a Canadian. After spending almost $50 million on player salaries, the Blue Jays won the World Series in 1992 and 1993.

While professional sports teams were almost exclusively male, both female and male athletes won international honours in individual sports, bringing home medals in a variety of events at Olympic, Special Olympic, Commonwealth, and Pan-American games and world championships in individual sports.

SPORTS AND SOCIETY

For many Canadians, the country's most inspiring athlete had never attempted to win any competition. In April 1980, Terry Fox, a 21-year-old Vancouver student who had lost a leg to bone cancer, began a run across Canada to raise funds for cancer research. After five months of running almost 40 kilometres per day on his Marathon of Hope, Fox was forced to give up his run at Thunder Bay when doctors found that the cancer had spread to his lungs. He died in June 1981, but the Terry Fox Run, an annual fund-raising event for cancer research, became one of the major participatory sports events in Canada. From 1985 to 1987, British Columbia wheelchair athlete Rick Hansen, inspired in part by Fox's achievement, dramatized the oft-ignored capabilities of people with disabilities by circling the globe in his wheelchair on his Man in Motion World Tour.

For Fox, running was a means to a noble end, but running was also big business. As in many other sports, the desire to win often led athletes and coaches to cheat. A steroids scandal rocked Canada after sprinter Ben Johnson was stripped of a gold medal at the Seoul Olympics in 1988. In the media circus and official inquiry that followed, Canadians learned that many athletes used performance-enhancing steroids. Questions of amateurism that had plagued earlier international competition seemed rather quaint as sports took on a big-business atmosphere in which millions of dollars in endorsements could await Olympic gold medallists. Canada's reputation in running rebounded with Donovan Bailey's convincing 100-metre win in the 1996 Atlanta Olympics.

While many young Canadians dreamed of becoming sports celebrities, studies suggested their chances were best if they were Anglo-Canadian males with professional or white-collar parents. The costs involved in training athletes who could compete in national and international events excluded most working-class children. Girls faced particular challenges as sexual segregation continued to make sports a largely male preserve. Attempts by girls and women to share the same opportunities as boys were mightily resisted. In 1985, the Ontario Hockey Association (OHA) barred 13-year-old Justine Blainey from participating on a leading boys' hockey team. Several courtrooms and thousands of dollars later, Justine got her wish in 1987, but the OHA continued to grumble that the bodychecking and slapshots of the boys' league made the inclusion of girls inappropriate.

While sports for youngsters were supposed to be about fun, they sometimes became a nightmare. In 1997, Sheldon Kennedy, a former member of the Swift Current Broncos, a junior team, who had made it to the NHL, revealed that in the late 1980s the Bronco coach had sexually abused him on hundreds of occasions. It soon became clear that Kennedy was not his only victim and that coaches for other teams had also sexually abused players. The hockey scandal followed revelations about sexual abuse of boys and girls in other sports, alarming parents and sports authorities at a time when more and more children were becoming involved in organized sporting activities.

Canadians in the post-war period spent a great deal of money and time as sports spectators, both at children's and professional games. But attending sports activities and participating in them were two different stories. In the early 1970s, it was estimated that 90 percent of adults did not do the minimum amount of exercise recommended for protection against heart disease and stroke. While Canadians were living longer, poor nutrition habits, lack of exercise, and smoking were ending many lives prematurely and restricting the lives of many other Canadians who survived cancer, heart attacks, or strokes.

Increasingly, the federal government, aided by campaigns of nutritionists, physical education specialists, and physicians, encouraged Canadians to rethink their lifestyles. Urged on by a federal body called Participaction, which placed clever advertisements on radio and television, previously indolent Canadians took up jogging, enrolled in aerobics classes, swam, or at least took an occasional long walk. The physical fitness craze meant new business for leisure industry operators from ski hills to fitness clubs.

Health consciousness helped stimulate interest in sports. It also sparked anti-smoking campaigns. By the 1990s, the intrepid smoker stood out in the snow or rain during a coffee break at most workplaces, public buildings, and halls of education. Airlines banned smoking altogether, and intercity buses, once thick with smoke, became havens for non-smokers. In most cities, restaurants were divided by law into smoking and non-smoking sections, and some city councils legislated smoking out of all establishments where food was served. The percentage of adults who smoked dropped by half between the 1960s and the 1990s, but today young people continue to begin smoking at rates similar to those that prevailed when their parents' generation was young.

The diets of many Canadians have changed and are now more likely to meet Health Canada's requirement for "balanced" eating. Consumption of red meat, one of the items linked by physicians to cardiovascular problems, fell, and the cattle industry changed breeding habits to develop leaner meats. The focus on diet, however, had its seamy side. Social images, especially for young women, created the view that the ideal body was fat-free, an unhealthy suggestion that led to a rise in anorexia and bulimia, with associated risks of death by starvation in a prosperous society.

More commonly, unhealthy diets that ignored nutritionists' guides for getting all necessary vitamins and minerals were pedalled by diet gurus out to make a buck at the expense of women and sometimes men who were misled by the pervasive images that "fat is not where it's at." Social class was a big factor in people's response to new ideas of healthy living. Surveys suggested that the working class and the poor had less time and money to devote to "participaction" and that in any case, they often regarded the new opposition to smoking, drinking, and relaxation as an attack on the few pleasures in their lives.

Conclusion

In the last quarter of the twentieth century, Canada became a more multicultural and pluralist society. It was also forced to respond to the demands of groups whose voices had long been submerged. Native, women's, environmental, and gay rights struggles resulted in legal victories and greater self-confidence on the part of groups that had suffered oppression in Canadian society. Growing self-confidence was also evident in many areas of Canadian cultural production. Whether these new trends will continue to animate Canadian social and political life is a question that only time will tell.

Notes

1 Paul Anisef, Paul Axelrod, Etta Baichman-Anisef, Carl James, and Anton Turritin, *Opportunity and Uncertainty: Life Course Expectations of the Class of '73* (Toronto: University of Toronto Press, 2000), 239–40.

2 John L. Steckley and Bryan D. Cummins, *Full Circle: Canada's First Nations* (Toronto: Pearson Education, 2001), 132.

3 Tony Clarke, *Behind the Mitre: The Moral Leadership Crisis in the Canadian Catholic Church* (Toronto: HarperCollins, 1995).

RELATED READINGS IN THIS SERIES

From *Nation and Society: Readings in Post-Confederation Canadian History*

Tania Das Gupta, "Political Economy of Gender, Race, and Class: Looking at South Asian Immigrant Women in Canada," 452–65.

Margaret E. McCallum, "Rights in the Courts, on the Water, and in the Woods: The Aftermath of *R. v. Marshall* in New Brunswick," 466–76.

From Primary Documents CD-ROM, Volume II

On Abortion
Lesbians Fight to Keep Kids
Indian Amendment Act, 1985
Read No Evil, Watch No Evil

SELECTED READING

On immigration, see the works cited in Chapter 18 and Daiva K. Stasiulis and Abigail B. Bakan, *Negotiating Citizenship: Migrant Women in Canada and the Global System* (Toronto: University of Toronto Press, 2005).

On Native peoples, apart from the works cited in Chapter 18, see William C. Wicken, *Mi'kmaq Treaties on Trial: History, Land and Donald Marshall Junior* (Toronto: University of Toronto Press, 2002); John L. Steckley and Bryan D. Cummins, *Full Circle: Canada's First Nations* (Toronto: Pearson Education, 2001); Peter Kulchyski, ed., *Unjust Relations: Aboriginal Rights in Canadian Courts* (Toronto: Oxford University Press, 1994); Patricia Monture-Angus, *Thunder in My Soul: A Mohawk Woman Speaks* (Toronto: Fernwood, 1995); Geoffrey York, *The Dispossessed: Life and Death in Native Canada* (London: Vintage, 1990); James S. Frideres and René R. Gadacz, *Aboriginal Peoples in Canada: Contemporary Conflicts*, 6th ed. (Toronto: Prentice Hall, 2001); and Ken Coates, *The Marshall Decision and Native Rights* (Montreal: McGill-Queen's University Press, 2000).

On religion, see Reginald Bibby, *Restless Gods* (Toronto: Novalis, 2004); Terrance Murphy et al., eds., *A Concise History of Christianity in Canada* (Toronto: Oxford University Press, 1996); and John Stackhouse, *Canadian Evangelicanism in the Twentieth Century* (Toronto: University of Toronto press, 1993).

On the women's movement in Canada, see the works cited in Chapter 18. Sharon Rosenberg offers a thoughtful reflection on the Montreal Massacre in "Neither Forgotten nor Fully Remembered: Tracing an Ambivalent Memory on the Tenth Anniversary of the Montreal Massacre," in *Killing Women: The Visual Culture of Gender and Violence*, eds., Annette Burfoot and Susan Lord (Waterloo: Wilfrid Laurier University Press, 2006).

On the environmental movement, see Mary Richardson, Joan Sherman, and Michael Gismondi, *Winning Back the Words: Confronting Experts in an Environmental Public Hearing* (Toronto: Garamond, 1993); George N. Hood, *Against the Flow: Rafferty-Alameda and the Politics of the Environment* (Saskatoon: Fifth House, 1994); and John Dyson with Joseph Fitchett, *Sink the Rainbow! An Enquiry into the "Greenpeace Affair"* (London: Victor Gollancz, 1986).

On gay liberation and AIDS organizing, see Tom Warner, *Never Going Back: A History of Queer Activism in Canada* (Toronto: University of Toronto Press, 2002); Gary Kinsman, *The Regulation of Desire: Homo and Hetero Sexualities* (Montreal: Black Rose, 1996); and David M. Rayside and Evert A. Lindquist, "AIDS Activism and the State in Canada," *Studies in Political Economy* 39 (Autumn 1992), 37–76.

On cultural developments, see the works cited in Chapter 19, in addition to George Melnyk, *One Hundred Years of Canadian Cinema* (Toronto: University of Toronto Press, 2004).

CHAPTER 23

Canada in the Twenty-First Century

TIMELINE

- **2000** Jean Chrétien wins third majority government
- **2001** Suicide bombers crash four American airplanes; Parliament passes Anti-terrorism Act; Stockholm convention bans pollutants that contaminate northern food
- **2002** Parliament ratifies the Kyoto Protocol; Canada begins sending troops to Afghanistan; the United States "renders" Maher Arar to Syria; Romanow report on medicare
- **2003** Paul Martin becomes prime minister; the Canadian Alliance and Progressive Conservatives unite as the Conservative Party of Canada; Canada declines to join the American invasion of Iraq
- **2004** Stephen Harper becomes Conservative leader; federal election produces minority Liberal government
- **2005** Kelowna Accord on Native policy; national day-care policy
- **2006** Federal election produces minority Conservative government; Kyoto, Kelowna and day-care agreements sidelined
- **2007** Fourth Report of Intergovernmental Panel on Climate Change; federal government provides financial compensation to Maher Arar; federal–provincial conflict over equalization payments; Supreme Court ruling provides some Charter protection for trade unions; Commission on Accommodation Practices Related to Cultural Differences appointed in Quebec

I nuit are an ancient people. Our way of life is dependent on the natural environment and animals. Climate change is destroying our environment and eroding our culture. But we refuse to disappear. We will not become a footnote to globalization. Climate change is amplified in the Arctic. What is happening to us now will happen soon in the rest of the world. Our region is the globe's climate change "barometer." If you want to protect the planet, look to the Arctic and listen to what Inuit are saying.[1]

This warning was issued by the Inuit Circumpolar Council (ICC) to the Inter-American Commission on Human Rights in 2005, challenging the once-dominant view that economic growth and human well-being were partners. According to ICC chair Sheila Watt-Cloutier, climate change caused by unregulated economic development would destroy the Inuit culture, a culturebased on marine life. Species requiring sea ice, including polar bears, ice-dwelling seals, walrus, and some marine birds, faced extinction if global warming was not alleviated. The ICC spoke for 155 000 Inuit in Canada, Greenland, Alaska, and Russia, who saw global warming as both an environmental and a human rights issue. Their very survival as a people depended on a serious response to the threat of global warming.

Campaigns for public policies to arrest global warming formed only one part of the politics of protest in the early twenty-first century. While the issues—peace, the environment, and social justice—were not new, their context had changed since the end of the Cold War. The attack by Muslim extremists on the World Trade Centre in New York and the Pentagon in Washington on 11 September 2001 added another element of crisis as Canadians tried to sort out their role in the aftermath of these tragedies. With security trumping all other concerns, the United States, under the leadership of Republican president George W. Bush, embarked on wars against regimes in Afghanistan and Iraq. Canada managed to side-step the war in Iraq but became mired in a nasty battle in Afghanistan.

Meanwhile, the divided forces of economic liberalism and social conservatism united in a new Conservative Party under the leadership of Stephen Harper. The Conservatives emerged as leaders of a minority government following a national election in 2006. Although Harper was unable to move as quickly as he would have liked in curbing what he considered to be the excesses of his Liberal predecessors, he signaled his intentions by stepping up Canada's commitments in Afghanistan, cutting taxes, abandoning plans for a national day-care program, and calling for a second vote in the House of Commons on the issue of gay rights.

This chapter examines developments in Canada in the early years of the new century, which from close range seem to have ushered in a new era of uncertainty and set the stage for dramatic changes.

FORECASTS OF ENVIRONMENTAL CATASTROPHE

In February 2007, the Intergovernmental Panel on Climate Change (IPCC), created by two United Nations bodies in 1988—the World Meteorological Organization and the UN Environment Program—filed its fourth comprehensive report. It stated that the planet was experiencing continuous increases in temperatures on land, sea, and permafrost, a result mainly of the increased human production of greenhouse gases. The burning of fossil fuels, intensive agricultural practices, and deforestation had all contributed to global warming. In the millennium before the Industrial Revolution, the level of greenhouse gases in the atmosphere had been relatively constant at 280 parts per million, but as industrialization developed, carbon emissions rose to 379 parts per million by 2005. During the twentieth century, average global surface temperatures had increased by less than one degree but were predicted to rise 1.9 to 4.6 degrees by 2100. To prevent an even larger rise in temperature and drastic ecological consequences—including a rise in sea levels by seven metres with the melting of the Greenland ice cap—global emissions had to fall by 90 percent as soon as possible.

Although the Canadian government promised swift action, its commitment to a reduction in global warming was questionable. The Chrétien Liberal government signed the Kyoto Protocol in 1998 and it was

Born in Kuujuaq, Nunavik (northern Quebec), Sheila Watt-Cloutier lives in Iqualuit, Nunavut. She led the campaign that sparked global negotiations leading to the Stockholm Convention ban in 2001 on persistent organic pollutants that contaminated the northern food supply.
CP/Chris Windeyer

ratified by parliament in December 2002, but under pressure from industrial lobbyists, the Liberals relied mainly on voluntary cooperation by industry to meet Kyoto's goals. Predictably, there was little reduction in greenhouse gas emissions. The victory of the Conservatives led by Stephen Harper in January 2006 made environmentalists nervous. In opposition, Harper had denounced Kyoto as a socialist plot. In government, he continued to oppose the protocol but agreed that government action on global warming was necessary. In response to the IPCC report, the Harper government pledged $2 billion over five years to combat climate change, proposing long-term reductions in greenhouse gas emissions. For the 15 years until 2021, however, the focus would be simply on reducing the intensity, not the volume, of emissions.

Critics suggested that the Conservatives were too solicitous of the oil-sands companies. The oil sands were an environmental nightmare, since the process of separating tar from sand produced exceptionally high carbon emissions. Environmentalists called instead for an emphasis on renewable energy projects paid for by higher royalties on the oil and gas industries, improved fuel standards in transportation, and the refitting of energy-inefficient buildings throughout the country. Cities would have to become denser so that walking and cycling could replace motor vehicles as the main methods of transportation. Amid growing global concern about the effects of global warming, Canadian

Arctic Sovereignty

In the twentieth century, the chief threat to Canadian sovereignty in the North came from occasional forays of American icebreakers and nuclear submarines in the Northwest Passage. As global warming gradually reshaped the Northwest Passage into a potentially safe seasonal sea lane for commercial ships, Russia and the European Union sided with the American claim that no country could impose laws on transport through the "international" waters of the passage. Russia also laid symbolic claim to an economic zone in the region of the North Pole. While any claim to the barren pole might at one time have seemed pointless, estimates of untold mineral and energy riches beneath the Arctic ice, presumably more reachable as the ice thinned, changed the stakes.

Opponents of Canada's claims to northern islands and the sea beyond them emphasized that the Law of the Sea extended only 22.2 kilometres beyond each shoreline. Canada's traditional response was that the sea was frozen most of the year and that Inuit hunters made their livelihood from hunting on the ice floes during the long freeze. As the ice melted and the Northwest Passage became more navigable, this argument lost credibility.

Successive Canadian governments promised to bolster Canada's claims to the Arctic by building facilities in the region and strengthening Canada's Arctic research. The promises remained largely unfulfilled. In 2006, Stephen Harper pledged to build new Arctic icebreakers and a northern deepwater port. Experts on the region suggested that Canada take additional steps to win greater support for its claim of sovereignty by investing in scientific research to establish more clearly its claim to the sea areas bordering on recognized Canadian lands and demonstrating an ability to clean up oil spills, provide security against terrorist attacks, and protect threatened species in northern regions.

MAP 23.1 **The Northwest Passage**

governments continued to stall on the drastic measures required to address the looming environmental crisis.

"9/11" AND AFGHANISTAN

Perhaps the most ecologically destructive activities involve modern warfare. While North American territory had long been spared direct attack, the situation changed on 11 September 2001. Muslim extremists turned hijacked airplanes into gigantic bombs that they used to destroy the twin towers of the World Trade Center in New York and to inflict damage on the Pentagon. The bombers' goal was to punish Americans for their government's alleged role in supporting global anti-Islamic forces and for exploiting the resources of Arab countries for American financial benefit.

Canadians were saddened by the deaths of nearly 3000 people in the "9/11" attacks but were more restrained in their response than their southern neighbour. American president George Bush claimed that terrorists resented the democratic freedoms enjoyed by Westerners. Jean Chrétien, in contrast, suggested in a CBC interview on the first anniversary of the 9/11 attacks: "You cannot exercise your powers to the point of humiliation for the others . . . we're looked upon as being arrogant, self-satisfied, greedy and with no limits. And the 11th of September is an occasion for me to realize it even more."[2]

Six weeks after the suicide bombings, the United States invaded Afghanistan when its government refused to surrender Osama bin Laden, the leader of al-Qaeda, a terrorist organization that appeared to be responsible for 9/11. The Taliban, Islamic extremists who ruled Afghanistan, made no secret of the fact that they would do anything in their power to undermine Western domination anywhere in the world. Few people voiced concern about overthrowing such an aggressive regime. But Afghanistan was not the only Muslim country on Bush's hit list. In April 2003, the United States invaded Iraq to remove its dictatorial leader, Saddam Hussein, who, the Bush administration claimed, was stockpiling "weapons of mass destruction." Although the International Atomic Energy Agency cast doubt on this claim and the United Nations opposed military action, the United States led a coalition of countries, including Great Britain, into another war. When it seemed that Canada might join

the "coalition of the willing," Canadians took to the streets to protest. Two demonstrations in Montreal in the weeks before the invasion of Iraq, each with over 250 000 participants, helped persuade Prime Minister Chrétien to keep Canada out of the war.

Nevertheless, Canada's response to the terrorist threat was a military one. In February 2002, the Chrétien government committed 140 members of the Princess Patricia's Canadian Light Infantry as part of a Canadian undertaking to assist the American occupation and reconstruction of Afghanistan. When Canada was criticized in the United States for failing to support its closest neighbour and major trading partner in its invasion of Iraq, Chrétien tried to sooth ruffled feathers by stepping up Canada's military commitment in Afghanistan, where the Taliban was mounting stiff resistance against the invaders. Canada became a leading force in NATO's International Security Assistance Force, which worked with the new Western-friendly Afghan government to repel Taliban attacks. From mid-2003 to May 2005, nearly 2000 Canadian troops were stationed mainly in the area around Kabul. Only eight Canadian troops died in Afghanistan during that period, four as a result of American "friendly fire." When Canada agreed to send 1250 troops to the Kandahar stronghold of the Taliban in May 2005, casualties began to mount. By July 2008, 85 Canadians died in what turned out to be a protracted war.

A majority of Canadians, raised on the belief that Canada's major role in the world was peacekeeping, not fighting wars, found Canada's involvement in

Canadian soldiers try to cool off while doing their duties in Afghanistan.
Les Perreaux/CP Photo

Afghanistan troubling. They demanded that Canada leave Kandahar as soon as possible and consider leaving Afghanistan altogether or simply focus on reconstruction projects but not play a military role. When Stephen Harper became prime minister, he made it clear that Canada would not "cut and run" under his leadership. Public pressure forced him to try to encourage other NATO countries to replace Canada in southern Afghanistan by February 2009, the date Canada's original commitment would end, but there were no takers. When he hinted that it might be necessary for Canadian troops to stay beyond 2009, the Liberals, under their new leader, Stéphane Dion, pressed him to stick to the deadline. Although supporters of Canada's military commitment argued that the presence of Canadian troops allowed democratic forces to consolidate in Afghanistan, the reality was less than inspiring. Corruption, torture, and ethnic division were rife and the central government of the Islamic Republic of Afghanistan appeared to govern little beyond the capital city of Kabul. While the lives of some people in Afghanistan were improving, the unemployment rate in 2007 was 78 percent and life expectancy was 42.5 years.

Canada's booming military export industries, subsidized by the federal government, suggested that economic interests played a major role in determining whom Canada regarded as allies. From 2000 to 2006, Canada's second largest buyer—following the United States—of military supplies was Saudi Arabia, a country lacking both democratic institutions and rights for women. Egypt and China, two other countries with limited civil rights, were also customers for Canada's military industries. By 2006, Canada's military exports were about $2 billion, a sevenfold increase over the previous decade. According to the US Congressional Research Service, Canada is the world's sixth biggest international exporter of military products in the twenty-first century.

9/11, THE SECURITY STATE AND MULTICULTURALISM

If Canada's vaunted peacekeeping role was compromised after 9/11, so arguably was its commitment to human rights. The Anti-Terrorist Act, given royal assent in December 2001, amended several bills including the Criminal Code, the Official Secrets Act, the Canada Evidence Act, and the Proceedings of Crime (Money Laundering) Act to make it easier for the government to ban organizations it considered to be supporting terrorism. The powers of CSIS and the RCMP to acquire information and detain suspects were increased. Civil rights groups unsuccessfully protested clauses that made arrest without warrant possible and allowed judges to hold secret hearings. Only the combined votes of opposition parties in the minority parliament forced a reluctant Harper government to abolish warrant-free arrests and secret hearings when the act was reviewed in 2006.

Several arrests were made under the Anti-Terrorist Act. In March 2004, Momin Khawaja, a Canadian-born Ottawa software developer, was charged with membership in a terrorist group. In January 2008, he remained in prison awaiting trial. There were 17 more arrests in June 2006, this time in the Toronto area, with the individuals arrested charged with ordering tons of explosives in a plot to blow up Canadian institutions. No trial had been announced as of 18 months later.

Alleged terrorist arrests were not limited to Anti-Terrorism Act detentions. From 2001 to 2007, at least five people were jailed under security certificates—government orders for the detention of non-citizens resident in Canada and deemed a threat to Canadian security. Several Canadians were also arrested abroad because of reports from Canadian security organizations to their foreign counterparts. The most publicized case involved Maher Arar, an Ottawa telecommunications engineer. In September 2002, Arar was returning home from a vacation in Tunisia when American security officials took him into custody during a stopover in New York. The Americans, using erroneous information provided by the RCMP, accused Arar of having links with al-Qaeda. Though Arar was a Canadian citizen, the Americans deported him to Syria, his country of birth. This was an example of a practice known as "rendition," in which countries that had formally renounced the use of torture to extract information from potential informants contracted the torturing out to countries without such inhibitions. In Syria, Arar was tortured for over 10 months. While Canada initially offered only a mild protest of Arar's fate, official demands for his release toughened when Canadian public opinion was mobilized in Arar's favour. A government-ordered commission of inquiry concluded that the RCMP had misinformed the Americans about Arar and that he had never posed a security risk. In January 2007, the Canadian government offered substantial financial compensation to Arar, for whom recovery from the torture and allegations came slowly.

Other Canadian Muslims believed that the new emphasis in Canada on security over human rights had resulted in "racial profiling" in airport screening, employment, and efforts to find rental housing. Girls wearing hijabs (Muslim headscarfs) were sometimes barred from sports teams, while in 2007 several small towns in Quebec adopted codes of conduct for potential immigrants that included prohibitions against stoning and burning women, reinforcing a negative stereotype of gender relations among Muslims. Prime Minister Harper seemed to court xenophobic fears when he introduced legislation in 2007 that forbade voters from covering their faces. Elections Canada chief Marc Meyrand questioned this not-so-veiled attack on Islamic women who wore the veil. Over 80 000 voters in the previous election had voted by mail-in ballot and could not have been asked to show their faces.

Concern about "political Islamism"—that is, an effort to insert religion into politics—was rarely expressed before 9/11, but it became a cause for debate and action in the years following. In 2005, a heated debate ensued in Ontario about whether *sharia* law, or Islamic-based law, could be used in family court. Since the passage of the province's Arbitration Act in 1991, divorcing Catholic, Jewish, and Ishmaeli Muslim couples could elect to use faith-based tribunals to settle family law matters. But when devout Sunni Muslims in Mississauga asked for tribunals using *sharia*, the Arbitration Act became a flashpoint. The Canadian Council of Muslim Women opposed any foothold for *sharia* in Canada on the grounds that it represented a politicized and patriarchal view of gender relations that Muslim women seeking social justice rejected. Supporters of allowing *sharia*, in contrast, argued that it was a matter of civil rights that all religious groups must be treated the same under the law. Premier Dalton McGuinty's solution was to repeal the Arbitration Act.

In the emotionally charged aftermath of 9/11, Canada's liberal approach to multiculturalism began to show its limits. During the provincial election in Ontario in 2007, Conservative leader John Tory argued, with disastrous electoral impact, that the constitution-

Maher Arar speaks at a news conference in Ottawa in December, 2006, pointing to Justice Dennis O'Connor's report that vindicated Arar's claims that he had no involvement with terrorist activity. One month later, Prime Minister Stephen Harper announced a government apology and financial compensation for Canada's role in the American out-sourcing of the torture of Arar to Syria.
CP/Tom Hanson

ally mandated public support for separate Roman Catholic schools in the province should be extended to support faith-based schools of every kind. Opponents of extending funding to all religious-based schools defended public schools as keystones to the creation of social cohesion in a multicultural society, though they largely failed to engage the question of whether the existing separate schools prevented such cohesion or whether faith-based funding had created problems in the provinces that allowed it.

An undercurrent of discomfort with newcomers on the part of the majority also surfaced in the 2007 provincial election in Quebec. The Action Démocratique du Québec, which finished a close second, argued that Quebec was doing too much to accommodate immigrants and too little to encourage them to assimilate into the mainstream. Recognizing the vote-catching potential of this matter in a province where protection of Francophone culture was a major priority, Jean Charest, who emerged from the election with a minority government, appointed a commission headed by two highly acclaimed academics, Charles Taylor and Gerard Bouchard, to hold public hearings on accommodation practices related to cultural differences.

The questioning of Canada's relatively liberal approach to cultural diversity attracted much media attention, but a scholarly study of immigrant attitudes in 2007 concluded that multiculturalism in Canada did not threaten social cohesion. "For newcomers, we find little evidence of vast, enduring ethnic differences across a variety of social cohesion indicators."[3] Immigrants generally expressed pride in Canada and trust in its institutions.

ECONOMIC CHANGES

Canada's economy in the first decade of the twenty-first century seemed to go from strength to strength. Despite several setbacks, including a collapse in high-technology stocks in 2001 and an economic slowdown in the wake of 9/11, soaring commodity prices produced a job creation bonanza that brought the unemployment rate down to 5.8 percent in October 2007, the country's best performance since November 1974. The Canadian dollar reached US$1.08 one month later, a 50-year record, due in part to global increases in commodity prices, with the price of oil reaching all-time records, and the weakness of the US dollar.

Beneath the surface, the economy was less resilient than the one that had emerged in the aftermath of the Second World War. In that period, manufacturing had grown apace, though narrowly concentrated in central Canada. By contrast, in the early 2000s, the deindustrialization that had slowly begun in the 1970s accelerated, and central Canada bore the brunt of the job losses. From November 2002 to February 2007, about a tenth of all manufacturing jobs in Canada disappeared. Ontario lost 141 600 manufacturing jobs and Quebec lost 124 100, while the rest of the country had a net gain of 18 400 jobs. Over 300 000 jobs in auto assembly, auto parts, steel, electronics, shipbuilding, and other sectors disappeared, many lost to low-wage Third World countries. The high Canadian dollar combined with the prospects of cheap labour abroad gave many profit-seeking capitalists good reasons to close Canadian operations. By 2007, there was more new investment in the Alberta oil sands than in the entire Canadian manufacturing sector.

Due to high nickel prices, the economic picture looked rosy in Sudbury, and Alberta and Saskatchewan were flush with decent-paying, if short-term, jobs for construction workers, including workers flown in from other provinces, to build oil-sands projects and heavy oil upgraders. Tens of thousands of "temporary foreign workers" were brought in to fill employment gaps created by the boom in the commodities industries, particularly the development of the oil sands. Mining in British Columbia flourished. New Brunswick was planning to construct a new liquefied natural gas (LNG) terminal in Saint John and refurbish the Point Lepreau nuclear plant. Newfoundland and Nova Scotia, still reeling from the loss of much of the fishery in the 1990s, stood to gain billions in economic activity from the Hibernia and Sable Island energy projects, though neither provided more than 1000 jobs in the post-development phase. Quebec's manufacturing losses were partially offset by growth in the province's knowledge industries, including a large research sector in software and bio-pharmaceutical companies.

Foreign ownership of the economy persisted. According to the Corporations Return Act, foreign-based corporations controlled 21.2 percent of corporate assets and 29.2 percent of corporate operating revenues in 2005, earning 30.5 percent of corporate operating profits. Though the numbers had been stable since 2000, mergers of Canadian corporations with American corporations, including Molson Breweries with Coors and Domtar with Weyerhauser, further complicated the issue of "who owns Canada?" Over half of all manufacturing assets and just under half of oil and gas assets were American controlled. Among previously Canadian-owned companies that came under foreign ownership in the early twenty-first century were all the steel companies; metal-mining giants Alcan, Inco, and Falconbridge; Fairmont and Four Seasons Hotels; CP Ships; the Hudson's Bay Company; and Sleeman Breweries. Head office jobs and sometimes local operations disappeared altogether. When Molson Breweries workers went on strike in Edmonton in 2007, American management decided to simply close the Edmonton plant.

Canada's total exports in 2000 were equivalent to 45.6 percent of GDP, a steep rise from the period before free trade, to the delight of supporters of NAFTA. But that figure fell to 36.5 percent of GDP in 2006, less than it had been in 1994 when NAFTA was signed, even though energy exports had risen from 5.6 to 6.5 percent of GDP. The rising value of the dollar had reduced the international attractiveness of Canadian manufactured products and services. Imports declined

The Foreign Takeover of Canada's Steel Industry

Throughout the twentieth century, the steel industry remained under Canadian ownership. The steel plant on Cape Breton Island had been an exception, but in 1967, the provincial government, responding to the American owner's decision to close its Sydney mill, created a provincially owned company, Sydney Steel, to operate the plant.

Downsizing had occurred throughout the Canadian steel industry since the 1970s and the demands of the major steel union, the United Steelworkers, for greater capital investment in the industry and consolidation under a single Canadian owner, perhaps the federal government, fell on deaf ears. By the turn of the twenty-first century, the steel industry in Canada faced further difficulties. China had cornered about 30 percent of the global steel market and North American steel companies, faced with monopolistic suppliers and buyers, decided to pursue greater consolidation to maintain prices. The result was a series of mergers and buyouts. In contrast to the vigorous state response to foreign takeovers in the mid-twentieth century, federal and provincial governments refused to intervene as the sales listed below doomed prospects of a Canadian-operated steel industry:

– Sydney Steel, with 500 employees, was sold to Zoom Developers of India in 2001, which shut the plant and stripped its assets for overseas sales.

– Dofasco, Hamilton, with 11 000 employees, was sold in 2006 to Arcelor SA, Luxembourg.

– Algoma Steel, Sault Ste. Marie, with 3200 employees, was sold in 2007 to Essar-Global, India.

– IPSCO, Regina, with 4400 employees, was sold in 2007 to Sveskt Stal AB, Sweden.

– Stelco, Hamilton, with 5500 employees, was sold in 2007 to United States Steel Corp.

– Harris Steel, London, with 3000 employees, was sold in 2007 to Nucor, U.S.A.[4]

in turn, but only two-thirds as much as exports. Export industries paid wages 25 percent higher than the rest of the economy and many lost jobs were replaced by poor-paying service jobs.

Even resource industries sometimes faced restrictions in American markets despite the free trade agreement between Canada and the United States. The American government heavily subsidized agricultural producers, creating barriers for Canadian exporters of farm products. American lumber producers continued to successfully pressure their government to restrict imports of Canadian softwood lumber with devastating consequences for the Canadian lumber industry, particularly in British Columbia. In 2006, the Americans partially relented, signing an agreement with Canada that accepted free trade as a principle, but contradicted that principle by requiring that Canada impose an export tax on softwood exports when the price of the Canadian product fell below a set dollar value.

Unsurprisingly, Statistics Canada data suggested average Canadians were benefiting little from the energy-fuelled economic boom. The rich prospered while the middle-class and the poor fell further behind. In 2006, 16.2 percent of Canadians (excluding Treaty Indians), or about 5 million, lived on incomes below Statscan's low income cutoffs. Between 1980 and 2005, the top 20 percent of income earners added 16.4 percent to their earnings while the bottom

This open-mine pit forms part of the tar sands extraction in the area around Fort McMurray, Alberta, where tens of thousands of hectares of land had been dug up by 2008, with few prospects of dug-up areas ever being restored.
© Bob Anderson/Masterfile

20 percent lost 20.6 percent. Canada's top chief executive officers had earned $3.5 million on average in 1998; in 2005, that figure rose to $9.1 million. By contrast, the earning power of wages fell 2.85 percent during those years. This squeeze on wages likely contributed to political restiveness.

THE FEDERAL ELECTIONS OF 2000 AND 2004

The 2000 federal election suggested continuing regional patterns of voting. While the Liberals won only 40 percent of the vote, they had a comfortable parliamentary majority, winning 100 of 103 Ontario seats. This time, there was also a Liberal revival in Quebec, and the party won only one seat less in that province than the Bloc Québécois. But the new Canadian Alliance swept most everything before them in western Canada.

Shortly before the 2000 election, the Reform Party attempted to unite forces to the right of the Liberal Party by creating the Canadian Alliance. Stockwell Day, a former lay Pentecostal school administrator who had served as Alberta's provincial treasurer, was elected party leader. Well financed by Bay Street, Day tried to convince Canadians to adopt his national agenda of huge tax cuts, especially for the wealthy. The Liberals undercut his promised tax cuts with pledges of both tax cuts and modest increases in social spending, including transfers to provinces for health care.

After the election, the Canadian Alliance imploded in a nasty battle over the future of the party. Eventually, business supporters of the political right used a threat to pull the plug on campaign donations to leverage a merger of the Canadian Alliance with the Progressive Conservatives. Stephen Harper, the last Canadian Alliance leader, emerged as the leader of the new Conservative Party of Canada in 2004.

The Liberals had tried to restore their image as progressives after the 2000 election. Playing to Canadian concern about the erosion of medicare, Jean Chrétien appointed Roy Romanow, the former NDP premier of Saskatchewan, as a one-man commission to determine how best to ensure the health of Canadians. Romanow rejected conservative arguments that Canada needed a larger dose of private medicine, concluding that "medicare has consistently delivered affordable,

timely, accessible, and high quality care to the overwhelming majority of Canadians on the basis of need, not income. It has contributed to our international competitiveness, to the extraordinary standard of living we enjoy, and to the quality and productivity of our work force."[5] Romanow proposed a major injection of federal money into provincial medicare programs to compensate for earlier cuts. In 2003, a federal-provincial agreement provided the provinces with billions of additional federal dollars. There were no strings attached because in 2000, the federal government, eager for peace with the provinces, had agreed to the Social Union Framework, which largely reduced the federal role to providing untargeted funds to the junior level of government in broad areas such as health and social services.

Chrétien retired in 2003, and the Liberal Party chose Paul Martin as its new national leader and prime minister. The former owner of Canada Steamship Lines before becoming finance minister, Martin initially proved popular with Canadians. The relative fortunes of the political parties began to change in March 2004, when Auditor General Sheila Fraser revealed irregularities in a federal sponsorship program implemented by the Chrétien government after the 1995 referendum in Quebec. The program offered federal sponsorship of sporting and cultural events, mainly in Quebec, to foster greater support for federalism. Fraser suggested that perhaps $100 million of the $250 million spent by this program had been fraudulently diverted to Quebec-based advertising agencies tied to the Liberal Party with no obvious product provided in return. Martin promised to punish all wrongdoers, but many voters became disillusioned with his party.

Martin called an election for June 2004 and tried to discredit opponent Stephen Harper by pointing to his past opposition to federal social spending programs and his apparent support for two-tier health care, involving private insurance for those who could afford it alongside the public program. But the Liberals were reduced to a minority government with only 135 of 308 seats. The remaining party standings were Conservatives 99; Bloc Québécois 54; NDP 19; and Independents 1. An interesting feature of the election was the first credible showing in the popular vote for the national Green Party. Though failing to win any seats, it offered voters a peculiar mix of environmentalism and fiscal conservatism.

A New Era of Minority Government

Dependent on NDP votes to remain in office, Paul Martin faced a difficult challenge. In the spring of 2005, he acquiesced when the NDP demanded that his budget include funds for social housing, a program the government had ended in 1993, and other social programs, and that Martin abandon his planned corporate tax cuts. On other issues, such as continuing Canada's military commitments in Afghanistan, which the NDP opposed, he governed with the consent of the Conservatives.

Martin's overall strategy was to restore public confidence in his scandal-plagued party by focusing on social policy. He added billions to the federal contribution to provincial medicare programs and negotiated a modest federal-provincial agreement on day care that child-care advocates supported as a first step toward a national, universal day-care program. Responding to pressures from Native organizations, he also negotiated with the premiers and the leaders of the major national Aboriginal organizations for a $5.1 billion program of spending by the federal, provincial, and territorial governments to improve the lives of Canada's Native peoples. Martin demonstrated social liberalism by legalizing same-sex marriage against opposition from most Conservative MPs. He also tried to revive Jean Chrétien's plan to decriminalize possession of small amounts of marijuana but found insufficient support in his caucus.

By November 2005, the Liberal-NDP alliance had collapsed, and an election was set for January 2006. Stephen Harper tried to reduce voter skepticism that the Conservatives would shrink social programs by sticking to a few conservative promises. He would replace the promised day-care program with a grant to all families with children regardless of whether they put their children in day care. He would cut the GST from 7 percent to 6 percent immediately and later to 5 percent. His government would increase military spending but would also increase federal transfers to the provinces.

For weeks, Harper's promises excited little support. The sponsorship scandal issue had lost potency after an inquiry ordered by Martin exonerated him of any blame. But in late December, the question of the government's honesty was raised again in a press conference by Judy Wasylycia-Lees, the NDP MP for Winnipeg North. She had written RCMP commissioner Giuliano Zaccardelli about allegations that a government minister had tipped off some investors of government plans to reject new taxes on income trusts, a controversial form of corporate holding that offered lower corporate taxes. Remarkably, Zaccardelli responded that the RCMP had launched a criminal probe of these allegations. Within days, Liberal support began to sag. Eventually, the allegations were disproved, but damage had been done at a crucial moment in the election campaign. This unusual intervention of the commissioner of the RCMP in a federal election has yet to be explained.

The scandals hurt both the Liberals and the Bloc Québécois in Quebec, but they were not the only problem for the "governing" party. For over a decade, Quebec federalists had voted overwhelmingly for the Liberals, and separatists for the Bloc. Increasingly, however, nationalists in Quebec were rebelling against such limitations on their choices and neo-liberal values were engaging more support. The result was that 10 Quebec constituencies elected Conservatives in the 2006 election after being virtually shut out of the province since 1993.

On election night, the Conservatives carried 124 seats, the Liberals 103, the Bloc 51, the NDP 29, and Independents 1. Stephen Harper formed a minority government. For the next year and a half, his chief ally was the Bloc, which feared an early election. Compromising its liberal tenets, the Bloc voted to abandon the Kelowna agreement and the national day-care program on the grounds that Harper was shifting more funds to Quebec. By late 2007, the Bloc, recognizing that Quebec voters were abandoning their party, became strident critics of the Harper government, but the Liberals, performing erratically in the polls under their new leader, Stéphane Dion, refused to bring the government down and force an election.

Provincial Politics

The federal tilt to the right had echoes in some provinces. NDP governments were defeated in British Columbia in 2001 and Saskatchewan in 2007 by neo-liberal parties, and the Parti Québécois was ousted by the fiscally conservative Liberals in 2003. By contrast, the Manitoba NDP routed its opponents in several provincial elections, and the Ontario Liberals rode to power on a socially interventionist platform. While divisions among the major parties in the Atlantic provinces defied traditional notions of left-and right-wing ideologies, the continuing growth of the NDP as a political force in Nova Scotia demonstrated growing polarization in that province. In 2006 in New Brunswick and 2007 in Prince Edward Island, long-standing Tory governments were defeated by the Liberals, while in Newfoundland and Labrador the Liberals were up-ended in 2003 by the Progressive Conservatives.

Despite rhetoric in favour of environmental sustainability and reductions in greenhouse emissions, it was economic growth that motivated most provincial governments. Provinces with resource-based economies fared best in achieving this goal. Oil-rich Alberta led the pack. In 2005, Alberta paid off its last debts and began mounting budgetary surpluses. Most voters were pleased but critics argued that its low taxes, minimal unemployment, and debt-free status hid the government's failure to diversify the economy beyond petroleum.

By 2006, Saskatchewan was beginning to take the economic lead from Alberta and a year later provincial voters gave the reins of power to the Saskatchewan Party, a party formed in 1997 on the ruins of a scandal-plagued provincial Progressive Conservative Party. In British Columbia, the NDP had been reduced to a mere two seats in the 2001 provincial election. The party was in disarray after a scandal forced Glen Clark's resignation as premier in 1999. His successor, Ujjal Dosanjh, who took office in 2000, was Canada's first Indo-Canadian premier. Dosanjh proved unable to convince British Columbians that Liberal leader Gordon Campbell's promises to reduce taxes without cutting education and health services did not add up. In office, Campbell chopped provincial social programs considerably, sold BC Rail to Canadian National, privatized much of BC Hydro and health-care support, and stripped negotiated contract rights, creating a backlash that allowed the NDP to regain many of its lost seats in the provincial election of 2005. Successful in retaining a reduced majority, Campbell saw the writing on the wall and began to modestly re-invest in education and health and supported major infrastructure projects on the road to the 2010 Winter Olympics.

In Ontario, as well, a backlash developed against neo-liberal policies. The Mike Harris "commonsense revolution" of cuts in government spending went sour in the early 2000s after the deaths of seven people in Walkerton, Ontario, from drinking water contaminated with toxins. Spending cuts and contracting out in areas of traditional government regulation such as the safety of water supplies clearly carried dangers. A massive power outage in southern Ontario in the summer before the provincial election of 2003, coupled with increasing power bills a year earlier, damaged the campaign of Ernie Eves, Harris's successor, to gradually privatize Ontario Hydro. Dalton McGuinty's Liberals easily defeated the Conservatives in 2003. The

TABLE 23.1 Federal Transfers to Provinces and Territories per Capita and Total Dollars, 2007–2008*

Area	Per capita	Total transfers (in millions of dollars)
Nunavut	30 446	941
Northwest Territories	20 368	863
Yukon	18 862	590
Prince Edward Island	3 484	484
New Brunswick	3 369	2 529
Nova Scotia	3 006	2 814
Manitoba	2 999	3 552
Quebec	2 436	18 767
Newfoundland	2 325	1 181
Alberta	1 699	5 886
Saskatchewan	1 685	1 672
Ontario	1 636	20 984
British Columbia	1 589	6 958

Total federal transfers to provinces and territories: $67 010 000 000

*The figures include federal grants to provinces in cash or tax credits for the Canada Health Transfer, Canada Social Transfer, Equalization, and Territorial Formula Financing.

Source: Canada, Department of Finance, "Federal Transfers to Provinces and Territories," 26 July 2007, http://www.fin.gc.ca/FEDPROV/eqpe.html.

TABLE 23.2 Equalization Payments from 2006–2009 (in millions of dollars)

	NL	PE	NS	NB	QC	MB	SK	BC	ON	AB	Total
2006–07	632	291	1 386	1 451	5 539	1 709	13	260	0	0	11 281
2007–08	477	294	1 308	1 477	7 160	1 826	226	0	0	0	12 768
2008–09 projection	197	310	1 294	1 492	7 622	2 003	0	0	0	0	12 918

Source: Canada, Department of Finance, "Federal Transfers to Provinces and Territories," 26 July 2007, http://www.fin.gc.ca/FEDPROV/eqpe.html.

McGuinty government, despite campaigning on a platform of ambitious reforms, delivered little, pleading poverty. McGuinty's focus increasingly became the alleged federal plunder of Ontario finances. He claimed that Ontario residents were providing $23 billion more annually in revenues to Ottawa than they received in federal expenditures to the province. (See Table 23.1)

McGuinty's campaign for "tax fairness for Ontario" began after a federal deal in early 2005 with Newfoundland and Labrador and Nova Scotia to fully exempt offshore oil earnings from the federal equalization formula for eight years to spur long-term economic development for these two disadvantaged provinces. The Atlantic Accord was estimated to be worth at least $2.8 billion for Newfoundland and Labrador and one-third of that amount for Nova Scotia. Campaigning for office, Harper pledged that if equalization rates were increased, offshore oil revenues would be excluded in any new formula. When Harper increased equalization payments in 2007 (see Table 23.2), placing a cap on the increases that the Atlantic Accord could yield, Newfoundland and Labrador premier Danny Williams was outraged. His tough talk to Ottawa and his insistence on getting a good return for the province from the Hibernia oil developers, despite the companies' claim that the province was demanding too much from them, won him a resounding re-election victory in 2007. In contrast, Rodney McDonald, leading a minority government in Nova Scotia, made peace with Stephen Harper in October 2007 in return for assurances that the province would never receive less than the original Atlantic Accord had promised.

QUEBEC IN THE TWENTY-FIRST CENTURY

The changes in equalization payments in 2007 were designed to improve the standing of the federal Conservatives in Quebec. Harper's breakthrough in Quebec in 2006 came partly because of a promise to correct the alleged fiscal imbalance. Even under the old formula, Quebec was to receive an increase of about $900 million in 2007 over 2006, but the new formula gave Quebec an additional $700 million. Liberal premier Jean Charest, on the campaign trail, announced that the whole $700 million would go to tax cuts.

The winds of Quebec politics seemed to be blowing in every direction at once—left and right, nationalist and federalist. While separatist sentiment declined, the federalism favoured by most Francophone Québécois mostly involved federal redistribution of revenues to provinces and letting Quebec establish its own priorities without interference from Ottawa. Quebec led the country in many social programs, including day care and post-secondary tuition fees. Its Act to Combat Poverty and Social Exclusion, adopted in 2002, was the vanguard for provincial anti-poverty strategies in Canada, establishing clear guidelines and programs to significantly reduce levels of poverty.

Polls suggested the Québécois were more egalitarian than other Canadians, more willing to sacrifice economic growth to achieve ecological advances, and more pacifist. Despite such liberalism, mainly centred in Montreal, there was growing resentment with the high rate of provincial taxes relative to all other provinces. The Action démocratique du Québec (ADQ), which had won only marginal support in the 1990s when it focused on constitutional issues, became a major player when it championed tax cuts in the early 2000s. The combination of complaints about tax levels and the alleged unwillingness of minority groups to adapt to Québécois norms suggested a degree of angst in the province that contrasted with the optimism of the early René Lévesque days. The Quebec provincial election of 2007 reflected such anxieties, with the Liberals winning only a minority government and almost being defeated by the ADQ, and the Parti Québécois, viewed as the most social democratic party, reduced to third place.

NATIVE PEOPLES

While the provinces fought old battles with Ottawa, Native people continued their even longer struggle for recognition of their land titles and a decent standard of living. In 2005, the federal and provincial governments and the major national Aboriginal organizations agreed to additional programs of joint federal and provincial spending on First Nations health, education, and housing worth $5 billion over a 10-year period. The Conservative rejection of the Kelowna Accord after the 2006 election caused outrage on most reserves.

Continued federal unwillingness to expedite Native land claims was evident in February 2006 when Six Nations residents of Grand River occupied 40 hectares of land and blockaded roads and rail lines adjacent to the town of Caledonia, south of Hamilton, Ontario. They used this strategy to prevent development of a housing subdivision on land they claimed was theirs. The land had been granted to the Mohawk in 1784 as a reward for their armed support of Britain during the American Revolution. According to the protesters, it had been illegally alienated from Six Nations control in the 1840s. The division of jurisdiction and poor communication between federal and provincial governments contributed to the crisis, which lasted for 18 months. In other provinces, however, there were some treaty negotiation successes. The Tsawassen First Nation Agreement with British

A standoff in the southwestern Ontario town of Caledonia between Six Nations defenders of their people's traditional lands and non-Aboriginals who supported the development of a proposed subdivision that began in February 2006. In this picture, Six Nations protesters stand on top of their barricade moments before taking it down on May 23, 2006 in an effort that proved unsuccessful to persuade the federal government to negotiate Aboriginal demands.
CP/Nathan Denette

Columbia in 2006, the first federal-provincial-Aboriginal agreement for the province since the Nisga'a treaty in 1998, seemed to bode well for other negotiations under way in the province.

One sordid story in Canada's dealings with Aboriginal peoples had a partial resolution in 2007: the residential schools issue. Lawyers for most Natives suing for redress for their experiences in residential schools and government lawyers came to an agreement that the courts approved. The settlement provided $1.9 billion for "common experience" payments to residential school students, with $10 000 paid for the first year in a school and $3000 for each subsequent year. Those who had suffered sexual or serious physical abuses could receive between $5000 and $275 000, "or more money if they can show a loss of income."[6] The settlement also included $125 million for healing programs, $60 million for researching, documenting, and preserving survivor experiences, and $20 million for commemorative projects.

On June 11, 2008, Stephen Harper formally apologized in the House of Commons to former residential school students for the suffering they endured as a result of the government's policy of "assimilation." He noted, "We now recognize that it was wrong to separate children from rich and vibrant cultures and traditions, that it created a void in many lives and communities and we apologize for having done this."[7] Harper expressed the hope that a "truth and reconciliation commission" that the government had established to allow residential school survivors and operators alike to share their stories would play a role in healing the wounds left within Native communities because of the former policy of forcing Native children into white-run boarding schools. While Aboriginal organizations generally responded positively to Harper's historic apology, many Natives regarded the carefully delimited apology as insufficient. They suggested that what Harper had called "assimilation" was in fact an effort at cultural genocide and that the residential school policy was the tip of the iceberg of policies aimed at destroying the sovereignty of First Nations peoples. The apology would only be meaningful when all such policies had been jettisoned and First Nations communities had adequate territorial and financial guarantees to be able to recover from the consequences of several centuries of European colonial policies aimed at stealing their lands and marginalizing or erasing their cultures.

WORKERS AND TRADE UNIONS

Courts had traditionally been less supportive of trade unions than other groups seeking social justice. They maintained that the Charter right of association did not extend to the right to bargain collectively or the right to strike. Persistence paid off, however, when the Supreme Court in 2007 axed a British Columbia law that contracted out work in the health-care and social work sectors at the cost of thousands of jobs. The Health and Social Services Delivery Improvement Act of 2002 overrode existing collective agreements and ignored any need to consult with or give notice to unions. It affected transfers and multi-worksite assignment rights, contracting out, the status of contracted-out workers, job security programs, layoffs, and seniority rights. Wrote the Supreme Court: "The right to bargain collectively with an employer enhances the human dignity, liberty and autonomy of workers by giving them the opportunity to influence the establishment of workplace rules and thereby gain some control over a major aspect of their lives, namely their work."[8]

Though the court defended collective bargaining, it gave the BC government a year to negotiate with the unions. In 2001, the Supreme Court had ruled that Ontario legislation that excluded the province's 100 000 farm workers from the Ontario Labour Relations Act violated their rights of association and gave the Ontario government a year to amend its legislation. Harris responded by allowing farm workers to form associations without requiring employers to bargain collectively with them.

Agricultural labourers were among Canada's poorest workers. Usually immigrants with little English, their working conditions were often unsafe. Yet in 2006, only 5 percent were in unions, mainly in British Columbia, where an NDP government had granted them the right to unionize though denied them access to employment standards legislation, with sometime fatal consequences. Farm workers' plight demonstrated the uneven ability of trade unions to organize workers and protect their rights. The percentage of employees represented by a union had declined from 40 percent in the early 1980s to 29.7 percent in 2006. Women comprised a small majority of unionists, a change from earlier decades when men's rates of unionism dwarfed women's. The high rate of unionization in the public sector, where women dominated, gave women a slight advantage in winning unionization.

GAY RIGHTS IN QUESTION

Gay rights, which had been gaining ground since the 1960s, still had one hurdle to jump: the right of gays and lesbians to legal marriage. Although efforts to persuade legislators to make gay marriages legal had failed, court decisions beginning with the Court of Appeal for Ontario in 2003 determined that limiting marriage to heterosexuals violated equality provisions in the Canadian Charter of Rights and Freedoms. By the end of 2004, five other provincial and territorial courts had ordered governments to rewrite the definition of marriage to include heterosexuals and homosexuals. The Liberal government under Paul Martin also backed gay marriage, introducing a free vote on the matter in the House of Commons and asking the Supreme Court in 2005 to rule on the constitutionality of legislation that it had prepared to make same-sex marriages legal while allowing individual churches to determine whether or not they would recognize same-sex unions among their congregants.

For neo-liberals, many of them supporters of the Conservative Party, these legal advances were interpreted as posing a threat to the sanctity of heterosexual unions. During the 2006 election, Stephen Harper, who was a neo-liberal in social policy, pledged a Conservative government to a second parliamentary vote regarding gay marriage. By the time the second vote occurred in December 2006, over 12 000 same-sex marriages had been registered. In British Columbia that year, 3.5 percent of all marriages were of same-sex couples. Public support for same-sex marriages had increased substantially since the 2005 legislation had been proclaimed, so it was anti-climactic when Harper's bill to redefine marriage as the voluntary union of a man and woman was defeated by 175 to 123.

CANADIAN WOMEN IN THE TWENTY-FIRST CENTURY

Though women formed the majority of unionists, most trade union leaders, like most bosses, were men. In 2007, nine of 10 provincial federations of labour and the Canadian Labour Congress had male presidents, which put them on a gender par with Canadian corporations, in which a woman held the highest corporate position in only 7.3 percent of the biggest 500 companies in 2006. In politics, women did little better. After the federal election of 2006, 20.8 percent of MPs were women, a percentage unchanged in a decade. The ratio of four men to every woman prevailed in most provincial legislatures and municipal councils.

Though immigrant women were more likely than Canadian-born women to have a university education and second and third degrees, they were less likely to be employed. When they were employed, their incomes lagged well behind not only Canadian-born women but also men from the same immigrant background. Twenty-one percent of women of colour, including both immigrant and Canadian-born women, had a university degree in 2006. On average, they had far less success than white women with similar educations.

Although feminists could celebrate significant victories for women since the 1960s, income inequality still prevailed in the early twenty-first century.

Women's incomes from all sources, including government transfers, averaged only 62 percent of men's in 2006. Women employed full-time earned 72 percent of the earnings of men employed full-time. In Quebec, interestingly, where social policy had the promotion of women's equality in the workforce as a clear objective, the figure rose to 80 percent.

Single-mother families remained over-represented among families living in poverty. In 2003, when single-father families had a poverty rate of 13 percent, the comparable figure for single-mother families was 38 percent. Finding a male partner to share the work of raising a family sometimes only made matters worse. Demands made on women's shelters demonstrated the continuing scourge of violence against women, mainly perpetrated by intimate partners. A Statscan survey in 2004 indicated that the 473 shelters that provided statistics had provided refuge to 58 486 women in one year, of whom 76 percent had been victims of abuse.

The plight of non-profit social service agencies staffed by women and serving mainly women clients

MAP 23.2 **Canada in the Twenty-first Century**

demonstrated the gender insensitivity of most provincial and municipal governments. During the economic boom, such agencies struggled to find employees. With their restricted finances, the agencies often offered poverty wages to day-care workers, companions for the ill and disabled, and workers in women's shelters. The result was that non-profit agencies could not fill all positions, resulting in overwork and stress for those employees, overwhelmingly women, who persevered. Jan Reimer, coordinator of the Alberta Council of Women's Shelters and former mayor of Edmonton, noted that many women's shelter employees, after working long hours to make up for staff shortages, had to resort to food banks to insure that their own families did not starve.

Feminists argued that the neo-liberal economic agenda, coupled with the resurgence of conservative values about the appropriate role of women, made it difficult to achieve genuine equality in Canadian society. Against a backdrop of the war on terror in Afghanistan and Iraq and the global race for economic ascendancy, values of caring and cooperation assigned to women were trumped by supposed masculine traits of aggression and competition.

CONCLUSION

Canada's main challenges as the new century opened would have been unfathomable to the Fathers of Confederation, who had little concern about environmental threats, the politics of Afghanistan, or the rights of women, gays, and Aboriginals. Other issues confronting Canadians today have been present since confederation, including the balance of powers between the federal and provincial governments, the treatment of immigrants, and foreign versus domestic direction of the economy. Although many Canadians seem generally optimistic that despite their divisions, they can build upon their past achievements to create a more sustainable and harmonious society, they recognize that these goals can only be achieved in cooperation with other peoples in our steadily shrinking global village.

NOTES

1 Inuit Circumpolar Council press release, 7 December 2005, http://www.inuitcircumpolar.com/index/php?ID=316&Lang=En.

2 CBC News, http://www.cbc.ca/canada/story/2002/09/12/pm_reax020912.html#skip300x250.

3 Stuart N. Soroka, Richard Johnston, and Keith Banting, eds., "Ties that Bind? Social Cohesion and Diversity in Canada," in Keith Banting, Thomas Courchene, and Leslie Seidle, eds., *Belonging? Diversity and Social Integration in Canada* (Montreal: Institute for Research on Public Policy, 2007), 586.

4 *Globe and Mail*, 27 October 2007.

5 Roy J. Romanow, Commission on the Future of Health Care in Canada, *Building on Values: The Future of Health Care in Canada: Final Report* (Ottawa: Government of Canada, 2002), xvi.

6 "Official court notice" advertisement in the *Globe and Mail*, 27 April 2007.

7 "Text of the Apology," *National Post*, 11 June 2008.

8 Supreme Court of Canada, Decisions—Health Services and Support, Facilities Subsector Bargaining, http://csc.lexum.umontreal.ca/en/2007/2007scc27/2007scc2007.html.

RELATED READINGS IN THIS SERIES

From *Nation and Society: Readings in Post-Confederation Canadian History*

Reem Bahdi, "No Exit: Racial Profiling and Canada's War Against Terrorism," 494–511.

SELECTED READING

On the "discovery" of global warming, see Spencer Weart, *The Discovery of Global Warming* (Cambridge, MA: Harvard University Press, 2003) and Patrick Bond and Rehana Dada, eds., *Trouble in the Air: Global Warming and the Privatised Atmosphere* (Durban: Centre for Civil Society and Transnational Institute, 2005). Broader issues of environmental threats and environmental policy are tackled in David V. Bates and Robert B. Caton, *A Citizen's Guide to Air Pollution* (Vancouver: Greystone Books and David Suzuki Foundation, 2002); David R. Boyd, *Unnatural Law: Rethinking Canadian Environmental Law and Policy* (Vancouver: UBC Press, 2003); and Richard Heinberg, *Peak Everything: Wake Up to the Century of Declines* (Gabriola Island: New Society, 2007). On environmental struggles, see Bill McKibben, *Fight Global Warming Now: The Handbook for Taking Action in Your Community* (New York: Henry Holt and Company, 2007) and Mike Hudema and Jacob Rolfe, *An Action a Day Keeps Global Capitalism Away* (Toronto: Between the Lines, 2004).

Studies of the impact of 9/11 on Canada include Kent Roach, *September 11: Consequences for Canada* (Montreal: McGill-Queen's University Press) and Karim-Aly Kassam, George Melnyk, and Lynne Perras, eds., *September 11: Impact and Response* (Calgary: University of Calgary Press, 2002). For the impact of the "war on terror" on civil liberties, see Reem Bahdi, "No Exit: Racial Profiling and Canada's War Against Terrorism," *Osgoode Hall Law Journal*, vol. 41, No. 2 and 3 (2003), 293–317. A longer-term background on surveillance of citizens is provided in Gary Kinsman et al., eds., *Whose National Security? Canadian State Surveillance and the Creation of Enemies* (Toronto: Between the Lines, 2000) and Anna Pratt, *Securing Borders: Detention and Deportation in Canada* (Vancouver: UBC Press, 2005). Changing immigration policies after 9/11 are explored in Charles M. Beach, Alan G. Green, and Jeffrey G. Reitz, *Canadian Immigration Policy for the 21st Century* (Montreal: McGill-Queen's University Press, 2003). The anti-war movement that kept Canada out of Iraq is discussed in George Melnyk, ed., *Canada and the New American Empire: War and Anti-War* (Calgary: University of Calgary Press, 2004).

Dangers to Canadian economic sovereignty are outlined in Gregory J. Inwood, *Continentalizing Canada: The Politics and Legacy of the Macdonald Royal Commission* (Toronto: University of Toronto Press, 2005). Issues regarding the distribution of wealth and leisure in Canada are detailed in Lance W. Roberts, *Recent Social Trends in Canada* (Montreal: McGill-Queen's University Press, 2005) and Armine Yalnizyan, *The Rich and the Rest of Us: The Changing Face of Canada's Growing Gap* (Ottawa: Canadian Centre for Policy Alternatives, 2007).

On recent developments in Canadian politics, see Janine Brodie and Linda Trimble, eds., *Reinventing Canada: Politics of the 21st Century* (Toronto: Prentice Hall, 2003) and Michael Whittington and Glen Williams, *Canadian Politics in the 21st Century*, 6th ed. (Toronto: Nelson Education 2001). The complicated issues of equalization are discussed in Sujit Choudhry, Jean-François Gaudreault-DesBiens, and Lorne Sossin, *Dilemmas of Solidarity: Rethinking Redistribution in the Canadian Federation* (Toronto: University of Toronto Press, 2006).

Challenges of the modern workplace are outlined in Eric Tucker, ed., *Working Disasters: The Politics of Recognition and Response* (New York: Baywood Publishing, 2006) and D.W. Livingstone and P.H. Sawchuk, *Hidden Knowledge: Organized Labour in the Information Age* (Toronto: Garamond Press, 2004).

The continuing impact of social service cuts on women is detailed in Shelagh Day and Gwen Brodsky, *Women and the Canada Social Transfer: Securing the Social Union* (Ottawa: Status of Women Canada, 2007). Women's experiences in a changing labour force are the subject of Krista Scott-Dixon, *Doing It: Women in IT* (Toronto: Sumach Press, 2004). On the challenges facing immigrant women, see Daiva K. Stasiulis and Abigail B. Bakan, *Negotiating Citizenship: Migrant Women in Canada and the Global System* (Toronto: University of Toronto Press, 2005).

Population of Canada

Year	Population (in thousands)
1871	3 689
1881	4 325
1891	4 833
1901	5 371
1911	7 207
1921	8 788
1931	10 377
1941	11 507
1951	13 648
1956	16 081
1961	18 238
1966	20 015
1971	21 568
1976	23 550
1981	24 820
1986	26 101
1991	28 031
1994	29 036
1995	29 354
1996	29 672
1997	30 011
1998	30 301
2001	31 051
2006	31 613
2008 (July)	33 318

Source: Statistics Canada, CANSIM, Tables 075-0001 and 051-0001.

Prime Ministers of Canada

Prime Minister	Party	Term(s)
John A. Macdonald	Cons.	1 July 1867–5 November 1873
Alexander Mackenzie	Liberal	7 November 1873–8 October 1878
John A. Macdonald	Cons.	17 October 1878–6 June 1891
John Abbott	Cons.	16 June 1891–24 November 1892
John Thompson	Cons.	5 December 1892–12 December 1894
Mackenzie Bowell	Cons.	12 December 1894–27 April 1896
Charles Tupper	Cons.	1 May 1896–8 July 1896
Wilfrid Laurier	Liberal	11 July 1896–6 October 1911
Robert Laird Borden	Cons.	10 October 1911–12 October 1917
Robert Laird Borden	Unionist	12 October 1917–10 July 1920
Arthur Meighen	Unionist	10 July 1920–29 December 1921
William Lyon Mackenzie King	Liberal	29 December 1921–28 June 1926
Arthur Meighen	Cons.	29 June 1926–25 September 1926
William Lyon Mackenzie King	Liberal	25 September 1926–7 August 1930
Richard Bedford Bennett	Cons.	7 August 1930–23 October 1935
William Lyon Mackenzie King	Liberal	23 October 1935–25 November 1948
Louis St. Laurent	Liberal	15 November 1948–21 June 1957
John G. Diefenbaker	PC	21 June 1957–22 April 1963
Lester Pearson	Liberal	22 April 1963–20 April 1968
Pierre Elliott Trudeau	Liberal	20 April 1968–3 June 1979
Joe Clark	PC	4 June 1979–2 March 1980
Pierre Elliott Trudeau	Liberal	3 March 1980–30 June 1984
John Turner	Liberal	30 June 1984–17 September 1984
Brian Mulroney	PC	17 September 1984–25 June 1993
Kim Campbell	PC	25 June 1993–4 November 1993
Jean Chrétien	Liberal	4 November 1993–12 December 2003
Paul Martin	Liberal	12 December 2003–6 February 2006
Stephen Harper	Conservative	6 February 2006–present

Cons. = Liberal Conservative PC = Progressive Conservative

Source: Library and Archives Canada, *First among Equals: The Prime Minister in Canadian Life and Politics*, http://www.collectionscanada.ca/primeministers/h4-3000-e.html.

Index

École des hautes etudes, 145
École literaire de Montréal, 151
École Polytechnique de Montréal,
  145, 431
École sociale populaire, 142, 220, 262
Economic Council of Canada, 350
economic nationalism, 327–329, 396
economy (1867–1945)
  see also free trade
  of 1920's, 187–189, 191, 200
  agricultural industry, 81
  Atlantic provinces, 32, 33, 61, 92
  Great Depression, 207–213, 222
  Great War and, 164–166,
    176–177, 277
  manufacturing and construction,
    80–81
  measurement of, 79
  and the National Policy, 40, 77–78, 92
  recession (1913–1914), 70, 73
  trade deficit, 277
economy (1945–1975), 336–353
  see also welfare state liberalism
    (1945–1975)
  communications, 341–342
  computers, 342–343
  costs of growth, 345–346
  dependence on America, 324–325
  economic disparity, 349–351
  environmental costs, 347–348
  farming and fishing, 339–340
  the fifties, 338–339
  foreign ownership, 325
  resource industries, 340–341
  service economy, 343–344
  stagflation, 344
  trade union movement, 351–353
  wage and price controls, 344
  welfare and warfare economy,
    337–338
  working conditions, 346–347
  World War II, 277–278, 286
economy (1976–2008), 395–402
  Canadian foreign policy and,
    401–402, 446
  economic changes (2000–2007),
    448–450
  free trade, 395–399
  high-tech economy, 400–401
  inflation versus unemployment, 400
  jobless recovery, 399
  neo-liberalism, 394
  tax and income disparity, 400
Ed Sullivan Show, 331
Edison, Thomas, 158

Edmonton Oilers, 438
education
  see also university education
  1867 (pre-Confederation years), 12
  1867–1918 (industrial age), 45–46,
    47–48, 143–145
  1918–1939 (interwar years), 253–256
  1945–1975 (post-war years), 360–362
  1976–2008, 425–426
  agricultural industry, 242, 243
  faith-based schools funding, 447
  French language, 46–47, 144–145, 170,
    203, 254, 308–309
  Manitoba Schools question
    (1870–1896), 47–48
  of Native Canadians, 67, 368, 369
  New Brunswick schools (1871–1875),
    45–46
  of women, 130–132, 145, 456
Edward VII, King, 67, 152
El Alamein, 270
Eldorado Gold Mines, 212
Eldorado Mining and Refining, 325
election(s)
  of 1911, 69
  of 1917, 171
  of 1935, 222–223
  2000 and 2004, 450
  2006, 451
  in Confederation years, 24
electrical appliance industry, 190
emigration, 41, 97, 98–99, 188, 230, 424
Empire Day, 65
employment. *See* labour force
enfant martyre, 237
entrepreneurship, 87–88
environment
  economic growth and, 347–349,
    393, 442
  global warming, 432–433
  Greenpeace, 431–432
  movements (1970–2008), 431–433
  reform attempts, 121–122, 347
equalization grants, 304–305, 406–407,
  415, 453
Established Programs Financing,
  417–418
estate taxes, 351
*Ethical Reflections on the Economic
  Crisis*, 434
ethnic minorities. *See* visible minorities
eugenics, 120, 235, 361
Europe
  architectural influence, 149–150
  artistic influence, 154

Great War, 166–168
World War II, 265–266, 268,
  270–277
European immigrants, 100, 101–105, 357,
  230–231, 364–365
  see also Jewish immigrants
  Communist Party of Canada, 200
  and Roman Catholic Church,
    142–143
European Union (EU), 394
Evangeline (Longfellow), 46

F

Fairclough, Ellen, 299
families
  see also children; women
  1867 (pre-Confederation years),
    10–12, 13
  1867–1917 (industrial age), 90–91
  1919–1939 (interwar years), 240
  1939–1945 (World War II years), 286
Famous Last Words (Findlay), 381
Famous Players, 250
Farmer-Labour government,
  194–195, 203
Farmers' Creditors Arrangement
  Act, 222
Farmers' Platform, 180
farming
  see also agricultural industry
  1867 (pre-Confederation years), 8–9
  1867–1917 (industrial age), 90–91
  1919–1939 (interwar years), 240–243
  decline of traditional, 345
  political parties, 180, 194–195, 203
fascism, 217
fast-food industry, 339
Father Knows Best, 331
federal-provincial relations
  Charter of Rights and Freedoms,
    406–407
  and Confederation, 21, 23, 48–49
  cost-sharing programs, 304–305
  equalization grants, 304–305, 406–407
  federal cutbacks (1976–1999),
    417–418
  Medicare, 301–302
  patriating the Constitution, 406
  provincial rights versus progress,
    60–61
  transfer payments, 452–453
Fédération des femmes du Québec, 418
Féderation nationale Saint-Jean-
  Baptiste, 129

"AS IS" LICENSE AGREEMENT AND LIMITED WARRANTY

READ THIS LICENSE CAREFULLY BEFORE OPENING THIS PACKAGE. BY OPENING THIS PACKAGE, YOU ARE AGREEING TO THE TERMS AND CONDITIONS OF THIS LICENSE. IF YOU DO NOT AGREE, DO NOT OPEN THE PACKAGE. PROMPTLY RETURN THE UNOPENED PACKAGE AND ALL ACCOMPANYING ITEMS TO THE PLACE YOU OBTAINED THEM. THESE TERMS APPLY TO ALL LICENSED SOFTWARE ON THE DISK EXCEPT THAT THE TERMS FOR USE OF ANY SHAREWARE OR FREEWARE ON THE DISKETTES ARE AS SET FORTH IN THE ELECTRONIC LICENSE LOCATED ON THE DISK:

1. GRANT OF LICENSE and OWNERSHIP: The enclosed computer programs and any data ("Software") are licensed, not sold, to you by Pearson Canada Inc. ("We" or the "Company") in consideration of your adoption of the accompanying Company textbooks and/or other materials, and your agreement to these terms. You own only the disk(s) but we and/or our licensors own the Software itself. This license allows instructors and students enrolled in the course using the Company textbook that accompanies this Software (the "Course") to use and display the enclosed copy of the Software for academic use only, so long as you comply with the terms of this Agreement. You may make one copy for back up only. We reserve any rights not granted to you.

2. USE RESTRICTIONS: You may <u>not</u> sell or license copies of the Software or the Documentation to others. You may <u>not</u> transfer, distribute or make available the Software or the Documentation, except to instructors and students in your school who are users of the adopted Company textbook that accompanies this Software in connection with the course for which the textbook was adopted. You may <u>not</u> reverse engineer, disassemble, decompile, modify, adapt, translate or create derivative works based on the Software or the Documentation. You may be held legally responsible for any copying or copyright infringement that is caused by your failure to abide by the terms of these restrictions.

3. TERMINATION: This license is effective until terminated. This license will terminate automatically without notice from the Company if you fail to comply with any provisions or limitations of this license. Upon termination, you shall destroy the Documentation and all copies of the Software. All provisions of this Agreement as to limitation and disclaimer of warranties, limitation of liability, remedies or damages, and our ownership rights shall survive termination.

4. DISCLAIMER OF WARRANTY: THE COMPANY AND ITS LICENSORS MAKE <u>NO</u> WARRANTIES ABOUT THE SOFTWARE, WHICH IS PROVIDED "<u>AS-IS</u>." IF THE DISK IS DEFECTIVE IN MATERIALS OR WORKMANSHIP, YOUR ONLY REMEDY IS TO RETURN IT TO THE COMPANY WITHIN 30 DAYS FOR REPLACEMENT UNLESS THE COMPANY DETERMINES IN GOOD FAITH THAT THE DISK HAS BEEN MISUSED OR IMPROPERLY INSTALLED, REPAIRED, ALTERED OR DAMAGED. THE COMPANY DISCLAIMS ALL WARRANTIES, EXPRESS OR IMPLIED, INCLUDING WITHOUT LIMITATION, THE IMPLIED WARRANTIES OF MERCHANTABILITY AND FITNESS FOR A PARTICULAR PURPOSE. THE COMPANY DOES NOT WARRANT, GUARANTEE OR MAKE ANY REPRESENTATION REGARDING THE ACCURACY, RELIABILITY, CURRENTNESS, USE, OR RESULTS OF USE, OF THE SOFTWARE.

5. LIMITATION OF REMEDIES AND DAMAGES: IN NO EVENT, SHALL THE COMPANY OR ITS EMPLOYEES, AGENTS, LICENSORS OR CONTRACTORS BE LIABLE FOR ANY INCIDENTAL, INDIRECT, SPECIAL OR CONSEQUENTIAL DAMAGES ARISING OUT OF OR IN CONNECTION WITH THIS LICENSE OR THE SOFTWARE, INCLUDING, WITHOUT LIMITATION, LOSS OF USE, LOSS OF DATA, LOSS OF INCOME OR PROFIT, OR OTHER LOSSES SUSTAINED AS A RESULT OF INJURY TO ANY PERSON, OR LOSS OF OR DAMAGE TO PROPERTY, OR CLAIMS OF THIRD PARTIES, EVEN IF THE COMPANY OR AN AUTHORIZED REPRESENTATIVE OF THE COMPANY HAS BEEN ADVISED OF THE POSSIBILITY OF SUCH DAMAGES. SOME JURISDICTIONS DO NOT ALLOW THE LIMITATION OF DAMAGES IN CERTAIN CIRCUMSTANCES, SO THE ABOVE LIMITATIONS MAY NOT ALWAYS APPLY.

6. GENERAL: THIS AGREEMENT SHALL BE CONSTRUED AND INTERPRETED ACCORDING TO THE LAWS OF THE PROVINCE OF ONTARIO. This Agreement is the complete and exclusive statement of the agreement between you and the Company and supersedes all proposals, prior agreements, oral or written, and any other communications between you and the company or any of its representatives relating to the subject matter.

Should you have any questions concerning this agreement or if you wish to contact the Company for any reason, please contact in writing: Permissions, Pearson Education Canada, a division of Pearson Canada Inc., 26 Prince Andrew Place, Toronto, Ontario M3C 2T8.